# MOVEMENTS OF THE SPIRIT

Rev Dr John W. McKay

First published by The Way of The Spirit.
UK Registered Charity (No. 1110648).

info@thewayofthespirit.com
www.thewayofthespirit.com



ISBN: 978-0-9553650-4-1

Cover design: Jon Smethurst, Ezekiel Design

Printed in the UK by CPI William Clowes, Beccles, NR34 7TL

# Other Publications by John McKay

## Materials published by www.thewayofthespirit.com

**Books**

*The Way of the Spirit, A Bible Reading Guide and Commentary,* (4 vols.)
Published by Marshall-Pickering, 1988-90, Kingdom Faith, 1990-2001)
vol.1 *The Call and the Cross*
vol.2 *Times of Refreshing*
vol.3 *Heirs of the Prophets*
vol.4 *My Lord and My God*
Genesis, *2003*

**Courses**

*The Way of the Spirit, A Bible Reading Course.* Audio-book lectures and workbooks to go with the Bible Reading Guides to make a complete package for home and group study with optional tutorial assistance by correspondence.

**Booklets & Short Courses**

The Drama of Salvation, 1988
The River of God, 1989
The Lamb and the Dove, 1990
Visions of the End Times, 1991
Songs of Faith and Worship, 1991
It is Finished, 1991
When the Veil is Taken Away, 1994
The History of Heaven and Earth, 2001
Cherubim, Palm Trees and the Glory of God, 2001

**Teaching Audio Books**

*The Secret of the Lord*
*The Everlasting Covenant*
*The Prophetic Church*
*The Unseen Dimension*
*What happens when we die?*

**Old Testament Biblical Lectures**

| Title | Audio | Booklet |
|---|---|---|
| Genesis | ● | |
| Exodus | ● | |
| Leviticus | ● | |
| Deuteronomy | ● | |
| Joshua | ● | ● |
| Judges | ● | |
| Ruth Jonah Esther & Song of Songs | ● | |
| 1 Samuel | ● | |
| 2 Samuel | ● | |
| 1 Kings | ● | |
| 2 Kings | ● | |
| Prophets and Kings (1 Samuel-2 Kings) | ● | |
| 1 & 2 Chronicles | ● | |
| Lamentations Ezra & Nehemiah | ● | |
| Job | ● | |
| Isaiah 1-39 | ● | |
| Isaiah 40-66 | ● | |
| Jeremiah | ● | |
| Ezekiel & Daniel | ● | |
| Amos & Hosea | ● | ● |

**New Testament Biblical Lectures**

| Title | Audio | Booklet |
|---|---|---|
| Matthew | ● | |
| Mark | ● | ● |
| Luke | ● | |
| John | ● | |
| Acts | ● | |
| 1 Corinthians | ● | |
| 2 Corinthians | ● | |
| Galatians | ● | |
| Philemon Colossians & Ephesians | ● | |
| Hebrews | ● | ● |
| Revelation | ● | |

## Published Articles & Books

### Books

*Religion in Judah under the Assyrians*, SCM Press, 1973

*Psalms*, The Cambridge Bible Commentary, CUP, 1977 (3 vols., co-authored with John Rogerson)

*Revival Today*, Kingdom Faith Ministries, 1987

### Articles

"Pentecost and History" *The Spirit & Church*, Volume 3, Number 1, May 2001 pp113-128 Gospel Theological Seminary.

"The Experiences of Dereliction and of God's Presence in the Psalms: and Exercise in Old Testament Exegesis in the Light of Renewal Theology," *Theological Renewal* 12, 1979, pp. 18-24.

"Elihu – A Proto-Charismatic?" *Expository Times* XC.6, March 1979, pp. 167-71.

"My Glory – a Mantle of Praise," *Scottish Journal of Theology* 31, 1979, pp. 167-72.

"Psalms of Vigil," *Zeitschrift für die alttestamentliche Wissenschaft* 91, 1979, pp. 229-47.

"Is it Always God's Will to Heal?" *Way of Life*, The Church's Ministry of Healing, 1986, pp. 120-24.

"The Old Testament and Christian Charismatic/Prophetic Literature," *Scripture: Meaning and Method. Essays presented to Anthony Tyrell Hanson*, edited by Barry P. Thompson, Hull University Press, 1987, pp. 200-17.

"The Experiences of Dereliction and of God's Presence in the Psalms: and Exercise in Old Testament Exegesis in the Light of Renewal Theology," *Faces of Renewal. Studies in honor of Stanley M. Horton*, edited by Paul Elbert, Hendrickson Publishers, Massachusetts, 1988, pp. 3-13. (Reprint of article in *Theological Renewal* 1979, with minor modifications)

# Contents


ACKNOWLEDGEMENTS 9
NOTES FOR USING THIS BOOK 10
FOREWORD 12
PREFACE 14
AUTHOR'S NOTE 1 19

PART ONE – The Vision of a Prophetic People in Bible Times
1. From Adam to Christ 23
2. Samuel and Israel's First Prophetic Movement 26
3. Elijah, Elisha and the Sons of the Prophets 36
4. The Visions of the Great Writing Prophets 42
5. Jesus and the Prophetic Church 50
6. Prophetic Christianity – its distinguishing characteristics 59

PART TWO – The Prophetic Vision Fades in The Early Church
7. From Christ to Constantine 79
8. Prophetic Christianity in the Early Church 88
9. Montanism or the New Prophecy 102

PART THREE – The Conquest of Paganism in Late Patristic and Early Medieval Times
10. From Constantine to Hildebrand 135
11. Prophecy in the Dark Ages 149
12. Prophetic Ministries among the Celtic Saints 166

PART FOUR – Stirrings of Dissent and Prophecy in the Later Middle Ages
13. From Hildebrand to Luther 183
14. Prophecy in the Later Middle Ages 192
15. Mysticism in the Late Middle Ages 207

PART FIVE – A Moment of Prophetic Hope during the Reformation
16. From Luther to Fox 223
17. The Zwickau Prophets 234
18. The Bible and Revival 255

AUTHOR'S NOTE 2 269

PART SIX – Prophetic Awakenings in an Age of Religious Intolerance

19. From Fox to Wesley 273
20. Seekers and Quakers 284
21. The French Prophets in the Cevennes 307
22. The French Prophets in England 335
23. The Shakers or United Society of Believers 359

PART SEVEN – Prophecy and Revival in an Age of Revolution and Rationalism

24. From Wesley to Today 382
25. The Awakening of the Church in the Eighteenth Century 391
26. Edward Irving and the Catholic Apostolic Church 406
27. Church and Theology in the Nineteenth Century 422
28. Pentecostalism and the Full Blessing of Pentecost 445
29. Charismatic Renewal 467

PART EIGHT – Prospect and Conclusion

30. Where is the Spirit Leading us Now? 493
31. Pentecost and History 512
32. The End-Time Prophetic Church 524

EPILOGUE 533

BIBLIOGRAPHY 537

# Acknowledgements

Compiled over three decades by John McKay, earlier revisions of this work have formed the basis of lectures on Church History at: the University of Hull (1970 – 1983); Kingdom Faith Bible College (1985 to 2001); and latterly students of The Way of the Spirit Prophetic Bible Teachers' Course. The penultimate chapter of this book was published shortly after John's 'promotion to Glory' in the May 2001 edition of The Spirit & Church, Prophesy.

The teachings of John McKay continue to bless many today through the ongoing work of The Way of the Spirit Trust. The Way of the Spirit is also the title of a four part Bible reading guide published by John McKay in the early 1990's, the prequel to this work.

Special thanks are extended to all who contributed to this project in one way or another, in particular my thanks to John Fleetcroft, Tony Reynolds and John Taylor for their assistance in getting this work to press and to Jon Smethurst for the cover design.

I believe that John would have wanted primarily to dedicate this book to his family, and in particular to his beloved wife, Marguerite. Also he would have wanted to dedicate it to all the students of The Way of the Spirit who have faithfully studied the Bible.

In proofing, to retain the integrity and authenticity of this work, only minor edits have been made to the author's original words such as changing 'this century' to 'the twentieth century' for example. No interpretation or additions have been made, save for the foreword and epilogue, for which I thank Colin Urquhart and Richard George for their contributions in contextualising the relevancy of this work for today.

Praise the Lord!

*Iain McKay*
*6 May 2010*

# Notes for using this book

*1. Conventions*

Unless otherwise stated, translations of texts in Latin, Greek, French and German are my own.

Words in square brackets [...] are my additions. These are used for explanatory comments added inside quotations that are no part of the original quotation, e.g. for biblical references, or notes on word meanings, or alternative translations.

Round brackets () are used for comments that are part of the original quotation, for notes or parentheses by the original author.

Outside quotations only round brackets () are used.

In copying old English texts, I have often modernised the style to make reading easier:

(a) by removing the capitals that were frequently used at the beginning of nouns,

(b) by setting speech and citations in quotes instead of in italics,

(c) by updating punctuation, for example, making less use of commas and substituting full stops for semi-colons where they represent the start of a new sentence in modern usage,

(d) by occasionally altering archaic spelling, mainly for ease of reading (e.g. 'clothes' for 'cloaths', 'desert' for 'desart', 'ecstasy' for 'exstasie').

(e) Where I have substituted a modern English word for an older one, the original is given in square brackets following it.

---

*2. The terms 'Pentecostal' and 'Charismatic'*

These are capitalised when referring to the modern Pentecostal and Charismatic Movements or any related persons or matters: e.g. Pentecostal theology, Charismatics and non-Charismatics.

Otherwise, when used in a general sense, referring to pentecostal phenomena, charismatic personalities, and the like, they are spelt without capitals.

*3. Dates*

Many of the dates used in this book are open to discussion, particularly those relating to the times of the Bible and the early Church. The biblical dates are those in *The Way of the Spirit*. For the times of the Church, the dates are those in the *Oxford Dictionary of the Christian Church*, except that no indication is given when dates are approximations, whereas in the *Oxford Dictionary* these are preceded by 'c.' (= *circa*, meaning 'about').

Dates preceded by 'd.' are dates of death (d. = 'died')

# Foreword

Having worked alongside John McKay for several years, I know that he does not have any particular theological axe to grind as he presents this history of prophetic movements in the history of the Church. However, he does speak from personal experience of the Holy Spirit. It was that experience that transformed him from an academic theologian to someone who was able to communicate God's Word in a simple, forthright and yet profound way, much loved and appreciated by his students.

There are so many encouraging and uncomfortable truths that are stated clearly in this book, truths that Church leaders and theologians need to face at what is an extremely significant time in the Church's history. This book has been well researched and gives an amazingly wide perspective of the issues the church has needed to face prophetically in the past, and needs to address today.

Every believer is heavily influenced by his personal experience of God (or lack of it!), his experience of Church (whether good, bad or indifferent), and the particular theology to which he or she has been exposed. So it is refreshing to encounter the work of someone who has the competence to stand back and look objectively at the situation, from both an historical and contemporary perspective. It is an added bonus for a work of such scholarship to be so readable, riveting even.

John McKay wrote this book out of a firm conviction that he was doing so in obedience to the leading of God's Spirit and the end product bears the marks of being written under anointing. So this is far more than a history book, for it provokes the reader to look to the future, to understand where we stand now in God's prophetic purposes. John McKay rightly points out that with the increasing number of liberal, rational and anti-God philosophies of modern secular society, God continues to pour out His Spirit in revival power in many parts of the world. The words of Isaiah are relevant: "Who will believe our message and to whom has the arm of the Lord been revealed?" Where there is faith, God reveals His life and power, regardless of the unbelief evident in the world.

The Kingdom of God continues to advance and of the increase of His government there shall be no end! Throughout this book the reader has the conviction that despite the Church's chequered history, and regardless of believers' many failings (and the author faces both honestly), neverless God is in control not only of the Church, but of His purposes for the history of the world. Those purposes will prevail and God will have His way!

At a personal level, I believe those who read this book will discover or rediscover, their own destiny in God's purposes today; that they are numbered among a prophetic people that He is raising up to take their place in preparing for the Lord's return – whenever that may be!

*Colin Urquhart*

# Preface

As for so many others, so for me baptism in the Holy Spirit changed everything. I cannot, as some do, identify the event with conversion, for that took place sometime in my childhood and I was already active in ministry, but its effect was every bit as cataclysmic to me as Paul's encounter with the risen Lord at Damascus was to him. He was, of course, converted at that time and baptised in the Spirit three days later in the house on Straight Street, and when Ananias laid hands on him 'something like scales fell from his eyes' (Acts 9:18). My own experience of the Holy Spirit, though separated by many years from my first encounter with Christ, could well be described in the same language, a falling away of scales from the eyes, or, as Paul also described it later, the removing of a veil from the mind (2 Cor. 3:14-18). I quite simply saw everything differently, and that revolutionised my life and ministry entirely.

One of the early effects was seeing Scripture in a completely new light. That story need not be retold here; it has already been given in *When the Veil is Taken Away: Biblical Theology and the Spirit-filled Life*. Its fruit is amply seen in the four volumes of *The Way of the Spirit,* in the Bible Reading Course that goes with them, and in the new Bible study centres and groups it has generated.

I was also confronted with one large question. Why, since what I now saw was so clearly biblical, so central to the teaching of the Old Testament, of Jesus and of the Apostles, should it have taken till I was about thirty before I ever heard about such living and essential truths? Why were none of my clerical and theological friends telling me about such things beforehand and why were they not able to understand what I was telling them about afterwards? Why was there such ignorance in the churches, and, still more strange, even hostility on the part of some towards what was so obviously of the very essence of the gospel that told about the one, the Lord Jesus Christ, who came expressly to take away our sin and baptise us in the Holy Spirit?

Such questions sent me searching. The time was the early 1970s, when the Charismatic Movement in this country was still in its infancy. For those involved it was a season of spring-time freshness and evangelistic enthusiasm. Few were yet engaged in reflective, theological or historical assessment. A number of books did touch on the historical quest, but only in passing, in sketchy outline. What earlier Pentecostal works I could find then were mostly preoccupied with the recent story of Pentecostalism itself, and so my question remained unanswered. I could only glean the vaguest notions about what had happened to that vital river of life in the Spirit that Jesus had released. There was an eighteen hundred year gap between the end of the first century and the beginning of this that I could not properly fill and could not understand.

Somehow I never found satisfaction in the main explanation Pentecostals offered, that the fullness of life in the Spirit was lost at the end of the apostolic age and after a long hiatus was only now being restored in our own time, probably because it still left me with an unanswered question-mark over the eighteen-century gap. What did happen to life in the Spirit during those long ages of the history of the Church?

I thought it was because I was not myself a historian that I could give no answer, but when I started to read the Church historians I quickly discovered that they could give me none either. On the contrary, for the most part they showed no interest whatsoever in the question I was asking, let alone try to answer it. I therefore realised that if I were to persist in seeking answers I should have to do some historical study myself. That did not particularly delight me at the time for a number of reasons. My desire was to preach the gospel, not spend long hours in libraries, but the questions persisted, and were kept very much alive when others asked me about the same things. Furthermore, I had found the study of history at school a wearisome thing, with its long lists of kings and parliamentarians, of dreary wars and treaties, of tedious laws and reform bills. Church history at university hardly proved any more exciting, with its tortuous theological debates and definitions, its unending ecclesiastical wranglings and councils, its confusingly changing systems and doctrines. Coming to terms with all that was hard going. But still the questions persisted and, strangely, when I addressed myself to them and began to search for the answers, it did not prove at all as dull as I had anticipated. On the contrary the quest proved surprisingly exciting.

Now I was searching for something living. I had found the life of God for myself, and wanted to know who else had. The story was suddenly alive, for it was about people and about my God. Just as the Spirit had brought life to my reading of the Bible, so now also to my reading of history. That did not make the books that told me nothing about this new life any more interesting to read, but it did send me searching for sources that were so. And as I have shared my findings in the lecture room, I have found history becoming a most enjoyable subject to teach and the students have found it a most interesting one to study. With the Holy Spirit, it is not the same as it was in academia.

My studies have led me up some strange alleyways that are not even alluded to in the pages that follow. I have found the subject so vast that it could happily occupy many volumes, and so I have had to limit myself here to one or two central themes. The first, of course, is simply to trace the broad stream of pentecostal life down through the ages. To do that properly I have had to start with Samuel and the earliest prophetic movement in Israel, because the story is a continuous one, beginning long before the first Christian Pentecost, as indeed the early apostles themselves openly acknowledged (Acts 3:24-6). The biblical section is therefore partly a summary of volume three of *The Way of the Spirit* (*Heirs of the Prophets*), partly an expansion on it.

The second is that I have restricted myself largely to the history of movements and churches. To catalogue the lives of individuals would enlarge the work beyond reasonable limits and would also be a distraction from my central search. Just as today, many individuals have found new life in the Spirit, but have not thereby made any significant contribution to the church of their day or to the ongoing flow of history. They have generated no new movement and have stood aloof from what movements already exist, perhaps out of fear or embarrassment, but for whatever reason, while their experience may have enriched their own lives and ministries, they have not seen fit to encourage the same in others. By contrast, there have been those who have only been able to long for such things, or have no more than dimly perceived them, or because of the theological or spiritual impoverishment of the age or place in which they have lived have laid hold of them with imperfect understanding, and yet with what they have had they have spread an enthusiasm for life in the Spirit among their contemporaries that has impacted the church in their time and left a wake of spiritual ferment in history after them. Though they may not have been fully pentecostal by our definition today, and though their teachings may sometimes have been tinged with heresy, their heart was in the right place and their vision and aspiration was essentially for the same things, and so such men are of far more interest to us in this work than the occasional saint who spoke in tongues but never saw the need to encourage anyone else to do the same.

This book has therefore a very particular orientation. It is a history, not of the Church, nor of dissent, nor of revivals, nor of spiritual movements, but of specifically prophetic movements living in or longing for the blessing of Pentecost or the empowering of the Holy Spirit. The backdrop is indeed the church, dissent, revival and the like, and all that has to be reviewed in passing, but only in outline for the contextualisation of the movements we shall be studying.

This book is about a heart-longing after the full life of Pentecost in the Church as the apostles knew it. It is about the Spiritual Church, the mystical Church, the prophetic Church, the charismatic/pentecostal Church, the Church of revival life, the Church of the Spirit. Different people prefer different terminology, but the essence is the same.

Approaching history with these spectacles has led me to some surprising conclusions not normally voiced in Pentecostal circles. Protestants have been taught that the Reformation was the most significant event in the history of the Church after the apostolic age, and with that view most Pentecostals would entirely agree, adding, of course, that it is now surpassed by the phenomenal outpouring of the Spirit in our times. I therefore looked to the Reformation for first signs of a rebirth of the prophetic Church, but found only a quenching of it instead. To be sure, the recovery of the Bible and faith by the great reformers and the releasing of the Church from the shackles of Medieval Catholicism is not to be undervalued, but I found more evidence of prophetic sensitivity in the Medieval Church than I ever had expected, I discovered that the pivotal point in this history lay a full century later, after the dust of the Reformation had settled, when the European wars it generated were over, when men had grown tired of the doctrinal wranglings it aroused and once more began to hunger for deeper, more spiritual things. Hence the main division is in the middle of the seventeenth century.

This has been an interesting work to do. Because of my lack of training in the field of history, it has taken me a long time to dig out sources that most historians pass over unnoticed. Many of these had to be translated or updated, for they are generally unavailable to English readers today. For those interested, I have set my translations of the more important of these in an additional volume.

This work has taken me many years to complete, far more than I originally imagined it would. That is partly because life in the Spirit has been so full that I have had to write it in a very busy context of teaching and preaching, as well as producing other urgently needed books and manuals on the Bible and ministry. During these years others have written and published on related fields. There has been an increasing interest in most of the subjects I have dealt with and today there is much more source material available. This has made me wonder whether it is still worth publishing, but I do believe this volume has a contribution to make. I therefore submit it to public readership with a degree of apprehension, in the hope that others more competent than I will take up the challenge and produce something fuller and better.

I offer it as a work that I have thoroughly enjoyed doing, one that has given me great satisfaction and a good sense of fulfilment, and I pray that you, the reader, will find as much gratification in using it as I have had in researching and writing it. God bless you as you read on, and may he fill you with the same hope and joy as those you will read about, as they have known and experienced when they have opened their hearts and minds to the fullness of the Holy Spirit available to them through the sacrifice of his Christ and the promise of the Father.

*John McKay*

# Authors Note 1

**All the Lord's People Prophets?**

God's Spirit and his Word are like two hands he uses to perform all he has to do in relation to mankind and his world. Both were operative in creation and have been active in all history ever since. There have, however, been times when they have been more noticeably at work among the Lord's people than at others, and particularly when he has raised up prophets, people he has empowered with his Spirit to speak his word. Our intention is to scan history for traces of movements of such prophets and see how they relate to all that is happening in our churches today.

Moses once said, 'I wish all the LORD's people were prophets and that the LORD would put his Spirit on them!' (Num. 11:29) Our story takes us from that primitive longing to Israel's prophets foretelling its fulfilling, and on into the prophetic ministry of Jesus and the New Testament Church. The early church experienced the power of the Spirit to the full, but it slowly lost sight of its dynamic down the long ages of the medieval Church when it lay for the most part forgotten. However, not entirely so, and in the fires of revival in the post-Reformation centuries its vision was increasingly recaptured until the Pentecostal history of our own times in which we live in increasing measure in the good of it all once more.

Our primary purpose in tracing this story will be to show not only how God has never left himself without a prophetic witness in the Church, but more importantly how as Christians today we are heirs of Israel's ancient prophets and how akin our faith and our experience is to theirs and to that of their New Testament successors.

Our aim is to study individual prophetic movements, but their stories need to be read against the wider background of both secular and Church history. To that end each part of this book opens with a simplified overview of the main events of the times it covers.

PART ONE

# THE VISION OF A PROPHETIC PEOPLE IN BIBLE TIMES

The story we are about to tell is of a vision unfolding and coming to birth. The vision speaks of the Church of the Spirit, of a body of believers filled with the power and virtue of God's Holy Spirit, living the good and godly life he intended for man from the very start and equipped with his grace and gifting to do so.

No human birth is ever painless. Neither was the birthing of the Spiritual Church. The story is one of hope rising and falling, of great encouragements and great disappointments, of wonderful successes and disastrous failures. It tells of a struggle to get born, of the birth pangs of the Church of Christ.

But it is also the story of God's wonderful grace lavishly showered on the undeserving. Left to man himself it could never have happened, but God repeatedly repainted the vision through his prophets and performed great wonders through other men of the Spirit, until in the end he sent his own Son and through him brought the vision to fulfilment.

The story is a familiar one, but it is retold as the first part of this book so that its prophetic emphasis may be clearly grasped, since that is foundational for understanding the history of the Church of the Spirit after the time of the New Testament.

A fuller account of the thesis in this chapter is found in *Heirs of the Prophets*, which is volume 3 of *The Way of the Spirit.*

# 1
# From Adam to Christ

Any survey of the Bible's story must be selective. What follows is merely an outline of its main drift highlighting those aspects of it that are important for understanding the work and message of the Old Testament prophets and their successors in the Christian Church.

*Paradise Lost (Genesis 1–11)*

When God made the earth, 'he saw that it was good . . . very good' (1:4,10,12,18,21,25,31). Eden's Garden was a place of rustic idyll and harmony, a kind of everyman's Paradise. But man chose ways other than God's and lost it. Consequently sin, suffering and death multiplied, until 'God saw how corrupt the earth had become' and 'his heart was filled with pain' (6:12,6). The Flood expressed his judgment, but sin continued to multiply, culminating in the Babel fiasco which resulted in total alienation of man from both God and his fellow men.

*God's Covenant with Abraham—his Call and Promise (Genesis 12–50)*

About 2,000 BC God called Abraham, promising him land and descendants, and through them restoration of blessing to 'all the families of the earth' (12:1-3). Abraham responded in faith by moving to Canaan, but there he had to learn, through various trials, to continue to trust God's promises. They were partially fulfilled when children were born, but faith remained a challenge for them too and the Genesis story ends with them in Egypt, out of the land of promise. Nevertheless, the book does close on a note of hope with Joseph on his death-bed reminding his brothers of the promises God gave to their great forefather (50:24).

*God's Covenant with Moses—the Call to Obedience (Exodus – 1 Samuel)*

About 1,500 – 1,300 BC God called Moses and through him brought the Israelites out of Egypt. At Sinai he gave them his Law by which they might live in blessing through obedience. After much rebellion and a disciplinary forty years in the wilderness, Joshua successfully led them into their promised inheritance in Canaan. But in the period of the Judges that followed they went after other gods and found themselves oppressed by enemies, ending up enslaved again, this time by the Philistines. Once more, however, we see signs of hope as God's Spirit begins to stir in men raising up revival preachers (prophets: Samuel and others) and even a charismatic king (Saul)!

*God's Covenant with David and his New Covenant (1 Samuel – 2 Kings)*

The Israelites had hoped a king would solve their problems, but Saul's reign ended in tragedy. Hence, about 1,000 BC, God called David. To him he promised peace, greatness and for his descendants eternal rule (2 Sam. 7). Initially he saw success when he established an empire and when the reign of his son, Solomon, recaptured many of the glories of Eden (1 Kings 4:20f). But Solomon and his successors repeatedly turned to other gods, and so the kingdom split and gradually disintegrated, until the Northern Kingdom (Israel/Ephraim) fell to the Assyrians in 722 and the Southern (Judah) to the Babylonians in 597. Jerusalem was destroyed in 587 and Israel found itself once more in exile, this time in Babylonia.

Towards the end of this period we hear again a voice of hope, of prophets speaking about another covenant, a 'New Covenant', by which man's heart would be changed through the working of God's Spirit. The new age of this covenant was to be inaugurated by a Spirit-bearing man, later known as Messiah (cp. Hos. 2; Isa. 9-12; 60-62; Jer. 31,33; Ezek. 36-37).

*The Close of the Old Testament Age (Ezra, Nehemiah, etc.)*

When the Persians overthrew the Babylonian Empire in 539 BC, Jews started returning to Israel and a community was restored around Jerusalem. Its initial enthusiasm was much encouraged by prophets, especially Haggai and Zechariah, though it saw no immediate evidence of the ancient promises coming to fulfilment. By 400 BC the voice of prophecy had fallen silent and Jewish religion became increasingly legalistic and ritualistic. After the Persians, the Greeks ruled Palestine, and then, after a brief spell of independence, the Romans took over in 63 BC. Despite the apparent delays and setbacks the Jews never believed God's promises had failed. After the prophetic age they simply settled down quietly to wait for their Messiah and the new age of the Spirit. Also, thanks to their exile,

Jews were now strategically placed in all major centres of civilisation, preparing the world for the coming of Christianity.

*The Dawn of the New Covenant Age of the Spirit (The New Testament)*

Jesus came, born of the Spirit, filled with the Spirit, teaching and performing wonders in the anointing of the Spirit, like one of the prophets of old, yet with a power and authority hitherto unknown to men. He gathered disciples, trained them in his gospel-message and prepared them for the moment when they would themselves be endued with the Spirit, that is, for the long awaited time of the fulfilling of the New Covenant promise proclaimed by the prophets of the Old.

After Pentecost, the disciples, now filled with the prophetic Spirit themselves and armed with God's word, carried Jesus' message and ministry through the ancient world.

*Paradise Regained?*

2,000 years have passed, Eden is not yet restored, history is littered with evidences of man's continuing unfaithfulness, and the record of the Church is not always good. Nevertheless, at the end of the first century, John was granted a vision in which he saw down the course of earth's violent history to God's final hour with the blessings of Eden fully restored and man in Christ reigning as he was intended to at the start. That vision continues to inspire, while the power of Word and Spirit that moved in prophets and lived in Jesus has surfaced again and again among the prophetically-minded people whose story it is our purpose to follow, and it still works in our times giving a foretaste of Paradise and heralding the final recreation of all things.

# 2
# Samuel and Israel's First Prophetic Movement

'As you approach the town, you will meet a procession of prophets coming down from the high place with lyres, tambourines, flutes and harps being played before them, and they will be prophesying. The Spirit of the LORD will come upon you in power, and you will prophesy with them; and you will be changed into a different person.' That was what Samuel said to Saul as he sent him on his way home after prophetically anointing him to become Israel's first king. (1 Sam. 10:5f)

It had been a strange few days for Saul. He was a farmer's son, a handsome young man, from the tribal area of Benjamin in central Palestine. The events of the past twenty-four hours were so astonishing they must almost have made him forget he had only been sent by his father to look for a few lost donkeys. He had taken one of the farm servants with him but, though they had scoured the region thoroughly, they had not found the strays. Soon they became concerned that father might stop worrying about the donkeys and grow anxious about their own welfare instead, and so they decided to head for home. It was then that it all began to happen, a strange sequence of coincidences—or were they really just coincidences?

It so happened that, at the point they took their decision to return to the farm, they were quite near the town where Samuel was staying. The servant suggested that as a last resort they might consult him about the lost asses, and when Saul objected that they had no gift to take him, the servant just happened to produce something appropriate from his purse. And so it was decided to seek out Samuel.

As they were going up the hill to the town the second "coincidence" occurred. They met some girls coming out to draw water from the well and on enquiring where Samuel might be found, were told they had arrived just at the right moment, in the nick of time to catch him before he went up to offer sacrifice, for it was some special festival day in that place. And sure enough, just as they entered the town, there he was, though apparently they themselves did not recognise him. Considerable, therefore, must have been their delight when, having approached this stranger asking for direction to the seer's house, he announced, 'I am the seer.' But what he said next must have completely astonished them. He had been expecting them, he knew who they were, told them before they could ask about the donkeys that they had already been found, intimated he had other important matters to talk to Saul about, and invited him to join him at the sacrificial meal, in preparation for which he had already instructed the cook to prepare a special joint for his visitor.

Saul must have been very surprised indeed, but then Samuel was well known in the land as a man of God who could see things that other men could not. That, after all, was why they had come to him in the first place. But God had other purposes. That night, after the meal, Samuel took Saul to his home and sat with him in his roof-chamber talking into the small hours of the morning. We have no record of their conversation, but we can guess from the context that Samuel must have spent most of that time unveiling God's purposes for Saul to become Israel's first king and preparing him for the role.

The first part of his preparation was entirely spiritual. Next morning Samuel conducted them to the edge of the town where he sent the servant on ahead. Then in secret he prophetically anointed Saul for his future leadership. Saul's mind must have been in a whirl of excitement, but surely also of doubts and questions. To reassure him Samuel gave him a couple of prophetic signs to show his words were true, then told him that at Gibeah, he would meet a band of prophets playing musical instruments and prophesying. Then God would do for Saul all he needed to do before he became king: equip him with his Spirit, empower him to prophesy and turn him into a different person.

And so it was. As Saul went on his way, these things came to pass just as Samuel had said. The Spirit came upon Saul that day and he prophesied with the prophets. Some bystanders who recognised him were astonished. When he arrived home he said nothing about these things to his family, perhaps because he was too embarrassed to tell them, perhaps because it was all so new and strange he did not know what to say, perhaps because Samuel had counselled him to keep silent. His uncle seems to have noticed something had happened to him, but when he quizzed Saul, he could get nothing out of him except that Samuel told him the donkeys had been found.

Charismatics will find many familiar traits in this story. Apart from the matter of the kingship, it could almost have been written about events that have happened in some of our own lives in recent years. We can feel completely at home with Samuel's band of prophets playing their revival worship-music and exercising their charismatic gifts. (Whatever 'prophesying' means exactly in 10:5,10, it is clearly akin to the kind of thing that occurs in Charismatic settings today. Peter also used the same word about the tongues-speaking at Pentecost in Acts 2:16f—though, of course, there is no evidence that anyone in Old Testament times ever spoke in tongues.) The reaction of the bystanders is typical of the surprise and even mockery that friends and religious people direct against charismatics (cp. Acts 2:13), and Saul's own reactions—the inner change of heart and personality, the hesitancy to speak amongst relations—all these are familiar to the experience of modern-day Charismatics. There is nothing at all surprising or unusual about any of them, not even about Samuel's prophetic foreknowledge and his late-night conversations preparing Saul for receiving the Spirit. Many today have lived through very similar experiences.

What is significant, however, is that these things were happening for the first time in biblical history. Here for the first time ever we encounter a band of prophets bearing some resemblance to a modern Charismatic group at worship.

In his sermon in Acts 3, Peter speaks of 'all the prophets from Samuel on' as if prophecy began in his day (v. 24). Certainly there were a few individuals who were known as prophets before him, such as Abraham (Gen. 20:7), Miriam (Exod. 15:20), Moses (Hos. 12:13) and Deborah (Judg. 4:4), but there is no earlier trace of anything like a structured prophetic movement and so it is with Samuel that our story must start.

*Samuel's Call and his Prophetic, Revival Ministry*

He must have been born about 1085 BC, in an age of severe moral and religious decadence. The active exercise of the priestly office at Shiloh, the central sanctuary for the tribes of Israel at the time, had passed from the hands of the old priest Eli to his sons, Hophni and Phinehas, who are described as 'wicked men; they had no regard for the LORD' (1 Sam. 2:12). They are remembered only for their irreverence, their disgusting gluttony and their immoral sexual relationships with other members of the temple staff (2:13-17,22-24). In them, however, we only see reflected a more widespread malaise that characterised the age in which they lived.

The triumphant success of Joshua's conquest of Canaan and the distribution of the land among the tribes of Israel lay well in the past. Succeeding generations had lost hold of the faith and vision that had inspired his armies and had gradually drifted into the immorality and paganism of their Canaanite neighbours. The results were disastrous. By the end of the period of the judges morale in the nation had virtually collapsed and there was nothing to halt the aggressive expansionist inroads of their Philistine neighbours. By the time Samuel was in his teens, probably about 1070 BC, they were able to inflict a resounding defeat on Israel's troops at a place called Aphek, in the wake of which Shiloh and its temple were destroyed and the central regions of the land brought under their domination and control (1 Sam. 4–6; cp. Jer. 7:12-14).

It was in that setting that Samuel became a prophet. Himself the son of devout parents, he was dedicated to the LORD in infancy and raised at the temple under the tutelage of the old priest, Eli. Though unable to control his own godless sons, Eli certainly did not approve of their ways. He did have a measure of godliness about him and seems to have been able to keep Samuel from their waywardness, for under his care the boy 'grew in stature and in favour with the LORD and with men'.

One day a stranger appeared at the temple, a 'man of God', they called him. He approached Eli with strange prophetic speech, the like of which Samuel had never heard because 'in those days the word of the LORD was rare; there were not many visions' (3:1). With words that he said were from God, he told of judgment coming on Shiloh's priesthood. They were harsh and frightening words, but they also told how God would raise up another, a faithful priest, who would act according to God's heart.

The effect of this strange visitation on the young Samuel must have been profound, and it was probably not long afterwards that he had his own prophetic visitation when, in his night vision, he heard the same message confirmed to him personally by the voice of God himself. In the weeks and months that followed the Lord continued to reveal himself to Samuel through his word and it was not long before he came to be recognised as a prophet himself. Soon his prophetic words were being carried through all Israel (3:1 – 4:1).

Meantime the Philistines continued pressing into the land. When the Israelites were routed at Aphek, the prophecy about Eli's line was fulfilled, for both his sons were killed and he himself died on hearing the news. The temple was destroyed, the ark of the LORD was captured, and Israel hit rock bottom (chs. 4–6).

Revival seldom comes in an instant. The groundwork for it is often laid by faithful preaching of the word, calling men back to

God in repentance. So it was with Samuel. His story tells of twenty years of ministry before revival eventually broke forth in full blossom. During that time Samuel preached continuously to 'the whole house of Israel', pleading with them to abandon their pagan ways and return to the LORD, promising them his blessings if they did so. That remains the primary message of revival preaching, as we shall see, the same in every generation.

Under the impact of his preaching Israelites came together from all over the land for a national camp meeting to pray for revival. There they witnessed a powerful miracle from God when a Philistine ambush was set in disarray by a sudden, very violent thunderstorm. The result of all that was that Samuel became more than a prophet and preacher. In those days when there was no other leader of stature, he inevitably became recognised as Israel's judicial and political authority as well, particularly in central Canaan. The impression we get of him is of a man with a magnetic personality, a fine sense of judgment and a rich charismatic endowment. Nevertheless, he had his critics and they wanted a king to succeed him.

### *Saul's Prophetic Anointing and his Kingship*

It is in the course of the debates and events leading to Saul's appointment as king that we meet the other prophets, Samuel's friends, the ones Saul encountered on his way home from visiting Samuel, among whom he received the prophetic Spirit himself, the members of Israel's first prophetic movement.

By the time he left them, Saul had himself become a prophet—hence the saying popular at the time, 'Is Saul also among the prophets?' (10:12). With respect to the kingship, however, he still had to bide his time, for when presented a little later at a national assembly, he received general, though not complete, approval (10:17-27). He therefore returned to his farming, but then came a moment of crisis and the Spirit of God moved in him so powerfully that he led the Israelites to a resounding victory, which set the final seal on his election as king (ch. 11).

The message of the story is clear: Saul owed his crown entirely to the Spirit, mediated to him by the prophets. They were the ones, Samuel first and then his friends, who roused awareness of the Spirit's action in his life, preparing him for the moment of Spirit-inspired action leading to his establishment as national leader. The first king of Israel was a prophet, the direct product of a prophetic movement of the day. Samuel's ministry had not only brought the nation to the point of revival, but had also effectively drawn together a band of persons of a kindred, prophetic spirit whose impact on society was being strongly felt in more ways than one.

Their influence continued to be strong in Israel. We see that in the story of Saul's downfall and the raising of David to replace him. Samuel made and unmade kings. When he anointed David he too received the Spirit, just as Saul had before him (16:13). It was therefore natural that later, when David had to flee from Saul, it should be with Samuel and his prophets that he first sought refuge (ch. 19).

Meantime, Saul's misery increased. A charismatic who had lost his endowment, he became moody, withdrawn, melancholic and tormented (16:14-23). Occasionally he erupted in displays of mad temper against David, who now had the favour of the prophets. Eventually he was found consulting a spiritualist medium, the very antithesis and counterfeit of everything that prophets stand for (ch. 28).

### *The Faith of the Prophets and the Degree of their Impact*

The impression is of a movement that was not particularly large. It looks like a little company Saul met at Gibeah (ch. 10), and the astonishment of the onlookers when he prophesied with them suggests the majority of Israelites remained uncertain about these strange prophets. Though Samuel's own influence was strong, he did not turn Israel into a nation of enthusiasts overnight. Far from it. Even his own sons did not walk in his ways (8:3). Nor were the political and religious problems quickly resolved. Philistine domination continued, Shiloh's temple was never rebuilt and the ark lay abandoned in a private home. Though there are some bright highlights, the nation was still not on its feet again. It is in that context this prophetic movement's impact is to be assessed. However, even if few, they were certainly not lacking in spirit, and that more than anything else is the key to the measure of their influence.

We noted earlier a broad affinity between their worship in 10:5-13 and prophetic worship today. We see them at worship again in 19:18-24. In both places it is said they were 'prophesying', though it is by no means clear what that signifies. In ch. 10 they did so accompanied by musical instruments and in ch. 19 the effect of their worship was to cause others to fall to the ground. In both places this prophesying is attributed to the direct action of God's Spirit and those familiar with singing and falling in the Spirit today will no doubt readily draw parallels. There are, however, cultural and theological borders to cross in doing so, and it would not be right to make too much of such parallels, other than to note the broadly familiar atmosphere. Many of today's Charismatics would doubtless have found themselves very much at home among Samuel's men.

The conclusion is clear. Samuel's men were the prophetic products of a lively revival campaign in an age of decline. Lives were changed, miracles witnessed, enthusiasm openly expressed. They were intoxicated with God. When they assembled and worshipped they 'prophesied' together, thus affording each other the mutual encouragement of shared experience, which must have done a lot to strengthen their sense of solidarity, as it still does in Charismatic meetings today. Though few in number and scorned by many, they were resolute in faith and there was something contagious about their fervour. They were also blessed with a strong, stable leader of national standing and they delighted in keeping alive the stories of his great acts. Their contribution to history was ultimately far in excess of their numbers, not only in that they kept the faith alive in their generation, nor that the first kings of Israel rose from their ranks, but also that they laid the first foundations for all subsequent prophetic movements.

*Samuel's Story and Charismatic Biography*

Before moving on with the Bible's story, it is worth commenting a little further on this early movement, partly because in it so many of the patterns we shall find in later movements are already discernible.

We meet Samuel and his men through stories about them and are told hardly anything about their teaching, unlike the later prophets from Amos onwards. The stories tell of men who are charismatics, on fire with God's Spirit, led by a great revival preacher calling the people back to God, sometimes with miraculous demonstrations of supernatural power, sometimes with dynamic words inspired by God, sometimes with both. As we read them, it is good to bear in mind what kind of literature we are handling. Their nearest modern equivalent is found, not in history books, or secular biographies, or legends of ancient heroes, but in some of the Charismatic biographies found in our religious bookshops. These delight in the workings of God more than of men and tell their stories mainly for his glory. They focus on moments in a man's life when God has worked dramatically, usually starting with some account of how, in a setting of personal, spiritual emptiness and corresponding dryness in his church environment, the Spirit first began to work in and through him, then progressing to tell how his preaching subsequently became more effective, with the result that his hearers' lives were radically changed, some of them receiving the same spiritual anointing as he has experienced. Interwoven with that will be tales of signs and wonders adding confirmation to the witness of God's power in his life and encouraging others to respond to his preaching with the same kind of enthusiasm as he has himself.

The purpose in writing these biographies is normally to encourage those who know the power of such anointing to stand firm in their faith, and to draw those that do not closer to desiring and even experiencing it themselves. To be sure, the Old Testament prophet-stories are preserved as historical records of the words and deeds of the prophets, but as we read them we sense that same delight in the workings of the Spirit as we do in reading their modern counterparts. They are stories written by prophetic men about prophets to encourage other prophetic men and to testify to the workings of God's Spirit through the prophets for the benefit of the rest of God's people. The later prophets sought to draw men back to God by writing down the prophets' teachings, the earlier prophets sought to do the same by writing down the records of his revival power working through them.

*Prophecy and Revival*

The first prophetic movement, like so many later ones, was born in a cradle of decline, at the end of the period of the judges, a time of loss of vision, religious decadence and political instability. But even in that darkest hour God was at work preparing some to lead his people back to himself. And, in the power of the Spirit, they brought revival. Samuel spent his life's energies to that end, knowing revival was the nation's only answer. He therefore knew the absolute necessity for Saul to catch the same revival spirit before becoming king. If the revival impetus was to be maintained, Samuel's successor had to be a revivalist/prophet/charismatic like himself. Hence the events of chs. 9–11 must have given him some measure of satisfaction, but equally we can understand the degree of his distress when Saul began to let go of that revival dynamic (15:34f). Fortunately he was able to ensure that David got hold of it at an early stage in his life (16:1-13), and it seems that unlike Saul he never let it go. And no more clearly is that seen than in the way David encouraged the use of music in worship.

*Revival and Worship*

Down the centuries of Christian history hymn-writing has regularly gone hand in hand with revival. At times when men have discovered

God afresh, there has usually been a fresh burst of praise that has issued in a flood of new songs. So it was in the Wesleyan revival of the eighteenth century, so also in the nineteenth century during the campaigns of Sankey and Moody, then again at the beginning of the twentieth century in connection with the Pentecostal revival, and then with the growth of the Charismatic Movement.

Something similar seems to have happened in Samuel's Israel. One of the reasons why the psalms are so firmly associated with David, apart from the fact that he is said to have written some of them, is that it was during his reign that public worship in Israel was first expressed in music and song (1 Chron. 15:16; 16:4-7,39-42; 23:30, 25:1,6f). And that too could well be one of the effects of Samuel's revival.

David's biographer includes a few of his songs in his life story (2 Sam. 1,22,23), but apart from that only mentions his musical skills at the beginning, soon after he introduces him to us (1 Sam. 16). At that stage David was closely associated with Samuel and his prophets, who themselves enjoyed worshipping with music (1 Sam. 10:5). Before their time there is no record of any public or corporate worship accompanied by music in the Old Testament. Yes, there were poems and songs written and sung by individuals, such as Moses or Deborah (Exod. 15; Judg. 5). Moses even composed one the Israelites had to learn by heart to help them remember how God had cared for them, but we do not know if it was ever intended to be sung corporately in public worship (Deut. 31:19; 31:30 – 32:43). The law says nothing about music in worship and so the impression we get is that it was an innovation of David's day, with its origins lying back in the outburst of prophetic praise that accompanied Samuel's revival. Some of his psalms we still sing today might even have originated in that flood of new songs associated with the prophetic revival of his childhood days.

*The Political Impact of Revival*

Revival, however, is not just about songs. The effect of Samuel's prophetic preaching was to put fibre and vision back into the lives of the Israelites, so that in the generation after him David was able to establish the kingdom as a small empire of some standing in the ancient world. The ark was restored to the proper care of priests in a new sanctuary in Jerusalem (2 Sam. 6) and in the reign of his son, Solomon, a proper temple was built to house it (1 Kings 6–9). By that time the mood had changed radically from depression to optimism. National hope now found its focus in the new Davidic monarchy that had proved so successful under God and to which God promised even greater things (2 Sam. 7). The work of Samuel's men in generating all this should not be underestimated. Nor should the encouragement we may take from their example when we become engaged in prophetic revival ministry ourselves.

## 3

# Elijah, Elisha and the Sons of the Prophets

There continued to be prophets in Israel after Samuel, but their stories are not always particularly memorable. An explanation is not hard to find: their revival work was done, the kingdom was established, and so their voice became eclipsed by that of the palace. Whereas Samuel had made kings, prophets now attended David at his court. Gad became known as 'David's seer' (2 Sam. 24:11) and Nathan was readily at hand to be consulted when David was toying with the idea of building a temple (7:1-3). We even find Nathan at the end of David's life actively participating in the political wrangling that attended the succession of Solomon to the throne (1 Kings 1).

To be sure, there were a few who acted in a memorable way. Nathan spoke out against David's seduction of Bathsheba (2 Sam. 12) and Gad challenged him about his census of fighting men. Ahijah of Shiloh encouraged Jeroboam to rebel against Solomon and establish an independent northern kingdom, while Shemaiah restrained Rehoboam, Solomon's son, from retaliating (1 Kings 11–12). An unnamed 'man of God' condemned Jeroboam for setting up sanctuaries with bull-images and one called Jehu denounced his son for continuing to patronise them (1 Kings 13 & 16). Early in the following century another called Hanani was put in prison for challenging King Asa of Judah about his unfaithfulness in the later part of his reign (2 Chron. 16:7-10).

Some of the prophets clearly never lost sight of the basic principles that had called them into being in the first instance, and so there were those that did see positive fruit in national revival on a number of occasions. At the beginning of his reign Asa led the people of Judah back to faith in a memorable work of revival, in which he was encouraged by a prophet called Azariah (2 Chron. 15). His son, Jehoshaphat, was advised and confronted by prophets on several occasions (2 Chron. 18–21). But on the whole the movement seems to have settled into a kind of stagnant respectability, even enjoying considerable royal patronage, so much so that Jehoshaphat and Ahab were able to summon about four hundred of their prophets for advice on one occasion. Even then there was frustration that a 'prophet of the Lord' could only be found in Micaiah (1 Kings 22). It is hardly surprising the movement made little history for a century or more.

All that changed when Ahab ascended the northern throne in 874 BC. His wife, Jezebel, was an ardent devotee of the Canaanite gods, Baal and Asherah, for whom she erected a sanctuary in the capital, Samaria (1 Kings 16:32f), and in whose service she retained 850 pagan prophets (18:19). Worse still, she sought to silence the opposition—which was voiced mainly by Israel's own prophets, many of whom were forced into hiding as a result (18:4). So thorough was her persecution that Elijah at one point thought he was the only true prophet left (19:10,14). For the first time in its history the very faith of Israel was in danger of being extinguished. The crisis was different from that of Samuel's day, but the ultimate danger was not entirely dissimilar, and again it was the charismatic enthusiast who responded to the challenge and saved the day.

*The Revival Ministries of Elijah and Elisha*

Jezebel's chief opponent at first was Elijah. He is remembered most for his exercise of miracle-working power: effectively pronouncing an extended drought in the land, supernaturally providing food for a widow, then raising her son from the dead, and particularly for outmanoeuvring the Baal prophets on Mount Carmel by calling down fire from heaven (chs. 17–18). Such activities, coupled with his open criticism of royal policy (ch. 21), scarcely endeared him to Jezebel, from whom he spent much of his time in hiding. But to the prophets he championed he was nothing less than a giant, one who like Moses spoke with God himself on the holy mountain (ch. 19).

Elijah was not, however, the only prophet to speak out against Ahab and Jezebel. Micaiah, for example, had the reputation of one who never prophesied good about him and found himself put in prison as a result (ch. 22). But by far the most famous of the regime's opponents besides Elijah was his disciple, Elisha, about whose ministry many spectacular stories are preserved (2 Kings 2–9 & 13): how he sterilised the putrid wells of Jericho, cursed the jeering youths of Bethel, prophesied a miraculous flood to confound the armies of Moab, created a wondrous supply of oil to clear a widow's debts, like Elijah raised a dead boy to life, neutralised poison in a pot of soup, fed a large gathering with inadequate food supplies, healed a

Syrian commander of skin disease, caused an axe-head lost in the river to rise to the surface, caused blindness to fall on a troop of Syrian invaders, and how his prophesying helped in lifting the siege of Samaria. Then even in his grave chance contact with his corpse restored a dead man to life.

Perhaps the most consequential of all his actions, however, was not a miracle, but his sending a fellow prophet to anoint one of the army officers, called Jehu, to be king over Israel and to commission him to suppress the pagan house of Ahab, still actively ruling in the persons of King Jehoram, Jezebel the queen-mother and some seventy other sons of Ahab. Jehu responded with enthusiasm and quickly engineered the extermination of the whole royal family, together with all Jezebel's retinue of Baal priests (chs. 9–10). Hence the battle for the faith that had been spear-headed by the prophets for many years was finally won by the sword of a man who, like Saul, David and Jeroboam, had been roused to the task by the prophets themselves. This was to be the last occasion in Bible times, though not the last in history, that a prophetic movement would advocate the use of military force for the defence of the faith.

*The Sons of the Prophets*

In the course of these stories we find little windows through which we glimpse the life-style of the prophets of this age. They were known as 'the sons of the prophets'. They came together in some kind of fellowship structure to share their lives as they pursued their common vision. At least some of them lived in community (2 Kings 6:1-7) and shared common meals (4:38-44). Perhaps some were unmarried, as Elijah and Elisha seem to have been, but not all, for we read about their widows and children (4:1-7). Groups of them were found at large towns, such as Jericho and Bethel (2:3,5), though Elijah and Elisha themselves moved quite freely around the country, as Samuel had done. They called Elisha 'My lord' (6:5) and were said to 'sit before him' (literally meaning 'be taught by him'; NIV translates 'meet with him' – 4:38). However, it is unlikely that his authority rested on anything other than recognition of his personal charismatic endowment, which he had amply demonstrated from the moment his own master, Elijah, had been taken from him, when he divided the water of the Jordan before their very eyes (2:12-15).

The overall impression is of groups of like-minded people living or congregating in different parts of central Palestine, seeking to cultivate some kind of communal existence, presumably focused on their prophetic worship (which is nowhere described), and visited from time to time by the man they recognised as their leader. We have no statement of their beliefs, but it is clear that they were Israel's charismatic enthusiasts. Though we lack enough detail to make a full comparison, the picture is reminiscent of Samuel and his men, and in many ways bears comparison with revival communities and fellowships today. Again, though we are shown nothing of their worship, the story about Elisha calling for a minstrel to calm his anger and put him in the right mood for hearing God's word (3:14f) does remind us of Samuel's men prophesying to the accompaniment of their musical instruments and also compares well with present-day Christian experience of the prophetic word being received most readily in the setting of worship (cp. 1 Cor. 14).

*False Prophets*

A little more must be said about ninth-century prophecy. It would be wrong to leave the impression it was a uniform revival movement. Not all prophets were members of the Elijah-Elisha group. There were the pagan prophets, of course, and solitary prophets like Micaiah, but there was also Zedekiah's group of four hundred mentioned in 1 Kings 22 (and perhaps other similar groups) who were apparently quite happy to be the king's yes-men. This was an age in which the problem of distinguishing the true voice of God from the false must have been acute, as is amply illustrated from the account of the confrontation between Zedekiah and Micaiah. Not only did Micaiah give a prophetic word that contradicted Zedekiah's, but even claimed the LORD had shown him that Zedekiah was prophesying under the impulse of a lying spirit. Quite naturally Zedekiah was indignant and the king, having no other standard by which to judge, heeded the majority. This failure to distinguish the true from the false was to cost him his life.

The problem was even more intractable than 1 Kings 22 might suggest. It is understandable that the king, or anyone else with no personal prophetic experience, should have some difficulty in discerning the true word of God, but should not one who was himself a prophet have a greater degree of spiritual perception? In theory, yes, but in practice it was often otherwise, as is evidenced by the story in 1 Kings 13, which tells how a man of God who had just pronounced an absolutely authentic word from the LORD was himself subsequently deceived by a false word from an older prophet who also claimed his inspiration was from the LORD.

The problem of true and false prophecy is a continuing one. The Old Testament does suggest a few guide-lines for approaching it, such as: that the prophetic word should not contradict the received traditions of the faith (Deut. 13:1-5), that the prophecy which does not come to pass should be rejected as false (Deut. 18:21f), that a true prophet speaks not visions from his own mind, filling his hearers with vain hopes, but only visions that issue from his having 'stood in the council of the LORD to see or to hear his word' (Jer. 23:16-18), and that his life style should be that of a holy man of God and not self-seeking (Mic. 3:5,11). Useful as these criteria are, it is clear that more were needed. We shall be returning to this subject again, because it arises afresh with every new move of prophecy.

*The Prophet's Authority*

A prophet might sometimes declare his own conviction about the authenticity of his word by alluding to the means by which he received it: for example, by stating quite bluntly that God had spoken to him personally and using such phrases as 'the LORD has spoken it' or 'thus says the LORD' (1 Kings 14:11; 20:13); by telling of visions, like Micaiah's (22:19-22), or of angelic communications, like Elijah's (19:5-7); by simply indicating that he knew the operation of the Spirit or the hand of God upon him (2 Kings 3:15). Later movements sometimes appealed to their miracles as witnesses to their message, and although this is not done overtly by the Old Testament prophets, their collections of miracle stories must surely have afforded added testimony to the worth of their utterances.

Certainly many in Israel, from king to commoner, came to regard the prophets with an awesome respect. They were people who seemed to stand very close to God—'men of God' they were often called—and while contact with them could bring great blessings, such as the gift of a child (2 Kings 4:16ff) or a supernatural provision of food (1 Kings 17:14-16), it could also be dangerous, as some discovered in most costly ways (2 Kings 1:9-16; 2:23-25). Some sought their blessings or consulted them for guidance (e.g. 1 Kings 14:1-16), but others, even those very close to them, feared their holiness and the judgment of God it might bring on them (1 Kings 17:18). Others, of course, regarded them with disdain, dismissing them as madmen (2 Kings 9:11).

*Prophetic Behaviour*

Some of the scorn they suffered was doubtless generated by observation of their unusual behaviour, particularly in worship. Here we have to resort to a measure of speculation, because the only group worship described is the frenzied, orgiastic incantation of the Baal prophets in 1 Kings 18:26-28 and the corporate 'prophesying' of Zedekiah's four hundred while he spoke the word either holding or wearing iron horns that were supposed to symbolise the bull-like strength with which the Israelite armies were to defeat the Syrians. It would be wrong to deduce the behaviour of 'the sons of the prophets' from the actions of these prophets and false prophets, as some have wanted to do.

On the other hand, most prophetic movements have left accounts of unusual experiences and activities, such as visions, auditions, strong emotional sensations, trances, utterances in unknown languages, exuberant singing and shouting, dancing, jumping and the like. As we shall see from the surveys that follow in this book, these tend to be governed to some degree by social context and to vary from movement to movement, but aa tend to be fairly stereotyped within any one movement. Doubtless the ninth century prophets had their own stereotypical actions and manifestations, though we cannot now say what these would have been.

*Summary and Conclusion*

Probably because of Samuel's personal influence, the prophets enjoyed royal patronage from the beginning, and therefore a considerable level of social acceptance. This continued association with the court, even if not always on the happiest of terms, must have done much to promote their growth over the years, but the mantle of respectability equally did much to blunt their impact and led many into false ways. By the ninth century the number of prophets in Israel had certainly increased, but also the fighting spirit in many of them had cooled as they took comfortable refuge in their charismatic communities. The pattern is still a familiar one in prophetic churches today.

Nevertheless, because of their spiritual understanding and heritage of enthusiasm, the prophets were the ones best prepared for the day of crisis and when it came they rose to the occasion, or at least some of them did. Not only did they witness revival in the nation as a result, but also something of a revival among themselves. Their spiritual boldness won them the reputation of preservers of Israel's faith, God's front-line warriors in the holy war against paganism, religious apathy and all decadence. It was a role they delighted to play, as the tales of their heroes so fondly portray, but then it is the role to which charismatics are called in every age, which is why we find in them such kindred spirits even after almost three thousand years.

# 4
# The Visions of the Great Writing Prophets

In another book on prophecy this would be by far the longest chapter, but our concern here is with prophetic movements, not the details of each individual prophet's teaching. Our problem is that while there is evidence of a continuing wider movement of prophets in and after the eighth century, it is not entirely clear how the great writing prophets related to them.

*The Last Traces of Israel's Wider Prophetic Circles*

The movements in Samuel's and Elisha's days were mostly active in the northern half of Israel. Amos, the earliest of the writing prophets, also ministered in the north and spoke respectfully of the prophets he knew in the mid-eighth century, as men raised up by God, to whom he revealed his purposes (2:11; 3:7). However, he denied that he belonged to their circle himself, claiming that his own background was entirely secular and that the LORD called him to prophesy quite independently (7:14f). Hosea, also a northern prophet, likewise spoke appreciatively of the prophets as the mouthpieces of God's judgment and the teachers and protectors of Israel's faith (6:5; 12:10-14), though he was also critical of some of their shortcomings (4:4-6). When the North fell to the Assyrians in 722 BC, many of these prophets must have died or been taken into exile, but some of them doubtless found refuge in the South and may have been among those anonymous prophets who spoke out against the abuses of Manasseh's reign in the early half of the seventh century, paying for their boldness with their lives (2 Kings 21:10-16). Not in vain, however, for Manasseh's grandson, Josiah, led the nation in reform and revival after his death, and that may well have been the fruit of their earlier prophetic witness (chs. 22–23).

In sharp contrast, the great southern prophets have little that is complimentary to say about the wider circles of prophets in Jerusalem and Judah. Micah pours scorn on their greedy, money-seeking ways and their empty utterances (Mic. 3:5,11); Isaiah speaks of prophets who teach lies (Isa. 9:15); Jeremiah declares that they are ungodly men, caring little about increasing paganism and injustice in the land and uttering words that are no more than thoughts of their own minds, men with no revelation, prophesying lies (Jer. 23:9-40); Ezekiel dismisses them similarly as 'foolish prophets who follow their own spirit and have seen nothing' (Ezek. 13:3). One of the recurrent themes in their criticisms is that the prophets give too many encouragements of the wrong sort, crying 'Peace' when there is no peace (Mic. 3:5; Ezek. 13:10), saying 'Is not the LORD among us? No disaster will come upon us.' (Mic. 3:11), filling people's minds with empty hopes (Jer. 23:16), for example, by encouraging the exiles in Babylon to expect they would be free to return to their homes within two years (Jer. 28:11; 29:8f). Of course, that was what the priests of Jerusalem loved to hear, because it bolstered up their own dogma that Jerusalem, as the seat of the Davidic kings and the place of the temple, was under God's eternal protection (cp. Psalms 2, 46, 48). These prophets do not at all look like the successors of the zealotic Elijah or Elisha. History would produce more prophets like them, who succumbed to ecclesiastical or political pressure to prop up a one-sided theological view-point, the party line, at the expense of calling men into a new relationship with God.

*The Great Classical Prophets and the Earlier Prophets*

It is debatable how far we can speak of the succession of writing prophets as a movement. They were certainly not a coherently organised group with recognised leaders as the older prophets had been. Some of them did gather disciples of their own who collected and edited their sayings: for example, Isaiah had his followers write down his words and keep them, and Jeremiah's scribe, Baruch, even copied down his oracles at his dictation (Isa. 8:1,16; 30:8; Jer. 36:2-4,32). However, there is no evidence of any significant interplay between the major prophets themselves, or their followers. Occasionally the same oracle may appear in two prophetic books (e.g. Isa. 2:2-4 = Mic. 4:1-3), but otherwise the prophets made no reference to each other's ministries or teaching. (In Jer. 26 it is not Jeremiah himself, but some elders and the editor that make mention of Uriah and Micah.) And so, if we are to speak of a movement at all, it must be mainly one of thought or revelation, not an organisation.

The writing prophets are not to be thought entirely distinct or different from the earlier prophets. Their experiences were similar and clearly belong to the same continuum of religious tradition. The accounts of their experience of God are every bit as striking as those of Samuel or Elisha. Jeremiah speaks of a fire burning in his heart and of limbs shaking like a drunken man's (Jer. 20:9; 23:9); Ezekiel of falling to the ground, being lifted up in the spirit, feeling the hand of God upon him, and the like (Ezek. 1:28; 3:12,22); Micah of being 'filled with power, with the Spirit of the LORD' (Mic. 3:8). Amos saw awesome visions of locusts, fire, a plumb-line and summer fruit, signifying messages about judgment (Amos 7–8); Isaiah had a remarkable visionary encounter with God in his heavenly throne-room (Isa. 6); Ezekiel was granted most dramatic and majestic visions of God's glory (Ezek. 1–3, 8–11, 43–44); God revealed himself to Habakkuk as a mighty warrior, so vividly that he all but collapsed at the sight (Hab. 3). Not only did they see visions, but they also spoke with God: Amos became a prophet when God ordered him to 'Go, prophesy' (Amos 7:15); Hosea was specifically commanded to marry his prostitute-wife (Hos. 1:2); Jeremiah even argued with God over his call (Jer. 1:5-10) and spoke about hearing God's word in his heavenly council, as Micaiah had (23:18). Like the earlier prophets, they were men called and sent by God, his messengers, bearers of the divine word, with the same zeal for God and for the urgent revival needs of his people. Hence they met with the same mixture of respect and scorn—heeded by kings, as were Isaiah and Micah (Isa. 37; Jer. 28:9f), yet mocked, persecuted and murderously hounded, like Isaiah and Jeremiah (Isa. 28:9f; Jer. 26, 37f). These were clearly men of the same spirit as their prophet forebears.

The main difference between the earlier prophets and them is that the former were remembered mostly for their wonder-working feats and revival ministries, while few of their sayings have survived, whereas the latter seem to have performed few miracles and their books are cherished almost exclusively for the teaching they contain. Their main concern was to share their revelation, rather than their experiences. It is not that they thought experience unimportant, but theirs was primarily a movement of word or message, and so it is to that that we must now turn.

*The Message of the Prophets*

First and foremost, their word was a denunciation of sin and a call to repentance, or a recall to the standards set down in the ancient laws of Moses. They criticised the religious establishment for maintaining outward displays of piety that corresponded little with the inner lives of the worshippers: plenty of rituals, offerings, songs, prayers and festivals, but little morality or social concern (Isa. 1;

Amos 5). Samuel had played the same tune, but then prophecy is basically a protest against laxity and decadence in the church in every age.

Their vision was by no means limited to the church. More often their word was addressed to all who would listen, sometimes to kings, leaders and private individuals, again like the older prophets, but mostly to all 'Israel' or 'Judah'. Predominantly they spoke of sin and punishment, or of repentance and hope. Thus Amos inveighed against injustice and corruption, while Hosea bewailed Israel's unfaithfulness in turning to other gods. Both of them warned of fearful judgment that must result in the form of enemy invasion, but they also saw beyond that to a future restoration with exiled captives returning to rebuild their ruined homeland. Hosea in particular spoke of that coming age as a time when God's people would have a new intimate relationship with him, when they would become totally faithful and would truly 'know the LORD' (Amos 9 and Hos. 2).

Their prophecies of judgment were vindicated when the North fell to Assyria in 722 BC, but their message, speaking both judgment and hope, continued to be heard through their successors in the South. Isaiah in particular, while warning Judah that her behaviour would bring the same kind of disaster as Israel had suffered, went on to tell of a purified remnant surviving the judgment and of a new day of light and joy for the faithful when a son of David, endowed with the (prophetic) Spirit, would lead them into an age of paradisal peace and blessing (Isa. 9, 11, 32). Jeremiah, who cherished a similar hope (Jer. 30–33), spoke of the need for a profound change in human hearts before it could be realised. He fully recognised this was not a change men could effect themselves, but one that would have to be wrought by God. However, the day was coming, he said, when God would make a 'new covenant' with his people. He would put his law within them, 'write it on their hearts'. Then they would all know the LORD in a perfect relationship based on forgiveness and obedience (Jer. 31:31-4).

Ezekiel went one step further. During his ministry the predicted judgment on Judah which took place when Jerusalem fell to the Babylonians in 597 BC, and so in the latter part of his book he concentrates on the coming new age. He too saw a change in man's heart and, like Jeremiah, that it would be God's doing, but he added the insight that it would be wrought by the operation of the Spirit: 'I will give you a new heart and put a new spirit within you; I will remove from you your heart of stone and give you a heart of flesh.

And I will put my Spirit in you.' (Ezek. 36:26f) In saying that Ezekiel was to all intents and purposes telling that the renewed people of the coming age would themselves possess the prophetic Spirit. Something similar is found in the book of Isaiah, which tells, not only that Messiah will be endowed with the Spirit (Isa. 11:2; 42:1; 61:1), but that there will be a more general outpouring of the Spirit from on high for all God's people (32:15; 44:3). The point is made much more bluntly in Joel 2:28f:

*And afterwards,*
*I will pour out my Spirit on all people.*
*Your sons and daughters will prophesy,*
*your old men will dream dreams,*
*your young men will see visions.*
*Even on my servants, both men and women,*
*I will pour out my Spirit in those days.*

The clear vision of Israel's prophets was that their experience of God would be shared by all his people, in some measure at any rate. It is touching to think that well before their day the longing that it might be so was already expressed when Moses once said to Joshua, 'I wish all the LORD's people were prophets, and that the LORD would put his Spirit on them!' (Num. 11:29). Moses would have been thrilled to hear the good news Isaiah, Ezekiel and Joel had to tell.

*Prophecy after the Exile*

By the time of the exile the prophetic vision was almost complete. In the day of crisis, when the nation was being plunged into darkness without any hope, the prophets had laid a foundation of faith for the future. The devastation of exile was not the end. God would remain true to his ancient promises. One day he would send his king (Messiah), regather his scattered people and give them a new start, released from the sin that had undermined their faith and equipped with his Holy Spirit. This vision for the future spiritual age was probably one of the main reasons why their sayings were preserved, assuring faith for the future of a beleaguered people. A few post-exilic prophets added the finishing touches, and then the voice of prophecy fell silent round about 400 BC.

Though warnings about the consequences of sin were still heard, the main drift of post-exilic prophecy was to offer encouragement, as, for example, when Haggai and Zechariah exhorted the leaders and people in rebuilding the temple. The word they spoke to spur them on to faith focused largely on the future glory of Jerusalem as God's holy city, where he would be known to be personally present among his people and where he would be seen to reign as king over the earth. Its population would increase greatly and become highly blessed with prosperity, long life and happiness, while pagan nations would come there seeking the LORD and bringing him tribute. (See Zech. 8, for example.) Such pictures are found also in the earlier writing prophets, but the post-exilic prophets seem to focus more attention on them.

Their vision is essentially that of Eden's blessings restored to the LORD's people in the end-time, and as such is of the very essence of biblical hope. It is part of a prophet's calling to remind the faithful of this hope and so encourage them in their walk with God. Sometimes a distant vision is what they highlight most, sometimes it is the more immediate or intermediate future, but the overall sequence is basically the same:

1. in the present time God must act in judgment to deal with sin,
2. in the longer term he will introduce a new age in which his Spirit will be given to change the course of history radically,
3. in the end he will restore the world to its original goodness.

Prophets since biblical times have continued to emphasise the various aspects of this vision, though sometimes focusing attention more on the eternal states, sometimes more on the historical outworkings. Though the prophetic movements we shall be looking at in this book were generally more preoccupied with establishing the work of the Spirit now, thoughts of end times were seldom far from their consciousness.

'Surely the Sovereign LORD does nothing without revealing his plan to his servants the prophets,' said Amos. All the revelation needed to prepare for Christ's coming had been given by the end of the fifth century and prophecy had dwindled to extinction. There were some who tried to perpetuate the prophetic gift, but Zech. 13:2-6 portrays them as men without true vision who resorted to empty practices, such as wearing hair-cloth garments and indulging in the laceration rituals of paganism. They are dismissed as false prophets, the last representatives of a dying movement clutching at useless straws. By the time the author of 1 Maccabees told how Judas Maccabeus delivered the Jews from their Greek persecutors in the second century BC, prophecy was a thing of the past, for he wrote of Israel's suffering in 161 saying it was 'worse than any since the day when prophets ceased to appear among them'

(9:27). Nevertheless, the final prophetic vision had told of a future rebirth of prophecy associated with the coming of Messiah and its last utterances had foretold that he would be preceded by a herald, identified as Elijah (Mal. 3:1; 4:5). The Gospel tells how these things came to pass.

*The Prophets and Revival*

The impact of the prophets' teaching in their own time (as opposed to their long-range vision) varied greatly from prophet to prophet and from age to age. Amos and Hosea were not well received by their contemporaries and saw no revival—only their warnings coming to pass in the fall of Samaria in 722 BC. Isaiah and Micah, on the other hand, lived in an age of revival in Judah, during the reign of the good King Hezekiah. He led the nation back to God and re-established worship and faith sufficiently to enable his people to stand firm on the day Jerusalem was surrounded by the armies of Assyria (2 Kings 18–19). At that time Isaiah preached faith and the king heeded him, unlike his father, Ahaz, to whom Isaiah had preached the same message (Isa. 7, 36–37). Isaiah's part in this revival is unquestionable.

In the following century, Jeremiah and his contemporaries, Zephaniah, Nahum and Habakkuk, did not see the same results. They also called for repentance and faith, but their words were mostly rejected, so much so that Jeremiah found himself constantly persecuted and eventually imprisoned for his message. He too called for a return to God but, like Amos and Hosea in the north before him, had to watch God's hand of judgment descend when Jerusalem was taken by the Babylonians in 597 and destroyed by them in 587 BC. He was as much a revival preacher as Samuel, Elijah, or Isaiah, but his age would not receive him, and so had to bear the consequences of its rejection of the word of God.

The teachings of Isa. 40–55 must have stirred positive faith and hope among the exiles, for many of them came back to Judea after the Babylonian Empire was overthrown and the Persians allowed the exiles to return home. When this initial enthusiasm began to flag, two prophets, Haggai and Zechariah, roused their leaders, Zerubbabel, the Governor, and Joshua, the High Priest, to renewed faith and vision, which led to the temple being rebuilt and its regular worship restored.

Whether they saw the effects of their prophesying in revival or in judgment, the heart of the writing prophets was always the same, to see the LORD's people return to him in repentance, faith and obedience, and so be saved from the consequences of their sin. They were truly the heirs of Samuel and Elijah in the work of revival for their time.

*Conclusion*

Down the several centuries of their history, the Old Testament prophets established their own special ethos with certain recognisable patterns of speech and behaviour. There was, of course, no uniformity, but through all their differences, and even disputes, we see something distinctive that clearly marked them off from the prophets of other nations, like the Baal prophets with their frenzied dances (1 Kings 18:26-28), or the Babylonian soothsayers reading signs from animal entrails (Ezek. 21:21), or the mediumistic witch of Endor summoning up the spirits of the dead (1 Sam. 28). Any such activities among the prophets of Israel were constantly regarded as aberrations. These were men of a different order altogether, calling their people back to God in repentance, urging them forward into revival, and assuring them of a glorious future with him. They were distinct in the ancient world, and the treasuring of their words and deeds hallowed their spirit for posterity, setting standards from which no future prophetic movement could ever greatly diverge. And their own vision was that some such movement as theirs would again arise in Israel.

By the fourth century enough had been revealed to prepare for that next phase of history and so the prophetic voice fell silent while men waited and other preparations took place. The Babylonian exile left Jews scattered all over the ancient world. Judah passed from the Persians to the Greeks in the fourth century BC and was ruled first by the Ptolemies of Egypt and then by the Seleucids of Syria, who proved particularly oppressive. But it gained a measure of independence in the middle of the second century under the Maccabees, and then came under Roman rule in 63 AD.

The Greeks gave the world a common language and culture which, together with the peace and religious toleration enjoyed in the early years of the Roman Empire, made conditions ideal for the spread of the gospel. Furthermore the event of the exile so confirmed the message of the prophets that by New Testament times most Jews had learned its lesson well and now held firmly to faith in the one God and his ways of righteousness. But above all they became a waiting people, waiting quietly for the coming of their Messiah and the outpouring of the Spirit in the promised New Covenant age. By Jesus' day the work of preparation was truly complete.

# 5

# Jesus and the Prophetic Church

The long period of waiting after the post-exilic restoration ended dramatically just before the birth of Christ. The story is best told by Luke. He is perhaps the most enthusiastic of all the New Testament writers about the overtly prophetic aspects of early Christianity, which he clearly presents in his Gospel and in Acts as the prophetic movement of the new age of the Spirit foretold by the Old Testament.

### *Fresh Stirrings of the Spirit*

The story begins with an angel appearing to the priest Zechariah, announcing he is to become father of a prophet-son who 'will be filled with the Holy Spirit' and will go 'in the spirit and power of Elijah' to herald the Lord's coming (Luke 1:13-17; cp. Mal. 3:1f; 4:5f). This 'vision' (1:22), remarkable in itself, but particularly so in an age when such things were thought to belong to the distant past or some dreamed-of future, was quickly followed by what can only be viewed as an amazing new release of spiritual and prophetic activity.

The same angel visited Mary announcing the conception of Jesus—by the working of the Spirit (1:26-35). When Elizabeth heard Mary's news she blessed her, 'filled with the Holy Spirit' (1:39-42). Then Mary praised God in words vividly reminiscent of the song Hannah, Samuel's mother, sang in those ancient days when the first prophetic movement was being birthed (1:46-55; cp. 1 Sam. 2:1-10). Zechariah too was 'filled with the Holy Spirit and prophesied', recalling the message of the olden prophets and describing his newborn son as one like them, 'a prophet of the Most High' (1:67-79). Angels appeared again to bring shepherds to the manger, which reminds us how Joel's prophecy said the blessings of the new age would be, not just for a select few, but for all people, for sons and daughters, old men and young, servants both men and women, all of whom would see visions and dream dreams (2:8-20; Joel 2:28f).

Then, finally, when Jesus was presented at the temple on the eighth day, old Simeon, who had been shown by the Holy Spirit he would see the Lord's Christ before he died, was waiting for him with the Holy Spirit upon him. Inspired by the Spirit to come to the temple at that very hour, he gave thanks and prophesied about Jesus' ministry and his agony (2:22-35). Also waiting at the temple was an aged widow called Anna, whom Luke describes as 'a prophetess', and she too gave thanks to God (2:36-38). Of the boy Jesus himself, Luke tells only that he 'grew and became strong; he was filled with wisdom, and the grace of God was upon him,' and that he 'grew in wisdom and stature, and in favour with God and men,' in much the same way as Samuel had done in his childhood (2:40,52; cp. 1 Sam. 2:21,26).

Here at last, after so many long years, the Spirit was stirring in Israel once more, just as in former times, granting the same visions, encouraging the same modes of worship and prophetic expression, enabling the same kind of personal growth. And it was all happening in the way the earlier prophets said it would: first the herald coming in the spirit of Elijah, the Spirit visiting all sorts of people, and the leader of the new age, the man of the Spirit, the young Jesus, quietly being prepared for the great work that lay ahead of him—just as it had been with Samuel, the founder of Israel's whole prophetic history.

*The Herald and the Prophet's Call*

Malachi had prophesied that God would send the prophet Elijah as the herald of his coming (Mal. 3:1; 4:5), and in accordance with that word came John the Baptist 'in the spirit and power of Elijah', announcing himself as 'a voice of one calling in the desert, "Prepare the way for the Lord."' (Luke 3:4) He wore a camel's hair coat and a leather belt, as Elijah had done (Matt. 3:4; 2 Kings 1:8), and like his prophetic predecessors preached a strong message of repentance, criticised the religious authorities for their sham faith, urged social justice and care for the needy, and told his hearers they would soon receive the long-awaited, promised Holy Spirit from the hands of the one whose advent he had come to herald (Luke 3:3-18).

John, however, was not the founder of the new prophetic movement, only its herald. The Old Testament prophets had said the new age would be inaugurated by a descendant of David, himself richly endowed with God's Spirit. And so it was with Jesus. At the Jordan he was given the Spirit from heaven (3:21f); and immediately, now 'full of the Holy Spirit', he 'was led by the Spirit' in the desert for forty days where his calling was tested. Then, 'in the power of the Spirit', he returned to Galilee for his most remarkable preaching career (4:1-15). Luke sums it all up beautifully elsewhere:

> *. . . how God anointed Jesus of Nazareth with the Holy Spirit and power, and how he went around doing good and healing all who were under the power of the devil, because God was with him.*
>
> (Acts 10:38)

Jesus was the most successful, charismatic, revival preacher Israel had ever known. The crowds loved him and came from far and wide to hear him. But he knew the nature and source of his strength, that it was prophetic and was from the Spirit. Hence, on returning to his home synagogue in Nazareth he taught that he was personally living in the fulfilment of the prophecy of Isa. 61:1, that 'The Spirit of the Lord is on me, because he has anointed me to preach good news to the poor . . .', and the outcome of his visit was the sad admission that 'no prophet is accepted in his home town' (4:16-30). Of course, Jesus was much more than a prophet, for he was Messiah and Son of God. But as such, his ministry was also that of a man empowered by the Spirit, a prophet. That is the clear witness of both Luke and Jesus himself.

It was Jesus' experience at the Jordan that launched him into his prophetic career. There is no evidence that he exercised any prophetic ministry before that event, but he certainly had a whirlwind ministry after it. His baptism experience ranks alongside the call visions of the great Old Testament prophets.

*Jesus' Prophetic Ministry*

Jesus now knew his calling was prophetic, and so too did most others. They disputed the claim that he was Messiah, but virtually everyone agreed he was a prophet (Mark 6:4-16; Luke 9:7-9; Matt. 16:13f; 21:46). After raising the widow's son at Nain the crowd cried out, 'A great prophet has appeared among us' (Luke 7:16). We hear a Pharisee questioning, 'If this man were a prophet, he would know . . .' (Luke 7:39). Jesus was heard saying of himself, '. . . surely no prophet can die outside Jerusalem' (Luke 13:33). The crowd on Palm Sunday recognised him as 'the prophet from Nazareth in Galilee' (Matt. 21:11). The soldiers at his scourging mocked his ministry with the taunt, 'Prophesy to us' (Matt. 26:68). And after the resurrection the two on the road to Emmaus spoke of him as 'a prophet, powerful in word and deed' (Luke 24:19).

He had a prophet's power to read men's secret thoughts (Mark 2:8; 9:33; 12:15), or to discern the future, particularly as it related to his own suffering and death (Mark 8:31; 9:31; 10:39) and to the fate of his people and the city of Jerusalem (Matt. 24). His miracles were demonstrations of the same prophetic power as we read about among the Old Testament prophets, only much more powerful, many of them having close parallels in the ancient narratives, for example:

- feeding the multitudes (Mark 6:30-44; cp. 2 Kings 4:42-44),
- healing the sick (Mark 1:40-5; Luke 17:11-19; cp. 2 Kings 2)
- exercising power over the waters (Mark 4:35-41; 6:45-52; cp. 2 Kings 2:8,14; 6:1-7),
- raising the dead (Mark 5:21-43; cp. 1 Kings 17:17-24; 2 Kings 4:32-7).

He demonstrated a prophet's authority in his teaching, speaking not with the learning of a scholarly exegete, like the scribes of his day, but with the authority of one who knew his message came straight from God (Matt. 7:29; Mark 1:22). We must note, however, one significant difference: the prophets prefaced their utterances with 'Thus says the LORD', whereas he as Messiah introduced his words with 'I say to you'.

*Jesus Prepares his Disciples to become Prophets*

Clearly Jesus' contemporaries, his own disciples, the gospel writers and even his enemies recognised him as a prophet, though it is in Luke that this aspect of his mission is most strongly highlighted. There we see Jesus, not only conducting his own prophetic ministry, but also preparing his followers for the same work. Hence, after their early training he sent out the Twelve on mission to heal and to preach (9:1-6). Then later he sent out seventy others and, when they returned rejoicing at the success of their mission, Jesus was overjoyed. 'I saw Satan fall like lightning from heaven,' he exclaimed, and together with them he rejoiced 'full of joy through the Holy Spirit', praising and thanking his Father for the success of his trainees to date (10:1-24). Next we hear him encouraging them to prepare for receiving the Spirit themselves, to persist in seeking and asking the Father for this gift, making the point strongly that it is very much the Father's will to give it (11:1-13). Then finally, just before his ascension, he tells his disciples the time they have been waiting for, which the Old Testament prophets foretold and for which he has been preparing them, has now come: 'I am going to send you what my Father has promised; but stay in the city until you have been clothed with power from on high.' It is little wonder that they returned to Jerusalem so excited (24:49-53).

In Luke's presentation of the Gospel in particular Jesus comes as a prophet whose ministry, even from his very conception, has the purpose of ushering in the new age of the Spirit and bringing it to fulfilment in the lives of his followers. The first Israelite prophets had sung and worshipped to the accompaniment of lyres, tambourines, flutes and harps (1 Sam. 10:5); these latter-day prophets-to-be returned to Jerusalem after their Master's departure 'with great joy. And they stayed continually at the temple, praising God.' (Luke 24:50-53) Their joy was still only a first foretaste of something fuller to come, but the same joy in the Spirit had been known in Israel since the day John the Baptist leaped for joy in his mother's womb (1:44) and Mary sang her song of rejoicing (1:47), since Elizabeth and her kinsfolk rejoiced (1:50) and the angels proclaimed 'good news of great joy that will be for all the people' (2:10). Jesus himself had been 'full of joy through the Holy Spirit' (10:21) and his disciples too had known great joy (10:17). Indeed Jesus had urged them to 'rejoice and leap for joy', even in persecution (6:23). We trace a persistent thread of joy running through Luke's Gospel, but then these were exciting days, when such preliminary tinglings of charismatic joy were about to give way to the full prophetic movement that was the early Church.

*Jesus' Disciples become Prophets*

Luke's second volume, the Acts of the Apostles, is amongst other things very much an account of the acts or doings of God's latter-day prophets. Right at the start he reminds us that these were men Jesus had been preparing for the moment when they would receive 'the promise of the Father' and 'be baptised with the Holy Spirit' (Acts 1:1-5; RSV). As it had been for Jesus, so also for them the Spirit would mean 'power', by virtue of which they would become his 'witnesses' (1:8). The Old Testament prophets had foretold that his day would come; the New Testament prophets would bear witness that his day had arrived.

Their moment came at Pentecost, when God visited them amid wind and fire, not unlike Moses and Elijah on Mount Sinai/Horeb (Exod. 19:16-20; 1 Kings 19:11f). 'All of them were filled with the Holy Spirit and began to speak in other tongues as the Spirit enabled them' (Acts 2:1-4). Speaking in tongues is not known to have been part of the experience of the Old Testament prophets, but that is probably because it signals, in the crossing of language barriers, the reversal of the curse of Babel (Gen. 11:1-9), and since the power of the curse was not broken until Christ died (Gal. 3:10-14), certain blessings were not available to men in pre-Christian times, tongues presumably being one of them. Anyhow, the effect was that 'God-fearing Jews from every nation under heaven . . . hear them declaring the wonders of God in our own tongues' (Acts 2:5-11). When asked what this meant, without hesitation Peter defined it as prophetic activity, or more precisely as the latter-day prophecy foretold by Joel (Acts 2:14-21), emphasising the point particularly by adding to Joel's words a second 'and they will prophesy' at the end of verse 18, and then ending his sermon with a reminder that the promise is for all men everywhere who will receive it (2:38f).

The story of Pentecost recalls several prophetic moments in the Old Testament, like the occasion in the wilderness when God poured out his Spirit on Israel's elders and they prophesied and Moses wished all God's people could experience the same (Num. 11:24-29), or when the Spirit came upon Saul in the company of Samuel's prophets and the onlookers were astonished or mocked (1 Sam. 10:9-12). Then afterwards the lifestyle of the early Christians began to look more like that of the ancient prophets: they seek each other's company and establish a form of communal living, as in Elisha's time (Acts 2:42-5; 4:32-5); like Samuel's followers they come together for worship, apparently of a happy, praise-orientated kind, though sufficiently unusual for most observers to stand aloof from it (2:46f; 5:12f); their ministry is attended by 'many wonders and miraculous signs', just like Elijah's and Elisha's (2:43; 5:12,15f); and their preaching quickly stirs up opposition and persecution, as often happened also in Old Testament times (4:1-3; 5:17-40).

Peter could hardly have put it more bluntly when he announced that the new proclamation of the disciples stood firmly in the tradition of 'all the prophets from Samuel on' and that his hearers, if they would but accept it, were 'heirs of the prophets' (3:24f). And indeed, the story of early Christianity as told by Luke in the chapters that follow is very much a tale of men filled and led by the Holy Spirit, as we should expect in a history of the acts of prophetic men.

*Prophetic Leadership in the Early Church*

One of the chief signs of the Church's prophetic character is seen in its admiration for strong, charismatic leaders and personalities. The Old Testament prophet-stories were mostly hero stories, and so, in a sense, are the stories in Acts, especially in the first eleven chapters.

The earliest ministry of Peter and John is remembered for a miracle of healing they wrought (3:1-11) and for the unnatural courage with which they preached in the temple and conducted themselves before the Sanhedrin (3:12 – 4:22).

Stephen is revered as 'a man full of God's grace and power' who 'did great wonders and miraculous signs among the people' and whose preaching was so dynamic that his critics 'could not stand up against the wisdom or the Spirit by which he spoke', but had to seek recourse to crying 'Blasphemy' and hailing him before the council, as both Jesus' and Jeremiah's opponents had done (6:8-15; cp. Jer. 26). Furthermore, his preaching was, in the best prophetic tradition, highly critical of the contemporary religious leadership (7:51), and in his last moments he was granted a vision of heaven with which any Old Testament prophet would have been greatly pleased (7:55f).

Philip's ministry in Samaria was so powerfully attended by 'miraculous signs' that even the local magician was 'astonished' (8:4-13). It was well remembered how he had converted the treasury-minister at the Ethiopian court thanks to the leading of an angelic vision (8:26-40), and like the good prophet he was, he eventually raised a family of four daughters to be prophets themselves (21:8f).

Paul (or Saul) was called to faith like a prophet from the start. He heard God's voice personally on the Damascus road; he was first ministered to by Ananias, who was himself led to Paul by a vision, and through him was filled with the Spirit; and he was so powerfully moved that straight away he began to proclaim his new revelation in Damascus with a prophet's boldness and with startling effect (9:4-25).

Peter's personal ministry was also very much in the power of the Spirit. He healed a man who had been bed-ridden for eight years and raised a dead girl to life (9:32-43); he was granted a vivid vision that prepared him for receiving the first Gentile convert into the Church (10:1-16); then, when he had preached to this Gentile, a Roman centurion called Cornelius, he witnessed him and his household being filled with the Spirit (10:17-48).

Because of his special gifting Joseph was nicknamed Barnabas, 'Son of Encouragement'. Encouragement was the primary function of prophecy in the early Church (4:36f; cp. 15:32; 1 Cor. 14:3). He is also described as 'a good man, full of the Holy Spirit and faith', whose ministry was so rich that the church at Antioch quickly became too large for him to manage single-handed (11:19-26).

The first Christian leaders were clearly prophets. Luke leaves us in no doubt about that whatsoever.

*Prophetic Giftings and Ministries in the Church*

The prophetic Spirit was not the exclusive possession of a few leading personalities. The promise of the Father was for all his people (Acts 2:39); it was expected that all believers should be baptised in the Spirit. Thus, when Peter and John discovered that the Spirit had not been given to Philip's converts in Samaria, they 'placed their hands on them and they received the Holy Spirit' (8:14-17). Likewise, Paul laid hands on some converts at Ephesus and 'the Holy Spirit came on them, and they spoke in tongues and prophesied' (19:1-7). Though the word 'prophesy' is not used in the account of Cornelius' baptism in the Spirit, it is said that he was 'speaking in tongues and praising God' and that his experience was identical with that of the disciples at the first Pentecost. The Spirit of prophecy was indeed for all men, even Gentiles (10:46; 11:15,18).

There was also a special gift of prophecy besides this more general endowment with the Spirit. In Barnabas' church at Antioch there were leaders who were especially recognised as 'prophets and teachers' (13:1). Jerusalem also had its prophets; two of whom, Judas and Silas, were sent to Antioch after the council that met to discuss the status of Gentile converts. We are told that they 'said much to encourage and strengthen the brothers' (15:22-32), presumably by using their prophetic gifts which, according to 1 Cor. 14:3f, were given precisely for that purpose.

Another group of prophets had also visited Antioch earlier, when one of their number, Agabus, caused quite a stir by predicting 'that a severe famine would spread over the entire Roman world' (11:27-30). We meet Agabus again at the home of Philip and his four prophet-daughters in Caesarea, where he forewarns of Paul's arrest (21:10f). His speech and his actions are entirely reminiscent of the Old Testament prophets: in his 'The Holy Spirit says' (or 'Thus says the Holy Spirit') we hear a clear echo of the more ancient 'The LORD says' (or 'Thus says the LORD'). The symbolic binding of his hands and feet has several Old Testament parallels—for example, in Ahijah of Shiloh rending his new coat (1 Kings 11:29-32). Furthermore, it is remarkable how readily and how seriously his hearers responded to his words on the earlier occasion by starting a famine relief fund and on the later by pleading with Paul to postpone his visit to Jerusalem. The New Testament Christians clearly held their prophets in high esteem.

In prophetic communities today respect for spiritual gifting commonly governs the ordering of leadership structures. So too, it seems, in the early Church. Whilst a three-fold governmental system of overseers, elders and deacons was to emerge early, it was interlaced with a more prophetically cast five-fold one of apostles, prophets, evangelists, pastors and teachers. The forms may have varied from place to place, but certainly at Antioch, Corinth and Ephesus the authority of prophets ranked highly, perhaps only second to that of apostles (Acts 13:1; 1 Cor. 12:28; Ephes. 4:11). That in itself is further witness to the prophetic nature of early Christianity as a whole. A prophetic movement must inevitably accord the highest status to those who show the greatest superabundance of prophetic endowment.

*Heirs of the Prophets*

Because of space we have restricted ourselves to Luke's accounts for the most part, but in the pages that follow we shall range more widely. However, already we can see that the early Christians considered themselves, to use Peter's phrase, 'heirs of the prophets'. Their experience, lives, giftings, ministries and proclamation unanimously testify to that fact, the fuller implications of which we must pause for a while to review before proceeding further with our history.

John the Baptist summed up Jesus' ministry in two brief statements: 'Look, the Lamb of God, who takes away the sin of the world!' and 'he will baptise with the Holy Spirit.' (John 1:29,33) It is the united witness of all four gospels that the ultimate purpose of Jesus' ministry, once he had dealt with sin by his sacrifice on the cross, was to baptise men with the Holy Spirit. Luke reminds us that that was 'what the Father promised', and his story of the early church shows that that was precisely what they enjoyed. Cleansed from sin, made acceptable in the presence of their God, endued with the Holy Spirit, they became the prophetic movement of the new age that would release a floodtide of evangelistic and revival power in the same flow as their Old Testament prophet-forebears, but far exceeding anything that either they or indeed anyone in the world to that date had ever known.

# 6

# Prophetic Christianity – its distinguishing characteristics

We are now in a position to review some of the main patterns in Israelite and early Christian prophetic faith. It is important to take time to do so at this point, since the biblical patterns largely determine the character, history and teachings of the post-biblical movements we shall be studying.

We have seen that the faith and experience of the earliest Christians were continuous with those of the Old Testament prophets. We have also noted differences. Rather than suggesting any contrast between the two movements, these also testify to continuity because most of them can be explained in terms of fulfilment, that is that the Old Testament prophets looked forward to what New Testament Christianity became. The faith and flow are one; the experience and proclamation, while sometimes the same, are often necessarily different. But they are not in conflict with each other. They are entirely complementary—it is all one. It is in recognising that fact, that Christianity is the fulfilment of the Old Testament prophets' hope and vision, that we discover the distinctiveness of Christian prophetism, that characterises most later movements.

*The True Church of the Spirit: Heirs of the Prophets*

The general prophetic endowment of the earliest Christians differed little from that of the Old Testament prophets. Only tongues is significantly new, but even that is sufficiently of the same mould to be subsumed under the general heading of prophecy, as Peter's statement at Pentecost made clear (Acts 2:16-18). Tongues apart, there is, as we noted, much similarity between the events described in Num. 11 and Acts 2, or between the prophetic gatherings of 1 Sam. 10 & 19 and Christian assemblies described in Acts. Apart from tongues and their interpretation, all the gifts listed in 1 Cor. 12 can be illustrated from the prophetic sources of the Old Testament. The early Christians were without doubt 'heirs of the prophets', and the consequences of that fact were far wider than the exercise of spiritual gifts.

Because the prophets had foretold it all, prophetic Christianity must inevitably regard itself as the true Church of the Spirit, which is indeed one of the cardinal claims every prophetic movement makes. The early Church saw itself as this new people of the Spirit, the fulfilment of the ancient hope that some day all the LORD's people would be prophets, and so expected all its members to be baptised with the prophetic Spirit.

Though Old Testament prophets from time to time assembled in groups or lived in communities, they never sought to establish a separate prophetic church. They were always a movement within Israel, and could never have been anything more, for their perspective was different from the Church's. Their purpose was to prepare for what was to come, whereas the Christians could announce that it had arrived and invite men to attach themselves to it. Yet in order to do so, they had to believe they were indeed the long-awaited, peculiarly prophetic people with their own distinctive identity.

Such self-understanding no doubt made it easier for the Church to break with its Jewish roots when the time for that came. Since then, tension between charismatic and traditional religion, and a tendency to separate from the established, non-charismatic church have been regular marks of prophetic Christianity—which, of course, results from its claim to be the true Church of the Spirit, the end-time race of prophetical people, foretold by and in the tradition of Israel's ancient prophets.

Coupled with this conviction that they were the prophesied end-time people of God went a zeal for evangelism which is largely absent from the Old Testament. The Israelite prophets were not afraid to tell of their visions, but there is no indication they regarded it as a matter of urgency to convert their hearers into prophets. They challenged men to change their ways, to seek good, to pursue righteousness, to have faith in God and to hope for the future, but not to seek a filling with the Spirit for themselves (except, perhaps, Ezek. 18:31). That was for the age to come. Christian prophetism, by contrast, was an expansionist movement, regarding it as a matter of primary importance that its converts received the prophetic Spirit themselves. Here again we encounter what will be seen as an essential characteristic of every subsequent prophetic movement in history.

*Spiritual and Natural Men: the Prophetic Attitude to Spiritual Matters*

The New Testament Christian is one to whom the Spirit of Christ has come and who has therefore, in John's language, been born again of the Spirit, or born of God. He has also been filled with, or baptised in, the Spirit and has consequently experienced the operation of spiritual gifts in his life and ministry. But perhaps most significant of all is a total change in his appreciation of spiritual things, resulting in a completely new way of looking at life and the things of God, and usually leading to the emergence of a new personality.

In 1 Cor. 2 Paul draws a distinction between two kinds of wisdom: 'men's wisdom' (v. 5) and 'God's secret wisdom' (v. 7). The former is the common learning of mankind that can be acquired by teaching and study, the latter is a more ancient wisdom (v. 7), the very 'thoughts of God' that can be learned by no human means (v. 11), but is only revealed by his Spirit (vv. 10, 12) to those who are capable of understanding it (vv. 6, 14). It is to enable them to appreciate this divine wisdom that men are given the Spirit in the first place, for he alone can teach them its truths, since he alone knows them (vv. 11-13).

Though the word 'prophet' is not used in this chapter, we could reasonably paraphrase its teaching by saying that no one can properly appreciate prophetic insight and experience except one on whom the prophetic Spirit rests. The supernatural wisdom imparted by the Spirit in this way is concerned with the significance of Christ (v. 2) in the total, primordial plan of God (v. 7) and the interpretation of the gifts he gives to believers (v. 12). That is, it enables men to understand how the purposes and promises of God in the Old Testament find their fulfilment in Christ and in the Church which experiences the spiritual or prophetic blessings of the last age that has now dawned with him.

In 2 Cor. 3 Paul makes the distinction even more explicit when he contrasts Jewish and Christian appreciation of the Old Testament. The Jew, he says, reads his Bible with a veil over his mind and that veil is only removed through Christ, 'whenever anyone turns to the Lord' (vv. 14-16). But then, he says, 'the Lord is the Spirit,' and all this 'comes from the Lord, who is the Spirit' (vv. 17f). Since this enlightenment can only be given by the Spirit, it belongs exclusively to those who receive the Spirit from Christ, to those who permit the Spirit to form in them 'the mind of Christ' (1 Cor. 2:16). Paul uses the term 'spiritual' (*pneumatikos*) to describe Christians who are thus enlightened, and he contrasts them with others he calls 'natural' (*psychikos*—NIV 'without the Spirit'), those whose understanding of the world and religion is according to their own human wisdom (2:14f).

Such Christian self-understanding is akin to that of the Israelite prophets, who also drew a contrast between the so-called insight of those who 'speak vision from their own minds' (Jer. 23:16), or who 'prophesy out of their own imagination . . . and have seen nothing' (Ezek. 13:2f), and their own awareness of spiritual truth, spiritual experience and God's overall plan for the history of his world. Jude similarly warns against the teachings of those 'who follow mere natural instincts and do not have the Spirit' (v. 19).

We shall later see how strongly this contrast between spiritual and natural men continues to be part of the vocabulary of prophetic movements throughout history.

*Prophetic Attitudes to Human Learning*

Paul was insistent that his preaching was not with 'eloquence or superior wisdom . . . that your faith might not rest on men's wisdom, but on God's power' (1 Cor. 2:4f), and he advised the Colossians to 'See to it that no one takes you captive through hollow and deceptive philosophy, which depends on human tradition . . . rather than on Christ' (Col. 2:8). He also urged Timothy to 'Turn away from godless chatter and the opposing ideas of what is falsely called knowledge' (1 Tim. 6:20).

Some of these admonitions may be interpreted in the light of debates with early Gnostic heretics, but the attitude of admiration for supernatural wisdom they convey is not unlike that implied when some Jews said of Jesus, 'How did this man get such learning without having studied?' (John 7:15), or when the Sanhedrin wondered at the untutored boldness of Peter and John (Acts 4:13), or when the Jews were outmanoeuvred by Stephen, by 'his wisdom or the Spirit by whom he spoke' (6:10).

The wisdom of God that is prophetically imparted, as we have already noted (1 Cor. 2), gives a profound insight into the meaning of the Scriptures (2 Cor. 3), reveals the glory of Christ and leads into all the truth (John 16:13f). But once a man has grasped that kind of knowledge, conventional philosophical and theological disputation grows pale beside it. The prophet's need is to proclaim his vision, not to indulge in mental speculations. But to those with no such revelation his attitude looks very much like anti-intellectualism.

*The Spiritual Church and Prophetic Attitudes to Established Religion*

Old Testament prophets and New Testament believers had much in common in their attitudes to the established religious systems of their day. Just as the prophets from Samuel on preached against decadence in the sanctuary, so Jesus, in the style of Jeremiah, marched into the temple declaring that God's 'house of prayer' had been turned into a 'den of robbers' (Matt. 21:13; cp. Jer. 7:11). Just as the prophets had condemned the excessive, yet empty, ritualism of the sanctuaries, so Jesus denounced the scribes and Pharisees for the hypocrisy of their legalistic beliefs and practices (Matt. 23).

In these denunciations both the older prophets and Jesus applied the same kind of criteria for their judgments. Samuel wanted obedience rather than sacrifice (1 Sam. 15:22), Amos asked for justice rather than festivals and offerings (Amos 5:21-24), Isaiah sought care for the fatherless and widows rather than assemblies and prayers (Isa. 1:12-17), and Jesus looked for inner purity and concern for the need of others rather than outward displays of religiosity (Matt. 6, 23). The message is the same throughout: it is the things of the Spirit working in the inner man that really count, not the external appearances.

The true concern of prophets is, of course, to reform and revitalise the religion of their day, but in most ages their conversation inevitably sounds like little more than polemic against the establishment, and so it calls forth the same kind of wrath that was directed by the priest of Bethel against Amos (Amos 7:10-13), or by the priests and prophets of Jerusalem against Jeremiah (Jer. 7, 26), or by the chief priest and elders of the people against Jesus (Matt. 26:3f).

The impression of criticism or even arrogance in their preaching is further heightened by the fact that members of prophetic movements tend to heed charismatic leaders more readily than institutional authorities. They do so believing they are obeying the voice of God (= prophecy) rather than the voice of man (= the establishment). This often creates a theology of lay authority, which they support by such arguments as the New Testament priesthood belonged to Christ (Heb. 4:14, etc.) and passes through him to all believers (1 Pet. 2:5; Rev. 1:6; 5:10; 20:6), or that the Church chose as its leaders men who were known by their charismatic presence to be 'full of the Spirit and wisdom' (Acts 6:3).

### *The Prophet's Pursuit of Holiness: Ethics and The Spiritual Life*

To prophets the establishment is over-concerned with the things of this world, with outward displays of religion and with ways of life bolstered up with frail human philosophical arguments which look pallid to them in the light of their superior vision, their appreciation of the true wisdom of God, and their grasp of the real religion of the

Spirit. But it is not only on the institutional church that they are hard, for they also lay very heavy demands on themselves.

Jesus told his disciples that their righteousness must surpass that of the Pharisees and the teachers of the law (Matt. 5:20), that not only must they not kill, but they must love their enemies and not even be angry with their brothers (5:22,44), that not only must they not commit adultery, they must not even look lustfully at a woman (5:27), and so forth—indeed that they must 'Be perfect, therefore, as your heavenly Father is perfect' (5:48).

Paul in his epistles leaves no doubt whatsoever that he too believed Christians should be of exemplary character, 'holy and pleasing to God' (Rom. 12:1), not gratifying the desires of the flesh, but living a life of 'love, joy, peace, patience, kindness, goodness, faithfulness, gentleness, self-control' (Gal. 5:16,22), pursuing only whatever is true, noble, right, pure, lovely, admirable, excellent or praiseworthy (Phil. 4:8).

The Israelite prophets made similar high moral demands. Amos urged men to 'Seek good, not evil, that you may live' (Amos 5:4,14); Hosea and Jeremiah firmly upheld demands of the Ten Commandments (Hos. 4:2; Jer. 7:9); Zephaniah urged his hearers to 'Seek righteousness, seek humility' (Zeph. 2:3). Micah put it this way: 'He has showed you, O man, what is good. And what does the LORD require of you? To act justly and to love mercy and to walk humbly with your God.' (Mic. 6:8)

The Old Testament prophets gave their moral teaching along with a great deal of criticism of popular misbehaviour, which was a repeated cause of tension between them and the establishment. But Jesus' teaching pleased the scribes and Pharisees no more. We shall presently see how similar high morality is characteristic of most prophetic movements, and that it regularly caused the same kind of tensions.

The cause of tension is not so much a conflict between different moral codes as a clash between the prophet's desire to pursue holiness and the churchman's to adhere to an ethical system. Prophetic holiness is God's law written on man's hearts by the Spirit of God himself, something Christians experience after conversion and baptism in the Spirit (Jer. 31:33; Ezek. 36:26f; 2 Cor. 3:3). Ethical morality is of a different order, something created by and learned from men. It is external to oneself, codified in written documents. It can be debated and modified by the will of men according to the need of the times. Holiness, by contrast, is absolute. It cannot be modified or debated, but only sought after and learned by drawing closer to God and walking intimately with him in the Spirit. It is the very character of God himself and, like his wisdom, it can only be learned from the internal operation of his Spirit in a Christian's life. A prophet can have no dialogue with those who seek to modify God's standards of holiness, in compromise with the customs or culture of the age in which he lives. Many in the establishment feel uncomfortable with such apparently extreme attitudes.

*Spiritual Warfare: the Battle with Evil*

The power of evil is never underestimated in Scripture. And it is always dealt with in one way—by warfare. In Old Testament times, because the battle was to establish a territorial foothold for the kingdom in Canaan, the immediate enemy was Canaanite. Dialogue with its indigenous paganism was absolutely forbidden. Only one course of action was permitted in regard to that: total eradication. Paganism is religion and so the battle was inevitably with people. Frequently it became vehement and bloody. The alternative was toleration of practices that undermined God's holy demands. Israel did compromise and its history proved just how devastating the effects of that could be.

In the New Testament a different atmosphere predominates. Unlike Elisha who sent Jehu to slaughter the house of Ahab, Jesus blessed the peacemakers (Matt. 5:9), told his disciples to 'Love your enemies and pray for those who persecute you' (5:44), and warned them that 'all who draw the sword will die by the sword' (26:52). Nevertheless, the battle continued unabated. Only now it moved to a more universal plane, for the very power of evil itself became manifest when Jesus' ministry began. From that time on the battle was directed against Satan and his minions more than against men, for it was the very purpose of Jesus' ministry to see him defeated and men released from his domination. Like everything else we have looked at so far, the dimension in which the prophetic battle operates is spiritual rather than natural. But it does not therefore cease to be personal. Paul tells the Ephesians to 'Put on the full armour of God, . . . stand against the devil's schemes,' and resist 'the flaming arrows of the evil one,' to take 'the sword of the Spirit, which is the word of God,' and contend 'not against flesh and blood, but against the rulers, against the authorities, against the powers of this dark world and against the spiritual forces of evil in the heavenly realms' (Eph. 6:10-17).

Christian prophets are engaged in as fierce a battle as were the Israelite prophets, only at a different level. The Old Testament has no stories of battles with the demonic, but the ministry of Jesus cannot be told without them. The old battle against the Canaanite baals and their devotees has now moved to the level of confrontation with all the hellish powers that fight against the purposes of God. Like God's supernatural wisdom, this warfare is meaningless to the natural man, but is actively engaged in by all who are baptised in the Spirit. Men without the Spirit understand it so little that they regularly explain away the very existence of Satan and the demonic as primitive or mythological concepts.

Since by his death and resurrection Jesus released all who have faith in him from Satan's domination, for those in Christ the outcome of the battle is a foregone conclusion. In this new age of the Spirit the power of evil has already been broken. And so Jesus tells his disciples how he 'saw Satan fall like lightning from heaven' and he gave them 'authority to overcome all the power of the enemy' (Luke 10:18f). Most later prophetic movements take up the spiritual battle of the New Testament Church with renewed fervour, while movements that resort to the kind of warfare that the Old Testament prophets encouraged are rare in the annals of Christian prophetism.

*Spiritual Worship: Life in the Spirit versus Religion*

We have already noted that prophetic attitudes to established religious practice are not always particularly tolerant ones. One of the areas of strongest contention is worship. Jesus himself spoke of a different kind of worship that would be 'in Spirit and in truth' (John 4:23f) and no prophet is ever satisfied until he knows that his worship is of that nature.

New Testament Christianity was a matter of great joy and rejoicing. That, as we have seen already, is the uniform witness of Luke's Gospel. But perhaps the fullest account of the joy that attends the Spirit's presence is found in Jesus' last discourse in John 14–17. Here the joy is more mature than the childlike exuberance we find in Luke, for it is constantly coupled with 'peace', but it is not for that reason by any means a diminished joy: 'I have told you this so that my joy may be in you and that your joy may be complete' (John 15:11). In speaking of his imminent departure and death and of his sending the Spirit, Jesus tells the disciples 'You will grieve, but your grief will turn to joy . . . you will rejoice, and no one will take away your joy' (16:20,22). And then he urges them to 'Ask and you will receive, and your joy will be complete' (16:24).

There are many matters discussed in John 14–17, but the dominant theme is the coming of the Spirit, and through his presence the mutual indwelling or abiding of the Christian in Christ and Christ in him. It is in that context and in that experience that the Christian comes to know this promised joy and peace (esp. 15:1-11). Old Testament prophets had their joyful moments; Christians had the same. But these also tell of a continuing and maturing joy for everyone that the Old Testament prophets could only look forward to as a mark of the new age that for them was still to come (Isa. 9:3; 35:1,2,10; 61:7; 65:18f; etc.).

Joy is part and parcel of what it means to be a member of the end-time community of the Spirit and therefore is a notable feature in the worship and the life-style of every prophetic community. At its richest it is a response to awareness of the Spirit's moving in one's inner being or in the assembled body of believers. At its feeblest, it is but a memory of such times. It is a cause for sadness when a prophetic group that has known such things but has lost the Spirit's fire seeks to recreate the atmosphere of them by emotional means that are neither 'in Spirit' nor 'in truth'. But at least they have known the truth, of which natural religion is quite unaware.

*Prophetic Understanding of History: Urgency of the End-Times*

There was a sense of extreme end-time urgency in New Testament Christianity. It was very much in the style of the pre-exilic prophets that Jesus foretold the desecration and destruction of the temple, the fall of Jerusalem with its attendant horrors and the imminent sufferings that would herald the final day of judgment, the day of the coming of the Son of Man. In each of the chapters that contain the parallel accounts of his sayings on these matters (Matt. 24; Mark 13; Luke 21) it is recorded that he encouraged his hearers to expect the predicted events to happen in their own near future (Matt. 24:34, etc.).

The same sense of end-time urgency is found also in some of Paul's letters. In 1 Cor. 15:51f and 1 Thes. 4:15-17 he writes as if the return of Christ and the general resurrection of the dead could happen during the life-time of some of his readers. It seems that a number of Thessalonian believers were so thrilled by their new-found faith that they even believed the final day of the Lord had already come and that they were now living in the full light of its eschatological grace (2 Thes. 2:2).

This kind of thinking is found in many prophetic movements throughout history. Paul's response to the Thessalonians was that the end, though certainly to be expected at any moment, had not yet come, since a number of events, of which Jesus also spoke, had to happen first (2 Thes. 2:2-8; cp. Matt. 24, etc.)

The sense of end-time urgency reflected in these early attitudes seems to have faded in some measure with the passage of the first generation of Christians. Again we shall see that in most prophetic movements the sense of expectancy is at its highest during the first flush of charismatic enthusiasm and, as the latter dwindles, so also does the former. But similarly, whenever the one is rekindled, so also does the other tend to be. Hence towards the end of the first century we find that sense of imminence once more vitally present in the prophetic writings of the book of Revelation (Rev. 1:1; 22:6,20)

*The Exercise of the Gift of Prophecy: Edifying the Church*

Since the New Testament contains no book or collection of utterances of the early Christian prophets comparable with the Old Testament prophetical books, some scholars have searched its pages for traces of primitive prophecies, though with no certain results. However, the lack is not entirely surprising. Since early Christianity saw itself as *the* end-time Church, its founder, Jesus, was believed to have said about all that there was to say by way of additional revelation. His was the final word of God to man. He was *the* great Prophet, and any prophet after him must be limited to proclaiming his message anew, or to strengthening the faith of those who had believed in it. Hence, while his sayings were carefully collected and preserved, those of his early followers have been largely forgotten.

But the difference between the old and new prophets is more than just the kind of books they wrote. When the Old Testament prophets called for reform and warned of judgment, they were preparing Israel for a coming day of visitation and ultimately a better future. Their ministry was therefore a public one, as also was that of Jesus, who addressed his words to all who had ears to hear. The Church continued to have the same function, but now it had a new message as well, for the prophesied day of Christ had arrived. Its main role was therefore to call people to Christ and urge them to heed his words. That was done by witnessing and evangelism. Its prophecy, for the most part, now became a word to the Church itself, the new Israel of faith.

There are some instances of prophecy speaking to outsiders, though only in an incidental way, similar to what happened in 1 Sam. 10 & 19. Thus the crowd was moved by the disciples' declaration of God's praise in tongues on the day of Pentecost in Acts 2, and in 1 Cor. 14:24 Paul mentions the effect prophesying could have on an unbeliever who chanced to hear it, but there is no example in the

New Testament of any prophetic utterance specifically addressed to the unconverted.

When Paul urges the Corinthians to eagerly desire the gift of prophecy, he does so on the grounds that it 'edifies the church' (1 Cor. 14:4f), and he speaks of it as functioning entirely in the context of public worship (1 Cor. 11:3-15; 14:1-39). Indeed he makes the point quite bluntly: just as the use of tongues is good for edifying the speaker himself, so prophecy edifies the church. Tongues, if interpreted, can have a similar effect, as also can other revelatory gifts. Indeed, his portrait of an early church meeting is one in which 'everyone has a hymn, or a word of instruction, a revelation, a tongue or an interpretation,' and in which 'two or three prophets should speak' (1 Cor. 14:26,29). He even says 'you can all prophesy' (v. 31), and with that leaves us in no doubt whatsoever that at church meetings prophetic gifts were expected to be used. Their purpose was always 'for strengthening, encouragement and comfort . . . that the church may be edified . . . that everyone may be instructed and encouraged' (vv. 3,5,31).

Indeed, after reading 1 Cor. 14, it is almost impossible to imagine early Christian worship without the operation of spiritual gifts. But then, when prophets come together it is almost inevitable that they should prophesy. Was not that what Moses and Joel longed to see? It is what men have continued to long for and what has been resurrected in prophetic circles down the ages of history ever since.

*The Problem of True and False Prophecy*

In every age when the prophetic gift has revived, the Lord's people have been confronted with the need for clear discernment between true and false prophecy. John urged his readers to 'test the spirits to see whether they are from God, because many false prophets have gone out into the world' (1 John 4:1). What worries him is not so much the impact they will have on the world as on the churches. If they are the same as those he calls 'antichrists', they were erstwhile church members themselves (2:18f). Similarly, Jesus was concerned lest they might 'deceive the elect, if that were possible' (Mark 7:15), though the addition of the word 'even' to this saying in Matthew suggests they also had a wider audience (Matt. 24:24). However, the fact that such prophets could 'come to you in sheep's clothing' (Matt. 7:15) implies that they had access to the congregations and operated under the guise of authentic prophets in that setting. More light is shed on this aspect of false prophesying in a passage in Hermas' *Shepherd* discussed in the next chapter.

The resurgence of false prophecy in New Testament times, of course, adds further witness to the authentic prophetic nature of early Christianity and affords yet another point of comparison with Old Testament prophecy. The problem of how to handle it had not been properly resolved in ancient Israel, but the New Testament contains a number of hints that some persons at any rate in the early Church believed they had the ability to discern the true from the false. Thus Paul advised the Thessalonians, 'Do not put out the Spirit's fire; do not treat prophecies with contempt. Test everything. Hold on to the good. Avoid every kind of evil.' (1 Thes. 5:19-22). However, in 1 Cor. 12:10 'distinguishing between spirits' is coupled with prophecy as one of the gifts of the Spirit, indicating that Paul believed discernment operated on similar principles, that is, that it was a supernatural endowment like prophecy itself.

Other criteria are also given for testing prophecy. Jesus said prophets would be recognised by their fruit (Matt. 7:16) and pointed out that signs of obedience to the will of God are a better indication of authenticity than prophetic utterances and miracles, even if spoken and performed in his name (7:21-23). *The Didache,* discussed in the next chapter, expands on this method of discernment, which is not in essence very different from that proposed in Deut. 13 and elsewhere in the Old Testament.

Very similar also is John's suggestion that the prophetic spirit will be seen to be of God if it 'acknowledges that Jesus Christ has come in the flesh' (1 John 4:2). No true prophet would deny the divinity of Christ or the doctrine of his incarnation. After all, that is precisely what Christian prophecy is all about, the strengthening of faith in Jesus, and hence the encouragement and upbuilding of the Church.

In our historical study we shall see how disastrous it has proved when men have failed to test prophecy according to scriptural principles.

*Prophecy Remains All-Embracing*

Israel's prophets sometimes spoke directly to their national leaders about moral and political affairs urging political action; sometimes they addressed the whole community on social and religious topics as well, generally calling for repentance; sometimes they spoke mainly to the faithful about vision for the future, encouraging them in faith for the approaching new age. While prophecy in the New Testament is primarily for the faithful, the Church, to encourage them to hold fast to the good they have now received, it still retains its earlier interests. It has the same basic purpose: not just to announce earlier prophecies now fulfilled, but to make social, political, moral and religious proclamations, and to direct attention forward to a further coming new age, the end of all things when God will usher in a new heaven and a new earth.

Revelation, the only book in the New Testament to call itself 'prophecy' (Rev. 1:3; 22:7,10,18f), illustrates this well. Its present political, moral and social message is evident in its warnings to the churches and in the fate it envisages for the Roman Empire as a consequence of its decadence and its oppressive heartlessness. Its end-time message is one of encouragement to the faithful to stand firm in the face of persecution, knowing that the Lamb has conquered, that Satan has been thrown down from heaven aware that his days will be short on the earth, that the Lord our God the Almighty reigns, and that the vision of the kingdom of God proclaimed by the prophets of old already operative in the Church is hastening to its final fulfilment.

Again, like Old Testament prophecy it still calls for obedience (22:7) and righteousness (22:11), still holds the threat of judgment (22:18f) and promises blessings on all who respond to its message (22:17), still asserts the trustworthiness of its own utterances (22:6), and still expresses urgency in its vision for times yet to come (22:12,20).

All of this is in the same flow as Old Testament prophecy, only much more developed. Prophetic utterances of later movements maintain the same momentum. Many of them focus strongly on the vision of the millennial reign of Christ and his saints preceding the final judgment of God in ch. 20, but that is only a reapplication of the older vision of a new Israel that is so much a feature of late pre-exilic and post-exilic prophecy. It was this continuing future expectation in New Testament prophecy that enabled later prophets to proclaim the inauguration of that further final stage in history and the nearness of the end of all things again in their own day. Prophecy in the Church clearly remains recognisable in all its essentials as prophecy, still very much in the Old Testament mould.

*The Nature of Prophetic Inspiration*

This subject also requires some comment, particularly in view of the debates about the prophetic phenomenon that ensued in the history of the Church. In the Old Testament the prophets used formulae like 'Thus says the Lord', but they never discussed the nature of prophetic inspiration. Certainly some of them spoke of having been in God's council to hear his word and others spoke of their visions of God, but no explanation is ever offered for the fact, for example, that Jeremiah does not speak in the style of Ezekiel, or that Hosea's phraseology and ideas are recognisably different from those of Amos or Micah. In other words, the Old Testament contains no discussion about the relationship between the human and the divine in prophecy, except with respect to false prophecy.

The New Testament, however, has two passages that suggest the matter was certainly being discussed in the early Church. 2 Pet. 1:20f firmly asserts that 'no prophecy of Scripture came about by the prophet's own interpretation. For prophecy never had its origin in the will of man, but men spoke from God as they were carried along by the Holy Spirit.' Prophecy is not just preaching, or reading the signs of the times, or the fruit of meditation, or anything else that rests on human ingenuity and intellectual capability. In theory, within the limits of this definition, a child might prophesy, as happened in some later movements.

On the other hand, this definition does not suggest that prophecy was externally-controlled automatic speech. It is the men, not their lips, that were moved by God. On that topic Paul says, 'The spirits of prophets are subject to the control of prophets. For God is not a God of disorder but of peace' (1 Cor. 14:32f). Prophecy is a 'gift' to men, and is therefore something the prophets themselves use, not something that uses them. That is to say, there is a marked human element in prophecy.

It is God's word, certainly, but uttered by men. Hence it is essential to recognise, as Paul says, that 'we know in part and we prophesy in part' (1 Cor. 13:9). Nevertheless, prophecy is an important gift—Paul even says the most important (1 Cor. 14:1)—for the upbuilding of the church, and so is not to be despised (1 Thes. 5:20). It is, however, to be used with care and testing. Some later prophetic movements found themselves in very difficult circumstances through failure to recognise this cautionary truth that New Testament Christians had so clearly grasped.

The prophetic writings in the Bible itself must be viewed somewhat differently, even though the same criteria apply to assessing them and though they also reveal the individual personalities of the prophets themselves in considerable measure. They have stood the test of time and have been fully recognised by the Church as authentically inspired of God in a manner that is quite unique. They are thus accepted as sacred scripture in a way that personal and community prophecies today never can be.

*Conclusions*

The above is by no means a complete catalogue of the distinguishing marks of prophecy and prophetism, but it is sufficient as a measure against which to set the movements we shall be studying here. Not all characteristics are found in every movement, but sufficient are to enable us to distinguish between tendencies that are prophetic and those that are not. In today's Pentecostal, Charismatic and Revival churches the picture is much more complete, but we are sometimes hampered in studying earlier movements through scarcity of good source materials, and so it is often important to measure more by general impression than by statistical methods. If the broad portrait painted above is kept in focus, assessment and evaluation become much easier.

# PART TWO

# THE PROPHETIC VISION FADES IN THE EARLY CHURCH

It is one of the most common misinterpretations of history today that the prophetical gifts were given from heaven to enable the Church to become established and then were withdrawn after the death of the apostles at the end of the first century. This doctrine is known as cessationism (on the grounds that the gifts have 'ceased' to function). The first traces of it are found in the fourth century, in the writings of Chrysostom and Filastrius. The most influential exponent of it was Augustine in the late fourth and early fifth, though his opinion changed, for in the latter part of his ministry he was more than happy with, indeed adamantly insisted on, the open exercise of gifts in his church at Hippo in North Africa.

The cessationist argument has continued to prove popular. It appeals to those who do not want to have anything to do with prophetic religion, but it is without foundation in the New Testament itself and it misrepresents what actually happened in history. Its proponents appeal to a few passages like Paul's statements in 1 Cor. 13, that our prophecies and tongues are 'in part' or 'imperfect' and so will cease when the perfect comes, and that is commonly defined as the Bible, which they say perfectly encapsulates the word of God in a way no charismatic prophecy ever can. The argument looks convincing, but it cannot stand. Paul is not making a contrast between spoken prophecy and a written book, but between two levels of spiritual perception. That is made very clear by the fact that among the imperfect gifts he also lists 'knowledge', which cessationists conveniently choose to overlook. Perfect spiritual perception has clearly not yet arrived, and so the prophetical gifts are still as useful as ever.

There are other equally untenable arguments that are used, but the more basic fact is that in history the gifts were never withdrawn from the Church. To be sure, there were long stretches of time when men chose not to use them, whether through ignorance or by deliberate choice but, as we shall see, traces of them can actually be found in most ages of Christian history, even the darkest, and repeatedly there has surfaced a longing in the hearts of faithful believers for their fuller restoration.

The cause of their disuse has not been God's intention, but man's weakness. It is essentially the same story as the one we have traced through the Bible. God intended man should live in Eden; it was man who lost it all. And that is the continuing story of revivals and all God's workings among men. God gives, man spoils, God restores. It creates a graph of peaks and troughs, though one that does rise overall, since it is God's purpose that it should. God took Abraham to Canaan, but his descendants ended as slaves in Egypt; under Moses and Joshua he took them back to Canaan, but there they turned to other gods and became prey to every plundering nation around them; he raised up Samuel and David to bring them back to himself, but in the heyday of Solomon's reign they spoiled it again. And so the story continues, through the revivals of Asa and Jehoshaphat, of Elijah and Elisha, of Hezekiah and Josiah, all of which were followed by a turning again to pagan ways and consequent disaster.

In the same kind of way, in New Testament times, the explosive, life-giving ministry of Jesus and the Apostles was followed at the end of the century by encroaching spiritual apathy, which was clearly not God's purpose, as the letters in Rev. 2-3 most clearly attest. The call then was to return to 'your first love,' to 'Repent and do the things you did at first,' to 'Strengthen what remains and is about to die.' (2:4f; 3:2) And that is always God's call, not to accept any decline in spirituality, but to return to the spiritual heights, to the prophetic faith of the men of revival and the primitive pentecostal life of the first Apostles to whom Jesus taught the way.

The present work of the Holy Spirit is to restore in us the vision of what we have lost in the past so that we can regain the life of Eden and enter into the fullness of the life that Jesus came to bring. That is the first purpose of prophecy, for 'the testimony of Jesus is the spirit of prophecy' (Rev. 19:10). Men mostly get in the way and spoil the work. The call of Jesus is for us to co-operate in it, not find excuses for creating our own ways of doing things. And the purpose of prophecy is to remind us of the way, so that we can sustain our co-operation in it. Cessationist teaching only undermines that purpose, which is entirely of God.

To say these things, however, is not to give blanket approval to everything that has happened under the name of prophecy. It is equally important to remember that prophetic enthusiasts are commonly their own worst enemies. The greatest dangers to prophetic Christianity have come, not through pagan persecution, nor even through ecclesiastical suppression, but through its adherents own excesses. That, of course, has added fuel to the cessationists' fire. They can quite rightly point to charismatic disasters and triumphantly declare, 'That is not of God!' Paul could have done the same at Corinth, but he did not. Instead, he spoke to correct and restore balance. He appealed to them, not to reject the gifts, rather to 'eagerly desire' them, but at the same time he challenged them to 'follow the way of love' and to do everything 'in a fitting and orderly way' (1 Cor. 14:1,40). That is how we must continue to view the Spirit's work. Today's prophets, for all their faults, failings and imperfections, are still God's front-line fighters. They need to be encouraged and corrected, not dismissed.

The story of the prophetic in the early Church is not one of withdrawal of the gifts, but of their functions being overtaken by other, more human means of operating, followed by a diminishment in understanding of their nature and purpose. Then came the first charismatic revival in the latter half of the second century. Most of it was perfectly orthodox, but some of it ran to excess, at least in the estimation of some of the influential church leaders of the time. The reaction caused such a setback in Christian thinking that it effectively sent the prophetic flow of Christian life out into the fringes of church life—in some places extinguishing it altogether. And these effects lasted for hundreds of years, only to be properly reversed in our own time.

# 7
# From Christ to Constantine

The history of the early Church is one of rapid expansion, with opposition and persecution. That is the flavour of its story in Acts, and it continued in much the same vein, though on a wider canvas, over the next three centuries until Constantine and his successors established Christianity as the state religion of the Roman Empire. In New Testament times the growth was unquestionably prophetic, but it gradually became less so. After a remarkable charismatic revival in the late second century, it settled into a more ecclesiastical mould, though certainly not lacking in fibre and faith.

*Church Growth and Opposition in New Testament Times*

The combined stories of growth and persecution start right at the beginning. Jesus, because he came as King of the Jews, had limited his own mission to 'the lost sheep of Israel' and had similarly instructed his disciples not to 'go among the Gentiles or enter any house of the Samaritans' (Matt. 10:5; 15:24). But after his resurrection he commissioned them to 'go and make disciples of all nations', to be his 'witnesses in Jerusalem, and in all Judea and Samaria, and to the ends of the earth' (Matt. 28:19; Mark 16:15; Acts 1:8), commanding them first to wait for the coming of the Holy Spirit, 'the gift my Father promised' (Luke 24:49; Acts 1:4f).

On that day, the day of Pentecost, when the Spirit descended on the waiting company, they were able to witness immediately to men of every nation gathered for the festival in Jerusalem, and in that setting Peter announced the birth of the Spiritual or Prophetic Church of the last days (Acts 2:16-18).

From that point the apostles' preaching quickly brought a large harvest of Jewish souls into the kingdom of God. But when there was new growth, they ensured that it had the same pentecostal anointing as their own. Peter ended his first sermon by offering his hearers and their families the promised gift of the Holy Spirit (2:38f), and his second by offering them the inheritance of the prophets (3:25). When they chose new leaders in the church they had to be men noted for their spiritual endowment (6:3). When a new church grew in Samaria, the apostles ensured that it was fully blessed with the Spirit (8:15-17). It seems to have been part of the apostles' duty to make certain that the early Jewish church in Jerusalem, Judea and Samaria was thoroughly pentecostal.

The picture continues to be the same when their wider missions set the Gentile harvest in motion. Under Peter's ministration the first Gentile convert was born into the kingdom in a wonderful pentecostal outpouring (10:44-47). When Paul was prophetically appointed to his calling as a missionary to the Gentiles, he was filled with the Holy Spirit (9:17). His first evangelistic tour was initiated thorough prophecy (13:2), and the report of the council that followed it was carried to the churches by two prophets, Judas and Silas (15:32). From the brief notice of Paul's first encounter with some converts in Ephesus we see how foundational baptism in the Holy Spirit was to him in a new church (19:1-7). The same emphasis, of course, comes through many of Paul's letters to the churches.

The early church clearly held fast to its pentecostal vision. Its growth was also exceedingly rapid, so much so that about twenty years after the crucifixion it was being said that Christianity was turning the world upside down (Acts 17:6). The story of Acts climaxes with the gospel being preached in Rome itself ten years later.

Equally swift were the persecutions, first by the Jews, then later by the Romans. Very early the Sanhedrin authorised the arrest of Peter and John, and the purges of Saul which led to Stephen's martyrdom (Acts 3-7). In 43 AD Herod had James the Apostle executed and Peter was arrested for a second time (Acts 12). Paul suffered a lot at the hands of the Jews all through his missions (Acts 13-14, 16-17, 21-28). It was on the related issue of Jewish-Gentile tensions inside the Church itself that he had to defend his mission when the first major council of Christian leaders was convened in Jerusalem in 48 AD (Acts 15).

In 62 AD the Chief Priest ordered the stoning of James ('the Just'), Jesus' brother, head of the church in Jerusalem, but Jewish persecution was abruptly halted soon after that when the Palestinian Jews revolted in 66 AD against the Romans, who responded in turn by attacking Jerusalem. In 70 AD, after a three-year siege, they took the city, plundered it and set it on fire.

*The Beginning of Persecution by Rome*

About this time, just after the history in Acts ends in the mid-60s, Christianity and Judaism separated and came to be seen as two distinct religions. Shortly before the outbreak of the Jewish War the church in Jerusalem, encouraged by a word of prophecy,[1] removed itself from the city to a town called Pella in Transjordan and thus escaped the massacres of 70 AD. A few years earlier, in 64, the Roman authorities first showed that they too now recognised Christianity as a separate faith. Earlier, in 49 AD, the Emperor Claudius had made no distinction, but simply drove all the Jews from Rome, both Christians and non-Christians, when disturbance arose among them on account of Christ.[2]

By contrast, when a large part of the city of Rome was destroyed by fire in 64 AD, Nero, pinned the blame quite firmly on the Christian community, thus initiating the first official Roman persecution of the Church, in which many were brutally tortured and killed and in the wake of which Peter and Paul were both martyred in Rome in 67 AD.

After Nero's death in 68 the Church enjoyed some respite, until Domitian, towards the end of the century, required Christians to acknowledge him as 'Lord and God'. Further suffering ensued, including John's exile on the island of Patmos (Rev. 1:9). Then in the early second century, about 112, we find Trajan writing to Pliny, governor of Bithynia, permitting persecution 'for the name'. Nero and Domitian had found other reasons for persecuting; Trajan's decree permitted persecution simply for being called Christian. And so it was to continue intermittently, though with increasing intensity, over the next two centuries. Among those martyred in Trajan's time were Simon, the second Bishop of Jerusalem, an aged cousin of Jesus, and Ignatius, Bishop of Antioch (37-107), whose teaching helped to establish the authority of the bishops in the early Church.

Some respite followed in Hadrian's time (117-38), towards the end of which attention switched again to the Jews. In 132 they rose in rebellion in Palestine under the leadership of one, Bar-Kochba ('Son of the Star'), who presented himself as their Messiah. The Christians in Judea suffered again at the hands of the Jews during

---

1. 'Moreover, the people of the church at Jerusalem, in accordance with a certain *oracle* that was vouchsafed by way of revelation to approved men there, had been commanded *to depart from the city* before the war, and *to inhabit a certain city of Perea*. They called it *Pella*. And when *those who believed in Christ* had removed from Jerusalem, as if holy men had utterly deserted both the royal metropolis of the Jews itself and the whole land of Judea, the Justice of God then visited upon them all their acts of violence to Christ and His apostles, by destroying that generation of wicked persons *root and branch* from among men.' (tr. H. Lawlor & J. Oulton, Eusebius, *Ecclesiastical History* III.5.3.)
2. Acts 18:2; Suetonius (*Claudius* 25.4) said the Jews rioted 'at the instigation of Chrestus', and presumably Chrestus is a Latin rendering of Christ.

this uprising, but after it was quashed in 135 the Jews were expelled from Palestine and Jerusalem was turned into a Roman city, renamed Aelia Capitolina. It was not until recently, in 1948, that the Jews were again allowed to return to their ancestral homeland.

*Church Growth and Development in the Second Century*

Unfortunately we know virtually nothing about the Church's history during the thirty years after the end of Acts, but when it re-emerges into the light at the beginning of the second century we see that it has grown and spread rapidly throughout the Empire, in some regions quite extensively. When Pliny became governor of Asia, the size and impact of the Christian presence there perplexed him considerably and it was mainly that that caused him to write to Trajan asking whether and how to persecute.

Growth brought other problems besides opposition. The multiplying of conversions and churches highlighted the need for sound teaching and for good control over what was taught. Lack of either resulted too easily in departures from the doctrine of the apostles and the consequent growth of heresy. Hence the earliest post-biblical writings, from the end of the first and the beginning of the second centuries, lay much emphasis on the need for strong church discipline and firm systems of leadership. To that end the orders of bishop (overseer), presbyter (elder) and deacon (assistant) were now recognised as the Church's main governmental structure, with a clear mandate to maintain sound teaching.

Other traditions were also beginning to emerge at this time, such as growing reverence for Sunday and Easter, and accepted forms for worship and celebration of the Eucharist, though it was to take another two hundred years and more before any universal agreement was reached about any of these matters. The Church also continued to maintain a high moral profile and a strong, aggressive zeal among its members, but, sadly, we detect occasional signs of decline in the tone of its spiritual life (cp. Rev. 2-3). The Church that was thoroughly charismatic at its birth and as it first spread through the Gentile world, by the early second century was no longer so obviously alive in its exercise of spiritual gifts. Nevertheless, by the end of that century Christianity had spread throughout the whole of the Roman Empire and its episcopal structures were quite well established everywhere.

*Heretics, Apologists, Theologians and Schools*

The main heresies the Church had to deal with in the first two centuries are collectively described as Gnosticism. The Gnostic systems varied a great deal, but their adherents all believed in hierarchies of intermediate heavenly beings between God and man, Christ usually coming somewhere in the middle. Among their most famous teachers were Cerinthus (c. 90), Basilides (c. 125), Valentinus (c. 140) and Marcion (c. 140-55).

The task of opposing these, as well as appealing to the civic authorities against persecution, and seeking to establish firm doctrine and practice in the churches, dominated the writings of the second century Church fathers. Among the best known of these was Justin Martyr, a Palestinian philosopher, who, after his conversion, wrote several apologies in defence of Christianity, one addressed to the Emperor, another to the Roman Senate, and another to a Jew called Tryhpo. He was martyred about 160 AD. One of his most outstanding pupils was Tatian, who came from Assyria. He also wrote an apology, addressed 'To the Greeks'. In Gaul, Irenaeus, Bishop of Lyons (120-202), wrote extensively to oppose Gnosticism and all heresy, appealing to good biblical foundations. His work was also constructive in seeking to explain some of the foundational doctrines of the faith and so he is often regarded as the first of the great theologians of the early church.

Explaining the faith to a Greek-thinking world in which Hebraic thought seemed strange became one of the main preoccupations of the third century church. Among the most outstanding leaders in this work were two men from Alexandria, Clement (150-215) and Origen (185-254), who applied the Greek Platonic philosophy, for which the university of Alexandria was famed at the time, to the interpretation of the faith. Their system proved very attractive and established an approach to the Bible that persisted throughout the Middle Ages. Its extensive use of allegorising and spiritualising interpretation, however, tended to remove the reader from the plain meaning of the text and thus obscured some of the truths that are foundational to prophetic faith. Part of the work of the sixteenth-century reformers was to recover that plain meaning for the faithful.

In Carthage, Tertullian (160-225), laid the first foundations for Latin theology, but he was a lawyer by profession, not a philosopher, and his writings, particularly on the Trinity, are more practical than fanciful. Round about the year 200 he became a Montanist.[3] Also in Carthage, but a little later, Bishop Cyprian (martyred 258), probably did more than anyone else to see episcopal authority finally established.

---

3. See below, p. 102.

Over in Italy, Hippolytus (170-236), probably the most important theologian in the Roman Church in the third-century, wrote a massive work called *Refutation of All Heresies*.

Through the work of such men, well-known schools of theology began to emerge as centres of Christian learning, the best known of them in Carthage, Alexandria, Caesarea (where Origen finally settled) and various places in Asia Minor.

*The Faith of the Martyrs and the Conquest of the Roman Empire*

Persecution started afresh in the middle of the second century and continued in waves of varying but increasing intensity until the early fourth. The martyr stories, of course, make both horrific and heroic reading, but their details are not our concern in this book.[4] What is important, however, is to recognise the change in spirituality they wrought. Martyrdom came to be regarded as a Christian's highest calling and those who so died came to be venerated as heroes of the faith. The accounts of their sacrifice were written down and cherished as encouragements to the faithful.

Sporadic persecution had continued regionally, but the philosopher-emperor, Marcus Aurelius, again made it imperial policy for a while during his reign (161-80). Among the more memorable martyr stories from this period are those of Polycarp, the aged and saintly bishop of Smyrna, in 155, and of the martyrs of Lyons in 177. After a further period of relaxation, persecution erupted once more at the beginning of the third century, during the latter part of the reign of Septimus Severus (193-211). This time the imperial fury was felt most severely in North Africa where the martyrs, mainly new converts, included Leonidas, Origen's father, in Alexandria, and the lady Perpetua and her maid, Felicity, in Carthage, the tale of whose martyrdom is particularly moving.

After Severus the churches enjoyed some forty years of respite, interrupted by a brief and limited persecution under Maximinius (235-8). Christians were now found in all levels of society, some of them serving in high positions in government and at the imperial court. Most emperors were simply glad of their service, occasionally taking active measures to ensure their protection. Then quite suddenly the persecutions erupted again in two quite brief, but exceedingly fierce and bitter outbursts, the first in 250 when Decius (249-51) tried to strengthen Roman unity on the basis of Emperor worship, and the second in 257 when Valerian (253-60) sought to close the

4. Ed. J. Stevenson, *A New Eusebius*, pp. 18-20, 31-41, 285-9. Foxe's *Book of Martyrs*.

churches, forbid Christian worship and confiscate their properties. These two persecutions, though brief, are among the bloodiest in history. But the next emperor, Galien (260-8), restored the stolen properties and the Church again enjoyed imperial favour for most of the rest of the century, apart from one brief moment under Aurelian (270-5). It was during Valerian's persecution that Cyprian, Bishop of Carthage, was martyred, and also Sextus, Bishop of Rome.

The last and by far the most intense and violent persecution was that instituted by Diocletian (284-305) towards the end of his reign and continuing into the reign of his successors, from 303 to 311. It is particularly memorable to the English, because it produced their first martyr, St. Alban. Imperial edicts withdrew the protection of citizenship from the Christians, ordered the demolition of all their churches, and commanded the burning of all Bibles. This, however, was to be the final fury before the end, which came quite suddenly, first when Galerius (305-11) issued an edict of toleration in 311 and then finally when Constantine became emperor (312-37) and published his famous Edict of Milan in 313, officially ending all persecution of Christians in the Roman Empire.

Apart from one movement known as Montanism, which we shall look at in detail presently, there were no recorded prophetic revivals during the age of persecution, but evangelistic zeal was far from weak and the Church continued to grow. Doubtless one of Christianity's strengths actually came through persecution, for as Tertullian once said, 'The blood of the martyrs is seed.' Though persecution in the early days was sporadic, it later became governmental policy and was systematically organised. The end result was purification of the Body of Christ. Christians were almost to a man totally committed to the faith and martyrdom became their greatest act of witness—so much so that many came to see martyrdom as their ultimate vocation and therefore viewed those who fled into hiding or exile as traitors.

In North Africa, where the persecutions became particularly severe, those that had stood firm in their time of trial later refused to join hands with the rest, who had fled or renounced their faith. When persecution eased off after 311, they formed themselves into a separate church, known as Donatist. Their rigid stance caused great heartache and further suffering among the churches in Africa, and so they themselves suffered further persecution at the hands of the state. The schism was finally condemned at the Council of Carthage in 411, but it persisted until finally suppressed by the Islamic invaders of North Africa in the seventh and eighth centuries.

Their fervent spirit, troublesome as it proved to the rest of the church, bears witness to the zeal of the faithful that enabled Christianity to survive in persecution and indeed to grow until it conquered the empire.

*The Vision of the Church of the Spirit*

The greatest danger to the vision of a spiritual Church came not from persecuting Jews or pagans, but from inside the Christian community itself. Despite Jesus' own vision of a world-wide Church and his commission to take the gospel to all nations, the day the gospel began to spread beyond the security of the Jewish cradle into the Gentile world, the spiritual Church encountered its first opposition. The enemy was tradition.

When Peter went to Cornelius, the defenders of tradition rose up in indignation, and Peter had to plead the cause of Pentecost (Acts 10-11). When Paul went out into the Gentile world he had to battle for the freedom of the Spirit (Gal. 2), because the same hackles were raised once more (Acts 15). Had Peter not stood firm before the other apostles and the church in Jerusalem, and had Paul not also stood firm at Antioch, the Church might well have become little more than a sect of Judaism, buried under a blanket of tradition.

What Paul fought for so hard was again in danger only twenty or thirty years after his martyrdom. According to the letters to the churches in Rev. 2-3 zeal was diminishing considerably and so the appeal at the end of the first century was already for revival. This time it was internal failings rather than external pressures that had caused the decline, for the repeated call is to repentance.

The second century produced some excellent leaders and writers. But as time passed their attention was increasingly taken up with internal issues. The early apologists who defended the faith so enthusiastically before Jews and pagans were gradually superseded by the anti-Gnostic theologians who were necessarily preoccupied with issues of orthodoxy, matters of belief and doctrine. Prophetic zeal slipped slowly into the background, giving way to the very formalism in religion and laxity in morals that Paul had fought to avert. The vision of the Church of the Spirit faded correspondingly—that is until the end of the century when the Montanist movement brought it right to the fore again in a wave of prophetic revival.

Like the Judaisers in Paul's day, the churchmen objected and this time proved too strong for the revivalists. Though the Montantists found a defender of stature in Tertullian, he was not able to achieve what Paul had done, and the movement, once it had been branded heretical by the bishops and councils, quickly lost credence. The triumph of the orthodox was to mean the suppression and virtual loss of the vision of the spiritual Church for many centuries. The issue caused a flurry for a time, but the Catholic Church was far too much occupied with other matters to sustain the dialogue, and so the prophetic Church was soon forgotten, or regarded as a thing of the past.

As doctrinal, ritual and theological issues increasingly occupied the minds of churchmen, Christianity became correspondingly more academic and religious. Virtually all the Church councils of the fourth century, after Constantine became Emperor, were called to deal with such issues. The battle Paul won in the first century had been lost by the fourth. Orthodoxy had surely triumphed. To any observer at the time, indeed over the following thousand years, it would have seemed that the Church of the Spirit was little more than a memory of history. But God had not forgotten it. A battle was lost and won, the lines of victor and vanquished were drawn for a time, but the war had not ended. The prophets were still there, albeit underground. They would raise their heads again from time to time …

But now we are passing beyond the period that immediately concerns us. First let us look more closely at the story of the prophets in the early church before we progress any further.

# 8

# Prophetic Christianity in the Early Church

Tracing the history of prophetic Christianity becomes increasingly difficult as we progress through the records of the first three centuries, quite simply because they have little to say on the subject. They also lack the enthusiasm for such things that we found in the writings of Luke, Paul and John. Though spiritual gifts continued to be recognised and used, by the early second century Christianity as a whole was ceasing to be self-consciously prophetic.

There are many reasons for the change, some of which we have already noted. The displacement of charismatic ministry by institutional, authoritarian government led to the prophetic task of speaking 'to men for their strengthening, encouragement and comfort' (1 Cor. 14:3) becoming the preserve of the bishops and their clergy. The concentration on the formulation of doctrine, made essential at the time to control proliferating heresy, subordinated pastoral concern for fullness of life in the Spirit to theological concern for correctness of belief. Christian understanding of 'faith' gradually changed, so that it became acceptance of credal statements about the nature of God, Christ and the Church, instead of the open trust in Jesus and the power of God's Spirit that enabled signs and wonders to follow those who believed. Equally disastrous was the disrepute brought on spiritual giftings through failure to deal conclusively with the problem of false prophecy.

The gifts never passed entirely from the Church. In some places they dwindled into relative disuse, in others they were deliberately suppressed, in yet others they persisted in some measure with a different understanding of their function. The process of change was fairly protracted before the fixed attitude of the medieval Church finally emerged.

*The Persistence of Prophetic Christianity in the Second Century*

The early Church fathers do not often make mention of prophetic activity in their writings, though in a handful of scattered texts they do acknowledge its existence, and that usually with approval. Though exercise of the gifts was clearly in decline, they were still held to be of God, and some of the fathers even seemed proud to point out that they were still found in the churches.

Justin Martyr, writing shortly before his death in 165 AD, in discussion with a Jew named Trypho, argued that the exercise of spiritual gifts among the Christians of his day showed that they had passed from the Jewish people through Christ to the Church and that the Church must therefore be the true heir of the Jewish prophetical Spirit:

> 'The prophetical gifts remain with us even to the present day. From that fact you ought to recognise that the gifts which were found among your people in ancient times have now been transferred to us.... it had to be that these gifts should be withdrawn from you [the Jews], find rest in him [Christ], and become once more, as was prophesied, gifts which, from the grace of his Spirit's power, he gives to those who believe in him, according as he reckons each man worthy of them.... And there are indeed to be found among us both women and men who possess the gifts of the Spirit of God.'[5]

At one point Justin says that the Christians using these gifts are those who are 'worthy' to do so:

> 'they are also receiving gifts, each one as he is worthy. For one receives the Spirit of understanding, another of counsel, another of strength, another of healing, another of fore knowledge, another of teaching and another of the fear of God.'[6]

He does not explain what he means by the word, but in it we detect overtones of an emerging doctrine of merit, the very thing Paul opposed in Galatians (cp. Gal. 3:1-5). The gifts may be the same, but the understanding of them has somewhat changed.

Irenaeus, Bishop of Lyons, writing about 182-88, speaks with highest approval of the regular exercise of a whole range of gifts in the churches of Gaul, but he also gives the impression that these gifts, though widely and openly used, were for the most part the reserve of a few enthusiasts, whom he reverentially calls 'those who are truly his disciples'.

5. Justin, *Dialogue with Trypho* 82, 87f.
6. *Dialogue* 39.

> 'Those who are truly his disciples, receiving grace from him, perform miracles in his name to the benefit of others, each according to the gift he has received from him. Some most surely and truly drive out demons, so that those who have been purged of the evil spirits very frequently become believers and join the Church. Others have foreknowledge of things to come; they see visions or have the gift of prophetic utterance. Others by the laying on of hands heal the sick and make them well again. Also, as I have already mentioned, dead men have been raised and have remained with us for a number of years. And what else can I add? It is not possible to list the number of gifts that the Church throughout the whole world has received from God in the name of Jesus Christ.'[7]

*Spiritual Christians and Spiritual Leaders*

The respect with which Irenaeus views the charismatics in the churches is explained even more fully when he applies the terms 'perfect' and 'spiritual' from 1 Cor. 2 to them.

> 'The Apostle says, "We speak wisdom among the perfect." [1 Cor. 2:6] The ones he calls "perfect" are those who have received the Spirit of God and who through the Spirit of God speak in all languages, just as he also used to do himself. In the same way we also hear many brethren in the Church who possess prophetic gifts, and speak through the Spirit in all kinds of languages, and bring to light the secret things of men for their good, and declare the mysteries of God. The Apostle also calls these men "spiritual"—they are spiritual because they partake of the Spirit.'[8]

His use of this terminology highlights the shift that has taken place since apostolic times. When Paul wrote to the Corinthians, the distinction he was drawing was between non-Christians, whom he called 'natural' (*psychikoi*) because they did not have the Spirit of Christ, and the Christians, who were 'spiritual' (*pneumatikoi*) because they did. Irenaeus, in contrast, now uses it to distinguish between two categories of Christian. Paul used it of all Christians, because in his day all of them were 'spiritual', or prophetical, anyhow. But with the waning of charismatic Christianity, the term can now only apply to those that still stand in the prophetic tradition of

---

7. Irenaeus, *Against Heresies* II.32.4.
8. *Against Heresies* V.6.1.

the apostles. This is a distinction Paul would hardly have envisaged in his time, but it is the one that was to be applicable in every future age until our own.

Much as Irenaeus may have esteemed the 'spirituals', by his day they were clearly a minority and held no position of authority in the churches. It had been different in New Testament times. In the first post-apostolic decades leadership in the Church had continued prophetic. Eusebius makes reference to two early prophets named Ammia and Quadratus, whom he lists alongside Agabus, Judas, Silas and the daughters of Philip, and he adds 'there were many others besides these who were known in those days [for their prophetical gifts], and who occupied the first place among the successors of the apostles.'[9]

*The Ministry and Authority of Prophets*

The high esteem with which prophets were held in early post-apostolic times is perhaps best illustrated in the *Didache,* a small handbook on morals and church practice, dating from the late first or early second century. Prophets are mentioned in four of its chapters.

Ch. 11 is concerned with the status of itinerant prophets who, like other missionaries, are to be received 'as Christ', though not without caution, since there were also plenty of false prophets around.[10]

Ch. 13 deals with the 'true prophet who wishes to settle down among you'. Unlike the itinerant, he is to be maintained by the church. But more than that, he is to have the status that the chief priest held in Jewish society and so is to receive all the offerings of first-fruits and the tithes that old Israel had been commanded to take to the sanctuary. What precisely his function in the congregation was is not very clear.

Ch. 10 says he is to offer the prayer of thanksgiving at Communion and by virtue of his special prophetic endowment is not to be restricted by prescribed formulae when he prays. Otherwise no duties are specified.

Ch. 15, however, suggests he must have had some kind of presidential and pastoral role, for it likens his function to that of bishops and deacons.

The implication of all this is that, though Paul could earlier rank prophets next to apostles in the church, not every congregation at the end of the first century had its own prophet. Ch. 15 urges:

9. Eusebius, *Ecclesiastical History* III.37.1 & V.17.2-4.
10. See further below, pp. 93, 94.

'Appoint for yourselves bishops and deacons ... For they also perform the service of the prophets and teachers for you. So do not despise them, for they are your honourable men along with the prophets and teachers.' The prophetic office still had the edge over the bishopric in the thinking of the author, though he clearly recognised it was a declining office.

It is commonly held that *The Didache* originated in Syria, where the main centre of Christianity was at Antioch. There the leadership of the church in New Testament times was in the hands of 'prophets and teachers' (Acts 13:1). It seems this system persisted into the second century in the region.

*Outstanding Prophetic Leaders*

A few second century bishops were noted for their prophetic anointing. Polycarp, bishop of Smyrna, is said to have foreseen his own martyrdom in a vision and to have shown other signs of prophetic gifting.[11] Melito, bishop of Sardis, was considered by Tertullian to be a prophet[12], and Eusebius said that he 'lived altogether in the Holy Spirit'.[13] Perhaps the most notable of all is Ignatius, bishop of Antioch, who was the leading protagonist of the episcopal system at the beginning of the second century. If Jesus' disciples had appreciated the need for prophetic zeal to maintain their missionary impetus, Ignatius felt that the greatest need of his time was for strong, authoritative leadership in the churches to maintain unity and orthodoxy in the face of rapidly proliferating heresies. Now what is particularly interesting is that in one of the letters he wrote on the eve of his martyrdom in 107 AD he claimed that his teaching about the authority of the bishop was itself based on prophetic inspiration:

> 'When I was among you I cried out, I spoke with a loud voice, with the voice of God: "Give heed to the bishop and the presbytery and deacons." But there were those who suspected that I said this because I knew beforehand about the division that some persons had caused. But he for whom I am bound a prisoner is my witness that I did not learn it from any human being. It was the Spirit who was preaching, saying these words: "Do nothing without the bishop; keep your flesh as a

11. *Martyrdom of Polycarp* 5 & 7.
12. Jerome, *Lives of Illustrious Men* 24.
13. *History* V.24.5.

temple of God; cherish unity; shun divisions; be imitators of Jesus Christ, as he also was of his Father."'[14]

In the course of the second century the episcopal leadership completely overtook the charismatic. Prophecy by then had become the possession of a few enthusiasts, Irenaeus's 'spirituals'. Though it carried no divisive overtones in Irenaeus' thinking, this term that Paul had once applied to all Christians was presently put to entirely sectarian use by the Montanists. Some such development, however, was virtually inevitable, for Christianity itself had to all intents and purposes ceased to be a prophetic movement.

*The Continuing Problem of False Prophecy*

False prophecy proved to be just as intractable a problem to the Christian Church as it had been to ancient Israel. Its early existence is attested, as we have noted, in the New Testament itself, and at the end of the second century Irenaeus can still write about

> 'false prophets who, though they have not received the gift of prophecy from God and though they do not fear God, pretend to give prophetic utterances, motivated perhaps by the prospect of empty glory or by the hope of some personal gain, or even in some other way under the influence of an evil spirit. Their words are lies against God.'[15]

He also gives an interesting example of one such prophet at work, an otherwise unknown heretic, called Marcus:

> 'It seems likely that he possesses some demon as a familiar spirit by whose power he appears able to prophesy himself and by whose power he enables others to prophesy, that is those he considers fit to be partakers of his grace. He devotes himself particularly to women ... If the woman replies, "I have never at any time prophesied, and do not know how to prophesy," ... he says to her, "Open your mouth, speak whatever occurs to you and you will be prophesying." She then, vainly puffed up and elated by his words, inwardly excited by the expectation that it is she herself that is to prophesy, her heart beating violently, reaches a pitch of daring at which she utters some nonsense as it happens to occur to her, all of it as empty as it is daring, just as might be expected from one

14. Justin, *To the Philadelphians* 7.
15. *Against Heresies* IV.33.6.

heated by an empty spirit… . Thereafter she reckons herself a prophetess and thanks Marcus for giving her a share of his own grace.'[16]

*Discerning True and False Prophets*

The main preoccupation of Didache 11 is with distinguishing the true from the false prophet, particularly if he is a hitherto unknown itinerant visitor. Strangely, despite Paul's injunction to test 'everything' (1 Thes. 5:21) and John's caution to 'test the spirits to see whether they are from God' (1 John 4:1), it prohibits subjecting 'any prophet who speaks in the Spirit to a test or critical examination,' and declares that any attempt to do so must be regarded as unforgivable sin. The tests it does advocate are moral and doctrinal rather than spiritual, similar in some respects to those approved in the Old Testament.

A true prophet is recognised by the degree to which his character and way of life are those of the Lord. He should not make himself a burden to the congregation by staying for more than a couple of days, and when he leaves he should take only enough food to sustain him till he finds fresh lodging. He should certainly never ask for money. Similarly, his actual prophesying should show no signs of selfish interest. Thus if, in the Spirit, he asks for money, it should be only that it may be given to the needy. Furthermore, his teaching should conform to the Church's doctrine and his own practice should also conform to his teachings.

The most thorough attempt to deal with the problem of false prophecy in the Church is found in Hermas' *Shepherd*, a book that was very popular in its day, written some time between 90 and 150 AD. In a section known as 'The Mandates', Hermas is granted revelations by the Shepherd, an angelic instructor, who teaches him lessons for the edification of the Church. The eleventh mandate is devoted entirely to the subject of true and false prophecy, but its value also lies in the fact that it is both the fullest account of early Christian prophecy extant and, apart from 1 Cor. 14, the only text that gives any picture of how the gift operated in church meetings.

Like Didache 11, it suggests that truth is best determined by observation of the prophet's way of life. But it goes a little further when it also claims that the difference will be manifest from the prophet's behaviour before the assembled church at prayer. In conformity with the New Testament, it sets the true gift wholly in the

16. *Against Heresies* I.13.3.

context of congregational worship, and it equally maintains that the prophet who gives private teaching or prophetic consultations to enquirers must be dismissed as false. In contrast with the New Testament and the Didache, prophets are nowhere recognised as church leaders. Hermas accepts only the episcopal system of government. The prophets are solely charismatic functionaries and their value to the Church lies entirely in the exercise of their prophetic gifts in the gathered meeting.

*Prophetic Scenes from Hermas*

The Shepherd shows Hermas a portrait of the false prophet addressing his clients. He describes a scene like an ancient schoolroom, with a false prophet occupying the teacher's chair and people sitting on a bench in front of him. These, he says, are Christians who are not strong in their faith, but rather double-minded, and they come to the prophet in much the same way as pagans go to consult a soothsayer, hoping they will learn what is going to happen to them. The prophet, who 'has no power of the divine Spirit in himself', basically tells them the kind of things they want to hear anyway. 'He is empty himself, the people who come to him are empty and the answers he gives them are empty too.' He simply preys on and feeds their empty human longings. Some of his answers do prove true, however, because the devil uses him to deceive and destroy the righteous. Those who are strong in their faith know better than to consult such a person, but the double-minded run after him for his divinations. The whole thing is no better than pagan idolatry. The Shepherd comments at this point:

> 'One does not enquire of any spirit that has been given by God [in the sort of way that one would enquire of a soothsayer]; it has the power of the deity and says all that it does of its own accord, because it is from above and partakes of the power of the divine Spirit. But the spirit that one consults and which speaks to flatter human desires is of the earth and is mindless; it has no power. Anyhow, it does not speak at all unless it is consulted!'

In answer to the question, 'How then shall a man recognise which is a true and which a false prophet?', the Shepherd says,

> 'You must estimate the man who possesses the divine Spirit from his way of life.' The true prophet will be gentle, peaceable and humble, he will keep away from evil and the vain desires

of this world, and he will not seek riches, indeed will even make himself poorer than the rest of men.

Thus far the test is like that suggested in the Didache, but the Shepherd also goes on to discuss how the gift will operate in a church meeting, and at this point we find ourselves back in the world of Paul in 1 Cor. 14:

> 'He will give no reply to anyone who comes to enquire for an oracle, nor will he speak when he is alone (the Holy Spirit does not speak just whenever someone wants him to do so), but he will speak when God wants him to speak. When the man who has the divine Spirit comes into an assembly of righteous men who have faith in the divine Spirit and the men of that assembly offer prayer to God, then the angel of the prophetic Spirit that is allotted to him will fill the man and he now filled with the Holy Spirit will address the congregation, speaking whatever the Lord wishes him to speak. This, then, is how the Spirit of the Godhead will show himself.'

For the rest the Shepherd simply expands on these things he has already said. The false spirit is earthly, from below; the Spirit of God is heavenly, from above. The man with the earthly spirit is proud, self-seeking, always wanting the most important seat, pushing himself forward, a great talker, a seeker of luxury, indeed fraudulent, and even looking for payment for his prophecies. He avoids the assembly of the righteous, preferring the company of the weaker brethren who will listen to him, in whose company he is like one empty jar among other empty jars, speaking empty words to empty people, but

> 'when he comes into an assembly full of righteous men who have the Spirit of the Godhead and they offer prayer, that man finds himself empty. The earthly spirit flees from him in fear and he is left dumbfounded, utterly shattered and quite unable to speak.'

The Shepherd says the difference between the two spirits is easily discerned if you bear in mind the distinction between the earthly and the heavenly, from below and above, from the devil and from God. What is from below has no power, what is from heaven has God's power. Contrast the uselessness of trying to pierce the sky by throwing a stone or squirting water up at it with the dramatic effect of a small hailstone falling on one's head or water dripping on a stone.

'The smallest things falling to the earth from above have great power. So also the divine Spirit coming from above is powerful. Put your trust in that Spirit, but keep well away from the other.'

*Opinions about the Nature of True Prophecy*

The last paragraph in Hermas suggests persistence of the view expressed in 2 Pet. 1:21 about the inspirational character of prophecy, that men were moved, not by any human impulse, but by the Holy Spirit to speak from God. The church fathers never discuss the nature of Christian prophetic inspiration (except in relation to Montanism, see ch. 3), but their comments on Old Testament prophecy indicate that many of them regarded the prophet as a passive instrument in the hands of the Spirit.

Theophilus of Antioch speaks of them being

'transported by the Holy Spirit ... inspired and made wise by God ... taught by God ... that they should become instruments of God and hold the wisdom that comes from him, through which wisdom they spoke.'[17]

Other writers compare the prophets with musical instruments. Athenagoras speaks about

'the Spirit of God who moved the mouths of the prophets like musical instruments,' saying that 'they found themselves lifted in ecstasy above the normal functioning of their minds as the Divine Spirit stirred in them, the Spirit making use of them as a flute-player breathes into a flute.'[18]

Justin Martyr compares them with stringed instruments. He believes that they

'taught us nothing from their own private fancy ... had no need of rhetorical art ... but to present themselves pure to the energy of the Divine Spirit, in order that the divine plectrum itself, descending from heaven, and using righteous men as an instrument like a harp or lyre, might reveal to us the knowledge of things divine and heavenly.'[19]

17. Theophilus, *To Autolycus* II.9.
18. Athenagoras, *A Plea for the Christians* 8 and 9.
19. Justin, *Exhortation to the Greeks* 8.

Hippolytus uses the same image:

> 'They were like musical instruments and the Word which was always within them and at one with them was like a plectrum. When they were moved by him, the prophets announced whatever God wanted them to say. For they did not speak by their own power—let there be no mistake about that—nor did they declare whatever they wanted to themselves. But first of all they were endowed with wisdom by the Word, and then were carefully instructed about the future by means of visions. Finally, when they were fully convinced by these communications, they spoke out those things which had been revealed by God to them alone, but which were concealed from other men.'[20]

It is, of course, uncertain how far some of these writers had experienced Christian prophecy in the churches and whether they would have described contemporary prophets in the same way. The Montanists held similar views about their prophets, but already by their time, and increasingly because of their activities, these views were being disputed by the champions of orthodoxy and ecclesiastical order.

*Decline of Prophetic Christianity in the Third Century*

At the end of the third century Eusebius wrote as if he were no longer aware of any active exercise of prophetic gifts in the churches with which he was familiar. In his history he introduced some of Irenaeus' statements about them with the comment, 'he shows that manifestations of divine and miraculous power continued to his time in some of the churches,' and he rounds off his citations with the further remark, 'So much in regard to the fact that various gifts remained among those who were worthy until that time.'[21]

On the other hand, Novatian, a Roman presbyter (martyred 257/8), wrote about the middle of the century in his study of the Trinity, that the Holy Spirit

> 'is he who places prophets in the Church, who instructs teachers, inspires tongues, gives power for healing, does wonderful things, gives discrimination of spirits ... and thus makes the Lord's Church everywhere to be mature and complete'[22]

---

20. Hippolytus, *Treatise on Christ and Antichrist* 2.
21. *Ecclesiastical History* V.7.1 & 6.
22. Novatian, *On the Trinity* XXIX.

About the same time, Origen, in a work (c. 247 AD) he published against Celsus, a bitter critic of Christianity, cited Celsus' own description of some prophets he had encountered in Phoenicia and Palestine, though he refused to give any credence to these reports himself. The report is, however, vivid and mostly quite credible:

> 'There are many—they bear no names—who very readily prophesy both inside and outside temples whenever they can find any excuse to do so. Some of them go about begging, wandering around cities or army-camps. They pretend to be moved as if acting under divine inspiration. A typical, common utterance for any one of them would be: "I am God (or the Son of God, or the divine Spirit). And I have come, for already the world is being destroyed and you, O men, will perish because of your iniquities. But I want to save you, and you will see me again when I return with heavenly power. Blessed is the man who has worshipped me now. But I will cast fire on all the rest of you, on cities and countryside alike. Men who do not understand the penalty they are having to pay will repent and groan in vain, but those who have put their faith in me I shall preserve for ever." Having enunciated these threats, they then proceed to add incomprehensible, incoherent and totally obscure utterances, the meaning of which no reasoning person could discover. The words are not clear and do not add up to anything, and so they afford every fool or impostor an opportunity to turn them to his own advantage in whatever way he wants.'[23]

Some have said these prophets Celsus met were Montanists, but it is just as likely they were the last representatives of the itinerant prophets of the late first and early second centuries we read about in the Didache and Hermas. They still speak 'as from God', are apparently still familiar with the gift of tongues, still afire with evangelistic zeal, and still preaching a basic gospel message with a strong end-time flavour. They are also still respected in the congregations, for Celsus notes that among their fellow Christians they are accorded the same kind of honour as the Old Testament prophets whose predictions 'are considered wonderful and unchangeable' (VII.3).

Despite Origen's unwillingness to credit Celsus' reports, he does actually admit the continuing existence in his time of some prophetic activity. Pointing out that the apostles' preaching could not have had the impact it did without signs and wonders, he adds,

23. Origen, *Against Celsus* VII.3 & 9.

> 'Even yet traces of that same Holy Spirit that appeared in the form of a dove are preserved among Christians. They drive out demons, they perform many acts of healing and they are able to see, as the Word wills it, certain things that relate to the future.' And he explains that it is still largely because of such charismatic ministry that people in his own time come to faith, knowing the potential cost in terms of persecution and even death. 'We know lots of stories,' he says, 'that would illustrate this, but if we were to write them down, even though we were present and saw the events for ourselves, we would simply expose ourselves to open ridicule from unbelievers.' (I.46)

*The Disappearance of the Prophetic Gifts from the Church*

Clearly in some places prophetic Christianity persisted beyond the second century. Even at the end of the third there is still evidence of continuing regard for prophets in some of the churches, as an Egyptian papyrus of about that date suggests:

> 'and that man being filled with the Holy Spirit speaks as the Lord wills, the spirit of the Divine nature will thus be manifest. For the spirit of prophecy is the essence of the prophetic order, which is the body of the flesh of Jesus Christ, which was mingled with human nature through Mary.'[24]

By and large, however, by the fourth century charismatic Christianity had become a virtually unknown entity in some parts of the Church. Writing at the end of that century, Chrysostom comments on 1 Cor. 12:1ff thus:

> 'This whole passage is exceedingly obscure; and the obscurity is occasioned by our ignorance of such things which, though they were common in those days, are no longer happening in our own.'[25]

Writing about the same time as Chrysostom, Filastrius, bishop of Brescia, in his arguments against Montanism, expresses what would appear to have become the commonly accepted theological teaching about prophecy in the Church of his day:

> 'There are some who insist that prophets are an every-day phenomenon and who forecast that prophecies will continue to be uttered. They do not seem to know that "the law and the

24. *Oxyrinchus Papyrus* V.
25. Chrysostom, *Commentary on 1 Corinthians.*

> prophets were until blessed John the Baptist" [Luke 16:16] and that the complete and utter end of the law and the prophets came with the presence of Christ.'[26]

Such teaching remains fairly standard in many evangelical and other church circles even today.

It is about the same time that we find the first instance of an apparently spiritual gift of speaking a recognisable foreign language being treated as evidence of demonic activity. This is a gift that is recognised today, when authentic, as one form of speaking in tongues (technically referred to as *xenolalia).* Jerome tells a story about a man who knew only French and Latin being found possessed of a demon, he says, because he spoke in fluent Syriac. He goes on to tell how the demon left him when commanded to do so and how the man expressed strong gratitude for being delivered.[27]

The prophetic movement that had begun with such zest at the first Christian Pentecost now lay well and truly buried. Ecclesiastical orthodoxy had no place for it any more and would repeatedly drive it out to the fringes of church life, into the sects and underground movements—that is, until our present century. It is often said that Montanism was responsible for bringing it into disrepute. There is certainly, as we shall see, much truth in that statement, but hardly the whole truth, for already by the time Montanism made its entry on the stage of history, prophecy, though by no means extinct, was no longer a vital force in the Church.

Charismatic gifts did continue in use among Christians, with full respect and approval from the authorities in many cases, for we still read about healings, exorcisms, words of wisdom and revelation, miracles, and the like. But when we do, they tend to be associated with some outstandingly holy individual, such as Gregory Thaumaturgus ('the Wonder Worker', 213-70), Bishop of Neocaesarea in Pontus, to whom many outstanding miracles are attributed, and particularly in the following centuries among the Desert Fathers and others like them, mainly ascetics and monastics. What was lost from the Church, however, was the understanding that Christianity itself was in nature prophetic. Consequently, the gifts passed from common use and any attempt to suggest they should be revived in that way was regarded as heretical and so quickly suppressed.

26. Filastrius, *On Heresies* 78.
27. Jerome, *The Life of St. Hilarion* 22.

# 9
# Montanism or the New Prophecy

To this point we have been able to study the history of prophetic faith mainly through the eyes of enthusiastic or sympathetic writers. In contrast, most of our information about Montanism comes from the pens of antagonists whose purpose was to discredit the movement. While there were doubtless grounds for some of their criticisms, we must be cautious how we use their writings for historical reconstruction. Some of the more extravagant accusations, for example, concerning Montanus' suicide, or about gambling and the use of eye-paint among his followers, or about the sacrifice of infants at their services, are clearly based on nothing but scandalous rumour. But then, such polemic is often more useful to opponents than verifiable facts are. Furthermore, prophetic phenomena tend to generate excessively heated animosity in any age, and in such an atmosphere truth can sometimes be difficult to discern.

*The Early History of the Movement*

Montanism appeared on the historical scene during the latter half of the second century. It takes its name from its founder, Montanus, though ancient writers also refer to it under a variety of different headings, the main ones being 'New Prophecy', and the 'Phrygian' or 'Cataphrygian' heresy, after its place of origin and main centre of influence, Phrygia in Asia Minor (central Turkey today).

It was there in Phrygia in 172 AD (or perhaps 15 years earlier—the date is uncertain) that Montanus, a recent convert, first began his prophesying. Among his earliest followers were two well-to-do ladies, called Priscilla (or Prisca) and Maximilla. Doubtless their patronage did much to promote the movement, though perhaps not precisely in the way Jerome suggests when he wrote that

> 'Montanus, that mouthpiece of an unclean spirit, used two rich, upper-class ladies, Prisca and Maximilla, first to bribe the churches with their wealth and then to pollute them with his heresy.'[28]

---

28. Jerome, *To Ctesiphon* 133.4.

However, it is at least as much for their prophetic giftings as for their wealth that they are remembered. Alongside Montanus they became the movement's chief leaders, if indeed they did not ultimately overshadow him.

Historians of the past have often said that the New Prophecy was a child of its pagan environment in Phrygia, a wild region with correspondingly barbaric religions—mystery cults, ecstatic forms of worship, orgiastic rituals and fanaticism—hence one of the most likely places for an outburst of excessive enthusiasm in the Church. Supporting that opinion is a tradition preserved in a late fourth century document, *A Dialogue between a Montanist and an Orthodox*, that Montanus was himself a pagan priest before his conversion.[29] Be that as it may, the modern tendency is more to set Montanism against the background of the Christianity of the Asian churches themselves where there was already a strong prophetic tradition represented by such persons as Ammia of Philadelphia or Melito of Sardis, and where there was also a living apocalyptic tradition, represented particularly by the book of Revelation. Since John the Apostle spent his later years in Ephesus, both his Gospel and Revelation were already part of the Asian churches' heritage, and many of the Montanists' idiosyncrasies find echoes in these two books. For example, they preferred the title 'Paraclete' when referring to the Holy Spirit, using the Greek word *parakletos* from John's Gospel, usually translated 'Comforter' or 'Counsellor' in our English Bibles (John 14:16,26; 15:26; 16:7).

Whatever the influences behind his teaching, there is little doubt that it was Montanus' prophetic activities that first drew attention to himself. Our main source of information is a strongly antagonistic, anonymous writer of the late second century, cited by Eusebius in his *Ecclesiastical History*. He tells how he first heard of the movement when he was visiting Galatia and 'found the church there greatly agitated' by it.

It all started, he tells us, in a village called Ardabau in Mysia on the Phrygian border. There Montanus, recently converted, was baptised in the Spirit, spoke in tongues and prophesied. The writer puts it in a much less approving way, saying Montanus allowed the adversary to enter into him

> 'and he became beside himself, and being suddenly in a sort of frenzy and ecstasy, he raved, and began to babble and utter

29. P. de Labriolle, *Les Sources de l'Histoire du Montanisme*, p.103.

strange things, prophesying in a manner contrary to the custom of the Church handed down by tradition from the beginning.'

The reaction of those who heard him, as at Pentecost in Acts 2, was very mixed. Some said he was possessed of a demon and tried to prevent him from speaking; others began to follow him and were themselves baptised in the same Spirit,

> 'with the result that he could no longer be restrained and silenced. The devil ... stirred up two women besides [Maximilla and Priscilla], and filled them with the false spirit, so that they spoke in a frenzied, unreasonable and strange manner ... And the spirit pronounced those blessed who rejoiced and glorified in it, and puffed them up by the grandeur of its promises.'

The number of Phrygians who followed him was small, we are told, but they were quite outspoken,

> 'and the arrogant spirit taught them to revile the entire universal Church under heaven.' The response of the Church, after a great deal of consideration and debate, was equally uncompromising, 'for the faithful in Asia met often to consider this matter, and examined the novel utterances and pronounced them profane, and rejected the heresy, and thus these persons were expelled from the Church and debarred from communion.'[30]

Despite his comment about the small following, it seems fairly clear that Montanus' impact was both immediate and extensive. By the end of the century his teachings had found root in Syria in the East, where they were being condemned by Serapion, bishop of Antioch[31], and North Africa in the south, where Tertullian became the leader of a Montanist church. In the west, as early as 177 they were being discussed in Gaul, where the churches had heard 'the disciples of Montanus, Alcibiades and Theodotus were beginning to win a wide reputation for their prophesying' and 'disagreements about these persons' had erupted. They formulated their own statement about the matter and sent it along with letters written by the martyrs of Lyons to the brethren in Asia and Phrygia, and also to Eleutherus, bishop of Rome, 'negotiating for the peace of the churches'.[32]

---

30. *Ecclesiastical History* V.16.7-9.
31. *EH* V.19.1.
32. *EH* V.3.4.

The debate continued in Rome itself for several years. It is uncertain what effect the apparently conciliatory, if not favourable, letters of the martyrs had on Eleutherus, who was bishop from 177 to 192. Tertullian tells us one of the Roman bishops, probably Eleutherus' successor, Victor (192-202), was on the point of granting his approval to the movement when a certain Praxeas, himself a heretic, persuaded him against doing so, pointing out that his predecessor had already condemned it. The account of this episode is of particular interest since it is told from a Montanist standpoint.

> 'He [Praxeas] did not have the love of God, for he successfully fought against and squashed God's spiritual gifts. For at that time the bishop of Rome was already in the act of recognising the prophecies of Montanus, Prisca and Maximilla, and by that act of recognition would have brought peace to the churches of Asia and Phrygia. But this man [Praxeas], by making false assertions about the prophets and their assemblies, and by quoting the decisions of the bishop's predecessors, forced him to withdraw the conciliatory letters that he had already sent out and to withdraw from his purpose of sanctioning the spiritual gifts. Thus Praxeas at Rome effected two pieces of the devil's business: he drove out prophecy and brought in heresy, he put the Paraclete to flight and crucified the Father.'[33]

By the third century the Roman attitude had hardened irrevocably, for Jerome tells us that in the next episcopate after Victor's a certain 'Gaius, under Zephyrinus, bishop of the city of Rome [202-17], delivered a very impressive disputation against Proclus, a follower of Montanus, accusing him of rashness in the way he defended the New Prophecy.'[34]

*Opposition and Struggle for Acceptance*

It was principally in Phrygia itself that Montanism flourished and there, as elsewhere, it also failed to find acceptance in the churches. Some of the Asian bishops set themselves to refute the heresy openly, though with little immediate success. Eusebius' anonymous source tells of

> 'eminent men and bishops, such as Zoticus from the town of Cumana and Julian of Apamea, who were prevented by

33. Tertullian, *Against Praxeas* 1. Praxeas' heresy was that he maintained the unity of the Godhead so strongly that he taught the Father suffered in the crucifixion, hence Tertullian's accusation that he 'crucified the Father'.
34. Jerome, *Lives* 59.

> Themiso and his followers from opening their mouths to refute the false spirit that was deceiving the people.'[35]

Quoting another writer, Apollonius, whose work he dates forty years after Montanus' first prophesyings, Eusebius relates, perhaps referring to the same incident, that on one occasion

> 'in Pepuza when Maximilla was pretending to prophesy, Zoticus tried to refute the spirit that was working in her, but was prevented by her partisans.'[36]

In a similar vein he cites a tradition from Apollinarius, who was writing about the same time as Apollonius, that

> 'the blessed Sotas of Anchialus wanted to cast out Priscilla's demon, but the hypocrites would not let him.'[37]

The Montanists clearly stood by their prophets!

It is perhaps a sign of the movement's vigour that by the end of the century it had roused the Asian bishops to summon a general council, for the first time, apparently, since the days of the apostles (Acts 15). Again our information comes from Eusebius, quoting his anonymous source:

> 'The faithful in Asia met often and at many places throughout Asia to consider the matter, and after examining the new teachings pronounced them profane. They rejected the heresy, and so the followers of Montanus were expelled from the Church and excluded from its communion.'[38]

Alongside the verbal disputes and the episcopal and synodical denunciations, the movement stimulated a flurry of publication. Eusebius quotes extensively from the polemical writings of his anonymous author, from Apollinarius, bishop of Hierapolis, and from another writer, Apollonius, of whom we know very little.[39] He also refers to a treatise against Montanism by a certain Miltiades[40] and mentions a work *On Conduct and Prophets* by Melito of Sardis, which may have been composed in the same polemical style.[41] Jerome adds the name Rhodo to this list of critical writers.[42] These

---

35. *EH* V.16.17.
36. *EH* V.18.13.
37. *EH* V.19.3.
38. *EH* V.16.10.
39. *EH* V.16-18; cp. Jerome, *Lives* 26, 40-41.
40. *EH* V.17.1.
41. *EH* IV.26.2.
42. Jerome, *Lives* 37, 39.

authors were all roughly contemporaries at the end of the second and the beginning of the third centuries.

On the Montanist side for the same period Hippolytus mentions 'an infinite number of books' deriving from Montanus, Priscilla and Maximilla themselves[43], but we have no idea what was contained in them. Collections of their sayings must have circulated in the Phrygian churches. Eusebius' anonymous source contains a reference to a work by a certain Asterius Urbanus, from which he quotes one of Maximilla's prophecies[44] and Epiphanius probably had recourse to some such anthology for the various oracles he cites.[45]

None of these works has survived, nor have the 'seven books against the Church in defence of Montanism' written by Tertullian, six of which were apparently *On Ecstasy* and the seventh a discourse *Against Apollonius*, the critic mentioned above.[46] Several of his other Montanist writings have come down to us and, though these are mostly on matters of personal and church discipline[47], they are almost entirely preoccupied with the defence of his teachings against the polemic of the orthodox, and so provide further indication of the heat the movement generated.

Considering that so many books were being written and that later writers continued to deal extensively with the matter, it is strange that so few stories about its founder-prophets have survived, like the charismatic hero-stories of the Old and New Testaments, and indeed of most later movements. But this silence may be no more than a comment on the thoroughness of the orthodox in suppressing Montanist literature. Besides the traditions mentioned already, what material we do possess is of questionable reliability. Apollonius levels the following accusations:

> 'these first prophetesses themselves, from the time they were filled with the Spirit, left their husbands. So did not those who called Prisca a virgin speak falsely? … does a prophet dye his hair? Does as prophet play at gaming tables and dice? Does a prophet lend money at interest?'[48]

It is just conceivable that the charge of abandoning husbands reflects something of the movement's insistence on chastity within

43. Hippolytus, *Refutation* VIII.12.
44. *EH* V.16.17.
45. See below, p. 109.
46. Jerome, *Lives* 24, 53.
47. See below, p. 109.
48. *EH* V.18.3,11.

marriage[49], but it is quite clear that Apollonius was on the whole making the most of scurrilous, market-place gossip.

A similar judgment must be passed on Eusebius' anonymous author's description of Montanus' and Maximilla's deaths, as indeed he suspected himself, for he writes:

> 'Report has it that they were both driven by the maddening spirit to hang themselves, though not at the same time. It is a widespread report from the time of each of their deaths, that they died in this fashion and so ended their lives in the same way as the traitor Judas ... At any rate, this is how they say it happened; but then we did not see it and so cannot pretend to know what really transpired.'[50]

Even more fanciful is the account of the death of one of their close associates called Theodotus, to whom reference has already been made.[51] Of him it is said that

> 'on one occasion, going into an ecstasy and entrusting himself to the deceiving spirit, he found himself being lifted up, raised towards the heavens, only to be whirled to the ground and die a miserable death.'[52]

These are hardly the kind of source materials that historians delight to use!

*Montanism's Dispensationalism and its Trinitarian Theology*

It may have been Montanus' charismatic activities that first attracted public attention, but they would not have caused the commotion they did by themselves, for the prophetic gifts, though diminished in use since New Testament times, were still known and accepted in the second century Church. Rather, it was the interpretation the Montanists put on his prophesyings that caused the real problem. They taught that divine revelation began in Old Testament times, increased under Christ and the apostles, and now reached its peak in the age of the Paraclete that had dawned with the ministry of Montanus.

Their tripartite view of the work of salvation is most clearly summarised in a letter written by Jerome about 382-5:

49. See below, pp. 119, 123.
50. *EH* V.16.13-15.
51. See above p. 104.
52. *EH* V.16.14.

> 'I must confute their open blasphemy when they say that God first wanted to save the world through Moses and the prophets; that since he was not able to fulfil his purpose that way, he took a body through the virgin and in Christ, under the form of the Son, he preached and underwent death for us; and that when he was not able to save the world by these two steps, in the end he descended by the Holy Spirit on Montanus and those demented women, Prisca and Maximilla. So they maintain that the castrated and emasculated Montanus possessed a fullness that Paul did not have, for he said, "We know in part and we prophesy in part," and "now we see in a mirror dimly".'[53]

Jerome's summary also suggests that in his opinion they held unusual views about the relationship between the persons of the Trinity. Indeed, he puts it more bluntly in the same letter:

> 'We distinguish the Father, the Son and the Holy Spirit as three persons, but unite them as one substance; they follow the doctrine of Sabellius by forcing the Trinity into the limits of a single person.'[54]

Didymus of Alexandria, writing about the same time as Jerome, also thought their Trinitarian beliefs were peculiar:

> 'The Phrygians do not baptise in the name of the three holy *hypostases*, for they believe that the Father, the Son and the Holy Spirit are the same.'[55]

He even maintained that this teaching was based on a prophetic utterance of Montanus himself:

> 'They declare that the three divine hypostases are contained in one person, for Montanus, they say, announced, "I am the Father and the Son and the Paraclete".'[56]

However, others of the fathers held that their views about the Trinity, indeed about most aspects of theology, were perfectly orthodox and that their deviation lay mostly in the areas of church discipline, charismatic enthusiasm and their supplementary teachings about Montanus as the bringer of the new age. Epiphanius, another contemporary of Jerome, writes:

---

53. Jerome, *To Marcella* 41; cp. 1 Cor. 13:9,12.
54. *To Marcella* 41.
55. Didymus, *On the Trinity* II.15.
56. *Ibid.* III.41.

'The Cataphrygians, as they are called, accept all the same Scriptures, both Old and New Testaments, and they agree about the resurrection of the dead. But they claim that they have a prophet in one called Montanus and that Priscilla and Maximilla are prophetesses. By following these persons their thinking has become distorted. True, they think the same as the Holy Catholic Church about the Father, the Son and the Holy Spirit, but following erroneous spirits and demonic doctrines, they have separated themselves from us, saying that we too should be receiving the gifts of the Spirit.'[57]

A similar opinion is expressed by Filastrius, who also belongs to the same late fourth century period:

'The Cataphrygians, who live in the province of Phrygia, accept the prophets and the law, they confess the Father, the Son and the Spirit, they look for the resurrection of the body, all things to which the Catholic Church also subscribes. However, they also proclaim that certain of their number are prophets, namely Montanus, Priscilla and Maximilla, persons whom neither the prophets nor Christ foretold. They further add that the fullness of the Holy Spirit was not handed on through the blessed apostles by the gift of Christ, but they reckon that it was imparted through those false prophets of theirs, and they, thanks to these false prophets and false teachers, separate themselves from the Catholic Church.'[58]

About 150 years earlier Hippolytus also wrote in the same vein:

'The Phrygians … are heedlessly swept onwards, by the reliance which they place on these impostors [Priscilla, Maximilla and Montanus]. And they allege that they have learned something more through these than from law and prophets and Gospels. But they magnify these wretched women above the Apostles and every gift of Grace, so that some of them presume to assert that there is in them something superior to Christ. These acknowledge God to be the Father of the universe, the Creator of all things, similarly with the Church, and they receive as many things as the Gospel testifies concerning Christ. They introduce, however, the novelties of fasts, and feasts, and meals of parched food, and repasts of radishes, alleging that

57. Jerome, *Against Eighty Heresies* 48.1.
58. Filastrius, *On Heresies* 49.

> they have been instructed by the women. But none of them assent to the heresy of the Noetians and affirm that the Father himself is the Son.'[59]

It would indeed be strange that Tertullian, one of the most orthodox Trinitarians of all time, should have espoused the Montanists' cause, if their doctrines had been as heterodox as Jerome and Didymus suggest. The solution to the apparent confusion seems to lie in recognising that by the end of the fourth century there was no longer complete uniformity of doctrine among them. Indeed, Hippolytus' last sentence indicates that diversity was already entering the movement at the beginning of the third, and his witness to that fact is corroborated by Pseudo-Tertullian, an anonymous author of the third century whose work is attached in some manuscripts to the end of Tertullian's treatise *On the Prescription of Heresies*:

> 'theirs is not a uniform doctrinal system. For there are those that call themselves followers of Proclus and others that are known as followers of Aeschines. They have one blasphemous doctrine in common and another that they do not share, one peculiar to themselves. The doctrine they have in common is that while they would certainly say the Holy Spirit was in the apostles, they would say the Paraclete was not. According to this doctrine they maintain that the Paraclete has spoken things through Montanus that are additional to the revelation through Christ in the gospel—indeed not only additional, but also superior and more significant.'[60]

*Montanism as the End-Time Church of the Spirit*

It is in the very nature of a prophetic movement to have a sense of end-time urgency. At first the prophets may simply proclaim that urgency as the message of the Spirit to the whole Church, but sooner or later it crystallises in a belief that the prophetic movement itself embodies the true Church of the last age of the Spirit. Teaching about a third state or era of the Spirit was only properly formulated in the twelfth century, but already something of the attitude underlying it, as we saw earlier, was found in the post-Pentecost teaching of the New Testament Church, and now is strongly represented in Montanism. With its exodus from the cradle of the Catholic Church its end-time views helped to create an eclecticism that had conse-

59. Hippolytus, *Refutation of All Heresies* VIII.12.
60. Pseudo-Tertullian, *Against All Heresies* 7.

quences for both personal behaviour and communal practice. If Montanists believed 'that now Montanus has come they have the perfection of the Paraclete'[61], then somehow they had to show evidence of that spiritual perfection in their church system and in exemplary moral conduct.

End-time expectation was very strong, in the early days at any rate. For example, Maximilla is on record as having said,

> 'There shall be no further prophetess after me, but the end will come.'[62]

And the Montanists, believing Christ's return to be imminent, nominated a village in Phrygia called Pepuza as the site where the New Jerusalem would shortly come down from heaven (cp. Rev. 21:10). This quite naturally evoked a few sneers from the orthodox; Cyril of Alexandria mockingly called Pepuza 'a most insignificant little hamlet in Phrygia'.[63] But that little hamlet quickly became the sect's chief centre, a place to which Montanists flocked in preparation for the end[64], and there, so Jerome tells us, they established their own hierarchical system of authority:

> 'they put first the patriarchs of Pepuza in Phrygia, then second those they call stewards [*cenones*], and then the bishops are relegated to the third rank, almost the last.'[65]

Some further glimpses of their early administrative and evangelistic machinery at Pepuza are provided by Eusebius' various sources. They apparently had some kind of central fund, maintained by the contributions of their members, not all of whom were particularly wealthy; so we gather from some comments about it by Apollonius who uses its existence to prove their prophecy not authentic, arguing that while

> 'the Lord has said, "Take no gold, nor silver, nor two coats" [Matt. 10:9], they gather their gain not only from rich men, but also from the poor, and orphans, and widows.'[66]

It seems that Theodotus, whom we have already met[67], administered this fund in the early years, for he is called their 'first financial

61. Didymus, *On the Trinity* 41.2.
62. Epiphanius, *Against Eighty Heresies* 48.2.
63. Cyril, *Catechetical Lectures* 16.8.
64. Cp. Apollonius in *EH* V.18.2.
65. Jerome, *To Marcella* 41.
66. *EH* V.18.4,7.
67. See above, pp. 104, 108.

administrator [*epitropos*]'[68], and it appears that it was used, in part at any rate, to support the evangelistic ministry of the movement:

> 'Montanus appointed money-collectors, devised a scheme for receiving gifts under the name of "offerings", and provided salaries for those who preached his message.'[69]

Perhaps some of their money helped finance the publication of evangelistic tracts, for Apollonius, in his tirade against their supposed avarice, mentions that a certain

> 'Themiso ... imitated the apostle by composing a catholic epistle to instruct those whose faith was better than his own.'[70]

Of course, we cannot tell how far these administrative arrangements applied outside Phrygia, or how long they continued in operation, but perhaps we can detect behind the abusive phraseology of the critics something of the spirit of eschatological zeal that encouraged the Montanists to contribute in this way to the work of their church, like some poverty-stricken Macedonian Christians also did in an earlier age, even beyond their means (2 Cor. 8:2f).

According to several reports, they also developed their own distinctive rituals, though no reliable account of these has come down to us. All that we have is a handful of ridiculous rumours about 'cutting the throats of wretched little children, and chopping them up into unholy food, for the purpose of their so-called mysteries'[71] rumours about which Jerome wrote, 'I prefer not to believe these scandalous accusations; all that talk about blood-letting may be entirely untrue.'[72]

However, we do have more trustworthy information about some of their religious observances. These were mostly of an ascetic sort, such as might be thought to convey an image of spiritual excellence befitting the church of the last days. Thus, for example, Jerome remarks,

> 'We, in common with everyone else, observe the apostolic tradition of keeping one Lenten fast in the year, but they keep three, as though three saviours had suffered!'[73]

---

68. *EH* V.16.14.
69. *EH* V.18.2.
70. *EH* V.18.5.
71. Cyril, *Catechetical Lectures* 16.8.
72. Jerome, *To Marcella* 41.
73. *To Marcella* 41.

In addition to fasts, Hippolytus also lists 'novelties of feasts, and meals of parched food, and repasts of radishes'.[74]

Alongside such food laws and astringent rituals they established a system of excessively puritanical morality, one particularly notable aspect of which is seen in their refusal to permit second marriages, not only for divorcees, but also for a Christian whose spouse had died. Jerome describes their views thus:

> 'While we do not encourage second marriages, we do allow them, since Paul bids the younger widows to marry. But they think second marriages so utterly sinful that they regard anyone who enters into them as an adulterer.'[75]

More than that, the Montanist Church did not look lightly on backsliders who failed to maintain its high moral standards. According to Jerome, Montanus taught it was

> 'impossible to renew again through repentance those who have crucified to themselves the Son of God, and put him to open shame.'[76]

And in disgust at the hardness of this teaching, he wrote:

> 'Perish Montanus and his mad women! Montanus who would hurl the fallen into the abyss that they may never rise again. Every day we all sin and make some slip or other. Being then merciful to ourselves, we are not rigorous towards others.'[77]

He also pointed out that their hard beliefs about the impossibility of second repentance created an atmosphere of smug self-righteousness among them:

> 'they close the doors of the Church to almost every sin, whereas we read daily, "I desire the repentance of a sinner rather than his death," [Ezek. 18:23] ... But they are so rigid—not that they do not also commit serious sins themselves. The difference between them and us is that they in their self-righteousness blush to confess their sins, whereas we do penance for ours and so more readily obtain pardon for them.'[78]

Charismatics in other ages have also been criticised for an apparent lack of sin-consciousness, but they have normally explained that

74. Hippolytus, *Refutation of all Heresies* VIII.12.
75. *To Marcella* 41.
76. Jerome, *Against Jovinianus* II.3.
77. Jerome, *To Pammachius* 2.
78. *To Marcella*, 41.

themselves in terms of a new awareness of holiness, purification, or sanctification as a consequence of the Spirit's presence in their lives. Perhaps a Montanist would have expressed it similarly. Anyhow, the attitude is recognisably part of the ethos of the end-time Church of the Spirit. To the enthusiast it is an expression of victory over and freedom from sin, to the onlooker it spells bigotry. Montanism differs from other movements only in its formulations, not in its basic attitude, which is entirely comparable with the high moralism of the Old Testament prophets, or the perfectionism of Jesus' Sermon on the Mount, as well as with similar views held among later prophets who have also regarded themselves as members of a latter-day Church of the Spirit.

*The Prophetic Sayings of Montanus*

Most of the prophets' sayings have been preserved by critics simply because they embody some teaching that was thought heretical. A few others have survived in the writings of Tertullian. Perhaps the most striking are those by Montanus that speak of the Trinity:

> 'I am the Lord God, the Almighty, dwelling in man.'[79]
>
> 'I am neither an angel, nor a mere human messenger, but I am the Lord God, the Father, who have come.'[80]
>
> 'I am the Father, and the Son, and the Paraclete.'[81]
>
> 'I am the Father, and I am the Son, and I am the Paraclete.'[82]

On the basis of the first two of these sayings, Epiphanius believed that 'Montanus said he was the Father himself', but it is unlikely that that is what Montanus actually intended. When a prophet speaks, he frequently uses the divine 'I', as did Isaiah, for example, when he said, 'I, even I, am the LORD, and apart from me there is no saviour.' (Isa. 43:11) This form of speech is common among prophets in every age and points to their belief that God has spoken to reveal himself or his will through them, not that they claim to be God. It is rather the declaration of the source and authority of the words they speak. Neither Didymus nor the author of the *Dialogue* level the same charge, but on the basis of the sayings they cite simply accuse Montanus of bad Trinitarian theology, of compressing the three persons of the Godhead into one.

---

79. Epiphanius, *Against Eighty Heresies* 48.11.
80. Epiphanius, *Against Eighty Heresies* 48.11.
81. Didymus, *On the Trinity* III.41.1.
82. *Dialogue between a Montanist and an Orthodox*, de Labriolle, Sources, p. 97.

It is with the third person of the Trinity that Montanus is more properly associated. Some of the later fathers state quite bluntly, as does Theodoret, for example, that he 'called himself the Paraclete'.[83] In the *Dialogue* the Montanist uses the title 'Montanus the Paraclete', and a late fourth or early fifth century inscription from Numidia contains the peculiar Trinitarian formula: 'in the name of the Father and of the Son and of the Lord Montanus'.[84]

It is, however, to be questioned whether Montanus himself would have approved of such language. Certainly no utterance that might suggest so has survived, and if he had said such things, his critics would surely have used them as fuel for their fires. Probably nearer to the original truth is the more tempered account of Didymus that the Montanists 'try to show that Montanus possessed the perfection of the Paraclete'.[85]

Be that as it may, it is this notion of fullness or perfection that predominates in the debates about their teaching on the age of the Paraclete. The Montanist in the *Dialogue* argues,

> 'We also say that the apostles had something of the Spirit, but not that they had the fullness of the Paraclete … that the apostles had the guarantee of the Spirit, but not its fullness.'[86]

He supports his view by appealing to 1 Cor. 13:

> 'It is our faith in St. Paul that encourages us to accept Montanus as having the perfection of the Holy Spirit, that is the Paraclete. For Paul himself said, "When the perfect comes, that which is in part will pass away" and "we know in part and we prophesy in part".'[87]

The orthodox, of course, argues that the perfect will only be realised in the age to come, but for the Montanist that age had already begun with Montanus.

*The Prophecies of Maximilla*

The prophetesses shared something of Montanus' uniqueness. Though they are never identified as closely with the Paraclete as Montanus himself, there is one saying of Maximilla's that uses language akin to that of Montanus' Trinitarian sayings. Apparently with reference to her treatment in the churches, she said,

---

83. Theodoret, *Compendium of Heretical Fables* III.1.
84. *CIL* VII.1.2272; cp. de Labriolle, *Sources*, p.195.
85. Didymus, *On the Trinity* III.41.3.
86. de Labriolle, *Sources*, pp. 103f.
87. *Sources*, p. 93.

'I am driven away from the sheep like a wolf. I am not a wolf. I am word and spirit and power.'[88]

Some have thought her 'word and spirit and power' allude to the Son, the Holy Spirit and the Father respectively, but the equation is not at all obvious. The three terms more naturally suggest different aspects of the Spirit's action in prophecy. Maximilla was claiming nothing more than a prophet's relationship with her God.

She herself defined the relationship thus:

'The Lord sent me as a party-leader, instructor and interpreter in this work, this profession of faith, this covenant, as one under compulsion, whether willing or unwilling, to make known the knowledge of God.'[89]

A further brief word, 'Hear not me, but Christ'[90], may be interpreted in the same vein, indicating her conviction that, while Christ spoke through her, she was herself just an ordinary and fallibly human prophet. Alternatively, if these words are regarded as a message from the Spirit speaking through her, rather than Maximilla speaking of herself, they must be interpreted differently, perhaps in the light of John 16:13f, that the Spirit speaks not of himself, but to glorify Christ. On the basis of these sayings we can conclude no more than that Maximilla believed herself a prophetess and leader in the movement.

There is, however, one further utterance of Maximilla's that shows her prophesying was thought in some way unique, even within Montanism itself:

'There shall be no further prophetess after me, but the end will come.'

Epiphanius, who quoted this prophecy, argued that it proved Maximilla a false prophet, simply because it was not fulfilled.

'This woman,' he wrote, 'said that the end would come after her, and this has not happened. Instead several emperors have come and gone and a considerable space of time has elapsed. Indeed something like 290 years have passed until this present time.'[91]

---

88. *EH* V.16.17.
89. Epiphanius, *Against Eighty Heresies* 48.13.
90. *Ibid*. 48.12.
91. *Ibid*. 48.2; the figure is grossly inaccurate, since Epiphanius was writing about 375-7 AD.

This word raised a further puzzle. Epiphanius noted earlier how it was integral to Montanist teaching 'that we too should be receiving the gifts of the Spirit'[92], and so he queried,

> 'If it is essential that the charismata be appropriated and that they be found in the Church, why should they have no more prophets after Montanus, Priscilla and Maximilla?'[93]

A similar question was asked by Miltiades, one of the authors Eusebius quotes, more than 150 years earlier:

> 'if ... the women who accompanied Montanus received the gift of prophecy, let them show who among them received it from Montanus and the women, for the apostle thought that the prophetic gift should continue in the whole Church until the final coming. But they have no one to show us, even though it is already about fourteen years since the death of Maximilla.'[94]

Was Montanism then a prophetic movement in the sense that its founders were prophets, while its adherents were only in some diluted sense charismatics? On the basis of the evidence so far it might seem so. After all, plenty of other movements had their outstanding founder-figures whose prophetic endowment was quite unique, men like Samuel and Elijah, as well as others we shall encounter in later times, who in different ways stood out over the movements they led or founded. None the less, their followers were still prophets, even if the leaders were charismatic giants. So it appears to have been in Montanist circles too. Certainly Tertullian, who alone provides us with an inside view of the Spirit's workings in a Montanist church, gives several examples of prophetic and visionary experiences in his congregation.[95]

*Priscilla's Prophecies*

Only three of Priscilla's sayings have survived. Tertullian quotes her as having said about those who do not believe in the resurrection of the flesh:

> 'They are flesh, and they hate the flesh.'

Presumably this was intended to mean something like 'They live their lives in the flesh, but paradoxically they hate the flesh, because

---

92. See above, p. 110.
93. *Ibid.* 48.2.
94. *EH* V.17.2-4.
95. See below, p. 126.

they deny it a resurrection.'[96] Apart from offering some insight into one aspect of Montanist theology, that does not shed much light on its prophetic mentality, but a second one quoted by Tertullian does.

While arguing that chastity in marriage contributes greatly to a clear conscience, thus enabling men to offer pure prayers to God, he writes:

> 'The message is preached by the holy prophetess Prisca, that a holy minister knows how to minister holiness, for she says, "Those who seek chastity find [an inner] harmony and they see visions and with heads bowed they hear distinct voices, as saving as they are secret."'[97]

What is particularly striking is the atmosphere of quiet implied in these words as a proper context for prophetic experience—striking because it contrasts markedly with the image of frenzied ecstaticism critics have led us to associate with Montanist prophesying. In fact Tertullian's evidence is all in that quieter vein. Doubtless a movement so widespread experienced much diversity in its activities.

Priscilla's third extant saying is one that evoked sneers among her critics because of its eschatological teaching. She said,

> 'Christ came to me in the likeness of a woman, wearing a shining robe, and he endued me with wisdom and revealed to me that this place [Pepuza] is holy and that here Jerusalem would come down out of heaven.'[98]

We know through Apollonius that Montanus himself was the originator of the Pepuza/Jerusalem tradition, for he wrote that he

> 'named Pepuza and Tymion (small towns in Phrygia) "Jerusalem", because he wanted to gather people to them from all quarters.'[99]

Presumably, therefore, putting the two statements together, it was Montanus who called Pepuza 'Jerusalem' because he had selected it as the movement's headquarters, then sometime later Priscilla introduced the eschatological dimension with her vision.

### *The Nature of Montanist Prophesying*

It was the way in which the Montanists prophesied rather than the content of their prophecies that created the greatest opposition

96. Tertullian, *On the Resurrection of the Flesh* 11.
97. Tertullian, *On Exhortation to Chastity* 10.
98. Epiphanius, *Against Eighty Heresies* 49; Epiphanius was not entirely certain whether the author of this revelation was Priscilla or another called Quintilla.
99. *EH* V.18.2.

among the orthodox. The criticism levelled against them was that they prophesied 'in ecstasy'. The term 'ecstasy' in these discussions is used in a fairly technical sense, not in the way we commonly use it today. The Greek word it translates, *ekstasis*, is made of two parts: *ek* meaning 'out of', and *stasis* 'standing' or 'state'. It thus denotes a spiritual state or experience of standing apart from or outside one's normal, human faculties, generally unaware of one's environment, and being caught up in the realm of the Spirit. Today we would perhaps more readily use the expression 'in the Spirit'. The debate centred around whether a prophet should speak 'in ecstasy', as Montanists obviously did quite regularly[100], or afterwards once he had regained the use of his normal senses.

One of Montanus' few extant sayings explains how prophecy worked in this way:

> 'See, man is like a lyre and I fly over him like a plectrum. The man sleeps, but I am awake. Behold, the Lord is the one who stirs men's hearts to ecstasy and gives them [new] hearts.'[101]

We have no clear evidence whether Old or New Testament prophets ever spoke in ecstasy, but the explanation from Montanus is hardly distinguishable from that offered by other second century writers, like Justin, Athenagoras and Hippolytus, when they discussed biblical prophesying, using even the same musical analogies.[102] However, by the beginning of the third century a fairly rigid view was being formulated in opposition to the Montanists.

The earliest example comes from around 180-90, the opinion of a certain Alcibiades (or Miltiades—the reading is uncertain), quoted by Eusebius:

> 'a prophet ought not to speak while in ecstasy … but the false prophet speaks in a state of ecstasy, in which he shows himself to be without shame or fear. He begins by suppressing his conscious thoughts and passes on to a state of delirium in which he has no conscious control.'

The writer goes on to argue that none of the New Testament or early Church prophets behaved in such a fashion.[103]

100. Though not always, as the example of a prophetess in Tertullian's congregation telling her vision after the service clearly demonstrates (see below, p. 126) . See also below, pp. 312, for fuller discussion of the subject in connection with the French Prophets who prophesied in ecstasy in later times.
101. Epiphanius, *Against Eighty Heresies* 48.4.
102. See above, p. 98.
103. *EH* V.17.1-2.

Epiphanius argues round the subject at considerable length[104], firmly stating that

> 'it is in full possession of his powers of reasoning and intelligence that the true prophet speaks and gives utterance from the Holy Spirit, pronouncing everything in a steady, clear voice.'[105]

Several other similar pronouncements followed throughout the third and fourth centuries. For example, Didymus wrote:

> 'If we leave the sphere of normal human activity and enter into an ecstatic relationship with God, we remain in control of our senses towards you, for divine ecstasy has no madness in it, only sober rationality. So we should pay no attention to those of the Phrygians who say that the apostles and prophets became ecstatic to the point of losing their reason.'[106]

Jerome produced the same argument several times in the course of his writings on the prophets. For example, in the prologue to his *Commentary on Nahum* he wrote:

> 'He [Nahum] does not speak in ecstasy in the way that Montanus and Priscilla and Maximilla rave. The book of his prophecy contains the vision of one who understands all that he is saying.'[107]

It is unfortunate that Tertullian's six volumes *On Ecstasy* have not survived, for without these we have no statement on the subject from the Montanists themselves, and so it is impossible to judge how far their critics have accurately represented their experience—or indeed whether they have understood it at all. Whatever their opponents said, the Montanists certainly respected their prophets, and perhaps none more than Tertullian, himself a theological giant in the early Church.

### *Tertullian on Progress and Revival*

If we are to see Montanism as a movement akin to Old or New Testament prophetism, we have to find in it a reforming or revivalist heart, crying out in reaction against growing laxity among the Lord's people. From Tertullian's writings we get the clear impression that

---

104. *Against Eighty Heresies* 48.3-7.
105. *Ibid.* 48.3.
106. *Commentary on 2 Corinthians* 5:12
107. Cp. also his commentary on Ephes. 2:3 and the prologues to his Commentaries on Habakkuk and Isaiah.

it did have that heart, though none of its critics ever hint that it was revivalist in outlook, either with respect to its religious zeal or to its ethics. To them it presented itself entirely as a movement for the propagation of a supplementary revelation.

It has to be admitted that to some degree Tertullian did understand its claims in the same way himself. In his thinking Montanism was indeed new—'New Prophecy'—and its status could be illustrated by likening Christian history to natural growth and development:

> 'So too it is with righteousness [= Christianity], for the God of righteousness is the same as the God of creation: to begin with it was in a rudimentary state, expressed in a natural fear of God; then it advanced through the law and the prophets to infancy; then through the gospel it blossomed into the fervour of youth; and now through the Paraclete it is settling into maturity.'[108]

Despite these progressivist views, there is also a strongly reactionary flavour in his extant writings. These are mostly occupied with defending the more puritanical observances of Montanism, but in so doing he seldom appeals to prophetic revelations for his authority. Not that he never does so, for he refers to the teaching of the Paraclete on most subjects, but for the greater part he prefers to present his arguments on grounds that the Catholics could also accept. He writes on one occasion,

> 'Let us leave aside any mention of the Paraclete—since he is really a supporter of our cause!—and let us look through the ancient Scriptures, the documents we have in common.'[109]

It may be that these are simply the necessary tactics of disputation, and that in the end Tertullian must take refuge in what the Paraclete had said through Montanus and the prophets, but they do give his writings something of a revivalist flavour.

The same spirit of reaction and revivalism breathes through his repeated contrasting of Montanism's higher spirituality and its more stringent morality with the worldliness of the Catholics. This is perhaps nowhere more evident than in his constant use of the term *psychici,* which Paul applied to those who did not appreciate spiritual gifts.[110] To Tertullian the Catholics are the *psychici,* not just because of their failure to accept Montanist prophecy, but also

108. Tertullian, *On the Veiling of Virgins* 1.
109. Tertullian, *On Monogamy* 4.
110. See above, p. 90.

because of their more feeble and 'fleshly' moral attitudes. He argues the point thus:

> 'Among us, who can justly claim the title 'spiritual' because of our recognition of the spiritual gifts, self-control is as religious as licence is shameful … But since the *psychici* do not receive the Spirit, they take no pleasure in the things of the Spirit. So, as long as they take no pleasure in the things of the Spirit, they will take pleasure in the things of the flesh, because they are contrary to the things of the Spirit.'[111]

Montanism may be based on new revelation, but for Tertullian it is also essentially an appeal to the rest of Christendom to become what he believes the New Testament truly wants it to be, both in spirit and in practice, that is a good, old-time, revival movement. Indeed, in his writings the Paraclete's work is as much to do with moulding Christian behaviour, as with doctrine. His function is

> 'to give direction about discipline, to lay open the Scriptures, to reshape the mind, and to bring advancement to better things.'[112]

*Tertullian's Montanist Spirituality*

Our concern here is not to examine Tertullian's arguments about fasting, chastity, veiling of virgins, avoidance of public shows, refusal of second marriages, and the like, but to glean from his writings some glimpses of the charismatic aspects of his own personality and of his Montanist church.

He was born about 160 AD and was brought up a pagan in the city of Carthage, where he was given a good Roman education. After his conversion he wrote many apologetic, polemical, doctrinal and ethical works that have exercised an immense influence on the development of Western Christian theological thinking. He became a Montanist about 200 and thereafter used his pen almost entirely for the defence of the New Prophecy he now espoused.

It is usually argued that Montanism in North Africa must have been considerably less fanatical and extravagant than in Phrygia, otherwise a man of Tertullian's stature would never have joined the movement. There are some conjectural grounds for supposing that this opinion may be correct, though there is no material evidence to support it, and certainly Tertullian himself always held the

111. *On Monogamy* 1.
112. *On the Veiling of Virgins* 1.

Phrygian prophets in the highest esteem, speaking, for example, of Priscilla as 'the holy prophetess' and quoting her teaching as authoritative.[113] But it was not without some sadness that he had to leave the Catholic fold, or, as he puts it, 'was separated from the *psychici* because of my acknowledgment and my defence of the Paraclete.'[114]

He continued to plead that his beliefs were still the same as theirs:

> 'We share with them the law of peace and the name of brotherhood. They and we have one faith, one God, the same Christ, the same hope, the same baptismal sacraments. Let me say it once for all: we are one Church.'[115]

Even if the Catholics could not reciprocate this sentiment in its entirety, it does accord in many ways with the things some of them were saying, as also does the following:

> 'This is the reason why they reject the new prophecies: not because Montanus, Priscilla and Maximilla proclaim a different God, nor because they separate Jesus Christ from the Godhead, nor because they overturn any rule of Christian faith or hope, but because they clearly teach that one should fast more often than marry.'[116]

Two particular phrases that Tertullian used, 'because of the Paraclete' and 'because one should fast more often', give us the measure of his Montanist values. Montanism to him was perfectly orthodox Christianity realising its full spiritual and ethical potential. And it was both aspects of that potential, not just the charismatic, that he believed were being suppressed in the churches.

> 'You erect boundary posts round God,' he wrote, 'and so fence in his discipline as much as his spiritual gifts. In that way you put an end equally to his duties and to his benefits.'[117]

Doubtless many Catholics were more spiritually and morally aware than Tertullian was prepared to concede, but the sadness for him was that his championing of this movement for spiritual and moral renewal drove a wedge between himself and them. Nevertheless, despite his protests, we do not get the impression that he was too

---

113. See above, p. 92.
114. *Against Praxeas* 1.
115. *On the Veiling of Virgins* 2.
116. *On Fasting* 1.
117. *On Fasting* 11.

greatly upset by the division. His attitude seems to have been that the Catholics were the losers anyhow, that theirs was the limited perception of unspiritual men, whilst he had discovered the kind of Christianity the New Testament itself describes.

*Tertullian on Prophetic Ecstasy*

He certainly believed the charismatic aspect of Montanism was entirely concordant with New Testament experience and so he found in it a strong apologetic weapon. In his work against the heretic, Marcion, he challenged him to produce evidences of prophetic activity among his followers:

> 'Let him show me some prophets, ones that have spoken, not by human senses, but by the Spirit of God, that have foretold things to come and have revealed the secrets of the heart. Let him produce some psalm, some vision, some prayer (only let it be one given by the Spirit, in an ecstasy, that is, without the usual operation of the mind), or let him produce any instance of interpretation of a tongue he may have encountered… . Now all these evidences can be produced from my side without any difficulty.'[118]

Though nothing of his works *On Ecstasy* has survived, we get a glimpse of his views on the subject in this passage just cited, but even more fully in another where he discusses the account of Christ's transfiguration in Luke 9:28-36:

> 'Peter said, "Let us make three tabernacles, one for you, and one for Moses and one for Elijah." But he did not realise what he was saying. How did he not realise? Was this just a matter of a simple mistake? Or is the explanation the one that we uphold in our defence of the New Prophecy, namely that ecstasy, in which one's normal mental faculties are suspended, is concordant with the operation of grace. For when a man is rapt in the Spirit, especially when he beholds the glory of God, or when God speaks through him, he inevitably loses the customary operation of his senses—is bound to, indeed, because he is overshadowed with the power of God. (There is some dispute between ourselves and the *psychici* about this.) Now, it is easy to prove the rapture of Peter: for how could he have recognised Moses and Elijah, except in the Spirit?'[119]

---

118. *Against Marcion* V.8.
119. *Against Marcion* IV.22.

*Prophetic Gifts in Tertullian's Congregation*

We catch further glimpses of Montanist ecstasy in some passages where Tertullian gives examples of prophetic gifts in use among members of his congregation. The total impression is not at all of the frenzy that its critics suggest, but then it is just possible that the prophets of Phrygia were a little more excitable than in North Africa. Tertullian's accounts are also valuable as little windows on the life and worship of the Montanist churches.

In the course of his argument about women veiling their heads, he tells how one of his flock had a vision in her sleep of an angel scolding her for failing to wear her veil.[120] In another place he tells of a Christian lady becoming possessed after visiting the theatre and having to be delivered of the demon, who claimed he entered her quite righteously, since, he says, 'I found her in my domain'. In the same place he speaks of another woman who died after visiting the theatre, but who first was shown in a dream her burial shroud and the reason for her judgment.[121]

Perhaps the most fascinating tale he tells is found in a work he wrote on the corporeal nature of the human soul:

> 'In our congregation today we have a sister whose lot it is to receive gifts of revelations which she experiences in the Spirit by ecstatic vision during our sacred worship on the Lord's Day. She holds converse with angels, sometimes even with the Lord; she sees and hears mysterious things; she discerns what is in some men's hearts; she receives medical instructions for those in need. Be it as the Scriptures are read, or the Psalms sung, or the sermons preached, or the prayers offered, so on any of these occasions the subject matters are supplied for her visions. Perhaps, while this sister was in the Spirit, we were discussing something or other to do with the soul. After the services are over and the congregation has been dismissed, she is in the regular habit of telling us the things she has seen (for her visions are reported with the greatest of care so that their veracity can be tested). She said, "Amongst other things I was shown a soul in bodily form and a spirit appeared, not a void and empty illusion, but one that looked as if it could be held by the hand, delicate and translucent, of an ethereal colour, and with a completely human form." This was her vision and

120. *Veiling of Virgins* 17.
121. *On the Shows* 26.

> God is her witness; and the apostle [Paul] is himself a sufficient pledge that there would be spiritual gifts in the Church.'[122]

This story is of particular interest, first because it shows us a context in which the prophetic gift was used, one that is recognisably the same as that in 1 Cor. 14, in the *Didache* and in Hermas' *Shepherd*, namely the body gathered for worship; and second, because it indicates that the visions were not simply accepted with unquestioning enthusiasm, but were tested by submission either to the congregation as a whole, or to its leaders. Of course, it is not possible to say whether such careful procedures were followed in other Montanist churches besides Tertullian's, but they clearly bring Montanist prophesying, 'new' though it may have been, within the general context of New Testament and early Christian prophetic activity. Indeed, had later movements been as careful to observe the same scriptural principles, some of the excesses of history might have been avoided.

*Prophetic Confirmations of Montanist Theology and Ethics*

If Tertullian's writings convey an impression of prophetic activity that is much quieter in mood than that portrayed by Montanus' critics in Phrygia, what he says about the prophets' teaching differs very little from this. He even shared the Phrygian views about the end-times and the New Jerusalem, though he never actually mentions Pepuza in connection with it. His millennial teaching is neatly summarised in one passage:

> 'We confess that a kingdom has been promised for us on earth, though before heaven and in a different state of existence, that is to say after the resurrection it will be let down from heaven for a thousand years in the form of the divinely-built city of Jerusalem… . Ezekiel knew about it and the apostle John saw it. Furthermore, the word of the New Prophecy that is part of our faith attests to it. It foretold that as a sign, before the city is finally made manifest, people would see a picture of it. This prophecy has been recently fulfilled during an expedition to the East.[123] For it is reported even by heathen witnesses, that a city appeared suspended in the sky over Judea every morning for a period of forty days and that the outline of its walls

122. *On the Soul* 9.
123. The expedition of Severus against the Parthians.

> would fade as the day advanced, though sometimes it would vanish instantly.'[124]

Tertullian tells, like Paul before him (cp. 2 Cor. 3), how the Spirit, as well as encouraging strong morals and inspiring New Prophecy, also gives fresh, clear insight into the meaning of Scripture, how

> 'he has now got rid of all the old ambiguities and arbitrary explanations by his clear and easily understood interpretation of the whole mystery through the New Prophecy that is flowing down from the Paraclete. If you draw from its fountains, you will not be able to thirst for any other doctrine, nor will you be consumed by any feverish questionings.'[125]

Similar testimonies are regularly given by charismatics and prophets in our own time.

It has to be admitted that occasionally the revelations and interpretations we encounter are somewhat partisan, favouring Montanist views, of course. One good illustration of this is found in Tertullian's arguments about second marriages (which the New Testament does actually permit, even if hesitatingly; cp. 1 Tim. 5:14):

> 'If Christ abrogated a law that Moses had commanded, on the grounds that 'it was not so from the beginning' (see Matt. 19:8) … why may not the Paraclete abrogate a concession that Paul granted, also on the grounds that second marriage was not from the beginning … The New Law abrogated divorce, the New Prophecy abrogates second marriage.'[126]

A further aspect of the Paraclete's work was strengthening the faithful in the face of persecution and martyrdom. It may be that *The Passion of Saints Felicity and Perpetua,* which is a contemporary story of martyrdom in Carthage at the beginning of the third century, is a Montanist work, possibly edited by Tertullian himself. Certainly its spirit of endurance is one that he greatly applauded and that he believed was a gift of the Spirit himself, for he wrote,

> 'We are not asked who is prepared to follow the broad way, but who the narrow. That is why the Paraclete is needed, for he is the one who leads into all truth and who encourages to total endurance. Those that have received him will not even know

124. *Against Marcion* 3.24.
125. *On the Resurrection of the Flesh* 63.
126. *On Monogamy* 14.

> how to flee in persecution or how to buy it off, for they will have in them him who stands by us both to speak for us when we are interrogated and to support us in suffering.'[127]

Finally we must note Tertullian's doctrine of the Church. Authority to him was not just a matter of institutional hierarchy, but of the Spirit, as witness these words addressed to the bishop of Rome:

> 'Then show me, apostolic Sir, prophetic evidences, so that I may recognise your divine endowment; prove to yourself the power of remitting such sins… . You reply, "But *the Church* has the power to forgive sins." This I do recognise and accept, even more than you do, for I have the extra authority of the Paraclete himself saying through the new prophets, "The Church has the power to forgive sins …" Accordingly, the Church will indeed forgive sins; but it will be the Church of the Spirit that will do so by means of a spiritual man, not the Church that consists of a number of bishops. For right and judgment belong to the Lord, not to the servant, to God himself, not to the priest.'[128]

The logical corollary to that is a doctrine of the priesthood of all believers, which is exactly what Tertullian himself said:

> 'Are not we laymen priests? It is written, "He has made us a kingdom and priests to his God and Father." … Where three are, even though they be laymen, there is the Church. For each individual lives by his own faith, and there is no respecting of persons with God, since it is not the hearers of the law that are justified, but the doers, according to what the apostle says. So if you have the right of a priest in your own person …'[129]

Similar sentiments have been shared by prophetic persons in every age and have therefore found expression in most prophetic movements in history. Some movements, like Irvingism in the nineteenth century, did develop strong priestly systems, but for the most part the prophetic Spirit has sat loose to hierarchical structures. Be that as it may, Tertullian's own church seems to have been orderly and well-organised, and prophetic utterance in it was carefully supervised and vetted by the leadership. But then, we hardly get the impression that Tertullian would have been happy in a worship setting

127. *On Flight in Persecution* 14
128. *On Modesty* 21.
129. *On Exhortation to Chastity* 7.

that was little better than a free-for-all. He was too much the prophet like St. Paul for that.

*Sectarianism and Decline*

It would be interesting to pursue the later history of Montanism in the same detail, but it must suffice to make no more than a few observations.

We find very little about the Montanists in late third and early fourth century writings, but they appear again in anti-heretical writings of the late fourth, and there we discover that by that time they had split into several factions. We meet them under various names, such as Priscillianists, Quintillianists, Tascodrugites, Artotyrites, Alogoi and Tertullianists. Some of these names suggest that they fell foul to the temptation that had confronted the Corinthian church in New Testament times, to venerate charismatic heroes too highly and elevate them to positions of leadership that proved divisive.

We also hear of doctrinal differences, disagreements about the Trinity[130], or about the status of St. John's Gospel, or about the materials to be used in the Eucharist. There was a lot of debate among Catholic writers about their methods of dating Easter, about the validity of their unorthodox baptismal rites, and about their attitudes to women in ministry. It would seem that with the passage of the decades the same thing overtook the Montanist Church as the New Testament Church: their attention became diverted from matters spiritual to matters ritual, doctrinal and ecclesiastical. We should therefore expect to find evidence of a change in their attitude to spiritual gifts, but our sources are largely silent on these issues. It was mainly their rituals and doctrines with which the orthodox concerned themselves.

At the end of the fourth century Epiphanius wrote as if the gifts of the Spirit were still a living part of their system[131], but he also described one interesting ritual of theirs that could suggest some of their charismatic activities at any rate had become stereotyped and pressed into a ritual mould, similar to the sort of thing we shall see happening among the Shakers and the Irvingites in later times:

> 'Often in their assembly seven virgins dressed in white robes will come carrying torches and they will come and prophesy before the congregation. They display a kind of enthusiasm

130. See above, p. 109.
131. See above, p. 110.

> that deceives the people present and makes them weep. They shed tears as if they were conducting a service of sorrow and penitence for sin, and by their behaviour give the impression they are weeping over the life of mankind.'[132]

Whether the prophetic gifts continued to flourish or not, Montanism itself did not die easily. Repeated episcopal denunciations and conciliar decrees did inhibit its growth, but it remained deeply implanted in Asia Minor in particular, despite persecution, until the sixth century.

*Conclusion: the Heritage of Montanism*

Paradoxically the heritage of Montanism appears to be the exact converse of its hope, for the Montanist experience probably contributed much to the disappearance of prophecy from the early and medieval Church. Already in the second century spiritual gifts were becoming rare for other reasons, but the branding of Montanism as heretical sounded their death-knell. Soon the Church became convinced that prophecy as known in Old and New Testament times had entirely ceased[133], and such has remained the opinion of orthodoxy right down to this present day.

132. Epiphanius, *Against Eighty Heresies* 49.1.
133. See above, p. 93.

## PART THREE

# THE CONQUEST OF PAGANISM IN LATE PATRISTIC AND EARLY MEDIEVAL TIMES

Our understanding of history depends very much on the sources we use and on the presuppositions we bring to their interpretation. It is possible to sustain two very different views of the period we are about to review. To begin with it was the age in which the Church won Europe from paganism in the teeth of the most terrible and violent opposition. It was also the age in which great thinkers hammered out the meaning of its main doctrines, great pastoral leaders gave structure to its means of caring for its members, and great saints gave their lives for the conversion of the heathen. Spiritually it was also an era of great richness, when the Church's main forms of worship evolved, and did so without eradicating freedom of expression in praise, prayer and other aspects of devotion, when there was a great openness to the supernatural among the Lord's people, with high expectation of healing and the miraculous. In many ways these were centuries of great richness.

Yet they were also times of great emptiness with respect to pentecostal expectation. Throughout the long millennium after the demise of Montanism the Church was almost entirely preoccupied with matters of ecclesiastical and political authority, theological debate and definition, and moral and spiritual discipline. Prophetic freedom came to be looked on as an aberration and as evidence of a heretical tendency which was not to be tolerated. Only a small handful of texts offer any information that even hints at the existence of prophetic movements or tendencies before the twelfth century. These early records tend to use the most abusive language in their descriptions of the heresies in question, so much so that it is not always clear whether they do in fact cloak allusions to prophetic activity at all. Again, the movements of which they tell were all highly localised, and even if they be correctly adjudged prophetic, the conclusion remains that this was an age in which the pentecostal fervour of the early New Testament Christians or the prophetic enthusiasm of the Montanists was virtually unknown and would have been far from acceptable in the Catholic Church.

Before examining the remaining traces of these things, we need a brief overview of the history of the Church during these long centuries. They are certainly not lacking in interest and bear clear evidence of much zeal among the followers of Christ.

# 10
# From Constantine to Hildebrand

Constantine's arrival in Rome heralded a change of startling proportions for Christians. Overnight they were lifted up from being a persecuted people to become the leading religion of the empire. They had grown both in faith and numbers throughout the age of persecution, but now they began to grow in power beyond all former expectation.

*The Imperial Church in the Fourth Century*

The age of persecution was already ending before Constantine became Emperor, for Galerius had issued a decree of toleration in 311. But it was Constantine's Edict of Milan two years later that put the final seal to it.

Under his rule the Church became established and in the course of his reign church buildings were restored and endowed, pagan temples were closed or turned into churches, official worship became Christian, clergy got the privileges formerly allowed to pagan priests, and some outstanding Christians became the Emperor's advisers. Sunday became an official day of rest, and the whole ethos of the state became more Christian; for example, crucifixion was abolished, slavery made more humane, and the gladiatorial games were suppressed.

Now that it had imperial backing, Christianity began to spread not only in court circles and among the aristocracy, but also more widely in the rural areas too. There were obvious benefits for the Church in that, but inevitably it became more worldly as many now joined it for the wrong reasons. Pagan influences also began to creep in and the state began to exercise control in Church affairs.

However, one of the greatest bonuses was that the zeal of those wholly dedicated to the Lord could now be channelled into evangelistic work, and so Christianity started to spread more purposefully beyond the boundaries of the empire, into Mesopotamia, Armenia, Arabia, Ethiopia, Germanic Europe, and elsewhere

The other main channel into which enthusiasm flowed was the birthing of monasticism. The movement started with individuals withdrawing to remote places in order to spend their time more fully with the Lord. Tradition dates the start of it all about 320, when one called Antony retired to a cave in Egypt and others began to follow him. Though it seems there were already others before him, he is remembered as St. Anthony, Father of Monks (died 356). It took another two hundred years before monasticism became recognisable in anything like the forms with which most people are familiar today, but in that time it produced some very colourful and interesting characters, particularly among those known as the 'Desert Fathers', to whom we shall return later.

Further highlights of the fourth century were the Councils of Nicea in 325 and Constantinople in 381. The first was called to deal with the problem of Arianism, a heresy that undermined belief in the full divinity of Christ. Arius (250-336) taught that Christ, though higher than man, was lower than God and therefore not eternal, but had a beginning in time. The Council condemned his teaching and promulgated the Nicene Creed. The second Council condemned another heresy, Apollinarianism, so called after its proponent, Apollinarius (310-390), Bishop of Laodicea, who taught virtually the opposite of Arius, that Jesus was not a man, but God in human form.

A number of outstanding theologians and churchmen were involved in these debates. In Egypt, Athanasius of Alexandria (296-373) was Arius' main opponent and wrote extensively on the nature of Christ. In the Eastern, Greek-speaking part of the Church, Gregory of Nyssa (330-95) and Basil of Caesarea ('the Great', 330-79) were both keen exponents of Nicene doctrine; Eusebius of Caesarea (260-340) wrote the first proper history of the early Church. In the Western, Latin-speaking sector, Hilary of Poitiers (315-67) also wrote on Church history and was another anti-Arian theologian; Ambrose of Milan (339-97), a strong champion of orthodoxy, stood firmly for the authority of the Church over the state, even rebuking the Emperor and causing him to do public penance. The fourth century is known as the golden age of the Church Fathers.

Imperial Christianity was threatened temporarily when Julian ('the Apostate'), Emperor in 361-3, tried to revive paganism. By that time, however, the Roman Empire had become well and truly Christian in ethos. In 330 Constantine founded the city of Constantinople, by the entrance to the Black Sea, to be his new Christian capital. The long-term result of that was that the Empire became divided, with two capitals, and then in 364 with two emperors,

Valentinian in the West at Rome, and Valens in the East at Constantinople. The division was to affect the Church every bit as much as the state.

*The Close of the Patristic Age of the Church in the Fifth Century*

The phrase 'Patristic Age' refers to the time of the great writing Fathers of the Church in the second to fifth centuries. The end of this age marks the transition to Medieval Christianity.

Most of the writings of the Fathers were called forth by debates about doctrine and the need to combat heretical teaching. In 431 the Council of Ephesus condemned Pelagianism, the teaching of Pelagius, a British monk who lived in Rome and then in North Africa at the beginning of the century. He held that man must take the first step towards his salvation by his own effort, without divine grace, and that he was himself responsible for his good and evil deeds. A modified version of this heresy developed later (Semi-Pelagianism) holding that while God's grace is needed, man takes his own first steps to salvation, and that was condemned in 529 at the Council of Orange. The Council of Ephesus also passed sentence on Nestorianism, the heresy of Nestorius (died about 451), who said there were two separate persons in Jesus Christ, one divine and the other human, that is as opposed to the orthodox teaching that Jesus was one person with two natures. Then in 451 the Council of Chalcedon denounced Monophysitism, a heresy that believed Jesus had only a divine and not a human nature. It was this council that drew up the famous Chalcedonian Definition of Faith, which is still read in some churches today.

The doctrinal issues of the first five centuries focused mainly on explaining the Trinity and the Person of Christ. Some of the confusion was caused by the fact that one half of the Church communicated in Greek and the other in Latin, but most of it resulted from trying to interpret Hebraic biblical teaching to a world dominated by Greek philosophical thinking and to a Church that no longer understood the pentecostal dimension.

Outstanding among the writers and theologians of the period were, in the Eastern Greek-speaking Church, John Chrysostom (347-407), Patriarch of Constantinople, a Bible preacher whose writings are still read today, and Cyril (died 444), Bishop of Alexandria, an anti-Nestorian writer. The West produced Jerome (342-430), the biblical scholar who made the Latin translation of the Bible known as the Vulgate, which has been the version authorised by the Catholic Church down to our own time, and perhaps the most famous of them all, also Augustine (354-430), Bishop of Hippo in North Africa, the father of Western Church theology.

The influence of Augustine was immense. In his own day most of his energies were occupied in opposing three different heresies, but in doing so he elaborated theological systems that have massively governed the thinking of churchmen ever since. The first of these heresies was the Manichean, a dualist belief that the source of evil was in a spiritual power opposed to God. Augustine taught that God, who made everything, made it all good, and that evil results from the exercise of free-will by fallen men. The second heresy was the Donatist, which was creating deep division in North Africa at the time.[134] Out of his polemics with its supporters came our Western theology of Church and sacraments, and also his teaching that the civil power could be God's rod of correction in punishing and suppressing heresy (a doctrine used later to justify the actions of the Inquisition and the execution of many critics and reformers). The third heresy was Pelagianism, the denial of original sin. Out of his debates with its adherents he developed his well-known teachings on the fall of man, original sin and predestination that had a great influence on Calvin and several other reformers and so are still authoritative among many Christians. Augustine's teaching influenced the whole course of theological thought right down through the Middle Ages and still carries weight today.

It was not only for its theologians that the century was particularly noted. Monasticism was also spreading, albeit still raggedly. In Egypt many more withdrew to join the Desert Fathers in their caves and other remote places on the wilderness fringes. In Syria some strange and very austere ascetic practices developed, such as wearing heavy chains, or living exposed to all weathers like the animals. But strangest of all were the 'Pillar Saints', men who erected pillars and lived on top of them, the most notable being Simeon Stylites ('Simon of the Pillar', 390-459), who built his first pillar in 423.

Church politics also increasingly occupied the minds of Christians. As the theological and Christological disputes continued, it became more and more difficult for the Latin and Greek churches to agree on points of doctrine and practice, and so the gulf between Eastern and Western Christianity grew. The political division of the empire, of course, added to the sense of separation, and that was soon to lead to the emergence of Orthodoxy in the East and Catholicism in the West.

---

134. See above, p. 85.

Also on the political front, we now see considerable growth in the authority of the Bishop of Rome. The most famous of this age were Innocent I (402-17), Celestine I (422-32), and particularly Leo I ('the Great', 440-61), who, at a time of international turmoil and instability, sought to strengthen the Church by energetic central government, and so firmly established the authority of the Papacy over the Western Church and also in considerable measure over the state.

*The Sack and Fall of Rome*

It was not the affairs of churchmen and theologians that most occupied the minds of men in the middle of the fifth century, but the growing threat to the empire from northern tribesmen. The southward movement of barbarian hordes from central Asia, known generally as Huns, created massive disruption among the north European tribes and in turn put pressure on them to move southwards. This led to successive invasions of Italy and the ultimate overthrow of the Roman Empire. Rome itself was taken and plundered by Alaric the Hun in 410, and again in 455 by Genseric the Vandal. Then finally, in 476, the German King Odoacer took Rome, dethroned the Emperor, and declared himself 'King of Italy'. From that date the Western Roman Empire was no more.

At the time there were many pagans who claimed that the Roman Empire fell before the barbarians because Christianity had undermined its military resolve. There was some justification for their assessment, for in its later years some of the Christian emperors were feeble puppets in the hands of bigots, women and priests. The rot, however, had set in right at the beginning, with Constantine himself. While Christians were grateful to him for ending the persecutions, and though he did accept and patronise their faith, it seems he overlaid its worship with elements drawn from his own pre-conversion devotion to the Roman Sun-god, Sol Invictus, whose image he had stamped on his coins alongside the cross. Compromise was thus built into the Roman Church from the start, and so it continued, influencing not only churchmen, but statesmen as well. The Christianity of Rome in the early fifth century was certainly not that of the early Church and so was quite unable to impart the strength the state needed to withstand the barbarians. The Rome taken by Alaric, who was himself a Christian anyway, even if a heretical one, was already half pagan. While many Christians were horrified and distressed at its fall, Augustine, who also stood in awe at the event, regarded it as an act of divine judgment on a system already riddled with paganism.

Nevertheless, despite their failings, many of these later Roman Emperors were personally responsible for the continued growth of Christianity in the empire. Unlike their pagan predecessors, who sought to eradicate faith by persecution, they mainly operated through processes of governmental debate and legal decision. That in itself involved them in inevitable compromises, but on the whole the policy worked, and by the time Rome fell most of the major cities were centres of Christianity. Paganism still lingered in the rural areas (which is where the word comes from: the Latin *paganus* means 'countryman'), but for the most part Christianity had triumphed in the Roman Empire in the fifth century.

### *The Dark Ages—Sixth to Eleventh Centuries*

The five centuries between the fall of Rome and 1,000 are usually referred to as 'the Dark Ages'. The barbarian invasions from Northern Europe were followed by the conquests of Islam in the East and South, and these were in turn followed by the Scandinavian (Norse, Viking, etc.) invasions in the North. It was a time of spiritual turmoil, political anarchy and cultural eclipse. About 800 Charlemagne actively extended the sway of Christianity and did restore stability for a time, but the fuller recovery of Western European civilisation had to wait until the pagan invaders had been more thoroughly converted and most of Europe was Christian, in name at any rate. However, certain significant developments did take place in the Church during these years. Most of the evangelistic work was done through the monasteries.

### *Missionary Monks*

This was the age of the great missionary monks: of Patrick (c. 389-461), the missionary bishop in Ireland who became the nation's patron saint; of Columbanus (c. 543-615), an Irish monk who carried the gospel through Gaul (France) as far as Switzerland and north Italy; of Columba (c. 521-97), first Abbot of Iona in western Scotland; of Aidan (d. 651), who evangelised widely in the south of Scotland and the north of England; of Cuthbert (634-87), Abbot of the monastery at Lindesfarne and missionary bishop in the north-east of England. These were all monks of Celtic origin or affinity.

The Roman form of Christianity came to England with Augustine, first bishop of Canterbury (d. 605), who initiated the conversion of the southern part of the country. From there it spread northwards and overtook the old Celtic system, and then southwards into northern Europe. Its greatest luminary was undoubtedly Boniface (c. 680-754), an English missionary who gave his life to the conversion of the tribal peoples in Germany and North Europe with phenomenal results, establishing the Roman Church there very firmly. The works of Willibrord (658-739) in Frisia and Denmark and of Anskar (801-65) in Denmark and Sweden were exceedingly powerful in their day, though the Scandinavian lands relapsed completely into paganism afterwards, coming properly to faith only after the tenth century.

The outstanding work of Martin (c. 315-397) in Gaul belongs to an earlier period than any of these but, through the continuing influence of the monastery he founded at Tours, it laid the groundwork for many of the missions of the later medieval monks.

The missionary work of the medieval monks was regularly attended by manifestations of miraculous activity and other evidences of the use of spiritual gifts. They were truly, or at least many of them were, the early medieval charismatics. However, they were so fully occupied with their tasks of evangelism and pastoral care that they had little leisure for writing and theological reflection.

### *Platonism and Neo-Platonism, the Ground of Medieval Theology*

Only two names stand out for mention as noteworthy theologians in the Dark Ages, one at the beginning of the era, Boethius (480-524), a neo-Platonist, the other an Irishman from the brief time of respite under Charlemagne, John Scotus Erigena (John the Irishman, 815-877), who, despite his name and origin, lived and worked in Paris, another neo-Platonist who sought to explain Christianity in terms of Greek philosophical concepts.

Plato was a Greek philosopher (427-347 BC) whose teaching had a wide influence in the Greek-speaking world. It was known in Judaism through the writings of Philo in the early first century AD and was later made popular in the Christian Church, mainly through the work of two Alexandrians in the early third century, Clement and Origen.[135] Plato's fundamental theory is that behind this world of sense and every-day experience there exists another, higher world of 'ideas' or 'forms', in which is to be found the changeless, eternally good form or essence of all observable phenomena. By laying hold of these eternal forms, the soul of man is lifted above the changeableness of this world and finds its true identity and well-being.

135. See above, p. 83.

Neo-Platonism is basically a recasting of Plato's teaching in a more closely co-ordinated system with a more directly religious purpose. It was elaborated by Plotinus (205-70), a pagan philosopher, and taught by him in his own school in Rome. It was further developed by his friend and disciple, Porphyry (c. 232-303), in opposition to Christianity, and then again much later by Proclus (d. 485), the school's last well-known master. It views the universe as a hierarchy of existence. At the top there is the One or the Good, the first principle, infinitely simple and pure. Beneath it is a world of intelligible ideas, beneath that the World Soul, and then finally the material world in which the creatures, that issued from the One originally, have an existence of their own. Though separated from their source in the One, they remain united with it and desire to return to it. Salvation for man, therefore, is to break his ties with the external world and flow back into the One.

The world-views of Plato and Plotinus stayed foundational in European thinking right through the Middle Ages, up to the twelfth century when they were largely overtaken by the philosophical system of Aristotle. But even after that they persisted, and are still influential in some circles today. Although the two systems, the Platonic and Neo-Platonic, differ in detail, their essential suppositions agree, and so as their ideas became diffused in general use, it was not always possible to distinguish the precise source of inspiration in the teaching of the Church.

The great Cappadocian theologians of the fifth century, Basil of Caesarea, Gregory of Nazianzus and Gregory of Nyssa, were all inspired by Neo-Platonism. Boethius' treatise, *On the Consolation of Philosophy*, in which he describes how the soul attains to the knowledge of the vision of God through philosophy, became very popular and was translated into Anglo-Saxon by King Alfred. The extensive works of Augustine are entirely penetrated by Neo-Platonism, and that above all else ensured its continued influence in the Church down through the Middle Ages and beyond. Equally significant are the writings attributed to Dionysius the Areopagite (Pseudo-Dionysius, c. 500), which present a mysticism based on a synthesis of Neo-Platonism and Christianity. They were translated from the Greek into Latin by John Scotus Erigena in the ninth century and, together with Augustine and Boethius, inspired almost all the mystic speculation of the Middle Ages.

While the reinterpretation of Christian doctrine into Platonic categories resulted in a departure from purely biblical modes of expression, and thus blocked the restoration of any pentecostal understanding of the faith, it did enable a widespread spiritual movement that was in many ways quite close to biblical prophecy, though with a somewhat different self-awareness. It encouraged Bible teachers, especially in Alexandria, to look for different levels of meaning, spiritual included, behind every biblical statement, and it thus encouraged praying people to seek after spiritual experience, particularly for unity with the divine One (mysticism). Medieval Christianity did have a high spiritual content.

*Gregory the Great and the Vision of a Christian Europe*

When the Roman Empire collapsed, Europe plunged into a chaos of tribes and peoples squabbling and fighting with each other, with no central, stabilising voice among them, that is apart from the Church. Christianity was by this time strong in most parts of southern Europe, while in central and northern regions a number of tribes were already Christian, and through the work of the missionaries others were to become so. The Church therefore had the unique opportunity of becoming a unifying force in the West, and that opportunity was seized upon by one of the most outstanding of the early medieval Popes, Gregory I ('the Great' 590-604), a man with a wide, European vision. He was the one who properly established the rule of the Papacy over the Western churches, and who energetically promoted the evangelisation of heathen Europe. To achieve these objectives, but for other reasons as well, he also encouraged the growth of monasticism.

Already in 529, before Gregory's time, an attempt had been made to bring some order to the monastic system through the proclamation of the Rule of St. Benedict. That had led to the emergence of the first of the great medieval orders, the Benedictines, with their code of poverty, chastity and obedience. They were very active in the work of evangelising Northern Europe and establishing Christian forms of culture everywhere they went. Gregory's encouragement gave their work a powerful boost and soon their monasteries were to be found everywhere, centres of evangelism, social care and education.

Among his other achievements, Gregory was responsible for promoting ideas about images, purgatory and transubstantiation that would later become standard doctrines in Catholicism. He also established strong political status for the Papacy by becoming the effective ruler of Rome and district. And it was he who, in 596, sent Augustine to England, where he became the first Bishop of Canterbury.

Gregory's work in strengthening the Church came none too soon. Shortly after his death, a far greater threat to Christian civilisation than the tribal chaos of Europe arose in the East with the birth of Islam.

### *The Rise and Spread of Islam*

The traditional date of the birth of Islam is 622, the date of the *Hegira,* when Mohammed had to flee from Mecca, the town of his birth, to the neighbouring city of Medina. In the following ten years before his death, and even more so afterwards, Islam spread rapidly through Arabia itself, then on into Persia and India in the East, to Palestine, Syria and Asia Minor (modern Turkey) in the Middle East, to Egypt and across North Africa in the South, and over the Straits of Gibraltar into Spain in the West. In 732, at the Battle of Tours, Charles Martel and his Frankish army halted its progress any further into Western Europe, but now most of the earliest Christian world lay in its grip. Christians suffered under their rule in different ways: enforced conversion, death, enslavement and the diminished status of second-class citizens paying heavy taxation. Because of its disunited and half-pagan condition, it took another three centuries before Europe was able to react more positively.

One of the main reasons why the Christian regions of the ancient world in the south and east of the old Roman Empire were so easily overrun by the Muslims is the same as the reason why the northern parts fell so readily to the pagan tribes of Europe three centuries earlier, namely that the influence of the churches, which should have been putting fibre into the muscle of the state through strong prophetic witness, was weakened through compromise, ecclesiasticism, division and corruption.

### *Charlemagne and the Holy Roman Empire*

However, God has never left his people or his purposes to sink without hope, and his usual way of redress has been to raise up a strong leader who will act as deliverer. That was his way with Samuel and Elijah in ancient Israel, and with Wycliffe and Luther much later in Europe. In this age it was Charlemagne, or 'Charles the Great' (742-814), grandson of Charles Martel. He was King of the Franks, a Germanic tribe controlling a large part of France. After conquering the Saxon lands to his east and driving the Islamic Moors back into southern Spain, he made himself master of most of western Europe, from northern Spain in the west, through France and Germany to Austria in the east, from the Netherlands in the north to Italy in the south. In Rome, on Christmas Day, 800, the Pope proclaimed him Charles Augustus, Holy Roman Emperor, successor to the great rulers of the old Empire.

He reigned over his wide dominion with great wisdom. As well as conqueror, he was a reformer, legislator and a keen patron of education and the Church. Some measure of unification came to the nations of Europe with the founding of the Holy Roman Empire and Charlemagne's rule restored stability for a time, for he established a strong central administration in his realm. Also, in the encouragement he gave to learning and culture, through the much-needed reforms he effected in the Church, and by governing through courts and councils with a mixture of civilian and church members, he probably did more than anyone else to set the Church back on its feet. It was that as much as anything else that caused the Pope to confer on him the title 'Holy Roman Emperor'.

The Empire continued to function after Charlemagne's death, though his successors were not able to maintain the same measure of control in Europe. The office therefore became elective, the Emperor being chosen by seven princes who bore the title 'Elector'. At times his headship was little more than nominal, at others quite strong. He was recognised as titular head of European Christendom and was therefore respected for the honour of his title, though seldom able to command obedience among the imperial states. Nevertheless, some of the emperors were powerful men and did exercise political leadership, as, for example, at the time of the crusades, when some of them played a strong leading role. Down to the Reformation there was constant rivalry, sometimes open warfare, between the emperors and the Popes over which of them really ruled Europe, and the heyday of the Church's power came in the twelfth century when Gregory VII (Hildebrand) was able to compel the Emperor's submission.

The title continued in use, held latterly by the rulers of Austria, but the Empire itself had become little more than the relic of a bygone age when the last Emperor was deposed by Napoleon in 1806.

*Western Catholicism and Eastern Orthodoxy*

This attempt to re-establish the Western Roman Empire had far reaching consequences in the history of the Church. The Eastern imperial capital, Constantinople, was still the seat of government for Eastern Christendom. Because of a mixture of political, linguistic and cultural differences, the churches of East and West had been slowly drifting apart from each other in many ways. And now, with the Church in the West politically allied to the Holy Roman Empire, the rift between Eastern and Western Christendom began to widen. The final break came in 1054 when the Pope excommunicated the Patriarch of Constantinople and the separation between Western Catholicism and Eastern Orthodoxy was made absolute.

The differences between the two churches are many, the greatest of them being aesthetic and spiritual, and therefore difficult to describe in one short paragraph. Only by attending an Orthodox Church service can one begin to catch anything of the flavour of Eastern faith and worship. There you will find no seats, since the congregation stands for worship. You will see paintings of saints (called 'icons') on the walls with people praying in front of them; in the Catholic Church the saints are portrayed by images. Whereas the Catholic priest conducts most of the Liturgy from an open sanctuary, the Orthodox priest does so out of view behind a decorated screen known as the 'iconostasis'. Most of the service will be in Greek, just as it used to be in Latin in Catholic churches until fairly recently, and where Catholics use unleavened wafers for communion, the Eastern churches use common bread. The ways of the priests are also different in the two churches. They dress and groom themselves differently and while Catholic clergy have to be celibate, the Orthodox have to be married. The head of the Catholic Church is known as the Pope, of the Orthodox as the Patriarch. However, the point of division is not ritual or practical, but doctrinal. And the dispute centres on a matter most Christians today would regard as trivial. In the Latin creed it is stated that Spirit 'proceeds from the Father and the Son'; the Orthodox say the Spirit 'proceeds from the Father' alone. The Latin for 'and the son' is *filioque,* and it was dispute over that one word that finally split the two churches apart.

*Prophecy and Revival*

These centuries were not particularly marked for revival or the prophetic. There are only a few local movements with prophetic traces that we know anything about, and even then we know very little, for the records about them are, as we shall see, highly critical. The main developments in the 'dark ages' were the spread and organising of monasticism, the evangelisation of Europe, mainly through the monasteries, the extension of Papal authority over the West, the development of Church Law, the Latin Liturgy, the Calendar of festivals and saints' days, and so forth, everything that led to the full flowering of ecclesiasticism and medieval piety in the West and the growth and establishment of Byzantine Christianity (Orthodoxy) in the East.

The main area of prophetic activity was in northern Europe. The international upheavals of the fifth to seventh centuries not only redrew the map of the nations, but shifted the religious balance of the lands of the old Empire, which inevitably affected the prophetic dimensions of Christian faith. When the eastern and southern Mediterranean lands became Islamic, freedom for prophetic expression was restricted totally and evangelism became well nigh impossible. The conquerors of Italy at the end of the fifth century were themselves Christians, and so in most of southern Europe the Church, for the most part, remained free to develop along the lines it had already been following. Evangelism was therefore mainly a matter of gathering the remaining unconverted into already established churches and planting new ones to cope with continuing expansion.

The story of northern Europe was very different. There the invaders were entirely pagan and so evangelism had to be aggressive and seen to be powerfully effective. Without the miraculous working of the Holy Spirit it would have been impossible to win the Saxon and the Germanic tribes for Christ. The stories of the northern monks and missionaries is a rich store of prophetic narrative, but even so, the faith they established never demanded that their converts became charismatics themselves. The gifts were primarily weapons for the evangelists to use in the work they were called to do.

In the Church in the southern European and Mediterranean regions that remained in Christian hands after the onslaught of Islam there was little evidence of charismatic enthusiasm in this period. One notable exception is found in Simeon 'the New Theologian' (949-1022), Abbot of St. Mammas at Constantinople, who was probably the most outstanding of the Byzantine medieval mystics. He clearly taught about the importance of experience of the Holy Spirit, of the charismatic over the institutional. However, he never started any prophetic movement, nor was he allowed the freedom to do so.

### *The Triumph of the Church in Europe*

The period reached its climax for the Church in the time of Pope Gregory VII, the only Pope better known by his family name, Hildebrand (1073-85). Under him the political authority of the Papacy was firmly established. He carried out extensive reforms, lifting the standard of morals and morale among the clergy. It was he who first enforced the rule of celibacy for priests, already widely practised but not compulsorily. But his major achievement was in freeing the Church from the domination of the state, ending the appointment of bishops by kings, insisting that priests be tried in ecclesiastical, not secular, courts, and refusing to allow his bishops to pledge feudal allegiance to their sovereigns. He found himself in an open conflict of wills with the Emperor, Henry IV. Henry persuaded the German bishops to vote for his deposition; Hildebrand retaliated by excommunicating him and absolving all his subjects from their pledge of allegiance to him. Henry capitulated and Papal power remained virtually absolute throughout the next century and beyond.

In Europe the Christian Church now reigned supreme, totally victorious over the forces of paganism that earlier sought to destroy it. But it was its very strength, expressed in its organised political systems and its regulated liturgical piety, that above all obstructed the expression of any Holy Spirit enthusiasm, affording it no more place than it had found in the Church of its early medieval forebears, perhaps even less.

By contrast, the story of the Church from Constantine to Hildebrand reveals a strange mixture of openly acknowledged prophetic ministry and rigorously suppressed prophetic enthusiasm.

# 11
# Prophecy in the Dark Ages

After the Montanist crisis, spiritual freedom and prophetic experience came to be viewed with suspicion. Also, because of necessary preoccupation with heresies that multiplied as the Church expanded, some of which we have mentioned in passing, the authorities became increasingly wary of anything that did not conform to the patterns then becoming established in belief and practice. There was much debate at first about how to deal with heretics. Some held they should be forcibly brought into line, others that they should be won back by preaching and argument. When the government decided to use force on the Donatists in North Africa, Augustine, Bishop of Hippo, was at first opposed to it, but soon he came to see it as little different from discipline used with recalcitrant children, necessary for their ultimate well-being. Increasingly the whole Church came to think likewise, and so as the Middle Ages progressed it became regular practice to suppress any movement that looked heretical both swiftly and ruthlessly, and to destroy all traces of its teaching.

As a result it is with a sense of tedium and frustration that today we search through early medieval records for some rare glimpses or hints of movements that might be called prophetic, that is, in the sense that they believed their purpose to be, in part at least, the propagation of prophetic faith. Even when we do find an odd text that looks anything like relevant, whatever glimpses it offers tend to be obscured by the abusive, polemical style of its author. And besides, these few texts all describe local movements that had little lasting influence on the wider Church. This was clearly an age in which the prophetic fervour of the New Testament Christians or the Montanists was either unknown or unacceptable in the Catholic Church.

*The Spiritual Vitality of the Early Medieval Worship*

Despite the pentecostal vacuum, spiritual gifts and phenomena were far from unknown during the Middle Ages. If anything they abounded more than at almost any other period in the Church's history before our own time. The rationalism of the Enlightenment had not yet made belief in the supernatural unfashionable. It would be entirely possible to compile an extensive catalogue of prophetic experiences from the legends of individual saints and from the monastic chronicles. In fact there is so much resource material that we could be utterly swamped by it, and anyway the task of filtering out the authentic from the legendary would be exceedingly tedious.

In the realm of worship, the age of the Fathers is noted for a rich variety of expressive styles. Liturgical forms were now emerging, but worshippers could also be quite spontaneous in calling out praises and thanksgivings. Sighs, tears and laughter were frequently heard during services, sometimes very loudly. For example, Augustine tells how, in response to a healing that took place in his church,

> 'Such wonder rose up from men and women together that the exclamations and tears seemed as if they would never come to an end ... (They) shouted God's praises without words, but with such a noise that our ears could scarcely stand it.'[136]

The allusion to praises without words probably refers to a form of worship that seems to have been similar to the corporate use of tongues in our own time. In Augustine's day, and indeed right through the Middle Ages, such worship was known as 'jubilation'. It was found in both private and congregational use, and even had a recognised liturgical setting. Before the reading of the Gospel in the Eucharist, it was common for the congregation to sing 'Alleluia' and to extend the last 'a' into a spontaneous song without words, sometimes lasting quite a long time.

It commonly expressed great joy and an ecstasy of spirit that could not be restricted to words. Augustine describes it thus:

> 'Where speech does not suffice ... they break into singing on vowel sounds, that through this means the feeling of the soul may be expressed, words failing to explain the heart's conceptions ... should we not sing the jubilation out of heavenly joy, what words cannot express ... You already know what it is to jubilate. Rejoice and speak. If you cannot express your joy, jubilate: jubilation expresses your joy.'[137]

---

136. Augustine, *City of God* 22.8. The information and quotations relating to jubilation in this section are taken from E. Ensley, *Sounds of Wonder. Speaking in Tongues in the Catholic Tradition*, Paulist Press, New York, 1977.
137. Augustine, *Commentary on the Psalm 97*, 4 PL 37, pp. 1254-5.

Again he says,

> 'He who sings a jubilus does not utter words; he pronounces a wordless sound of joy; the voice of his soul pours forth happiness as intensely as possible, expressing what he feels without reflecting on any particular meaning; to manifest his joy, the man does not use words that can be pronounced and understood, but he simply lets his joy burst forth without words; his voice then appears to express a happiness so intense that he cannot formulate it.'[138]

Others besides Augustine write about this spontaneous worship in speech without words. Jerome mentions it in the fifth century, Cassiodorus in the sixth, Isodore of Seville in the seventh. Apparently it was a widespread form of prayer used in many settings besides the liturgy. Jerome mentions farmers in the field and little children praying in this way, others tell of sailors and river-boatmen. It was a widely used song of joy.

There was much variety in the jubilation. It could take the form of improvised psalm singing or, at the opposite extreme, of bodily gestures without any words. Though it was often a spontaneous expression of joy, it could also be entered regardless of feelings; for sometimes Augustine and others had to exhort their people to jubilate. But all that came to an end in the ninth century when this improvised jubilation ceased to be a regular part of the liturgy. More fixed and stereotyped modes of worship then became the established norm and the spontaneous expressions grew less marked.

Nevertheless, jubilation in wordless praise survived in other ways. It continued among the mystics in particular, and occasionally among others. Thomas Aquinas says, for example,

> 'The jubilus is an inexpressible joy which is not able to be expressed in words but even still the voice declares this vast expanse of joy.'[139]

And Teresa of Avila writes,

> 'Many words are spoken, during this state, in praise of God, but, unless the Lord himself puts order into them, they have no orderly form. The understanding, at any rate, counts for nothing here; the soul would like to shout praises aloud, for it

138. *Commentary on Psalm 99*, 4 PL 37, p. 1272.
139. Aquinas, *In Psalterium David*, on Ps. 32:3.

> is in such a state that it cannot contain itself—a state of delectable disquiet.'[140]

Nowhere is it said that jubilation is speaking or singing in tongues, but the implication of the texts is that the two are at least closely related and no doubt often were the same. Over the first nine hundred years of its existence the Church in many places continued to worship God in ways that prophetic Christians from our own century would have found quite understandable.

*The Prophetic Experiences of Saints, Hermits and Monks*

Hundreds of utterances from the early monks and hermits in the deserts of Egypt, Syria and Palestine are preserved for us in a collection known as *The Sayings of the Desert Fathers* (*Apophthegmata Patrum*). Most of these are in the form of words of wisdom, some very brief like proverbs, others longer containing wise teachings and insights, usually spoken privately by a spiritual father to his sons or disciples in the ascetic life. They come from the lips of people who did not seek experience, but rather spurned it. They believed their calling was to pursue self-effacing, sacrificial love, to renounce themselves, take up their cross and follow Jesus. They never delighted in what happened to them personally, but sought rather to deny all that, so that the imprint of the image of Christ might be the only thing seen in them.

They were men committed to living near God, and other Christians knew it. Hence they were frequently sought out by the needy, who often received help from them in the form of heaven-inspired words of wisdom. Living as close to God as they did, they exercised quite regularly the gifts we today refer to as word of wisdom, word of knowledge and prophecy. They knew well the ways of spiritual warfare, of revelation and vision, of healing and miraculous power. That was simply the spiritual atmosphere they lived in, but they never gloried in these things, nor did they set themselves to seek after them. They were men set on seeking God for himself. Of St. Anthony, the first and best known of the Desert Fathers,

> 'Some say … that he was "Spirit-borne", that is, carried along by the Holy Spirit, but he would never speak of this to men. Such men see what is happening in the world, as well as knowing what is going to happen.'[141]

140. *The Autobiography of St. Teresa of Avila*, ed. By E. Allison Peers, Doubleday, New York, 1960, p. 164.
141. *Sayings of the Desert Fathers*, translated by Benedicta Ward, Mowbray, 2nd edn., 1981, p. 7.

Athanasius wrote a biography of St. Anthony containing many stories about the saint's confrontations with the powers of darkness, but he equally applauds the harshness with which he treated his body, even rejoicing in the fact that he never bathed or washed his feet.[142] Such stern ascetic attitudes encouraged the view that physical pain and suffering were spiritually advantageous, a veritable sharing in the sufferings of Christ. From there it is a short step to believing illness has redemptive value, which indeed became the teaching of some—a far cry from the faith for healing encouraged in Scripture. There are, to be sure, several passages in the New Testament that encourage the subjection of the flesh to the Spirit (e.g. 1 Cor. 9:27), but the Desert Fathers took this teaching to extraordinary limits of excess.

Their intention was good enough, to eradicate all personal pride, but even that led to perversion, to a view that exercising spiritual gifts, which they did frequently, was also a potential stimulus to pride and so to be discouraged except in cases of unavoidable necessity. These views were carried into Western monasticism through the writings of John Cassian (360-435), a monk from the East who settled in Gaul and wrote two books, the Institutes, setting out his rules for the monastic life, and Conferences, recounting his conversations with the great leaders of Eastern monasticism. Benedict made much use of these when he drew up his own rules, which became foundational among the Benedictines and then also among the other orders of the West. Yes, the gifts continued in use, but mainly among the ascetics, who now viewed them as valid enough, but potentially dangerous to their growth in humility and their search for spiritual perfection.

*Macarius the Great and Simeon the New Theologian*

Quite different, indeed strikingly so, and particularly interesting for us here, though from the same ascetic background as the Desert Fathers, is one known as Macarius. There were several outstanding men of that time who bore the name, such as Macarius of Alexandria, but the one to whom we refer is traditionally known as Macarius the Great (or Macarius of Egypt, 300-90), the author of a collection of *Fifty Spiritual Homilies*[143].

Most of the asceticism of the Desert Fathers, as we have seen, was self-imposed, but Macarius' teaching, though from the same mould

142. Athanasius, *Life of St. Anthony the Great*, chs. 39-42, 47.

143. G.A. Maloney, *Intoxicated with God*, Dimension Books, 1978. There is some debate whether the author of these *Homilies* was actually Macarius of Egypt, or some otherwise unknown Macarius who may have lived in Syria.

and expressing many of the same views, was actually quite different. His great theme was the need for the presence of the light of God in the soul of man through the indwelling of the Holy Spirit to enable him to live the holy and blessed life. He taught that, as we give ourselves totally to Christ, we receive our baptism in the Holy Spirit. This experience, he says, highlights our consciousness of sin, the centrality of Christ and the love of the Father, brings great peace and joy, and has as the sign of its operation the gift of tears. The Desert Fathers were convinced that that gift was given to keep them from sinning. The culture and language may be different, but the experience of the Spirit looks very close to what we find today in Charismatic Christianity.

Macarius taught that the gift of the Spirit was God's eternal and unchanging purpose for man, from the beginning, for him now, and perfected in the end:

> 'When God created Adam, He did not furnish him with material wings as birds have, but He prepared for him the wings of the Holy Spirit. The same He plans on giving him at the resurrection, to lift him and direct him wherever the Spirit wishes. These wings the Saints already now are deemed worthy to possess to fly up mentally to the realm of heavenly thoughts.
>
> 'For Christians live in another world, eat from another table, are clothed differently, enjoy different enjoyment, different dialogue and a different mentality. Because of all this they exceed all other men. This power already they are considered worthy to enjoy in their souls through the Holy Spirit. Therefore also in the resurrection their bodies will be worthy to receive those eternal blessings of the Holy Spirit. They will be permeated with that glory which their souls in this life have already experienced.'[144]

Macarius taught that this gift of the Spirit was not simply good, but necessary for living a holy life:

> 'The soul has need of a divine lamp, namely, the Holy Spirit who puts in order and beautifies the darkened house. The soul needs the shining Sun of justice which illumines and shines upon the heart. It also has need of weapons by which it can conquer in war.'[145]

---

144. *Intoxicated with God, p.61.*
145. *Ibid.*, p.78.

He spoke of Spirit-filled Christians as 'perfect'[146], having a glory and anointing unknown to the rest of mankind:

> 'Perfect Christians, who are considered worthy to reach a degree of perfection and to come close to the King, are continually dedicated to the cross of Christ. Just as the anointing in the times of the prophets was considered absolutely as a most precious thing since kings and prophets were anointed, so also now spiritual persons, who are anointed with a heavenly anointing, become Christians by grace, so that they too become kings and prophets of heavenly mysteries.
>
> 'Indeed, these are sons and lords and gods ... How much more do all, who have been anointed in mind and the interior man with the sanctifying and joy-giving, heavenly and spiritual "oil of gladness" (Heb. 1:9), receive the sign of that kingdom of imperishable and eternal power, namely, "the pledge of the Spirit" (2 Cor. 5:5).'[147]

Macarius tells that this anointing is so wonderful that

> 'If a man has a great thirst and he is given a pleasing drink, then, as he begins to taste of it, the more he wants to have it, the more eagerly he drinks of it. So is the taste of the Spirit, it can hardly be stopped or satisfied.'[148]

And so he urges us to plead with God for the gift:

> 'Let us, therefore, beg God, seeking and praying Him to gift us with the treasure of the Spirit in order that we may be empowered to walk in all of His commands without blame and purely and to fulfil every justice asked of the Spirit with purity and perfection by means of the heavenly treasure which is Christ.'[149]

He does teach that the Holy Spirit is received by faith but, in keeping with the ascetic context of his day, also says that we must strive to prove ourselves worthy and exercise our wills accordingly:

> 'The person that wishes to come to the Lord and to be deemed worthy of eternal life and to become the dwelling place of Christ and to be filled with the Holy Spirit so that he may be

---

146. The language is reminiscent of Irenaeus's; see above, p. 90.
147. *Intoxicated with God*, p.110.
148. *Ibid.*, p. 122.
149. *Ibid.*, p. 124.

able to bring forth the fruits of the Spirit and perform the commandments of Christ purely and blamelessly, ought to begin first by believing firmly in the Lord and giving himself completely to the words of his commands and renouncing the world in all things so that his whole mind may be taken up with nothing ephemeral.

'And he ought to persevere constantly in prayer, always waiting in faith that expects His coming and His help, keeping the goal of his mind ever fixed upon this. Then he ought to push himself to every good work and to doing all the commandments of the Lord because there is sin dwelling within him.

'Thus let him strive to show humility … Let him not seek honour or praise or the glory of men … But let him have always before his eyes the Lord and His commands, wishing to please him alone … let him accustom himself to be merciful, compassionate and good according to his power …

'Above all, let him take the humility and conduct of the Lord, His meekness and conversation, as his model by ever remembering Him. Let him continue incessantly in prayers, always beseeching and believing that the Lord may come to dwell in him and may perfect and give him power to accomplish all His commands and that the Lord Himself may become the dwelling place for his soul.

'And thus the things he now does with effort of a reluctant heart, he may perform one day willingly, accustoming himself always to the good and remembering the Lord and waiting for Him always in great love.

'Then the Lord, seeing such an intention and his good diligence, how he strives to remember the Lord and always seeks to do good and is humble and meek and loving, how he guides his heart, whether he wishes or not, to the best of his ability with force, has mercy on him and frees him from his enemies and the indwelling sin. He fills him with the Holy Spirit.

'And gradually without force or struggle he keeps all the Lord's commandments in truth. Or, rather, it is the Lord who keeps in him His very own commandments and then He brings forth the fruits of the Spirit purely.

'It is, however, necessary at first for one coming to the Lord to force himself thus to do good and even if he should not in his

> heart be so inclined, he must constantly await His mercy with unshakened faith ...
>
> 'And so, God, seeing him striving so and pushing himself by determination, even if the heart is unwilling, gives him the authentic prayer of the Spirit, gives him true charity, true meekness, "the bowels of mercies" (Col 3:12), true kindness, and, simply put, fills him with the fruits of the Spirit.'[150]

Present-day teaching would lay more emphasis on receiving purely by faith alone, but even so there are plenty who, though they express that view, would still act in something like the way Macarius advised and would encourage others to do likewise, holding that our actions demonstrate to God the seriousness of our intention and prayer.

Macarius' writings were widely read among Eastern Christians in the Middle Ages and later, and were particularly influential among the mystically minded in the Byzantine, Syrian and Slavic branches of the Church. The one who was probably most influenced by his works was the eleventh century mystic, Simeon the New Theologian.[151] The writings of both men are of interest in that they testify to continuing prophetic activity in the Eastern churches, but neither Macarius nor Simeon led prophetic revivals in their time. If our Macarius was Macarius the Great, then it is known that he was leader of a colony of monks in the desert of Scetis, which became one of the main centres of monasticism in Egypt, but even then there is no evidence that they sought to restore the whole Church to prophetic faith. Simeon had other problems to handle. He too led a community of monks, in Constantinople, but far from generating any prophetic movement, his teaching roused such fierce opposition that he was deprived of his appointment in 1005 and driven into exile in Asia. The writings of both Macarius and Simeon continued to be influential long after their time.

In Europe Macarius' *Homilies* found a new lease of popularity among the Pietists of seventeenth century Germany and France[152], and in England they exercised a strong influence on the Wesleys. Samuel Wesley was particularly fond of them and his son, John, even made his own translation of some of them. Thus, while Macarius may have started no major prophetic movement in his own time, he did initiate a school of thought and faith that influenced

---

150. *Ibid.*, pp. 128-9.
151. See above, p. 153.
152. See below, p. 393.

churchmen with prophetic and revival leanings for well over a thousand years, and still does so today.

*The Evangelistic Monks of Europe*

Somewhat different from the Desert Fathers, though also ascetic in their ways, were the monks who evangelised Northern Europe. They too sought to live close to God, but were inevitably much more actively involved in the affairs of men. Their spiritual diet was frequently less meditative and more energetic. As they invaded the darkness of paganism with the light of Christ, they regularly witnessed miraculous signs and wonders confirming the word they preached. Every abbey in Europe must have had its stories to tell. Some of the most popular were clearly mythical, like tales of saints subduing dragons, but there are also plenty of others that are entirely credible in the light of the New Testament and contemporary pentecostal experience. Some of the miracle stories told by Bede, for example, are very similar to what we might find in modern Charismatic biographies, allowing, of course, for the difference in cultural context. He tells how Bishop John of Beverley cured a young man of dumbness, prayed for a girl with a badly swollen arm, healed a woman who had suffered for forty years with some 'acute complaint', restored a paralysed and dying servant-lad, brought back from the brink of death one of his clergy who cracked his skull when he fell from his horse.[153]

Besides healings, the stories of the medieval saints are replete with miracles, exorcisms, prophecies, visions, battles with demons, and the like. The often quite dramatic and spectacular tales of the Celtic saints of Scotland are still taught to school-children as part of their Scottish heritage. The restoration of Iona Abbey has rekindled interest in its founder St. Columba and the account of his life by Adamnan is well padded with tales of the miraculous (including the driving away of a water monster from Loch Ness by the sign of the cross). The Pictish King Brude, who may have had some earlier Christian influence on his life but was still surrounded by pagan magicians, is said to have been greatly impressed by Columba's miraculous powers.

However, despite the existence of so much miracle-working and prophetic activity among the monks, none of it belongs properly in the field of our present study, for nowhere was it ever preached, as in the New Testament, that all Christians should be baptised in the

153. Bede, *A History of the English Church and People*, Penguin, 1968, pp. 271-9.

Holy Spirit and exercise spiritual gifts. Although they were themselves familiar with the prophetic, the monks never taught, as Paul did, that these things were to be earnestly desired by other believers. They neither expected general outpourings of the Spirit, nor that their converts should become prophets. To them such experiences represented God's working in the lives of particularly holy men. As among the Eastern Desert Fathers, Christian living for them was more concerned with subduing the flesh and pursuing the way of humility. There was no pentecostal expectancy in it at all. For traces of that we have to turn elsewhere.

Part of the reason for this lack of prophetic expectancy was theological. The thinking of the Medieval Church was in some ways dominated less by Biblical thought forms than by Neo-Platonic philosophy, which viewed the supernatural as a changeless, eternally good 'form' or essence that lay behind all observable phenomena. Augustine of Hippo, whose teachings were so strongly influential, was himself a neo-Platonist, and so he applied these views to his understanding of the miraculous. His opinions changed in the course of his life, from a stance that the gifts had been discontinued by his own day to one that enthusiastically affirmed the healing ministry of the Church. By the time he wrote The City of God he was insisting that regular testimony be given in church by those who had been miraculously healed, and he listed a whole array of quite spectacular healings he knew about personally. But because he believed this eternally good essence lay behind everything physical, and hence that sanctity could emanate from both sacred persons and objects, he was as much at home with healing through sacraments, contact with the relics of saints and pilgrimages to sacred places, as he was with healing through prophetic gifting and personal ministry. The Church of the Middle Ages was therefore fully open to healing and the miraculous but, because of its philosophical foundations, its practices frequently tended to drift away from recognisable biblical methods and shade over into the superstitious. It would not, therefore, be right to classify all of its beliefs and practices as prophetic, that is in the New Testament sense of exercising pentecostal gifts by faith in the operation of the Holy Spirit in the life of a believer. The gifts were often genuine enough, but the understanding of them, moulded as it was by the philosophy of the day, prevented the growth of any hope for a new age or Church of the Spirit.

*Possible Local Prophetic Movements*

Nowhere in the records of the Medieval Church do we find any writings by members of prophetic movements themselves, only by their critics and opponents. If there were such people who wrote about their ways, their writings have long since been lost or destroyed. The only texts we now have were written by men who did not understand the pentecostal dimension and therefore treated anything prophetic as either a heretical aberration or as diabolically inspired. However, it is possible that underlying some of them are echoes of authentic Christian prophetic activity. Interpretation of our sources for this period must inevitably be tentative.

*A Prophet from Bourges*

Gregory, Bishop of Tours, tells of an unnamed wandering preacher of his own time in the sixth century who made a forceful impact in the South of France.[154] His heretical career began after what could be interpreted as an event of Spirit-baptism, though, if that is right, the experience is crudely parodied in the telling:

> 'A certain man of Bourges, as he himself afterwards related, went into a glade to cut wood required to finish a certain work, when a swarm of flies encompassed him, in consequence whereof he was as one mad for the space of two years.' Gregory's deduction is naturally that the experience was of the devil, but then some of Jesus' contemporaries thought he operated under the demonic control of Beelzebul, whose name may be translated 'Lord of the Flies'.

Gregory's story of what followed has traits that look fairly typical of a revival movement. After travelling round the towns near Bourges the prophet went to the province of Arles, where 'he clad himself in skins and gave himself to prayer like a holy man' and there he began his prophesying. He then moved on to the region of Javols, but by this time his ministry seems to have turned his head, for there, accompanied by a woman he called Mary, he began 'to profess himself the Christ'. Nevertheless, he exercised a powerful ministry and large crowds 'flocked to him, and brought their sick before him, who, by laying on of hands, he restored to health.' His grateful followers gave him many rich gifts, and he 'distributed these things among the poor, prostrating himself upon the earth, pouring forth prayers'—all, says Gregory, simply to beguile them. Gregory passed a similar verdict on his prophesyings:

154. Gregory of , *The History of the Franks* X.25. Translation from M. Dalton, Clarendon Press, 1927, vol. 2, pp. 461-3.

> 'He foretold the future, and to some he announced coming sickness, to others losses; only to few did he promise good fortune to come. All these things he did by diabolical arts, and I know not what cunning tricks.'

However, there were plenty who saw something of God in all he was doing, for

> 'And a vast multitude of the people was led astray by him, and not merely the uneducated, but even priests of the Church; more than three thousand persons followed him.'

Though the account is totally disparaging, the details about the heretic's abnormal ecstatic behaviour, miraculous healings, utterances about the future and his personal magnetism all suggest we are here dealing with a prophetic personality. More than that, the development of his ministry prompts comparison with other prophetic leaders. His progression from charismatic at Bourges to itinerant preacher in the neighbourhood, to prophet at Arles, to Messiah in Javols is reminiscent of Montanus' ascent from ecstatic to Paraclete, or in later times Ann Lee's elevation from prophetess to Messianic Mother.[155] There is also the possibility of an echo of Priscilla or Maximilla in his Mary, and the criticism that he used his offerings to sway potential converts recalls similar accusations levelled against the Montanists. Again, like Montanus, he very rapidly attracted a large following, and that not simply among the uneducated peasantry.

Gregory goes on to tell that his movement became aggressive, that he turned into a kind of sixth-century Robin Hood, robbing the rich to give to the poor, and that he began to demand reverence from all and sundry at sword-point. He was finally killed by one of the bishop's men at Anicum in Le Velay when it seemed he was about to attack the bishop's palace. His Mary was tortured into confessing that he was a trickster, but many of his followers continued faithful to his teaching for some time after, and indeed continued to make disciples, it seems.

A couple of sentences in the closing part of Gregory's record suggest that this movement tried to foster some kind of charismatic or ecstatic experience among its converts, and that therefore it may have been, however heretical its doctrine, a full-blown prophetic movement, not just a heresy led by a strong personality.

155. See pp. 362, 485.

First, when he arrived in Anicum before the bishop's residence, he 'sent before him, as messengers to announce his arrival, naked men, who leapt and performed antics as they went.' Whether Gregory was crudely exaggerating their behaviour or not, the impression is of some kind of ecstatic activity, and not surprisingly it evoked the same kind of reaction as did the behaviour of Samuel's prophets or the Apostles at Pentecost, for the bishop was 'astounded at these doings'! Second, we read that after the prophet's death, 'throughout all the land of Gaul there arose many, attracting to themselves by such deceptions weak women who in a frenzy proclaimed them (the prophet and his Mary) to be saints.' Clearly ecstaticism was widespread among the prophet's followers.

It is unfortunate that we possess so little information about this movement. It is interesting for a number of reasons, partly just because it is unique in its time, partly because it looks akin to Montanism, of which it could even have been a late offshoot in a region where Montanism did take root, but also because it is reminiscent of Old Testament prophetism in its warlike aspects which are paralleled again in the history of European prophetic movements only among the Huguenot Prophets of the late seventeenth century, whose home was in the same general region of Southern France. However, comparisons can be no more than superficial, for we know so little about this earlier movement owing to the meagre and biased nature of our source.

*Thiota of Mainz*

The annals of the monastery at Fulda in Germany contain a brief account of the prophesyings of a woman called Thiota (or Theuda) who, in the year 847 'caused considerable disturbance with her prophecies' in the countryside around Mainz[156]:

> 'For she gave out that she had knowledge of several things that are known only to God, as if they had been supernaturally revealed to her, and particularly that she knew the date of the consummation of the age. She foretold that the last day would fall during that very same year. The consequence was that many of the common people, both men and women, were smitten with fear and came to her bearing gifts and commending themselves to her prayers. And, what is more serious,

156. The Annals of Fulda of the year 847 AD. Text: *Monumenta Germaniae Historica. Scriptorum* I, ed. G.H. Pertz, Hanover, 1826, p. 365.

> some men in holy orders set aside their Church doctrines and followed her as if she were a teacher appointed by heaven.'

However, despite the prophesyings, there is no indication that Thiota tried to introduce her followers to any kind of personal prophetic experience, which probably explains why the annals are able to assert confidently that her influence died when she was publicly flogged for having 'recklessly usurped the ministry of prophecy.' A truly prophetic movement turns its adherents into prophets themselves and is not so easily suppressed by the removal of its leaders, as we have seen in the case of the prophet from Bourges. In Thiota and her following we have probably little more than an example of the kind of popular millennialist excitement that is recurrent in all periods of the Church's history.

*Leutard of Châlons*

According to Ralph Glaber, a historian of the eleventh century, another movement with some prophetic traits appeared in France in the year 1,000, but this time further north, around Châlons. It was led by a local peasant named Leutard, who, though not called a prophet in the text, experienced and taught things that suggest he could have been one. To begin with, he must have told his disciples about an inaugural Spirit-baptism, though we can only guess what might have happened from Ralph's abusive parody of the event, which is remarkably similar to Gregory of Tours' account of his prophet's initial experience:

> 'One day he was working alone in the country finishing off some job or other. Tired out by his labours, he fell asleep and had a vision in which it seemed as if a great swarm of bees entered his body through his private parts and then as they rushed out through his mouth with a terrific noise, tormented him with numerous stings. After they had tortured him in this way for some time, they seemed to speak with him and command him to do many things impossible for men to perform.'[157]

The consequences of this experience were certainly dramatic. We are told that he went straight home and dismissed his wife 'as if he were effecting the separation by command of the Gospel', and then went to the church where he broke the crucifix. His sermons were remembered for their excessive length and their pseudo-intellectualism,

157. Ralph Glaber, *A History of his Time* II.11. Text: PL 142, cols. 643-4. See also Wakefield and Evans, *Heresies*, pp. 72-3.

and his teaching for its polemic against tithes and its selective use of Scripture. His following, unlike that of the man of Bourges or Thiota, was apparently all among the common people whom he held with his claims to prophetic inspiration:

> 'But he managed to persuade them—such is the peasant mentality, always susceptible to persuasion—that all these things were being done as the result of a miraculous revelation from God.'

Then, when the local bishop had him denounced as a heretic, he lost his popular support and committed suicide by drowning himself in a well.

If Ralph's lurid description of Leutard being invaded by bees is a parody of his claim to baptism in the Spirit, then it is likely that he was something of a prophet, but there is nothing to indicate that he tried to teach prophetism among his followers. Like Thiota's, his movement seems to have crumbled at his death. He was probably little more than a local iconoclast and reformer, inspired by his own charismatic experience, but not really appreciating its wider significance and potential.

*Tanchelm of Flanders*

At the beginning of the twelfth century heretical movements started to spring up in many parts of the Continent and some of these may have had a prophetic aspect about them, though there is no clear evidence to that effect in the ancient sources. The nearest approximation to a hint of prophetic activity is perhaps contained in the story of a heretic called Tanchelm, who flourished in Flanders in the years 1112-15. He apparently claimed equal status with Christ on the grounds that he too possessed the fullness of the Spirit:

> 'he declared that if Christ is God because he had received the Holy Spirit, he himself was no less God in exactly the same way, inasmuch as he had received the fullness of the Holy Spirit.'[158]

It is tempting to draw comparisons with Montanus, the prophet from Bourges, or the eighteenth century Shaker leader, Ann Lee, all of whom claimed some unique relationship with God because of their prophetic experiences. Also, like them, he denounced the Catholic Church and founded his own,

158. Cited from a letter written by the Canons of Utrecht to the Archbishop of Cologne. Translation from Wakefield and Evans, *Heresies*, pp. 98-100.

> 'holding that the Church consisted only of himself and his followers; … he sought to limit the Church … to Tanchelmites alone.'

However, we know nothing else that suggests anything particularly prophetic about Tanchelm's sectarian career. We are only told about gross blasphemies he is said to have committed, such as parading himself with all the pomp of a monarch, betrothing himself to a statue of the Virgin Mary, or dispensing his bath water to his followers as a sacrament.

*Conclusion*

The conclusion is manifest, that movements for the reviving of prophetic consciousness were exceedingly rare in the period between the fourth and twelfth centuries. We find only scattered evidences of personal prophetic anointing and leadership, and even then, because of the polemical style of the historians, it cannot be certain that they were prophetic at all. Nor is it clear whether the followers of those with such anointings also became prophets or simply accepted the doctrinal teachings of their leaders. If the latter, the texts we have looked at do not witness to the existence of any prophetic movements. Unfortunately our source information is too sparse and ambiguous to permit any proper judgment.

Towards the end of the twelfth century that all began to change, for then we begin to find clear evidences that seeds containing a prophetic germ were being sown, seeds that were to sprout and flower in the thirteenth. Nevertheless, the earlier period, though it produced few, if any, self-consciously prophetic movements, was by no means devoid of prophetic faith. Most of that was found, as we have noted, in monastic circles, and probably nowhere more manifestly than among the Celts of Britain and Northern Gaul.

# 12
# Prophetic Ministries among the Celtic Saints

'Celtic' is the name applied to the ancient peoples of Britain and Ireland whose descendants today live spread out up and down the western parts of the British Isles and north-west France, driven there by the movement of peoples in the fifth and sixth centuries. Their ancestors came to mainland Britain and Ireland from Europe in pre-Roman times, but after the Romans withdrew from Britain further invaders from northern Europe, the Angles, Saxons and other tribes, pushed these older Britons westward into Wales and Cornwall and then overseas into the part of France the Romans called Armorica, which then became known as Little Britain, or Brittany. Meantime the Celtic Scots from northern Ireland colonised the mainland of Kintyre and the islands up the west of the land we consequently call Scotland today.

*The Beginnings of Celtic Christianity*

Although the Christian faith came to Britain in Roman times, the Celts remained for the most part pagan until the missionary endeavours of their monks led to their conversion in the fifth and sixth centuries. The work of these men among their own people was very thorough, so much so that it created a strong home base from which many of them travelled widely over land and sea searching for lost souls. Hence they became major participants in the work of winning the tribes of pagan Europe for Christ.

The origins of Celtic monasticism are quite obscure, though it is likely that their earliest inspiration came from the East, since their customs show a much greater affinity with the ways of the Desert Fathers than with those of the monks of Latin Europe. It seems that the channel of mediation from the East may have been Martin of Tours, who was acquainted with its systems. The monastery he founded outside the city after he was made Bishop of Tours in 372 became one of the most important centres of evangelisation and the spread of monasticism in Gaul (France), but it, and other abbeys founded from it, also exerted some influence on the faith that came to Britain. Scotland and Ireland in particular owe some considerable thanks to him and other early French monks for the encouragement they gave to their first missionaries. Ninian (360-432), the earliest of Scotland's missionary monks, spent some time with Martin himself at the monastery in Tours on his way north from Rome after he had been commissioned for the work in 394. On arrival, he established his famous church at Whithorn by the Solway Firth, the 'Candida Casa' or 'White House', and from it travelled widely preaching the gospel and planting churches among the Britons in the south-west and the Picts in the north-east. In his later life he dedicated the church to St. Martin and in later generations it continued as a place of learning for many of the Celtic monks from Ireland, who may therefore well have learned Martin's monastic ideals there.

Ninian's work in Scotland was followed shortly after by the ministry of Patrick (389-461) in Ireland. Born of Christian parents on mainland Britain or Gaul, he was seized at the age of sixteen and sold as a slave in Ireland. After six years he escaped and spent several years training for ministry in a French abbey, probably at Lérins, whence he returned to Ireland in 432 as a missionary bishop with a vision to win the country for Christ, which he certainly did with great success, especially in the north. In 444 he founded the cathedral church in Armagh and made it the administrative centre for the Irish Church. Probably through continuing contact with the monasteries of Gaul, Patrick encouraged study, asceticism, monasticism and mission. The Celtic Church that emerged was totally missionary in its orientation and was led by monastic abbots rather than diocesan bishops.

*The Missionary Monks*

From Ireland, more than a century after Ninian, the work of the gospel in Scotland was given a fresh boost when Columba (521-97), crossed the Irish Sea with a small band of twelve monks, 'twelve disciples as his fellow-soldiers'[159], in 563. The pattern was that of Christ and his disciples and was repeated in many other Celtic missions. They made the journey in a flimsy open boat called a coracle, a wooden frame covered with animal hides, and established a community on the little island of Iona off the west coast of Scotland. From that base he and his monks travelled over the western

159. Adamnan, *Life of Columba* 106b.

mainland and islands founding churches, further monastic settlements and mission stations, traversing pagan tribal regions that even the strong Roman armies had found too inhospitable to colonise. The monks of Ireland and Iona also ranged much more widely, risking their lives in journeys across the wild northern seas in their flimsy craft in search of lost souls, travelling by about 700 as far north as the Orkneys, Shetlands, the distant Faeroes, and even Iceland.[160] Others journeyed into England and Wales, over into Europe, to Gaul, Switzerland, Germany and Italy. One of the best known of these was the Irish Columbanus (c. 540-612), who, setting out from the monastery at Bangor in Ulster, travelled through Brittany into Gaul, where he established a work at Fountaines. Expelled by the king of the region because of his outspokenness on religious, political and moral issues, he founded another monastery on the Rhine, and in his later years moved on into North Italy where he founded the famous monastery at Bobbio.

Peregrination, as such journeying was then called, was of the very essence of life and ministry to these Scots/Irish monks. Many of them engaged in it, taking Abraham as their example, encouraged also, no doubt, by the folk movements of the time, when the Celts spread themselves out along the western seaboard, and the Scots from Ireland settled in south-west Scotland. The initial wandering of the monks was therefore among kindred peoples, though, of course, they ranged much more widely in the end, as the missions of men like Drostan, Colm, Fergus, Moluag and Maelrubha among the northern Picts, Aidan among the Angles of Bernicia in the east, and the followers of Columbanus among the Gauls clearly attest. Among these was Gall (c. 550-645), one of Columbanus' twelve missionary companions who separated from him and settled in Switzerland, where the monastery at St. Gallen beside Lake Constance, according to tradition, dates back to his time.

Also outstanding among the Celtic missionaries were the Welsh saints, such as Samson (c. 490-565) from the monastery of Llantwit in South Wales, who, after travelling through Cornwall, crossed the channel and settled in Brittany where he founded the monastery at Dol. Hélier, also from Llantwit, went to Jersey, where his memory is preserved in the name of the island's capital. By far the most famous of the Welsh, of course, was David (d. c. 601), the nation's

160. 'In the year 825 the monk Dicuil described an island lying to the north of Britain and said, "there are many other islands in the ocean to the north of Britain ... On these islands hermits who have sailed from our Scotia (Ireland) have lived for roughly a hundred years."' (E. de Waal, *A World Made Whole*, p. 63.)

patron saint. His mission work was mainly in Wales itself, where he is said to have planted twelve monasteries. Though many tales were told about him, most of them seem to be quite legendary. It appears that he eventually settled in an abbey he founded himself at Mynyw (Menevia), where he modelled the community's life on the extreme asceticism of the Egyptian monks.

From manuscripts preserved at St. Gallen we gather that Celtic pilgrim monks became common figures on the continent after the sixth century, travelling in companies, carrying long walking sticks, leather wallets and water bottles, with their heads shaved in a different style from the Latin priests, clad in rough garments, and yet with excellent mastery of the languages of the regions they traversed, preaching the gospel with great fervour.[161]

The settlements they established in their Celtic homelands were marked, after the patterns of the Egyptian desert, by severe simplicity, little colonies of self-denying, hard-working men, scattered over the country. Each brother lived in a separate hut or 'cell' within the compound, but the monastery was certainly not a place of retreat for solitaries. Its purpose was to provide a home base for those called to preach the gospel among the heathen. Though they were fervent, devout, and strictly ascetic, the monks were first and foremost missionaries. They travelled widely among the different tribes, preaching in hamlets and settlements where no missionary had ever been before and, after spending weeks or months in this work, they returned to base for rest and refreshment, to prepare themselves for their next evangelistic sortie.

### *Celtic and Roman Christianity*

In the second half of the seventh century everything began to change for the Celtic Church. At that time conflict with the Roman Church came to a head and the Celtic system was overtaken by the Continental. Its monks then became subject to the rules of the Benedictine Order which encouraged them to give up their peregrination and settle in their monasteries. Apart from that the Viking invasions began to make travel more dangerous anyway. However, by then the Columban monks and the Brito-Pictish missions of Ninian, Kentigern (Mungo) and others had between them brought most of Scotland subject to the reign of Christ. Similarly the work of Patrick's successors in Ireland and of David (d.c. 601) and his fellow

161. W.M. Macpherson, *Materials for a History of the Church and Priory of Monymusk*, Aberdeen, 1895, p. 9.

monks in Wales, of whom Teilo, Deniol and Asaph are perhaps the best known[162], had made both these lands essentially Christian.

One of the most famous of the Columban monks was Aidan (died 651), who evangelised widely in the south of Scotland and the north of England. King Oswald of Northumbria sought refuge on Iona after the defeat of his father and was there converted to Christ. On regaining his kingdom he invited missionaries to come from Iona and instruct his heathen subjects in the faith. The result was that in 635 Aidan made his headquarters on the island of Lindesfarne and from there travelled widely setting up many missionary stations in Northumbria. His work was continued later in the century by Cuthbert (died 687), who also became Prior and then Bishop of Lindesfarne. In the next century the best known monastic of Northumbria is 'The Venerable' Bede (673-735), who spent his life from his early teens in the monastery of Jarrow. He is best remembered as a biblical scholar and historian, whose *History of the English Church and People* is our main source of information about the spread of Christianity in England up to his time. However, by his day the Roman system had conquered.

The conflict came to a head after Aidan's death. Celtic monasticism and the forms of Christianity that went with it were quite different in character from those that developed in Europe under Roman supervision. The Latin form was imported into southern and central England through the work of Augustine (d. 604), the first Archbishop of Canterbury, who was sent there as a missionary from Rome in 596-7. He was followed by Paulinus (d. 644), first Bishop of York, who was also sent from Rome with a similar commission, to further the work Augustine had started. Inevitably the two forms clashed. The Roman Church operated through dioceses overseen by bishops and parishes ministered to by priests. The Celtic system knew nothing of dioceses or parishes, but was administered from its monasteries, with the abbot, rather than the bishop, being the supreme authority over the dependant priories and churches founded by his monks.[163] Though the differences were quite profound, the main contention arose over the date of Easter, about which the Irish and Roman traditions disagreed. The matter was finally settled at a synod held in 664 at Whitby, at the convent of the famous

---

162. It is told of David that on a pilgrimage to Jerusalem, he 'was baptised in the Holy Ghost and spake in tongues as in the days of the apostles.' (D. Pawson, *Fourth Wave*, Hodder & Stoughton, 1993.) However, the whole tradition of this journey is of questionable historical value.

163. In the Celtic system, the bishop was either the abbot himself, or a member of the abbey community, subject to the abbot.

Abbess Hilda, at which the Northumbrian King Oswy, Oswald's brother and successor, agreed to adopt the Roman system, from which point the Church in England came uniformly into line with Rome. The Scottish, Welsh and Irish churches followed later, after much resistance.

*Celtic Spirituality*

Celtic spirituality is in many ways closer to the prophetic than other medieval forms. To the Celtic monks the veil between earth and heaven was very thin.

> 'In them we encounter people of whom very often almost humanly impossible things are related. They see visions, talk with angels, repulse demons, stop rivers in their courses, raise the dead, tame fierce beasts. The supernatural is always breaking in. They are men of power. Miracles are recounted as though they are the most natural of daily occurrences.'[164]

In his major work, *De Natura Divisione*, John Scotus Erigena, the Celtic theologian, taught that God is in all things and is the true essence of all things. One of his favourite words was 'theophany'. For him the world is theophany. Things are not external to God. With him 'making' is the same as 'being'.[165]

This awareness of the intertwining of nature and the divine cannot be mistaken for primitive, superstitious animism or pantheism, for it is clearly and firmly embedded in sound Trinitarian and Christ-centred theology, with an excellent appreciation of creation, sin, salvation, Christ's incarnation, heaven and hell. If anything their theology is free of the medieval accretions that the reformers found so repulsive in the Roman system, such as worship of the Virgin, belief that souls could be relieved of suffering in Purgatory through the prayers of the faithful, the doctrine of transubstantiation, and recognition of Papal authority. Celtic Christianity grew up a strictly native growth, with the influence of Rome practically unfelt.

Most of the 'lives' of the saints that have survived were written long after their time, several centuries later in the majority of cases. Their primary purpose was not so much to present historical biography as to highlight the sanctity of the monk by emphasising his devotion to the life of self-denial and by cataloguing the miraculous wonders that attended his ministry. Over the intervening centuries,

164. E. de Waal, *A World Made Whole*, p. 48.
165. De Waal, p. 75. See above, p. 142.

fact and fable often became confused and a desire to venerate the saint inevitably led to a heightening of the miraculous. These lives are therefore mainly viewed as reflecting the popular, superstitious piety of the age in which they were written and not as the most reliable sources of information about the saint himself. However, some earlier lives from the seventh century have also survived. For example, Jonas became a monk at Bobbio only three years after Columbanus's death in 612 and started to write his life soon after that, obtaining his material from the saint's companions, thus providing an invaluable contemporary insight into what mainland Europe owed to the Irish monks. Similarly the life of Samson was written about 610 or 615, not long after his death, again giving us lively contact with the missionary work of the Celtic Church in Wales, Cornwall and Brittany in his own day. While Adamnan wrote his life of Columba about 690-5, a century after the abbot's death, he tells us that his sources included earlier writings and testimonies of 'informed and trustworthy aged men,' and so it provides us with a wholesome sense of the early Celtic missions in Scotland. With such narratives we are indeed much nearer to the historical saints and their companions.

From them we see clearly that the Celtic monks knew a greater degree of personal freedom than was permitted in the Roman orders, where the rule of community loomed much larger. If a monk believed God was calling him to go on pilgrimage or mission, he was generally free, indeed encouraged, to do so. Similarly he was free to leave the community and seek solitude on some small island or remote mainland place for whatever length of time seemed right to him. Such a lone place, whatever its nature, they called a 'desert', presumably after the example of the Egyptian and Syrian monks with whom they shared so much in common. A monk who had withdrawn to such a 'desert' was expected to return with new spiritual wisdom and power, and so the needy would often seek him for prophetic counsel or miraculous aid. Living in personal contact with the world of the Spirit was of the very essence of his monastic calling. Samson and Columbanus both sought out caves where they could withdraw to be alone with God. Columba had a small oratory on the little island of Hinba to the south of Iona where he regularly sought solitude.

One of the main results of all this was that the work of the Celtic monks took on a strong prophetic quality. To be sure they saw plenty of signs and wonders, healings, miracles of provision and protection, nature miracles, exorcisms, raising the dead, and such like, but many of these were shot through with a prophetic quality, being often effected as a result of spiritual guidance, wisdom or insight. Nowhere is that better seen than in the life of St. Columba.

*The Prophetic Ministry of St. Columba*

The restoration of Iona Abbey in the twentieth century has generated a great deal of interest in its founder, Columba, with the result that several books about him and translations of his life story have been published in recent years.[166] Adamnan, his biographer, was born twenty-seven years after the saint's death in 597 and later became Abbot of Iona himself. His book is well padded with tales of the miraculous and the prophetic, but it is fairly free from the obviously legendary and quite unbelievable accretions that are found in some later lives of the saints.

Adamnan takes particular note of the interrelationship of the miraculous and the prophetic in Columba's ministry on several occasions. In telling of water drawn from a rock, a miraculous provision of fish, increased fertility in a herd of cattle, and a number of other miracles, he comments on how it was prophetic foreknowledge that led to their performance in the first place (57a, 61a, 67b, 69a). But more than that, the whole of Adamnan's *Life of Columba* is the account of a ministry based on strong prophetic gifting. He divides it into three books, the first containing

> 'prophetic revelations; the second, divine miracles effected through him; the third, appearances of angels, and certain manifestations of heavenly brightness above the man of God' (3b).

It is in recounting the deeds of the second part that he comments on the prophetic quality of the miracles. Columba is portrayed as a man in close communion with the world of the Holy Spirit and the angels of God, who hears and sees what mortal eye cannot, and who repeatedly receives wisdom, revelation, direction and guidance in the manner of the Old Testament prophets or the New Testament apostles.

Adamnan is keenly aware of the comparison himself and comments on it at one point, saying that Columba's wonder-working ministry secures him a place

166. The translation used here is A.O. & M.O Anderson, *Adomnán's Life of Columba*, from which all quotations are taken. References are to page and column in the original Latin manuscript, the system used in the Andersons' book.

> 'in common with the prophets Elijah and Elisha; and a like share of honour with the apostles Peter and Paul and John; and a glorious eternal place in the heavenly land, among both the companies, namely prophets and apostles, as a man prophetic and apostolic' (79a).

Indeed the *Life* as a whole reads much like the stories of these two prophets in the books of Kings and of the apostles in Acts. In his preface, Adamnan summarises thus (6a – 10b):

> 'By virtue of prayers and in the name of the Lord Jesus Christ he healed people who endured the attacks of various diseases.
>
> 'He, one man alone, with God's aid repulsed innumerable hostile bands of demons making war against him, visible to his bodily eyes, and preparing to inflict deadly diseases upon his community of monks; and they were thrust back from this our principal island.
>
> 'With Christ's help, he checked the raging fury of wild beasts, by killing some and strongly repelling others. Swelling waves also, that once in a great storm rose like mountains, quickly subsided at his prayer, and were stilled. …
>
> 'At other times also, through his prayers, winds unfavourable to voyagers were changed to favourable ones. …
>
> '… He restored to life—and this is a major miracle—the dead son of a believing layman, and gave him back alive and unharmed to his father and mother.
>
> 'At another time, in his youth, when … the necessary wine for the most holy mysteries was lacking, by virtue of prayer he changed pure water into true wine.
>
> 'Sometimes also there appeared to certain of the brothers, on various different occasions, a great light of heavenly brightness poured out upon him, either in the darkness of night or in the light of day.
>
> 'He was held worthy to receive in shining light the sweet and most pleasant visitations of holy angels.
>
> 'Often, by revelation of the Holy Spirit, he saw the souls of just men borne by angels to the height of heaven; and time and again he beheld other souls of the wicked being carried to hell by demons.

> 'Very often he foretold the future rewards of many who still lived in mortal flesh, of some happy, of others sad.
>
> 'And in the terrible crashings of battles, by virtue of prayer he obtained from God that some kings were conquered, and other rulers were conquerors. This special favour was bestowed by God …
>
> '… he began from his youthful years to be strong also in the spirit of prophecy; to foretell future events; to declare absent things to those present, because though absent in the body he was present in spirit, and able to observe what took place far away …'

*The General Expectation of Prophetic Gifting*

In his fuller account of these things Adamnan occasionally notes that other monks also participated in some of the prophetic giftings, but he never suggests that they were expected to experience them merely by virtue of being Christian. They were clearly expected to aspire to them, particularly through time spent in some 'desert' and through seeking God's presence in holy and devout living. The prophetic is always the potential, though not always realised. Those that did attain to it in significant measure tended to become abbots, bishops, missionaries, founders of monasteries and the like. Of Samson it is written,

> 'And, by him, God gave sight to many who were blind, and cleansed many who were leprous, and cast out devils, and saved very many from the error of their way.'[167]

It was his wonder-working that won over the hostile king and queen of Brittany and persuaded them to grant him freedom to establish his monastery at Dol.[168] It was Columba's exercise of the same power that so greatly impressed the Pictish King Brude, with the result that

> 'throughout the rest of his life, that ruler greatly honoured the holy and venerable man, as was fitting, with high esteem' (83a).

Similar tales adorn the life of Columbanus, though his holy anointing angered rather than impressed the local king and queen he had to

167. T. Taylor, *The Life of St. Samson of Dol*, p. 39, sect. XXXVII.
168. Taylor, pp. 53-8, sect. LIII-LIX.

deal with in Gaul and resulted in his deportation. Miracle stories are, of course, greatly multiplied in the later lives of the saints, but in these earlier narratives the constant emphasis is that such things were as signs following upon a holy life, not experiences sought after. The primary call of the monk was to emulate the piety and devotion of these saints, and what is admired most about them is not what God did through them but how they abandoned themselves totally to God with whole and undivided heart in a walk that was personally most demanding, albeit highly fulfilling. Adamnan's description of Columba's character in this respect is highly telling:

> 'he could not pass even the space of a single hour without applying himself to prayer, or to reading, or to writing or some kind of work. Also by day and by night, without any intermission, he was occupied with unwearying labours of fasts and vigils that the burden of each several work seemed beyond the strength of man. And with all this he was loving to everyone, his holy face ever showed gladness, and he was happy in his inmost heart with the joy of the Holy Spirit.' (4b – 5a)

The ethos is again similar to that of the Eastern Desert Fathers, who accepted the miraculous and the prophetic as part and parcel of their lives as Christians, but who sought personal holiness rather than the gifts.

Monastics in the Roman orders continued to cherish stories of the miraculous among the saints (and to embellish them), though they mostly lost hold of the living sense of the supernatural that so strongly characterised Celtic spirituality. True, there were always clear instances of the same rich endowment, but their frequency was reduced with the passage of time, which is perhaps one of the reasons why the lives of the saints became more and more fabulous. Once the prophetic and miraculous ceased to be part of the everyday living experience, it became little more than the material of romantic dreams, shot through with unreality. The atmosphere among the early Celtic missionaries was entirely different. To them the supernatural was in the very air they breathed.

They were not, for all that, a prophetic movement in the same sense as the early Christian Church was, for, as far as we know, they had no pentecostal expectation and never taught that all converts should be baptised in the Holy Spirit and then exercise spiritual gifts. Their approach was much more that of the Eastern Desert Fathers, which held that engagement with the supernatural resulted from a life of total devotion and ascetic dedication.

Nevertheless, their experience of life in the Spirit regularly matched that of the early Church and of the modern Charismatic, indeed frequently outshone them.

*The Achievement and Passage of the Celtic Church*

The Columban monks reclaimed the pagans of the farthest Hebrides for Christ, sent their ambassadors to establish the faith as far north as Iceland, and planted Christianity in every glen and bay where they could assemble a congregation. Meantime the Irish and the Welsh monks crossed over into Europe, founding abbeys as far away as Switzerland, the Rhineland and Northern Italy.

The conditions they encountered were often far from friendly, as the history of Columbanus in Gaul so vividly illustrates. The paganism of the northern Picts also generated considerable hostility, for it was a kind of fetichism which saw the air, the earth, the water, and all natural phenomena inhabited by malignant beings who were always bent on working evil. Its spiritual leaders, named druadh, or sorcerers, exercised great influence among the people and were by no means kindly disposed to the new preachers. They exercised their witchcraft to benefit those who sought their assistance or to injure those to whom they were opposed.

To combat these forces as effectively as they did, they had to be men of supernatural empowering and to be able to demonstrate that they were so in the working of miraculous signs and wonders. But by determined faith, persistent seeking after the presence of God, strong perseverance and heroic evangelism, the Scots and Irish monks won through, aided only by the Holy Spirit at work within them and the mutual encouragement they afforded one another—certainly unaided by the Roman bishops, from whose domination they long remained free, even after the Northumbrians had submitted to their rule. Columba brought this independence with him. For many generations Iona was the centre of northern Christendom, and Columba, as chief abbot, was to all intents and purposes looked upon as its head during his lifetime. The Celtic missionaries gave their allegiance to him, not the Bishop of Rome.

The time of Celtic ascendancy in Northumbria goes down in history as a golden age of saintliness in England, and yet it was the North of England that first capitulated to the Roman pressure from Kent, at the Synod of Whitby in 664. Colman, the leader of the Scots delegation at the synod, and his brother monks refused to abandon the traditions and customs of Iona and withdrew from the debate. Adamnan did become a convert to the Roman uses and, when he was Abbot of Iona from 679 to 704, tried to persuade his clergy to adopt them, but without success. To them Roman direction was quite pointless.

The conversion of the Northern Picts by the Columban missionaries had been followed by a century and a half of peace between Picts and Scots, and throughout that whole period the Celtic Church was to all intents and purposes the national Church in Scotland. But the Roman faction kept up its pressure until, about 710, Nectan, King of the North Picts, accepted the Roman usages, and then the monks of Iona had to yield. Some time later he ordered all the Columban clergy to conform or leave the country, and the primacy of Iona came to an end. Many of the Columban clergy preferred exile. The Celtic customs and liturgies were rigidly suppressed and are not heard of after 730.

The Picts conquered Dalriada (roughly Argyll) in 736 and ruled over the Scots for most of the following century. Then came the Viking devastation. Between 794 and 825 Iona was ravaged at least five times by the Norsemen, and then again in 877. At the end of the century, when the calamity was over and the ruined churches and monasteries began to be rebuilt, the Celtic Church in Scotland was little more than a memory. Columba's successors sought shelter in the monasteries of Ireland, and when next we hear of Iona, in the twelfth century, it is the site of a convent of Cluniac monks of unknown foundation.

In 843 the Scots king, Kenneth MacAlpine, conquered the Picts and united his people with them to form a single kingdom in Scotland for the first time. He built a new cathedral church at Dunkeld, dedicating it under the name of St. Columba, and that became the nation's religious centre, until about 903, when it too was laid waste by Norsemen. In 1057 Malcolm Canmore killed Macbeath and took the Scottish throne, just nine years before William the Conqueror took the English one. The effect on Scotland was every bit as radical as that on England, thanks largely to Queen Margaret, the saintly English wife Malcolm married in 1070. Her influence finally broke the isolation of the Scottish Church and brought it fully into line with the Roman system. The land was carved into Catholic dioceses, cathedrals and abbeys were built in the Roman style, and so the process continued until the Reformation. The Celtic faith was now well and truly buried in Scotland.

In Ireland the Celtic Church paid scant regard to the decisions of Whitby. It was only after the Norman Conquest of England that the

Irish showed any inclination to seek a closer union with the rest of Christendom. Various steps were taken at a number of synods in the twelfth century, but it was the English conquest of Ireland in 1172 that expedited the process. English bishops were appointed to a number of Irish sees, but even so the Irish Church retained a strong individuality and continued to sit loose to Papal authority.

The process also took a long time in Wales. There it was a piecemeal affair, various regions submitting at intervals to Canterbury after the eighth century. The last to submit was the Bishop of St. David's, who was finally compelled to do so in 1203.

*Conclusion*

The history of the Celtic Church vividly illustrates the struggle men of the Spirit face in seeking to remain free when confronted by the crushing might of the politico-ecclesiastical system urging them to conform. The Celtic monks may not have been active proponents of pentecostal Christianity, but many of them were living examples of it, as their records so clearly attest. They had freedom to withdraw to some 'desert' and enjoy private, spiritual communion with the Lord, to go out on mission wherever the Holy Spirit might lead them, to establish communities of sympathetic brethren, to preach the gospel, heal the sick and worship God as they were led to do so, to enjoy visions and revelations, to cherish encounters with angels, to hear God for themselves and prophesy as the Spirit enabled them. They were free from the restrictive rules of the Continental abbeys and the authoritative oversight of diocesan bishops. Given the cultural limitations of monastic and ascetic vocation, they were free to follow the Spirit. Indeed, the system was too free for the Catholic monolith to tolerate its continued existence. Like the Spiritual Franciscans at a later date, they had to be brought into line. The same restrictive hand that arrested Jesus, imprisoned the apostles, quenched the spirit of the Montanists, and silenced the later medieval voices of dissenting prophecy, operated here also with terrifying effectiveness. That hand still exercises its suppressive power. The pressure to conform is still one of the greatest obstacles prophetic Christians have to surmount.

The record of the late patristic and early medieval Church is truly impressive. Yes, compromise, political ambition, and much else sullied and obscured the pure faith of the gospel, increasingly so with the passage of the centuries. Yes, the sharp prophetic thrust of the apostles was blunted by the overlay of theological reinterpretation in terms of Platonic world views, by mounting pressure for central ecclesiastical control, and many other factors. Nevertheless, it was this same Church that drove back the boundaries of paganism and won Europe over for Christ, doing so against overwhelming odds. But as we have probed beneath the surface, we have seen that there were indeed fairly strong prophetic elements to be found, particularly among the enthusiasts of the age, those who were prepared to abandon all for the sake of the gospel and the salvation of the lost. These enthusiasts were the monks, hermits, ascetics and missionaries who roamed through the nations preaching, teaching, healing and driving out demons. In many ways the degree of heroism and prophetic anointing displayed by these early evangelists puts many of our modern Charismatic heroes right into the shadows. Much as we are rediscovering the wonder of Pentecost today, the history of these early times clearly shows that not many of us have reason for proudly dismissing the Dark Ages and the centuries that immediately preceded and followed them as of little or no account in the history of prophetic faith.

# PART FOUR

# STIRRINGS OF DISSENT AND PROPHECY IN THE LATER MIDDLE AGES

It is a strange and paradoxical fact that the high point of political power, when a nation or governmental system seems at its strongest and most unshakeable, is often its time of greatest vulnerability. So it was with the Catholic Church in the later Middle Ages. It had conquered the religions of Europe, it reigned supreme over kings and nations, it brooked no rivals. Yet it was then that it had to deal with mounting unrest and opposition, among both churchmen and statesmen. Finally the Reformation shook the system to its very roots. It had become a monolith, a monopoly exercising dictatorial power, which could have been for the good, had it not increasingly let go of basic biblical values.

For churchmen the nub of the problem was that the Church had come to claim for itself saving and sanctifying powers that belonged to Christ alone, such as the forgiveness of sins and the gift of the Holy Spirit; for statesmen the dispute was mainly over the extensive political power the Church exercised through property and land ownership and through taxation. Inevitably any prophetic voice speaking for basic biblical values and Christ-centred truth was most unwelcome and quickly suppressed.

In the thirteenth and fourteenth centuries a new spirit began to emerge in Europe, giving birth to a whole plethora of sects, heresies and dissenting movements. Amongst these, but also in certain Catholic circles, dissatisfaction with the medieval Church found expression in a variety of ways, including a new interest in eschatology and a desire for a more spiritual expression of the faith. The eschatological hope focused on the expected dawn of a new era in history, the age of the Spirit and of the spiritual Church. The search for present spiritual reality culminated in the flourishing of mysticism. Though these centuries produced no movement that compares closely with the prophetic Christianity of the early Church or with the Pentecostalism of more recent times, they did witness the rebirth of many of the hopes and experiences that are the basic and essential ingredients of charismatic/prophetic faith.

# 13
# From Hildebrand to Luther

This period is sometimes called 'the age of faith', for through much of it the Church reigned supreme, and men did believe in God and the working of the supernatural. The memory of their devotion is magnificently preserved in the great cathedrals of Europe, most of which were founded or built in these times and remain today as testimonials to a faith that ranked the worship of God above all else. It is also known as 'the age of chivalry', when the brute values of paganism were overtaken by the finer sentiments of Christianity. And the memory of all that is well preserved in the castles that were built at the same time as the cathedrals and in the legends of knights in armour that are still told to our children today. The heritage of the later medieval Church is still very much with us.

There is, of course, another side to the story, one that highlights the increase of non-biblical beliefs and superstitious practices in the Church, and emphasises the slavish conditions of serfdom and the immoral aspects of conduct among feudal lords and barons. We must, however, beware of the mistake many Protestants and Pentecostals make in assessing the faith of this era, the mistake of dismissing the good because of the bad and ending with a totally negative view of an age in which there was also much that was positive. Nothing is ever perfect in history.

*The Power of the Church in the Twelfth and Thirteenth Centuries*

The later medieval period was certainly the 'Age of the Church'. Thanks mainly to the work of Hildebrand the political authority of the Papacy was firmly established over the kings and rulers of Europe. The culmination of Papal power that started with him continued over the next hundred years and more, with the Catholic Church reigning supreme, particularly during the rule of Innocent III, from 1198 to 1216.

At his enthronement Innocent claimed for his office a status and authority over every other human institution, with 'the right of finally disposing the imperial and all other crowns.' And he was able to implement it! He chose and installed Otto of Brunswick as Emperor, and later deposed him for insubordination. He assumed the government of the city of Rome, exercised effective authority over the King of France, and compelled King John of England to surrender his crown and receive it back as the Pope's subject.

The Popes continued to exercise this kind of authority throughout most of the thirteenth century, though not quite at the same level as Innocent had done. The result was that voices of dissent were easily silenced. This Church, with its organised political systems and its regulated liturgical piety, had no place for any prophetic movement or activity. These times were certainly not noted for prophetic action, though it was in them that the first of such voices were raised. In spite of the Church's great political strength, and partly in reaction to it, the next two centuries were to witness a remarkable stirring of dissent all over Europe and an equally remarkable upsurge in longing for a new 'age of the Spirit'.

*Crusaders and Friars*

The history of the twelfth and thirteenth centuries is dominated by the Crusades to win back the birthplace and first lands of ancient Christendom, but these are a story in themselves and cannot occupy us in any detail here. The first major crusade in 1095 culminated in the capture of Jerusalem in 1099 and the establishment of a European-style feudal state in Palestine which lasted for almost two centuries. However, several further crusades had to be fought during those times, mainly to hold on to what had been gained, but with progressively negative results. The second crusade, in 1146-8, was to protect Jerusalem, but the city finally fell to Saladin in 1187. That resulted in a series of further crusades over the next forty years to win back the city. The third (1189-92), in which one of the leaders was King Richard I of England ('The Lion Heart'), failed to recapture Jerusalem. The fourth (1201-4) got diverted before it even reached Palestine, having to turn aside to protect Constantinople from the Turks. In the fifth (1219-29) the Holy Roman Emperor, Frederick II, won back Jerusalem, Jaffa, Bethlehem and Nazareth, but Jerusalem was lost again in 1244, finally so until 1917. Two further crusades, in 1248-54 and 1270-2, were complete failures, and by the end of the century Palestine was once more firmly back in Islamic hands.

Though they were costly in lives and ultimately failed in their purpose, the crusades did give an outlet for enthusiasm that was otherwise largely lacking in Western Christendom in this age. The main alternative was still in monasticism, but much of the evangelistic fire had gone from the abbeys, which were themselves badly in need of revival. It was for that very purpose that the Cistercian order was founded in 1098, to revive the Benedictine disciplines that had fallen into decline. A fresh breath of revival Spirit came to the system in 1209 when the Franciscan Order was founded by St. Francis of Assisi (1181-1226), and in 1215 when the Dominican Order (the 'Black Friars') was founded in Spain by St. Dominic (1170-1221). Both the Franciscan and Dominican friars were evangelistic preachers. There were some charismatic off-shoots from the Franciscan movement, particularly among those that came to be known as the Spiritual Franciscans, while mysticism flourished among the Dominicans, especially in Germany.

*Dissenters, Theologians and Prophets*

With the dawning of the twelfth century there came stirrings of dissent all over Europe, veritable fore-rumblings of the Reformation. Some of these resulted from rediscovery of the Bible, which generated a longing for a gospel of saving faith and for holier ways of living. The results were not so much pentecostal as puritanical. Two movements in particular stand out for mention. We first encounter the Cathars or Albigensians (both words mean 'Puritans' or 'Purified Ones') in Southern France about 1170. They made full use of the New Testament and outspokenly opposed Roman ways. Though some of their teachings were heretical, they represented something of the discontent and longing that were to grow and finally break surface in the sixteenth century. About the same time, 1170, we also for the first time meet the Vaudois or Waldensians, the followers of Peter Waldo of Lyons (died 1217). He translated the Bible into Provençal and, as Wycliffe was to do in England a century and a half later, sent out Bible preachers armed with it. These, 'the Poor Men of Lyons', travelled widely in Southern France preaching their dissenting gospel. Unlike the Cathars, they were not heretics, and if anything their work was hindered rather than helped by them, for they had to spend much time opposing their teaching. Both groups were severely persecuted by the Catholics. The Cathars were brutally massacred, and have long since disappeared from history, but some Waldensians managed to find refuge in the mountains and valleys of northern Italy where communities of their descendants are still found today.

In the field of theology, though the systems of thought were largely fixed in this age, it was not an entirely dull season without any creative thinking. The debates were not about the Trinitarian and Christological doctrines that so occupied the early Church, but more about the relationship between faith and reason in Christian thought. Among the most influential writers of the age were Anselm (1033-1109), Archbishop of Canterbury, who taught that we can only understand the things of God if we first believe: 'I believe in order to understand'. Peter (1079-1142), founder of the University of Paris, pleaded for the primacy of reason and even reasonable doubt: 'By doubting we enquire, by enquiring we reach the truth.' But it was Thomas Aquinas (1225-74) whose teaching on the subject became most influential in the long run, though he himself had a personal encounter with God in his later years and in the light of it dismissed the whole system he had created (usually referred to as Thomism) as of little value. He taught the primacy of reason in theology, and reason for him meant the system of thought based on the Greek philosophical teachings of Aristotle.[169]

Other theologians, like Bernard (1090-1153), Abbot of Clairvaux, discussed the relationship between the grace of God and our free will. Among them was John Duns Scotus (1264-1308), who taught the primacy of the will. Peter (1100-60), catalogued the main teachings of the Church in his *Sentences*, which became the standard theological textbook in the seminaries of the day. And then, with best English common sense, William of Ockham (or Occam, 1300-49), proposed one of the handiest ever solutions to theological debate (still commonly referred to as 'Ockham's Razor'), namely, that 'the simplest explanation is the best.'

The writings of these men represent the flowering of medieval theology, most of which was tied to the Greek philosophical systems of Plato (before Aquinas) and Aristotle (after Aquinas). In them we see early traces of the free thinking that was to blossom in the so called 'Enlightenment' of the Renaissance that accompanied the Reformation and has ever since formed the framework of almost all Western thinking.

Also influential, but in a very different way, and more pertinent to this history, were the writings of a Calabrian (Spanish) Cistercian monk, Joachim of Fiore (or Flora, 1132-1202), who taught about a coming 'age of the Spirit'. As we shall see later, the basic interpretation of history he outlined has become axiomatic in almost every prophetic movement since his time, although it was also found much earlier among the Montanists. Similar teaching was being

169. See further below, p. 192.

propounded soon after his death, in 1209-10, by Amalric of Bena, a lecturer at the University of Paris, who started a prophetic revival movement in and around the city, but it was quickly stamped out by the Church authorities. Joachim's teaching also made a strong impression among the Spiritual Franciscans. In 1254, one of them, Gerard of Borgo San Donnino, published his *Introduction to the Eternal Gospel* which roused a great deal of end-time excitement. He said the new age of the Spirit would begin in 1260, and so sects expecting its arrival began to appear, such as the Apostolic Brethren in North Italy and the Beguins in Southern France. Though not charismatic, they were looking for a new outpouring of the Spirit as at the first Pentecost. They were all hounded to extinction and never saw their hopes fulfilled.

*The End of the Middle Ages, the Fourteenth and Fifteenth Centuries*

For the Church these were times of unrest and schism throughout Europe. Not only did the dissenting movements continue to grow, even in spite of severe persecution by the Catholic authorities, but the Church itself was torn apart from inside and its authority rapidly eroded.

The decline began when Boniface VIII became Pope in 1303. He made the same high political claims as his predecessors, but found them largely ignored. He failed to prevent Edward I of England from taxing the church and clergy, and when he quarrelled with Philip IV of France, the King went to war against him, arrested him and put him in prison. From 1305 the Papal seat was removed to Avignon and the Popes were chosen and appointed only with the approval of the French monarch. In fact, the Church now found itself with two rival Popes, one in Rome and the other in Avignon, and it continued that way for the next seventy-two years, till 1377. This period is often referred to as 'the Babylonish Captivity' of the Church.

After 1377, when the Papacy was restored to Rome, the Popes continued to make high claims for themselves, but were generally unable to enforce them. Part of the reason for their loss of authority was that the split between Rome and Avignon led to the appearance of rival Popes, a problem that was only resolved after the Council of Constance in 1414 when the claims of four rivals were considered and dismissed. But other things were not well with the Papacy at this time either. The stories of corruption and moral laxity at the top are often told and do not make edifying reading, but sadder still are tales of the same abuses throughout the whole Roman Church, among bishops, clergy, monks and nuns. Dissenters, of course, made much of these things to support their views. Among them Rome was commonly referred to as Babylon and the Pope as Antichrist. By the end of the fourteenth century the Church was badly in need of, and very much ready for, reformation.

However, despite decline, the Church still exercised extensive political power throughout Europe. Furthermore, as one of Europe's largest estate owners it had the right to considerable income from taxation, that is besides the taxes it demanded of governments as their due to the Body of Christ. The Church was exceedingly wealthy and exceedingly powerful. It therefore had a strong authority in most parliaments, law courts, civic councils and places of commerce, which made it difficult for dissenters to find any protection either inside or outside the Church. That is, until the fourteenth century.

*The Early Reformers, Wycliffe and Hus*

The first important break came in England. At the time England was at war with France, and so the removal of the Papacy to Avignon caused more than a ripple of concern among the ruling English lords. Though they gave their support to the Pope in Rome, they were not entirely happy about the enormous amount of English money that went in taxes to the Vatican. It was badly needed at home to finance the war effort, and anyhow there was also a niggling suspicion that some of it was being redirected to help fund the armies of their enemies. However, Canterbury demanded that the Church taxes be paid and there seemed to be no way out of this ridiculous knot.

The solution was provided in the teachings of an Oxford don called John Wycliffe. Today he is remembered almost entirely for his work as Bible translator, but his translation work was made possible because his political statements won him friends in parliamentary circles who were able to protect him from the wrath of the Church until just before he died. He held that the authority of the Church's leaders depended, not just on their office, but also on how they conducted themselves in it. Hence priests, and even the Pope himself, could lose their authority under God if they did not live up to their high calling, and then the civil leaders had every right to overrule them. Particularly valuable was the patronage he received from the most powerful noble of the time, John of Gaunt, Duke of Lancaster, who rescued him on more than one occasion.

Wycliffe also argued, however, that the same law applied equally to the secular authorities, and he even went as far as to say that the common people could in extreme circumstances be used by God to remove them from power. Wat Tyler and the leaders of the Peasants' Revolt in 1381 were inevitably encouraged by this teaching, which was further developed and popularised in a more extreme version by a priest called John Ball, who taught the equality of bondsmen and gentry. He is perhaps best remembered for his preaching on the rhyme,

'When Adam dalf (delved) and Eve span,
Who was then a gentilman?'

He was imprisoned in 1376 and released by the rebels in 1381, but he was captured and executed the same year, after the insurrection had been suppressed.

Wycliffe's translation of the New Testament was published in 1384, and was the first complete English Bible. After his death the Church tried to destroy all the copies of it they could find, but Wycliffe had been a teacher as well as a translator. He had trained his students as preachers and sent them out, like Peter Waldo's Poor Men of Lyons, to travel through Britain and teach the nation the gospel. These Bible preachers were known as Lollards and thanks to their faithful work throughout the following century Britain was exceedingly well prepared for the Reformation when it did come. Already it had a strong Bible-believing movement that had spread everywhere.

One of Wycliffe's most outstanding admirers was Jan Hus, who translated and disseminated Wycliffe's gospel with great effect in Bohemia. He was arrested and burnt as a heretic in 1415, but by then he had sowed the seed and thus prepared many hearts in Europe for the Reformation that was to follow a hundred years later.

### *Mystics and Prophets at the End of the Middle Ages*

The fourteenth was also the century that saw the flowering of mysticism in Europe, especially in Germany, Spain and Britain. The best known among the Germans were Master Eckhart (1260-1327), John Tauler (1300-61) and Henry Suso (1295-1366), in Spain Catherine of Sienna (1347-80), and in Britain Richard Rolle (1295-49), Walter Hilton (died 1396), Julian of Norwich (1342-1413+) and the anonymous author of *The Cloud of Unknowing*. Although most of them experienced God in ways familiar to prophetic people, they tended to be fairly solitary figures with no identifiable movement of like-minded people gathered around them. There was one group that stood out as an exception, one of particular interest in the history of prophetic movements. That was a Rhineland mystical movement known as the Friends of God, and they, though not pentecostal in our modern sense, did display many of the characteristics familiar to us today.[170]

The fifteenth century produced two outstanding prophetic personalities. One was Joan of Arc, the 'Maid of Orleans', who, guided by her 'voices', led the French armies to victory in some campaigns against the English during the Hundred Years' War, but she was captured, tried and burnt as a witch and heretic at Rouen in 1413. The other was Savonarola, a Dominican who, through accurately prophesying some major military and political events, rose to power in Florence, where he established a puritanical Christian state for a brief time, but his prophecies were not approved in Rome and his rule was too severe for the Florentines. He was arrested, tortured and hanged as a heretic in 1498.

We end our survey of the Middle Ages at 1453, the year Constantinople fell to the Turks and became Istanbul, the Muslim capital of the Turkish Empire. That event is commonly held to mark the end of the period of the Medieval Church. Certainly it was definitive in Eastern Church history, but in the West, as we have seen, the Roman Catholic Church was already in decline and reforming zeal was rising to the surface all over Europe.

*Summary and Conclusion*

When we reviewed the earlier part of the Middle Ages, from the fifth to eleventh centuries, we saw that though it was not completely devoid of prophetic awareness, it was not a time of much prophetic expectancy for the reviving of pentecostal faith in the Church in general. Other matters had occupied the attention of the medieval Church very fully, and so it continued into the era we are now studying: the growth of the monasteries, the conversion of Europe, the political triumph of the Papacy, the suppression of heresy, the disputes between East and West, the rise and spread of Islam, the crusades, and much else besides.

After the fall of Rome the power of the Church and the Papacy had kept on growing until the Pope virtually ruled Europe, but now, in the heyday of its strength, the system it had created began

170. See below, p. 211.

to creak and crack as voices of dissent multiplied throughout the later Middle Ages, until finally it was thrown into turmoil by the Reformation in the sixteenth century.

The vision of the Church of the Spirit was largely forgotten and any dissenting movements that might have resurrected it were quickly and efficiently suppressed. But the voice of dissent increased from the twelfth century onwards, producing strong movements that prepared the way for the changes that were to take place at the Reformation, in particular the Waldensians in southern France and north Italy, the Lollards in England and the Hussites in Bohemia. There were also those inside the Catholic Church itself who sought for something better and whose voices were heeded by many, adding to the longing for a more spiritual Church, amongst whom the most influential were some of the medieval mystics and the disciples of St. Francis and Joachim of Fiore. The prophetic vision may have dimmed in the Middle Ages, but it was not forgotten.

# 14
# Prophecy in the Later Middle Ages

As we have seen, the thirteenth was a century of stirrings and spiritual awakenings in many parts of Europe. The age of the crusades was not yet over, but crusading enthusiasm waned progressively and finally died in the 1270s. Christians seeking spiritual fulfilment began to look elsewhere, some to the new dissenting movements that were springing up in different places, some of them biblical in their basis, like the Cathars and the Waldensians in Southern France and North Italy. North European movements had more of a mystical flavour. Among the better known were the Béguines and Béghards of the Netherlands and the Rhineland, semi-religious communities devoted to communal life, contemplation and philanthropic work, especially among the sick and the needy. Also widespread were the Brethren of the Free Spirit, a variety of mystical sects with little central organisation, claiming to be independent of the Church's authority and living in the freedom of the Spirit. However, none of these held views about Christianity that could be said to have been charismatic, prophetic or pentecostal.

*The Theological Context of Greek Philosophy*

A large part of the reason why the pentecostal voice was silent or silenced in the Middle Ages was lack of a theological framework to comprehend its views and experiences. Most medievals just would not have understood the language and concepts of New Testament and present-day prophetic Christianity. Before 1200 the dominant world view was that of the Greek philosopher, Plato, in the light of which all biblical revelation was understood and interpreted, and that, as we have seen, encouraged views about prophetic matters that found no proper parallels in Scripture.[171] After 900 the teachings of another ancient Greek philosopher, Aristotle, were being introduced into Europe through the Muslims and Jews of Spain and south Italy. His approach was thoroughly logical and rationalistic,

---

171. See above, p. 141.

explaining reality in terms of what could be experienced with the senses, without reference to a personal God. This philosophy proved exceedingly popular, but it presented a serious challenge to the Church.

Various writers tackled it in the twelfth and thirteenth centuries, but the one who produced the most thorough reappraisal of Christian teaching in the light of it was Thomas Aquinas. He taught that while philosophy is based on information available to all men through observation, theology depends on revelation and what can be deduced from it. The result was that the material and supernatural worlds came to be seen as two separate and distinct realms of existence, interacting with each other only occasionally. Since Christians in the medieval Church believed that that interaction resulted mainly through the prayers of the saints and the Virgin Mary, who operated in the spiritual realm anyhow, the new theology proved totally acceptable. The problem for prophetic understanding was that it held no appreciation of the commingling of the spiritual and the material that the doctrine of Spirit-baptism demands, and it understood faith for miracle-working as something exercised by saints, angels and others living in the spiritual world, rather than the believing expectancy of men living in this world, as is foundational to biblical teaching and all charismatic Christianity.

Aquinas published his arguments in two books, *Summa Theologiae* and *Summa Contra Gentiles*, which together made up one of the most complete encyclopaedias of Christian thought ever written. They were not accepted without much debate, but in due course they gained nearly total prominence in Catholic thought.

### *The Spiritual and Prophetic Influence of Francis and Joachim*

Meantime, in a totally different and unrelated context a remedy for the prophetic problem was being prepared in the twelfth century and that was to enable a first expression of charismatic life early in the thirteenth. The man who did the theological spadework was a Spanish monk, Joachim of Fiore.[172] He elaborated the doctrine that history falls into three great stages: the age of the Father, that is the Old Testament dispensation of the Law; the age of the Son, which is the New Testament dispensation of the Gospel continuing through to the Church of his own day; and the age of the Spirit, which he reckoned was about to begin in 1260. In the first age the letter ruled, in the second there was a blend of the letter and the Spirit, in the

172. See above, p. 186.

third the Spirit would alone prevail. This last age would see the spiritual renewal of the Church, and the conversion of the world to a 'spiritual Church' through the zeal of a new religious order of men that was soon to appear. The most striking characteristic of this new age would be personal direct access to God by his Spirit, which would release men from their dependence on the letter of Scripture and the machinery of the Church.

The other pivotal figure in the history of matters spiritual in the thirteenth century was St. Francis of Assisi. The son of a wealthy merchant, he gave up everything to follow Christ after a revelation he had in a church near Assisi where he heard the Lord's commission to his disciples to leave all and go preach the gospel addressed personally to himself. He is remembered for his generosity, his simple faith, his great joy, his love and humility, and above all his passionate devotion to God. He was a man who knew the freedom of spirit, joy in God and faith in Christ that is common among charismatics. He was not himself a preacher of things pentecostal, but the quality of his life and faith were similar, and he quickly attracted to himself a band of like-minded followers, men who knew God in the Spirit and were drawn to living an evangelistic and spiritual life. In 1209 the Pope recognised them as a new religious order, the Franciscans.

After Francis' death in 1226 the order began to experience tensions between those who wanted to organise along the lines of other monastic orders and those who longed to retain the freedom in the Spirit that had characterised Francis' earliest band. The latter became known collectively as Spiritual Franciscans, but they never found approval in the Church because of their unwillingness to submit to the legalistic regulations required for religious orders. Some of them were hounded, arrested and executed as heretics, but the rest of the Franciscan order survived with the full approval of the Church. Some prophetic tendencies developed in Spiritual Franciscan circles, particularly where Joachim of Fiore's teaching was absorbed among them.

Joachim died in 1202 before his ideas had properly taken root, though perhaps we see his views already reflected about 1210 in the claim of the Amalricians to be the Church of the Holy Spirit. In the ensuing decades his apocalyptic vision increased in popularity, particularly among the Spiritual Franciscans who began to regard themselves as Joachim's new order of men. One of their number, a certain Gerard of Borgo San Donnino, gave new impetus to Joachim's ideas with the publication of his *Eternal Gospel* in 1254 and, as the year 1260 approached, end-time excitement increased. Visionaries preaching penance abounded in Provence and flagellants appeared on the streets of Italy, South Germany and Bohemia scourging themselves in penitential processions. Several new sects were birthed at this time, the most interesting for our purposes being the Apostolic Brethren, and a little later the Beguins of Southern France. But before we consider either of these we must first take a look at the earlier movement, the Amalricians.

*Amalric and the Amalricians*

Amalric of Bena (French *Amaury de Bène*) was a lecturer at the University of Paris who was condemned by the University in 1204 and by the Pope in 1205. His main tenet was 'that every man ought to believe, as an article of his faith without which there is no salvation, that each one of us is a member of Christ'[173], but the charge on which he was condemned was for propagating pantheistic doctrines. He died the following year, and a very short time later, in 1209/10, a fairly numerous sect bearing his name was discovered in Paris and the neighbouring dioceses, one that bears a clear prophetic stamp. Its adherents combined Amalric's pantheistic doctrine, that God is to be found in human lives rather than in the remote heavens, with a tripartite view of history, similar to that held by the Montanists a thousand years earlier[174], in which they distinguished the ages of the Father, the Son and the Holy Spirit.

They held that

> 'the Father has worked under certain forms in the Old Testament, to wit, those of the Law; the Son likewise has worked under certain forms, such as the Eucharist, baptism, and the other sacraments. Just as the forms of the Law fell away with the first coming of Christ, so now all the forms in which the Son has worked will fall, and the sacraments will come to an end, because the person of the Holy Spirit will clearly reveal himself in those in whom he is incarnated.'[175]

Believing that this third age had already begun with the Spirit becoming incarnated in them, they held that they were free from all the restraints of the Old Testament's law and the Church's formalism. Hence they recognised no priestly hierarchy, though one of their number, 'William the Goldsmith', was known as 'their prophet',

173. *Gesta Philippi Augusti* by Guillaume le Breton, cited here from R.M. Jones, *Studies in Mystical Religion*, p. 179.
174. See above, p. 108.
175. Caesar of Heisterbach, *The Dialogue of Miracles* V.22. Translation of this and the following excerpts are taken from Wakefield and Evans, Heresies, pp. 260-1.

and so presumably exercised some kind of charismatic leadership among them. Similarly they spurned all the forms and paraphernalia of church worship and occupied themselves, it seems, largely in the mystical pursuit of the Spirit's inner presence and in the sharing of their visionary experiences.

Much of our information about them comes from the writings of Caesar of Heisterbach, a Cistercian monk of the same period. In a work known as *The Dialogue of Miracles* (c. 1223) he gives us an account of how the movement was discovered. His list of its more influential members includes the names of several churchmen and masters of Paris University, indicating that theirs was no mere movement of peasant gullibility such as Leutard's is said to have been. Indeed, it was when a certain Master Ralph of Namur discovered how many important people had become involved that the Church first took notice.

The story goes that this Ralph was approached by William the Goldsmith, who claimed he had been 'sent by the Lord' to convert him. When Ralph heard of their doctrines and the extent of their membership, he was horrified, but to gain access to William's society he pretended to be convinced. Caesar tells us,

> 'the worthy man realised the imminent danger to the Church and that he alone was capable of investigating their wickedness and obtaining their conviction. He adopted a kind of subterfuge in saying that a revelation from the Holy Spirit had come to him in regard to a certain priest, who might preach their doctrines with him.'

Ralph next reported to the Church authorities and they commissioned him and his friend to infiltrate the sect in order to discover as much as they could about it. This they undertook with zest, maintaining a kind of prophetic charade, the account of which gives us some idea of the sort of worship practised by the Amalricians, not entirely unlike charismatic worship today:

> 'In order to persuade the heretics to trust him completely, Master Ralph would sometimes, with uplifted face, pretend that his soul was wafted to heaven. Afterward, in their private meetings, he would recount some of the things he said he had seen and would vow to preach their faith publicly, day in and day out.'

Ralph and his companion had to spend three months travelling through the dioceses of Paris, Langres, Troyes and the province of

Sens before they had met all the members, for the movement had become quite extensive in a very short space of time. As soon as Ralph had collected sufficient names, he submitted his report to the Bishop of Paris and there followed the inevitable arrests, inquisition, torture and burnings—even the exhumation of Amalric's body for removal from consecrated ground.

Without doubt the Amalricians were men with strong prophetic leanings. Not only were they mystics and charismatics, but they also had a view of the end-times that followed closely in the Old Testament, New Testament and Montanist traditions, affirming belief in the proximate advent of a final age of the Spirit and viewing themselves as the nucleus of that new age. They did not propound this doctrine as simply a matter of philosophical speculation or interpretation of Scripture suitable for discussion, but also as revealed truth.

Apparently in 1209-10 they were prophesying that the age of the Spirit would arrive in all fullness within five years, or as a thirteenth century tract, *Against the Amalricians* puts it, 'In five years all men will be "spirituals".'[176] They also prophesied that it would be preceded by various judgments, as Caesar relates:

> 'William also prophesied that within five years these four plagues would occur: first, one upon the people, who will be destroyed by famine; the second will be the sword, by which the nobles will kill each other; in the third, the earth will open and swallow up the townspeople; and in the fourth, fire will come down upon the prelates of the Church, who are members of Antichrist.'

Caesar adds a remark that recalls some of the comments about Maximilla's prophecies a thousand years earlier[177]:

> 'But thirteen years have gone by and not one of the things has happened which that false prophet predicted would happen within five years.'

Besides the mystical, charismatic and eschatological aspects of their beliefs and conduct, the Amalricians shared all the anti-clerical, anti-ritual, anti-establishment attitudes of prophetical men. Caesar tells us that to them 'the pope was Antichrist, Rome was Babylon.' That and several of his other notes, such as that 'they said that to erect altars to the saints and to use incense before sacred images was

176. J.B. Russell, *Religious Dissent*, p. 87.
177. See above, p. 116.

idolatry,' suggest comparison with the Old Testament prophets who criticised abuses in the sacrificial worship of the temple. And like their prophet forerunners, the Amalricians also believed the inner experience of the Spirit was the only thing truly worthwhile. Hence they envisaged an alternative charismatic community, which they saw led by seven prophetical men through whom chiefly God would speak, one of them being William the Goldsmith himself.

Like many other prophetic movements their vision was expansive and their purpose evangelistic, but their attitude sectarian. They were not simply reformers or critics of the existing system, but members, as they believed, of the true Church of the Spirit, and therefore living under compulsion to call others, like Master Ralph, into membership of their community.

Again, the tenacity with which they held their faith was characteristically prophetic. Caesar speaks of their stubbornness before the inquisition and the unrepentance with which they faced the executioner. We may compare, for example, Tertullian's earlier comments about similar steadfastness that the prophetic Spirit inspired in Montanists facing martyrdom, or the unflinching dedication with which the French Prophets went to the torture chamber and death in later times.

One point at which they digress significantly from the main tradition of Old Testament and Christian prophecy was in the pantheistic interpretation they gave to their experience of the Spirit. Believing that 'God is everywhere' and that 'all things are in the essence of God', they held that to be one of the 'spirituals' was to have grasped the truth about his universal Spirit working within, rather than to have been granted some additional spiritual endowment. That is, their view of their own prophetic faith was that it was more a matter of spiritual appreciation than of external inspiration.

This kind of thinking is also reflected in their doctrines of hell, heaven and eternal life, all of which they regarded as present spiritual conditions:

> 'Hell is nothing other than being ignorant. Heaven is understanding the truth. To understand the truth is the only kind of resurrection there will be.'[178]

Again their doctrines, according to their critics at any rate, led them into libertine ways, which stand in sharp contrast to the rigorist moralism of the main Judeo-Christian prophetic tradition, and if

---

178. *Against the Amalricians.*

these reports are to be trusted, they stand at this point much closer to other mystical groups of their own age that were influenced by the Free Spirit heresy.

None the less, even these heretical teachings find some echoes in other ages among charismatics, who have sometimes paid more attention to the immanent divine than to the transcendent, for whom present appreciation of truth has often loomed much larger than post-resurrection hope, or among whom plainly immoral action has sometimes been justified by reference to the Spirit's guidance.

The Amalricians were a unique sect in their day. Though they rapidly increased in numbers, in true prophetic fashion, embracing all sections of society, they were rigorously hounded and suppressed by the authorities. In consequence, it is not possible for us to trace any history of their development after 1210, but it is interesting to note the growth of not entirely dissimilar mystical groups in the Rhineland, Italy and Southern France in the following century. Of course it is impossible to prove any connection, but one cannot resist speculating that the Amalrician heritage might have been ultimately more extensive than our sources suggest.

*Joachim and the Spiritual Church*

The vision of a future coming era, or presently beginning one, in which the Spirit of God has full and free expression in the lives of the faithful is, as we have already seen, a recurrent ingredient in the expectation of prophetic movements. It appeared in various forms in the teaching of the Old Testament prophets, the New Testament Christians, the Montanists and the Amalricians. Among the later, post-New Testament prophets the tendency was to identify this age of the Spirit as a third phase in the history of faith, the first being the age of the Father, or the Old Testament dispensation of the letter of the Law that required obedience from men, and the second being the age of the Son, or the New Testament dispensation of the Gospel that was characterised by a blend of letter and Spirit and found its expression in the forms and observances of the Church of the day.

There is little evidence that this kind of thinking held any wider appeal for Christians in the Middle Ages until Joachim of Fiore began writing about it towards the end of the twelfth century. His elaboration of the doctrine is considerably more detailed and carefully thought out in relation to Scripture and contemporary history than anything we find among the Montanists or the Amalricians, and therein perhaps lay much of its fascination for Christians of his own day, as well as in his suggestion that the third age was about to begin in the not too distant future.

He also proposed, in a more practical vein, that the spiritual renewal of the Church and the conversion of the world to the 'spiritual Church' of the new age would be brought about through the zeal of a new order of monks that was soon to appear. The most striking feature of his third age, of course, was to be the full liberty of the Spirit, releasing men from their dependence on the letter of Scripture and the forms of the Church and permitting them personal, direct access to God by his Spirit—all things the Old Testament prophets had foretold and the earliest Christians had already enjoyed.

It has often been thought that the Amalricians held their views about history as a result of Joachim's influence, but not all scholars would agree. The problem is that when Joachim died in 1202 his ideas had not yet gained wide popularity and it was only a short time after that date that the Amalricians were propounding their doctrines. However, in the years that followed, Joachim's vision did dramatically increase in popularity, especially among the Spiritual Franciscans, many of whom came to regard themselves as members of Joachim's new religious order. But after the fashion of the time, their spirituality tended to find expression in the cult of holy poverty rather than in charismatic modes.

Nevertheless, their end-time expectation was strong, especially since 1260 was widely favoured as the date for the inauguration of the age of the Spirit. In 1254 Gerard of Borgo San Donnino, himself a Spiritual Franciscan, injected new momentum into this enthusiasm with his book, *The Eternal Gospel*. Although 1260 passed without the expected shift of the ages taking place, new dates were soon forthcoming and in the decades that followed new sects appeared, one of which was known as the Apostolic Brethren.

### *The Apostolic Brethren*

Sometimes referred to as the Pseudo-Apostles, the Apostolic Brethren were created and led initially by an unlettered North-Italian peasant called Segarelli, and then, when he was burned as a heretic in 1300, by one named Dolcino, who suffered a similar fate in 1307 after an abortive attempt to establish a sort of millennial kingdom in the mountains near Novara.

The focus of their faith was the life of holy poverty, which they believed freed them from the control and restraint of all religious and legal institutions. They were not a prophetic movement and there is no evidence of the pursuit of prophetic experience among them, as among the Amalricians. None the less, their expectations do bear some resemblance to the kind of theology that undergirds many prophetic movements, and though extremists of their sort, their teaching usefully illustrates a kind of spiritual hope that was current in that period in circles far beyond their own. They saw the experience of the Spirit and his gifts in the pentecostal sense as something that belonged to their future, yet to be granted them in the new age of the Spirit they believed was about to dawn (the fourth age in Dolcino's scheme). They therefore considered that their present purpose was to gather a people in readiness, waiting for this new outpouring of the Spirit, which would be just as on the apostles of old.

> 'Dolcino said that then all Christians would enter an era of peace when there would be one holy Pope, one not chosen by the cardinals, but miraculously sent by God … Under that Pope would be those who belong to his Apostolic Order along with others of the clergy and the religious orders who chose to join them … and then they would receive the gift of the Holy Spirit just as the apostles in the primitive Church had done, and then they would bear fruit in others even to the end of the world.
>
> 'Then he, Dolcino, and his followers among the Apostolic congregation would be set free everywhere and all spiritual persons who were in all the other religious orders would then be united with this Apostolic Brotherhood and would receive the gift of the Holy Spirit and in this way the Church would be renewed. Then when the wicked had been destroyed, they would reign and bear fruit to the end of the world.'[179]

In the meantime, while they waited for this new age to begin, the Apostles believed, like the Montanists and Amalricians before them, that, in contrast with the Roman Church which they denounced as corrupt and devoid of spiritual authority, they themselves alone embodied the nucleus of the Church of the future, the true spiritual Church:

> 'that all the spiritual power that Christ gave to the Church from the beginning has been transferred to the sect of those who call themselves the Apostles or the Order of Apostles.

179. Bernard Gui, *De secta illorum qui se dicunt esse de ordine Apostolorum*. Text: L.A. Muratori (ed.), *Racolta degli Storici Italiani* IX.5, pp. 21-4.

> They describe this sect as the spiritual congregation sent by God and chosen in these last days.'

Joachim's own ideas were not developed as a polemic against the Church of his day or as a basis for the establishment of an alternative faith. His was rather a theory about how the Catholic Church would change in the future, and as such was not condemned by Rome. The interpretation of his teaching among the Apostolic Brethren, however, stands as a further illustration of a tendency towards introversion and sectarianism we have observed in some of the prophetic circles and end-time movements we have already reviewed.

*The Beguins of Southern France*

The Beguins provide another example of this same tendency. They are to be distinguished from the Béguines and Béghards of the Netherlands and elsewhere. Both groups espoused the ideal of holy poverty and were profoundly influenced by the Spiritual Franciscans. But the northern groups, though frequently accused of Free Spirit heresy in the fourteenth century, were mainly orthodox and in some ways show affinity with the Friends of God[180] who are occasionally confused with them. The Beguins of southern France (hereafter simply 'the Beguins'), on the other hand, were condemned as heretics in 1319, some two years after their existence was brought to the notice of the Catholic Church. Their ideal was set by St. Francis himself, but their 'prophet' was a certain Peter John Olivi, from whose writings they learned the Joachimistic doctrine of the three ages. Olivi, who died in 1298, was himself a Spiritual Franciscan, not a Beguin, but his influence was considerable in both movements.

The Beguins believed Olivi had 'received his knowledge by revelation from God' and circulated collections of his sayings among themselves as inspired writings. A disciple of Joachim, he further developed his theory of the three ages, but differed from him in his attitude to the Roman Church, which was similar to Dolcino's or the Amalricians'. He applied to it the title Tertullian had used over a thousand years earlier, namely 'the carnal Church' (*ecclesia carnalis*), though he outdid all his Montanist predecessors by identifying it as 'Babylon, the great harlot'.[181] His Beguin disciples, of course, saw themselves, like the Montanists before them, as the nucleus of 'the spiritual Church', the Church which was to be blessed with the Spirit in the new age about to dawn.

---

180. See below, p. 211.
181. Olivi, *Liber Sententiarum* 302.

> 'They believe that the teaching of Brother Peter John Olivi was altogether true and catholic and that the carnal Church, that is, the Roman Church, was the great harlot of Babylon, destined to be destroyed and cast down. Also, they distinguished as it were two churches: the carnal Church, which is the Roman Church, with its reprobate multitude, and the spiritual Church, composed of people whom they call spiritual and evangelical, who follow the life of Christ and the apostles. The latter they claim, is their Church.'[182]

However, the Beguins, unlike the Montanists, but like the Apostolic Brethren, were not a prophetic movement. For them the age of the Spirit had not yet dawned. They believed that they were still living in the last (seventh) phase of the era of the Son, and so they are more properly regarded as a sect waiting for a new outpouring of the Spirit than a movement of prophets seeking to propagate prophetic experience. Nevertheless, their theology and modes of expression show many points of similarity with thinking and attitudes found among the Montanists, and indeed in most other prophetic circles down the centuries.

> 'And some of them teach that upon those men, the spiritual and evangelical elect through whom the spiritual Holy Church will be founded in the seventh and last era, the Holy Spirit will be poured out in abundance greater than, or at least equal to, its outpouring upon the apostles, Christ's disciples, on the day of Pentecost in the primitive Church. They say that it will descend upon them like a fiery flame of a furnace and, as they anticipate, not only will their souls be filled with the Holy Spirit, but also will they feel its dwelling within their bodies.'

*Conclusion*

Joachimism and Franciscanism produced no prophetic movement as such, but they did create an outlet for the aspirations of the prophetically inclined. They reflected the longing of their adherents for the sort of spirituality that the first century Christians had grasped, but that the medieval Church had stifled. Joachim's ideas have continued to influence Christians over the centuries, but the fact that almost every prophetic movement since his time has thought itself to embody the end-time Church of the Spirit in some

182. Bernard Gui, *The Conduct of the Inquisition of Heretical Depravity* IV. Translation of this and the following texts from Wakefield and Evans, *Heresies*, pp. 413, 419, 424, 425.

way probably tells us more about the essentially prophetic quality of Joachim's own vision than about his direct influence in subsequent ages, for the ideas he popularised were already, as we have seen, a regular feature of prophetic thought from earliest times, even if only in embryonic form.

The suppression of the Spiritual Franciscans reminds us of the similar fate that befell the Celtic Church, a process that was only completed in Ireland and Wales a short time before Francis came on the European scene. Neither movement was prophetic in the strong sense we are using in this book, but both provided a hospitable context for prophetic activity. In both cases the pressure to conform proved too strong, but the power of the ecclesiastical bureaucracy was weakening now and the day when prophetical men and women would be free, or at least more free, was swiftly approaching.

*POSTSCRIPT: The Cathars and the Heresy of Spirit Baptism*

We cannot finish our survey of the thirteenth-century movements without some comment on the Cathars, or Albigensians. They were a puritanical movement, not a prophetic one, and their teaching was really quite heretical, but they did pray for baptism in the Holy Spirit, which is of some interest here.

Catharism flourished in various forms through north and central Italy, the south of France and the Rhine Valley from the eleventh century to the fourteenth. Their heresy was that they taught a form of dualism: that all matter is evil, and so Christ's body could not have been material, for if it had, it too would have been evil. It must have been a mere phantom, cloaking, they went on to say, the highest of the angels, who brought salvation by his teaching, not his death and resurrection. They therefore held that Christianity had to do with more pure and spiritual things than church ritual and practice, and that for them meant adherence to a strict code of morality and asceticism. In their membership they distinguished two classes. The one they called 'perfect', those who received the *consolamentum*, or baptism in the Holy Spirit by the laying on of hands, and thereafter lived the ascetic life. The others were 'believers' who lived ordinary lives but undertook to receive the *consolamentum* at some later date, particularly if in danger of death.

It is their teaching on baptism in the Holy Spirit that is of interest to us. Some of it has a surprisingly modern ring, bearing in mind that their presuppositions were so different from our own. Consider, for example, their argument from Scripture.

> 'They have openly confessed also that besides water, they baptise and have been baptised with fire and the Spirit, adducing that testimony of John the Baptist who, while baptising in water, said of Christ, "He shall baptise you in the Holy Spirit and fire"; and in another place, "I baptise with water; but there hath stood one in the midst of you, whom you know not," as though he were to add: "He will baptise you with another baptism beyond that with water." That such baptism should be performed by the imposition of hands they have sought to show by the testimony of Luke in the Acts of the Apostles who, in describing the baptism which Paul received from Ananias at Christ's command, made no mention of water but only of the imposition of hands... . Anyone among them who is thus baptised they refer to as "Elect", and say that he has the power to baptise others who shall be found worthy, and to consecrate the body and blood of Christ at his table... . They give no credence to our baptism.'[183]

Baptism in the Holy Spirit was received through the laying on of hands with prayer. Some Cathars debated whether the laying on of hands was itself of any value, because the hand, being material, was inherently evil, but the majority practised it anyway. They believed that the rite also imparted the forgiveness of sins and salvation, so long as the person laying on hands was not himself living in any mortal sin at the time.

> 'The imposition of the hand is called by them the consolamentum, spiritual baptism, or baptism of the Holy Spirit. According to them, without it mortal sin is not forgiven, nor is the Holy Spirit imparted to anyone; both of these occur only when the rite is performed by them... . This imposition of the hand is performed by at least two persons, and not only by their prelates, but by those under them, even, in case of need, by Cathar women.'[184]

We have one quite full description of how they prayed for people to receive this baptism:

> 'They perform the ceremony of this sacrament, after a large number of brothers and sisters have assembled, by calling into

183. From a letter by Eberwin, prior of Steinfeld, to Bernard, Abbot of Clairvaux, concerning some heretics at Cologne, 1143/4. Translation from Wakefield & Evans, *Heresies*, p. 130.
184. Rainerius, *Summa on the Cathars and the Poor of Lyons*, 1250. Translation from Wakefield & Evans, *Heresies*, p. 331.

> their midst the man or woman who, after one year's probation, is to receive it. There, one of the aforesaid officials or some other person especially qualified by age or wisdom utters a long prayer.'

He then preaches him a sermon about commitment, etc., and asks if he is willing to comply. When he agrees to do so,

> 'the senior prelate holds the text of the Gospels over his head and all the brethren gathered there come forward, each to put his right hand on the believer's head or shoulder. Then the prelate who holds the Book speaks these words, "In the name of the Father, and of the Son, and of the Holy Spirit; and after repeating the Lord's Prayer seven times, he proceeds to read the Gospel of John which is chanted in church at Christmas, which is, "In the beginning was the Word," and so on.'[185]

185. James Capelli, *Summa Contra Haereticos*, about 1240. Translation from Wakefield & Evans, *Heresies*, p. 303.

# 15

# Mysticism in the Late Middle Ages

In the fourteenth century mysticism came to full flower in the lives of certain individuals and in the blossoming of various mystical groups in different parts of Europe. The precise relationship between mystical, charismatic and prophetical religion is much debated. There are considerable areas of overlap between them, particularly in their attitudes to illuminism, or the interior life of prayer and contemplation, but they are quite sharply distinguished from each other by certain differences of emphasis. For example, the mystic tends to have less interest than the prophet in the end times, or in communicating messages from God. Again, it would be generally true to say that prophetical religion tends to be more aggressive and evangelistic in character, generating the kind of contagious enthusiasm that produces movements and sects, whereas mysticism is gentler and more introspective, creating groups more by mutual attraction of like-minded persons than by intentional outreach. The term 'charismatic' acts as something of a bridge between the two, though perhaps it inclines more to the prophetic than the mystic.

On the whole, however, the three should understand each other well. They all speak the same basic language and enjoy the same quality of experience of God in the Spirit. The truth of that is witnessed in our own day by a revival of interest in the writings of medieval and other later mystics generated by the Charismatic Movement. Particularly popular from the fourteenth century are *The Cloud of Unknowing* (an anonymous work), Julian of Norwich's *Revelations of Divine Love*, Richard Rolle's *The Fire of Love* and Walter Hilton's *Ladder of Perfection.* Also very popular are the writings of the seventeenth-eighteenth century Quietist, Madame Guyon, and other post-medieval writers like Fénelon, Francis de Sales and William Law.

*What is Mysticism?*

In broad general terms, mysticism is a seeking after knowledge of God through personal religious experience. The seeking is primarily by prayer and contemplation and the experience can range from occasional spiritual awareness to a more permanent relationship with God that is often called 'mystic union' or 'mystic marriage'. The experience of God is often accompanied by visions, revelations, heavenly messages, trances, dreams, ecstasies, and the like, though some mystics hold that such things are hindrances to pure union with God and are generally said to cease when one attains the highest state of marriage. Mystics usually say the true value of all this is not in the experience itself so much as in its results in producing the fruit of humility, patience, endurance, love, etc.

All seeking after God arises out of a spiritual hunger in the human soul. Augustine's famous cry,

> 'O God, Thou hast made us for Thyself, and our hearts are restless till they rest in Thee,'

sums that up perfectly (*Confessions*, 5th cent.). Mystic seeking is very different from theological enquiry which tries to understand with the mind. Its heart is love rather than intellect. It is more a heart-longing akin to a lover's longing for a loved one. The author of *The Cloud of Unknowing* puts it this way:

> 'By love may He (God) be gotten and holden; but by thought never.... Therefore, if thou wilt stand and not fall, cease never in thine intent, but beat evermore on this cloud of unknowing that is betwixt thee and thy God with a sharp dart of longing love.'

His expression, 'cloud of unknowing', refers to the fact that God is unknowable to the intellect, and his thesis is that only a heart reaching out to God in longing love will ever pierce through it to reach him.

The mystic believes the search will always be fruitful, because God, who is himself love, is more than willing to respond to the love of one who loves him; or, as William Law wrote in *A Serious Call to a Devout and Holy Life* (18th cent.),

> 'The sun meets not the springing bud that stretches towards him with half the certainty as God, the source of all good, communicates Himself to the soul that longs to partake of Him.'

Belief in the unfailingness of God's love is the basis of all mystical hope. It is the ground of faith and all true experience of God. Jan van Ruysbroeck, a fourteenth century Flemish mystic, in *The Seven Steps of the Ladder of Spiritual Love*, had God say to the Christian,

> 'Why are you so anxious? I am enfolding you with all My love and care. There is no more possible love in existence than that which I am giving out to you now. How is it that you have so little faith? How is it that you do not understand? I am appealing for your love in return. I am asking you to pay your debt, and to love the Love that ever loves you.'

That is the main thing God asks of those who would pursue the mystic way, to love him in return. But there is a strong insistence that the love be directed to him himself, not to his gifts, or his blessings, or any other thing. Hence the author of *The Cloud of Unknowing* wrote:

> 'Lift up thy heart to God with a meek stirring of love; and mean Himself and none of His goods.'

The seeker after God is bidden to consider himself and his personal needs as of little or no importance, and to abandon himself in complete trust into the hand of God who best knows how to lead and help him. The words 'meekness', 'humility' and 'abandonment' are used frequently. In the seventeenth century a semi-mystical movement known as Quietism developed around such thinking, teaching that only action inspired and directed by God is of any worth, while action initiated by man is worthless in God's eyes. Probably the best known exponent of the movement, whose writings are widely read by Charismatics today, is Madame Guyon. She was helped and encouraged by François Fénelon, Archbishop of Cambrai, whose teaching on the subject is well summarised in his *Christian Perfection*:

> 'Let God do all that He wishes with us ... To want to serve Him in one place rather than in another, in one way and not another, is to want to serve Him in our own way, and not in His ... O man of little faith! What are you afraid of? Let God act.'

Similar sentiment was found among mystics in the fourteenth century who also sought to become so united with God and abandoned to his will that they would become malleable instruments in his hand. For example, an anonymous writing known as the *Theologia Germanica* puts it thus:

> 'I would fain be to the Eternal Goodness what his own hand is to a man.'

The condition they sought after was not, however, a passivity of inaction as in some oriental religions, but rather a loving, submissiveness to God that would issue in their total co-operation with his will.

The basis for such abandonment was a total trusting in God's sovereignty. Seeking after a mystical encounter was never a means of escaping from the hard realities of life into a world of super-spiritual unreality, but rather a means of personal strengthening to live amid this world's sin and suffering, knowing that God is greater and more powerful than the worst that man can do, that in the end his will will conquer.

All that is beautifully expressed in one of Julian of Norwich's better-known statements:

> 'It behoveth that there should be sin; but all shall be well, and all shall be well, and all manner of thing shall be well.'

She learned the greatness of God's power and love for us personally in one of her revelations in which she saw Jesus holding something the size of a hazel-nut in his hand and gazing at it with eyes of complete love. As she contemplated the vision, wondering what its significance might be, she tells us she had the following conversation in the Spirit:

> '"What may this be?" I thought. And it was answered generally thus: "It is all that is made." I marvelled how it might last, for methought it might have suddenly fallen to naught for littleness. And it was answered in my understanding: "It lasteth, and ever shall last for that God loveth it." And so all things have their Being by the love of God. In this little thing I saw three properties. The first is that God made it; the second is that God loveth it; the third is that God keepeth it.'

Charismatics of a more passive and contemplative inclination would find themselves totally at home among mystics, others of a more active and evangelistic bent would find themselves quite restless. Some would find almost total satisfaction of spirit, others would find only frustration. Mysticism is less embracing than prophetism, though clearly it does overlap with it in considerable measure. However, it is among them in the fourteenth century that we find the nearest thing to a prophetic movement in that age.

### *Forerunners of Fourteenth Century Mysticism*

It should be noted that in the above survey no mention has been made of Neo-Platonism, and yet almost all the medieval mystics explained their revelations in terms of its systems. Indeed it is commonly acknowledged that the foundations of European mysticism lie in the Neo-Platonism of Augustine, Boethius and Pseudo-Dionysius in the fifth century, channelled through men like John Scotus Erigena, who made the works of Pseudo-Dionysius available in the West by translating them into Latin in the ninth century. Neo-Platonism encouraged men to seek release from this lower, created world and to pursue union with the unchanging One in the superior world of eternal reality, which alone offered satisfaction. However, it is also important to remember that the true heart of mysticism is not a desire to understand a conceptual entity, but a passionate devotion to Jesus, and it is that that emerges most strongly in their writings. Their true source was the Bible, their heart longing was for God, their entire love was for Jesus, their contextual language was Neo-Platonism. The philosophy is only the framework of their age, the contemporary means of explaining the mystery.

Thus Bernard of Clairvaux, whose teaching, with all its Neo-Platonism, dominated the twelfth century, was concerned above all else to know Jesus Christ and him crucified and spoke about the soul espoused to Christ. Along with Hugh of St. Victor in Paris, he is among the earliest of the great Western mystics. From the same century the Rhineland Benedictine Abbess, Hildegard, and Elizabeth of Schönau, another Benedictine, have left us accounts of their visions, entirely Christ-centred.

The thirteenth century witnessed a much fuller blossoming of mysticism, particularly in the new Franciscan and Dominican circles. The Franciscans flourished mainly in Italy and southern Europe, the Dominicans in Germany and the north. It was in the latter group that the movement flourished most fully, mainly among the nuns, the best known of whom are Mechthild of Magdeburg, Mechthild of Hackeborn and Gertrude the Great, all of whose mysticism is full of the most tender emotion towards their Lord, just like that of Bernard and Francis before them.

Out of this mainly Dominican background came the full flowering of medieval mysticism in central and southern Germany in the fourteenth century, giving birth to a widespread movement that was known as the 'Friends of God'.

### *The Mystical Experiences of the Friends of God*

The title 'Friends of God', or *Gottesfreunde*, applies to a group of mystics in the Rhineland and Switzerland in the fourteenth century. They were not a sect, nor an organised movement, but 'a fairly definite type of Christianity that found its best expression in persons of the prophet-class.'[186] For the most part they remained within the Catholic fold, though some of them did become organised into separate societies. One of their better known writings is an anonymous mystical work known as the *Theologia Germanica,* which Martin Luther republished two centuries later, but their main sources of inspiration were the teachings of three well-known mystics: first Master Eckhart, an outstanding Dominican preacher of the early part of the century whose teaching was condemned by the Pope shortly after his death; second Johann Tauler, one of the movement's most outstanding luminaries, a Dominican at Strasbourg, himself strongly influenced by Eckhart, whose sermons were extremely popular at the time and later held in high esteem by Luther; and third Henry Suso, also a pupil of Eckhart, a Friend of God and a Dominican, whose *Little Book of Eternal Wisdom* was widely popular and much admired by Thomas à Kempis a century later. At first the movement was mainly centred on southern Germany, but as the century progressed it spread northwards where one of its most famous children was the Flemish mystic Jan van Ruysbroeck.

The Friends of God formed themselves into small groups around local spiritual leaders. Though there was little organisation, the movement was given coherence and recognisable identity by the work of itinerant 'prophets', by the literature it produced and by a constant interchange of letters and visitors.

The prophetic/charismatic strain among the Friends of God is perhaps best illustrated in a work entitled *The Book of the Master* (mid-fourteenth century). Traditionally it has been interpreted as a piece of biographical literature, the Master being identified with Tauler and the other main figure in the story, an unnamed 'Friend of God from the Oberland', the Master's spiritual instructor, with Nicholas of Basel, a well-known itinerant Béghard preacher of the day who was burned as a heretic in Vienna in 1395. However, it is also widely held that the book is not a biography at all, but a mainly fictitious narrative written to illustrate the kind of thing the Friends of God believed could and did happen among them when the Spirit of God was given freedom to work his will.

> 'It is a telling, concrete illustration of the ruling idea of the Friends of God that a divinely instructed layman, who has attained the highest stage of mystical experience, "speaks in the place of God" and has an apostolic authority which puts

186. R.M. Jones, *Mystical Religion*, p. 242.

him above any priest or doctor who has only the authority of ordination or of scholarship.'[187]

*The Story of the Master and the Friend of God*

The Master was an outstanding and learned theologian who attracted large crowds whenever he preached. One visitor in his audience, the anonymous Friend of God from the Oberland, having listened to several of his sermons, personally requested one on the subject of the highest spiritual life attainable on this earth. The Master objected that a mere layman would not be able to understand a subject like this properly, but delivered the sermon none the less. The Friend then approached the Master with these words,

> 'You are a great scholar, and have taught us a good lesson in this sermon. But you yourself do not live according to it… . in the life which you now have, know that you have no light, but are in the night. You can indeed understand the letter, but have not yet tasted of the sweetness of the Holy Ghost.' (Bevan, pp. 15,17.)[188]

The Master was naturally taken aback by this apparently impertinent accusation, but he asked the Friend to relate what he knew of the spiritual life, whereupon the latter told his own story. He had tried hard in the manner of the times to bring his flesh into subjection with many austerities, when on one occasion, he recounts:

> 'I had been so chastising myself all night, that my eyelids closed from very weariness, and I fell asleep. And in my sleep it was as though a voice spoke to me and said, "You foolish man, if you are bent on killing yourself before your time, you will have to bear a heavy punishment. But if you suffer God to exercise you, he could exercise you better than you by yourself, or with the devil's counsel."' (Bevan, p. 47)

Troubled by his dream he consulted a hermit who urged him to take the advice seriously. This he did, not without difficulty, and at the moment of surrender to God, it happened, as he puts it himself:

> 'In that same hour God showed his mercy upon me, so that my mind was filled with light and clearness. And in that same hour it seemed to me that my natural reason was gone from

187. Jones, *Mystical Religion*, p. 263.

188. All citations from the story are taken from Mrs. Bevan's translation, *Three Friends of God*. Page references in brackets after quotations relate to this book.

> me, and I had an understanding far above it. The time seemed all too short to me. I saw that it was a supernatural and mighty wonder wrought by God, and I could have cried with St. Peter, "Lord, it is good for me to be here!" … in that self-same short hour I received more truth, and more illumination in my understanding, than all the teachers could ever teach me from now till the Judgment Day by word of mouth, and with all their natural learning and science.' (Bevan, pp. 50-1)

The Master was suitably impressed, and even more so when the Friend went on to describe some of the miraculous consequences of this experience in his life, giving this remarkable story as one illustration:

> 'There was,' he said, 'a heathen, who was a very kind-hearted man, and often cried to Him who had made, as he believed, both himself and all the world; and said, "O Creator of all creatures, I have been born in this land. Now the Jews have another faith, and the Christians another. O Lord, who are over all and have made all creatures, if there be now any faith better than that in which I have been born, or if there be any other better still, show it to me in what way you will, so that I may believe it, and I will gladly obey you and believe." Now, behold, dear sir, a letter was sent to that heathen, written by me, a poor sinner, in such sort that he came to the Christian faith, and he wrote me a letter back again, telling what had befallen him. Dear sir, can you instruct me how I should write to a heathen far away in a heathen land in such fashion that the heathen should be able to read and understand it, and make the letter such that the heathen should come to the Christian faith?' (Bevan, pp. 52-3)

This tale evoked from the astounded Master the confession,

> 'Dear son, these are the works of the Holy Ghost. God is wonderful in all His works and gifts. Dear son, you have told me very strange things.'

Thereupon the Friend pressed home his argument:

> 'Wherefore then do you not believe that the Holy Ghost is speaking to you at this moment through me, a poor sinner and unworthy man, and is minded to speak to you?' (Bevan, p. 55)

At length the Master was persuaded to admit his own spiritual poverty and submitted himself to the Friend's guidance and tuition.

He was instructed to withdraw from his over-busy life and in solitary meditation to shed his self-love and seek humility. His strange new ways resulted in the loss of his former friends, but he was urged to see that as a blessing which would result in his having confidence in none but God alone. For two years he pursued his ascetic way in the face of increasing hardship, scorn, ill-health and despair, till one night,

> 'as he lay there, thus weak and stricken down with sorrow, but fully awake, he heard as it were a voice speaking to him and saying, "Trust in God, and be at peace, and know that when He was on earth as a man, He made the sick, whom He healed in body, sound also in soul."
>
> 'Straightway when these words were spoken to him, he lost his senses and reason, and knew not how or where he was. But when he came to himself again, he was filled as it were with a new strength and might in all his being, and those things which aforetime were dark to him were now clear to him.' (Bevan, p. 68.)

When the Friend heard of the Master's experience, he commented,

> 'Dear sir, you must know that you have now, for the first time, received the true gift of God's grace, And I tell you of a truth, that now, for the first time your soul has been touched by the Most High. And know that the letter which has slain you, also makes you alive again, for it has now reached your heart in the power of the Holy Ghost. Your teaching will now come from the Holy Ghost, which before came from the flesh. For you have now received the light of the Holy Spirit by the grace of God, and the Scriptures which you already know will now be made clear to you, for you will have an insight that you never had before.' (Bevan, p. 69.)

The Friend continued,

> 'For, as you know, the Scripture sounds in many places as if it contradicted itself, but now that you have, by the grace of God, the illumination of the Holy Spirit, you will perceive that all Scripture has the same intent. You will now understand that it does not contradict itself. And you will also be able rightly to follow the example of the Lord Jesus. You ought now to begin to preach again, and to show to others the right path to eternal

> life. And know that now, one of your sermons will be more profitable than a hundred aforetime, and the people will receive more fruit therefrom. But it will be most especially needful that you keep yourself humble, for you know well that he who carries a great treasure exposed to view, must ever be on his guard against thieves. I tell you truly, the Devil is in great terror when he perceives that God has bestowed on any man the noble and precious treasure of His grace, and the devils will set all their arts and wisdom to work to rob you of this costly gift. Wherefore look wisely to your goings.
>
> 'Now, dear sir, it is no longer needful for me to speak to you as a teacher, as I have done hitherto, for you have now the right and true Teacher, whose instrument I have been. To Him give ear, and obey Him in all things.' (Bevan, pp. 70-1.)

The Master now announced that he would preach again, but when he began to deliver his first sermon, he was so overcome with tears and emotion that he was quite unable to preach. More than ever he was now the laughing-stock of the people, but he was given permission to attempt a second sermon. He took as his text, 'Behold the Bridegroom cometh; go ye out to meet Him.' (Matt. 25:6) As he developed his theme of the Bridegroom's (Jesus') great love for the Bride (the Christian), he included these words which must presumably be taken as a reflection of his own experience:

> 'And on this great day of His espousals, the Bridegroom sheds forth by the Holy Ghost the torrent of divine love upon the Bride, and this love flows out unto the Bridegroom, insomuch that the Bride loses herself and is intoxicated with love, so that she forgets herself and all creatures also, and beholds the Bridegroom only.
>
> 'And this Bride is a true worshipper, for she worships the Father in the Holy Spirit. In this marriage-feast is joy upon joy, and there is therein more peace and joy in one hour, than all the creatures can yield in time or in eternity. The joy that the Bride has with the Bridegroom is so measureless, that no senses or reason can apprehend it or find it.' (Bevan, pp. 80-1.)

As he spoke these words, a man cried out with a loud voice, 'It is true!' and fell down as if he were dead. And after the sermon there were counted some forty dazed persons, twelve of whom also lay still on the ground as if dead. (Bevan, pp. 81f.)

From that time on the Master increased in power and reputation, particularly among the lay folk. But his reputation among the clergy was not at all enhanced by his experience, for he found himself increasingly impelled to criticise the evils and corruptions of the Church.

*The Illumination of Henry Suso*

If *The Book of the Master* is really just an illustrative story, Elizabeth Staglin's account of the life of Henry Suso is not. Suso, like Tauler, was one of the most brilliant luminaries among the Friends of God. He was born about 1295 and, after a somewhat turbulent childhood, was settled in a Dominican convent at Constance at the age of thirteen. The following record of events in his eighteenth year has much in common with the accounts of the experiences of the Master and of the Friend of God from the Oberland and, like them, shows traits familiar from the testimonies of prophets and charismatics in every age. Thus while it is itself a particular, biographical narrative, it may correctly be regarded as exemplifying the kind of experience that the Friends of God sought to encourage and delighted to recount.

> 'And it came to pass that one day when he was eighteen years old, he went alone into the chapel, when all the monks were at dinner in the refectory. And he stood there utterly dark and miserable, for he was weary of all things, and he knew not where to go for help or comfort.
>
> 'And it was to him at that moment, as though a Presence were with him, and a sudden light and glory filled his soul, and he saw and heard in his innermost heart that which no tongue can tell, and no heart of man can conceive. And his soul was filled with longing, and yet was satisfied, and thirsted no more, and all the things that he had desired were now as nothing to him, and all his desire for them had passed away. Whether it were day or night he knew not, for he had tasted of the sweetness of the eternal life, and he knew that He who was present with him, was the Lord.
>
> 'And thus he remained lost in joy and rest, and he said to himself, "If this is not heaven, I know not what heaven can be, for all that could be suffered here below were small and even as nothing, to him to whom eternal gladness such as this is, shall be given."

> 'And when he came to himself, he seemed to himself as a man who had come from another world. And he fell down, and he sighed in his heart a fathomless sigh, and he said, "O my God, where have I been? Where am I now? O Thou blessed of my heart, this hour shall never pass away from me for ever and for ever." And he went on his way, and no man saw or knew that he was another man. But his heart and soul were filled with the heavenly wonder, and with the glory that he had seen, and he was as a box which has been filled with a sweet perfume, and the odour is left behind, when the perfume is poured out. And from that moment of heaven, his heart henceforward longed with a deep desire after God.' (Bevan, pp. 307f)

### *A Prophetic Movement?*

Many of the traits of prophetic movements are clearly discernible in the literature of the Friends of God. First, there is the obvious delight in ecstatic experiences and in tales of miracles and visions, particularly those of their great charismatic leaders. Also notable is the lay-orientated, apparently anti-clerical, anti-establishment and anti-intellectual attitude that goes naturally with prophetic enlightenment. Furthermore, the highly moralistic flavour of their writings and the conviction that theirs was the only fully Christian experience recall some of the attitudes we have noted pervading the thinking of prophetic movements in other times. Then there is their evangelistic purpose to bring others into their prophetic experience of God in the Spirit that is so clearly illustrated in the *Book of the Master*.

However, they were never properly a prophetic movement, for the focus of their interest lay firmly in their present, mystical experiences. They put no great emphasis on millennial hope and did not cast themselves in the guise of the end-time Church of the Spirit. Consequently they lacked that involvement in politics, whether of Church or state, that we regularly find among prophets with their vision of an alternative society made up of Spirit-filled people of God. Hence, though some of their more extreme adherents did break away from the Catholic Church, for the most part they never considered themselves a separate people or movement.

### *Conclusion*

If the later Middle Ages produced no fully prophetic movement, it certainly gave birth to movements that were prophetically inclined in the quality of their aspirations and experiences. Perhaps some amalgam of the end-time zeal that inspired the heretical offshoots of Joachimism with the mystical fervour of the Friends of God might have generated the right atmosphere for the conception of proper prophetic growth, but geographical, sociological and political dislocation did not yet allow for such a marriage, which had therefore to wait for a later day.

PART FIVE

# A MOMENT OF PROPHETIC HOPE DURING THE REFORMATION

The Reformation was both a protest against the established religious and political system of the medieval Church and also a renewing of reasonable, personal faith in God. It was largely prompted by the rediscovery of the Bible, long withheld from the people by a church that had substituted its own authority for that of Scripture. *Sola Scriptura* ('by Scripture alone') as the authoritative measure of faith, became one of the watch-cries of the reformers.

Another was *Sola Fide* ('by faith alone'). The Medieval Church had set itself between the believer and God. Forgiveness could only be had through a priest; God was to be approached through a priest or a saint; grace was received through the sacrament; instruction was obtained from the Church's creeds and conciliar decrees. The Church stood firmly between a man and his God at every turn. The reformers discovered, by contrast, that they could approach God for themselves, thanks to the sacrifice of Christ on the cross, by personal faith in his atoning work, and that that was the only way to approach him, by faith alone.

The Reformation also brought Christians a new freedom of thought. They were no longer required to give unquestioning credence to Papal utterances and non-scriptural doctrines, but were free to weigh everything in the light of scriptural revelation for themselves. This was not a replacing of faith by reason, but the permitting of a reasonable approach to faith.

And politically, the Reformation created new national identities, enabling states and nations to break free from the old Papal domination that sought to subordinate every church and government to its own overriding authority. In every land that accepted Protestantism a national church emerged, entirely independent of Rome.

For the history of prophecy the Reformation is both an encouragement and a disappointment—an encouragement because it laid the foundation of faith and scriptural understanding necessary in the long run for the erection of a prophetic structure, a disappointment because it quenched the prophetic voice in its own time. Although some of the reformers, including Luther himself, found their early inspiration in the writings of the mystics, the edifice they built stood aloof from such tendencies and quickly became quite dry and doctrinaire.

# 16
# From Luther to Fox

It is common to date the beginning of the Reformation as 31st October, 1517, the day Martin Luther nailed a document containing ninety-five theses or statements to the door of Wittenberg Cathedral. Over the next ten years the movement swept through northern Europe, totally altering the course of both ecclesiastical and secular history.

*Forerunners of the Reformation*

The Reformation was not, however, conceived and birthed in one day. We have already noted earlier stirrings of dissent from the twelfth century onwards. The Albigensians or Cathars, in their pursuit of a purer and more spiritual faith, repudiated the authority of the Roman Church, but were wiped out in a massive blood-bath of persecution. Their contemporaries, the Waldensians, preached against Roman doctrines on the basis of Scripture, but they were driven out of France into hiding in the mountains and valleys of North Italy.

Over a hundred years later, in the fourteenth century, John Wycliffe also attacked many of the Roman doctrines. He criticised the monastic system, particularly its mendicant (begging) friars. He opposed the Pope's political authority in England and even went as far as attacking the central doctrine of Catholicism, transubstantiation, the belief that in the mass the bread and wine change their substance to become the actual body and blood of Christ. Had he lived elsewhere in Europe, Wycliffe would have suffered the same fate as the Cathars, the Waldensians and many others who were persecuted to extinction, but he survived because he was protected by some of England's strongest nobles, partly because they were glad of his teaching as a bolster to their own rebellion against paying taxes to the Pope. His Bible translation and the continuing missionary work of his students, the Lollards, helped to lay a strong foundation in England for the reforms that were to follow a century and a half after his death in 1384.

Jan Hus, his disciple in Bohemia, was not as fortunate as Wycliffe. He was arrested treacherously and burnt as a heretic in 1415, but was equally effective in disseminating dissenting doctrine, so much so that the whole country was aroused in a movement of nationalistic and reforming fervour quite unique in its age. Again Catholic military force won the day, but his heritage lingered in the hearts of many all over Europe.

The last major outburst of reformation zeal in the fifteenth century was in northern Italy, in Florence, where Savonarola by his fiery prophetic preaching succeeded in establishing a puritanical dictatorship not entirely unlike the system Calvin created at Geneva in the following century. However, it did not last long, for Papal denunciation resulted in his arrest and burning in 1498, less than twenty years before Luther pinned up his theses in Wittenberg.

There were many others, some of them less well known today, who also helped pave the way for the Reformation in the Church. Some fourteenth century mystics made notable contributions. Eckhart's teaching, condemned after his death, left a profound mark in pre-Reformation Germany. It strongly influenced Tauler and his sermons helped to mould Luther's thinking. As important as any of these was a movement in the Church, originating in the Netherlands, known as the *Devotio Moderna* (Modern Way of Serving God) or 'Brethren of the Common Life'. It was founded by a mystic called Geert de Groote, encouraged by his friend Ruysbroeck, and so had direct links with the Friends of God and the general flow of late medieval mysticism, though de Groote gave it a flavour that was less other-worldly and more practical than its forerunners. It was a semi-monastic group dedicated to spiritual discipline and education, founding schools and producing books. Many of the Brethren and those educated by them left their mark on history. Two of its most famous protégés were Thomas à Kempis, author of *The Imitation of Christ*, and Desiderius Erasmus, who 'laid the egg that Luther hatched'.

As the fifteenth century dawned the Roman Catholic Church, though at its lowest ebb in history, seemed entirely secure. It had learned how to suppress heresy successfully. Its power was unchallenged. 'Now nobody contradicts, no one opposes,' was the opinion expressed at the Fifth Lateran Council in Rome in 1512.

*The Renaissance*

Other forces were also at work, and had been for many decades. Though universities had been founded at places like Paris, Oxford,

Cambridge, Naples, Prague, Cologne, Heidelberg and Vienna, they gave no encouragement to open enquiry. They taught rhetoric, logic and some mathematics, but in a closed system in which the philosophy of Aristotle was regarded as the ultimate authority in almost every branch of knowledge. Though Aristotle was a Greek of the fourth century BC and all teaching and writing were in Latin, no interest was shown in the classical literature of ancient Greece or Rome. It was a closed system dominated by the Church and free enquiry was not welcomed. At the University of Paris Abelard taught for a while in the twelfth century that we are not to believe just 'because God has said it, but because we are convinced by reason that it is so,' but he was forced by the Church to recant his opinions. Similarly in England in the next century Roger Bacon, who among other things speculated about travel by sea, land and air in transport operated by mechanical engines, suffered imprisonment for his free thinking.

The first breakthrough came in the fourteenth century with the publication in Italy of Dante's *The Divine Comedy*, which, while firmly set in the context of religion with its review of Hell, Purgatory and Heaven, is none the less full of natural, human and political interest. After him came Petrarch and Boccaccio with their interest in the classics of Rome and Greece. Then, after the Turks took Constantinople a hundred years later, large numbers of Greek teachers sought refuge in the West and the door swung wide open to the art, literature, drama, philosophy and culture of the ancient world, which was much freer and far more rationalistic than anything known in Europe at the time.

The dissemination of this new learning was, of course, greatly helped by the invention of printing. It is perhaps significant that Guttenberg's first printed books appeared at Mainz only three years after the fall of Constantinople. Suddenly everything began to happen. Art started to break loose from the regulated style of the medieval Church with its stiff, formalised depictions of the saints, and men began to explore modes of painting that were more true to nature and more expressive of life, culminating in the great artistic works of the sixteenth century by men like Michaelangelo, Raphael and Leonardo da Vinci.

Leonardo was also a scientist, a naturalist, an architect and an engineer. He was one of the earliest of a whole new breed of men of science, like Copernicus, who taught that the earth moved around the sun; Tycho Brahe, the astronomer; Kepler, who described the motion of the planets; Galileo, who invented the telescope; and Isaac Newton, who described the laws of gravity and motion.

Galileo, for reasserting the teaching of Copernicus, was severely opposed by the Church and forced to recant his opinions, and that was as late as the early seventeenth century.

In Italy the Renaissance produced great works of art and literature. While Northern Europe also had its great poets and literary men like Thomas Moore, Christopher Marlowe, William Shakespeare, Ben Johnson and John Milton, and its great artists, particularly in the Netherlands, the emphasis there was on the whole more academic, religious and practical. This was first seen in a work by Erasmus called 'In Praise of Folly', which was highly critical of the Roman Church, but more importantly in his publication of the New Testament in Greek, thus providing access to an original language edition for reforming translators like Martin Luther to work with. In the north the Renaissance awoke a new interest in the Bible, in good education, and in a search for truth and sound faith.

The late fifteenth century was also the great age of discovery, when voyages of exploration began to open up the New World. The Portuguese led the way with their exploration of the coast of Africa, and they were soon followed by the Spanish. From these two nations Columbus sailed to the West Indies in 1492 and Vasco da Gama round the Cape of Good Hope to India in 1498. In 1519 Magellan rounded the southern tip of South America and crossed the Pacific where he was killed by natives in the Philippines. Some of his crew were able to continue and complete the first ever voyage round the world.

While the Medieval Church was rigorously holding on to its stiff and tired systems, the world was beginning to awaken to new and exciting discoveries on every front. The events of the last half of the fifteenth century, after the fall of Constantinople in 1453, changed the heart of Europe irrevocably. With the introduction of the printing press and the discovery of the New World, perspectives shifted. As new vistas opened, men began asking new questions, not just about politics, technology and exploration, but also about the doctrines of the Church, the workings of the universe—indeed about almost everything.

The Reformation had become an inevitability. Once it started, about 1520, its progress was swift. By the middle of the century the whole of northern Europe had turned Protestant.

### *Martin Luther and the Reformation in Germany*

Luther was born in 1483, the son of a poor Saxon miner. After receiving a village education, his father sent him at great expense to himself to study at the University of Erfurt. He became an Augustinian monk in 1505 and in 1512 a doctor of theology and professor of biblical studies at the University of Wittenberg. While preparing to give lectures there on Romans he came to realise that our salvation is a matter of faith, not works or church tradition.

A month before he pinned his famous ninety-five theses on the cathedral door, Luther had another set of theses printed and circulated, ninety-seven of them, against the use of Aristotle's works, arguing that his ethics were not Christian, unbiblical, indeed utterly heathen and contrary to faith. Students, he claimed, would be better employed reading their Bibles or the works of Augustine, and so he had Aristotle removed from the syllabus at Wittenberg University, together with the writings of other Greek philosophers and Peter Lombard's *Sentences*, which was still the standard theological text-book of the day. In doing this he struck at the very roots of the Thomist system of theology, established and unchallenged since the thirteenth century.[189]

A year before that Luther had published his first book, entitled *A German Theology* (*Theologia Germanica*).[190] This was an edited version of a manuscript by a German mystic whom he called 'the Frankfurter'. While studying the medieval theologians he had come to be particularly impressed by the works of Tauler and others in his circle of mystical friends, so much so that he ranked this book that he published next to the Bible and Augustine, saying he knew of none better for learning the nature of 'God, Christ, man, and all things.' What particularly attracted him to the mystics was their teaching that man had to pass through the anguish of spiritual rebirth before he could enter into the blessedness of knowing God and enjoying union with him.

This shift from a faith founded on philosophy to one based on experience reflected in these writings links Luther in his early years with the continuum of prophetic tradition we have been tracing in this book. The revival among Lutherans that took place in the late seventeenth century was essentially a return to this position. However, as the reformation ran its course, much of the personal, mystical heart of these early years got lost, buried under doctrinal disputes and political wrangles that effectively stifled it. The change must have happened quickly, for it was only 1522 when Luther met the Zwickau Prophets, just four years after he published a second

189. See above, p. 169.
190. See above p. 212.

edition of the *German Theology*, and by then he had come to have little patience with mystical language.

Foundational as were the theological shifts and insights in Luther's early life, it was none of these that sparked off the Reformation, though they did, of course, shape the new forms that emerged from it. No, the process started in a very different way. In 1517 a Dominican friar called John Tetzel came selling indulgences from the Pope, Leo X, to raise money for completing the work on St. Peter's Church in Rome. An indulgence was a certificate that bestowed pardon for sin on the holder, and on any friends or relatives, living or departed, for whom it was purchased, and that without confession, repentance, penance or absolution by a priest. Tetzel said, 'As soon as your coin clinks in the chest, the soul of your friends will rise out of purgatory to heaven.'

Luther thought the system irrational, and so nailed his protest on the church door, calling for some open debate on the matter. He argued that while it made sense that an indulgence could excuse a sinner from a penance imposed by the Church, it could not excuse him from punishment by God or remove the guilt of his sin. There was nothing new about this argument. Erasmus and others had said the same before him, but there was something about the way Luther said it, or about his personality, that alarmed the Pope, who therefore summoned him to Rome, where he would probably have been burnt as a heretic. But Luther had influential friends in high places, as Wycliffe had had in his day. Frederick, the Elector of Saxony, whose subject he was, refused to let him go. In 1520, after many controversies and the publication of many pamphlets that made Luther's teaching known all over Germany, Pope Leo excommunicated him and demanded that Frederick hand him over for trial. Frederick protected him instead and Luther defiantly burnt the Papal bull of excommunication (document sealed with the Pope's *bulla* or seal) at the gates of Wittenberg before a gathering of university and town people, thus renouncing the authority of the Roman Church.

In 1521 the Holy Roman Emperor, Charles V, summoned Luther to appear before a Diet or Supreme Council of German rulers at Worms. Luther went, and standing before the Emperor and his princes, when asked to recant, said these famous words,

'Here I stand, and can do no other. So help me God. Amen.'

On his way home Luther was arrested by some of Frederick's soldiers and taken for his own safety into hiding in the castle of the Wartburg in Thuringien. He remained there in disguise for almost a year while the storms raged outside in Germany. He used this time fruitfully by translating the New Testament into German and by keeping in touch with other reforming leaders by letter. He returned early in 1522 to take up the reins again just in time to save the movement from potentially dangerous excesses.

Compared with reforms in other parts of Europe, Luther's were fairly moderate. One of his associates, Carlstadt, would have had a totally lay church, but Luther retained an ordained ministry with regulated forms of worship and a fairly high doctrine of the Eucharist. To him the words of Christ, 'This is my body,' meant the bread was more than a mere symbol. Again, when there was mounting pressure for adult believer's baptism, he held fast to his own belief in the efficacy of the faith of parents and godparents in infant baptism. Not everyone was happy with the limitations he set. Denmark, Sweden and Norway, at this time one kingdom ruled by Christian II, accepted the Lutheran form of Protestantism quite early, but elsewhere in Europe a different form was to prevail.

*Calvinism in Switzerland, France, Holland and Scotland*

About the same time as Luther was attacking indulgences in Wittenberg, Ulrich Zwingli was quite independently opposing remission of sins offered through pilgrimages at the shrine of the Virgin at Einsiedeln. He broke away from Rome in 1522 and began to organise the Reformation in Zurich along more radical lines than in Wittenberg. His work was cut short by the outbreak of war between Catholics and Protestants in Switzerland, when he was killed in battle in 1531. All was not lost, however, for three years later Calvin arrived in Geneva to take up leadership of the work there.

Jean Calvin was a Frenchman. In 1512 another Frenchman, Jacques Lefevre, had written and preached on justification by faith, a doctrine that became central in all the reformed churches. At first the French, both at court and among the people, were divided about the new teaching, sometimes favouring it, sometimes not, and sometimes with strong feelings on both sides. In 1572, on August 24th, St. Bartholomew's Day, the movement was almost dealt a death-blow when thousands of Protestants were massacred, but it did survive, though now definitely in a minority and suffering much persecution, yet continuing to be influential. In 1598 an edict of toleration was issued, the Edict of Nantes, allowing the Protestants freedom to worship in their own style everywhere, except within five miles of Paris. The persecution abated, though it did surface locally from time to time, until Louis XIV revoked the

Edict in 1685 and open persecution began again in earnest. The French Protestants are known as Huguenots.

In the earlier stages of these troubles, Calvin was forced to flee from France and seek refuge in Switzerland. In 1534 he settled in Geneva where he committed his principles of reformed Christianity to writing in his famous *Institutes of Christian Religion*. Before long he became virtual ruler of the city, taking charge not only of its religious affairs, but also of its education, commerce, and everything else. There he was able to work out his principles of a Christian state in a practical, political setting. Public worship was compulsory, society was organised on an efficient basis, immorality was severely punished, secular entertainments were prohibited, and life in the city became thoroughly puritanical.

Calvinism produced a race of hard-working, sturdy, self-reliant people, known for their industry, strength and vigour of character, but not for their colourfulness. The same character emerged in all the societies that adopted this faith—among the French Huguenots, the Dutch Protestants, the Scottish Presbyterians and the English Puritans.

The people of the Netherlands were influenced by Calvinism quite early, but they were severely persecuted for it by the Spanish who ruled the region at that time. It finally became established there in 1600 after a long and bitter war lasting forty years, which won them freedom of both government and religion. Holland then became Protestant, but Belgium remained predominantly Catholic.

Probably the greatest success story for Calvinism comes from Scotland. There the Reformation made very slow progress at first because both church and state were ruled by unbending Catholics, Cardinal Beaton and Mary of Guise. However, the cardinal was murdered and Mary died about the same time. She was succeeded by the young Mary, Queen of Scots. But John Knox also returned from exile in Geneva and took up leadership of the Protestant cause in 1559. With his fiery, uncompromising preaching and his dogged determination, he turned the tide so effectively that within a very short time, despite continuing opposition from the Queen, Calvinism became thoroughly established in Scotland, as it still is today in the Church of Scotland (Presbyterian).

*The Reformation in England*

In England things happened quite differently and produced yet a third type of Protestant Christianity, namely Anglicanism. Even before the Reformation there were many in England who, through the preaching of the Lollards, were already reformed at heart. The groundwork had been done and so, when Henry VIII broke with Rome in 1533, there were many who welcomed the change. Several churchmen and scholars had also absorbed the teachings of the Continental reformers, particularly the Lutheran ones, and were more than ready to see them applied, none less so than the Archbishop of Canterbury himself, Thomas Cranmer, who immediately set about putting the services into English, thus giving us our first English Prayer Book.

The progress of the Reformation in England was much more political than in Europe. The immediate pretext for separating from Rome was the Pope's refusal to grant Henry a divorce from Catherine of Aragon, the sister of the Holy Roman Emperor, Charles V, who actually held the Pope his prisoner at the time and so had little freedom to heed Henry's request anyway. Up to this point Henry had strongly opposed the Reformation, so much so that in 1521 the Pope had awarded him the title 'Defender of the Faith', but now he declared himself head of the Church in England. He had his churchmen produce English services and an English Bible that had to be made available to the public in every parish church. Clergy who refused to give him their allegiance were dealt with summarily, including Thomas More and John Fisher, who were executed in 1535 and are now remembered as saints and martyrs by the Catholic Church. Then in 1536 the dissolution of the monasteries and the transfer of their wealth to the crown began. Despite all that, Henry never was a Protestant at heart, and so the religious reforms proceeded with many restraints during his lifetime.

The main reforming influence in England was more Lutheran than Calvinist, and therefore fairly moderate. However, there were also the extremes, and the subsequent history of the Church in England is a sorry tale of swings in both directions, mainly according to the whims of the monarchs, with a lot of bloodshed from time to time. When Henry died in 1547, he was succeeded by Edward VI, who furthered the cause along with Cranmer, but his reign was brief, ending in 1553. For the next five years Queen Mary ('Bloody Mary') tried to restore Catholicism by the old way of persecution. Most of the main Protestant leaders were martyred at this time, including Cranmer himself, as well as the famous Oxford martyrs, Latimer and Ridley. Peace was restored in 1558 when Elizabeth I came to the throne and Protestantism was re-established, becoming the Church of England in the basic form it still has today, somewhat pragmatic and not exactly a vibrant catalyst for revival.

*The Counter-Reformation*

It was not long before the Catholic Church awoke to the need to see itself reformed too. At the beginning of the sixteenth century the whole of Europe had been uniformly Catholic, ruled from Rome. Now at least half of Europe had rejected Catholicism and in an accompanying wave of nationalism each country had also appropriated the right to govern itself without reference to Roman oversight. The need for action was clearly urgent.

In 1545 Pope Paul III summoned the Council of Trent to put right the abuses that had caused the Reformation. The council met off and on over the next eighteen years, bringing together bishops and abbots from all over Europe. The reforms were very conservative, but the atmosphere in the Catholic Church changed, and many improvements resulted.

Not all the changes were for the best. The medieval Church had allowed a good measure of spiritual freedom to those with a strong awareness of the supernatural, and hence a fair degree of openness to the prophetic and the miraculous, so long as they did not disturb the structure and presented no challenge to hierarchical authority. Reaction to the Reformation caused the Council, quite understandably, to seek greater control, but that inevitably resulted in increased rigidity. Over the following centuries, as the Church continued to lose ground in the face of growing secularism and to lose its territorial holdings and its political privileges, the system only got tighter, tending more and more to formalism and to the development of a faith based mainly on rules and formulas. The consequence has been little room for any prophetic movement to develop within Catholicism, not until very recent times when the Charismatic Movement broke out in the Catholic Church in the 1960s. Examples of prophetic spirituality were, of course, still to be found, but they have tended to be individual rather than corporate.

Every bit as significant as the Council itself was the emergence of the order of Jesuits. It was founded in 1534 by a Spaniard called Ignatius Loyola to fight Protestantism. It was different from other religious orders in that it had no special dress, or homes, or duties, but it did demand a very strict discipline, an intense loyalty to the Church and a strong evangelistic zeal. It was effective in winning back many Protestant districts to the Catholic faith and in carrying Catholicism into other parts of the world. At a time when Protestants were still trying to establish themselves in Europe, Jesuits and other Catholic missionaries were carrying Christianity to China, India and North and South America. One of the most famous of their missionaries was Francis Xavier (1506-52), who worked mainly in India.

*Persecution and War, the Heritage of the Reformation.*

Much of the inspiration for both the Counter-Reformation and the Jesuit movement (the Society of Jesus) came from Spain. It was also in Spain that Protestantism was most effectively suppressed, mainly by persecution and torture through the agency of the infamous Spanish Inquisition. Similar tactics doused the Protestant fire in France and Italy, but nowhere as effectively as in Spain, except perhaps in Bohemia, the land of the early reformer, Jan Hus.

Sadly the clashes led to warfare and bloodshed all over Europe, leaving a massive blot in the history of Christendom. The Dutch Calvinists, after a prolonged struggle, won their independence from Philip of Spain between 1560 and 1600. In France, the Edict of Nantes in 1598 secured a measure of toleration for the Huguenots, but that was only after a wave of horror was sent rippling through Europe by the terrible massacre of St. Bartholomew's Day, on 23-24 August, 1572, when somewhere between five and ten thousand of them were slaughtered. In Germany, in the Thirty Years War (1618-48), the Catholic Emperor Ferdinand II fought to bring the new Protestant states back to Catholicism, but the war ended when the Lutheran King of Sweden, Gustavus Adolphus, intervened on the Protestant side. At the end of it Germany was divided up into Catholic and Protestant states much as before the war.

These wars were fought with a ferocity that reflects very badly on the Christianity of the day. They left Europe, and particularly Germany, in a state of considerable depression from which it took a long time to recover. The Peace of Westphalia that ended the Thirty Years War fixed the Catholic and Protestant boundaries in Europe. It is usually taken as the end-point of the Reformation period. Europe had entered the sixteenth century a Catholic continent, but by the end of it almost all Northern Europe was Protestant.

# 17
# The Zwickau Prophets

While the Reformation changed the face of Christendom throughout Europe, it did not make the Church prophetic or charismatic. It did re-establish a strong personal faith and spirituality, but not of the sort that we find in charismatic circles. If anything there was an antipathy to things prophetic among the reforming leaders, and it was that that surfaced in Luther's conversations with the leaders of the only movement at the time that showed any potential for having a positive influence in a prophetic direction.

Since Luther was familiar with and much influenced in his early years by the writings of some of the medieval mystics, he was at first open to the present possibility of prophetic gifting. However, he drew back from that position after encountering the Zwickau Prophets. He met them at a time when he found himself compelled to lay a restraining hand on some of the reformers who seemed to be running into excess and he felt obliged to curb their activities also. Luther had a derogatory name for extremists and he used it of the prophets unhesitatingly: *Schwärmer* (enthusiasts). He most frequently applied it to the Anabaptists and others who were involved in the Peasants' Revolt, though he also used it quite widely to express his disgust at all forms of enthusiasm he considered excessive. The same attitude remains among Lutherans today, causing a considerable blockage among them to things pentecostal and charismatic.

The stance on prophetic gifts that emerged among the leading reformers was that they belonged to the first ages of the Church and had now no part to play. This opinion was held partly in reaction to the superstitious view of miracles in the Medieval Church, but also because the new thinking of the Enlightenment was founded on Aristotelian rationalism, which held that true knowledge could only be deduced by our five senses. While faith did have spiritual connotations in Luther's teaching, it came more and more to be identified with beliefs and doctrines. Faith as experience gave way to faith as doctrine, particularly in the Calvinistic churches where preaching came to be regarded as the main purpose of ministry. Calvin himself argued strongly against any continued use of miraculous gifts. For example, discussing the anointing of the sick for healing, he wrote,

> 'But that gift of healing, like the rest of the miracles, which the Lord willed to be brought forth for a time, has vanished away in order to make the new preaching of the gospel marvellous for ever. Therefore, even if we grant to the full that anointing was a sacrament of those powers which were then administered by the hands of the apostles, it has nothing to do with us, to whom the administering of such powers has not been committed.'[191]

The main Reformation churches offered no warm, welcoming cradle, but rather a hostile environment, for any infant prophetic movement. And as at the beginning, so for the most part it has continued until very recent times.

*The Early Prophets in Zwickau, Thomas Müntzer and the Anabaptists*

The story starts in a town called Zwickau, a thriving commercial centre in southern Saxony. Despite its prosperity Zwickau had a large, dissatisfied lower class among whom the influence of late medieval heresy was strong. Luther's reforming ideas reached the city in 1518 and won swift approval there, so much so that within two years a supporter of his teaching, Thomas Müntzer, was invited to serve as pastor there. He proved too outspoken, however, and found a great deal of opposition among the wealthy burghers, with the result that he increasingly gravitated towards the more sympathetic lower classes.

There he met a weaver called Nicholas Storch, who was exceedingly well versed in Scripture and who spoke of obtaining illumination, not only from the Bible, but also through special revelations. Müntzer, who was familiar with the works of Tauler, was suitably impressed and began to attend Storch's house-meetings, where he was introduced to the Zwickau Prophets. His association with them was short-lived, however, because increasing opposition to the very radical reforming demands of his pastorate caused him to flee the city in April, 1520. After he left, the antipathy he had engendered was redirected against his erstwhile prophet-associates, many of

191. Calvin, *Institutes*, book IV, ch. xix, sect. 18.

whom were also compelled to seek refuge in flight. As they scattered they naturally carried their prophetic message with them, but without continuing leadership and coherent organisation, their voice became dissipated and soon fell silent.

For the most part the prophets were absorbed into the wider Anabaptist movement that was flourishing at the time. Indeed they are sometimes thought of as its founders, but that is hardly correct, even though Müntzer became one of the movement's leaders in Germany and the prophets themselves did have Anabaptist leanings. But the history of the Anabaptists is another story.[192] They were so called ('re-baptisers') because of their teaching on adult believer's baptism. They are not directly related to the English Baptists, though some of their pacifist and 'inner light' teachings did reappear among the English Quakers.

Though he attended their meetings in the early days in Zwickau, Müntzer was never himself a leader among the prophets. After his expulsion from the city he tried to establish his radical church in several other places, but was driven from each. In the end, in 1525, he gave his support to the Peasants' Revolt, placing himself at the head of their army. But that very year he was defeated in battle, captured and executed.

Back in Zwickau, late in the year 1521, the prophets were summoned to appear before the town magistrates. About mid-December three of them, Thomas Drechsel, Marcus Thome (nicknamed Stübner) and Nicholas Storch himself, fled the city and made their way to Wittenberg, the heart of the Reformation in Germany. It is largely because of their contacts with the reforming leaders there that we know as much about them as we do. In fact, we have very little information about their earlier days in Zwickau itself.

Since the movement only lasted a few short years, it is reasonable to assume that for the most part its teaching as heard in Wittenberg in 1522 would have differed little from the teaching Müntzer heard among them in Zwickau some two years earlier, though on some points, as we shall see, it seems reasonable to infer a degree of development. Nothing that the prophets themselves may have written has survived, but the extant sources, despite their generally critical attitudes, are very informative and give a lively impression of the movement, its leaders and its teachings.

192. See further below, p. 273.

*The Prophets' Vision to Establish a New Society of the Spirit*

The fullest record of the activities and views of the Prophets is given in a biography of Philip Melanchthon written by Joachim Camerarius, the reformer who reorganised the Universities of Tübingen and Leipzig on Lutheran principles in the 1530s and '40s. He was a personal friend of Melanchthon, who himself was one of the more moderate reformers at Wittenberg and who had probably more to do with the prophets than any of the other leaders there. According to his account, the Zwickau Prophets, like every other prophetic movement before them, believed themselves to be the end-time Church of the Spirit, a doctrine that for them had immediate implications that were equally religious, political and social.

He tells how Storch, like so many other reformers, attacked the Catholic Church, calling on his followers to deny it was the Church of Christ and leave it to set up the true Church. But he went even further, says Camerarius, demanding the changing of the whole state system. He maintained it was corrupt to the core, its chief offices held by

> 'men who were strangers to religious piety and the practice of honesty and virtue, men who privately served their own greed instead of the public interest.' The prophets therefore believed that God 'had decreed the destruction of this ruling class and the elevation of a new class of men endowed with innocence, justice and sanctity.'

Since they regarded themselves as the nucleus of this new society God was creating, they sought to establish its moral and social principles among themselves right from the start.

> 'For the purpose of establishing this society and securing its growth, they taught the necessity of exercising care and diligence in the rearing of children. And so they urged that no one ought to marry a wife by whom he was not certain he would be able to raise godly children that would be pleasing to the eternal God and that would become elect members of the community of the kingdom of heaven.'[193]

Furthermore, it seems Storch eventually claimed he would occupy the throne of this latter-day kingdom himself,

> 'for he was heard to say that once when he was asleep he saw a vision of the angel Gabriel flying to him and standing beside

193. Joachim Camerarius, *Vita Philippi Melanchthonis*, 1604 and various later editions. References here are to the 1655 edition, in which the above is found on pp. 43-4.

> him. Gabriel mentioned several things to him that Storch thought should not yet be publicly told, and then he said this: "You will be set on my throne." And that has been interpreted that the leadership of the new state that was shortly to come into being was promised to Storch.'[194]

Melanchthon wrote to Camerarius about Storch's vision in a letter dated 17th April, 1525,[195] but we find no hint of any allusion to it in the records of the prophets' earlier conversations with the reformers at Wittenberg in 1522. A more tempered description of his role given by Melanchthon elsewhere, commenting of 1 Cor. 14:15, probably reflects his earlier, or perhaps more publicly expressed, view about the significance of his leadership:

> 'He used to tell that angels of visible form had often spoken with him and had foretold to him that he would be the leader of a renewal of the churches. He would speak about worship in the manner of enthusiasts and would say that there was a new righteousness and a heavenly light in men's hearts, and that there was a new movement or blowing [of the Spirit].'[196]

Storch's elevated claim to kingship conforms to a pattern we have noticed in some earlier movements. The vision of a new Church and a new social order is a familiar feature in all prophetic teaching from Old Testament times onwards. But in addition to that we have also noticed an occasional tendency among Christian prophets to see that vision being realised or inaugurated through particular personalities of their own time. For example, quasi-Messianic qualities were attributed to Montanus and later to the sixth-century prophet of Bourges. Of course, no two movements are identical and to Christian prophets the claims of Jesus should always remain unique, but this pattern we observe from time to time suggests that Storch's claims for himself are symptomatic of this same tendency to promote the charismatic leader to some status of elevated, even cosmic, importance. The tendency is perhaps an exaggerated version of that in the church at Corinth in New Testament times, which elevated Peter, Paul and Apollos to virtual equality with Christ (1 Cor. 1:12), but history has repeatedly adjudged it an aberration and distortion of prophetic faith, the true function of which is to glorify Christ alone (John 15:26; 16:14).

194. Camerarius, *Vita Melanchthonis*, p. 48.
195. See *CR* 1, cols. 739f.
196. Melanchthon, *Commentary on 1 Corinthians*

Despite Storch's progressivist views, the principles by which he sought to direct the course of the renewal seem to have been thoroughly conservative and biblically orientated, for according to one report, he structured his movement's leadership on patterns established in the Gospels.

> 'In this way Storch's fellowships (*secta*) developed and their name became a by-word. Furthermore, when they had grown in numbers, as it is publicly rumoured, they elected and assembled from among their fellowship twelve apostles and seventy-two disciples.'[197]

Whatever Storch may have thought about his own standing within the movement, he certainly believed his latter-day Church would recapture the life-style of New Testament Christianity, and particularly in its charismatic aspects.

*The Spiritual Experiences and Theological Attitudes of the Prophets*

> 'They also boasted of a special gift of God exercised in their meetings, that of being able to predict future events and disclose secret knowledge, a gift exceptional and wholesome in itself, which is properly known by its Greek name, 'prophecy'. Many of them have experienced marvellous visions in the quiet moments of sleep, and others, though only a few, have also had some kind of visions while awake. It has also been known for women to prophesy in such a meeting.'[198]

The spiritual experiences of the prophets were apparently no different from those of charismatics in other ages and so need little comment here, beyond noting, perhaps, that they would clearly have felt at home with the congregational worship described by Hermas, or with the experiences of some of the members of Tertullian's church.[199]

Similarly, the reference to women prophesying in their assemblies, whilst contrary to all the conventions of the age, is in accord with New Testament practice and also finds parallels in the history of all prophetic movements. We have some information about one of their prophetesses, the wife of a certain Caspar Teucher, the master-builder in the renovation of St. Mary's Church in Zwickau.

---

197. J.K. Seidemann, *Thomas Müntzer*, 1842, p. 110; cited in P. Wappler, *Thomas Müntzer in Zwickau und die 'Zwickauer Propheten'*, p. 32, n. 127.
198. Camerarius, *Vita Melanchthonis*, p. 44.
199. See above, pp. 129, 202.

According to entries in the record-books of the town council, she caused considerable disturbance with her public utterances, on one occasion even delivering an address from the pulpit of the church itself, for which she was, of course, censured by the council fathers.[200]

Thus far our picture of the Prophets corresponds well with models we have discerned in earlier times, for example, in their elevation of charismatic personalities, their view of themselves as the uniquely true church, their end-time vision, or their evangelistic zeal, as well as in their delight in mystical experiences. They also expressed strong anti-establishment, anti-clerical, anti-ritual sentiments that find many parallels in the teachings of the Old Testament prophets, or of Jesus himself, as well as of later movements, and these attitudes are reflected in the lay-church atmosphere of Storch's meetings, where the desire of the prophets was to hear the voice of the Spirit first and foremost, uttered by whomsoever, lay or otherwise.

*Divine Inspiration and the Practices of the Church*

Similar sentiments are reflected in their anti-sacramentalism. Commenting on 1 Cor. 14:15, Melanchthon wrote that Storch

> 'so exaggerated the enthusiastic aspects of religion that he saw little value in the sacraments and simply rejected them as human traditions.'

In that we hear, perhaps, an echo of Hosea's cry, 'I desire mercy, not sacrifice, and acknowledgment of God rather than burnt offerings' (Hos. 6:6). But we also get the impression that the Zwickau Prophets went further and became so excessively caught up in their spiritual experiences that they tended, according to some of their critics at any rate, to belittle all tradition, scriptural as well as ecclesiastical. That was their greatest mistake, leading directly to the elevated claims of Storch and to their ultimate rejection by the reformers.

Several texts point to this conclusion. For example, Nicholas Hausmann, a pastor in Zwickau, in a letter written two days after the event, gave an account of an examination of some of the prophets conducted there on 16th December, 1521.

> 'About sixteen people,' it reads, 'among whom were two females, presented themselves and were duly examined. Without any pressure we learned of some surprising and unchristian usages. It was noted in particular that some of

200. Wappler, p. 46.

> them doubted that the faith of the Godparent availed for the child at baptism; that some believed that baptism should be spiritual; that some spoke as if the Sacred Scripture lacked power for the work of teaching men, saying that men must be taught only by the operation of the Spirit, otherwise if God had wanted men to be taught through the Scriptures, he would have sent us a Bible from heaven. They also held that prayer should not be offered for the dead—and other cruel and ugly things.'[201]

*Divine Inspiration and the Preaching of the Church*

We have no earlier evidence of the attitudes just outlined, but others like them appear in some later writings, for example in a letter believed to have been written by Johann Agricola, one of the Wittenberg reformers, in 1525.

> 'Certain prophets came to Wittenberg teaching a new kind of doctrine. First, they scorned the power of the human voice to propagate the word of God, as they had been deliberately taught to do in presenting their teaching, the gist of which was that they should reject the performance of ceremonials, should read the sacred books, consult the oracles of the prophets, trust in the promises of God, reckon it wrong that we have been redeemed and saved by Christ's blood—not to deny that entirely, nor yet to press it strongly, indeed not to say anything about it at all, but rather to point out that we must set Christ and the Gospel aside and listen to the voice of God the Father in our hearts. They taught that no one was worthy of God unless in a vision he had either seen God with his eyes, or heard him with his ears, or felt him in his heart.'[202]

Of course, holding such views as these, they had a very low estimate of the preaching in the churches of their day, as witness the following extract from a more formal presentation of Storch's teaching by one called Marcus Wagner, based on information he says he obtained from another, Johann Chiomusus, who apparently knew Storch quite well.

> 'Where the Spirit is not present, word and sound, noise and voice can achieve nothing at all. My voice may go forth like the

201. Nicholas Hausmann, 18th Dec., 1521. See T. Kolde, 'Ältester Bericht über die Zwickauer Propheten,' *Zeitschrift für Kirchengeschichte* 5, 1881, pp. 323-5. Cp. Wappler, pp. 47f.)
202. A. Brecher, 'Johann Agricola (?) an Reusch.' *Zeitschrift für historische Theologie* 1872, pp. 404f.

> peal of a bell and return not thither, but the Spirit is creative, living and active. So it is wrong that you should be directed to churches made of wood and stone, and that you should be required under threat of excommunication to appear in them every Sunday and on work-days to hear their word. It is not God's word, but loud noise and din. Don't you think that God ought to have a different word from that, one that he will reveal to you through the Spirit? … the external, audible word that the priests utter is not God's word, but their own. Indeed you should hear God daily, in the way he spoke himself with Adam in Paradise, direct from heaven, as he appeared to Moses in the bush, and as he associated with Elijah and Elisha.'[203]

*Divine Inspiration and Human Learning.*

In a similar vein, they also had a fairly low opinion of human learning, though they apparently prized the support of such academics as did espouse their cause!

> 'Storch himself pretended that he was lacking in any kind of formal education—or perhaps he really was—and claimed that he had attained wholesome knowledge by divine inspiration. None the less, they were eager that there should be some educated persons in their number. One called Marcus [Stübner] stands out among them. He claimed that it had been given to him as an exceptional gift from God that he should excel in interpreting and explaining what is written in the Sacred Scriptures. He had once been a student at the University of Wittenberg. But he had given up his studies, either before or after he entered their society. For this requirement was in their laws: that one should not devote oneself to the study of the arts or literature and that one should not seek skill in knowledge and learning from any source other than from the generosity of the Eternal God, who has no need at all for man's efforts to help him.'[204]

The majority of these opinions find echoes in the teaching of other prophetic movements. For example, Peter followed the guidance of his vision at Joppa, though it contradicted everything he had hitherto held sacred in his Jewish tradition (Acts 10); Tertullian was prepared to accept the authority of the Paraclete when that contradicted the

203. Marcus Wagner, *Einfeltiger Bericht*, cited in Wappler, pp. 85f. This is an excerpt from a fuller account he gives of Storch's teaching.

204. Camerarius, *Vita Melanchthonis*, p. 47.

teaching of Paul on the question of marriage; the Friends of God thought little of preaching and scholarship that was not founded in mystical illumination. The difference among the Zwickau Prophets seems to have been that they failed to maintain a healthy balance between their illuminations and other aspects of their Christian heritage. The consequences were disastrous, of course. Their visions, unlike those of the Friends of God, or some of the earlier prophets, quickly ceased to be Christ-centred. They became pallid and trivial, much to the disgust of Melanchthon and Luther, who were, as we shall see, surprised at the inanity of some of them. Also, without the checks of Scripture and history, their visions were open to all kinds of weird interpretations, culminating almost inevitably in Storch's self-aggrandisement. By contrast, Peter, Paul, Tertullian and the like were at pains to uphold their received traditions and to establish their prophetic teachings as scripturally orthodox.

*The Illuminist Teachings of the Prophets*

The Zwickau Prophets seem to have looked to the Rhineland mystics, rather than to Scripture, to explain their prophetic experience. In an account of an interview he had with Stübner, Luther complains about his lack of reference to Scripture and his use of 'wondrously obscure terminology' to support his cause. Johann Agricola also speaks about the prophets using

> 'a vocabulary the like of which had not been heard in the hundred years before them ... wonderment, removing the coarseness, contemplation, long suffering, sprinkling, to be rescued from the creatures, to have no images, extended longing, unto the righteousness of God, the straight righteousness of God—and countless other expressions.'[205]

As to their contemporaries, so equally to us today the precise significance of some of these expressions is far from self-evident. Some were used among the fourteenth century mystics to denote stages of spiritual progression from sin and ignorance, through dissatisfaction with self, to longing for God. Müntzer certainly used them again in the sixteenth century and may have been himself largely responsible for introducing them to the prophets, though in

205. A. Brecher, pp. 404f. The terminology is difficult for us to understand today because its mystical meaning was peculiar to the prophets themselves. Even in their own day it was difficult enough, for Luther himself could make little sense of it all. See *Wider die himmlischen Propheten, von den Bildern und Sakrament*, 1525, *WA* 18, 137 & 138 (Luther deutsch 4, p. 149 & 150). See also below, p. 249.

a letter to Luther, written on 9th July, 1523, in which he was trying to patch up his relationship with the reformer, he disclaimed any sympathy with the jargon:

> 'You complain that you feel nauseated by some of their jargon; I suppose you refer to phrases like "patient waiting," or "constraint of mind," or "aptitude." Most honourable father, I know that the rule of the apostles instructs me to "shun godless babblings and what falsely passes for knowledge" (1 Tim. 6:20). Believe me, I shall say nothing unless I am able to corroborate it with a most obvious and appropriate text.'[206]

Luther's attitude was that mystical language and prophetic experience, however elevated or profound, are of no value without the corroborating voice of Scripture. By the time Müntzer wrote his letter, the prophets had become a symbol of excess (*Schwärmer*) to Luther. They on their part, of course, had considered Luther's reforms far too limited, claiming that it was not plumbing the depths of spirituality that they themselves had tapped in their prophetic experience.

> 'They claimed special illuminations, revelations and inspirations, or private conversations with God. We ourselves have listened to one such impostor, Nicholas Storch, ... deceitfully boasting that angels had appeared to him in visible form and had prophesied that he would be the renewer and reformer of the churches. He would add that the purge of doctrine begun by Luther was not yet penetrating to the living sources and that it was not being set on true foundations. There were many who were loudly and violently expressing the same sentiment at that time.'[207]

One wonders whether they might have created a better impression with Luther, and even made some significant contribution to the progress of the Reformation, if, as well as being excited by their inspirations, they had only heeded the voice of other men of God a little more carefully. The question is largely speculative, but it does require us to turn our attention to their conversations and encounters with the reformers at Wittenberg.

### *The Prophets in Wittenberg*

Nicholas Storch, Thomas Drechsel and Marcus Thome (Stübner)

206. 'Müntzer to Luther,' 9th July, 1523. See ed. G. Franz, *Thomas Müntzer, Schriften und Briefe*, Quellen und Forschungen zur Reformationsgeschichte 33, Gütersloh, 1968, p. 391.
207. Melanchthon, *Commentary on Matthew* (7:15). Latin text: *CR* 14, cols. 766f.

arrived in Wittenberg in December, 1521, at a time of considerable upheaval and disturbance. Luther was in exile in the Wartburg, Carlstadt was about to celebrate the first Protestant Communion on Christmas Day, and the zeal of some of the reformers for purging the churches of images and the like was beginning to excite violence in the streets of the city. None the less, the prophets did gain a hearing, particularly from Melanchthon, who was impressed by their sincerity. On 27th December, he wrote as follows to Frederick, the Elector of Saxony:

> 'Many different and dangerous dissensions about the Word of God have been stirred up in the city of Zwickau. There have been men imprisoned there for teaching some new doctrine. Three of the originators of these disturbances have fled to this place, two of them weavers, men of little education [Storch and Drechsel], and the third a scholar [Stübner]. I have given them a hearing, and it is astonishing the things they tell about themselves: that they have been sent by the clear voice of God to teach, that they hold intimate conversations with God, that they see into the future; in short, that they are as prophets and apostles. I cannot easily tell you how I have been moved by these men. I can certainly see strong reasons why I should not want to despise them. For it is clear on many counts that there are some spirits in them, but whose spirits no one besides Martin is going to be able to judge easily.'[208]

Melanchthon also wrote a briefer note to similar effect to Spalatin, Frederick's tutor, on the same day[209], and then on 1st January, 1522, at the Elector's request for further information, he and Amsdorf, another of the Wittenberg reformers, submitted fuller reports. These deal most fully with the prophets' views on infant baptism, but they also provide some information about their prophetic claims. This correspondence also reveals something of Frederick's anxiety at the thought of more trouble in Wittenberg and the reformers' fears that he might use force to deal with this new movement, for they emphatically counsel that the prophets' teaching should be given a proper hearing and dealt with on rational grounds.

> 'Nicholas Storch came to me one day in the church of St. John the Evangelist in Wittenberg with two of his associates and told me how some dissension had arisen at Zwickau, especially

208. 'Melanchthon to Frederick, Elector of Saxony, 27th December, 1521,' *CR* 1, cols. 513f.
209. See *CR* 1, cols. 514f.

with respect to the baptism of infants and the question of vicarious faith, and said that they were appealing to Dr. Martin on the matter. I was particularly interested in what one of the three, called Marcus Thome, had to say. He told me how he, and Storch likewise, had had remarkable, vivid and clear conversations with God, and henceforth would preach only when and whatever God commanded him to preach. I have observed this much about him, that he has got the right sense of the Scriptures as relates to the primary and most important articles of the faith, although he has a peculiar way of expressing himself.

'I had some discussion with this Marcus about six months ago [i.e. when he was a student at Wittenberg], but he did not say anything to me at that time about heavenly conversations. So I have thought the matter over and over to myself, especially since they indicated it had stirred up such an uproar at Zwickau, and could stir up trouble again. But I came to the conclusion that since such dissension has not been silenced by force in recent times, but through writings and by the judgment of spiritual men, the judgment of Dr. Martin would be particularly valuable in this matter, and especially since they themselves appealed to Dr. Martin.'[210]

Amsdorf's letter is in the same vein, but the Elector's reply shows less sympathy for the prophets and a degree of irritation at the insinuations that he might use force. It seems, however, that Melanchthon's and Amsdorf's fears were not without foundation, for on 17th January Luther wrote to Spalatin,

'I do not want them jailed … Please see to it that our Sovereign does not stain his hands with the blood of these new "prophets" from Zwickau.'[211]

*The Movement spreads and Melanchthon loses sympathy*

The real cause of the worry, apart from the reports of the commotion their teaching had caused at Zwickau, was the fact that the prophets had begun to make an impact at Wittenberg, not only with Melanchthon, but in wider circles in the university and the city, according to Camerarius, at any rate.

---

210. 'Melanchthon to Frederick, 1st January, 1522,' *CR* 1, cols. 533f.
211. *LW* 48, pp. 380f.

> 'This disastrous cancer began to spread throughout Germany [after the prophets' expulsion from Zwickau], perniciously creeping little by little and gathering strength as it progressed. No one tried to stop it or direct its course ... Storch wandered around the countryside. He never stayed very long in any place, but strenuously pursued those policies that he had conceived in his own mind. But Marcus, whether at Storch's instigation or by his own choice, stayed at Wittenberg for some time. I saw him there myself and had several conversations with him. Philip Melanchthon took him to stay at his house ... And so he enjoyed Philip's hospitality, but that in no way hindered him from visiting other people, and he led several through to his way of thinking. The most important of these was Martin Cellarius [one of Melanchthon's own pupils who had become a teacher at Wittenberg] ... So when Marcus had won him over as a friend, associate, helper, companion and indeed as a leader, he virtually made him second in command of the movement at Wittenberg, where everything was more difficult in those days because of people's fickleness and hastiness resulting from their yearning after new ideas. And now the doctrine was no longer just whispered, but loudly and openly preached.'[212]

Meantime, Melanchthon, at first favourably impressed by the prophets, was becoming disenchanted with them and so more ready to adopt Luther's hostile attitude. Increasingly he found their illuminism rather shallow and even tiresome. Camerarius tells the following story, which illustrates the process very well indeed.

> 'Philip Melanchthon was entertaining Marcus [Stübner] at his home ... On one occasion Philip was engaged in some piece of writing and Marcus, who happened to be sitting opposite him, gradually became drowsy as he sat in the silence with his own thoughts. His head sank down onto the little table at which he was seated and he fell fast asleep. Not long after he woke up, looked at Philip and suddenly asked him what his opinion of John Chrysostom[213] was. Philip agreeably answered that he held him in esteem, though he did not much like his verbosity. Then Marcus said, "I have just seen him in purgatory with a sad expression on his face." At first Philip laughed at this, but presently he went away saddened at such inconsistency in him

212. Camerarius, *Vita Melanchthonis*, pp. 47f.
213. Fourth/fifth century theologian, Bishop of Constantinople. See above, p. 137.

> that he should have made reference to purgatory, the existence of which they had completely refuted in their other discussions.'[214]

In the end, feeling himself quite unequal to the task of handling the prophets, Melanchthon appealed to Luther for help.

*Luther's Views before he met the Prophets*

In March 1522, Luther left his place of exile in the Wartburg to take up the reins again and bring some moderation to the reforms that were in danger of running into excess. The information he had been receiving about the prophets had already made him suspicious about their claims before he returned to Wittenberg, but now the urgency of the situation was only highlighted with further reports of their successes, particularly of the impression they were making on Carlstadt and another called Zwilling who, in Luther's estimation, were already showing too much zeal for overthrowing the old regime. The development of Luther's opinions is amply illustrated in two of his letters. The first he wrote to Melanchthon from the Wartburg on 13th January, and its tone, though critical, is not at all damnatory.

> 'Since they [the prophets] bear witness to themselves, you do not need to accept them straight away. Remember John's advice, that the spirits are to be tested [1 John 4:1]. If you cannot test them, then you have Gamaliel's advice, that you postpone judgment [Acts 5:34f]. So far I have heard nothing they have said or done that Satan could not also do or imitate.'[215]

Luther's second letter, which he wrote to Nicholas Hausmann in Zwickau on 17th March, almost immediately on his return to Wittenberg and before he had actually met with the prophets, shows a very different attitude:

> 'The "prophets" who came from your [town] are striving for peculiar things; they are pregnant with monstrosities I do not like. If these should be born, they will cause no small damage. Their spirit is extremely deceitful and specious.'[216]

In the months after Luther's return he met Stübner, Storch and Drechsel in turn and by the end of the year he had effectively

---

214. Camerarius, *Vita Melanchthonis,* p. 50.
215. 'Luther to Melanchthon,' from the Wartburg, 13th Jan. 1552. *LW* 48, pp. 365f.
216. 'Luther to Nicholas Hausmann,' 17th March, 1522. *LW* 48, p. 401.

silenced the voice of prophecy. The outcome of these interviews is not at all surprising, since he was clearly predisposed to reject their claims from the start, while they equally clearly had no intention of relinquishing or modifying their vision.

*Luther's Interview with Stübner*

Several descriptions of Luther's meetings with the prophets are extant, each providing some little extra piece of information or elaboration. Camerarius gives a very full account of his encounter with Marcus Thome. He tells how Marcus was encouraged by his fellowship in Wittenberg to seek an interview with Luther, which Luther agreed to, though he was not too happy about it. Marcus brought with him his disciple, Cellarius, and someone else; Luther invited Melanchthon.

> 'Luther listened quietly as Marcus gave an account of his views. When he had finished speaking, Luther, thinking that it would be pointless to argue against such absurd and silly opinions, admonished them in this way: they should see what they were arguing for; none of the things they had mentioned were supported by appeal to sacred Scriptures, but were either the inventions of inquisitive imaginations or even the mad and dangerous ruminations of a deceitful and fraudulent spirit.
>
> 'At that point Cellarius raised his voice and expressed considerable indignation that Luther should dare to suspect such a thing in a holy man. He accompanied his vocal expressions with some wild gestures, pounding the ground with his feet and banging on the little table in front of him with his hands.
>
> 'But Marcus was a little more restrained and, as you may know, said, "Luther, I am going to show you that it has been revealed to me by the Spirit of God what thought you have in your mind. It is this: that you are beginning to incline to the opinion that my teaching is true." As Luther himself said afterwards, he was in fact entertaining precisely that thought, so he retorted, "The Lord rebuke you, Satan."
>
> 'After that Luther did not think of holding any further discussions, but sent them away uttering their threats and boasts. They promised all sorts of things about the miraculous achievements by which they would prove their case, but he simply said, "The God whom I venerate and worship will have little difficulty in preventing your signs from working

> themselves out in the way you describe." They left the city that day and went to Chemburg, a place over five miles away ...'[217]

The meeting certainly did not leave Luther with any improved impression of the prophets. Fairly soon after it, he wrote to Spalatin, on 12th April,

> 'Their spirit is excessively proud and impatient, for it is incapable of producing persuasive arguments, but demands to be believed with a complete authority at its first utterance and is unwilling to discuss or debate anything ... I at length bade them prove their teaching, which vaunts itself in excess of and in contradiction to the Scriptures, with miracles. They refused to perform miracles, but instead threatened that I should one day be compelled to believe them. One of them, Master Martin [Cellarius], though no one bade him speak or asked him anything, fumed and growled and raved so much that he afforded me no opportunity to speak. So I dismissed them and strongly forbade their god to perform any miracles without the consent of my God.'[218]

Further reports of this meeting with Stübner and Cellarius are found in the records of Luther's conversations with his students at table, where a few additional pieces of interesting information emerge, illustrating further the mind of the prophets.

> 'Marcus approached me with the most pleasant conversation and manners, which, however, lacked reference to Scripture. So I said to him, "I shall not agree with you nor believe you unless you perform signs." He said, "You will see signs in the next seven years!"—and presently the peasants' revolt followed. Amongst other things he said that he could immediately see in a man's face whether he was godly or ungodly and not one of the elect.
>
> 'This fellow used wondrously obscure terminology: state of sinfulness, state of discontentment, state of boredom. When I asked him how he could be understood when he spoke like that, he replied that he revealed such information to students who had the aptitude or talent for it. When I asked him about my talent, he told me that I was in the first stage of mobility and would next enter the first stage of immobility where he

217. Camerarius, *Vita Melanchthonis*, pp. 52ff.
218. 'Luther to Spalatin,' 12th April, 1522. *WA* II (*Briefwechsel*), no. 472.

> was himself. And then he wrote letters and exhortations to me from Chemburg with more persuasive language, but at that point I bade him a final farewell.'[219]

*Comment*

From these accounts we note several familiar characteristics of prophetic Christianity, and some common aberrations too. Luther's notes about lack of reference to Scripture confirm our earlier observation about the prophets' over-preoccupation with their visions, and that is a recurrent failing among prophetic people. Their prediction of political turmoil is typical of prophetic utterances from Old Testament times to the present day and has nothing unusual about it. Nor has the ability to detect godliness in a person's face, which can also be illustrated from various prophetic sources and may be associated with what Paul calls the gift of discernment (1 Cor. 12:10).

The teaching about progression from one stage of spiritual experience to another, or of progression into full prophetic illumination, is also found in the writings of other prophets. Some prophetic groups, it is true, speak more of an abrupt experience of baptism in the Spirit, but as we have noted, the Zwickau Prophets were in many respects the successors of Tauler and the medieval mystics, and their teaching about the soul's progress from sin through various degrees of dissatisfaction to yearning for God and full enlightenment is well illustrated, for example, in the story of the Master among the Friends of God.

*Luther's Interview with Nicholas Storch*

Luther's conversations with Storch himself seem to have been largely occupied with the subject of baptism. Some of our sources imply that the prophets saw little necessity of water-baptism at all, or indeed for any of the sacraments; others suggest that the dispute was only about the efficacy of the faith of Godparents in infant baptism. Probably the opinions of the prophets themselves were divided on this issue. All that Luther tells us is that 'Storch himself strongly ridiculed the notion that a handful of water could save men, and I did not achieve anything by saying that this water was sufficiently efficacious for working salvation on account of the related word of God that would command this and perform it.'[220] It

219. *WA* II (*Tischreden*), no. 2837a.
220. *WA* II (*Tischreden*), no. 2060.

would seem that Storch, like Stübner, was also unwilling to heed arguments based on Scripture alone.

*Luther's Interview with Drechsel*

This meeting was much less consequential and almost entirely occupied with Drechsel relaying a vision which is slightly differently described in the different sources, though the following account of it by Luther gives a sufficient impression of its content and theme.

> 'He [Drechsel] said, "My Father has sent me to you."
>
> I asked him, "Who is your Father?"
>
> "God," he replied.
>
> I retorted, "He is my Father too. So we are brothers. What message do you bring from our common Father, then?"
>
> "That God is exceedingly angry with the world."
>
> 'He added that he had seen a certain large house in which many people were sitting together drinking, and that God had come and stood before them threatening them with two fingers. He said that it was through this vision that he had been shown his message. I told him that I knew all that before, but if he had some new insight for me, something that was not generally known, then he should tell me about it. I pointed out that it is recognised in all the Scriptures that God is angry with the world. At that he went away, angry that I should be contemptuous of his warning.'[221]

*What became of the Movement?*

After these encounters we lose sight of the prophets. Camerarius says he knows nothing more about them. He does, however, tell us that Cellarius moved to Prussia where, in 1525, he was still adhering to and writing about their cause, but that soon afterwards, seeing how it was to all intents and purposes defunct, he married and settled down to a quiet life. Commenting on 1 Cor. 14:15, Melanchthon notes that 'Storch eventually became a fugitive in Central Germany,' but earlier, in 1525, he must still have been actively involved in propounding his views, because in April of that year Melanchthon wrote to Camerarius questioning whether Storch was involved in

221. *WA* II (*Tischreden*), no. 2060.

the peasant unrest. He also added, 'He promises himself world dominion and they say that within four years it will be that he will have control of affairs, will establish his new religion and will give the reins of state into the hands of holy men.'[222]

We know nothing at all about the fates of Stübner and Drechsel, though Müntzer, who had broken with the prophets and followed his own line of reform, was eventually captured and executed as one of the leaders of the peasants' revolt.

It is difficult to assess the size and impact of this movement. Sixteen persons appeared before the magistrates in Zwickau on 16th December, 1521, but presumably they were only a few of the movement's leading personalities, since several had already fled the city by that time. As time went on they were able to appoint a leadership and ministry group of 'twelve apostles and seventy-two disciples,' so we are told.[223] We know that Stübner had a congregation in Wittenberg early in 1522, for it was they who urged him to seek the interview with Luther. Camerarius certainly suggests that their growth was both rapid and extensive.

Perhaps it would be nearest the truth to think of a fairly small movement, but one with a forceful voice that spread its influence far wider than mere consideration of its numbers might suggest, somewhat like Samuel's little groups of prophets in early Israel.

On the other hand, their story is probably one of the most inglorious in the history of prophecy, for it stands as an object lesson about the consequences of heeding inspirational experiences at the expense of Scripture and history. This was certainly one of the main weaknesses Luther detected in their teaching, as is made evident in the reports of his interviews with Storch and Stübner. It is surprising that it should have been so, for Stübner was a scholar and therefore well versed in Scripture, while Storch, although an untutored weaver, had a knowledge of the Bible that impressed Melanchthon. Like prophets in other times, they must have treasured the Bible in so far as it witnessed to the same kind of experience of God as they themselves had discovered. But, in the excitement of their new mystical awareness, they must have become puffed up with their visions, just like some of the early Christians before them (Col. 2:18), and so failed to observe the scriptural injunction to test everything, and particularly to see that their insights accorded with the biblical revelation itself.

---

222.
223. See above, p. 239.

The Rhineland mystics, their forerunners in the faith, were seldom confronted with this problem, because they did not, for the most part, reject the traditions of the Church. The Zwickau Prophets, on the contrary, were the spiritual casualties of an age of transition. Ideally Christian prophecy is a matter of order, encouragement and peace (1 Cor. 14). The turbulence of the early 1520s was too inhospitable an environment for its purer forms of expression to flourish. Perhaps it had to end in excess.

# 18
# The Bible and Revival

The story of the Bible makes a book in its own right, but its recovery was one of the main contributions the Reformation made to the flow of the history we shall be following in the rest of this book, and so it is important that we tell some of it. Since our main concern is with movements of the Spirit, our focus must be limited to the story of its revival impact in history, to times when reading it or from it has caused men to discover afresh the life-giving power of the Spirit and draw them together in movements of spiritual revival. To trace that story properly we have to go right back into the times of the Bible itself.

*The Written Word in Bible Times*

From earliest times the Israelites recognised that God's words had life-giving power: 'They are not just idle words for you—they are your life' (Deut. 32:47). Heeding them was of paramount importance, because obedience would bring life-giving blessing, disobedience the curse of death (30:15-20). The Israelites were therefore commanded to teach them to their children and have them regularly rehearsed at certain festivals, so that they and their children would learn to fear the Lord and live long under God's blessing (6:2; 31:9-13). Likewise, the king was instructed to write out his own personal copy of God's word, read it every day and live in obedience to its commands, so that his reign might be long-lived (17:18-20). This life-givingness associated with the written, read, or rehearsed words of God in the Old Testament is basically the same as the life-generating power of God's own utterance at creation, or in the New Testament of the teaching of Jesus, who said, 'The words I have spoken to you are spirit and they are life.' (John 6:63) The expectation of Scripture itself is, therefore, that its words should release power for revival (= restoration of life).

We see examples of this principle in operation in Old Testament history. Joshua and Solomon were both told, like the king in Deut. 17, that regular study of the Law would ensure their continuing success in leadership (Josh. 1:8; 1 Chron. 22:12f). The basic rule is spelt out in Deut. 30: obeying the word leads to blessing and life, disobedience to curse and death (vv. 11-20), returning to the Lord (repentance) and obeying to restoration (vv. 2f).

While there are many stories of returning and revival in Israel, two are outstanding as instances of that resulting from Scripture-reading. The first is in 2 Kings 22-23 and 2 Chronicles 34-35. It tells how the High Priest found a copy of 'the Book of the Law' while repairs on the temple in Jerusalem were being carried out by the godly King Josiah in the eighteenth year of his reign (622 BC). During the reigns of his two predecessors, Judah had slipped away from God and turned progressively to worshipping pagan images. The Bible (Law) had clearly become a forgotten book in that time, because when Josiah heard it read he was horrified to learn how far his people had fallen from its standards and how great God's wrath must be against them as a result. After consulting a prophetess who affirmed the word he had read, he summoned a national assembly in the temple so that it could be read to the whole people. The consequences were phenomenal: the people pledged themselves to keep the law; the temple purge which was already under way was given new impetus; it was extended to the city and its suburbs, then to the rest of the land; another national assembly was called, this time for the biggest Passover celebration in Israel's history since earliest days. Here was surely a move of God in revival power, and it resulted from a simple reading of Scripture by one whose heart was devoted to seeking God.

The second instance is recorded in Nehemiah 8. The year is 445 BC and the scene is the autumn festival of Tabernacles. Thirteen years earlier the Persian emperor, concerned about the decadent state of religion in Judah, had sent Ezra, a priest and scribe, with instructions to teach the Law to the people and revive their faith, lest 'there be wrath against the realm of the king and of his sons' (Ezra 7). Nehemiah had arrived earlier in 445 and rebuilt the city walls amazingly rapidly. And now the people were assembled for the feast. Ezra mounted a pulpit and read to them from the Book of the Law 'from daybreak till noon', then sent Levites among them to interpret and instruct them further. The scenes that day were dramatic. What should normally have been an occasion of festival joy suddenly turned to one of people weeping everywhere as they heard the Law read, so much so that the Levites had a struggle to get them to return to proper observance of the feast. Day after day, throughout the whole seven days of the festival, Ezra continued to read the Law to them. On the twenty-fourth day they reassembled for a gathering that was attended by deep repentance and confession of sins, culminating in the making of a covenant to observe the Law again. Clearly Scripture reading could have profound effect.

In the New Testament we see the same principle at work. Jesus' own teaching, though never a bare reading or exposition of Scripture passages, was entirely based on their message, for he saw his ministry as fulfilment of all that was written in them. He considered it important that his disciples should take the same view, and so we see him, on the eve of his ascension, opening their minds so they could understand the Scriptures and see how the gospel was entirely concordant with them (Luke 24:44-9).

That became the message of the apostles, 'that Christ died for our sins according to the Scriptures, that he was buried, that he was raised on the third day according to the Scriptures' (1 Cor. 15:3f). Christian preaching in the early Church was thoroughly Bible-based. Peter's sermons in Acts 2, 3 & 10 preach Jesus altogether from the Old Testament, Stephen's speech in Acts 7 is little more than a review of the Israel's history, and Paul spent much of his time 'proving from the Scriptures that Jesus was the Christ' (Acts 18:28).

*The Bible in the Early Church*

In New Testament times the Scriptures were hand-written on scrolls of bulky papyrus or parchment. Unlike our modern books with thin paper pages and highly condensed printed text, these were not easily portable. Isaiah, for example, made up one complete scroll in itself and that one scroll would have been clumsier than a whole Bible is today. From about the second century Christians began to use the codex, a form of book with pages which was easier to handle than the scroll. Far fewer people could read or write than today anyway and so Bible teaching had to be mainly by word of mouth rather than by reading.

Gospel preachers and teachers were greatly helped by the fact that throughout the Roman Empire people spoke one of two languages, Latin in the West and Greek in the East. Greek was the official language in Palestine, the heritage of the earlier Greek Empire that had ruled there since the mid-fourth century BC, and already in the last two centuries BC the Old Testament had been translated into Greek. Greek was therefore the main language used by New Testament evangelists and writers.

The Greek Old Testament was not simply a translation of the Hebrew Bible, though for the most part it was. It also contained a number of books and parts of books that are not found in the Hebrew text, such as 1 & 2 Maccabees, Judith, Tobit, Ecclesiasticus, Wisdom of Solomon, and extra chapters in Jeremiah, Esther, Daniel and 2 Chronicles, books and chapters that today we collectively refer to as *The Apocrypha*. This Greek Bible is known as *The Septuagint*, meaning 'The Seventy', after a tradition that it was translated by seventy-two Jewish scholars in Egypt with miraculous accuracy.

The importance of all this for our purposes is simply to note that the Bible of the early Church was not the same as that used in reformed churches today. Because of the widespread use of Greek in the Roman Empire, the Church quickly came to use this larger Greek Bible rather than the smaller Hebrew collection that the Jews agreed on in the last decades of the first century AD. In the sixteenth century the Protestant reformers mostly opted for the smaller Hebrew Bible, partly because some of the Apocryphal writings seem to be of questionable value. The Catholics and the Orthodox have never given up their older, larger Bibles. The Orthodox still use the Septuagint unmodified, the Catholics until recently have used a Latin translation of it known as The Vulgate. Anglicans have, as in many other things, sought a middle way, permitting the reading of the Apocrypha for edification, but not for doctrine.

It took many years before the Church agreed on the shape and content of the New Testament as we know it today. Though the gospels, epistles, Acts and Revelation were all written in the first century, it was not till the fourth that final agreement was reached about which of them should be considered sacred Scripture, at the Councils of Laodicea in 325 (later modified slightly in 363) and Carthage in 397. The details of the debates need not concern us here. In fact they still continue among scholars and theologians, and also to a lesser extent in certain church circles. However, unlike the Old Testament, agreement among Christians about the shape and size of the New Testament is virtually unanimous.

The greatest challenge to the Bible in the early Church came from two sources, Greek Philosophy and the superstitious beliefs of contemporary religion. Paul urged Timothy and Titus to ensure the teaching of true doctrine. As the Church spread into the world of Graeco-Roman paganism, the need for sound biblical teaching became all the more urgent. Untaught converts too easily fall foul to any heretical or strange doctrines that may come their way. The truth of that is well illustrated in the syncretistic beliefs and practices in many African tribal churches today. As experience of Christ is interpreted in terms of thought forms that are already familiar,

Christian truth becomes buried under a morass of pagan thinking. One early example of this process is Gnosticism, which interpreted Christianity in terms of a multiplicity of divine levels and beings and a quest for knowledge (Greek gnosis). Marcion, an influential second-century Gnostic, made one of the earliest statements about what the New Testament should contain, and he was happy only with an edited version of Luke's Gospel and ten of Paul's letters. The other apostles and evangelists, he claimed, had been blinded to the truth, and their writings should therefore not be read.

As churches continued to multiply, it became more and more urgent to have an agreed Bible, one Christians could read for themselves. Agreement was reached about the shape of the New Testament at the end of the fourth century, and it was about the same time that an authorised translation was first made into Latin, when about 384 Pope Damasus instructed Jerome to produce a fresh, revised translation.

*Bible Translation in the Middle Ages*

At that time several translations were either available in other languages already or about to become so. In the Eastern Orthodox stream several translations were made that are still in use in their churches today. One of the earliest of these was a Syriac version known as the *Peshitta*. Work began on the Coptic version (Egyptian) in the third century. Translations in their own languages in Ethiopia, Armenia and Georgia in the fourth and fifth centuries are also still used among the Orthodox in these lands. The Russian Orthodox use a ninth century translation in Old Slavonic made by St. Cyril, for which he had to invent the alphabet Russians still use, known as Cyrillic. Other less well known translations were made, even one in Chinese in the seventh century.

In Europe local translation was more sporadic and less enduring. The Goths whose invasion brought about the downfall of Rome had a translation made by a missionary among them called Ulfilas, but only fragments of it remain. No European native language translations from earlier than the twelfth century have survived, apart from a Frankish translation of Matthew made in 758.

In England Aldhelm, Bishop of Sherborne in Dorset, made a translation of the Psalms about 700. About the same time, at Jarrow in Northumbria, Bede ('The Venerable') was working on a fuller English Bible when he died translating John's Gospel in 735. Alfred the Great, King of the West Saxons at the end of the ninth century, undertook some translating himself, and in the tenth Aelfric, abbot of Eynsham, near Oxford, translated the first seven books of the Old Testament and the four Gospels (the Wessex Gospels). English renderings are also found between the lines of Latin text in the Lindesfarne Gospels and the Rushworth Gospels, illuminated manuscripts from the same general period.

Not all of these works have survived. They were written in Anglo-Saxon, which is very different from modern English. That only began to develop properly after the Norman Conquest in 1066. A monk called Ormin produced a poetical version of the Gospels and Acts about 1200 in the new language. A few other verse and prose translations of parts of the Bible were made over the following two centuries, some of them for the exclusive use of monks and nuns.

Perhaps more translations were made than have survived, but even in their own time they were not very widely used, partly because copies of them were so costly to produce, partly because very few people could read anyway, but mainly because the Vulgate reigned supreme in the Western Church. It was originally intended to be a Common Language Version or People's Bible (Latin *vulgus* means 'common people'), but with Papal authorisation it soon became the main translation in use. The result in the long term was that, as Latin fell increasingly into disuse after the collapse of the Roman Empire, the Bible became for most Christians an unknown book.

Nevertheless, its message and stories continued to be taught by word of mouth by those who knew them. Sometimes they were recited in verse form, or accompanied by singing, or presented in drama, or in art. Church wall-paintings depicted scriptural scenes and passion-plays became popular in the later middle ages, but perhaps the most common way of teaching Scripture was in poetry and song. One of the most famous Bible bards was Caedmon, a cowherd at Whitby Abbey in Yorkshire in the middle of the seventh century. One night in a dream he received the gift of song and in the course of his life sang the whole Bible story from creation to the last judgment. Even though his biography belongs to the earlier part of the Middle Ages, parts of it are worth retelling because they give us a good flavour of how the Holy Spirit ensured that the Bible was taught in these times.

> 'It sometimes happened at a feast that all the guests in turn would be invited to sing and entertain the company; then, when he (Caedmon) saw the harp coming his way, he would get up from table and go home.
>
> 'On one such occasion he had left the house in which the entertainment was being held and went out to the stable, where it

> was his duty that night to look after the beasts. There when the time came he settled down to sleep. Suddenly in a dream he saw a man standing beside him who called him by name. "Caedmon," he said, "sing me a song." "I don't know how to sing," he replied. "It is because I cannot sing that I left the feast and came here." The man who addressed him then said: "But you shall sing to me." "What should I sing about?" he replied. "Sing about the Creation of all things," the other answered. And Caedmon immediately began to sing verses in praise of God the Creator that he had never heard before.... When Caedmon awoke, he remembered everything that he had sung in his dream, and soon added more verses in the same style to a song truly worthy of God.'

Next morning he told his superior what had happened. After much testing his gift was recognised to be of God. He was taken into the community and

> 'instructed in the events of sacred history. So Caedmon stored up in his memory all that he learned, and ... turned it into such melodious verse that his delighted renderings turned his instructors into auditors. He sang of Israel's exodus from Egypt, the entry into the Promised Land, and many other events of scriptural history. He sang of the Lord's Incarnation, Passion, Resurrection, and Ascension into heaven, the coming of the Holy Spirit, and the teaching of the Apostles. He also made many poems of the terrors of the Last Judgment, the horrible pains of Hell, and the joys of the Kingdom of God, by which he sought to turn his hearers from delight in wickedness and to inspire them to love and do good.'[224]

*The Reforming Power of the Bible*

The New Testament played an important part in the puritanical and anti-Catholic preaching of the Cathars in western Europe in the twelfth and thirteenth centuries. In the same period, the founder-leader of the Waldensians, Peter Waldo of Lyons, translated the New Testament into Provençal for his itinerant preachers ('the Poor Men of Lyons') to use.[225] They travelled extensively in the south of France and the north of Italy and their work established a reforming church that had considerable impact in its own time, so much so

224. Bede, *A History of the English Church and People*, Penguin Books, 1968, pp. 251f.
225. See above, p. 185.

that it was severely persecuted by the Catholic Church. There are still some Waldensians found in Italy today.

Powerful as the impact of these European movements was, a full century and more was to pass before the main thrust towards the Reformation came through the work of the Oxford scholar, John Wycliffe (1330-84).

*Wycliffe and the Lollards*

Wycliffe was a theologian and philosopher, but, as we noted earlier, also very much concerned with the affairs of state, and so gained for himself some influential friends at court who later supported and protected him when the Church turned against him. His great passion was that England should learn the laws of God, which were hardly known because the Church kept them locked up in its Latin Bible. With the help of some of his students, he set himself the mammoth task of seeing it rendered into English. His translation was made from the Latin Vulgate, not the original Hebrew and Greek, but it was a careful translation and was the first complete Bible ever made available in English. The work was finished shortly before he died in 1384, but, since printing had not yet been invented, every copy had to be hand-written and was therefore quite costly. However, it proved highly popular and many copies were produced, despite the fact that the authorities opposed its circulation.

It was not just the translation the Church disliked, but Wycliffe's reforming teaching that went with it. He saw no reason why the government should pay taxes to an ecclesiastical system that was corrupt. That pleased some statesmen, but, of course, angered the churchmen. He also attacked the Church's doctrine of the Eucharist (transubstantiation) and taught that the true Church was made up of God's people, not a system of priests. These views found their way into marginal notes in some manuscripts of his Bible, which certainly did not help to endear it to the churchmen. Wycliffe's views were too strong for his time. Gradually he lost the support of his influential friends and the Church authorities forced him to leave Oxford. In 1382 he retired to his parish at Lutterworth in Leicestershire where he continued his Bible work, but he died a sick man two years later.

Wycliffe's work might have died with him, had he not in his lifetime taught his disciples so that they could propagate his teaching after him. Like their master, these travelling Bible-teachers and preachers, 'the Lollards', believed that the Bible should be available to everyone and that the first task of a priest was to teach it. The movement spread quickly and by the end of the century had grown into an organised group with a clear mission, their own ministers and committed supporters. They were opposed by the Church, of course, but they also lost the favour of the state, because some of them were suspected of being involved in the Peasants' Revolt in 1381. In 1408 a decree was issued forbidding anyone either to translate the Bible into English or to possess a translated copy. The word was proving too powerful and had to be suppressed.

But it was too late. Despite persecution, some of it bloody and severe, Lollardy continued to prosper in certain regions, creating a substantial body of people prepared for the Reformation in the following century.

Wycliffe's influence was not only at home. Some of his students came from Europe and carried his reforming gospel home with them. The most outstanding of those influenced by him was Jan Hus, a priest, teacher and preacher at the University of Prague in Bohemia (Czech Republic). He was ordained in 1401 and very quickly his Bible preaching became immensely popular. He rapidly became a national hero, but his attacks on the corruptions of the Church led to his arrest and martyrdom in 1415. His followers continued the work of translation and as a result a Czech New Testament was printed in 1475. His martyrdom roused national indignation among the Czechs who established the Hussite Church. It dominated Christian life in Bohemia until Catholicism was forcibly restored by the Austrians after 1620.

The Reformation that swept Europe in the 1500s was built on this platform which was itself constructed on the Bible. Such is the power of the Word of God to change lives, churches and nations.

*Bible Translation during the Reformation*

The details of the story of Bible translation in Reformation and post-Reformation times need not occupy our attention too much here since they were only marginally related to our search for things prophetic. On the other hand, it is important to be aware of something of the story, for every prophetic movement since the Reformation has had Bible teaching at its heart. But for the open Bible, it is unlikely that the movements we shall be reviewing in the following pages would ever have been. The word continued to have its powerful impact. However, to follow that story further we need no more than a very brief review of the continued history of translation work.

The story of the Bible's impact was totally transformed with the introduction of the printing press in the middle of the fifteenth century. Bibles became more plentiful, more portable and cheaper to buy. The process of printing was pioneered by Johann Guttenberg in Mainz and the first major book to come off his press, in 1456, was the Latin Vulgate. By the end of the century translations in German, Italian, Czech, Dutch and Catalan (in Spain) had all appeared.

The first printed English Bible was a relative latecomer on the scene, mainly because the law forbade translation. Though William Caxton set up a printing press at Westminster in 1483, it was not until 1526 that Tyndale's New Testament was printed, and even then it had to be produced on the Continent, at Worms, near Mainz, and smuggled into England. However, his work did mark a new departure in Bible translation. Earlier translations were all made from the Vulgate, but the Jews had printed a Hebrew Bible in 1488 and the Dutch scholar, Erasmus, a Greek New Testament in 1516, thus making the Bible widely available in its original languages. Tyndale used Erasmus' work for his New Testament translation. It was denounced by the English Church authorities who publicly burned as many copies as they could find.

Tyndale's response was to have more printed and smuggled into the country. He was arrested at Antwerp in 1535 and held prisoner for seventeen months then burnt as a heretic in the autumn of 1536, praying as he died, 'Lord, open the king of England's eyes.' It is one of history's sad ironies that, unbeknown to him because of his long confinement, King Henry VIII's eyes had already been opened and an English Bible was in circulation with his consent. This was Coverdale's revision of Tyndale's own work, in which he had completed the translation of the Old Testament (1535).

Though the Vulgate continued in use in the churches, a new edition of Coverdale's Bible appeared in 1537 with the inscription, 'set forth with the Kinges most gracious lycence', permitting its free use in private. Two years later, in 1539, a further revision was published, the Great Bible, or Cranmer's Bible, issued this time with the king's order that a copy of it be set in a convenient place in every church, where every Christian could have ready access to it. This was the first Bible printed in England itself.

In 1553 the Queen, Mary Tudor, tried to stop the printing and reading of Bibles as part of her drive to restore Catholicism, but translation and revision work was continued by refugees in Switzerland. In 1560 they published the Geneva Bible. It was the first to be printed with chapter and verse divisions. It was also the first to be set in Roman type, and so was smaller, more easy to handle and cheaper. It was very popular among Puritans, but not among English churchmen, because its margins carried some extreme anti-Catholic notes that were highly critical of the established church and the government. It was nicknamed 'the Breeches Bible' because its rendering of Gen. 3:7 said Adam and Eve sewed fig leaves together and made themselves breeches.

The Bishops' Bible was published in 1568, a further revision without the anti-establishment notes, for use in the Church of England, but it never proved as popular as the Geneva Bible. Then finally in 1604 King James commissioned a team of scholars to produce a new translation to replace both the Bishops' Bible and the Geneva Bible, one that he could authorise for common use in the churches of his realm. It appeared in 1611 and is referred to as the King James or Authorised Version (though it never was properly 'authorised'). Its original printings contained a translation of the apocryphal books, but they are now omitted. It has enjoyed almost four centuries of popularity, and even though its language sounds old-fashioned now, it is still one of the most widely used translations in the world today.

Now that the Bible was available in English, Catholics were beginning to read it, and since the only translations available were Protestant, some of them highly so, the Catholic Church decided to produce its own one. That appeared in 1609 and is known as the Douai Bible. It was translated partly at Rheims and partly at Douai in France. It was a very literal translation of the Latin Vulgate. After some revision in the eighteenth century it became the official version of the Roman Catholic Church.

*Bible Translation in Modern Times*

Changes in the English language and the discovery of ancient manuscripts of the Hebrew and Greek texts, many of them centuries older than those used by the Reformation translators, including most recently the Dead Sea Scrolls which include Hebrew manuscripts of Old Testament books from before the time of Christ, have prompted further work to be done in more recent times.[226]

226. The manuscript tradition used by the King James translators is usually referred to as the Textus Receptus, or Received Text. Like the Vulgate in the Catholic Church, the Authorised Version has become hallowed by long use among English- speaking Protestants, so much so that today there are those who argue that the Textus Receptus should be treated with the same reverence, as though both it and the Authorised translation made from it are themselves the infallible word of God. A lot of very heated debate is carried on around this matter in certain circles, though most Christians are quite unaware of it and are simply glad to have the more readable and understandable modern translations. The debate becomes quite complicated and need not detain us here. Despite all the criticisms it levels against modern translations, they are serving a good purpose in making the word of God available to thousands who would never read it in the English of the seventeenth and eighteenth centuries which is so difficult for many to understand today.

The first revision, known simply as the Revised Version, was published in 1881-5 in England, and an American counterpart, the Standard Version, appeared in 1901, but neither was widely used. The first real breakthrough in modern translation came with the Revised Standard Version, another American work, and it has proved immensely popular, not only with Protestants, but also with Catholics, so much so that a Catholic edition of it was published in 1965, and an edition acceptable to both sides, known as the Common Bible, in 1973.

All these translations, from Wycliffe down to the RSV, have been basically revisions of earlier ones in the same flow. In the century, however, there have been some significant departures from this long-standing tradition in Bible translation. A large number of translations have been made by private individuals, among the most popular being R.F. Weymouth (1903), J. Moffatt (1913 & 24), E.J. Goodspeed (1923 & 27), Ronald Knox (1945 & 49), J.B. Phillips (1947-57), K. Taylor (Living Bible, 1971). Most of these seek to be fresh and easily readable, without being tied to the style of the older versions. Other modern translations have been produced by panels of scholars and these have also sought to be free from the restrictions of the Tyndale-Authorised tradition. The translators have started afresh from the Hebrew and Greek texts, drawing on the earlier and more reliable versions of these we now have, and have produced works that are in flowing modern English, though each has its own aims and characteristics.

The New English Bible was among the first of them to be published, with the New Testament in 1961 and the complete Bible in 1970. It was intended to be in modern English, but some of its language is quite stilted and academic, and its theological leaning is fairly liberal.

About the same time, in 1966, the Catholics produced the Jerusalem Bible, which has also proved quite popular among Protestants.

The Good News Bible came out in two parts, the New Testament in 1966 and the whole Bible in 1976. It is written in fairly simple, non-technical English so that it can be easily read by non-Christians, people with little education and those for whom English is a second language. It has proved immensely popular, especially among young people.

The New International Version appeared in 1973, a translation made by a team of evangelical scholars, most of them in America. It has proved highly successful among the evangelicals for whom it is intended.

Something now had to be done for those who were finding this departure from the Authorised tradition unacceptable. In 1983 the Revised Authorised Version, or New King James Version, was published in the style of the old 1611 version, but in modern English. It has become a strong rival to the NIV.

And most recently, in 1989, the New Revised Standard Version appeared, a fresh translation using non-sexist language wherever possible, for example 'child' instead of 'son', 'humankind' instead of 'mankind'.

In addition to all these English versions there are now translations available in all the main languages of the world and in many of the minor national and tribal languages. Most of these have been produced in the past two hundred years, made necessary by the thrust of world-wide missionary activity that followed in the wake of the revivals of the eighteenth century. At first they were the work of individual missionaries, but more recently they have tended to be produced by various Bible societies that came into being in the nineteenth century, such as the British and Foreign Bible Society, the Netherlands Bible Society, the American Bible Society, the National Bible Society of Scotland. About sixty such national Bible Societies have now joined forces under the banner of the United Bible Societies, and an organisation known as the Wycliffe Bible Translators was founded in 1934 to see the Bible translated into the thousands of languages that are still without it.

More translation work is being done today than ever before in history. The Bible that has had such an impact on the history of the Church and the world since the time of the ancient scrolls in the days of the kings of Israel still has its ancient power, to bring life to men who do not yet have it in Christ their Saviour.

## HISTORICAL OUTLINE OF BIBLE TRANSLATION

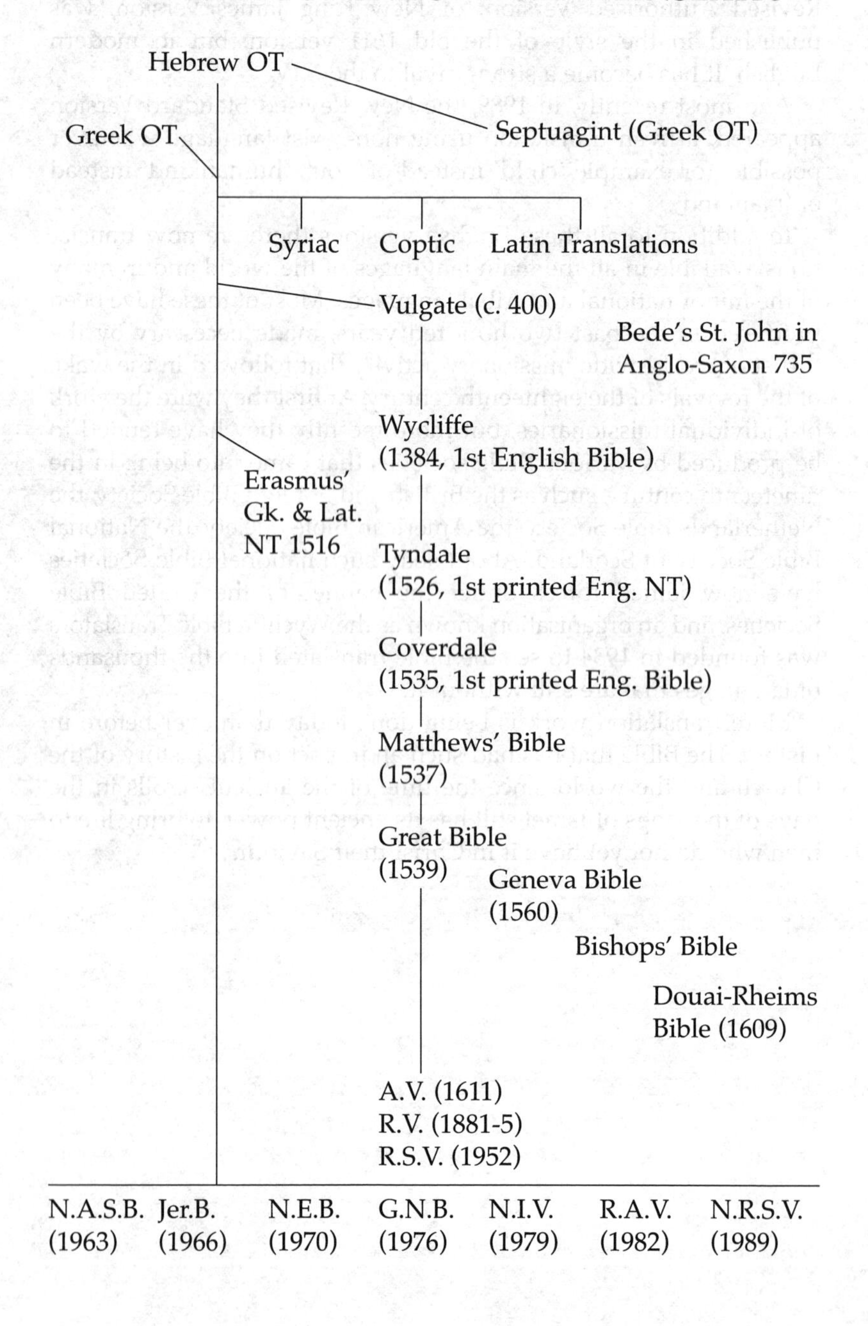
Hebrew OT
Septuagint (Greek OT)
Greek OT
Syriac
Coptic
Latin Translations
Vulgate (c. 400)
Bede's St. John in Anglo-Saxon 735
Wycliffe (1384, 1st English Bible)
Erasmus' Gk. & Lat. NT 1516
Tyndale (1526, 1st printed Eng. NT)
Coverdale (1535, 1st printed Eng. Bible)
Matthews' Bible (1537)
Great Bible (1539)
Geneva Bible (1560)
Bishops' Bible
Douai-Rheims Bible (1609)
A.V. (1611)
R.V. (1881-5)
R.S.V. (1952)
N.A.S.B. (1963)
Jer.B. (1966)
N.E.B. (1970)
G.N.B. (1976)
N.I.V. (1979)
R.A.V. (1982)
N.R.S.V. (1989)

# Authors Note 2

**All the Lord's People Prophets?**

So far we have asked the question and showed how from the beginning there was always the potential for it to receive an affirmative answer. We then saw how the affirmation did indeed come, first in prospect through the Old Testament prophets, and then in fact through the ministry of Jesus and the early Apostles. However, after the first flush of pentecostal enthusiasm in the early Church, while many Christians continued to enjoy the fruit of prophetic anointing, the majority by late Roman times had lost sight of the Church of the Spirit. The vision was recaptured and revived periodically by a few individuals and groups in the Middle Ages, but Church thinking then was for the most part locked up in Neo-Platonic categories that allowed little place for a biblical understanding of the Spirit's work. In the course of the Renaissance and the Reformation that stranglehold was broken and many Christians began to look at the Bible with fresh eyes, thus preparing the way for the rediscovery of prophetic faith.

The rest of this book tells how the foundational prophetic potential in Christian faith has been rediscovered since the Reformation and has progressed towards fulfilment in more recent times. Beginning with the quiet longings and prayers of the English Seekers in the seventeenth century, we shall trace the story of the turbulent prophetic proclamation of George Fox and the early Quakers in England, the militant Prophets from the South of France who followed them at the beginning of the eighteenth, and the Shakers who were born out of an amalgam of both and took their gospel from England to America, where it flourished for a while in the nineteenth century, but died out in the twentieth.

We then trace the parallel, and much more successful stream, that started in seventeenth century Germany and was known as Pietism, how it helped to spark off the revivals in England and America in the eighteenth and led in the nineteenth to a growth of longing for Christian perfection or holiness and for the restoration of primitive apostolic Christianity in which the power of the Holy Spirit was so evidently at work. We shall then see how the prayers of those who sought such things were answered dramatically at the beginning of the twentieth century and how Pentecostalism has grown to embrace about a third of all Christians alive today.

While it cannot yet be said that all the Lord's people are prophets, the momentum in that direction is greater today than at any time since the first century. The potential is truly there, and it is being rapidly fulfilled. But none of this, as we shall see, is without a greater and fuller purpose.

PART SIX

# PROPHETIC AWAKENINGS IN AN AGE OF RELIGIOUS INTOLERANCE

Something new started to happen in the seventeenth century, a stirring of prayer and an awakening of faith that initiated a process towards a move of God every bit as powerful and far-reaching as that which gave birth to the Reformation. This is the point at which we start our history of the present-day Pentecostal revival, with the expressed longings of the Seekers, a largely nameless people, who began to seek and pray for it to come into being.

The Reformation had spread swiftly, like a mighty river in flood, sweeping whole communities in northern Europe into one of the three main forms that Protestantism took, Lutheran, Calvinist (Reformed), or Anglican, and releasing Christians everywhere into a fresh revelation of faith and a wonderful rediscovery of the Bible. Its early years were marked by great gospel enthusiasm, so much so that it could well have led Europe directly into revival and a world-wide thrust of evangelism. But it did neither, for it was itself tarnished by strife, compromise and intolerance, and sadly the churches that emerged in the latter half of the sixteenth century bore little reflection of that first zeal.

The reformers argued not only with their Catholic opponents, but also among themselves, mainly over doctrinal issues, such as the Eucharist and baptism, and matters of church order. Fear lest excess might spoil what they were achieving, or even spark off military reprisals, restrained some of them and compelled moderation in their reforms. But the consequence of their compromise was that the new churches became official state churches, just like the Catholic Church had been before them, though much more academic and doctrinaire, and every bit as intolerant.

The new system had little place for the prophetic or the miraculous. Indeed, it positively quenched any momentum in that direction and produced a doctrinal and religio-political structure that excluded it. The Protestant churches ran quickly into dryness, leaving plenty for men of a prophetical bent still to do.

Late in the first half of the seventeenth century their prayers, those of earnest seekers, began to rise to heaven; about the middle of the century a first spring of Holy Spirit-inspired proclamation burst forth in England; by the end of it a prophetic fountain was pouring out of France and a mystical flowing had started again in Germany; then suddenly the flood broke in the mighty revivals of the next century, preparing the way for the movement towards the massive Pentecostal outpourings of our own time.

# 19

# From Fox to Wesley

The aridity of the Protestant churches in the early seventeenth century was not entirely the fault of their members at the time, but also the heritage of their founders in the century before. Opportunities for prophetic revival had not been lacking at the time of the Reformation, but they were not taken up, rather firmly suppressed.

### *The Quenching of Prophecy at the Reformation*

Both Luther and Calvin were keen students of Augustine, from whom they gained many rich insights into salvation through God's grace. However, in reaction to the unbiblical and superstitious views of the medieval Church relating to miracles through relics, pilgrimages, invocation of the saints and the like, they rejected his later teaching about healing and charismatic giftings in favour of his earlier view that the gifts were given to empower the Church in its first, formative years. Calvin argued often against any continued ministry of healing or the miraculous after apostolic times. He wrote, for example,

> 'That gift of healing, like the rest of the miracles, which the Lord willed to be brought forth for a time, has vanished away in order to make the new preaching of the gospel marvellous for ever. Therefore, even if we grant to the full that anointing [of the sick] was a sacrament of those powers which were then administered by the hands of the apostles, it has nothing to do with us, to whom the administering of such powers has not been committed'[227]

Luther's views, though generally more moderate than Calvin's, became in this respect quite similar. As we have seen, he was much influenced by the German mystical tradition in his earlier years, but his encounters with the Zwickau Prophets and his dealings with the Anabaptists caused him to turn away from things prophetic, which

227. *Institutes*, IV.19.18.

he lumped together with all other forms of excess under the heading he used to describe any who exhibited extraordinary enthusiasm, *Schwärmer*.

Protestants, out of veneration for their founding fathers, have generally accepted their views without asking too many questions. Nowhere, however, was the reformers' antipathy to 'spiritual' Christianity made more evident than in their treatment of the Anabaptists.

The Anabaptists were among many in Europe who thought the reforms were not thorough enough. The name embraces a number of different Continental groups that, among other things, upheld believer's baptism and refused infant baptism. Besides Müntzer's following, which died with the suppression of the Peasant's Revolt, there was a group led by Balthasar Hübmaier in Switzerland and South-West Germany, another in Moravia under the leadership of Jacob Hutter (the Hutterites), one in North-West Germany under Melchior Hoffman, and yet another that tried to set up a Kingdom of the Saints at Münster under a Dutchman called Jan of Leyden, whom they acknowledged as 'King Emmanuel'. Both the Catholics and the Protestants sought to suppress these movements by force and much blood was shed. Thousands were put to death in the persecutions.

The various groups emphasised different doctrines, some excellent, others strange. Jan of Leyden's group brought terrible disrepute to the movement by practising polygamy, but it was eradicated after the siege of Münster. Menno Simons worked to rescue the Anabaptist cause in Holland and his following survives today among the Mennonites, a politically pacifist and theologically liberal church found mainly in Holland, Germany, Canada and the United States. Anabaptism was found in England in the sixteenth century almost exclusively among refugees from Europe.

Some of their views may have been strange, but their basic tenets were similar to those held by many Christians today. They said that the sprinkling of infants had nothing to do with biblical baptism, that it was not a baptism at all, and so they did not like the name 'Anabaptist' (Rebaptiser) that was given to them. They also held that the Church of Christ was not an organisation governed by men, but a body of believers, an assembly of those born again in Christ. Some of them taught that Christians should be guided, not by human dictates, but by the 'inner light' of Christ, or the direction of the Holy Spirit, a doctrine that surfaced again with great power in England in the teaching of George Fox in the next century.

The movement spread rapidly and groups appeared all over Europe. They were not charismatics, but some of them did provide the kind of illuminist context in which prophetic faith could have been fostered. However, Luther, Zwingli and Calvin all denounced them as dangerous schismatics, and even approved of the way they were dealt with by persecution. At the beginning of the seventeenth century there was little evidence in Europe of anything that could be identified as the Church of the Spirit. Protestantism was well and truly established, but equally the prophetic voice was well and truly stifled.

*Sectarian Heresy in England before the Seventeenth Century*

The heretical movements that plagued the Catholic Church in Europe from the twelfth century onwards had no serious counterparts in England, where Christianity remained fairly solidly orthodox throughout the late Middle Ages. In the early fourteenth century a religion of the Spirit surfaced in the wave of mysticism that rippled through the country but, like the majority of their contemporaries in Germany and elsewhere, the English mystics either remained devoted to the Church, as did Julian of Norwich, for example, or else, like Richard Rolle, or the author of *The Cloud of Unknowing*, they did not present their spiritual awareness as something that made them hostile to the Church.

The teachings of Wycliffe and his Lollards produced a change of climate in the second half of the century, and their dissenting voices echoed round England throughout the fifteenth, for the most part underground, preparing the way for the English Reformation. Even so, the Catholic Church was still able to maintain its authority and sustain uniformity of religion.

Everything suddenly changed when Henry VIII broke away from Rome in the 1530s. The monasteries and their orders, that had dominated English life for centuries, were dissolved and their properties were seized by the crown. Parish churches changed almost overnight from Latin Mass shrines to English preaching houses. The Bible, that had been locked away from the people for so long, was made available in the vernacular in every parish church in England. And all worship was conducted in English.

After the brief reaction in the 1550s, when Queen Mary tried to restore Catholicism, Elizabeth I saw the Church of England firmly established in the Anglican form it has had ever since. Though the majority of Englishmen accepted the new system, many others, who became generally known as Puritans, were not happy with the compromise it entailed. The consequence was continuing religious unrest, persecution now being directed against those who refused to conform to the new Anglican code, whether Puritans inside the church or Catholics who stood outside it. To be sure, the Bible was now an open book, but the religious and political domination of the state church remained. Orthodoxy had been redefined, but it still demanded uniformity of religion, just as the old Catholic system had done, and was still prepared to persecute in order to establish and sustain it. At the end of the sixteenth century there was little place for any sectarian voice.

However, the Reformation had brought another form of change as well, not one of externals and structures, but an inner and spiritual one, of freedom to seek after personal faith. And that encouraged many to continue searching for even freer forms of belief and practice. Europe and Britain differed slightly in how they dealt with this new freedom. In Europe there was far greater emphasis on uniformity of doctrine and there men died for their beliefs. In Britain the emphasis was more on uniformity of practice, and it seems men were generally much more free to question and hold their own beliefs, so long as they accepted the outward forms and disciplines of the Church. Either way, the new teaching from the Bible was now heard in most pulpits as men everywhere began to discover the great reforming truth of salvation by faith in Christ alone. Though the Church in its revised form retained its pre-Reformation status as an institution of the state, it could no longer claim the saving authority the old Catholic system had appropriated for itself. Christianity came more and more to be understood as a matter of personal relationship between the individual and his God. It was therefore inevitable that conflict should erupt, and when it did in the next century Church and state were unable to contain the spiritual explosion.

*England in the Seventeenth Century*

At the beginning of the century England had three distinct groupings of Christians. First there were the Romanisers, who sought reunion with the Catholic Church and who held power for a short time during Mary's reign. Then there were the Anglicans, who were happy with the moderate reforms accomplished mainly in the reigns of Henry VIII and Elizabeth I. And third, there were the radical Puritans who wanted a Calvinistic establishment as in Geneva and Scotland.

This was not an age noted for religious or political toleration. Puritans, because they were highly critical of what they considered laxity in the Church of England, suffered a lot of persecution. Their hopes for toleration rose for a while when James I, himself a Scottish Presbyterian, became king of both nations in 1603, but it was not long before they were disappointed. The only real concession he gave them was a promise to authorise the 1611 translation of the Bible. He too sought to impose Anglican uniformity, and so many of his citizens began to cross the Atlantic in search of freedom to live and worship as they saw right, among them the 'Pilgrim Fathers' who sailed to New England in the 'Mayflower' in 1620. After Charles I became king in 1625 the persecution of Puritans intensified and the court became more and more Catholic in ethos. The exodus to America increased yearly and for a moment it seemed the Catholic party might have won. But now other forces were also at work.

These tensions, coupled with political strife between Charles I and Parliament, led to the outbreak of the English Civil War. That lasted seven years, from 1642 to 1649, ending with the execution of Charles and the establishment of the Commonwealth and Protectorate, when the Puritans ruled England under Oliver Cromwell until 1658 and then under his son Richard until 1660. In typical Puritan style, Cromwell's rule was strong and efficient, with the result that England came to be feared and respected abroad.

The English, however, had no great liking for the Puritan government he imposed on them, and so they invited Charles II, the exiled heir to the throne, to return and restore the monarchy. During his reign (1660-85) the Anglican Church was re-established in its moderate form. His son and successor, James II, ruled foolishly for three years, trying to imitate the despotic style of government of the grand monarchs of Catholic Europe, seeking also to restore Catholicism, but England would no longer tolerate such behaviour. In 1688 he was deposed and his daughter, Mary, who was married to William of Orange, was invited along with her husband to take the throne, but on strict condition that the Church of England be recognised as the state church. The following year an Act of Toleration was passed, ensuring that every man in Britain should be relatively free to worship God in his own way. Locally, Christian enthusiasts would still suffer for their faith, and it would take another hundred and fifty years before all penalties against Catholics and Dissenters were finally removed, but the change in governmental policy marked the end of persecution by the state for failure to conform, and Christians everywhere were released to listen more closely to the voice of the Spirit.

*Sectarianism and Dissent in Britain*

During the course of the seventeenth century three main streams emerged in Puritanism: Presbyterian, Congregational and Baptist. The Presbyterians wanted a form of church government akin to that established in Scotland. The Congregationalists, or 'Independents' as they were also called, sought independence for each local congregation. The main plea of the Baptists, who had managed to establish themselves early in the century, was for adult believer's baptism. Their first church was started in England in 1612.

Before 1688 these were all considered parties within the Church of England, but after that date they were recognised as 'Dissenters', allowed to organise themselves independently and granted freedom to worship in their own way. It was during the years of the Civil War that some of the leading Puritan divines met at Westminster and drew up their famous 'Westminster Confession of Faith' and the Longer and Shorter Catechisms, still regarded as foundational in Presbyterian and Congregational circles, and also now in the United Reformed Church, which represents a union of the two.

About the time of the Commonwealth a plethora of new movements and sects appeared, particularly on the Puritan wing of the church. Few of these were welcomed by any of the main streams and some were persecuted as heavily by the Puritans as by the Anglicans. In a book published in 1646, entitled *Gangroena* (Gangrene), Thomas Edwards, a Presbyterian, described a hundred and seventy-six of them, what he called 'errors, heresies, blasphemies'. Some were well enough known in their day, like the Ranters, who were antinomian free-thinkers, and the Fifth Monarchy Men, who supported Cromwell for a time, believing they were helping him to usher in the millennium (the 'fifth monarchy' of Dan. 2:44). Others were ephemeral and made little impact.

Among these more fringe sects were several that inclined to illuminist teachings about the inner, guiding light of the Spirit, or to related doctrines about fullness of the Spirit, such as the Anabaptists and the Familists, both of which came to this country from the Continent. But nowhere among them all was there any movement that could properly be called prophetic or charismatic. One, however, that did become very widespread and provided an excellent context for such a faith, was that known as the Seekers, which we shall look at more closely in a moment.

More important for our purposes than any of these, apart from the Seekers, was the emergence of the Quaker movement, or the

Society of Friends, towards the end of the Civil War. George Fox, its founder, started his highly unorthodox, revival preaching in 1647, suffering frequent imprisonments as a result. He and his followers enjoyed some moments of freedom in the 1650s, during the Commonwealth when the Puritans ruled England, though even then they suffered greatly. After the restoration of Anglicanism under Charles II in 1660, life became increasingly difficult for them, but they continued to grow both in numbers and influence, until they eventually gained their freedom along with everyone else in 1689.

*The Church in Europe in the Seventeenth Century*

European Church history in the 1600s is blemished by the bitter wars of religion in the first half of the century and by the severity of continuing persecution in the latter half. The century opened in an atmosphere of spiritual truce in some areas. The Peace of Augsburg in 1555 had secured recognition of Lutheranism (but not Calvinism) in the parts of Germany where it had become established. Protestantism and Catholicism were both tolerated in Switzerland and Poland. In Holland Catholicism, Lutheranism, Calvinism and Anabaptism were all permitted. Catholics and Calvinists coexisted in France, but Catholicism was forbidden in Scotland and England, while Protestantism was banned in Spain and Italy. The lines had been drawn, but an underlying unease remained, surfacing from time to time in local tensions and skirmishes.

The issues at stake in the Thirty Years War that started in 1618 were a complex mixture of the religious and the political, so much so that, although the initial conflict was one between Catholics and Calvinists, the lines of allegiance were not always clearly drawn. When the Catholic troops of the Holy Roman Empire were winning their initial victories, sweeping all before them, Lutheran Saxony did not come to the aid of the Protestant states, not until it was itself invaded much later in the war. Help came first from the neighbouring Protestant states of Bohemia, Austria and Denmark, though to no avail. But then Lutheran Sweden entered the fray and the tables began to turn. Perhaps most surprising of all was the part played by Catholic France. Abetted by the Pope himself, it gave its support to the Protestant coalition, but its purpose was more political than religious, namely to prevent the Holy Roman Emperor, the Spanish Ferdinand II, from becoming too powerful.

Though religious considerations clearly diminished as the war proceeded, they were certainly not forgotten, and the treaty that ended the war in 1648, the Peace of Westphalia, resettled the borders of Protestant and Catholic power within the various nations and states as they had been in 1624. The consequence was religious liberty for each state, but not yet for individuals, at least not in most countries.

The war had been fought with horrifying bitterness and it left massive devastation in the heart of Europe. German unification was for the time being made impossible, but the various states now began to build despotic regimes within their own borders. Spain, though diminishing in power and prestige abroad, became more dictatorial at home. But it was France that emerged from the war as the most powerful and the most absolutist of the nations of Europe, attaining the peak of its splendour during the long reign of Louis XIV, 1643-1715.

The greatest loser after the war was probably the Pope. As the states of Europe, both Catholic and Protestant, strengthened themselves in despotic independence, his voice carried less and less weight, indeed went largely unheeded. Outside Italy the Catholic national churches became virtually independent of the Vatican and a variety of different attitudes to dissent developed as history moved into and through the eighteenth century. While the Spanish Inquisition continued to torture and burn, Austria and Tuscany eventually allowed almost total freedom of worship. But it was France, even though it was Europe's hot-bed of rationalism and socialism in the 1700s, that now set the course of Roman orthodoxy, and it continued to do so right up till 1815. Its record is a strange, sad and sometimes violent mixture of tolerance and intolerance.

The Protestant churches after 1648 settled down to develop in relative peace, but the war had left many countries in a low and depressed condition. During the fighting both sides had been so occupied with the struggle that neither had found much space to think of higher spiritual things and, now that it was over, morale in the churches, instead of starting to rise, began to sink even further. The same was true in England after 1688. The struggles were largely over, but the churches, established and dissenting alike, sank into formalism and lost their impact among the people at large. Moral and social standards declined correspondingly and the nation was in danger of sinking into apathy, inefficiency and corruption.

However, God had other plans. Thanks to an awakening of zeal among a handful of Christians early in the eighteenth century, revival began to spread in Germany, the American Colonies and Britain (a united nation, under a single monarchy since 1603, and now with a common parliament at Westminster since 1707). The story of these revivals belongs in the next chapter, but it may be noted here that they brought Protestant Europe, Britain and America back to God, put fibre into their churches and governments, led to the foundation of several missionary societies, and through them to the expansive evangelism of the nineteenth century.

Since our study is mainly concerned with movements of prophetic faith, we shall only touch the fringes of these great revivals in this book. Our quest, however, is not unrelated to them. They did not appear unheralded. Much of the preparatory work was done by prophetical men and movements in England, France and Germany that shook the increasingly sterile and complacent churches and societies of Britain and Europe from the middle of the seventeenth century onwards. We shall see, for example, that the strange activities of the French Prophets in London did much to prepare England for the shock of the revival preaching that came with Wesley and Whitefield. Their story starts in 1685 when the French Protestants lost the liberty of worship they had enjoyed for almost a century, but we must start our own story earlier than that, with the radical preaching of George Fox and the prayers of those Seekers who before him called out to God in longing for the birthing of a true Church of the Spirit.

In this age of intolerance none of these movements had an easy time. Theirs was a costly witness, but it helped to break the religious mould that bound the churches and helped to get the Lord's people ready for the great awakenings that were soon to follow.

*Continuing Intolerance in the Eighteenth and Nineteenth Centuries*

After a time of bitterly harsh persecution at the end of the seventeenth century, life became easier for Protestants in France, though locally they still suffered from sporadic outbreaks of hostility. And it continued so until after the Revolution. The German states became more tolerant, Spain less so. Generally speaking, those nations that opened themselves to the waves of rationalism and industrialisation that began sweeping through Europe in the eighteenth century became more tolerant, those that retrenched behind barriers of tradition less so.

In Britain the Act of Toleration gave legal recognition to dissenters, but it took much longer for popular religious attitudes to change. In Scotland the Act was followed by severe repressive action against the Episcopal Church, but the motives for that were as much political as religious, since the Episcopalians gave their support to the

Jacobite uprisings of 1715 and 1745 and it was only after these had been squashed that conditions started to ease. In England political considerations became less important once the threat of foreign interference was removed, after the monarchy and the government were established in Protestant hands. Then, by the time the Roman Catholic Relief Act of 1829 was passed, permitting Catholics to hold public offices and sit in Parliament once more, the mood had so moderated that only a handful of churchmen objected, and only verbally. Interests had radically changed by the early nineteenth century, for Church politics had been overtaken by the politics of industry and commerce. The cut-throat competition was no longer between denominations, but between financiers and industrialists.

That, however, did not eradicate all persecution. There remained a grave suspicion of anything that seemed strange or extreme, anything that smacked of 'enthusiasm', which was viewed as a fearful thing in itself, and a sufficient charge on which to hale anyone before a church court or council. Besides, there were still civil laws that could be invoked to have enthusiasts sent to jail or punished, such as those relating to Sabbath breaking, blasphemy, disturbance of the peace, or inciting to riot. They were applied from time to time, though with decreasing frequency.

Sometimes, of course, men have taken the law into their own hands and caused religious enthusiasts to suffer terrible acts of violence. That has been particularly true in America where, right down into the twentieth century, we read of churches being burnt, people beaten or driven from their homes, and even murdered. The early Pentecostals suffered much in those ways, but today the mood is somewhat different. The most widespread form of persecution now is either pagan or political, just as it was in Roman times, coming not from churchmen threatened by extremes, but from rulers seeking to impose their own form of political uniformity. The toll of Christian suffering under Communism is immeasurably greater than any in past history, but that too has had its day in most places. Though there is still persecution by atheistic socialists, the main thrust of oppression now comes from petty dictators, grass-roots pagans and Islamic fundamentalists.

The movements we shall study in this section were all birthed amid persecution of the older, more religious sort. That too is still found in our time, particularly in certain Catholic and Orthodox settings. The effect it has generally had on prophetic movements has been to drive them in on themselves, to make them self-protective and therefore ultimately exclusive, which is always the converse of their original hope and vision. In the long run, that has meant their influence has been less extensive and lasting than it could have become in other circumstances. None the less, they are all part of the same general prophetic tendency that has led to the explosive growth of Pentecostalism in our day.

# 20
# Seekers and Quakers

While the Reformation produced no prophetic movement in Britain, about the time of the Commonwealth, alongside the churches and the many new sects, though no part of any of them, there were found all over the land groups of men and women who had set themselves to wait for the advent of a new Church of the Spirit. They were not themselves a church, a sect, or even an organisation, for they had no bureaucracy, no buildings and no leaders. Rather they were a movement, or perhaps better, an expression of a tendency. In their day they were commonly known as 'Seekers'.[228]

*The Seekers and their Expectation of a New Church of the Spirit*

The Seekers were not charismatics, but they did have positive prophetic hopes and aspirations. They were essentially a mystical, rather than a prophetic movement, in many respects similar to the late medieval German 'Friends of God'[229]. As their name suggests, they had not yet attained the assertive assurance of prophets; their faith was a kind of precursor to that, a seeking after a form of Christianity embracing some such experience of God as prophetic men enjoy.

Their hope was essentially a criticism of and a reaction to the arid formalism and doctrinal intellectualism of the churches of their time but, unlike many others, they expressed their hope in the language and theology of prophetic men. Most of the typical traits of charismatic Christianity that we have noted repeatedly throughout the history of the Church are reflected in the texts that describe their faith, such as yearning for spiritual power and the miraculous, contrasting the carnal and the spiritual, revivalistic zeal for a New Testament expression of Christianity, expectation that a new age of the Spirit is about to dawn in the Church, requirement of high morality among spiritual men, lay-orientated worship, scattered assemblies, anti-

---

228. An excellent and well illustrated account of the Seekers is found in R.M. Jones, *Studies in Mystical Religion*, ch. 19, from which most of the passages cited here have been culled.
229. See above, p. 211.

sacramentalism, and the like. All that is missing is the free recording of visions, prophecies and other such phenomena, which, of course, were the very prophetic experiences they were seeking.

It would be misleading to leave the impression that they were simply seeking experiences, for what they were looking for was a new church, the true spiritual Church. The existing churches, they held, did not have the substance of real Christianity about them, but only the external forms. Hence they did not see it as their calling to establish any church themselves, for that would only create another form, a mere empty shell. The 'Gospel Church', they believed, would be born by the supernatural power of God, and it would be recognised by the miraculous signs that would attend it and by the prophetic endowment of its leaders. Their role was therefore simply to watch and wait, to be 'upper-room Christians' like the early disciples before Pentecost (Acts 1:13).

*Contemporary Accounts of Seeker Faith*

To get the most useful impression of this movement it is probably best to let the original texts speak for themselves. Some of them are critical, but they do at least convey the sense of the movement's aspirations. A very full account of their views is given by a contemporary author, called John Saltmarsh, in a book with the delightful title, *Sparkles of Glory*.

> 'The Seekers find that the Christians of Apostolic times were visibly and spiritually endowed with power from on high and with gifts of the Spirit, and so were able to make clear and evident demonstration of God in the Churches, and all who administered in any office were visibly gifted. All was administered in the anointing or unction of the Spirit clearly, certainly, infallibly. They ministered as the oracles of God. But now in this time of apostasy of the churches, they [the Seekers] find no such gifts, and so they dare not meddle with any outward administrations, dare not preach, baptise, or teach: they find in the churches nothing but the outward ceremony of all administrations, as of bare water in baptism, bare imposition of hands in ordination, etc. Therefore, they "wait" for power from on high, finding no practice of worship according to the first pattern. They wait in prayer, pretending to no certain determination of things, nor to any infallible interpretation of Scripture. They wait for a restoration of all things and a setting up of "Gospel Officers",

"Gospel Churches", "Gospel Ordinances", according to the pattern in the New Testament. They wait for an apostle or some one with a visible glory and power, able in the spirit to give visible demonstration of being sent.'[230]

Other writers were perhaps less sympathetic in their observations, but still conveyed a good sense of their views and activities. Richard Baxter, a prolific Puritan writer, said they

'taught that our Scripture was uncertain; that present miracles are necessary to faith; that our ministry is null and without authority; and our worship and ordinances unnecessary or vain; the true Church, Ministry, Scriptures and Ordinances being lost; for which they are now seeking.'[231]

Another less well-known writer, Thomas Edwards, told of a certain Mr. Erbury, who

'has fallen to many grosse errors and is now a Seeker and I know not what ... He said that within a while God would raise up apostolical men, who should be extraordinary to preach the Gospel ... He spake against gathering in churches and said that men ought to wait for the coming of the Spirit, as the Apostles. In a private meeting, the main scope of his exercise was to speak against the certainty and sufficiency of the Scriptures.'[232]

These comments about the loss of the true Scriptures and about the uncertainty and insufficiency of the Scriptures are probably exaggerations or misunderstandings of Seeker teaching, which is perhaps better expressed by Saltmarsh's comment above, that they were 'pretending to no ... infallible interpretation of Scripture,' that is, that they would not accept any existing human interpretation of Scripture as certain, sufficient, or infallible. The only certainty they were prepared to acknowledge, it seems, had not yet been revealed. That, after all, was what they were seeking.

*Seekers' Practice and their Impact*

We get some slight impression of their meetings from William Penn's preface to George Fox's *Journal*, where he wrote,

230. John Saltmarsh, *Sparkles of Glory*, London, 1648. This is a condensation of his account of the Seekers in pp. 214-21, cited from Jones, pp. 455f.
231. Richard Baxter's *Narrative of his Life and Times*, London, 1696, p. 76, cited from Jones, p. 458.
232. Thomas Edwards, *Gangraena*, 1646, p. 24, cited from Jones, pp. 457f.

> 'They sometimes met together, not formally to pray or preach, at appointed times or places, in their own wills, as in times past they were accustomed to do; but waited together in silence, and as anything arose in any one of their minds that they thought savoured of a divine spring, so they sometimes spoke.'[233]

We do not get the impression of a very large or forceful movement, but one that was fairly widespread, meeting in local groups of house-meeting size. Cromwell seems to have been impressed by their spirit. His favourite daughter, Elizabeth, Lady Claypole, had joined the Seekers and Cromwell wrote about her spiritual condition in a letter (1646) to her sister, Bridget:

> 'She sees her own vanity and carnal mind; bewailing it, she seeks after (as I hope also) what will satisfy. And thus to be a Seeker is to be of the best sect next to a finder, and such shall every faithful, humble Seeker be at the end. Happy Seeker, happy finder!'[234]

Had the Seekers encountered full prophetic or charismatic teaching, many of them would doubtless have seen in it the fulfilment of their hopes. As it was, some of them simply grew tired of seeking and waiting and returned to their local churches. Others turned to Ranterism, a kind of libertine, 'Free Spirit' heresy, a degenerate Christian aberration that William Penn called 'a monstrous birth'.[235]

*Seekers and the Early Quakers*

Many more of them found the satisfaction they were seeking in Quakerism, which though it was hardly what could be described as a charismatic or prophetic movement, did have prophetical qualities in its early days. For example, we read reports of Quaker meetings at which revivalist manifestations, such as falling or shaking, were witnessed and, although these are not in themselves evidences of prophetic activity, they are sometimes associated with the experiences of the prophets, as in the case of Samuel's men in early Israelite times, or later in the Shaker movement of the next century. Report has it that

---

233. Cited from the Eighth (Bicentenary) Edition of *The Journal of George Fox*, issued by the Society of Friends, London, 1902, vol. 1, p. xxv.
234. Thomas Carlyle, *Oliver Cromwell*, New York, 1897, vol. 1, p. 254, cited from Jones, p. 459.
235. On Ranterism, see most fully N. Cohn, *The Pursuit of the Millennium*, pp. 287-330.

> 'At first they did use to fall into violent tremblings and sometimes vomitings in their meetings, and pretended to be violently acted by the Spirit; but now that is ceased …'[236];

or again that

> 'Men, women and little children at their meetings are strangely wrought upon in their bodies, and brought to fall, foam at the mouth, roar and swell in their bellies.'[237]

The records of revival meetings in other ages carry similar reports, but what would have appealed to the Seekers even more than these would have been the news of visitations of the Spirit akin to that on the first Christian Pentecost, like one that took place at Malton in Yorkshire in 1652, when,

> 'at the time called Christmas, nigh two hundred Friends met to wait upon the Lord, and did continue three or four days together, did scarce part night or day I was with them, and twice the mighty power of the Lord was made manifest; almost all the room was shaken.'[238]

In his *Journal* George Fox cites several instances of meetings where he witnessed similar phenomena. Two occasions near the start of his ministry, both in Nottinghamshire, are particularly memorable, but we shall look at these more closely later.

The Seekers and the Quakers are of interest here, not just because they were prophetically inclined themselves, but because they paved the way for prophetic preachers who were to appear in England in the following century. They tilled the soil from which later prophetic groups were to sprout, but before we pursue that story any further we must first look more closely at the life, teachings and ministry of George Fox himself.

*Fox becomes dissatisfied with the religion of his day*

George was born in 1624, the son of devout Leicestershire weaver and a godly mother who showed much understanding for the 'gravity, wisdom and piety that very early shined through' him. He was apprenticed to 'a man, a shoemaker by trade, and that dealt in wool, and used grazing, and sold cattle.' His absolute integrity in

236. Richard Baxter's *Narrative of his Life and Times*, London, 1696, p. 77.
237. From a petition raised against the Quakers in Lancashire, cited from W.C. Braithwaite, *The Beginnings of Quakerism*, 2nd edn., Cambridge, 1961, p. 108.
238. From a letter by Richard Farnsworth to Margaret Fell, dated 7th January, 1653, cited from W.C. Braithwaite, p. 76.

everything was so consistent that 'people had generally a love to me for my innocency and honesty.' (pp. 1f)[239]

In his late teens he became seriously troubled in spirit. What he read in his Bible and what he believed about God did not marry with the conduct he saw among the churchmen of Leicestershire, not even among his Puritan friends and relations. In 1643, searching for something more, he left home and made his way to London, but, he says, 'I was under great misery and trouble there, for I looked upon the great professors[240] of the city of London, and I saw all was dark and under the chain of darkness.' (pp. 2f)

His search led him into some strange encounters with clergymen. He went to one

> 'ancient priest in Mancetter, in Warwickshire, and reasoned with him about the ground of despair and temptations; but he was ignorant of my condition; he bade me take tobacco and sing psalms ... Then I heard about a priest living about Tamworth, who was accounted an experienced man, and I went seven miles to him; but I found him but like an empty cask. I heard also of one called Dr. Cradock, of Coventry, and went to him. I asked him, the ground of temptation and despair, and how troubles came to be wrought in man ... Now, as we were walking together in his garden, the alley being narrow, I chanced, in turning, to set my foot on the side of a bed, at which the man was in such a rage as if his house had been on fire. Thus all our discourse was lost, and I went away in sorrow, worse than I was when I came. I thought them miserable comforters, and saw they were all as nothing to me; for they could not reach my condition. After this I went to another, one Macham, a priest in high account. He would needs give me some physic, and I was to have been let blood; but they could not get one drop of blood from me.' (pp. 4f)

These were agonising years, but they were not to last for ever. His release came in 1647, when he was about twenty-three.

*His Moment of Illumination*

It all started about the beginning of 1646 when he began to receive

239. Page references in brackets after quotations in the rest of this section refer to *The Journal of George Fox*, ed. by E. Rhys, Everyman Edition, 1924, pp.4f. In the text, reference is also made regularly to the date and location of events to help readers find the sources more easily in other editions of the *Journal*.
240. Up to the nineteenth century this term was commonly used of those who professed faith, particularly in revival circles and usually with critical overtones.

revelations—'openings' he called them. Approaching Coventry one day, 'the Lord opened to' him that, contrary to popular teaching that 'all Christians are believers, both Protestants and Papists,' making profession of faith in Christ was not enough, for men had to be 'born of God.' Another day

> 'the Lord opened to me that being bred at Oxford or Cambridge was not enough to fit and qualify men to be ministers of Christ; and I stranged [wondered] at it, because it was the common belief.'

That was soon followed by a revelation that turned him away from attending churches, which he then began to call 'steeple-houses':

> 'It was opened to me that God, who made the world, did not dwell in temples made with hands. This, at the first, seemed a strange word, because both priests and people used to call their temples or churches dreadful [awesome] places, holy ground, and the temples of God. But the Lord showed me, so that I did see clearly, that He did not dwell in these temples which men had commanded and set up, but in people's hearts … that His people were His temple, and He dwelt in them.' (pp. 5f)

Throughout the rest of the year he continued to have 'great openings', but no peace. 1647 began with him still wandering over the country, talking to many people with all sorts of opinions, but finding no help from any of them.

> 'I fasted much, and walked abroad in solitary places many days, and often took my Bible, and went and sate in hollow trees and lonesome places till night came on; and frequently, in the night, walked mournfully about by myself; for I was a man of sorrows in the times of the first workings of the Lord in me.'

However, there were moments of blessing too, when, he tells us,

> '[I] was sometimes brought into such an heavenly joy that I thought I had been in Abraham's bosom.' (pp. 7f)

At length he reached a point where he lost all hope that anyone could ever help him and was at an utter loss about what else to do, and that was his point of breakthrough:

> 'then, Oh then, I heard a voice which said, "There is one, even Christ Jesus, what can speak to thy condition," and when I heard it my heart did leap for joy.'

This experience was to prove determinative for all his understanding of the workings of God in the life of a believer. He tells us God showed him that he had had to find the answer this way so that he would know his faith was not dependent on any man, but only on God, and so that his love, his zeal and his gratitude would be directed to God alone. It was important that he was able to say, 'This I knew experimentally.' By way of explanation he added,

> 'Though I read the Scriptures that spake of Christ and of God, yet I knew Him not, but by revelation.' (pp. 8f)

Not surprisingly experience of God became an essential element in the gospel Fox preached, and so also in the teaching of the early Quakers. It was not that a man believed because he had read or heard the gospel that determined whether he was born of God, but that he knew it by the working of the Spirit within him. Quakers came to speak about this working as 'the Inner Light', 'the Inward Light', or 'the Light Within'. This is not just reason, or intuition, or conscience, but an almost tangible experience of the Spirit of God, usually accompanied by some revelation and some sensation, like the warming of the heart that Jesus' disciples knew at Emmaus (Luke 24:31f). Prophetic men know and understand what this is, and so with Fox's ministry we encounter the pentecostal Spirit once more, after a long gap since the time of the Reformation.

*His understanding is clarified by further revelations*

Fox now tells how he was shown the greatness of God's love that evokes wonder in man, the contrasting oppression of death and the Devil that causes despair, and the effectiveness of the power of God and the light of Christ in dealing with man's lost condition. It is perhaps best to listen to his own accounts of some of these revelations and let them speak for themselves.

> 'One day when I had been walking solitarily abroad, and was come home, I was taken up in the love of God, so that I could not but admire the greatness of His love. While I was in that condition it was opened unto me by the eternal light and power, and I saw clearly therein that all was done, and to be done, in and by Christ; and how He conquers and destroys this tempter, the Devil … and that all these troubles were good for me, and temptations for the trial of my faith … When at any time my condition was veiled, my secret belief was stayed firm, and hope underneath held me as an anchor in the bottom

> of the sea … But, oh! then did I see my troubles, trials and temptations more than ever I had done. As the light appeared, all appeared that is out of the light; darkness, death, temptations, the unrighteous, the ungodly; all was manifest and seen in the light. Then after this, there did a pure fire appear in me: then I saw how He sate as a refiner's fire and as fuller's soap;—then the spiritual discerning came into me, by which I did discern my own thoughts, groans and sighs; and what it was that did veil me, and what it was that did open me …
>
> 'Several things did I then see as the Lord opened them to me, for He shewed me that which can live in His holy refining fire, and that can live to God under His law. He made me sensible how the law and the prophets were until John; and how the least in the everlasting kingdom of God is greater than John …
>
> 'I saw also the mountains burning up, and the rubbish; and the rough and crooked ways and places made smooth and plain that the Lord might come into His tabernacle. I saw many talked of the law who had never known the law to be their schoolmaster; and many talked of the gospel of Christ who had never known life and immortality brought to light in them by it. Though the Lord in that day opened these things unto me in secret, they have since been published by His eternal Spirit, as on the house-top.' (pp. 9f)

Owning such revelations, George Fox was hardly going to be a preacher prepared to compromise. That indeed was the very thing that most people found so difficult about him, that he would not bend, even in the smallest matter. His 'Yes' was always yes, and his 'No' always no, as the gospel said it should be. He was to spend altogether six years of his life in prison, and almost every time he could have avoided it if he had been prepared to bend a little. Though his allegiance to the state was never really in question, yet he was gaoled because he refused to swear the oath of allegiance in court. On that matter he took his stance on the biblical injunction that he must not swear at all and that his Yes was sufficient proof of his allegiance. If the judges could not accept his word at that level, then he would certainly not compromise it. A man prepared to undergo suffering for his integrity over a matter like that was certainly not going to yield over more serious matters of faith and salvation.

*His ministry begins with great power*

Soon after his enlightening he was attending 'a great meeting' of Baptists and many others at Broughton in Leicestershire, when, he tells us,

> 'The Lord opened my mouth, and the everlasting truth was declared amongst them, and the power of the Lord was over them all.'

Shortly after that he

> 'saw the harvest white, and the seed of God lying thick in the ground, as ever did wheat that was sown outwardly, and none to gather it.'

Full of fire, he started to travel around the country preaching and very quickly he came to realise his ministry was going to cause 'a great shaking' among the Lord's people. Sitting one day, in 1648, in a house in Nottinghamshire, he saw

> 'there was a great crack to go throughout the earth, and a great smoke to go as the crack went; and that after the crack there should be a great shaking: this was the earth in people's hearts, which was to be shaken before the seed of God was raised out of the earth.'

And straight away be began to see that happen,

> 'for the Lord's power began to shake them, and great meetings we began to have, and a mighty power and work of God there was amongst people, to the astonishment of both people and priests.'

Shortly after, in Mansfield, he says,

> 'I was moved to pray, and the Lord's power was so great that the house seemed to be shaken. After I had done, some of the professors said it was now as in the days of the apostles, when the house was shaken where they were. [Acts 4:31]' (pp. 11-13.)

It was because of continuing experiences like this, both in individuals and at public gatherings, that his followers were soon to be called Quakers.

The effects were dramatic in other ways too, for

> 'many were turned from the darkness to the light within the compass of these three years, 1646, 1647, and 1648.'

His converts began to leave their churches and hold their own assemblies, and

> 'divers meetings of Friends, in several places, were then gathered to God's teaching, by his light, spirit and power; for the Lord's power brake forth more and more wonderfully.'

For Fox and these early Friends, as they called themselves, there was a sense of freshness about it all:

> 'All things were new, and all the creation gave another smell unto me than before, beyond what words can utter.' (pp. 14-16)

As well as conversions and bodily reactions, Fox also tells of miracles, healings, deliverance and the like. One of the first he records happened in 1649 at Mansfield-Woodhouse, where a doctor was trying unsuccessfully to bleed 'a distracted woman' who was bound and had to be held down by force.

> 'I desired them to unbind her and let her alone, for they could not touch the spirit in her, by which she was tormented. So they unbound her; and I was moved to speak to her, and in the name of the Lord to bid her be quiet and still; and she was so. The Lord's power settled her mind, and she mended; and afterwards she received the truth, and continued in it to her death.' (p. 26)

Such events were fairly regular in his early ministry:

> 'Many great and wonderful things were wrought by the heavenly power in those days; for the Lord made bare His omnipotent arm, and manifested His power to the astonishment of many, by the healing virtue whereof many have been delivered from great infirmities, and the devils were made subject through His name; of which particular instances might be given beyond what this unbelieving age is able to receive to bear.' (p. 26)

Needless to say, his ministry was not always welcomed, and right from the start he suffered persecution, sometimes very severe, so much so that he needed the reviving ministration of the Spirit himself. Following the healing at Mansfield-Woodhouse, he was so badly beaten that he

> 'was scarce able to move or stand … yet with considerable effort I got about a mile from the town, and then I met with some people who gave me something to comfort me, because

> I was inwardly bruised; but the Lord's power went through me and healed me.' (p. 27)

It was not the healing that caused the opposition, nor the shaking and other bodily responses to his preaching, so much as his uncompromising message that confronted ministers and their congregations with the challenges of a spiritual and prophetic gospel.

*Fox's teaching about the Spirit and his challenge to the churches*

Fox believed a true minister would have received his call and inspiration straight from God himself, because that call was to mediate between men and God. In his view, any Christian could receive this call and academic training was no substitute for it. What was of first and absolute importance was that a man be born of God and know it by his experience of the light of Christ and the power of the Spirit at work within him.

By contrast, the worldliness of the priests of his day caused him great agony of spirit. Whenever he heard the bells ringing to summon worshippers to the 'steeple-house', it struck at his heart, for he had little time for worldly worship, worldly priests, buildings where a bell was rung, 'just like a market bell,' to gather people to listen to the human learning of a priest who asked them payment for the privilege. True faith was not a matter of any of these things, but of 'the divine power and Spirit of God, and the light of Jesus,' freely given and freely received. That was available to all men everywhere, not just in ornate buildings or by a priest's university-training.

It was right at the start, when he was just beginning to see what the gospel was all about, that Fox realised the centrality of the Spirit in it. First, he saw that a Christian needs the Spirit to enable him to understand the Bible, and that without the Spirit he cannot possibly appreciate what it teaches, no matter how many academic qualifications he might have. This was one of his earliest discoveries:

> 'I saw that none could read John's [the Baptist's] words aright, and with a true understanding of them, but in and with the same divine Spirit by which John spake them ... none could know how death reigned from Adam to Moses, &c., but by the same Holy Spirit that Moses, the prophets, and John were in. They could not know the spiritual meaning of Moses', the prophets', and John's words, nor see their path and travels, much less see through them and to the end of them into the kingdom, unless they had the spirit and light of Jesus; nor could they know the words of Christ, and of His apostles,

> without His spirit. But as man comes through, by the spirit and power of God, to Christ who fulfils the types, figures, shadows, promises, and prophecies that were of Him, and is led by the Holy Ghost into the truth and substance of the Scriptures, sitting down in Him who is the author and end of them; then are they read, and understood with profit and great delight.' (p. 19)

Second, he saw an urgent need to call people out of the faithless steeple-houses they called churches, into the true Church of Christ 'made up of living stones, living members, a spiritual household.' Though this message naturally roused the leaders of both established and dissenting churches to indignation against him, there were plenty who were ready to listen, like the Seekers, who were already moving towards a religion of the Spirit. To them, Fox's teaching about the Church must have been like music in their ears, for the work of the Spirit was entirely central in his doctrine of the Church.

> 'But with and by this divine power and Spirit of God, and the light of Jesus, I was to bring people off from all their own ways, to Christ, the new and living way; and from their churches which men had made and gathered, to the Church of God, the general assembly written in heaven which Christ is the head of; and off from the world's teachers, made by men, to learn of Christ ... ; and off from all the world's worships, to know the Spirit of Truth in the inward parts, and to be led thereby; that in it they might worship the Father of spirits, who seeks such to worship Him; which Spirit they that worshipped not in, knew not what they worshipped. And I was to bring people off from all the world's religions, which are vain; that they might know the pure religion, might visit the fatherless, the widows, and the strangers, and keep themselves from the spots of the world; ... And I was to bring them off all the world's fellowships, and prayings, and singings, which stood in forms without power, that their fellowship might be in the Holy Ghost, and in the Eternal Spirit of God; that they might pray in the Holy Ghost, and sing in the Spirit, and with the grace that comes by Jesus; making melody in their hearts to the Lord, who hath sent His beloved Son to be their Saviour.' (p. 21)

To him it was fundamental that it is the Spirit that teaches us truth. A priest in Nottingham was once explaining that Scripture was the measure of truth, when Fox interrupted him: 'Oh, no, it is not the Scriptures,' he cried out.

> 'But I told them what it was, namely, the Holy Spirit, by which the holy men of God gave forth the Scriptures, whereby opinions, religions, and judgments were to be tried; for it led into all Truth, and so gave the knowledge of all Truth. The Jews had the Scriptures, and yet resisted the Holy Ghost and rejected Christ.' (p. 24)

To Pentecostals and Charismatics today such teaching is not strange, but in Fox's day it seemed so. The common view in Protestantism was the one expressed by Calvin, that the operation of the Spirit in prophetic gifting belonged exclusively to the first ages of the Church and was not continuous into modern times. The very fact that there were many seeking and praying for a restoration of pentecostal faith and that Fox had searched up and down the land without finding anyone who could tell him the truths he learned through his openings, these things are in themselves telling about the state of belief at the time. Fox's teaching therefore had something like the effect of an earthquake in his day. He declared boldly that as it was in Bible times, so it is still. The voice of the Spirit spoke then, and it is still his voice that speaks to the churches. He put it this way in a sermon he preached in 1673:

> 'Some have objected, that although Christ did speak both to His disciples and to the Jews, in the days of His flesh, yet since His resurrection and ascension He doth not speak now: the answer is, that as God did then speak by His Son in the days of His flesh, so the Son, Christ Jesus, doth now speak by His Spirit. Wherefore John saith in the Revelations, "He that hath an ear, let him hear what the Spirit saith to the Churches" (Rev. ii).' (p. 313)

Fox taught that the 'power of the Spirit' or 'light of Jesus' operated inwardly in the heart, just as it had for him in his early openings and continued to do throughout his life. It was this that Quakers have called 'the Inner Light', and it has become a distinctive of their faith, though the more quietist version of it that tends to be the norm today is not quite what it was in Fox's experience.

*Healing and Miracle Ministry*

Miraculous accompaniments continued to attend his ministry right to the end and are well documented in his *Journal*. A few instances will have to suffice as examples here.

At Twy-Cross in 1650 he visited 'a great man, that had long lain sick and was given up by the physicians,' and after he 'spake the word of life' and prayed for him he was restored to health. (p. 29) At a meeting in Arnside in 1653 a Prophet Myer had his lame arm restored when Fox spoke a word of command. 'His parents could hardly believe it; but after the meeting was done, they had him into a house, took off his doublet, and then saw it was true.' (pp. 81f.) In the same year he saw a mad woman in Carlisle, and another woman somewhere else, who was so 'distracted and very desperate' that she had attempted to kill her family, both restored to their proper senses. (p. 93)

Some of the healings he saw were very remarkable indeed, like that of a woman who was brought to him in Bishoprick 'tied behind a man, that could neither eat not speak, and had been so a great while,' or an eleven-year old boy in Hawkshead, lying helpless, dirty and unkempt 'in the cradle which rocked.' Three years later the boy's parents told him how they had found him after that playing in the streets and how he was now 'grown to be a straight, full youth.' (p. 93.) That healing made a considerable impact on the people of the neighbourhood, as did another at Baldock in Hertfordshire in 1655, when a godly Baptist woman was healed and started a meeting in her home, where 'many hundreds of people have met' since. (pp. 114f.)

Some of his most striking healings are recorded in the diary of his mission to America in 1671-3. There he saw a Friend who was thrown from his horse and broke his neck, raised from the dead, restored to full life and well-being (p. 293), a judge raised up from his sick-bed 'by the power of the Lord' (p. 296), and a woman who was out of her mind restored to her full senses (p. 306). Later, in Holland in 1677, 'there was a woman at the meeting who had gone fourteen years on her hands and knees, and through the wonderful hand and arm of the Lord was restored to her strength again, and can go very well.' (p. 342)

Wonderful as all these accounts are to read, it is obvious from the way Fox has recorded them that they gave him no cause for pride, but only for thankfulness to God. Once, when asked about his healings, he explained his attitude to them in this way, quite simply: 'I told him we did not glory in such things, but many such things had been done by the power of Christ.' (p. 299) George Fox was a humble man. He pointed men to Christ alone, never to himself or his ministry, powerful as it was.

*Quaking, Shaking, Falling, etc.*

Phenomena better known in later times of revival frequently

attended Fox's preaching, both at his public meetings and in personal encounters, bodily reactions to the power of God in his ministry. As we have seen, that began to happen right at the start, in some of his early meetings in 1647 in Leicestershire. It is often said that this was why the nickname 'Quaker' was given to his followers, though Fox himself gives another reason, that they were first called Quakers by Justice Bennet of Derby in 1650 'because we bid them tremble at the word of the Lord.' (p. 34)

Some of his accounts of shaking and falling make quite dramatic reading, at times also a little amusing. In 1652 he was arrested and taken before the magistrate at Patrington, near Hull. Not missing the opportunity, he found himself preaching to this justice and calling him to repentance. Thereupon, he tells us,

> 'As I admonished him, I laid my hand upon him, and he was brought down by the power of the Lord; and all the watchmen stood amazed.' (p. 54.)

After that he went to Tickhill, near Doncaster, where he was mobbed and horribly beaten by the priest and his congregation. He sought refuge with some Friends in the town, and then,

> 'the priest and people coming by the house, I went forth with Friends into the yard, and there I spake to the priest and people. The priest scoffed at us, and called us Quakers. But the Lord's power was so over them, that the priest began trembling himself; and one of the people said, "Look how the priest trembles and shakes, he is turned a Quaker also."' (p. 57.)

Two years later he found himself being taken as a prisoner to face trial in London, escorted by a certain Captain Drury, who had constantly mocked the Quakers and generally made life very miserable for him. That was until one day he

> 'came to me, and told me that, as he was lying on his bed to rest, in the daytime, he fell a-trembling, that his joints knocked together, and his body shook so that he could not get off the bed; he was so shaken that he had not strength left, and he tumbled off his bed, and cried to the Lord, and said he never would speak against the Quakers more, and such as trembled at the word of God.' (p. 106.)

The tremblings were not all individual, but sometimes affected the whole of the assembly. For instance, he tells of an occasion in Carlisle in 1653 when

> 'I preached the truth to the people, and declared the word of life amongst them. The priest got away, and the magistrate desired me to go out of the steeple-house. But I still declared the way of the Lord unto them, and told them I came to speak the word of life and salvation from the Lord amongst them. The power of the Lord was dreadful amongst them in the steeple-house, so that the people trembled and shook, and they thought the steeple-house shook: and some of them feared it would fall down on their heads.' (p. 87.)

Over the following centuries such events would become more and more commonplace in revival settings, but in Fox's day they were highly unusual. They would be seen again at the end of the century among the French Prophets and then in the next at Wesley's meetings and later on in Shaker meetings. Accounts multiply in the nineteenth century until today these things have become an accepted part of revival culture. Fox's ministry indeed represented a first breaking of new ground.

*Prophecy, Discernment and other Spiritual Gifts*

Revivals have not always given birth to prophetic movements, nor vice versa, but there should always be something prophetic in revival and something of revival in the prophetic, for the two have been interrelated since earliest Old Testament times. And so, although Quakerism itself never became a prophetic movement, prophetic anointing was evident in Fox's own ministry. He constantly attributed his actions to the inner promptings of the Spirit and taught his followers to seek the same direction for themselves.

In addition, he tells of occasions where he knew the biblical prophetic gifts were operating in him. The first time he makes conscious reference to that is in an account of a meeting in a village in Cumberland in 1653, where, he says,

> 'I cast mine eye upon a woman, and discerned an unclean spirit in her. And I was moved of the Lord to speak sharply to her, and told her she was a witch; whereupon she went out of the room.'

She was unknown to him before that, but, he discovered, well known in the neighbourhood as a witch. He goes on to comment,

> 'The Lord had given me a spirit of discerning, by which I many times saw the states and conditions of people, and could try their spirits.'

Then he tells of two other occasions when he had discerned women to be witches, and one when he had seen that another was a harlot, which led to her conversion:

> 'I cast mine eye upon her, and said, "Thou hast been a harlot"; for I perfectly saw the condition and life of the woman. The woman answered and said many could tell her of her outward sins, but none could tell her of her inward. Then I told her her heart was not right before the Lord, and that from the inward came the outward. This woman came afterwards to be convinced of God's truth, and became a Friend.' (pp. 85f.)

When he found prophetic gifting in others, he was open to listen to them and test their prophecies. One woman approached him in London in 1657, three years before the restoration of the monarchy, saying she 'had a prophecy concerning King Charles's coming in; and she told me she must go to him to declare it.' He cautioned her 'to wait upon the Lord and keep it to herself; for if it should be known that she went on such a message, they would look upon it to be treason.' But, he adds, 'I saw her prophecy was true.' (p. 175.)

He also tells how prophetic sensitivity once saved him from being arrested at a meeting Lancashire in 1663:

> '... they would have had me to stay their meeting next day; but I was much burdened in my spirit whilst I was in the house. It came upon me to go to John Blaykling's in Sedbergh, and to be next day at the meeting there, which is large, and a precious people there is. We had a very good meeting next day at Sedbergh; but the constables went to the meeting at Anne Auland's to look for me. Thus by the hand and power of the Lord I escaped their snare.' (p. 216.)

*On the absolute need for Christians to have the Spirit*

Fox never revelled in the outward manifestations or his own personal giftings. He was far too aware that they were from God, and so he viewed them with a mixture of awe and thankfulness. He never preached that men should seek after them or glory in them, but he did most emphatically preach the necessity for every believer to receive the Spirit of God for himself. Perhaps the best summary of his teaching on this matter is in his account of his defence at his trial in Lancaster court in 1652.

> 'That which I was moved to declare was this: that the Holy Scriptures were given forth by the Spirit of God, and all people

> must first come to the Spirit of God in themselves, by which they might know God and Christ, of whom the prophets and the apostles learnt; and by the same Spirit know the Holy Scriptures; for as the Spirit of God was in them that gave forth the Scriptures, so the same Spirit of God must be in all them that come to understand the Scriptures; by which Spirit they might have fellowship with the Son, and with the Father, and with the Scriptures, and with one another; and without this Spirit they can know neither God nor Christ, nor the Scriptures, nor have right fellowship one with another.'

That statement evoked a very strong reaction:

> 'I had no sooner spoken these words, than about half a dozen priests that stood behind me burst out into a passion; and one of them, named Jackus, amongst other things that he spake against the truth, said that the Spirit and the letter were inseparable. I replied, "Then every one that hath the letter hath the Spirit; and they might buy the Spirit with the letter of the Scriptures." This plain discovery of darkness in the priest moved Judge Fell and Colonel West to reprove them openly, and tell them, that according to that position they might carry the Spirit in their pockets, as they did the Scriptures. Upon this the priests, being confounded and put to silence, rushed out in a rage.' (p. 78)

Fox spoke with the same assurance and authority that is common among prophetic men. He knew his own place in Christ with absolute certainty and also that the source of that certainty was entirely the witness of the Spirit within him. The heart-longing behind all his preaching was that others might know the same assurance. That, of course, pleased those who longed for it too, but utterly annoyed others who did not have it. His conversation with the magistrates in Derby in 1650 is highly illuminating:

> 'At last they asked me whether I was sanctified. I answered, "Sanctified! Yes"; for I was in the paradise of God. Then they asked me if I had no sin. I answered, "Sin! Christ, my Saviour, has taken away my sin, and in Him there is no sin." They asked how we knew that Christ did abide in us. I said, "By His Spirit, that He has given us." They temptingly asked if any of us were Christ. I answered, "Nay, we are nothing, Christ is all." They said, "If a man steal, is it no sin?" I answered, "All unrighteousness is sin."'

For those who could accept it, the theology was sound enough, but that did not save him. The judges clearly did not appreciate the point, and so,

> 'when they had wearied themselves in examining me, they committed me and one other man to the House of Correction in Derby for six months, as blasphemers.' (p. 30f.)

Just as he taught that the Spirit was necessary to give assurance of salvation and sanctification to the individual, so also he preached that the Spirit was needed in the Church to make it as it should be, the Church of the Spirit, the Church of the Apostles, the Church of Pentecost. When he was in prison in Scarborough Castle in 1665, the governor

> 'brought two or three Parliament-men, who asked me whether I owned [recognised] ministers and bishops. I told them yes, such as Christ sent, such as had freely received, and would freely give, such as were qualified, and were in the same power and Spirit that they were in in the apostles' days. But such bishops and teachers as theirs were, that would go no further than a great benefice, I did not own; for they were not like the apostles.' (p. 240)

*Personal guidance and corporate authority*

Every movement that has encouraged openness to leadings of the Spirit has had to deal at some stage with the problem of false prophecy. Sometimes leaders themselves have become misguided into holding higher opinions of themselves or their ministry, as happened with Nicholas Storch, for example. Fox never had that problem personally, but one of his keenest supporters did

The year was 1656. James Nayler had already suffered greatly through long imprisonments and other ill-treatments when his head was turned by the acclaim directed toward him by a group of personal admirers. He set out to visit Fox when he was in prison, but was himself arrested and imprisoned at Exeter. Fox visited him there and tried to persuade him of his error, but to no avail. He was utterly fixed in his opinion. (p. 137)

On his release he went to Bristol where he rode into the town with his little band of followers crying 'Holy, holy, holy!' And casting down their garments before his horse. He was arrested, and when searched, was found to be carrying a letter saying, 'Thy name shall be no more James Nayler but Jesus.' He was condemned for blasphemy, and taken to London where he was pilloried and whipped. His tongue was bored through with a hot iron, his forehead was branded with a B for blasphemer, and he was imprisoned for the next three years. During that time he came to his senses, admitted his mistakes, was reconciled with Fox, and found his peace with God. In 1660 he was attacked by highwaymen and died.

This episode had a strong effect on Fox himself and on the history of the whole Quaker movement. Fox continued to urge men to heed the witness of the inner light within them, but it came to be seen as essential that they express their opinions among themselves and that their personal guidance be submitted to the collective voice of the Society. Six years after Nayler's death a letter was issued 'asserting the authority of a meeting to exclude from its fellowship persons who persisted in rejecting its judgment.'[241]

*Conclusion and Assessment*

His statements contrasting the church of his day with that of the apostles, like the one he made to the Parliament men at Scarborough Castle, link Fox over the centuries with Tertullian and the leaders of almost every other prophetic movement in between, who have distinguished between a spiritual and a carnal church. The biblical vision of the Church of the Spirit had neither died nor diminished and the spiritual dryness of the seventeenth century highlighted it once again. Fox's preaching sent a tremor running through that parched land of contemporary church life. To the establishment it seemed destructive, but there were plenty for whom it was good news, and Fox saw it himself, 'the seed of God lying thick in the ground.' All over the country there were groups of them, the quiet, faithful Seekers who were praying the pentecostal kingdom back into being.

The Quaker movement grew rapidly, as also did the persecutions. In 1656, Fox records,

> 'the Lord's truth was finely planted over the nation, and many thousands were turned to the Lord; insomuch that there were seldom fewer than one thousand in prison in this nation for tithes, and going to the steeple-houses, and for contempts, and not swearing, and not putting off their hats.' (p. 140.)

He tells that in the following year in Cumberland

> 'most of the people had so forsaken the priests that the steeple-houses in some places stood empty.' (p. 153)

241. Howard Brinton, *Friends for 300 Years*, London, 1952, p. 101.

While some Puritans welcomed the Quakers, and Oliver Cromwell was highly impressed by George Fox himself, the powers of the Commonwealth on the whole took a contrary stance, and the prisons were regularly well populated with Friends, some of whom died there for their faith. A brief moment of respite came when the monarchy was restored, but that was short lived, and if anything the persecution became even more severe. It was only after the Act of Toleration was passed in 1689 that any real freedom came to the movement, but even after that there were still local instances of persecution.

Whether it was the effect of persecution, or the greater establishment that came with the passage of the years, by the end of the century the spirit of the movement was not what it had been fifty years earlier. By then they had ceased to preach against the steeple-houses and become more occupied in commerce and absorbed in social issues. In 1682 William Penn sailed to America and established the new Colony of Pennsylvania, his 'Holy Experiment'. It was ruled by a Quaker parliament for almost three quarters of a century and its capital city, Pennsylvania, became the cultural centre of the New World. Quakers were also found in large numbers in many of the other Colonies and proved to be excellent citizens. But the pristine fire had gone. Early Quakers in America had been arrested, whipped, imprisoned and executed for their outspokenness. Now they were respectable, model citizens and the older prophetic preaching was conveniently forgotten.

The same happened in Britain. The Society of Friends has produced some eminent philanthropists and social reformers in its time, and has been involved in some wonderful works of mercy and charity, but it has stood firmly apart from charismatic and revival moves of the Spirit. Fox taught them to wait in silence for the voice of the Spirit, but it was never for the silence he was put in prison, but rather for his outspoken prophetic preaching. By the end of the seventeenth century Quakers had ceased to appear before the courts on such charges.

Though Quakerism never became a prophetic movement, and though the Seekers disappeared from history, they broke a mould that was in danger of becoming rigidly set. Right at the beginning of his ministry Fox saw that its effect would be like setting

> 'great crack to go throughout the earth, and a great smoke to go as the crack went; and that after the crack there should be a great shaking: this was the earth in people's hearts, which was

to be shaken before the seed of God was raised out of the earth.'

That was a true vision, for it described exactly what his ministry achieved—and that well beyond his own time. But for the crack he made and the shaking he created none of the other prophetic and revival movements that followed would have taken the course they did. He effectively broke up the soil ready for others to cultivate after him. His work marks a new beginning, the prelude to everything pentecostal that has happened since.

# 21
# The French Prophets in the Cevennes

It was in the south of France that the strong prophetic Christians Ireneus spoke about lived and where the martyrs of Lyons told of Montanist activity in the late second century, that the prophet from Bourges attracted his greatest following in the sixth, that the Poor Men of Lyons preached from Waldo's Provençal translation of the Bible in the twelfth, and that Joachim's prophetic views found expression in the Beguin movement of the fourteenth. And it was there at the end of the seventeenth century that prophecy flourished again, but in a manner unparalleled in the annals of Christendom. Perhaps it was, as some have said, the geographical isolation and scenic majesty of the mountain regions of the Cevennes, the Vivarais and the Dauphiné that encouraged separatist attitudes and mystical awarenesses but, for whatever reason, the region had a long history of dissent, not all of it prophetic by any means, particularly from the twelfth century onwards, so much so that by the sixteenth it had become one of the firmest strongholds of Calvinism in France.

By the end of the sixteenth century the French Protestants, popularly known as Huguenots, numbered somewhere between ten and fifteen percent of the total population of the country. In some regions they made up the majority, as in parts of Orléanais, Normandy, Navarre and the Dauphiné, as well as in various major cities. They had suffered some very severe persecution at the hands of the Catholic Church, but in 1598 the Edict of Nantes permitted them a degree of toleration. The peace that ensued was an uneasy one. Cardinal Richelieu, who was to all intents and purposes the ruler of France at the time of the Thirty Years War, saw them as a political threat to national unity and had the fortresses in their towns demolished. Nevertheless, they continued among France's most loyal citizens, and also provided some of their best soldiers, sailors and artisans. Then during the reign of Louis XIV, who believed he ruled by divine right and had greater pretensions to absolute authority than any other reigning monarch in Europe, pressure mounted at court for him to see France become an entirely Catholic nation, with only the one religion.

The pressure finally succeeded. The Edict was revoked in 1685 and open persecution began again in earnest. The history of the resulting carnage, torture, brutality and sheer inhumanity, even if it is lightened occasionally with tales of heroism, makes horrifying reading[242], but fortunately it is not our brief to retell that particular part of their history here. Suffice it to note that, in the years following the revocation, some three hundred thousand from the region sought refuge abroad, while thousands more died or were sent to the galleys. The toll of destruction and depopulation was so heavy that contemporary writers spoke of a once-populous and fruitful land reduced to a desert. Even today, almost 300 years later, the Cevennol region remains one of the most sparsely populated in France and thus continues to witness to this brutality of a past generation. It was in such conditions as these that the French Prophets took their origin.

*Our Sources of Information about the Prophets*

The Prophets' story has come down to us in two different versions that do not always agree. The Catholic is almost entirely antipathetic, generally rationalising and disparaging the prophetic phenomena and highlighting atrocities on the Huguenot side. Such are the writings of Fléchier, de Brueys and Louvreleuil, and modern readers will find something of their attitudes reflected, if somewhat modified, in Ronald Knox's *Enthusiasm*. On the other side are the testimonies of those who were themselves prophets or were involved in the movement, refugees whose reminiscences were published abroad by Pierre Jurieu in his *Pastoral Letters* of 1688-9, written and sent to encourage Huguenot refugees and to let the rest of world know about the sufferings of the Protestants in France. A slightly later edition of witness accounts was published by Maximillian Misson in his *Théâtre Sacré des Cévennes* in 1707, a work that appeared simultaneously in an English translation made by John Lacy under the title *A Cry from the Desart.*[243]

Since our intention is to gain insight into the mind and experience of the prophets themselves, rather than learn the opinions of antagonists, most of what follows here is based on the writings of Jurieu

242. Some accounts of it by Huguenot refugees are preserved in Jurieu's *Pastoral Letters*, 1688-9.
243. 'Desart' is simply the way Jurieu spelt the word 'Desert'.

and Lacy. Inevitably these have all the biases of committed persons, but Lacy informs us in his preface that every care was taken to avoid over-emphasising the miraculous and that each witness was urged 'to say no more than he was able, if legally required, to affirm upon oath before authority.' Such caution was needed at the time, for the wider circle of Huguenot emigrants living in London, where Lacy's translation was published, had little sympathy with the prophets' claims, as we shall discover in the next chapter. Whatever opinions we may form about these records, we must acknowledge our delight in their existence, for they are the first depositions of any prophetic movement since biblical times that have survived the vicissitudes of history.

*Sounds and Voices in the Air*

The first sign of spiritual stirring came fast on the heels of the revocation. Their churches closed, their pastors banished and their worship prohibited under severe penalty, Protestants in various places began to speak about hearing strange sounds in the air, sounds they took to be the voices of angels singing for them the psalms they loved but were no longer permitted to sing for themselves. Most of our information about this phenomenon comes from Jurieu's seventh *Pastoral Letter*, which is composed of accounts by witnesses, together with his own introductory remarks and comments. He opens his letter with the statement

> 'that in many places where there have been formerly churches, voices have been heard in the air, so perfectly like our singing of psalms, that they could not be taken for anything else.' (p. 143)

After a lengthy exhortation to the reader to maintain a balanced attitude to the miraculous, he goes on to tell that the aerial psalmody was first heard in the western province of Béarn, in the autumn of 1685, particularly in the town of Orthez, where it caused great popular excitement, so much so that the magistrates

> 'published an ordinance, whereby they forbade all persons from going out of their houses, or assembling themselves by night for hearing these voices.' (p. 150)

The beauty of the singing and the fact that it was heard mostly in the evenings, though also at other times of the day or night, are repeated topics for comment in the letters that Jurieu published. There is also much discussion about attempts to explain the sounds in terms of echoes or atmospheric disturbances, though the view of the writers that they are of heavenly origin is never in doubt. It also appears that some who heard them believed they were able to identify the particular psalms sung, though others had to admit less certainty:

> 'For my part I do acknowledge that I could not distinguish the words. I only heard a charming music, which represented to me a great number of voices that agreed exceedingly well.' (p. 154)

But all who heard the singing spoke of the same comfort and excitement they experienced in hearing it. One testified that

> 'multitudes of persons, who were ravished with the pleasant melody which they heard in the air … returned to their houses with great consolation' (p. 149),

another that

> 'more than fifty persons … who having heard it fell on their knees and wept through the joy they conceived to hear so incomparable a melody in the air.' (p. 158)

Experiences like these in a setting already highly charged with tension and emotion were hardly likely to pass without further consequences. By the end of the year reports of similar phenomena were heard elsewhere in the Cevennes, but the Cevennols, perhaps because they were naturally a more militant people, heard other sounds intermingled with the songs of consolation and praise. Sounds of drums and trumpets turned their heavenly music into war-songs of the celestial armies preparing themselves for the deliverance of the beleaguered saints. One of Jurieu's correspondents, who wrote about hearing voices, instruments and drum, commented,

> 'Can you imagine that we hear these voices night and day, that we can so much as doubt that they are troops of angels which God sends to us for consolation; to assure us that he has not utterly forsaken us, and that our deliverance is at hand.' (pp. 162f)

Soon it was said that thousands had heard the music and in many different places. In his *Reflections*, Jurieu published a report by one refugee pastor saying he had 'heard the sound of a trumpet, together with a harmony bearing resemblance to the singing of our psalms' in various places in the Cevennes, Upper Languedoc, the Dauphiné and the Savoie, and commenting

> 'that the trumpet sounds always as if an army were going to charge, and that the harmony is like a composition of many

voices, and of an infinite number of musical instruments, and that sometimes more and sometimes less ravishing … I do believe that the trumpet is a sign of a cruel war, that will be made in a little time; and that the harmony comes from the mouths of angels, who to put our enemies in the last confusion, thunder out the praises of God, at a time when these wretched men forbid it to Reformed Christians. This war will most probably be made against those who at this time make it against us in the most barbarous and unjust manner that can be.' (pp. 36-8)

Events were soon to show that the premonitions of the reformed were not unwarranted, though it was not the heavenly harmony, trumpet or drums that would incite the persecuted to rise in resistance. Their music was but an overture to an opera that was to be sung by rather different, more human voices.

*A Catholic's Account of the First Stirrings of Prophecy*

According to Catholic interpretation, at least as presented by de Brueys in his *History*, the outbreak of prophecy could be traced to the strange activities of a glass-blower called du Serre, who lived at Dieu-le-fit in Mont Peyrat in the Dauphiné. His trade took him on frequent journeys across the border to Geneva, and on one of these he obtained a copy of a work by Jurieu entitled *Accomplishment of the Prophecies, or the Approaching Deliverance of the Church*, in which he argued, on the basis of the book of Revelation, that the deliverance of the Reformed Church in France would be accomplished at the end of the decade. Fired by this hope, du Serre began to train some peasant children at his glass-factory in the art of prophecy, breathing into their mouths to convey the gift. Thus prepared, they were sent out preaching and so the contagion spread, especially among their own age group, until by the end of 1688, so de Brueys informs us, their numbers had swollen to some five or six hundred children who were prophesying in the same fashion.

De Brueys also gives his own description of their prophetic 'fits', saying that

'they came upon them with tremblings and faintings, as in a swoon, which made them stretch out their arms and legs, and stagger several times before they dropped down. They struck themselves with the hand, they fell on their backs, they shut their eyes, they heaved with the breast, they remained a while in trances, and coming out of them with twitchings, they uttered all that came into their mouths. They said they saw the heavens open, the angels, Paradise and Hell.'[244]

*The First Prophetess, Isabel Vincent, Shepherdess of Dauphiné*

It is uncertain how far de Brueys' account is to be trusted, for his sources were mostly confessions extracted under duress. Be that as it may, the Protestant version, as we would expect, entirely lacks the derogatory flavour of the Catholic. In the writings of Jurieu and Lacy the du Serre story has no part to play. To them the whole movement has a much more supernatural origin in the experience of a certain Isabel Vincent, sometimes referred to fondly as 'the Shepherdess of the Dauphiné', a peasant girl of about fifteen or sixteen, from the town of Saou in the Dauphiné. Her father was a weaver who had, like many others at the time, abjured the Protestant cause. He forced his daughter to attend Catholic Mass by beating her, but she fled to the home of her uncle, who was also her Godfather, and he gave her charge of his sheep and pigs. It was there that she became the first to experience the prophetic 'ecstasy' that was soon to become widespread.

Several accounts of her experiences and inspired sayings are extant, but perhaps the fullest is given by Jurieu himself in his *Reflections*. After some introductory remarks, he tells that on 12th February, 1688, 'she fell into an ecstasy,' which, he says,

> 'did not seem at first to be any thing else but a sort of apoplexy, or natural lethargy, into which she fell without any appearance of a violent motion. She returned out of it again after having been in it some hours, her health not being in the least impaired by it. In this first fit she neither said nor did any thing extraordinary. Upon the following night … she fell again into those fits, that have held her ever since that time. They did not seem to be any thing but a kind of profound sleep, out of which it was not possible to fetch her. They pulled her, they thrust her, they burnt her, yet nothing would wake her, so that she was in an entire and absolute privation of all sense, which is the true character of an ecstasy. In this condition she spoke …' (pp. 2f)

After some comments to the effect that she was totally illiterate, Jurieu tells us that after the first five weeks, during which the spoke in her ecstasies using her own local patois, the only language she knew,

244. Cited from Lacy, *A Cry from the Desart*, p. 6.

> 'the noise of this miracle being spread abroad, there came people that could speak and understand French. Then she fell a speaking of French, and that in as exact and correct a dialect, as if she had been brought up at Paris, and that in one of the families where they speak French best.' (p. 3)

Jurieu's account of her ecstatic behaviour has a more peaceful flavour than we might have expected after reading de Brueys.

> 'Her motions in delivery are not at all violent, neither does she use any strong agitation of her body. She puts her arms out of the bed, and with them forms certain graceful and well-ordered gestures. Her voice is clear and intelligible, but without affectation. She moves her lips, but it is but slowly, and without any appearance of convulsion. There have been some physicians to view and examine her in this condition, but they could observe nothing in her that savoured of any sickness or bodily infirmity … When she is come out of her ecstasies, she remembers nothing at all of what has passed, nor of what she has said. She affirms that she has slept well, and seems not at all tired after having talked sometimes three, four and five hours together, for her fits are of no less continuance. True it is that she speaks but by fits all this time, and her discourses are not always connected.' (pp. 5f)

This description reminds us of the debates about prophesying 'in ecstasy' among the Montanists[245] and suggests possible similarities between their and the French Prophets' experiences, a point that was not overlooked by critics of the movement at a later date. Jurieu makes no theological comment, but simply notes that the effect of her ecstasies was nothing but beneficial to Isabel herself.

> 'For in the beginning she was observed, after her waking, to return to her natural simplicity, and to the ignorance of a poor shepherdess, and of a country girl without any education, and whose instruction has been wholly neglected. But it is now apparent, by several relations, that her sentiment is become solid; nay, that she has something in her that even sparkles.' (p. 6)

Jurieu also provides fairly detailed descriptions of the nature and content of her ecstatic discourses. Re-emphasising that she was thoroughly illiterate, he tells that, after singing a psalm or uttering a prayer, she would speak at great length on matters of religion and faith,

245. See above, p. 125.

> 'not after the manner of preachers, or in a set method, but in a manner very singular, and always full of good sense; and it being out of the ordinary rules of method, it gives the greater character of divinity to what she says, for we do not find that inspired persons use to follow human methods in their discourses. Her expressions are always very vigorous and touching.' (p. 6)

The theme of her sermon might sometimes be Huguenot backsliding into Catholicism (her own father's sin), or matters of theological controversy between Catholic and Reformed. Her discourses made much use of Scripture and were, of course, totally critical of the Roman Church. Other frequent themes included the judgment of the wicked and the blessing of the faithful or the penitent.

> 'And her promises are not only general and indeterminate ones, but it is very certain that she has made some very particular predictions also.' (p. 5)

Jurieu gives no details about these predictions, but only mentions 'she has promised the church a very sudden deliverance' (p. 6), implying that that was one of her main themes, as indeed it was with most of the prophets who followed her. The same impression is conveyed in other accounts of her preaching published in his *Reflections*. The picture we get is of Isabel in her ecstasies singing psalms, uttering prayers and preaching fairly long sermons urging Protestants to renewed faith, warning them of the dire consequences of defection and encouraging them to hope for the future.

Her activity was abruptly curtailed when she was arrested at the beginning of June, some four months after her first ecstasy. Her interrogators tried every means to prove her an imposter, but her ecstasies continued wherever they put her. Eventually they transferred her to a convent near Grenoble, where they shaved her head, took away her clothes, exorcised her with holy water and put her in fear of her life. We do not know what happened to her in the end.

*The Spread of Prophecy in 1688*

In the months that followed Isabel's first ecstasies, prophetic enthusiasm spread widely and rapidly among the Protestants—as also did the persecutions. De Brueys may not always be the most reliable source, since his views are coloured by his own antagonistic stance, but Lacy seems to have thought his account of the spread of the movement sufficiently reliable to provide the following translation of some excerpts from his *History* in *A Cry from the Desart*.

> 'It is certain that from the month of June, *anno* 1688, unto the end of February following, there arose in Dauphiné, and then in the Vivarez, five or six hundred Protestants of both sexes, who gave out themselves to be prophets ... The sect of the inspired became in a trice numerous, the valleys swarmed with them and the mountains were covered ... This enthusiasm spread itself like a flood, with such a torrent, that a conflagration blown with a wind does not spread faster from house to house, than this fury flew from parish to parish ... the number of prophets was infinite ... there were of them many thousands.' (pp. 5f)

The tide of prophecy was, however, stemmed by the sheer brutality of the subsequent persecution. By the end of 1690 it seemed that mass execution and imprisonment had effectively broken its power. But the fire was not extinguished. It merely subsided for a while and remained smouldering, awaiting another day when it would burst into flame once more.

*The Second Phase in 1700—the Little Prophets*

The second wave of prophecy broke in the year 1700 and in a very short time 'the ecstasy' became as widespread as it had been before. It manifested basically the same characteristics as in 1688 and resulted in the same kind of persecutions, though this time it stirred the Protestants to armed resistance. The experiences of the prophets during this second outbreak are very well documented for us in the first-hand witness accounts published in Lacy's *A Cry from the Desart*, from which all the excerpts in the remainder of this chapter are taken.

One of the first things that strikes us on perusing Lacy's work is the generally youthful age of the prophets. Most of them were probably in their teens and early twenties, and a great number were mere children. We are reminded constantly that the children's utterances were supernatural, far beyond their intellectual capacities. For example, a certain William Bruguier says he once saw a boy

> 'aged about three, who was taken with the Spirit, and being flung to the ground, struck his breast with the hands with all his might; then I heard him say that he suffered much for the sins of his mother; he said that we were in the last times, that we ought to fight bravely the fight of faith, exhorting at the same time to repentance in general.'

He tells also of a four-year old girl

> 'who in my presence fell into the ecstasy, being also struck to the ground; she had near the same motions of body as the other; she spoke louder, in good French, as she could not out of that fit; she said the Church's delivery would soon be; she moved those present to a due regulation of life. Both this and the other infant used in their inspiration these words, "I say to thee, my child."' (p. 35)

James du Bois, another of Lacy's witnesses, claimed to have met about sixty children altogether, between the ages of three and twelve, who prophesied in a like fashion (p. 31), and there are many other similar accounts. Perhaps the most surprising is of a baby of thirteen or fourteen months, still 'in the cradle, which had never of itself spoken a word,' exhorting to repentance (pp. 14f). In a similar vein are stories about adults of childish mentality prophesying beyond their natural capability. A certain Mr. de Caladon tells of 'a poor changeling, a clownish wench of about forty,' of whom he said, 'I believe our mountains never brought forth a creature more stupid and silly,' prophesying in a manner described as 'really excellent.' He adds, 'This very Baalam's ass had a golden tongue when the heavenly influence made her speak.' (pp. 108f)

*The Physical and Emotional Aspects of the Prophetic Ecstasy*

Some of the accounts of the French Prophets' experience are indeed most remarkable. They remind us of the ecstatic activity among Samuel's men, among the Montanists and the followers of the prophet of Bourges, and they find later parallels among the Shakers and in certain contemporary Pentecostalist circles, particularly those influenced by the 'Toronto blessing'[246]. There is some question whether they are of themselves essentially prophetic, for examples of similar phenomena are found in the records of revival meetings throughout Christian history. However, there is an important difference between the prophetic and the revivalist experience, in as much as the former is a prelude or accompaniment to inspired utterance and tends to persist as part of the prophet's regular behaviour for months or even years, while the latter usually accompanies private religious encounters that last only for the duration of the revival meetings and may not issue in any utterance at all.

246. See below, p. 508.

Durand Fage describes how his prophetic experience began one afternoon, when, he says,

> 'I felt of a sudden a weight upon my breast, which for a moment stopped my breathing. At the same instant a flood of tears burst forth and I had power to speak no more … In that condition I continued about an hour and a half …
>
> 'About six o'clock the same evening, being at another house, I was surprised with a shivering all over me, and some agitation. The weight upon my breast was less than before, and here I found a gentle breathing springing up within me, whereat I was surprised a little, though I made no great reflection on it. At the same time my tongue and lips were of a sudden forced to pronounce words with vehemence, that I was myself amazed to hear, having forethought nothing, and no ways intending to speak. The things spoken by me were hortatory of repentance, and this lasted but three or four minutes. Presently after, I fell into a sort of swoon, which went soon over. Then I found a new fit of trembling that lasted but a small time, and after it I was wholly free and in my common temper.
>
> 'For a fortnight ensuing, I had continually sighings and a sort of starting that I could neither prevent or hinder. My mind was always lifted up to God.' (p. 60.)

Lacy's book is replete with such tales. One witness reckoned he had seen about four hundred instances of prophets experiencing

> 'agitations of the head, breast, stomach, arm, or otherwise, which attended their prophetic discourses.' (p. 23)

Violent as they appear to have been at times, it seems that their bodily agitations did not normally interrupt the flow of their discourses, for

> 'those who had the gift of preaching and exhortation were of a ready utterance and used a fluent eloquence, and after their first emotions (commonly not very great) during their discourses, with their eyes open, they had only some slight agitation, caused by the ardour of the Spirit's influence.' (p. 40)

However, there was probably a great deal of variety in the manifestations, as one observer records:

> 'These people had certain fits, which made them drop down, and during that had shakings of the head, breast and some-

times all over them, that were very surprising. There was not only different degrees of those emotions, but variety too. After some short agitations, they used to speak, some with interruptions and snatches of the breath, others evenly with facility and fervour.' (p. 107)

Others had similar tales to tell, and some of them spoke of the lasting duration of their prophetic gift. For example, Abraham Mazel, one of the Camisard warriors, later emigrated to Switzerland, where he was 'frequently blessed with the holy ecstatic visitations of God's Spirit' (p. 107), and John Vernett's mother continued to enjoy 'her gifts' after eleven years in prison (p. 13). It seems fairly clear that the ecstatic experiences of the prophets, whilst superficially similar to revivalist phenomena, were of a much more profound nature and had a much more lasting effect.

*The Experience of Elias Marion*

One of the longest depositions in Lacy's book is that of Elias Marion, who, with Durand Fage and some others, later became one of the leading apostles of the French Prophet movement in London. His story is particularly interesting because it illustrates how the bodily seizures could change, intensify and remain with the prophet over a long period of years.

He first encountered the prophets towards the end of 1701 when, at the age of twenty-two, he returned home after spending three years apprenticed to an attorney at law in Toulouse. After some initial perplexity about what he saw, he tells us that one day, while listening to one of the prophets speaking,

'I found within myself an unaccountable emotion, with a secret joy and sensation of the grace of God, so that methoughts I was even in heaven. A certain heat seized my breast and created me some oppression, which though it gave no pain, made me fetch deep sighs. My body was a little overset, and in this condition I continued more than a quarter of an hour, feeling little else of agitation.' (p. 83)

These were but first, preliminary stirrings in him. The story resumes one evening more than a year later, on 1st January, 1703, when he was at home with his father and two brothers several years his junior, both of whom had 'received the gift'. He tells us,

'I perceived of a sudden a great burning round my heart, that spread after over all my body; I was also a little oppressed at

> the lungs, that made me fetch deep sighs, but I suppressed them, what I could; some moments after, an irresistible force prevailed over me altogether, which made me cry out with interruptions of gulping like a hiccup, and my eyes poured out a flood of tears.' (p. 84)

With these tears came an overwhelming awareness of sin, but through them came also a sense of forgiveness.

> 'The night following I slept quietly, but upon awakening I fell into the like agitations, that ever since have taken me with the ecstasy, interrupted often with gulpings of the wind-pipe.'

So it continued two or three times a day for about a month, during which time Marion fasted and prayed and his 'consolation augmented from day to day'. After this month of 'silent ecstasies' he says he came to possess a 'happy satisfaction of mind.' Then he adds,

> 'I was altogether changed ... it pleased God to loosen my tongue and put his word in my mouth ... I will not pretend fully to express what was my astonishment and joy when I felt and heard flow from my mouth a stream of holy words, whereof my mind was no ways the author, and which ravished my ears to hear it.' (p. 85)

Soon after this Marion joined the Camisard troops in the hills where his ecstasies persisted and seemingly intensified, so much so that on one occasion, in anguish of mind, he found himself pouring

> 'forth tears of blood in great plenty. The blood was florid, as if spun directly from the veins, my clothes were stained with it and the earth likewise.' (p. 87)

After the war, Marion emigrated to London where his ecstasies continued unabated, though perhaps in a less dramatic manner, as we shall discover in the next chapter.

*The Inspired Utterances of the Prophets*

By far the most striking characteristic of their prophetic activity was neither the young age of the prophets nor the strangeness of their bodily and emotional experiences, but their inspired utterances.

For the most part, though by no means exclusively, their prophesyings amounted to little more than sermons in content, urging the hearers to amendment of life and renewed dedication of their reformed faith. But they differed from conventional Protestant sermons in several respects, not least in the powerful impact they made on their hearers. They were generally in French, which was not the natural tongue of the speakers, and in good prophetic style made free use of the divine 'I'. Normally the prophets would begin and intersperse their utterances with the words, 'My Child' (*Mon Enfant*), as their mode of addressing the congregation.

Apart from the need for repentance, the other main themes covered were the forthcoming vindication of the Huguenot Church and the relaying of visions or personal insights helpful to the assembled worshippers.

> 'They uttered large discourses, very pious and strongly hortatory of repentance. They had also predictions of the ruin of mystical Babylon, with assurances that the Church would speedily be delivered out of affliction … They always spoke good French in the inspiration, though they never could at other times. And during their discourses then they spoke in the manner as if the Divine Spirit had spoke in them, saying, "I tell thee, I declare to thee, my child," etc.' (p. 16)

The themes are similar to those that had been on the lips of Isabel Vincent more than a decade earlier and, judging by the various accounts in Lacy's book, they were widely cherished and regularly propounded at the prophet-meetings.

Far more dramatic than the sermon-type prophecies were the premonitory ones. The prophetic assemblies were usually held in secret, mostly at night, for fear of the persecutors, and quite often those gathered at them

> 'were forewarned and directed in a multitude of things relating either to their own particular conduct, or to the religious assemblies (held almost daily in secret) for their safety.'

Lacy's sources give several instances of congregations miraculously forewarned about the approach of the Catholic police. For example, James du Bois, whom we encountered earlier, told of a meeting he once attended in a house in Montpellier with fifteen present, during which

> 'a young woman named Bomelle, being amongst us, dropped into her ecstasy and said that we must disperse forthwith, for else we would be discovered. Some proposed to end first the psalm we had begun to sing, but she continued in the inspiration to urge us instantly to be gone, and hasting out herself, bid us follow, which they all did.'

He says he stayed in view of the house to watch, and sure enough the police arrived almost immediately to search it. (p. 33)

*The Experience of Jean Cavalier*

Equally striking are the examples of prophetic insight into the details of private lives. Although there are many of them recorded by Lacy, perhaps the most useful for our purpose are in the account of how Jean Cavalier became a prophet. It is worth giving a fairly full digest of his story. It contains so many incidental details about the prophetic assemblies, the preaching of the child-prophets and so forth, that we obtain from it quite a vivid picture of what a typical French Prophet meeting must have been like. Furthermore, this Jean Cavalier, who claimed to be a cousin of the famous Camisard leader of the same name, though there was some dispute about their precise relationship, eventually emigrated to England where, along with Marion and Fage, he became one of the leaders of the movement in England.

When he was fifteen or sixteen and 'not much given to devotion,' he was persuaded to go to a meeting in a barn where he was immediately captivated by the sight of 'a little boy lying on his back, with surprising agitations.' The sight frightened him a little, but not as much as when he heard the boy say that

> 'there was some persons in the company, who came in curiosity and with intent to scoff, and if they relented not, God would cause them to be known and exposed to shame.'

The boy, he continues,

> 'added more of the like import, and so exactly hit me that if he had known my thoughts he could not better have set me forth … so I hoped to escape … for I wished myself twenty miles off … I never was in such a pickle of fear.' (p. 37)

His attempts to escape were, however, foiled by another boy, who positioned himself between Cavalier and the door and, falling into 'violent agonies', said aloud that

> 'there was a certain person in the assembly disaffected, who intended to get away, and therefore the door should be watched to hinder him, lest he went and discovered [reported] the assembly.'

The crisis intensified, for the lad began

> 'to set forth most perfectly the imaginations that passed in my heart … he could not have done more without my name and surname, and laying hands upon me, he added many things tending to my conviction and humiliation before God, and persuading me to give him the glory.' (p. 38)

As we can imagine, Cavalier's 'inward terror increased mightily,' but even so, he could not help noticing the great piety and devotion in the utterances of the two boy-prophets. In this muddled state, his attention was caught by another prophet who had been preaching 'against the manners and corruptions of the age, against the idolatry of Papists, and all kinds of superstition and sin.' This third prophet

> 'all on a sudden stopped that discourse, and changing his voice, said there was a number of good people nigh at hand, who in looking for the assembly had mistook their way in the woods or fields, and to set them right, it was necessary some should go out of the congregation and trumpet out a psalm.'

Much to Cavalier's astonishment, some of the company did exactly as the prophet said and in a short time 'a good number of people joined them in the assembly.' (p. 39)

From that moment Cavalier's opinion of the prophets began to change.

> 'I thought the devil could not reprove vice in that manner, nor glorify the name of God as this congregation did. Such thoughts quieted my mind more than a little, and even gave me some joy.'

He now began to ask God to confirm for him whether the prophets' gifts were really from him or not. As his mind grew calmer, he became attentive to another youth who was speaking what he claimed was a word the Holy Spirit had put in his mouth for the consolation of the people.

> 'He spoke two full hours with a wonderful freedom and said so many excellent affecting things that the whole assembly fell into tears, and I among the rest. Nobody there slept, I am sure. The words of this little servant of God were not such as would permit it. None of them were lost, for they were all pertinent to the subject, all suited to the capacity of the good and simple audience, though at the same time sublime and heavenly. Where is the child able to perform such things? Everybody said this little youth could not read …' (pp. 39-40)

The theme of the sermon was just what Cavalier needed to hear at that point, emphasising God's mercy towards repentant sinners and the blessing that could be theirs. It dispelled all his doubts and effectively turned him to 'thirsting for the grace of God'. What happened next can only be described in his own words.

> 'When the sermon ended, there seemed a beating as of a hammer in my breast, which kindled a flame that took me and dispersed over all my veins. This put me into a sort of leaping which flung me down. I rose again without any harm, and as my heart was lifted up to God with unutterable fervour, I was struck a second time and my flame increased. My prayers grew also more ardent, speaking and breathing with mighty groans. Soon after, a third blow took me on the breast and set me all in fire. Some moments of respite intervened and then followed on a sudden violent agitations of the head and body, and like unto those I have had since unto this day. Those great agitations were very short, but the foregoing inward heat and twitchings continued. During all this I was employed in reflecting upon my sins. The liberties to which I was most addicted appeared heinous provocations and put me into a posture of mind I am unable here to describe.' (p. 41)

After the prophet had offered prayer, the congregation sang the Hundredth Psalm. Then the boy-prophet beckoned Cavalier to come to him and, still in the spirit, advised him to give thanks to God for the grace he had received and to continue in prayer until such time as it pleased God to 'put his word also into my mouth', warning him that that could take some time, since God had to do a transforming work in him first. The little prophet then pronounced a concluding benediction and dismissed the people with words of assurance that everyone at the meeting would get home safely.

Cavalier describes the subsequent changes that took place in his life very fully.

> 'I wept in secret continually at home, and the great agitations of body I had now and then several times flung me on the ground, or I was forced to stay upon something. Almost for nine months I continued in that condition, the hand of God often striking me before my tongue was loosed. 'Tis true on the other side, I experienced his consolations, for I readily yielded to the inward motions of the Spirit unto prayer, I immediately forsook my plays and usual diversions, and above all I found a perfect abhorrence of the train of public worship among the

> Papists, and of all that pageantry of the Mass, which delighted me before. I could hardly look upon their churches without shivering.
>
> 'At length, after about three quarters of a year's hiccough and agitation without speech, one Lord's-day morning, being at home in prayer, I fell into an extraordinary ecstasy and God opened my mouth. I remained then for 48 hours under the operation of the Spirit in different degrees, without eating, drinking, or sleep, and I spoke often, with more or less vehemence, according to the nature of the things spoken. They were in our family convinced by the extraordinary condition wherein they beheld me, and by the prodigy of my three days fasting (at the end of which I neither was hungry or athirst) that these sort of things must proceed from an Almighty Power. And as the words I spoke were good and holy, it was never imagined they could come from an impure author or cause.' (p. 43)

Like Elias Marion, Cavalier joined the Camisard armies. He served in his cousin's troop, but was taken prisoner. On release after the war he emigrated to London, where we shall meet him again in the next chapter.

*The Nature and Effect of the Prophetic Ecstasy*

Three significant claims are frequently reiterated in the testimonies collected by Lacy: first, that the prophecies were not 'framed' by their speakers; second, that after the ecstasy had passed from them, the prophets could seldom recall what they had spoken; and third, that their experience effected a change in their personality and lifestyle. Cavalier wrote,

> 'I here declare solemnly … that I am in no wise the framer of those bodily agitations I suffer in my ecstasies, I do not move my own self, but am moved by a power independent that over-rules me. And for the words that proceed from my mouth, I protest with the same awful solemnity, they are formed without my intention and glide forth of my lips without my direction, my mind no ways bearing any part in that marvellous operation by preceding forethought, or any attending will to deliver what I do at that instant.' (p. 44)

Similar statements were made about their experience by Durand Fage and Elias Marion (pp. 71f, 85f). Comments about the prophets' inability to recall their words and about their evident sobriety and devotion are also put most forcibly by observers. One wrote,

> 'In all places where the Spirit of God was diffused, those who received it in the manner above expressed, and such who frequented their discourses, became of a sudden new men, even such who before had been irregular. I asked several if they could repeat the things they had said in their paroxysm, who replied they could not do it.' (p. 26)

These and other like statements, such as Jurieu's about Isabel Vincent, suggest, as we have already remarked, some comparison with Montanist prophesying. Many distinguish between a more exuberant Phrygian and a relatively sober Tertullianist expression of Montanist prophecy, but some of the passages cited here indicate a similar variety in the French experience. There were those whose words came amid gulpings and hiccups and others whose ecstaticism was barely noticeable while they spoke. Nevertheless, both groups maintained that their messages came to them 'in ecstasy', and in that respect their experience differs from most present-day Pentecostal activity, and indeed from at least some of the New Testament Church's experience, of which Paul could write, 'The spirits of prophets are subject to the control of prophets' (1 Cor. 14:32). Montanist and Cevennol prophecy seem somewhat more spontaneous and uninhibited than their New Testament and modern Charismatic counterparts, though again there was and is variety in both of these also, as 1 Cor. 12-14 amply attests and as we shall see again in the final chapters of this book.

*Other Gifts among the Prophets*

As we have noted, prophets were healed and improved in health and mental sanity through their ecstasies, but we do not read about healing or deliverance ministries as such. Their stories are replete with accounts of the miraculous, but again we hear of no self-consciously miracle-performing ministries.

Similarly, we hardly hear anything about tongues or interpretation of tongues among the French Prophets, although these gifts were sometimes instanced. James du Bois testified,

> 'Several persons of both sexes I have heard in their ecstasies pronounce certain words which seemed to the standers-by to be some foreign language, and in effect he that spoke declared (sometimes) what his preceding words signified.' (p. 32)

The prophets did, however, like prophets in every other age, have many tales of visions and auditions, as du Bois also noted.

> 'I have seen at several times the persons inspired, of both sexes, in the time of their trances, have their eyes open and commonly lifted up to heaven, who said that they saw armies of angels, sometimes those angels engaged against armies of men and divers other things which I cannot distinctly remember.' (p. 32)

We have also already noted that they were very fully blessed with words of knowledge, spiritual insight, supernatural wisdom, premonition of danger and the like, often resulting in conversions or in their personal protection. Many of these gifts were to come even more dramatically to the fore in the Camisard wars, as we shall see in a moment.

*The Attitudes of the Persecutors*

Quite naturally, despite the repeated protestations of the prophets that their words and experiences were of divine origin, their critics and persecutors did their utmost to find demonic or purely human explanations in order to discredit the movement. David Flotard, another of Lacy's witnesses, gives an account of how a priest examined a six or seven year old girl and, being unable to find any human explanation for her prophecies, concluded

> 'the inspirations were of the Devil's contrivance to revive in France the expiring heresy of Calvin.' (p. 75f)

He then goes on to tell how the 'learned and famous college of physicians at Montpellier' conducted an examination into the possible physical causes of the prophet-children's bodily agitations and, finding no 'bodily distemper' in them, nor any other emotional, psychological, or rational explanation for their behaviour, were at a loss for an explanation, but

> 'thinking it necessary to make some report and judgment on the case, as it became them for their own reputation, a brand therefore must be fixed upon the inspired, and no better one could be found than that of "Fanatic".' (p. 76)

Flotard gives us an impressions of the extent of the movement at this time and a glimpse of how the Catholics tried to suppress it. He tells that

> 'some who set themselves to calculate the number of those persons computed eight thousand at the least in Languedoc. It was chiefly at the assemblies for worship that they appeared numerous. I saw them in troops carried to gaol in many places. Notwithstanding which hard usage, they seemed joyful beyond measure, singing anthems and directing up prayers to God continually.
>
> 'The prisons were in a little time so thronged with these poor creatures, especially children, they knew not what to do with them. So that there came an order from Court to release them and to commit no more, but instead thereof that the King's troops should put to the sword those who assembled for religious worship—which was executed to the uttermost ability of the heroic marshals of France.' (pp. 76f)

The prophets had broken once already under such pressure, but this time it was to be very different.

*The Outbreak of the Camisard Wars*

The reign of terror that followed the second outburst of prophecy was intense beyond comprehension. The massacres, executions and imprisonments cannot be numbered. When the prisons became full, the executioner was commissioned to thin their ever-swelling population. Whole villages were burnt to the ground and the land was laid waste, so much so that this 'land, so flourishing before the revocation, became a vast and mournful desert'[247]—hence the titles of Misson's and Lacy's books. In that setting the younger prophets gave way before older men whose words and visions breathed a sterner spirit, summoning the Protestants to arms for the defence of their lives and their faith.

On one level the story of the prophet armies makes stirring reading. It drew the attention of all Europe at the time. Their numbers never exceeded ten thousand, they were untrained, ill-equipped and grossly outnumbered, and yet they won victory after victory, and with such resounding success that after less than two years of fighting, their leader, Jean Cavalier, was able to negotiate a partial peace which conceded their liberty of conscience and worship. Historians accredit their successes primarily to their total dedication to their cause and to the fact that theirs was a kind of guerrilla war in mountain terrain which they, unlike the royal troops, knew

247. De Felice, *History*, p. 360.

intimately. However, the Camisards, as they were called, themselves attributed their successes from the very beginning to the leading and inspiration of the Spirit, and that to the extent that their own records, as preserved by Lacy, read like excerpts from the Book of Judges in the Old Testament.

At another level the story of the wars makes tedious reading. The battles were all local skirmishes, of which there were many, and we read of no overall plans of campaign or carefully co-ordinated tactical manoeuvres[248].

The uprising started in July, 1702, with an attack on the Abbot of Chayla's stronghold at Pont de Mont-Verd. According to Abraham Mazel, one of the leaders of the insurrection, the whole process was set in motion and guided by the Spirit. He tells that he had a dream in which he saw a garden with very fat black cattle feeding in it and was told to drive them away. Soon afterwards he

> 'received an inspiration which said that the garden was an emblem of the Church, that the great black oxen were the priests who laid it waste, and that I should have a call to drive away that sort of cattle.' (p. 101)

He says that a few days later the Spirit told him to prepare to take up arms and that a number of others had inspirations to the same effect. He then goes on to relate that at their gathering for worship on Sunday, 21st July, he was

> 'taken with the ecstasy and violent agitation, and was commanded in it to take arms forthwith without delay and go deliver our brethren, who by the persecutors were imprisoned at Pont de Mont-Verd.'

Accordingly, some forty men assembled the next night, apparently very poorly armed. They 'went all to prayers' and some of them 'were ordered by the Spirit' to go after dark into the village 'singing psalms, to go direct to the castle and deliver the prisoners.' They did so, their brethren were released, the castle was reduced to ashes, and the abbot, who had the blood of many Huguenots on his hands, was killed. The victory was, of course, ascribed entirely to God.

---

248. For those interested in such matters, the fullest accounts of the wars in English are given by Mrs. Bray and Charles Tyler. Mrs. Bray's book pays little attention to the tales of the supernatural that the prophets themselves told, but for our purposes it is the material she chooses not to notice that is of paramount importance, whereas the details about the progress of the wars are of no great significance. Mrs. E. Bray, *The Revolt of the Protestants in the Cevennes*, London, 1870. Ch. Tyler, *The Camisards*, London, 1893.

> 'They passed the remaining night in praises and acknowledgements for the success he had given to the first enterprise of his servants. And at break of day, we retired with songs and hosannas to the mountains.' (pp. 102f)

*The Organisation and Leadership of the Prophet Armies*

In the wake of this initial victory, resistance groups sprang up in various places in the Cevennes, each with its own leader. Little attempt was made to co-ordinate the activities of these guerrilla units, although their leaders did consult together wherever possible. According to the prophet-chroniclers, they spurned the military conventions of civil armies, preferring to organise themselves on the more biblical principles of holy war. The dedication and holiness of the troops, together with their openness to the leading of the Spirit, such as we see reflected in Mazel's account of the storming of the Abbot of Chayla's castle, were reckoned of far greater value than any structural organisation or skilled human captaincy.

Thus, for example, Durand Fage tells that the Camisards would seek the orders of the Spirit before any military undertaking, heeding even 'the inspirations of little children, and people never so simple,' although he admits that in Cavalier's troop, the one in which he himself served, 'the officers, and in particular Mr. Cavalier, were all graced with extraordinary gifts' and that Brother Cavalier (as he apparently preferred to be called) 'was obeyed more punctually than any king.' He describes Cavalier's leadership as follows:

> 'When a matter came under debate … lifting up his mind to God, the Spirit fell upon him, we found him under consequent agitations, and then resolved the point. It was somewhat wonderful in battles to observe him on horseback with a sword drawn and the Spirit's emotion on him, how he posted up and down to encourage and excite, giving orders often as surprising as wonderfully executed, and succeeding accordingly.' (pp. 69f)

*The Encouraging Power of Prophetic Inspiration*

Fage also describes how the same troops would have recourse to prayer on 'occasions of great moment', waiting until one or more of their number 'were taken with inspiration', and how they and their leaders would follow the guidance of the Spirit obtained in this way with complete dedication. However, he does admit that not everyone found this strange way of conducting military affairs readily acceptable, and mentions in particular new recruits 'who had not the inspiration themselves.' On the other hand, for those he calls 'the most faithful', the prophetic exhortations were of immense value in stirring them to deeds of fearless bravery.

> 'When the inspiration said, "March, fear not, obey my command, do this or that," nothing could dissuade from it. I speak of the most faithful, and who had best experience of the faithfulness of God. When the case was to be engaged in battle, I dare say for myself, if the Spirit had strengthened me with those good words, "Fear nothing, my child, I will preserve and stand by thee," I rushed into the midst of the enemy as if their hands had been paper and I were sheltered in steel. By the encouragement of such happy words from the Spirit of God, our boys of twelve years old laid about them on the right and left like valiant men. Those who had neither sword nor gun did wonders with a club, pitch-fork or sling. The showers of musket balls whistled in our ears, went through our hats and sleeves without terror. If the Spirit had said, "Fear not," a shower of bullets was but as one of common hail.' (pp. 70f)

Elias Marion likewise attributed the successes of the war entirely to the prophetic inspirations. It is worth quoting him at length, because he gives a vivid account of conditions among the troops in the hills during those days.

> 'It was only by the inspirations and their repeated orders that we began the war for the enjoyment of our holy religion. A small number of simple young people, without education and without experience, how could they have done so many great things without help from above? We had neither power nor counsel, but the inspirations were all our refuge and support. They alone chose our officers and commanders, and by them did they steer. They taught us the discipline of war. They instructed us to bear the first fire on the enemy on our knees, and to make our attacks upon them with loud chant of psalms for terror. They changed our fearful temper into that of lions, and made us perform gloriously …
>
> 'These did expel sorrow from our hearts in the midst of dangers from the enemy, as also when hunger and cold oppressed us in the caves and deserts. The most heavy cross we bore was a light burden, because the intimate communion the gracious God vouchsafed us afforded relief and comfort—this was both

our safety and happiness. Our inspirations instructed us to deliver our brethren out of prison, to know and convict traitors, to shun ambushes, to discover plots, and to strike down persecutors.' (pp. 97f)

*Warnings and Guidance from the Spirit*

The accounts in Lacy's book are replete with tales illustrating the kinds of guidance listed in Marion's last sentence. For example, one, Claud Arnassan, tells how Cavalier was once sitting in someone's house about to have a meal, when he was warned by the Spirit to be gone instantly, whereupon

> 'he rose up without eating, and as soon as we were out of doors, we had sight of three or four companies of the enemy who drew towards the house we left.'

Or again, he recounts how on another occasion Cavalier foresaw a battle that was about to take place and correctly foretold that in it he would have 'but one man slain and two wounded' (pp. 27f). Durand Fage tells a story about how Cavalier once had an enemy courier intercepted as a consequence of one of his inspirations. He also tells of an incident in which one of the many deserters from the royal armies that were constantly coming over to their side was discovered to be a traitor, thanks to 'several inspirations which plainly marked him out and declared him treacherous.' (p. 62)

The sources contain stories about miraculous guidance of an even more spectacular and directly supernatural nature. For example, Arnassan told of some forty persons who had lost their way to one of Cavalier's gatherings being guided by 'a light, like a large star, which advanced pointing to the place where the assembly was met.' (p. 27)

But even more startling is one very peculiar narrative found in the deposition of Jean Cavalier (not the Camisard leader, but his namesake whose story we recounted in some detail above), concerning a certain Brother Clary (or Claris). He records how at one of his cousin's assemblies this Clary 'was seized with ecstasy' and instructed to point out some traitors in the company, whereupon 'Claris, the agitations of his head and breast continuing, walked towards the traitors.' Some of the audience apparently objected that the whole demonstration had been prearranged 'to counterfeit a miracle', but Clary, to prove his truthfulness, spoke again in the Spirit, ordering a fire to be lit and declared that he would put himself into the midst of its flames which would have no power to hurt him. Despite many protestations, Cavalier had the fire prepared, and Clary

> 'put himself upon the top of the pile of wood, straight upright with his hands joined and lifted above his head. He was still in his ecstasy or agitations, and continued to speak in the flames ... though he continued at least a quarter of an hour in the flames, yet he came forth with hiccups and heavings of the breast upon him.'

We are then informed that no mark of the fire was found on him or his clothing, much to the relief of his wife and family who had stood by watching the entire bizarre proceeding. (pp. 49-52) A second account of this episode is given by Fage in his deposition. (pp. 64-6)

However we judge such tales, they at least attest to the fact that some of the prophets believed such things could happen, and they remind us of some of the feats of the prophets in Old Testament times, particularly Elisha. But even stronger echoes of the Old Testament are found in another story that Marion tells, one that reminds us of the account of Gideon's selection of his troops in Judges 7 and also of the regulations governing purity in the camp prescribed in Deut. 20 and 23.

> 'In the month of May, 1703, the troop of brother Abraham was incorporated with that of Castanett for some operations. Solomon Couderc (joint commander with Abraham), one of our most excellent preachers, and who had other great gifts, had order by inspiration to pass those two united troops in review, whereof several lived according to the fashion of the world and others had neglected the commandments given them. The Spirit therefore ordered Solomon to draw up this troop into a line (consisting between 400 and 500 men) and to separate those who were unworthy in it. Thus Solomon, under the operation of the Spirit and with the usual agitations, walked with his eyes open, intently viewing every man from one rank to another, and received secret intimations whom he ought to reject among them. He drew these out of line and ordered them apart to a place assigned them. These poor people obeyed with tears in their eyes and went to the place appointed and flung themselves to the ground upon the knee. Between sixty and seventy were thus set apart.'

Marion tells how relieved he was, being himself a commander, not to have to stand in the line and undergo this scrutiny, and then goes on to say that

> 'Solomon made, by his spiritual direction, a moving discourse to those whose good behaviour was thus approved, and presently after, by the same direction, caused those set apart to draw near. In this juncture the whole assembly burst into tears. He then proceeded to censure the guilty, the same overruling power continuing upon him, and made unto them very urgent exhortations. After this was done, he gave them the relieving news that their broken hearts were accepted of God and they were received to his mercy, whereupon everyone returned to his rank with tears of joy. Then Solomon concluded with an admirable prayer.' (pp. 86f)

*The End of the War and the Death of the French Prophet Movement*

In May, 1704, Cavalier succeeded in negotiating a kind of peace for the Huguenots, though Roland, the most outstanding of the Camisard leaders besides Cavalier himself, tried to prolong the war for a number of years after that date. Cavalier was given a colonel's commission in the King's army and, after serving with his troops for a time in Spain, he ended his life as Governor of the Island of Jersey. Sad to relate, the claims of respectability that went with his commission led him to deny his prophetic background, much to the dismay and annoyance of his erstwhile prophet-followers for whom he had once been a charismatic hero as eminent in their eyes as Samuel or Elijah had been in the eyes of the prophets of their day.

The history of the restoration of Protestantism in Southern France is dominated by the personality of Antoine Court, who considered it one of his primary purposes to suppress the voice of the prophets. It is not our intention to follow their story here[249], but suffice it to remark that he found himself in much the same position as Luther when he was confronted with the Zwickau Prophets. He did not have 'the inspiration' himself and he saw that it could lead to excesses when not restrained by the external controls of Scripture, doctrine and the Church. He was confronted with a phenomenon he did not understand and, like Luther in his similar setting, he effectively drove it from the Church, though not without a great deal of opposition. Once more the prophetic Church that was seeking to be born was suppressed by the arm of tradition.

*Assessment*

The French Prophets of the period from the revocation to the end of

249. See Tyler, *The Camisards*, pp. 223ff.

the Camisard Wars are virtually unique in history. They manifest few of the traits we have come to associate with prophetic movements, such as the evangelistic zeal and sectarian tendency associated with some form of belief that they were the nucleus of an end-time Church of the Spirit. In fact they seem to have developed very little at all in the way of a theology of their experience during these years. Certainly they predicted a better future for themselves, but theirs was the voice of a desperate, beleaguered Church, not of a movement seeking to reform existing Church systems or to establish any new Church. Their motivation was no Joachimistic vision of a new age of the Spirit, but simply the need to survive as a Protestant community.

Perhaps their closest counterpart in history is the prophetic movement that fought against the persecuting zeal of Ahab and Jezebel in the days of Elijah and Elisha. They too had to take to the hills and hide in the caves of the mountains (1 Kings 18:4); they too had to use their prophetic gifts to urge the zealous in Israel to wield their swords for the defence of their faith (2 Kings 9:4-10); they too wrote more about the wondrous deeds of their heroes than about any doctrines or teaching (2 Kings 3-8).

Nevertheless, with the more peaceful conditions that followed after the treaty of 1704, the prophets did turn their minds to other, more familiar matters. About the year 1715 a document that circulated in the Lower Languedoc declared 'God the Father had done his work, Christ had finished his, and it was now the turn of the Holy Spirit'.[250] However, it is in England rather than France that we must pursue the story.

250. Tyler, *The Camisards*, p. 237.

# 22
# The French Prophets in England

In the wake of the war in the Cevennes a number of Camisards made their way to London where there was already a sizeable community of exiled French Protestants. The prophets were well received at first, but the Huguenot churches in London and the English community itself soon began to feel troubled by their activities. The inevitable hostilities followed and the prophets, hounded from the capital, took to the provinces or went abroad, preaching their charismatic gospel as they went.

Their story is very mixed. It contains tales of profound faith, but also of utter naiveté; it reveals men of great dedication, but also of cowardly duplicity; it provides the usual round of exciting prophecies, visions, miracles and the like, but it also generated an almost endless series of tediously lengthy polemical and apologetic books and pamphlets. The prophets of Southern France had captured a vision that added vitality and heroism to their faith, much needed in their hour of crisis. In exile their vision remained and was caught by many who came into contact with them, but they had to find new forms of expressing it in the very different social climate of seventeenth-century England, and unfortunately, although essential truths relevant to all times and places lay at its heart, their re-expressions too often concentrated on the peripheral. The movement that had begun with the majesty of the inspired Camisard sadly declined in disrepute and eventually dwindled into oblivion.

*Handling the Contemporary Sources*

The prophets' story is perhaps best read in the French accounts of Ascoli and Vesson, or better still, especially for the earlier years, in Bost's edition of Marion's *Mémoires*. Although the prophets and their critics have left us a vast amount of literature in English, very little has been written about them in our language in recent times. There is a useful chapter in Knox's *Enthusiasm* and a fuller portrayal of them in the opening chapters of Symonds' *Thomas Brown and the Angels*, but both of these tend to rely on critical sources for their information, such as the writings of the Anglican clergyman, Nathaniel Spinckes, or the fascinating account of the movement by Samuel Keimer.

Keimer's work has to be read with caution. Spinckes made no attempt to hide his biases, but much of the time Keimer wrote as if objectively, though in fact from a stance of bitterness and self-pity. His sister was a prophet and he had himself been an active member of the movement, but because of debt incurred through careless business speculation, he found himself in prison and there he felt his prophet-colleagues let him down by failing to bail him out. The result was that he wrote partly to justify himself at their expense. The details he gives are often so spectacular that it is almost certain that he chose to emphasise some of the most ridiculous aspects of the prophets' activities. Symonds uses his work too uncritically.

The most important writings among the prophets themselves (apart from Marion's, which is in French) came from the pens of John Lacy and an Irish baronet called Sir Richard Bulkeley, both men of substance who devoted their entire energies to the movement. Other writings, of which there were many, will be referred to in passing. All in all we have a plentiful supply of source material for reconstructing the history and teachings of this movement.

*First Impact of the Prophets in London*

There were already some prophet-exiles in London before the war in the Cevennes started, but their impact was minimal until August and September, 1706, when three of those, whose depositions in *A Cry from the Desart* are cited in the last chapter, arrived in the city, namely Durand Fage, Jean Cavalier (namesake of the Camisard chief) and Elias Marion. They immediately set to prophesying in their accustomed vein, that God was preparing to work wonders to effect the triumph of his faithful servants, the fall of Louis XIV and the restoration of peace. At first their sincerity was applauded by the leaders of the French community and their fame spread rapidly, not only among the exiles, but in London as a whole. Bost writes:

> 'At that time God visited us often with his Spirit. Cavalier, who was lodging with his cousin, Allut … had (prophetical) warnings every day in his house … People came hurrying in crowds to hear him; his street was often full of carriages belonging to persons of quality.'[251]

251. Bost, *Mémoires*, p. 157.

However, in a very short time the applause gave way to condemnation. The respectable, long-established Huguenot community in London, with its church in the Savoy in Westminster, soon became uneasy about the prophets' peculiar behaviour. Already in September, Marion, Cavalier and Fage were being summoned before the French ministers to give account of themselves and of their prophecies, that had in the meantime been extended in scope to express denunciations of abuses in the churches of the exiles in the city of London itself.

A series of interviews at the beginning of October began amicably enough, but ended brusquely on the eighth. Then, on Sunday, 5th January, 1707, a public declaration was read from the French pulpits denouncing the prophets. It proclaimed their agitations to be nothing more than 'the effect of voluntary habit, over which they are entirely the masters, though in their fits they create a pretence of being agitated by a superior cause,' and it condemned their prophetic utterances as unworthy of the Holy Spirit because of their

> 'constant hesitations, infantile repetitions, a real jumble of words, gross contradictions, obvious lies, conjectures turned into predictions, predictions already proved false by the event, and moral lessons which one hears very much better expressed every day, lessons that have nothing new about them except the grimaces that accompany them.'[252]

*Mounting Opposition and Persecution*

The consequences of this declaration were disastrous for the prophets. Throughout the years 1707 and 1708 they were hounded from pillar to post, not just by the French exiles, but by the wider population of London amongst whom their prophecies were also causing quite a stir. Had the prophets been content, like the majority of present-day Charismatics, simply to meet in private and keep their prophesyings to themselves, they would probably have been left to their own devices. But, like many other prophets before them, they were inspired with an evangelistic zeal that drove them to broadcast their messages as widely as possible. Hence it is not at all surprising to discover that Marion's *Mémoires* contain several vivid accounts of mob violence in the streets and elsewhere.

One evangelistic method they employed was to hold meetings that were open to the public so that 'everyone was free to come and listen to the messengers of the Lord.' These meetings were often quite rowdy, for

252. Bost, *Mémoires*, p. 160.

> 'people certainly came in large crowds, but they came more to provoke ... not contenting themselves with their frightful booing, shouted all kinds of nasty names at us, continually pelting us with a shower of filth, with putrid dead dogs and cats, and often with stones.'[253]

On various occasions the prophets were haled before the civil authorities who clearly had little appreciation of the spiritual issues involved. Marion tells of one judge who taunted the prophets to prove the worth of their inspiration by predicting the outcome of Marlborough's campaign in Flanders, or by telling how much money he had in his pocket, to which they replied that they

> 'had nothing to say in answer to trivial questions of this kind, since the function of the Spirit of prophecy was to render witness to Jesus Christ.'

The answer was worthy of any New Testament prophet, but the point was entirely lost on the magistrate who simply dismissed the case as of no criminal consequence.[254]

However, not every confrontation with the law ended so amicably. On one occasion Marion and two others were pilloried in the stocks. Marion had a rather quaint inscription affixed over his head:

> *Elias Marion, Convicted for Falsely and Profanely pretending himself to be a True Prophet, and Printing, and Uttering many things, as dictated and revealed to him by the Spirit of God, to terrifie the Queen's people.*[255]

As well as violence and law-suit, the prophets had to face persistent mockery and ridicule, one fascinating example of which is given by the then Earl of Shaftesbury, who seems to have taken a bemused interest in their doings.

> 'I am told they are at this time the subject of a choice doll or puppet-show at Bart'lmy-Fair. There doubtless their strange voices and involuntary agitations are admirably well acted by the motion of wires, and inspiration of pipes.'[256]

*Growth of the Movement and its Literature*

The prophets did not simply take all this opposition and scorn sitting

---

253. Bost, *Mémoires*, p. 165f.
254. Bost, *Mémoires*, p. 164.
255. Symonds, *Thomas Brown*, p. 34.
256. *Letter concerning Enthusiasm*, p. 43.

down. They were men with a message, on fire with the Spirit, and were rapidly making converts, mostly among men and women of the artisan class. A select list of names drawn up by Keimer mentions merchants, an apothecary, a tallow-chandler, a shoe-maker, a watch-maker, and others of similar social status.[257] But they were also joined by persons of some social influence, like Thomas Dutton, a lawyer, or Dr. Emes, a surgeon. John Lacy and Sir Richard Bulkeley brought their considerable wealth to the movement's support, while Maximillian Misson, author, and Nicholas Facio, professor of mathematics from Geneva and long-standing member of the Royal Society in London, brought their learning.

Thanks particularly to the efforts of these men and a few others, the prophets responded to their critics in print. The first book appeared in April, 1707, under the title *Prophetical Warnings of Elias Marion, one of the Commanders of the Protestants, that had taken arms in the Cevennes: or discourses uttered by him in London, under the operation of the Spirit; and faithfully taken in writing whilst they were spoken*. This book was published simultaneously in French (*Avertissements prophétiques …*) and in the following years other similarly entitled works by Marion himself and by his associates were to appear with some regularity. They contained the oracles of the prophets—hundreds of them!—predicting blessings for the faithful and judgment on the apostate churchmen and corrupt citizens of the land. The aim of this literature was to warn men of judgment and urge them to repentance, but its effects were often simply to stir the flames of opposition even further.

Of an entirely different genre was Misson's *Théâtre Sacré*, which appeared along with Lacy's translation of it, *A Cry from the Desart*, about three weeks after Marion's *Prophetical Warnings*. In it were collected the accounts of many who had witnessed the prophetic activity in the Cevennes, its purpose being to vindicate the claims of the prophets in London.[258] Scores of other books and pamphlets followed from both sides, but the really decisive confrontations took place in the meeting of peoples, rather than on the printed page. And one of the most decisive of all was occasioned by the death of Dr. Emes.

*The Death and 'Resurrection' of Dr. Emes*

Dr. Emes fell ill at the beginning of December, 1707, complaining of

257. Hughson, *Copious Account*, pp. 77-81.
258. Cited extensively in the last chapter.

a violent headache, and on the 5th John Lacy was at his bedside prophesying,

> 'Fear not. Whatever I do for thy trial, thou art in safe hands. For if I command thy life away, yet I will restore it again. Here even in this house thou shalt return to thy dwelling-place.'[259]

Other prophecies were uttered to the same effect in the days following and when Dr. Emes died on 22nd December, he was apparently happy in the conviction that he was presently to rise again. The prophets were certainly confident of the outcome, and so, according to Keimer,

> 'instead of being laid out, as is usual for a dead corpse, he was kept hot in bed till he stunk so as there was scarce any enduring it, several imagining he would come to life again.'[260]

However, the doctor was duly buried on 25th in Tyndall's burying ground in Bunhill Fields, and on that very day one, John Potter, prophesied,

> 'The raising of the dead shall decide it, after some months being interred ... Yes, I will raise the dead. By the same power that I have raised up Jesus will I raise up that body now asleep. Yes, the same body, and the same face, tho' more lovely.'

In the days that followed, the number of months and the mode of the resurrection were all specified in prophecy. The first detail came through a twelve-year old girl, Anna Maria King, who revealed that the miracle would be performed 'by the hand of my servant Lacy.' John Potter added that Dr. Emes would

> 'come out of his grave without taking away the earth that lies upon him, and shall untie his shroud, and that not in private, but publicly, and in the sight of all.'

Then he rounded off his prediction with this very precise statement:

> 'Know ye the day in which my servant was interred? Five months from that day, the 25th day of May, you shall behold him rise again. The very hour that he was put in the earth shall he arise.'

---

259. The story is told fully by Spinckes, from whose book, *New Pretenders to Prophecy Examined*, all the unacknowledged quotes following here are taken, pp. 425-31. His selection of material and his choice of expression are clearly governed by his purpose to discredit the prophets, but his account is factual enough and seems sufficiently trustworthy, especially since he always cites his sources carefully for verification of quotations and detail.
260. Hughson, *Copious Account*, p. 27.

Tremendous excitement was engendered by these prophecies, which were reiterated and confirmed by the utterances of others in the movement. Spinckes tells us that some of them treated this whole matter as a touchstone of their credibility. Sir Richard Bulkeley apparently declared that he was treating the prediction of Dr. Emes' resurrection as 'one of those prophecies he calls decisive … wherein the truth of the prophet is certainly at stake,' while others, it seems, announced that 'they would own themselves deluded' if nothing came of it.

*Disillusionment and Decline*

The outcome did not match the expectation. Crowds gathered at Bunhill Fields to witness the great event. One estimate put their number at 20,000. Certainly there were enough of them to necessitate calling out the troops to keep order. But in the end the prophets' courage failed them. Spinckes comments wryly that Lacy

> 'was so far from calling Emes out of his grave, that he durst not so much as once appear there for fear of being insulted by the rabble upon his disappointment … poor Emes is still in his grave, and is like to continue there till the sound of the trumpet at the last day, all thoughts of raising him being given over long ago.'

The discredited prophets made a feeble effort to defend themselves with a 'weak and useless apology … under the title of *Squire Lacy's Reasons why Dr. Emes was not raised, &c.*'[261], but perhaps the best comment on this sad episode is that offered by Knox:

> 'There is, somehow, an intolerable bathos about the thought of all those heroic visionaries lying killed in action in the Vivarais, while the scattered remnants of the movement must assemble to witness the resurrection of Dr. Emes in Bunhill Fields.'[262]

The Dr. Emes affair was not unique. An even more bizarre attempt to predict both the death and the resurrection of a certain Stephen Halford of Birmingham is recorded in a letter written by his brother in 1708 and published by Spinckes in an appendix to his second polemical volume, *The New Pretenders to Prophecy Re-examined*. However, Mr. Halford failed to die at the appointed time, let alone

261. Spinckes, p. 431.
262. Knox, *Enthusiasm*, p. 370.

rise again, but his story caused little embarrassment at the time because it attracted little public attention. The Dr. Emes fiasco, on the other hand, did irreparable damage to the movement. The prophets had been steadily increasing in numbers to that point, but now all but the most dedicated fell away, thoroughly disillusioned.

*The Prophets after 1707—Continuing Scandal*

By the end of 1707 the movement had gathered many English converts and its leadership had passed increasingly into English hands. Although the designation 'French Prophets' persisted, many of the original French leaders, including Marion, began travelling abroad on missionary journeys. The names of John Lacy and Sir Richard Bulkeley now loom large in the movement's annals. Their stories make stirring, yet tragic reading, and stand as cautionary illustrations to any would-be prophet of the dangers of gullibility and extreme fanaticism left unchecked. They both gave much to the movement, and in its early, troubled days their encouragement and leadership earned them high esteem among their associates. Had they submitted their later leadings and inspirations to the judgment of Scripture and the scrutiny of their community in Christ, some of their excesses might have been avoided and the reputation of the prophets as a whole less tarnished.

As it was, the Dr. Emes affair was but a foretaste of other scandals to follow. Bulkeley fell under the spell of a certain Abraham Whitro, who preached (under inspiration, of course) a community of goods, that the rich should share their wealth with the poor. Despite opposition from other prophets, including Lacy, Bulkeley slowly divested himself of his considerable resources, but when he died in 1710, we are told, Abraham Whitro, his erstwhile missionary companion, began living the life of a rich gentleman, and no one doubted whence came his new-found prosperity.

The following year brought yet another scandal. Several of the prophets had entered into marriage bonds under the direction of the Spirit and with generally happy results, but in 1711 Lacy, who had earlier left his wife, married a certain young prophetess called Betty Gray. His action was not approved by the prophets and so he wrote an apologetic epistle in which he asserted that he had been guided by his inspirations and 'by a supernatural outward voice heard, that threatened me with eternal destruction and hell-fire if I disobeyed.'[263]

263. A copy of this letter is appended to Keimer's *Brand*.

One of the most serious set-backs had come at an earlier date. In Holland at the end of 1707 and again in London early in 1708, Jean Cavalier, the Camisard leader whose military exploits in the Cevennes had captivated the imagination of all Europe, betrayed his former prophet companions with a solemn denial of their and his own inspiration.

> 'Although his friends warned him and earnestly exhorted him to give glory to God ... he denied that he had ever been inspired, or that he had been guided in this war by inspirations, either his own or any one else's. He spoke about these matters with a great deal of contempt.'[264]

Extracts from the text of his declarations, together with copies of some letters in which he pathetically tried to justify his statements, are published by Bost in his edition of Marion's *Mémoires* (pp. 167ff). They make a sorry epitaph for the hero of the Camisard Wars, for they put Cavalier down in the annals of history as one who bought his respectability and fortune as Governor of Jersey at the expense of his own integrity and the reputation of his former friends and comrades-in-arms.

*Sober Lives or Bizarre?*

While the movement certainly had its excesses and aberrations, the total picture was generally a happier one. Doubtless many came to investigate its activities because of some fascination with the bizarre, but those who stayed were impressed by the sincerity, devotion and integrity of its members. Bulkeley wrote of them, and his testimonial finds many echoes in the writings of other prophets,

> 'I found them men of sober lives and conversations, such as heretofore frequented the assemblies for religious worship, men of good characters amongst their neighbours; in short, as far as man can judge (that knows not the heart) pious and devout Christians, and to have the fear of God before their eyes ... all practice what they profess in public, viz. a zeal for God and his holiness, and constant prayer and praises to him.'[265]

As we would expect, the critics had little to say about such matters as 'sober lives and conversations', and even occasionally tried to convey a contrary impression of loose morality. Doubtless there

264. Bost, *Mémoires*, p. 156.
265. Bulkeley, *Impartial Account*, pp. 6,7,11.

were occasional grounds for such accusations, but they do not appear to represent the norm at all. On the whole the French Prophets were the sort of men and women Bulkeley describes.

However, it was not so much the prophets' morals that the critics scorned as their grotesque bodily agitations, which, by all accounts would have been easy to lampoon:

> 'the shakings of their heads, crawlings on the knees, quakings and tremblings; their whistlings, drummings, trumpetings; their thundrings; their snuffling; blowing as with a horn; panting and difficulty of breathing; sighing and groaning; hissing; smiling; laughing; pointing with the finger; shaking the hand; striking; threshing; as likewise their perpetual hesitations; childish repetitions; unintelligible stuff; gross contradictions; manifest lies; conjectures turned into predictions; their howling in the assemblies like a dog, and being in all manner of disorder.'[266]

Keimer gives several vivid depictions of their agitations, but we must read his witness with some caution. For example, he says he saw Cavalier

> 'flung along upon the ground with a sort of violent force, showing several strange postures,'

and Lacy praying over a woman

> 'with his hands upon her head, uttering several sentences mixed with strange hiccups and shakings of his head forwards and backwards, his body it seemed to me jumping while he was speaking. Between every two or three words speaking, he cried, "Hoh, Hoh, Hoh, O—h, O—h, O—h," as if he were taking his last gasp.'[267]

These are actually some of Keimer's less spectacular accounts of the prophets' doings and so probably bear some relation to reality, though it is difficult to say how much.

### *The Agitations and the Spirit of God*

Whatever we make of these old records, the fact is that many of the antics they describe may be witnessed again today in certain charismatic and revival circles. The prophets themselves never denied or

266. Spinckes, *New Pretenders Examined*, pp. 499f.
267. Keimer, *Brand*, p. 6.

attempted to play down the reality of their agitations. On the contrary, they were to them the physical evidences of the divine activity in which they delighted, though they were usually thought of as a prelude to the more important utterance of the prophetic word. The gift was generally communicated through the laying on of hands.

Bulkeley gives a fairly full and informative account of the effects of the Spirit's entry in the prophet's life. He says that after the laying on of hands people generally received first 'the earnest of it, to wit, the agitations.' These, he says,

> 'do increase and vary progressively, till they come on to the opening of the mouth to speak by inspiration. They generally begin in the limbs, and then affect the lungs by a vibration of breathing ... some find great vibrations of the head, with some it is forwards and backwards ... with others it is in a horizontal motion, as a dog that turns his head when he comes out of the water.' He also describes 'an involuntary motion in the tongue ... the under jaw and the lips,' but adds that 'there is always a tranquillity of soul, and, for the most part, an elevation of it to God, that these are the most delightful minutes of their lives. And the more violent, the more inward joy; and these accompanied with better health than ever before.'[268]

Much of what Bulkeley wrote about the agitations corresponds with what was written about the prophets in the South of France, about the elegance of the discourses delivered in ecstasy, and the like, but he also distinguishes between two kinds of agitation: 'such as do only betoken the presence of a superior Spirit' and such 'as do seem to represent something to the imagination of those who behold them.' The second sort, he says,

> 'are called signs, and have a signification in them, and are commonly explained afterwards by the mouth of the prophet under inspiration.'[269]

That suggests they regarded these as something akin to the acted sign of the Old Testament prophets, though their signs were deliberate, rationally controlled actions, rather than bodily agitations.

One cannot but wonder whether Bulkeley and his associates were simply trying to extort meaning from actions that did not always have any particular message to convey. He writes, for example,

268. Bulkeley, *Answer*, pp. 104f.
269. Bulkeley, *Answer*, p. 31.

> 'The most general sign that all and every one of them have is that of shaking, some less and some more. And this the Spirit has explained to us to be the sign of what he is now going to do, what he has foretold in his word, and that they are sent before to warn of, to wit, he is coming "to shake terribly the earth".'[270]

The distinction Bulkeley draws between these two kinds of agitation is comparable to the distinction drawn today in Pentecostal circles between two kinds of tongue, the kind that signifies the presence of the Spirit and the kind that conveys a message requiring interpretation. But then, for the French Prophets their agitations had much the same kind of function as tongues has today, in that they viewed them as the most characteristic evidence of baptism in the Spirit. And therein lay the seed of similar problems and tensions. Bulkeley writes:

> 'I knew of several who earnestly desired the agitation, and constantly frequented the assemblies, and yet have them not, and others that never desired them, scarce ever saw them, and yet have been seized.'[271]

*Prophecy, Languages and Tongues*

Most of what was written about their forerunners in Southern France is equally applicable to the French Prophets in London. Their utterances were generally in the form of 'speeches, prophecies and exhortations,' usually beyond the intellectual capacity of the speakers 'to frame such,' and yet 'all conformable to truth and the word of God,' though unlike the Cevennols 'every particular person spoke in his or her own dialect.'[272]

Their style of utterance was similar, using the divine 'I' and the expression 'My Child.' Again, they could not normally recall what they had spoken and their manner of delivery was frequently broken 'thro' the interruptions of the agitations.'[273]

Besides the gift of prophecy, several writers make reference to 'the gift of languages' or 'the gift of tongues'.[274] However, this gift was apparently something quite different from that generally exercised in Pentecostal circles today, where tongues is predominantly identified

270. Bulkeley, *Answer*, p. 43.
271. Bulkeley, *Impartial Account*, p. 16.
272. Bulkeley, *Impartial Account*, pp. 8f.
273. Bulkeley, *Answer*, pp. 47f.
274. Bulkeley, *Impartial Account*, pp. 24, 29; Spinckes, *New Pretenders Examined*, p. 380.

with glossolalia, an unintelligible form of speech. Although the odd reference to glossolalia is found among the French Prophets, the gift of tongues is most commonly identified among them as xenolalia, the ability to speak a recognised foreign language in which the speaker has no naturally acquired aptitude. In the Cevennes this known language was mainly Parisian French, for there the prophets spoke to convey an urgent message and so their utterances were expected to be understood by at least some in their audience.

The same was the case in London, indeed so much so that when we do find an instance of what might be classified as glossolalia, the prophets felt obliged to extract some sense or meaning from the words. Durand Fage once prophesied (in French),

> 'My Child, I am going away to pour out my terrible judgments on my enemies, and my last sentence will be "Tring, trang, swing, swang, hing, hang!"'

Mr. Facio, who is said to have been adept in fifty-two languages, was puzzled by this utterance, but after prayer he felt it should not be dismissed as meaningless. He

> 'thought the words, or rather inarticulate sounds, might allude to the law among the Jews, not to exceed forty stripes in punishing some offences … and that the Holy Spirit condescended to express himself by the sound of blows, as a man, driving a wedge, cries "Ha! Ha!"'[275]

We do, however, read about some of the prophets' experiments with this gift that became quite pretentious, even eccentric, and certainly nothing to do with the impartation of an urgent message from God. Bulkeley tells how on one occasion, when he was travelling by coach with Lacy and Facio, 'the Latin impression' came on Lacy, who for over an hour translated for them whatever Latin passages were put to him, including excerpts from Ovid, Virgil, Lucretius and other classical authors. We are told he had never read any of these and had not read any Latin for twenty years, but now 'no sooner did we recite a line in Latin, but he recited the same in English.' Apparently he had experienced this 'Latin impression' on one or two other occasions also.

Bulkeley adds a similar note about having heard an attorney called Mr. Dutton, who knew no Hebrew,

275. Smedley, *History* III, p. 309, n.1.

> 'utter with great readiness and freedom complete discourses in Hebrew for near a quarter of an hour together, and sometimes much longer.'

Bulkeley admitted he was no Hebraist himself, but claimed to have sufficient acquaintance with the sound of the language to recognise it as Hebrew and to identify a number of the words spoken.[276]

*Prophecies and Blessings Taken Down in Writing*

We get the impression that such extravagances of xenolalia were fairly rare and that for the most part the prophets spoke in English or French, whichever was their own natural tongue, the utterances in French being translated for the benefit of those who spoke only English. For some reason, and uniquely so in the history of Christian prophecy, a great deal of importance was attached to having the utterances written down and preserved for private use or future publication. The prophets themselves, of course, could seldom recall what they had said, and since they spoke in a very broken fashion, their message was constantly in danger of not being heard properly at all if not taken in writing as it came from their lips. Keimer says that

> ''twas usual, those who took down in writing what was spoke, if it was in French, translated it, and read it in English to those present, and if desired, would write out copies of what was spoken, and particularly blessings, and give 'em the persons so desiring.'[277]

The 'blessings' he speaks about were described by Bulkeley as

> 'whatever is spoken in inspiration over the head of any particular person, whatever the contents of it be, whether consolation, reproof, or even threatenings.'[278]

Such blessings were apparently not given at every meeting—Bulkeley estimates about one in every four or five. They were similar to the words of reproof or consolation addressed to individuals at the prophetic assemblies in the Cevennes, such as those spoken by the boy-prophets Cavalier heard at his first meeting[279], except that in England they were less spontaneous, for they were normally

276. Bulkeley, *Answer*, pp. 92ff.
277. Keimer, *Brand*, p. 9.
278. Bulkeley, *Answer*, p. 95.
279. See above p. 322.

uttered only when a worshipper presented himself before a prophet seeking guidance. But following the earlier French custom, the guidance was acceptable whether it came through an adult or a child, a boy or a girl, a French speaker or an English one.[280]

Bulkeley gives several examples of personal blessings he had received when he presented himself. On two occasions he had received promises through different prophets that God would labour every day in his soul to make him a new creature. At another meeting he was forewarned of reproaches that were to come his way, and he tells us that a fortnight later a pamphlet was published in which he

> 'was treated more vilely than I believe ever any gentleman was in print.'

Again he recounts how

> 'a child, in ecstasy, instructed of my domestic affairs, and which are remote from this city, and such as prudence would have obliged me or anyone else to keep secret from the knowledge of others.'

And finally he tells that at

> 'a private meeting, where there happened to be blessings, I received a reproof for my vanity and love of the world.'[281]

*Other Gifts and Directions from the Spirit*

As in the Cevennes, and indeed as in any prophetic movement, a variety of gifts were exercised. Bulkeley lists

> 'an extraordinary spirit of prayer and praise to God, the gifts of prophecy, the gift of exhortation, the gift of discerning spirits, the gift of languages, the ministration of the same spirit unto others, and some earnests of the gifts of healing, all which were proofs that the Holy Spirit gave in the apostles' times.'[282]

One of the most useful gifts in the Camisard camp had been the ability to identify spies and traitors. A version of this gift persisted at the prophets' meetings in London. Bulkeley tells us that on several occasions when spies have come to their meetings hoping to find reasons for making mischief against them afterwards, he heard

280. Bulkeley, *Answer*, p. 96.
281. Bulkeley, *Answer*, pp. 95 100.
282. Bulkeley, *Impartial Account*, p. 29.

> 'one of the inspired call out to them by the name "Judas", and sometimes tell them even from whom they came, and their particular errand, and have so described them as has made them go off in the presence of all present.'[283]

Just as the armies in the Cevennes believed their movements were directed by the Spirit, so the prophets in England continued to acknowledge the same kind of spiritual leading, often in very similar settings. For example, Marion, recalling how he and several others were once compelled to leave London because of the persecution directed against them, tells that,

> 'under the direction of the Spirit we secretly sailed down the Thames ... On the day after our arrival at Northfleet, the Spirit came upon some of us in a quite extraordinary manner. The Spirit ordered us to return to London where our enemies were already crying "Victory", believing that we had fled ...We did exactly as he ordered us. When our enemies saw us, they gnashed their teeth, but they were allowed to go no further.'[284]

*Prophetic Inspiration and Human Wisdom*

As may be gathered from the preceding pages, there was a great deal of variety in the utterances of the prophets, for they touched on almost every aspect of daily living and theological belief. None the less, there are a number of recurrent themes that deserve further comment here, since they are of the fabric of most prophetic movements.

To begin with, there was a marked tendency among the French Prophets to hold their inspirations in greater esteem than natural reason and human learning. This attitude presents no problem so long as the spiritual and the natural agree, but unfortunately in prophetic circles the two tend to conflict quite frequently. We are reminded, for example, of Paul's contrast between 'men's wisdom' and 'God's secret wisdom' in 1 Cor. 2, or the disparagement of academicity among the Friends of God and the Zwickau Prophets.[285] Paul did urge that inspiration should be tested (1 Thes. 5:21), and other prophets, like Tertullian, for example, have done that carefully[286], but some less balanced groups have often failed to acknowledge this need, sometimes with disastrous consequences, as the con-

283. Bulkeley, *Answer*, p. 102.
284. Bost, *Mémoires*, p. 162.
285. See above, p. 243.
286. See above, p. 243.

frontations between Luther and the Zwickau Prophets amply illustrated. The French Prophets seem to fall too often into the latter category. Fage and Marion spoke of unquestioning obedience to the inspirations of the prophets in the Camisard camp, and the same unquestioning trust, it seems, was expected in England, even though the urgency of battle-field discipline was no longer with them.

Some of Lacy's utterances from the Spirit about inspiration and learning look very extreme, for example:

> 'Learning! Learning, that confounds the true knowledge of me. Multitude of reading to make men stupid ... The inspiration of the Almighty gives better understanding than all academies.'[287]

Or again,

> 'I do not teach by men's wisdom. I have no need of it. I did not use it in the first ages of my church ... Great words and empty sounds signify nothing. I can give to the weak a wisdom that all learning cannot contradict.'[288]

Perhaps it is unfair to judge a movement by the utterances of a man whose unquestioned following of his inspirations to leave his wife and marry another was not generally approved within the movement itself, but it is difficult to forget that others besides Lacy were enthused by the prospect of Dr. Emes' resurrection from the dead! The least we can say is that there was a tendency among some of the French Prophets to overestimate the value of their inspirations at the expense of basic scriptural revelation.

*Prophetical Warnings and Pleadings for Repentance*

A second recurrent theme in the prophets' teaching is that of imminent judgment. Here again the French Prophets join hands with every other prophetic movement that has emphasised the nearness of divine intervention to punish the wicked or terminate corruption. On the other hand, the French Prophets differ from all others, except the Old Testament prophets, in that they had their predictions written down, collected and published for all to read. Besides Marion's *Avertissements*, several other volumes of *Prophetical Warnings* by different prophets appeared, amongst which were three volumes by Lacy himself, dated 1707, the first entitled *The*

287. Spinckes, *New Pretenders Examined*, p. 468.
288. Lacy, *Prophetical Warnings*, p. 12.

*Prophetical Warnings of John Lacy Esq.*, the second and third *Warnings of the Eternal Spirit by the Mouth of his servant John, sirnamed Lacy.*

The oracles of the prophets are so many and often so long that it would be impossible to give more than the minutest selection from them. Spinckes made a useful summary by collecting a series of illustrative quotations from Lacy's writings. The style is reminiscent of some Old Testament prophecy, vivid, dramatic and urgent:

> '... concerning the terrible vengeance that should befall this city [London]. They confidently foretold, and with all the assurance that might be, that "the destroying angel should come and sheath the sword of his indignation in the bowels of those that would not hear; and the power of the Almighty should cause such echoes in this city, as that the city should tremble;" that "it was concluded, no revoke, no respite, the sentence was past, and a horrible tempest was to be poured out upon thee, O London! Smoke was to darken, aetherial fire to fall down, and ordinary flames to mount up ..."'

And so the warnings continue, page after page, interspersed with urgent pleas that the judgment was to fall speedily, 'in a very little time', starting in England, but spreading to other nations also. Sometimes they nominated dates when it should begin, 'at other times they expressed themselves in more general terms.'[289]

Coupled with this dramatic message of judgment were repeated exhortations to repentance and commitment, a theme recurrent in all evangelistic preaching, but not normally presented in the style we find in Lacy's *Warnings*. His language at times seems very impassioned and pleading, though its broken and repetitive style probably also reflects delivery under inspiration with accompanying agitations. Furthermore, they were delivered in very different settings, some in quiet private meetings, others at rather rowdy public gatherings. Though we cannot now tell how the words would have sounded to the original hearers, it is worth quoting two or three examples here simply to give some impression of their prophetic style.

> 'O ye hard hearted and unbelievers, fear, fear, fear. I am the Lord of the whole earth, who am come down to visit for iniquities, to pull down and to destroy, to purge away all hypocrites. I call you this day to repent. Choose. Own or deny.'

289. Spinckes, *New Pretenders Examined*, pp. 441f.

> 'O ye sheep of my flock. Oh come, come, come to your shepherd, who calls you from all the ends of the world. O ye sheep of Israel, ye lost wandering (sheep) come, come to your shepherd, your Lord, who was crucified by you. He comes (to call you). O don't harden your hearts as your fathers.'
>
> 'You are many of you beasts before me, and you have almost lost in my sight the distinction of rational creatures. You have only so much of my image left in you as will serve to survive in hell, if you repent not. For judgment am I coming down into this world.'[290]

*Encouragements for the Faithful and the New Church of the Spirit*

Of course it was not only sinners that the prophets addressed. Many of their words were spoken for the encouragement of the faithful. Again the biblical echoes are unmistakable in their style, as also is that sectarian sentiment we have noted in the teaching of most prophetic movements. A couple of brief illustrative examples will have to suffice here.

> 'I have chosen this place for my habitation, for my glory. I will not that you have any over you. I will preside over you. I will make my pleasure known to this people, for I have much people in this city, in this city. I will feed them with living streams.'
>
> 'I will watch over your assemblies. Oh, take heed that the word does not slip out of your hearts and thoughts. Oh, this is but preparatory to something, that shall be revealed in a short time. I shall never be weary of visiting you, if you be not weary of my visits. I leave you my benedictions.'[291]

Of course, the greatest encouragements for the faithful, as in every other prophetic movement before them, lay in their doctrine of a new age for the Church, of the imminent advent of the spiritual Church of which the prophets themselves were the present historical nucleus. Spinckes has once more provided us with a useful summary of their teaching on this subject, again in the form of a catena of quotations from Lacy's *Warnings*.

> '... they come to make way for a glorious state of the Church, far above what it has ever been, more adorned, more visited with the Spirit even than in the first planting of the gospel; a

290. Lacy, *Warnings* I, pp. 7, 7f, 16.
291. Lacy, *Prophetical Warnings*, pp. 8f, 16.

glorious reign upon earth; a kingdom to be ushered in with a great and terrible day; everlasting espousals to be between God and his beloved; a new creation with a seminal growing principle; a kingdom of Jesus Christ ... a glorious state of the Church, which is called Christ's kingdom; and yet it is to be ministered by the Holy Ghost; the restitution of all things to their original beauty ...'[292]

The French Prophets never established themselves as a dissenting sect or separatist denomination with an ecclesiastical system of its own. Theirs was to be a 'kingdom administered by the Holy Ghost', and so, like the Friends of God, the Zwickau Prophets and the Seekers, they remained a lay movement, fostering a kind of conventicle Christianity that has its best parallels in the house churches, Gospel halls and home groups of our own day, rather than in the hierarchical systems of the Montanists in the early Church or the Irvingites of more recent times.

*The Spread of the Movement at Home and Overseas*

Driven from London by the violence of persecution and by the disgrace consequent on Dr. Emes' failure to rise from the dead, the prophets took their gospel to other cities in the British Isles and elsewhere. Keimer mentions that 'some went to Bristol, Coventry, Worcester, Oxford, Cambridge, etc.; others went to Holland, Ireland, Scotland and Wales,' and comments, 'nor were they without success in their several progresses.'[293]

But what communities they did establish were always fairly small, though their enthusiasm and their reputation were usually more than commensurate with their size. Thomas Hearne describes the considerable interest that six of them aroused in August, 1709, at Oxford, where the Vice-Chancellor dismissed the 'vast crowds of people', including scholars, who gathered to hear them, and ordered them out of the town.[294]

Other missionaries travelled through Europe, particularly to areas where refugees from Southern France had settled and where events not unlike those in London had been occurring as well. Although these prophets ascribed the impetus for their missionary ventures entirely to the Spirit, their motives were doubtless mixed, for they were continentals themselves. In the latter part of 1711,

292. Spinckes, *New Pretenders Examined*, pp. 365f.
293. Keimer, *Brand*, p. 39.
294. Hearne, *Reliquiae Hearnianae* I, pp. 150f.

Allut, Marion, Portales and Facio journeyed across Europe visiting sympathetic communities and uttering their prophetical warnings as they went, starting in Amsterdam, then through Brandenburg, Berlin, Saxe-Hall, Leipzig, Coburg, Erlangen, Nurenburg, Schwabach and Ratisbonn as far as Vienna, whence they returned to London at the end of the year.

A further missionary journey in the following two years took them through Bohemia and Moravia to Budapest, Belgrade and Constantinople, after which Marion died in November, 1713, aged 35, while his companions went on to Rome. Their reception varied from place to place. For example, in Holland and Brandenburg at the beginning of their travels, they made little impression, whereas in Berlin they caused so much public excitement that they were taken before the council and banished from the city. On their third journey they were imprisoned twice.

*The Movement's Decline in England*

The mission in and around London, although much subdued by the events of 1707-8, did continue, sometimes with outbursts of surprising vigour and audacity. For example, Keimer tells how in 1711,

> 'James Cunninghame, Laird of Barns, a Scots prophet, came up to London, and was commanded to go to Paul's Cathedral, being told by the Spirit he should there prophesy.'

No sooner was the sermon ended and the blessing pronounced,

> 'than up starts J. Cunninghame, under agitations and with a very loud voice, distinctly utters the following warning …'[295]

The consequence, as may well be imagined, was a mob riot from which Cunninghame emerged somewhat bruised and beaten, indeed fortunate to escape alive.

But on the whole the temperature in London had considerably cooled since the riots of 1707-8. Bulkeley died in 1710 and Lacy's life took a quieter turn. In 1711 he published, jointly with John Potter, a further volume of *Warnings of the Eternal Spirit*, then in 1713 a lengthy work entitled *The General Delusion of Christians, touching the Ways of God's revealing Himself to and by the Prophets, evinc'd from Scripture and Primitive Authority*. By the time these works appeared, however, Lacy had already withdrawn from public view and soon

295. Keimer, *Brand*, pp. 54f.

thereafter he retired with his prophet bride, Elizabeth Gray, who interestingly continued to retain her maiden name, into Lancashire and virtual obscurity.

Although the excitement subsided, the movement lived on. As late as 1739, Wesley still found the prophets sufficiently numerous and influential in London and Bristol to want to visit their meetings 'to try the spirits'. Judging by his own account in his diary entry for Sunday, 28th February, that year, he seems to have been open-minded towards them at first. He says he visited them in a house in London with four or five of his friends. After a time, a young lady of about twenty-five entered and greeted them.

> 'Presently after she leaned back in her chair and seemed to have strong workings in her breast, with deep sighings intermixed. Her head and hands, and by turns, every part of her body, seemed also to be in a kind of convulsive motion. This continued about ten minutes, till, at six, she began to speak (though the workings, sighings, and contortions of her body were so intermixed with her words, that she seldom spoke half a sentence together) with a clear, strong voice ... She spoke much (all as in the person of God, and mostly in Scripture words) of the fulfilling of the prophecies, the coming of Christ now at hand, and the spreading of the Gospel over all the earth.'

She went on to plead with them to wait on God, watch and pray, and the like. Wesley says some of his friends 'were much affected, and believed she spoke by the Spirit of God.' But he was not so certain himself, thinking the bodily motions could have been contrived and that what she actually said could equally have been said by anyone well enough versed in the Scriptures.[296]

*The Heritage of the French Prophets*

It is manifest from Wesley's notes that the prophets were now little more than a shadow of what they had once been, a mere echo of bygone enthusiasm. The crispness had gone from their message, which was now reduced to a rehearsing of scriptural promises and a memory of things once uttered by Marion and his associates.

By the time Wesley visited Bristol in the summer, his attitude had completely changed and he denounced them as prophets who prophesy in the Lord's name, when he has not sent them. Possibly

296. Wesley, *Journal*, entry under 28/2/1739. His brother, Charles, had little time for them either, particularly after a rather frightening encounter he had with one of them in Wycombe. See below, p. 405.

he had become hardened towards them because they were stealing some of his converts, for he wrote in the same diary entry about 'one who "did run well", till he was hindered by some of those called French Prophets.'[297]

At Bristol he preached to the crowd that they should not let themselves be persuaded

> 'by appearances, or by common report, or by their own inward feelings; No, nor by any dreams, visions, or revelations, supposed to be made to their souls; any more than by their tears, or any involuntary effects wrought upon their bodies.'

Such things, he said, are

> 'in themselves, of a doubtful, disputable nature; they might be from God, and they might not.'

However, his general approach seems to have been that bodily paroxysms were to be condemned if they resulted from contact with the prophets, but welcomed if they resulted from his own preaching, for while he was saying these very things to the Bristol assembly, he approvingly records,

> 'one before me dropped down as dead, and presently a second, and a third. Five others sunk down in half an hour, most of whom were in violent agonies.'[298]

Wesley's Journal is well adorned with accounts of swoonings, tremblings and the like, and with records of healings, exorcisms and other wondrous manifestations. But as we have already noted, such phenomena are common by-products of revivalist fervour in every age and are not quite the same as their prophetic counterparts. Perhaps Wesley was aware of some such distinction, though he never said so. Yet paradoxically, it was perhaps the greatest legacy of the French Prophets that they, even more than the Quakers before them, prepared the people of England, by their strange antics and their charismatic enthusiasm, for the sudden and powerful impact of Wesley's and his contemporaries' preaching with its apparently similar initial effects.

However, the French Prophets had an even more clearly definable heritage in a yet stranger prophetic movement which started in Manchester not too much later in the same century, and to which we shall turn our attention next.

---

297. *Journal*, entry under 22/6/1739.
298. *Journal*, entry under 22/6/1739 also.

*Assessment*

One cannot but note the close similarity between the French Prophets and some of their Old Testament counterparts. Elisha and the ninth-century prophets encouraged war against the persecutors, Samuel's followers witnessed bodily motions and reactions at their meetings, the classical prophets had their words written down and published, most Israelite prophets gave themselves to urgent, public preaching of judgment and repentance, and so forth. The parallels are many.

The French Prophets are also close to other prophetic groups in a number of different ways. For example, their prophesying 'in ecstasy' has reminded us of the Montanists. In fact, in their own day the 'New Prophets Pretensions to Inspiration and Miracles' prompted a certain 'Lay-Gentleman' to write *The History of Montanism*, a work that is included along with Spinckes' earlier writing on the prophets in George Hickes' *The Spirit of Enthusiasm Exorcised*, 1709. Hickes' own view was that the gifts of the Spirit were for the first century only, a very popular view even today among those who do not like prophetic things.

The prophets' elevation of mystical inspiration above human learning has suggested parallels with the Friends of God and the Zwickau Prophets. And we have also noted in passing the whole gamut of doctrines that are usually associated with prophetic movements, such as belief in an imminent new age for the Church, lay-orientated theology, lack of interest in matters ecclesiastical and sacramental, criticism of contemporary Church life, missionary enthusiasm and a sectarian tendency that strangely does not set out to establish a separate sect, delight in the miraculous, and above all their total dedication and zeal for the gospel.

In some of these respects they had clearly moved away from their warrior predecessors in Southern France, who had had little freedom to concern themselves with either outreach evangelism or theological introspection, and yet they, of course, must always be more closely linked in ethos and vision with their immediate Camisard roots and with those ecstatic visionaries that sprang from the Huguenot soil after the Revocation. Indeed, in the French Prophets in England we have perhaps the most fascinating amalgam of diverse prophetic attitudes that history has ever produced.

# 23
# The Shakers or United Society of Believers

Whatever the more diffuse influence of the French Prophets on English religious society may have been, their most direct and lasting heritage is found in the United Society of Believers in Christ's Second Appearing, more popularly known as the Shakers. They flourished on American soil in mixed celibate, communal settlements during the nineteenth century, but these gradually dwindled away in the twentieth century. They are chiefly remembered for their highly successful communistic social organisation, their inventiveness and high standards of craftsmanship, their sobriety, hospitality and strict moral observances, and their strange forms of worship.

Songs, many of them with glossolalic expressions (tongues) incorporated in their verses, and ritual dancing, mostly in group formation, were regular features of their religious services. It is interesting to observe how these stereotyped forms gradually evolved out of originally charismatic worship inherited from their prophet-predecessors.

The later development of Shakerism as it unfolds in the United States is a fascinating story in its own right and deserves to be read. It has been told many times and is readily available to the English reader, but its details take us beyond the scope of our study, for by the mid-nineteenth century the prophetic strain in the movement had become either so formalised or else so confused with other things that it ceased to be properly prophetic in itself. Our main interest here is the movement's prophetic origins and its prophetic hope.

Shaker literature commonly traces the Society's origins to the activities and teachings of the French Prophets, mainly following the narrative in the opening chapters of the *Summary View of the Millennial Church or United Society of Believers (commonly called Shakers)*, which was a handbook on Shakerism, its history, practice and doctrine, published in 1823[299]. An abbreviated version of its

299. Page references in the paragraphs immediately following are to this source.

contents is available in Evans' *Compendium*, which is itself often little more than a verbatim rescript of extended sections from the *Summary View*. One of the most useful books published in recent years is *The Shakers. Two Centuries of Spiritual Reflection*, by R.E. Whiston, which is also referred to quite frequently here. It is an edited collection of original Shaker source materials and as such is exceedingly valuable for our purposes.

*Shaking Quakers, 1747-70*

The French Prophets are said to have prepared the way, not just with their physical agitations, but with their end-time preaching.

> 'They testified that the end of all things drew nigh, and admonished the people to repent and amend their lives. They gave warning of the near approach of the Kingdom of God, the acceptable year of the Lord; and in many prophetic messages, declared to the world, that those numerous scripture prophecies concerning the new heavens and the new earth; the kingdom of the Messiah; the marriage of the Lamb; the first resurrection, and the New Jerusalem descending from above, were near at hand, and would shortly be accomplished.' (p. 2)

The Shakers saw their own Society as the Millennial Kingdom thus heralded, but their own story only begins properly in 1747.

In that year a handful of Quakers living near Manchester, who were also

> 'endowed with the spirit of these witnesses [the French Prophets], were led by the influence of the Divine Spirit to unite themselves into a small society.' (p. 4)

We get the impression that there could have been as many as thirty of them altogether and they are said to have met in Bolton and Manchester. They were led by James and Jane Wardley, who 'were both sincerely devoted to the cause of God, and were blest with great manifestations of divine light.' James is reputed to have been 'greatly gifted in public speaking' and to have been 'remarkably clear, solid and powerful in his testimony against sin.' (p. 4)

His puritanical preaching was apparently matched by his and his wife's dress, deportment and manners, and in those respects he probably stood closer to his Quaker than his Prophet ancestors, though both movements championed righteous living in their own ways. The heritage of the Prophets is more clearly seen in their forms of worship, of which bodily movement was very much an integral part, in their openness to spiritual illumination and charismatic gifts, and in their eschatological preoccupations.

> 'This infant society practised no forms, and adopted no creeds as rules of faith or worship; but gave themselves up to be led and guided entirely by the operations of the Spirit of God. Their meetings were powerful and animated, attended with remarkable signs and operations, and with the spirit of prophecy and divine revelation. The manifestations of divine light in visions and revelations, raised in them the warning voice of God against all sin and every evil work. They boldly testified that the second appearing of Christ was at hand; and that the church was rising in her full and transcendent glory, which would effect the final downfall of Antichrist'

... all of which they said was already starting.

Their meetings were conducted much in the style of the French Prophets, but with a slightly different feel about them, coming perhaps from their Quaker background.

> 'Sometimes, after sitting awhile in silent meditation, they were seized with a mighty trembling, under which they would often express the indignation of God against all sin. At other times they were exercised with singing, shouting and leaping for joy at the near prospect of salvation. They were often exercised with great agitations of body and limbs, running and walking the floor, with a variety of signs and operations, and swiftly passing and repassing each other, like clouds agitated with a mighty wind. No human power could imitate the wonderful operations with which they were affected while under the influence of these spiritual signs. From these exercises, so strange in the eyes of mankind, they received the appellation of Shakers.' (pp. 4-5)

Like the prophets before them they were persecuted, their property was vandalised, they suffered various forms of personal abuse and some of them spent periods in prison. Shouting and dancing were hardly normal Sunday activities in eighteenth-century England and readily suggested the charge of Sabbath-breaking. But on the whole, the story of the Wardleys' society was not particularly dramatic, at least not until 1770, the year in which the Shakers believed the Millennial Church was born.

*The Illumination of Ann Lee, 1770*

Ann Lee was born in 1736. Her father was a blacksmith, poor, but honest and industrious. Since she was one of a family of eight, she received no formal education and could neither read not write. During her youth she was variously employed in a cotton factory, as a cutter of hatter's fur and as a cook in the Manchester infirmary. She 'was peculiarly distinguished,' we are told, 'for her faithfulness, neatness, prudence and economy.' She is also said to have been a particularly serious and thoughtful girl, 'not addicted to play, like other children,' but 'peculiarly favoured with heavenly visions,' and very conscious 'of the odiousness of sin, and especially of the impure and indecent nature of sexual coition.' (p. 6)

However, despite her feeling, which she often discussed with her mother, she was given in marriage to another blacksmith, called Abraham Stanley, by whom she had four children, all of whom died in infancy. They lived together in her father's home in Toad Lane, and it was during this period that she became acquainted with the Wardleys, at a time, we are informed, when she was overwhelmed with feelings of guilt and was yearning for release from the bondage of sin, often spending 'whole nights in labouring and crying to God for deliverance.' (p. 6)

She joined the Wardleys' society in 1758, when she was twenty-three, and there she 'found that protection which she had so long desired, and which, for the time being, was answerable to her faith.' And so she too became a prophet: 'she was baptised into the same spirit, and, by degrees, attained to the full knowledge and experience in spiritual things which they found.' (p. 7) But for Ann that was only the beginning. She was so obsessed with her consciousness of human depravity that she continued to cry out to God 'for deliverance from the very nature of sin,' asking him to show her 'the real foundation of man's loss.' (p. 8) And thus she 'laboured' for nine years, frequently refusing food and sleep in her anguish of soul, becoming very weak at times, but also being granted visions and insights that encouraged her in her search.

The culmination of her illuminations came in the summer of 1770, while in prison in Manchester on a charge of having profaned the Sabbath.

> 'She saw the Lord Jesus Christ in his glory, who revealed to her the great object of her prayers, and fully satisfied all the desires of her soul … the whole spiritual world seemed displayed before her … she had a full and clear view of the mystery of

> iniquity, of the root and foundation of human depravity, and of the very act of transgression, committed by the first man and woman, in the garden of Eden. Here she saw whence and wherein all mankind were lost from God, and clearly realised the only possible way of recovery.' (p. 9)

Prior to this time Ann had made it her custom to share her illuminations with the Wardleys and the other members of the society. But this time it was different. When she reported her latest vision, the gathering was so conscious of her spiritual endowment that they

> 'were filled with fear and trembling. They at once saw that the candle of the Lord was in her hand, and that she was able by the light thereof, to search every heart and try every soul among them.' (p. 9)

She had ceased to be a mere member of the group, but henceforth was recognised as Mother Ann, the one in whom Christ had chosen to manifest himself in his second coming.

They perceived that the Wardleys' society had been preparatory for that moment, fulfilling in those latter days the role of John the Baptist as the forerunner of Christ's appearing. Ann's baptism into their society had likewise been merely preliminary to her fuller baptism; by it she was

> 'prepared for the baptism of the Holy Ghost, and was made a fit vessel to receive the true Spirit of Christ, and to revive and bring light to his perfect law of righteousness for the direction and salvation of all souls who were willing to obey her testimony; and here commenced the real manifestation of Christ's second appearance.' (pp. 9f)

The Millennium was beginning!

*Founding the Millennial Kingdom*

Mother Ann now set herself to bear her 'testimony against the lustful gratification of the flesh' and to proclaim her gospel of latter-day celibacy. The little society entered directly into its age of miracles, the dramatic phase that is characteristic of the infancy of so many other prophetic movements.

We hear how Ann, though imprisoned for fourteen days without food or water, other than a little wine and milk secretly passed by a clay pipe through the keyhole of her cell door, walked healthily out of her cramped place of confinement that was designed to restrict any kind of movement; 'to the great surprise of her enemies, she was not only alive, but as well as before.' (pp. 11f)

Or again, we are told how on one occasion she spoke before her inquisitors in seventy-two languages. There is also an account of how the mob, having marched her and four of her followers out of town to stone them, were unable to hit any of them with the stones they hurled and eventually gave up and left them. In her own account, Mother Ann says,

> 'I felt myself surrounded with the presence of God, and my soul was filled with love. I knew they could not kill me, because my work was not done; therefore I felt joyful and comfortable, while my enemies felt distress and confusion.' (p. 11)

The Shakers' miracle stories are mostly tales of protection in persecution, though not only so. Perhaps their most dramatic story is of the intervention of two angels to protect the ship on which they sailed to America in 1774.

Throughout 1772 and 1773 the persecution subsided and Ann's little band enjoyed their faith in relative peace. But their public testimony also ceased and no significant addition was made to their numbers. Then came the momentous decision to emigrate and establish the Church in America. It came through Mother Ann, of course,

> 'by a special revelation … and at the same time, she received a divine promise, that the work of God would greatly increase, and the millennial church would be established in that country.'

When she told the society, the decision was 'confirmed by signs, visions and extraordinary manifestations' among them and it was opened to all in the group who were able and felt so led to accompany her. (p. 13)

On 19th May, 1774, Ann, her husband, her brother and seven others set sail from Liverpool and on 6th August they arrived at New York. Penniless, they spent the next two years in desperate poverty. Ann Lee's husband left her at this time, no longer able to accept the doctrine of celibacy, but her brother, William Lee, and her adopted son, James Whittaker, joined her in the leadership of the group. In the summer of 1776 they obtained the lease of a piece of land and settled in the woods seven miles from Albany where the village of Watervliet was presently to be built, and there they waited for the outworking of a promise Ann had received in vision while still in England, the vision that had turned her feet in the direction of America in the first instance. She said,

> 'I knew by the revelation of God, that God had a chosen people in America; I saw some of them in vision; and when I met with them in America, I knew them. I had a vision of America: I saw a large tree, every leaf of which shone with such brightness as made it appear like a burning torch, representing the Church of Christ, which will yet be established in this land.'[300]

For the fulfilment of that they would have to wait another four years.

Throughout this period the charismatic forms of worship were maintained, and even intensified by the excitement of their new-found gospel of which they were to remain an inseparable part. Evans tells us that during these early years,

> 'The exercises in their religious assemblies were singing and dancing, shaking and shouting, speaking in new tongues, and prophesying, with all those various gifts of the Holy Spirit known in the Primitive Church.'[301]

Unlike their prophet predecessors, these early Shakers left no written records, but once their church became established in America, that and many other things changed quite radically. One of their early American theological writings interprets their 'shaking' as a prophetic sign of God's visitation that would, they believed, soon shake the earth in judgment: 'The work which God promised to accomplish in the latter days, was eminently marked out by the prophets as a work of shaking ...' The text goes on to cite several confirming Bible passages, such as Isa. 13:13; Joel 2:16; Hag. 2:6,7,21 and Heb. 12:26.[302] That was just how the French Prophets before them had interpreted their shaking too.[303]

*The Early American Sequel*

Ours is but a story of beginnings. In the United States the movement made surprising progress, benefiting particularly from the waves of revival that were sweeping America in the late eighteenth and early nineteenth centuries, until their membership reached about six thousand about 1850.

The first of these revival occasions was in 1779-80, in the Pittsfield, Massachusetts area, when second-coming expectation

300. Evans, *Compendium*, p. 139.
301. Evans, *Compendium*, p. 128/132.
302. *The Testimony of Christ's Second Appearing*, 1810; see Sears, Gleanings, pp. 7f.
303. See above, p. 360.

ran high. To that point the little community at Watervliet had been viewed with considerable suspicion because of its strange religious behavioural practices, though some had been attracted to it, particularly by the personal magnetism of Mother Ann herself. While the opposition continued, some of those touched by revival came to investigate the community to see if there were anything of God in it and many were persuaded, particularly by what they saw of the gifts of the Spirit in operation among the Shakers, and also by their millennial proclamation. Nor were all of these converts simple, uneducated people. They also drew members from the artisan and professional classes, including an occasional minister from the main-line churches.

Suddenly, in 1780, the little band, that had grown little since its arrival in America, increased dramatically in numbers. James Whittaker preached the first public sermon in May, beginning the phase the Shakers called 'the Opening of the Gospel', and over the next few months many converts were made in the New York, Massachusetts and Connecticut region. During the next four years, 1780-4, Mother Ann and the Elders made several journeys in neighbouring states, establishing local believers in the faith.

The missionaries encountered a great deal of opposition and persecution, varying in nature and intensity from place to place. The War of Independence was at its height and, being Englishmen preaching pacifism, they were once arrested as British agents. In Massachusetts they were accused of breaking up families, preaching Romish doctrines of celibacy, and undermining the fabric of society with their views on the equality of men and women. Mother Ann was accused of witchcraft, harlotry, and the like. She and her followers were beaten and driven from their homes in many places. Then finally, after being dragged by the heels behind a wagon for several miles over icy roads, she died in September, 1784, exhausted by her labours.

Since William Lee had already died, James Whittaker now assumed the leadership. In the hope of securing peace from persecution, he called the Believers to form their own communities apart from their neighbours, the first of which established itself at New Lebanon, New York. When James died suddenly in 1787, his place was taken by Joseph Meacham, one of the leaders of the original Pittsfield revival. He headed up the ministry for the next ten years and during that time saw the work of establishing the new communities through to completion. Fresh outbreaks of revival in the 1790s ensured continuing growth and, as the revivals spread westward across the northern states, new communities began of appear in Ohio, Indiana, New England and Kentucky.

Under Father Joseph the charismatic spontaneity that had characterised Mother Ann's leadership began to give way to more regulated and doctrinal systems. The new communistic lifestyle required the making of rules for admission and membership, oversight and conduct, and inevitably also for worship. The view quickly developed that the communes, set apart from the world's people, were nurseries for Christian perfection, plantings of the Millennial Kingdom, and therefore had to be run in an exemplary manner. Joseph, therefore, anxious lest unstructured worship should lead to disorder, devised 'spiritual exercises', adaptations of folk-dances providing a context for ecstatic bodily movements, thus bringing them into a harmony suitable for communal participation. The formation dance continued to be one of the best known features of Shaker worship throughout the nineteenth century.

The greatest boost for the Shaker movement came at the start of the new century, with the great Kentucky Revival in 1801-5, where meetings were attended by physical and spiritual phenomena very similar to those experienced among the Shakers themselves. Vivid accounts of weeping, trembling, crying, falling, swooning, singing, shouting, whirling, rolling, twitching, jerking, barking, bouncing and other strange activities are found in almost all the records of this revival, as for example in the account by Richard McNemar, who became a Shaker himself.[304] This revival was no more prophetic or charismatic than Wesley's had been in England, but just as some of his converts, after encountering similar revivalist experiences, seem to have gravitated towards the French Prophets, so also many of the enthusiasts born of the Kentucky revival, who were not much welcomed back in their own churches anyhow, found themselves a new home among the Shakers. By 1820 there were seventeen Societies in eight States with a total membership of almost five thousand.

Life in the Shaker settlements was communistic. Because of Ann Lee's doctrine that the sex act was the source of all evil, the communities, though mixed male and female in composition, were totally celibate. Since they believed themselves to be the people of Christ's Second Appearing, they also pursued a life of astringent perfection, seeking to eliminate all greed and pride from among them through submitting themselves entirely to a rule of community of possessions, thus leaving little place for private ambition.

304. McNemar, *Kentucky Revival*, pp. 19-24, 63-8.

Under this system their settlements prospered greatly and so their high standards of living also proved attractive to some, though to others, of course, the cost of celibacy was equally a deterrent.

*Formalisation and Decline*

During the lifetime of Mother Ann, Shaker services continued much as they had been in England, resembling the meetings of their French Prophet forebears. The exercise of spiritual gifts was commonplace, including tongues, prophecies, visions and the like, accompanied with freedom of bodily expression. As well as interpreting their physical actions in terms of latter-day shaking of the heavens and the earth, they taught that the spiritual gifts found among them were also evidence of the end-times, that God was restoring his Church as at the beginning. But already in the first decades of the nineteenth century, while the theology remained, the spontaneity was beginning to give way to formalism.

Then came the 'Spiritual Revival', also known as 'Mother Ann's Work'. It ran from 1837 to 1847 and marked the main turning point in the history of Shakerism. Up to that date the movement was openly evangelistic, the public being freely invited to inspect their unusual forms of worship. But in those ten years the Shakers were caught up in a revival that was excessively charismatic, but one which also shaded off uncannily into spiritualism. Some claimed to be receiving ancestral and other spirit messages, and that, together with the introduction of mediumistic practices, led to a crisis of authority in the movement's leadership. In the end order was restored, but at the expense of the Spirit.

Afraid of such excesses, that could too easily and embarrassingly cross over into paganism and the occult, Shakerism became a much more formal and much less overtly enthusiastic movement in the second half of the century. The spontaneous, convulsionary behaviour now gave way almost entirely to their formation dancing, and the charismatic utterances to stereotyped, composed verses and songs with musical accompaniment, even sometimes containing lines written in 'tongues'.

After half a century of communistic institutionalisation and now with the need for greater control, the movement became increasingly introspective. It lost its evangelistic fervour, without which it was bound to die, particularly since it was an organisation dedicated to the principle of celibacy anyhow. Added to that, America was rapidly crossing over from being an agricultural to an industrial society. The income of the Shaker communes was mainly derived from its crafts and hand-manufacturing, which had enabled them to be totally self-sufficient in an agrarian setting, but these were no longer economically effective in an increasingly competitive manufacturing scene. The work and lifestyle of the communes that had once seemed so attractive now drew few to join them.

The story of late nineteenth and twentieth-century Shakerism has been one of decline to extinction. The first closure of a commune was in 1875. The next was in 1897 and others followed quickly after that. The poorer simply closed down, the more prosperous communities merged with each other. By 1920 only six were left. In 1938 Mother Ann's original settlement in Watervliet closed. In 1947, exactly two hundred years after the first meeting of the Shaking Quakers in Manchester, the mother Church at Mt. Lebanon closed. Only a memory remains.

*Jesus Christ, Mother Ann, and the Holy Spirit*[305]

Most books on Shakerism perpetuate a view that was only expressed by a few in the movement itself, and that only for a short period of time, during the 'Spiritual Revival' in the 1830s and '40s, that Mother Ann was the very incarnation of Christ, who, in his second coming, had chosen to appear in the form of a woman. The main Shaker teaching was quite different: that Christ had chosen to make himself known, not just in Ann Lee, but in their whole community of Believers (as the Shakers liked to call themselves). She was honoured as the one through whom this revelation was first granted, and she was their spiritual Mother because it all began in her. Through her testimony others were also brought into the same experience of Christ, not so much as individuals, but as a whole body. The emphasis was very much corporate, not just personal, and she was the first of the many who came to form the corporate unity. Though the expressions some of them used are often misleading in this respect, such as 'Ann The Christess', Shakers did not normally think of her as a new incarnation of Christ, or as a female Christ, but they did recognise her as the unique person chosen to inaugurate the awareness of his second coming.

One of the early Believers, Benjamin Whitcher, put it this way:

> 'Christ did indeed commence his second appearance, by his Spirit, in Mother Ann, to complete the work of salvation and redemption, according to his promise … that she and the first

305. For the best discussion of this aspect of Shaker belief, see R.E. Whiston, *The Shakers. Two Centuries of Spiritual Reflection*, Paulist Press, New Jersey, and SPCK, London, 1983.

witnesses did actually administer the only way of life and salvation, to all who believed and obeyed her testimony. … This saving grace of God, and these gifts of the Holy Spirit, have not been exclusively confined to Mother Ann, and the first witnesses with her; but by the same anointing Spirit and power have been transmitted, through them, to their faithful successors in the ministry …'[306]

Shaker doctrine was mainly based on spiritual experience. To Believers Ann Lee had experienced Christ come again, and through her witness so too had they. They rejoiced as much in their own experience as in hers. It had transformed her and lifted her into the perfection of Christ, but that was what it was also doing for them. Yes, there were those who exaggerated her status, equating her with Jesus, speaking of Christ incarnate again in a woman, using phrases such as 'Jesus the Word, Ann the Word' and 'Jesus the Father, Ann the Mother', but that was mainly by a minority during the excesses of the mystical revival after 1837, against which the movement as a whole reacted most strongly. The main Shaker view was that there was a tangible experience of Christ-come-again available to all believers.

'[Ann Lee] did not pretend that she was Christ; but only that through his spirit, the same divine anointing was revealed in her. We do not profess that Christ has made his second appearing in Ann Lee only. But as every new dispensation must have an agent, that first receives the spirit and revelation of the work to be performed thereby, and through the first agent, it must be transmitted to others, and none can be benefited by it but such as receive the same spirit by receiving their testimony; So Ann Lee, was the first chosen vessel, or agent to receive the true spirit of Christ, in his second coming; but a portion of the same spirit, must be in every member of the Church …'[307]

This experience was not entirely unlike baptism in the Spirit, but it was interpreted in terms of their millennial doctrine. Sometimes they spoke of Christ as though he were one distinct from Jesus, one more like the Holy Spirit; for example,

'Christ is not Jesus, but a Spirit that may be in each human soul as really, practically, as it was in Jesus.'[308]

306. Seth Wells, ed., *Testimonies*, 1827, p. 155. Cited from Whiston, p. 57.
307. Calvin Green, *Atheism, Deism, &c.*, 1830. Cited from Whiston, p. 80.
308. *The Shaker Manifesto*, 1882, XII.3, p. 50. Cited from Whiston, p. 136.

Paul also spoke of Christ something like this, as one who could be experienced in the same way as the Spirit, as 'Christ in you' (Rom. 8:10). The main difference is the context, which for the Shakers was entirely a matter of the Second Coming having already begun with the ministry of Mother Ann.

> 'The time is fully come, according to ancient prophecy, for Christ to make his second appearing, for the redemption of lost man. This is the Second Appearance of Christ, and we are God's true witnesses, through whom Christ has manifested himself, in this day of his second appearing; and the only means of salvation that will ever be offered to a lost world, is to confess and forsake their sins, take up their cross, and follow Christ in the regeneration.'[309]

Even Ann Lee's own experience was described as baptism in the Spirit, though with the difference that it was closely identified with Jesus' own experience at the Jordan:

'While lying in the Manchester jail … she saw, and experienced the manifestation of the baptism of the Christ Spirit—the same that made Jesus, the Christ; and the same that will make every man and woman Christ, when prepared.'[310]

Or again:

> 'Jesus appeared to her in person, and baptized her into and with The Christ Spirit, as John had baptized *him* … Evidently, the way to redeem humanity, as a whole, was thus to begin with one, *human* being, as a nucleus, for Christians to gather to.'[311]

But always their testimony was that they learned this doctrine through what they experienced, rather than from what they were taught:

> 'I know of a truth that Christ was manifested in her; because I know that I received the spirit of Christ through her ministration. I have obeyed her testimony and I have ever found the same spirit in all her successors, down to the present day.'[312]

It was certainly the manifestation of the spiritual gifts among them that drew people in the earliest days. Among a collection of testimonies of the early believers is one by a certain Samuel Johnson,

309. Giles Avery, ed., *Precepts*, 1816, p. 136. Cited from Whiston, p. 47.
310. *The Shaker* I.2, 1871, p.11. Cited from Whiston, p. 84.
311. *The Shaker* I.3, 1871, p.18. Cited from Whiston, p. 84.
312. *The Manifesto*, 1887, XVII.2, p. 35. Cited from Whiston, p. 85.

who tells how, in his searchings, 'I could not see how those who had not the Spirit of Christ, could be true ministers of the gospel.' When someone told him about the Shakers, 'that he had seen a people who had all the gifts of the apostolic church,' he says, 'I felt an evidence in my soul, by the sensible operation of Divine Power … and was fully convinced that it was the beginning of the second appearing of Christ, and the setting up of his Kingdom on earth.' And so he went to see for himself, was touched by their anointing in the same way as the Shakers were, and joined their community. He described it as 'the precious "unction of the Holy One," which is the baptism of the Spirit.' He told how that produced in him an understanding of 'the spiritual things of God, and many operations of Divine Power,' and a satisfaction that he had 'now lived to see the second coming of Christ, and the commencement of his Kingdom on earth,' that he had found 'a people so evidently filled with the Spirit of Christ, and so blessed with the Divine presence.'[313]

*The Pursuit of Holiness and Millennial Perfection*

Like most prophets before them, Shakers were devoted to the pursuit of moral perfection. To other prophets that has been understood as preparation for Christ's second advent, to the Shakers it was an integral part of their witness to the present inauguration of the millennial dispensation, of their proclamation that a significant transformation had been effected in them by a resurrection that had already begun.

Celibacy was understood by some as an aid to rejecting and resisting all the evil they saw devolving from the corruption of sexuality since Adam, by others more positively as a gift of the Spirit enabling them to embrace more readily the process of sanctification and divinisation in Christ. The Wardleys had advocated the principle of celibacy back in Manchester, and Ann Lee exhorted people to accept it. She is reported to have spoken

> 'to a number of married people as follows, "You must forsake the marriage of the flesh, and travel out of it, in order to be married to the Lamb; which is, to be married to Christ, or, joined to the Lord in one spirit."'[314]

Shakers did not condemn or object to marriage. It was simply how the world worked, and as such was 'the most fitting social relation for a worldly kingdom,' but it was, nevertheless, 'a worldly institu-

313. Seth Wells, ed., *Testimonies*, 1827, pp. 104-11. Cited from Whiston, pp. 51-5.
314. Giles Avery, ed., *Precepts*, 1816, p. 240. Cited from Whiston, p. 163.

tion,' which in their minds 'has no part nor lot in the kingdom of Christ.'[315] Did not Jesus himself say, 'The people of this age marry and are given in marriage. But those who are considered worthy of taking part in that age and in the resurrection from the dead will neither marry nor be given in marriage.' (Luke 20:34f) Mother Ann's own counsel was:

> 'Do not go away and report that we forbid to marry; for, unless you are able to take up a full cross, and part with every gratification of the flesh for the kingdom of God, I would counsel you, and all such, to take wives in a lawful manner, and cleave to them only, and raise up a lawful posterity, and be perpetual servants of your families; for, of all lustful gratifications, that is the least sin.'[316]

For those entering on the Shaker Way, celibacy was part of the process of mortifying the flesh, of purging of evil from their bodies, and of pursuing wholehearted dedication and holiness in the service of Christ. The cost was a high one, but they never watered it down.

The call to community was interpreted similarly. It had never been part of Ann Lee's vision that Shakers should live in communes. The process of establishing them only started after her death as a means of protecting Believers from the terrible persecution they were suffering at the time. But once established, a suitable theology was framed to encompass the system. It was never made a requirement that Shakers should live in the communes, and many continued to live privately, enjoying what was known as a 'full Gospel relation' in the Church. Their basic principle was one of freedom, which was itself a precious gift of God. Community living was a matter of choice. Children brought in by their parents were therefore free to leave or stay on reaching majority, and to take their inheritance with them. The system offered mutual support for Believers, but was never seen as a way of escape from the challenges of life. Personal problems, such as debt, had to be resolved before entry, not dumped on the community. Accepting a call to communal living was one more step in the process of self-mortification, growth in holiness and the pursuit of perfection.

*Early Shaker Worship*

Accounts of worship at early Shaker meetings clearly remind us of the French Prophet meetings, though with some variation. One of

---

315. *The Shaker Manifesto* XI.8, pp. 178-9. Cited from Whiston, p. 166.
316. Giles Avery, ed., *Precepts*, 1816, p. 233. Cited from Whiston, p. 163.

the earliest accounts dates from 1785, just after Ann Lee's death. The unknown author, not a Shaker himself, describes a meeting he attended.

> 'They were singing in this unknown language a very solemn tune, at the end of which they always begin again with Oh! And in such a loud and hollow note accompanied with a catching of the breath as if they were strangling and the most violent contortions of their whole body as cannot fail to shock every one who first sees them—'

There followed a sermon by one of the men, presenting the Shaker claim to be the way of salvation for the times of Christ's second coming and giving some justification from Scripture for their unusual bodily movements in worship: 'where St. Paul says he was with the brethren "in fear and much trembling" authorizes their shaking—"Turn ye and ye shall be turned" which is their apology for turning round on their heels—"Clap your hands and be joyful O ye people, shout for joy," "Praise God in the dance and with songs" which are also parts of their worship—'.

This concluding part of the sermon was obviously to prepare the visitor for what followed: 'solemn singing in that style for about an hour accompanying it with groaning sighing and shaking.' The preacher

> 'began to hum The Soldiers Joy, a country dance tune, and the whole assembly men and women began a violent dancing without any kind of order, the men keeping on one side of the room and the women on the other; during the dance one of the men who had lectured went over to the women's side and touched four of them, when they instantly began to turn round with a velocity that is really inconceivable to any one who has not been a witness to it ... for a space of eighteen minutes afterwards they went round with the same surprising velocity, until they were called off by a clapping of hands in which they all joined for a space of five minutes; they then began their solemn singing, then their jig and then clapped hands and continued at that kind of worship for some time—during one of their jigs the old man who had set them a dancing went dancing up to a likely young girl and held out his hand to her, as if to give something, when immediately she fell into such a fit of shaking as exceeded any convulsive fit I had ever seen and continued it for such a length of time that the exercise made

the sweat come from her face as if water had been thrown on her ...'[317]

As we have already noted, with the passage of time forms became more stylised at the public meetings, but Shakers seem to have maintained their freer ecstatic worship at other times. William Haskett, a critic of the movement, writing in 1828, tells of 'Quick Meetings' Shakers held near Christmas. These were closed to visitors (though he had observed one), meetings in which they could exercise all their gifts with total freedom. He says,

> 'The sisters began to talk in "unknown tongues." Then commenced a scene of awful riot. Now was heard the loud shouts of the brethren, then the soft, but hurried note of the sisters, whose gifts were the apostolic gift of tongues. These gently gestured their language, waved themselves backward and forward like a ship on the billows of a ceased storm, shook their heads, seized their garments, and then violently stamped on the floor. The exercise had lost its violence, and exertion grew faint; yet a continued din of frightful yells rendered the scene a scene of confusion, a scene of blasphemy, an awful scene. After, probably, three quarters of an hour had transpired, the members were called to order, and the meeting adjourned.'[318]

The period of Mother's Work from 1837 on saw a revival of the free whirling, shaking and singing in community worship, but the excesses of that period also brought a strong reaction, so that in the later part of the century worship became much more formal and structured.

*Assessment*

In the history of the Shakers we find echoes of tendencies we have traced in other prophetic movements, that is, quite apart from the more obvious similarities in their visions, revelations, inspired utterances and the like. For example, their naive confusion of prophetic revelation and spiritualistic practice reminds us how readily Saul, the erstwhile prophet, turned to a medium when he could find no help from the prophets of the Lord. Or again, their elevation of the charismatic leader to quasi-Messianic status recalls similar tendencies among the followers of Montanus, the prophet of Bourges and Nicholas Storch.

---

317. Untitled manuscript, 1785. Cited from Whiston, p. 271.
318. W. Haskett, *Shakerism Unmasked*, Pittsfield, Massachusetts, 1829, p. 189. See also *The Charismatic Movement*, ed. By M.P. Hamilton, Eerdmans, Grand Rapids, 1975, p. 83.

Their belief that Christ might manifest himself through a female in his second appearing, while unusual, was not entirely unique in the eighteenth century. The Southcottians and the Buchanites, for example, both imagined that Messiah had returned in female form[319], which is not, as we have seen, what the Shakers normally claimed about Ann Lee. Anyhow, the Shakers were alone among such movements in maintaining a prophetic profile as an integral aspect of their latter-day, Messianic church.

In their millennialism they have sometimes been regarded as the heirs of Joachimism, but our study thus far suggests rather that their views about the latter-day church were simply part and parcel of their prophetic tradition, held in common with almost every other prophetic movement before them.

And finally, formalisation of prophetic expression into stereotyped modes is a process that has been noted among others before them, as among the early Christians, the Montanists, the Quakers and the French Prophets. It is a familiar story: while the movement of the Spirit remains extrovert, enthusiastic and evangelistic, its prophetic expression is free and vital; but with institutionalism and over-concern for organisation, though the forms remain, the flow of the Spirit seems to dry up and the movement ceases to be charismatic at all. Such has been the fate of every movement we have studied so far, at least every movement that has been able to survive beyond its infancy. It is a pattern we shall see repeating itself again.

As an end-comment, we may note that the decline and near extinction of the movement was already foreseen as early as 1827, when a certain Daniel Merton prophesied:

> 'After great and peaceful growth, then change and decline ... Smaller and smaller shall you grow, fewer and fewer, till a child in its mother's arms can count the remnant, [then ...] A new opening of the Gospel—a far grander and more universal revelation of these and other sacred truths will come.'[320]

For sure, it was from their own stock that he was prophesying the fresh growth, but that was predestined to come in a very different way and from another river, at least in its prophetic aspects, namely through the Pentecostal outpourings of the twentieth century. Shakerism, flowing out of the Quaker and French Prophet movements, represented the last trickle of a prophetic stream that was born amid persecution in the post-Reformation churches of Britain

319. Harrison, *Second Coming*.
320. White and Taylor, *Shakerism*, 1905, pp. 369f. Cited from Whiston, p. 310.

and France. All three grew through infancy with a great evangelistic fervour, but a fervour that faded in each case within a couple of generations, partly because of the violence of the persecution they encountered, though for other reasons as well. The Quakers continued to expand their work by refocusing on matters commercial and social; the French Prophets turned inwards and became a dwindling fraternity of home-groups; the Shakers, though they tried to change, found themselves trapped in social structures that had worked for a while, but were pronounced irrelevant with the progress of time.

These movements did not leave any prophetic heritage in the churches at large, nor did they influence them in any way with their prophetic witness. Their hope and vision were that they would do so, even that the new modes they were introducing would entirely replace the old ones. But their stance in bearing that witness was always outside the churches. By contrast, the prophetic flow we enjoy today has come, not so much through men who have chosen to stand outside the churches, but who have borne witness both to them and inside them, yes sometimes calling men out of them, but also working alongside them and seeking revival within them.

### *Prophecy in the Post-Reformation Church - Review and Conclusions*

The history of the Church in Reformation and post-Reformation times was dominated by issues of church and state, denomination and dissent, doctrine and practice. Prophecy, as far as most people were concerned, was a very minor issue. Here we have had to focus on it because that is our purpose, but it would be wrong to leave an unbalanced impression. The Zwickau Prophets caused no more than a slight flutter in the progress of the Reformation in Germany; the Seekers were a quiet people that hardly anyone noticed; the French Prophets did hit the headlines at the time of the Camisard Wars and afterwards in England, but to most people they were little more than a passing wonder; the Shakers became well enough known in America, but their ways impinged little on the continuous flow of Church life in general. The history of the Church can be told without even mentioning any of these movements, as indeed it commonly is. The Quakers have continued to flourish, but have turned away from prophetic things.

What we have been tracing here is the story of a longing in the hearts of many of God's people seeking to find expression, breaking surface from time to time, but never quite making the mark. It is the story of a Church of the Spirit trying to come to birth, successfully appearing at certain times, but in its untutored infancy running into excess or error, or else into formalism and aridity, and therefore never lasting for very long.

Nevertheless, there has been evidence of a change since pre-Reformation times. There has been more freedom for such movements to find expression and even to survive for a time, particularly in the Protestant arena. In a way that is strange, for Reformation Protestantism, with its basically rationalistic doctrinalism, was actually a much more hostile environment for prophetic faith than medieval Catholicism had ever been, with its continuing openness to the miraculous and the supernatural.

Also, much more literature relating to these movements has survived for us to study. So far they have still made little or no impact on the Church at large, but in the next phase of our story that is all to change. The baby that struggled so hard to get born in the post-Reformation church has now grown and matured through the latter half of the twentieth century. But to follow the rest of its story we must first go back to Germany at the end of the seventeenth century.

PART SEVEN

# PROPHECY AND REVIVAL IN AN AGE OF REVOLUTION AND RATIONALISM

A fresh stirring of the Spirit started in Europe in the late 1600s, not only in Calvinist France, but also in Lutheran Germany. It quickly spread to Britain and America, and in the next century gave birth in both places to widespread, national revivals on a scale hitherto unprecedented in history since earliest times. These, in turn, gave birth to the missionary movements that proliferated in the nineteenth century, planting the gospel firmly in the new world that had been opening up to Europeans since before the Reformation.

All of that caused a deep longing to grow in many Christian hearts for a new empowering with the Spirit of God to further enable the work of revival and mission. As that work continued to expand, so the longing continued to deepen, until suddenly, at the beginning of the twentieth century, heaven stooped down and touched the faithful, satisfying their hunger with a new Pentecost. That launched a movement that has spread to embrace whole churches and denominations and has now touched at least one third of all Christians. It also gave such a boost to the work of mission and evangelism that massive national revivals are now running in many parts of the world. The Spirit of God is powerfully on the move today on a world-wide scale.

This is all somewhat different from the movements we have reviewed in earlier chapters. By comparison, they were fairly small and easily delimited. They had identifiable purposes that marked them off from the rest of the churches, and were generally looked upon with much suspicion. It is hardly possible to discuss the present Pentecostal move in the same way. Yes, it does have identifiable aims, but the movement is so embracing that these must be dealt with on the same level as the huge aims of Protestantism or Catholicism. It has been veritably described as a 'third force' in Christendom.

Since it is so extensive, it needs to be studied, not just in local context, but against the background of the whole history of the Church in our times. And because it has carried the gospel so massively into pagan communities over the past hundred years, it is equally important that we consider its growth against the background of world history as well.

The force of religious intolerance abated rapidly after about 1750, and so the revivals of more recent times have not been suppressed by persecution, at least not in the Protestant nations. To be sure, there has always been plenty of opposition, but the times have changed. In a context of continuing revival God has been raising up a prophetic Church—but for what purpose? In these times other enemies have arisen and they are threatening the work of God more virulently than any before them. But God has been raising up a new army of prophets to take their stand in this, the greatest battle the Church has ever had to fight in its history.

# 24
# From Wesley to Today

Up to the seventeenth or eighteenth century the history of the Church in Europe was inseparably intertwined with the history of the state, but in more modern times the two have increasingly separated. While our concern is not primarily with secular history, it is difficult to appreciate the story of the Church without some rudimentary knowledge of its broad sweep, for the past two to three hundred years have witnessed radical changes in the development of political and social structures, agriculture, industry and technology. If a first-century Roman had come back to life in England or France about the year 1750, he would have found little to surprise him in the industrial methods and social conditions of the time, but if he had come to life about 1850 he would have found himself in a totally unfamiliar world of industrial cities, factories full of complicated machinery and astonishing new methods of travel and communication. But let us go back a little way before we look at the changes.

*Grand Monarchy and Politics in the Seventeenth and Eighteenth Centuries*

The decline in power of the Holy Roman Empire and the Papacy after the Reformation led inevitably to the formation of strong independent monarchies throughout Europe. By the end of the sixteenth century France, Spain and parts of Italy were ruled by totally autocratic kings or princes. During the seventeenth and eighteenth the rulers of France, Prussia, Austria and Russia had established themselves in positions of considerable grandeur. The courts and palaces of Louis XIV in France (1643-1715), of Frederick the Great of Prussia (1640-88), of Peter the Great of Russia (1689-1725) and of Maria Theresa of Austria (1740-80) are all quite legendary for their wealth and magnificence. This was the heyday of grand monarchy in Europe.

In Britain, when the Stuarts tried to establish their courts along similar lines, that resulted only in the abolition of monarchy altogether and the establishment of the Commonwealth and Protectorate. After the monarchy was restored, when James II again tried to override the laws of the land, he also lost his crown, which was conferred in 1688 to William and Mary, and the Bill of Rights was drawn up defining the respective rights of king and subjects. From that point on it became impossible for English monarchs to attain the autocratic authority of the continental kings and for the next 150 years Britain was virtually ruled by the landed gentry.

The period after 1688 was one of much political change in Britain—in religious toleration, freedom of speech, evolution of newspapers, development of representative government, culminating in the Reform Bill of 1832 which finally thrust Parliament forward towards becoming the elective, democratic assembly we have today.

The only other country in Europe where absolute monarchy failed to take hold was Holland. After a long struggle for independence from Spain, Holland managed to establish itself as an autonomous republic in 1609 under the leadership of the Prince of Orange, one called William the Silent, who, though he held the military and executive power in the state, was limited in his authority by the States-General, which was a bit like the English Parliament.

Otherwise in Europe the great kings reigned supreme, in luxurious splendour in their grand palaces, right up to the end of the eighteenth century, and in some places beyond. These were not entirely peaceful years in Europe, and some fairly protracted wars were fought between the kingdoms: the Thirty Years War in the seventeenth century, the War of Spanish Succession at the beginning of the eighteenth, the War of Austrian Succession and the Seven Years War in the middle. The politics of these wars need not delay us, but it is worth noting in passing that, although they were fought in Europe, they led to the partitioning and repartitioning of the new world that was then opening up overseas in the Americas and the East. Britain emerged from its involvement in them with greatly increased imperial holdings, particularly in India and America, very much at the expense of the French.

*Three Revolutions that Changed the Course of History*

In the late eighteenth century three major revolutions shook the world: the American Revolution of 1775-83, the French Revolution of 1789-95 and the Industrial Revolution that started about 1760, spanned the following century, and has run on ever since.

*The American Revolution*

Also known as the War of American Independence, this was a revolt against the autocratic rule of England. America at the time was made up of thirteen Colonies spread out along its eastern seaboard, between Canada and Mexico. The Southern Colonies, Virginia, North and South Carolina and Georgia, contained large estates growing tobacco and cotton, worked by slave labour. The Northern or New England Colonies, Connecticut, Rhode Island, New Hampshire and Massachusetts, had been founded by Puritan refugees and their population was made up mainly of hardy and well-educated farmers. In the middle were the remains of old Dutch settlements, one Roman Catholic foundation, Maryland, and one Quaker foundation, Pennsylvania.

Distance from Britain, difficulties of communication across the Atlantic, grievances about taxation, removal of the threat of invasion on their northern border after the British took Canada from the French, and many other similar factors, generated a desire among the more independently minded pioneering settlers to run their affairs themselves through their own local legislative assemblies. Provoked by insensitive application of taxes on imports, they broke away in rebellion. At first they fared badly, but under the strong leadership of George Washington and with assistance from the French who were still smarting at the loss of Canada, they succeeded in winning their freedom.

Perhaps the most momentous event in the whole war was the promulgation of the American Declaration of Independence on 4th July, 1776. This document, the foundation charter of the United States of America, drawn up by Thomas Jefferson, established the principle of fundamental personal liberty, which included complete freedom of religion and would ultimately lead to the abolition of slavery. Britain acknowledged the independence of the United States seven years later, in 1783, and suffered no long-term ill effect from doing so. The effect on France, however, was devastating.

To begin with, the French could ill afford the financial and military assistance it gave to the colonists. But worse than that, their soldiers returned home with ideas of individual liberty for themselves which made them impatient with the restrictions of France's Grand Monarchy. The condition of life for the poorer classes in France was not good. They were heavily taxed and between them and the nobility a great gulf was fixed. The social system was still feudal, thought not entirely unenlightened. The condition of the French peasants was not as bad as that of the poor in Prussia, Russia, Austria, Italy or Spain. In all these countries the peasants were still serfs. Revolution erupted in France, not because the French were more oppressed than any others, but because they were sufficiently enlightened to realise the evils of the system under which they suffered.

Their enlightenment was further encouraged by the political and philosophical publications of some of their own citizens. Voltaire's satyrical pen, and the more studied work of Diderot and the Encyclopaedists, attacked many of the abuses of their age, but by far the most influential was the *Social Contract* by Rousseau, who argued that all present miseries were caused by priests and rulers, and that sovereignty should be exercised by the people. Their writings were widely read and discussed.

*The French Revolution*

It all began in an orderly enough manner with a meeting of the States-General in May, 1789, followed in July by the destruction of the Bastille, the great prison in Paris. By the end of the year feudalism had been abolished, along with all class and church privileges, and the famous Declaration of the Rights of Man had been made law, asserting that all men have equal rights and equal freedom in the state. The idealism was at first welcomed enthusiastically by many outside France as well as within, but it soon gave way to a measure of revolutionary violence that sent a shock-wave right across Europe. By 1793 the Reign of Terror, with its horrifying toll of executions and murders, was at its height, but when its chief architect, Robespierre, was deposed and himself executed in 1794, the violence began to subside.

Now other forces began to work in France. By 1793 the French army, inspired with revolutionary enthusiasm, had transformed itself into a force to be reckoned with. It had turned an invasion by Prussia and Austria and had itself occupied parts of their western territories. In 1796 the office of commander-in-chief of the French army in Northern Italy was given to Napoleon Buonaparte, then only twenty-seven years of age. His successes in Italy and then beyond into Syria and Egypt led to his promotion in 1799 to First Consul of France, and therefore its Governor. His conquests in Europe continued and in 1804 he had himself acclaimed Emperor. Between 1808 and 1810 he was at the zenith of his power, either ruling directly or holding in subjection most of Europe from Spain to the Russian border. But then the tide began to turn. The opposition of Britain, the antagonism of disaffected subject states, and his disastrous invasion of Russia in 1812 led to his downfall. In 1814 he was defeated, arrested and exiled to the island of Elba in the Mediterranean, but soon afterwards he returned to lead France again. He was finally defeated at Waterloo in 1815 and exiled to the remote island of St. Helena in the middle of the Atlantic Ocean where he died in 1821.

The details of the course of the French Revolution and the Napoleonic Wars are not of much importance in this history, but some understanding of the extensive impact they had on Europe is. Much of the map of Europe was redrawn after 1815 creating tensions that were to rumble on through the century, and many spheres of colonial influence changed, Britain gaining considerably by the acquisition of several French territories overseas. But much more significant than that, perhaps, was the effect the Revolution had on the thinking and philosophy of statesmen, churchmen, indeed almost everyone, in the rest of Europe.

At first the Revolution was acclaimed as an act of enlightenment, particularly in Britain which had itself overthrown its despotic monarchy more than a hundred years earlier, when James II was deposed and a much more democratic form of government was introduced in 1688 under William and Mary. British admiration, however, turned quickly sour when the revolution ran into excess, and particularly after 1793, when the French decided to work towards an invasion of England. It took longer for the admiration of the oppressed serfs and workers in the rest of Europe to turn. When the French armies invaded they were welcomed as liberators by the masses, for they came proclaiming their revolutionary doctrines of equality and freedom. But the oppressive deeds of the conquerors fell very far short of their high sounding words and by 1812 the ground-swell throughout Europe had reached proportions the French were unable to contain. Nevertheless, the seed-thoughts of freedom and social change had been sown and were now bearing their crop. The days of grand monarchy and feudalism were over for most of Europe. A new age, with its freedom of thought and hunger for social change, had dawned. Europe would never return to its old ways. The effects on church and society were to prove considerable.

While the American and French Revolutions were pursuing their course and filling the world with notions of freedom and equality, another revolution was taking place, one without the drama of wars and heroes, but one that was destined to affect the history of mankind far more profoundly than either of these other two.

### *The Industrial Revolution*

This revolution, usually dated from about 1760 and continuing over most of the following hundred years, was basically a transition from manufacturing goods on a small scale in cottage industries and home shops to producing them on a large scale in factories. The main reason for this transition was, of course, the invention of the steam engine. By the end of the century steam engines were more common than watermills in England and by the middle of the next Britain was crossed by a network of railways, as well as improved roads, bridges and canals, making transport and communication much speedier throughout the country. Steam-ships sailed the high seas reducing long voyages from several weeks to several days. International trade increased correspondingly, and Britain gained enormously from the change. This revolution was at its height while Europe was still torn by the French Wars and so most of the import and export trade came to Britain, but after the peace of 1815 Germany and France quickly adopted the new ways also.

Economically and politically the effects of the Industrial Revolution were exceedingly beneficial for the industrial nations. Their trading capabilities brought much wealth, though most of that went to the factory owners and industrialists, creating a new class of powerful capitalists and a new serfdom for the working classes. Workers had to live near the factories, and so long rows of closely packed tenement houses were built for them, creating new industrial towns and cities. Life in these was hard, with long hours, little pay, poor living conditions and often inhuman treatment by bosses. In some places the system was little better than slavery, involving women and young children as well as adult men.

Early attempts at securing better conditions for workers met with little success, but a new social ethic began to emerge as the century progressed. In 1848 Karl Marx published his *Communist Manifesto,* calling on workers of the world to unite, saying they had everything to gain and nothing to lose but their chains. In the same year revolution, mainly republican and democratic in its inspiration, though also influenced by the new socialism, broke in France, Germany and Italy, and ripples of the same were felt in several other countries in Europe, including Britain, which witnessed the great Chartist gatherings at this time. But it was all short-lived and brought strong reaction from most of the European governments, who then were swinging more to the right than to the left as they scrambled to build their industrial kingdoms and empires that were so much the mark of the later nineteenth century. France was restored to political dignity under Napoleon III, made Emperor in succession to his more famous uncle; Britain was attaining its imperial height under Queen Victoria; Germany was unified under King Frederick William IV of Prussia and then ruled by his iron Chancellor, Otto von Bismarck; and Italy at last became united as one nation under the Sicilian King, Victor Emmanuel II. The chief political mood of the age was nationalism, in the teeth of which communism had little hope of immediate success. It was not until 1917, when the Bolshevik government took control of Russia, that Marxist Socialism became established as a proper political system in any country.

Nevertheless, the socialist message did not go unheeded. In the second half of the century most European governments instituted programmes of reform, fearing that otherwise the socialist revolutionaries might rise up again in anger. Reform in Britain proceeded more gradually and without the violence often witnessed in Europe. The slave trade was abolished, the Poor Laws were improved, government was made more democratic, education became more readily available, trades unions were formed, and life for the workers generally improved everywhere. When the first Labour government came to power in 1924 it contained few if any Marxists. In the United States, thanks mainly to its vast wealth and resources, conditions never deteriorated enough among working people for Socialism to become a necessary political force.

*The Making of the Twentieth Century World*

The western mind today is radically different from that of the early eighteenth century. Not only have the revolutions of America, France, the Industrialists and the Socialists left their mark, but so also have wars and political intrigue. At the end of the Napoleonic Wars, in 1815, the four great world empires were the British, Russian, Austrian and Turkish. Over the next hundred years the Austrian Empire was dismembered and two strong new nations emerged in Europe with the unification of both Italy and Germany. The Turkish Empire also collapsed before European and Russian pressure to release the Balkan States, Macedonia and Greece into independence and, after the 1914-18 War, Turkey was reduced to a national state without any imperial holdings. Russia remained a feudal empire under the Tzars. The Communist revolution of 1917 brought radical changes in its internal history, though its international influence has remained exceedingly strong.

Elsewhere in the world the changes were every bit as radical. The British extended their colonial holdings considerably in the mid-nineteenth century, particularly in the Far East, in Australia and

New Zealand, India and Africa. Other nations besides the British also added to their colonies at this time, especially the French, Dutch, Belgians, Portuguese, Italians and Germans. The African story is perhaps the most dramatic. In 1850 it was still 'The Dark Continent', with a few scattered colonies and settlements on parts of its coasts, but otherwise, especially in its interior, quite unexplored, a mysterious continent inhabited by native tribes. Between 1850 and 1880 missionaries and explorers, like Livingstone and Stanley, made their historic journeys inland, followed shortly after by the armies of the colonising nations, who, by the end of the century, had carved up most of the continent between them.

Meanwhile new nations were awakening into independence and political significance. In the east Japan came out of its medieval seclusion and with amazing rapidity transformed itself into an imperial power with holdings in China and Korea. The Spanish Republics in Mexico and South America and the Portuguese Empire of Brazil came into being in the 1820s and the Dominion of Canada was created by the British in 1867. But by far the most important of the emerging new nations was the United States of America.

Probably no nation in the world has been so dramatically transformed by the Industrial Revolution as the United States. At the time the Americans gained their independence from Britain, they were no more than a group of trading and farming colonists spread out along the eastern seaboard. Then began the move inland, into the unexplored mid-west, a process that was phenomenally expedited by the development of steam transport. Americans did not have to seek an empire; they had one on their doorstep, new, largely unexplored and rich in natural resources.

As they penetrated westward new states were formed and brought into the Union, but there was one major problem. The southern colonial states were organised on the basis of slavery, whereas in the north slavery had been abolished since 1804. Some decision had to be reached about what form of society America should become. That led to war, the American Civil War of 1861-65, the result of which was that slavery was fully and finally abolished in America. The story of the subsequent development of the United States into a strong, industrial, technological and military power in the world hardly needs telling. The pioneering spirit of the Americans has lived on and made the nation what it is today.

*The Emergence of Global Man*

Today we speak of the Industrial Revolution as part of past history.

Now we talk about the Technological Revolution that has again radically changed the nature of life in our world. Gas, oil, electricity and nuclear fuel have superseded steam in most advanced societies. Life in the home and at work has been totally transformed by a vast array of highly sophisticated electronic, electrical and mechanical devices. A meal that once would have taken a whole day to prepare can now be produced in a matter of minutes. Consequently people now have much more time for leisure, for reading, education, sport, and the like. And since educational opportunities have improved so vastly, this technological and cultural progress continues to accelerate at an unprecedented pace.

Air flight has reduced international travel to a matter of hours instead of days or weeks. Radio, telephone and internet communication give us instant access to distant peoples. Daily papers and television broadcasts bring us news from around the world almost as soon as it has happened. And today we have the time and freedom to show more detailed interest. Our world has shrunk. Common concerns grip us in every nation: for controlling the population explosion, for minimising pollution of our air, land, rivers and seas, for preserving endangered species, for maintaining international peace, and so forth. There is a far greater sense of being part of global humanity than ever before.

And yet, much has not changed in man. War is still with us, only now its scale is vaster. Crime and brutality have certainly not decreased. Nationalism still sets people against people in bloody conflict. Selfishness still leads to acquisition of wealth at the expense of others. Marriages break up more readily than at any time in history. Thanks to medical progress people now live longer, but far too many have to be sustained with anti-depressant drugs and psychiatric care. Alcoholism is as rife as ever before, only now it is coupled with massive drug abuse. And in this age of technological sophistication more people than ever before visit mediums and magicians, astrologers and occultists. Man still has his spiritual emptiness. In that he has not changed. How then has the church been meeting his spiritual need?

## 25

# The Awakening of the Church in the Eighteenth Century

While political and industrial revolutions were shaking the world in the eighteenth century, another revolution was shaking the church, one that was to have equally far-reaching effects on social and governmental policies in the Christian world and also in new territories that knew nothing of Christ at all. The prophetic movements we have studied in this book so far had very little impact on either church or society at large, but the wave of revival that broke in the 1720s and '30s turned the Protestant Church and the nations it influenced back to their God on a massive scale. Very little in it was prophetic/charismatic, but it did lay the first foundation for what has become the Pentecostal Movement in our own time, and therefore forms an essential part of this study.

Although the French Prophet Movement belongs in the same century and flowed on into the Shaker Movement of the next, in ethos it belongs to the pre-revival history of the modern church. It did help to prepare the way for much that happened in the revivals in Britain later in the century, and the Shakers did glean most of their membership out of the American revivals in the early decades of the nineteenth, but in some ways they were relics of a past age of charismatic fervour and always stood apart from the main stream of the revivals that remoulded Protestant thinking. They were birthed out of Protestant-Catholic dispute in France and out of Puritan-Anglican dispute in England, and so belong more properly in the last chapter, as the last of the post-reformation movements with prophetic content.

While we must not view the great work that happened in the eighteenth century as something discontinuous with the past, for history is not like that, it was, none the less, a new thing that the Lord now did in his Church, coming like a fresh breath from heaven.

### *The Need for Revival*

While a far higher percentage of the population were church-goers then than today, the fire that had inspired the English and European reformers in the sixteenth century or the English and American Puritans in the seventeenth was burning very low.

In the American Colonies the early zeal of the Pilgrim Fathers, and the many Puritans who followed them after 1620, faded as commerce developed and wealth increased in the next generation. Though the earliest colonial Church was Anglican, under the jurisdiction of the Bishop of London, it was quickly outnumbered by the Congregational and the Presbyterian Churches formed by the Puritan settlers. Among these at first church membership depended on testifying to a saving experience of Christ, but with the cooling of evangelical zeal a decision of Synod in 1662 (the 'Halfway Covenant') opened the way for moral respectability to be considered a sufficient qualification. Soon preaching was moderated to suit, and before long there were unconverted ministers in the pulpits as well as unconverted members in the pews.

In Europe many Christians were simply tired. The Reformation had led churches and nations alike into long years of religious strife and warfare. After 1648, when the Thirty Years War ended and the fighting subsided, little remained of the evangelical fire of the great reformers and their sixteenth century followers. The emergent religious philosophy of the day was rationalistic deism, a belief that held God remote from the daily world of man, and so faith was increasingly seen as having little to do with experience, but more with sterile systems of belief. Protestantism became dry and doctrinal, little better than academic dogmatism, with much disagreement between its different factions, and many were quite simply losing interest in this squabbling religion.

In Britain morals were in a sorry state of decline. Corruption and nepotism were rife in government, obscenity in the arts, violence on the streets—historians often paint a portrait of Britain in the early part of the century that is far from attractive by any standards. And the churches at large, both Anglican and Non-conformist, tarred with the same deistic brush as their American and European counterparts, were doing little or nothing about it. To all intents and purposes they had gone to sleep. Anglicanism had become a largely irrelevant system, while the militant Puritanism of Cromwell and the fiery Quakerism of Fox were already little more than an echo from past history.

One of the reasons for this laxity in Britain was that the extreme swings of religion experienced in the seventeenth century, between Catholic and Protestant, with the wars and persecutions that attended them, had left most Englishmen cautious about enthusiasm. The memorable statement of Bishop Butler, that 'enthusiasm is a very horrid thing,' aptly sums up the prevailing attitude. Pursuit of moderation, however, issued in lifeless, compromising preaching and a consequent decline in moral, social and political values in church and society.

To be sure there were men of finer sentiment in every country, praying men and true men of God. But their voices were little heeded. The need for God to act grew more and more urgent with every passing year. When he did, it was through different channels in each country. Revival in America was nursed in a Protestant cradle that was mainly, but not exclusively, Calvinistic; in England it was born out of the established, Anglican Church, but it nurtured many groups that broke away into independence; in Europe the main influence was Pietism which had its roots in Lutheranism and the medieval mystics.

*First Stirrings in Europe*

German Pietism is usually associated with the name of Philip Jacob Spener, a Lutheran pastor, who ministered in Frankfurt, Dresden and Berlin in the last third of the seventeenth century. It has antecedents in the fourteenth century in the mysticism of Eckhart and Tauler, whose teaching so influenced Luther himself during his early years. Much of that had been made available again by Johann Arndt, who edited Tauler's writings for the German Lutheran community. In a work entitled *True Christianity*, which he published in 1606, he stated that the true basis of faith was the work of Christ in the heart of man, beginning with new birth, or mystical union with God, and leading to a sanctified life of active piety. His works were widely disseminated and became popular among later Pietists.

Spener's purpose, through promulgating these views, was to revive the Lutheran Church with evangelical fervour, to recover Luther's appeal to the heart, in an age when the reformer's teachings were hardening into rigid doctrines. To that end, he began to promote lay participation in Bible study, to teach the priesthood of all believers, to maintain that the practice of Christian truth was of greater importance than dogma, and to encourage the faithful to develop their inner spiritual life. Not only did he teach such things, but he also set about putting them into practice in his ministry. At Frankfurt he set up weekly house meetings for prayer, Bible study, and mutual encouragement in faith and Christian experience. His work did much to bring new life into the Lutheran Church in Germany, where it won wide support among pastors quite rapidly.

New hymns, particularly those of Paul Gerhardt, also did much to help spread the teaching, but the inevitable clash with orthodoxy also came quickly. The university of Leipzig expelled one of its lecturers, August Franke, for propounding Pietist doctrines, but he was appointed professor at the new university at Halle in 1692 and there continued to teach and write on the personal nature of faith. His influence on younger theologians and clergy was considerable and they helped to carry the movement even further throughout Protestant Germany. His main tenets were that the soul finds no true satisfaction in this world's pleasures and is empty until it responds to the call of God in repentance; the result is then conversion, followed by joy and assurance of faith, leading on to personal growth through perseverance in times of temptation and persecution.

As we shall see, this kind of teaching was to become foundational for Wesley's and other revivalists' preaching over the next two centuries, for Methodism and the Holiness Churches, for the Keswick Movement and for Pentecostalism. The arm of the German Pietists has been very far reaching, but its roots, as we have seen, reach far back too. In Germany itself Pietism influenced church thinking in a number of different ways. At Halle its teaching developed into a new doctrinal system and so lost its personal heart. However, in one place at least, its effects were exceedingly dramatic.

Jacob Spener had a wealthy godson called Nikolaus Ludwig, Count of Zinzendorf in Saxony. He became a strong proponent of Pietistic faith. In 1722 he found himself offering asylum on his estate to some refugees who had been driven by religious persecution from their homelands in Bohemia and Moravia. They were Hussites, a last remnant of the spiritual descendants of the fifteenth century reformer, Jan Hus, and so had a firm belief in the authority of Scripture, which they coupled with a strong sense of devotion to the community of believers in submission to its elders. They also laid much emphasis on worship, organisation and education. Their strength of character soon manifested itself as they set to constructing homes on the barren part of Zinzendorf's estate where they chose to establish their new community. They called their settlement *Herrnhut* ('The Lord's Watch'), since its site was on the *Hutberg* ('Watch Hill').

Count von Zinzendorf himself believed that the mark of true Christianity was a simple and childlike faith. He once wrote, 'He who wishes to comprehend God with his mind becomes an atheist.' He therefore found it hard when refugees of other Protestant traditions began to join the Moravian Brethren on his estate and bitter squabbles over doctrine broke out among the various groups. However, he gave himself to the task of peacemaking and reconciliation, with the result that on 12th May, 1727, the warring factions covenanted to seek the Lord together and from that point everything changed. For three months they prayed together and then, on 13th August, at a communion service, the whole congregation was reduced to tears as the Holy Spirit moved mightily among them. Within a fortnight the Spirit had moved through the whole community, young and old, and on 25th August they began a ministry of continual prayer that lasted for over a hundred years.

In 1731 they started sending out missionaries all over the world, and so became the first Protestants to embark on missionary work. Soon they had Moravian communities established in many parts of the globe, including missions in Pennsylvania and London, both of which were to play a significant part in the history of revival in Britain. We shall return to their part in the story later.

*The Great Awakening in New England*

At the beginning of the eighteenth century thousands of Germans arrived in the American Colonies seeking refuge from Catholic persecution. They were mainly Lutherans, but there were also Moravians and others, many of them already touched by the Pietist movement. This brought a new strain of faith into colonial Christianity, which had hitherto been mainly Calvinist, with the result that first tremors of revival were being felt in New Jersey in the 1720s. And then in 1734 the great wave began to break.

In 1727 Jonathan Edwards, a young Presbyterian minister, was appointed associate pastor to his grandfather, Solomon Stoddard, at the Congregational Church in Northampton, Massachusetts. In that same year he had a personal experience of God's sovereignty in which, he says in his *Personal Narrative* (1739),

> 'There came into my soul, and was as it were diffused through it, a sense of the glory of the Divine Being; a new sense, quite different from anything I ever experienced before.'

Throughout his subsequent ministry he always longed for his people to catch something of that same sense, 'a sense of the heart,' as he called it.

Stoddard died two years later, in 1729, leaving Edwards in sole charge. Under his preaching stirrings began in the church. Towards the end of 1734, because of some doctrinal discussion in the churches at the time, he preached a series of sermons on 'justification by faith alone,' through which one young woman was gloriously awakened. Observing the dramatic effects on her,

> 'a great and earnest concern about the great things of religion and the eternal world, became universal in all parts of the town, and among persons of all degrees and all ages.'[321]

Scenes of conviction, brokenness, tears and agonising over salvation, but also of joy, love and praise, were witnessed daily as the Spirit of God moved through the town.

> 'There was scarcely a single person in the town, either young or old, that was left unconcerned ... so that in the spring and summer following, anno 1735, the town seemed to be full of the presence of God.'[322]

The revival climaxed in 1735 and then, partly because almost everyone in Northampton had been awakened in it by then, partly because of reaction to the suicide of one eminent gentleman in the town, it subsided for a time. In the following years Edwards found himself writing many letters in response to enquiries, and so in 1737 he published a full account of the revival under the delightful title, *A Faithful Narrative of the Surprising Work of God*. 'Surprising' is without doubt the best word he could have used. The events of 1734-5 took everyone by surprise, Edwards himself, the New Englanders, indeed the whole Christian world. Nothing of this scale and nature had been known in the church, as far as anyone could tell at the time, since the days of the Apostles. Edwards' own sense of surprise runs through every page of his little book. The Lord was indeed doing a new thing.

In 1739 George Whitefield arrived from England and the fires were rekindled, this time to run throughout the whole of New England. Soon vast crowds of many thousands were gathering to hear Whitefield's preaching. Edwards quickly joined him and continued the work in the following years when Whitefield returned to England. The revival spread south beyond New England, into New York, New Jersey, Pennsylvania, Maryland and Virginia. It also crossed the denominations as ministers were awakened and led their people in revival themselves without the help of visits from men like Whitefield and Edwards, but the established Church of the Colonies (Anglican) was little affected. It is estimated that out

321. *Faithful Narrative*, p. 15.
322. *Faithful Narrative*, pp. 16f.

of a total population of 250,000 at the time, at least 50,000 were added to the Church.

One of the most brilliant luminaries born of the revival was David Brainerd, a great man of prayer, whose total devotion to Christ took him out of university and sent him as a missionary to the Red Indians. Though he died at the young age of twenty-nine, many wonderful tales are told of him, tales befitting any great saint.

Some of the enthusiasm aroused by Whitefield's campaigns in the early 1740s ran into excess, and many of the ministers who had supported him at first began to draw back, some even coming out in strong opposition against the revival. By the mid-40s it was a movement of the past, though its legacy in the churches remained. Then in 1750 Edwards was dismissed from his pastorate in Northampton, for reasons only secondarily related, because of his unwillingness to admit unbelievers to the Lord's Supper. He moved to a frontier church, where he stayed until 1757, when he was elected President of the College of New Jersey (now Princeton), but almost as soon as he arrived he died of smallpox, before he could enjoy his new appointment.

*Revival Comes to Britain*

Jonathan Edwards' *Faithful Narrative* stimulated many in England to start praying for revival on this side of the Atlantic, but, even before it was read in this country, God had already begun preparing his men. In the year the Northampton revival was at its height, 1735, the first pioneers of revival in Britain were being powerfully converted.

It was then that Howell Harris, a school teacher at Talgarth in South Wales, a young man in his early twenties, was dramatically converted out of a potentially dissolute life to become a fiery evangelical preacher, fearless and untiring. In 1739 he moved to North Wales where he continued his work in the same way. His preaching led to many conversions and the formation of small societies (home groups) of believers, which did much to help establish and sustain the revival. Later on they would form themselves into the Welsh Calvinistic Methodist Church.

Awakened about the same time was Daniel Rowlands, Anglican priest at Llangeitho in west-central Wales. His ministry continued until he died in 1790. Because of his deep pastoral care for his own people, he never left Llangeitho for long periods, but he extended the same care to the revived Christians and that did much to establish the renewed faith of the Welsh on a solid foundation.

It was in 1739 that the full blessing of revival was finally released in England. It started on Monday, 1st January, when John and Charles Wesley, George Whitefield and about sixty others were gathered at Fetter Lane, London. They had spent the night in prayer, then at about three o'clock in the morning the Lord visited them in such power, as at Pentecost, that many of them fell to the ground overwhelmed by awe in his presence. Shortly thereafter the revival preaching started, and it ran on for most of the rest of the century.

George Whitefield was the first of the English to be active in the open air preaching that became so characteristic of the revival. He was converted in 1735, the same year as Howell Harris, and was later to show the same fire as Harris and the same fearlessness in working for men's salvation. Son of a Gloucester innkeeper, he went to Oxford in 1732 where he met the Wesleys and joined their 'Holy Club'. He entered the Anglican ministry in 1736 and spent some time working with the church in the American Colony of Georgia. He returned to England in 1738, and the following year, soon after the January Pentecost, began preaching boldly in open places where people gathered—Moorfields, May Fair, Smithfield, Kensington Common and the like, some of them quite unsavoury at the time, but where lost souls could be found. Soon hundreds, even thousands, were flocking to hear him.

One of his early successes was in Bristol. He went there in February to preach to the miners who had never heard the gospel. By March his open-air congregation had swollen to two thousand, and then he invited John Wesley to join him. And so it was that in April Wesley had his first experience of the open-air preaching that would occupy him for the rest of his life.

In the same year Whitefield went over to Wales where he joined Howell Harris for a time in the Welsh revival. He returned to America in 1740 where Jonathan Edwards joined him in carrying the revival work through the whole of New England. Meanwhile disagreement with Wesley over his Calvinistic views caused a rift between the two of them that was never to be properly healed. Between 1741 and his death in 1770 he crossed the Atlantic several times and travelled extensively, preaching in New England, Wales, England and Scotland, adding further fuel to the fires of revival in each country. Perhaps the most remarkable of all his meetings was in Scotland in 1742, when he found himself preaching to crowds of twenty and fifty thousand at Cambuslang, near Glasgow, where two Scottish ministers, James Robe and William McCulloch had laid a good foundation in the months before his coming. The 'Cambuslang Work' was one of the greatest of all the revival gatherings in the whole century—certainly so in Wesley's estimation.[323]

*John and Charles Wesley*

Born and raised at the beginning of the century in the rectory at Epworth in Lincolnshire, John and Charles studied at Oxford in the 1720s. There, along with others, they formed the 'Holy Club' with the aim of improving and sustaining the spiritual life of its members. It was there that Whitefield met them. In 1735, the year of Harris's conversion and Whitefield's illumination, John Wesley, now an ordained minister in the Anglican Church, sailed to Georgia to work as a missionary, but he found the going very hard and so returned in 1738 saying, 'I went to America to convert the Indians; but oh, wretched man that I am, who shall convert me?'[324]

On the crossing, and also while in Georgia, he had had a number of encounters and conversations with Moravians and was greatly impressed by their seriousness of behaviour, their humility and their freedom from fear.[325] When he returned to England he was invited and went to a Moravian meeting in Aldersgate Street, London, where, while he listened to a reading from Martin Luther's Preface to the *Epistle to the Romans*, he says,

> 'I felt my heart strangely warmed. I felt I did trust in Christ, Christ alone for salvation; and an assurance was given me that he had taken away my sins, even mine, and saved me from the law of sin and death.'[326]

That was John Wesley's conversion (his brother's had taken place a few days earlier). Soon after it he made his way to Herrnhut and spent three months with the Moravian community on Count von Zinzendorf's estate. He returned to England greatly helped by them and encouraged. (He later explained that he did not join them because, among other things, he found their ways based too much on mysticism, rather than on Scripture.[327])

Then, on 1st January, 1739, at the Fetter Lane meeting, along with his brother, Whitefield and about sixty others, he experienced his Pentecost, which empowered him for the public, revival ministry he

323. *Journal*, 9th Dec. 1749.
324. *Journal*, 24th Jan., 1738.
325. *Journal*, 25th Jan., 1736.
326. *Journal*, 24th May, 1738.
327. *Journal*, 21st April, 1741.

was about to start and would continue with till his death at the age of 88 in 1791.

It was Whitefield who introduced him to open-air preaching, at Bristol. The two were very different from each other. Wesley was more refined, more meticulous, more of an academic and an administrator. Whitefield was the son of an innkeeper and so perhaps more accustomed to the rougher side of life, whereas Wesley was a clergymen's son, and therefore very much a churchman himself. Though hesitant at first, once released into ministry, he proved every bit as courageous as Whitefield and often saw more spectacularly emotional and spiritual evidences of divine visitation at his meetings, such as falling, swooning, groaning, and the like. Both men suffered persecution. They were pelted with rotten eggs, stones and other nasty missiles, and injured by them more than once. Wesley was almost murdered by a mob in Walsall in 1743. But both survived and, even though they did not minister together after their disagreement in 1740, they pressed on to take the nation for God.

When he died, Wesley is said to have covered 250,000 miles, preached 40,000 sermons, left about 140,000 Methodist members cared for by 1,500 itinerant preachers.

### *The Establishment of Methodism*

Other revivals have run their course and died. Wesley's continuing success lay in his ability to organise and in his writing. He was a prolific writer, both of books and tracts, and he published a regular magazine for his converts, the first Christian monthly. His brother, Charles, wrote over 7,000 sacred songs and poems, and the singing of his hymns did much to sustain the impact of revival everywhere.

John also organised his converts into local groups called 'Societies'. He remained an Anglican all his life and encouraged his followers to stay in their churches, but he did not leave them with nothing more than an unrevived church to attend. He put them into his societies, much as Howell Harris did in Wales, so that they could meet regularly to encourage one another in spiritual growth, in studying Scripture, in holiness of living, and in social activity in their communities, a bit like Spener and the Pietists did in Germany. As the movement spread, he introduced other co-ordinating offices and structures. His first 'Conference' met in 1744 and it became the movement's governing body, along with Wesley himself, of course. The societies nationwide were then viewed as a 'Connexion' and divided into local 'Circuits' under the care of 'Assistants' (later called 'Superintendents'), whose work was to travel round their circuits visiting and encouraging the societies.

Because of the split between Whitefield and Wesley, two brands of Methodism developed. Whitefield's followers became known as Calvinistic Methodists, Wesley's as Arminian Methodists.[328] Later in the century the Calvinistic societies came to be known as 'The Countess of Huntingdon's Connexion', because they received generous sponsorship from the then Countess of Huntingdon, Selina Hastings, who did much to introduce Methodism to the upper classes in Britain. The Arminians were known as 'Wesleyan Methodists', then later just 'Methodists'.

Methodism spread to America in the 1760s where, in 1784, it formed itself, against Wesley's wishes, into a separate Church led by bishops and became known as the Methodist Episcopal Church. In England Wesley refused to let his followers form a separate church, but in 1795, four years after died, they seceded from the Anglican fold.

*Revival Offshoots of Methodism in the Nineteenth Century*

A fresh wave of revival broke in English Methodism at the beginning of the nineteenth century. In the true style of Wesley himself it grew through out-door preaching and prospered greatly among the tough mining and other working-class communities. Its founder leaders were Hugh Bourne and William Clowes, both of whom were expelled by the Methodist Church, strange as it may seem, mainly because they preached in the open air. In 1807 they held the first ever camp meeting in Britain at Mow Cop, a hill-top village in Staffordshire, just north of Stoke-on-Trent. They learned about camp meetings from America, where they had been inaugurated only a few years earlier, and they proved phenomenally successful in drawing thousands to faith in Christ. In 1811, after the Methodist Church refused to accept some of their converts, they formed a separate denomination, known as the Primitive Methodists ('Prims').[329] They were persecuted just as Wesley had been, but they

---

328. The disagreement was basically about the issue of man's free will. Whitefield found himself at home with the Calvinistic views about election and predestination held by the American, Welsh and Scottish revival leaders. Wesley favoured the views of Arminius, a sixteenth-century Dutch theologian who fought to have the Reformed Churches accept that Jesus died for all men, not just for the elect, and that God's sovereignty was not incompatible with free-will in man.

329. Called 'primitive' because they believed they were following the primitive methods of preaching used by Wesley himself.

produced some powerful and fearless preachers and evangelists, so much so that by the end of the century they had well over two hundred thousand members in their churches. Their forceful witness helped considerably to stay the hand of violence in the nation. They also played a major role in the early trades unions, in sponsoring education and in the development of social action among the poor.

One of their most remarkable preachers was James Crawford, sometimes spelt Crawfoot. His 'enthusiasm' was not welcomed among the Methodists in Cheshire where he lived, and so he joined himself to the Primitives. He was well known as a teacher, and his home became a centre to which many gravitated to hear his message of 'full salvation', or new birth and second blessing. A humble man, he witnessed many healings and other miracles in his ministry, and his disciples, who also frequently had dreams and visions, came to be nicknamed 'Magic Methodists'.

Somewhat like the Primitives, another offshoot of Methodism were the Bible Christians, also known as the Bryanites, after their founder, William O'Bryan. He was a Wesleyan local preacher who, out of deep concern about the complete ignorance of the gospel in the villages, travelled widely in Devon and Cornwall. Expelled from the Methodist Church in 1815 because he refused to limit himself within the confines of his own circuit, he founded the first society of his new work at Shebbear in North Devon. Like Bourne and Clowes, he faced much opposition and persecution, but the movement grew and fifteen years later began sending its own missionaries overseas.

Perhaps the most fondly remembered of its local preachers was Billy Bray, son of a Cornish tin-miner, who became widely known and loved in the region. His style of ministry was highly colourful and totally idiosyncratic, but mightily effective. He lived entirely by faith and experienced the miraculous provision and workings of God repeatedly in his life. He made absolutely no attempt to conceal his Christianity. His loud 'Hallelujahs' could regularly be heard ringing far and wide over the open countryside as he travelled. He left many rejoicing converts and his story still is a great delight and wonderful encouragement to read.

Other splits led to the formation of the Methodist New Connection, the Independent Methodists, the Wesleyan Methodist Association and the Wesleyan Reformers, but a process of reunification started in the second half of the nineteenth century, and today all these bodies, including the Primitive Methodists and the Bible Christians, have joined together to form what is now known simply as the Methodist Church in Britain. The Calvinistic

Methodists in Wales, who were followers of Whitefield, rather than Wesley, still remain separate.

*The Wider Effects of Revival*

By the end of the eighteenth century the influence of revival was being felt everywhere. Thousands of church-goers came alive in Christ, thousands of unbelievers were gathered into God's kingdom, ministers were renewed in faith across all denominations, and so standards of worship, Scripture knowledge and pastoral care were raised everywhere.

Faith newly discovered is contagious. Many of the new converts became preachers themselves, eager to spread the gospel, not only at home, but also abroad. This led to the creation of the first Protestant missionary societies. The earliest was the Methodist Missionary Society, formed in 1786, initially to take the gospel to India. Then in 1792 William Carey founded the Baptist Missionary Society and went himself under its auspices to India. After that the floodgates began to open on to the mission field, from churches in America, Germany, France, Scandinavia and Holland, as well as from Britain. In England the London Missionary Society was formed in 1795, the Church Missionary Society in 1799, the British and Foreign Bible Society in 1804, the London Society for Promoting Christianity amongst the Jews in 1809, and so it has continued ever since.

The same zeal was also poured into evangelism and social works at home. Particularly outstanding was the work done by the Methodist Hannah Ball and the Anglican Robert Raikes in establishing Sunday schools, thus initiating a process that was to lead to the provision of the free education for everyone that we enjoy today. Appeals from Christians for humanity and social justice in the latter third of the century were to end in rousing William Wilberforce to campaign for the abolition of slavery in the early part of the next. Prison reform, poor relief, medical care, financial aid and the like were all born out of the Methodist/Evangelical Revival about the same time.

It is often said that, after the decline in religion and morals in the seventeenth century, it was revival that saved the Church in the eighteenth. But it is equally true that it saved our society. New voices with a finer social conscience were heard in Parliament, in offices of government, in the courts of justice, in the armed forces. The people of Christ were leaving their mark everywhere. The century that ended with France torn apart by revolution could well have ended the same way in Britain had the nation's heart not first been won for God. Most of the people touched by the field preachers were from the working classes and it was they who were to be herded together into the heartless factories and impersonal cities created by the Industrial Revolution. They could very easily have become the same angry and violent mob as in France, if they too had not been won over for God and the Church had not started to care for them as it did. History has much for which to thank the great revivalists of the eighteenth century. Their heritage still lives on, even down into our own time.

### *Revival and the Prophetic Church*

The Wesleyan revival produced no prophetic movement in its time. There were plenty of manifestations of the Spirit's presence at the meetings, when people broke down and wept under his convicting power, or rejoiced with unspeakable joy as they found release in salvation. In the nineteenth century the Primitive Methodists were familiar with gifts of spiritual insight, such as the ones Paul calls word of wisdom, word of knowledge and discernment of spirits, though they lumped them all together then and called them 'second sight'. Their noisy, lively worship even earned them the nickname 'Ranters', but neither they nor their Methodist fore-runners ever eagerly desired spiritual gifts (1 Cor. 14:1). Nor was it part of their self-understanding that they were forming a latter-day Church of the Spirit, nor promoting a Christianity marked by pentecostal experience or phenomena.

The same is true of Jonathan Edwards and those who worked alongside him in America. Edwards himself tells how he had to correct someone from the neighbouring town of South Hadley, one whom he actually found to be 'a pious man … and I believe none would question his piety,' whose 'delusion' and 'error' was that he was so thrilled with the revival that he thought it heralded a new age of the Spirit, for he

> 'was possessed with an opinion that it was the beginning of the glorious times of the church spoken of in Scripture … that there should be many in these times that should be endued with extraordinary gifts of the Holy Ghost.' After Edwards had put him right on the matter, he repented of his error and 'exceedingly laments the dishonour he has done to God.'[330]

When John Wesley encountered such things he also rejected them and warned his converts against them. He was no more keen on

330. *Faithful Narrative*, p. 96.

excessive beliefs and enthusiasms than Luther had been two centuries earlier. His brother, Charles, once stayed at the home of a French Prophet in Wycombe, but he found the experience quite frightening and ended up trying to drive demons out of him.[331] Soon afterwards John visited a French Prophet meeting himself 'to try the spirits,' but was not at all convinced.[332]

The French Prophet movement continued active past the middle of the century, no doubt gleaning some additional members from the revival in its early years, but it never fed anything into the revival, nor was it promoted by it. It was always something apart. The last remnants of the movement sailed from Britain because of persecution in the 1770s and became the Shakers of America. As we have seen, these did positively thrive on the back of revival in the United States, but they again were always a people apart, and so have dwindled away in the twentieth century without leaving any living heritage.

History has clearly shown that a revival is not a prophetic movement and that prophetic movements do not always generate revival. But, as we also saw in the first part of this book, that is not the biblical pattern. Biblical prophets were, and Christian prophets ought still to be, God's front-line fighters for and in revival. Not since the days of Montanism has it been fully so, not until our own century. However, in the revivals of the eighteenth and nineteenth the ground work was prepared and the seed was sown that enabled the full and proper marriage of prophetism and revivalism to be restored as it is today. These stories of the revivals of the past are therefore far from irrelevant to our history, for they laid the foundations for the greatest prophetic revival-movement since New Testament times. But before we trace that thread any further, we must first turn our attention to another prophetic movement that flourished in the nineteenth century and died in the twentieth.

331 Robert Southey, *The Life of Wesley*, p. 168.
332 *Journal*, 28th Feb., 1739. See above, p. 356.

# 26

# Edward Irving and the Catholic Apostolic Church

The name of Edward Irving was very widely known on both sides of the Scottish Border in the 1820s and '30s, but then largely forgotten until quite recent times, when there has been a renewal of interest in his life and work. Fortunately both his teaching and the movement he was mainly responsible for founding continued to attract sufficient interest to ensure a constant trickle of publications, some of which are recent enough to be readily available to English readers. Many of these are critical of the charismatic phenomena that flowered in Irving's church, though the trend today is to offer assessments in the light of modern Pentecostalism, and these are usually much more sympathetic. Indeed Pentecostal theologians today find themselves very much at home in Irving's writings. His light burned for a brief space of time, largely out of place in its own age, but a forerunner of the light that shines in our time.[333]

*Irving's Ministry in London in the 1820s*

Edward Irving went to London in July 1822, then only twenty-nine years of age and virtually unknown, to take up his first appointment as minister to a tiny congregation of fifty or so Scotsmen at the Caledonian Chapel in Hatton Gardens. He was an immediate success, and not only with his own flock, for crowds congregated to hear his flamboyant oratory. Within a year the Chapel, which seated five

---

333. Among the most useful recent works of that sort is Strachan's *The Pentecostal Theology of Edward Irving,* which, as the title suggests, concentrates on Irving's own teaching, and Graham McFarlane's *Edward Irving and his Christ and the Spirit*. They may be supplemented from Drummond's more cynical *Edward Irving and his Circle,* which contains extra biographical detail and extensive documentation of the charismatic gifts. Shaw's *The Catholic Apostolic Church* completes the picture with an account of the sequel to Irving's ministry in the church he helped to create. Mention must also be made of Whitley's brief, but highly delightful, account of Irving's life and teaching, *Blinded Eagle*. Since these works cite original sources at length, the reader is referred to them for the sort of fuller quotations provided in the earlier chapters of this book. Here we limit ourselves to a simple account of the Irvingite story.

hundred, could no longer contain his following. Plans were therefore made to build a new National Scotch Church in Regent Square and that was opened for worship in May, 1827.

Irving's audience was drawn from all walks of life, but much of it from the upper levels of society. He held scholars and parliamentarians, professional men and nobles, in rapt attention as he discoursed on faith and social righteousness. The crowds were drawn by his preaching, but they remained because of his deep pastoral devotion and commitment to them. Before coming to London, he had been assistant for two years to the remarkable Thomas Chalmers in Glasgow, where, through working among the city's poor, he discovered what it meant to be a quiet and faithful shepherd to God's people. Such he remained throughout his London ministry, even when fame and controversy laid their demanding burdens on him.

There is yet a third aspect to his ministry that calls for comment, besides his preaching and pastoral gifts. He was also a thinker and a theologian. Most of the prophetic movements we have studied had their genesis in some kind of revivalist fervour sparked off by reaction to an environment of religious decline or reformation and consequently drew their following mainly from the artisan or the working classes. Irvingism, by contrast, not unlike the Amalrician movement[334], had its roots in a theological quest and therefore attracted a great deal of support from professional men and women.

*Irving's Christology*

The two foci of Irving's theology in the 1820s were Christology and eschatology. On the former he taught that Jesus was a man like us in every respect, except that he did not sin (cp. Heb. 2:17; 4:15), which meant that he had all the same limitations and weaknesses as we have. Thus he was born with the same inherently sinful flesh as ours, but by his constant obedience to the Father, through the operation of the Holy Spirit in him, he did not commit sin and so defeated sin in the flesh, hence working our release from the power of sin.

Such views, though they might be accepted as orthodox in our day, earned him a great deal of criticism in his own. To some they seemed to suggest he was teaching that Jesus was a sinner, which, of course, he was not. In 1828 he published a book of sermons on the incarnation, which he hoped would prove to his critics that he was saying no such thing, but it only provided further fuel for their

334. See above, p. 195.

fires. By selecting a few sentences out of context, the Scots Presbytery of London, at its meeting in 1830, was able to denounce his teaching as heretical. That by no means brought the story to an end. Quite the contrary, for Irving thereupon withdrew himself from their jurisdiction and appealed to the General Assembly of the Church of Scotland, which considered his case in the following year.

We shall leave the further story of that aside for the moment. The point to note for the moment is that, although Irving had not yet formulated his pentecostal doctrines, his teaching about Christ left open the possibility of pointing to the Spirit as the answer to the question how Jesus was able to defeat sin in his flesh, if it were indeed the same flesh as ours, the flesh of fallen humanity.

> 'The point at issue is simply this: whether Christ's flesh had the grace of sinlessness and incorruption from its proper nature, or from the indwelling of the Holy Ghost. I say the latter. I assert, that in its proper nature it was as the flesh of his mother, but by virtue of the Holy Ghost's quickening and inhabiting of it, it was preserved sinless and incorruptible.'[335]

This doctrine was to prove pivotal in the birthing of prophetism at this time, as we shall see more clearly when we come to consider the spiritual pilgrimage of the first of the prophets, Mary Campbell.

*Irving's Eschatology*

If Irving's Christology ran counter to accepted opinions in his day, his views of the end-times were very much in conformity with those widely held among his contemporaries. The French Revolution and the Napoleonic Wars were in the recent past and questions about God's purposes in history were still very much in the air. At the end of 1826 he accepted an invitation from Henry Drummond, who was later to become one of the leaders of the Catholic Apostolic Church, to join a number of other churchmen for a conference on prophecy at his country seat at Albury.

This conference met annually for five years and agreed on a number of points, in particular that the chain of events leading up to the irruption of the Millennium, as described in the book of Revelation, had begun to unfold itself in 1793. That was the year of the Reign of Terror in France, which, they pointed out, was 1260 years (see Rev. 12:6) after 533, when the Emperor Justinian gave special recognition to the Papacy. In the year after the first Albury Conference, 1827,

335. E. Irving, *The Doctrine of the Incarnation Opened in Six Sermons*, 1828, p. 4.

Irving published a translation of a Spanish work entitled *The Coming of Messiah in Glory and Majesty*, which presented an interpretation of the sequence of events that would precede the Millennium that was subsequently to become very popular indeed.[336] Irving was clearly very much occupied with such matters, like so many other prophets that had gone before him.

*Irving's Teaching about the Spirit of God and the Love of God*

Irving's doctrine of the Spirit in the 1820s was also in some ways similar to that of his contemporaries, in as much as he did not expect the gifts of the Spirit to be operative again in the Church's history. He held that they had gradually disappeared from the Church with a decline of faith that accompanied the spread of Christianity in the Gentile world, and would not be restored until the Second Coming, though he admitted there was nothing in Scripture to say that they should not be operative in the Church now.

In 1828 Irving invited a young licentiate called Alexander Scott to assist him at the Regent Square church. Scott stayed with him for two years and during that period constantly affirmed his belief that the spiritual gifts ought still to be exercised. Irving's theological inclination was to agree, but his doctrine of history prevented him from doing so. None the less, Scott's views left their mark.

One further aspect of current theological debate that had an important part to play in the emergence of prophecy is found in the teachings of Rev. J. Macleod Campbell, minister of Rhu (or Row) in Dumbartonshire. The background is Scottish Calvinistic belief in predestination, which held that because God is utterly sovereign, our salvation is entirely a matter of his decision. It is solely by his determination that men are saved or not, and, since God is all-knowing, that decision is already predetermined. Our part is therefore to be thankful that we are of those he has elected to redeem.

While this teaching was intended to offer a sense of security to the elect, it frequently bred the opposite, since there were always plenty who were not sure, even though they were devoted church-goers, whether they were really of the number of the elect, that is, as opposed to the rest who were the damned. Against this background Macleod Campbell preached a strong gospel of the love of God, teaching that God's love was freely extended to all sinners, for whom repentance and forgiveness and salvation were therefore possible. His preaching brought an awakening to the West of

---

336. See below, p. 438.

Scotland, but in due course he was denounced as a heretic. Irving and Macleod Campbell were friends.

In these ways the theological scene was set for the birth of yet another prophetic movement.

*Clydeside, 1828-30*

Had it been left to Irving and Scott, or to Drummond and the Albury Circle, all of whom in their various ways were living in expectation of a new age for the Church, there would probably have been little more than theological discussions and inspiring sermons to report, like firewood prepared and arranged in the hearth, but unlit and without heat. The spark that kindled the flame was struck among working people far from London, in the West of Scotland.

In 1828 Irving was on tour in Central Scotland, preaching to large crowds as he went. When he was in the Glasgow area, he visited a friend and fellow-member of the Albury Conference, Robert Story, minister of Rosneath on the Gareloch. From there he went on to Rhu, on the other side of the Gareloch, where he met and established his life-long friendship with Macleod Campbell. It was on this trip also that he met Sandy Scott and invited him to become his assistant in London.

The visit was momentous for other reasons besides these. In Rosneath parish there lived a very devout family of Campbells in the farmhouse at Fernicarry. Robert Story published a book about one of them in 1829, Isabella, then recently deceased. In it he told of her intimate communion with God, an account befitting any great saint. She, however, is not the one on whom our story focuses, but her sister, Mary.[337]

Like most other people in those parts, she was familiar with Macleod Campbell's gospel of love, and very probably she had heard Irving when he preached at Rosneath in 1828. But the following year, she was housebound, 'lying ill with consumption.' In the autumn Scott came on a visit back home and went to see her. He spoke with her of his conviction that 'the spiritual gifts ought still to be exercised in the Church' and tried to explain to her 'the distinction between regeneration and baptism with the Holy Ghost.' But she, 'being a woman of very fixed and constant spirit,' was not persuaded. However, in December, while she was reading John 14-16, she saw everything in a new light, and firstly 'she saw there the

337. Irving's own account of Mary's story was published in *Frazer's Magazine* in January, 1832, pp. 754-61.

truth of our Lord's human nature,' that it was the same as ours and that his holiness was not inherent, but was derived from the operation of the Holy Spirit in him, just as Irving had been teaching for so long. But then she realised that if she and Jesus were really alike in that respect, then the works he did, she might also do, if the same Spirit were to dwell in her as it had in him.

Meanwhile, her health continued to deteriorate, despite her new-found excitement. Then on Sunday, 30th March, while she and a few others around her bed were praying especially for a restoration of the spiritual gifts,

> 'the Holy Ghost came with mighty power upon the sick woman as she lay in her weakness, and constrained her to speak at great length, and with superhuman strength, in an unknown tongue, to the astonishment of all who heard, and to her own great edification and enjoyment of God.'[338]

The scene now shifts to the other side of the Clyde, to Port Glasgow, where lived two brothers, James and George Macdonald, ship-builders, men of quiet and unobtrusive faith. Both claimed to have had a conversion experience in 1828, and their views were clearly influenced by the teachings of Macleod Campbell and Irving. They had a sister called Margaret who, like Mary Campbell, was bed-ridden, sick unto death. Some days after Mary's endowment, the Spirit came also on Margaret who spoke of the wonderful works of God for a space of two or three hours, as if the weakness were taken from her. When James and George came home for dinner, she spoke to them at great length and prayed for James to be endowed with the power of the Holy Ghost there and then. Almost instantly he said, quite calmly, 'I have got it.' He went to the window and stood there silently for a few moments, then turning to Margaret, he said, 'Arise and stand upright.' As he took her by the hand she rose up healed and joined them at table for dinner.

James then wrote to Mary Campbell telling her of what had happened to Margaret and commanding her also in the name of the Lord to arise. When she read the letter, she knew the power of the Lord was upon her, and she too rose up healed. A few days later, on Friday, 18th April, first George and then James spoke in tongues. The following evening they spoke in tongues and interpreted. The gist of the interpretation was, 'Behold he cometh—Jesus cometh.'[339]

338. *Frazer's Magazine*, pp. 759-60.
339. The full account is given in Robert Norton's *Memoirs of James and George Macdonald of Port-Glasgow*, 1840, pp. 107-11.

*Meanwhile in Regent Square*

Irving tells us himself that at the time of this Scottish Pentecost on Clydeside, his own congregation in London, under his guidance, was still bewailing their sins and the sins of their fathers that had caused the gifts to disappear from the Church, as he then believed, until the time of the Second Coming of Christ:

> 'Thus we stood, when the tidings of the restoration of the gift of tongues in the west of Scotland burst upon us like the morning star heralding the approach of day, and turned our speculations upon the true doctrine into the examination of a fact.'[340]

Just as persons of all ranks had flocked to hear the shepherdess of Dauphiné, so now they came to Mary Campbell and the Macdonalds, among them a party of six from the Regent Square church led by a solicitor, named John Bate Cardale. Irving heard their reports and those of others with a sense of excitement, but also with caution. He wrote:

> 'I felt it to be a matter of too great concern to yield up my faith to anything but the clearest evidence.'

In the following year he met the prophets himself, but by that time the reports reaching him had fully convinced him of the authenticity of their experiences. However, it was not simply reports from excited witnesses that swayed him. The 'fact', as he called it, did indeed agree admirably in his mind with the 'true doctrine' he had been propounding for so many years.

> 'The way had to be prepared by the full preaching of Christ's coming in our flesh, and his coming in glory—the two great divisions of Christian doctrine which had gone down into the earth out of sight and out of mind, and which must be revived by preaching before the Holy Spirit could have anything to witness to; for he doth not witness to any system of men … but to Jesus, who suffered with us in the flesh, who shareth with us his life and power, and cometh with us in glory.'[341]

Irving's theology had not only helped prepare the way for what had happened; it had also prepared him to oversee what was about to happen.

340. *Frazer's Magazine*, p. 755.
341. *Ibid.*

*Tongues and Prophecy in London, 1830-31*

After Cardale's party returned from Port Glasgow, several meetings were started in London to pray for the outpouring of the Holy Ghost. They were given a temporary boost by the miraculous cure of a certain Miss Fancourt in October 1830, but it was not till the thirtieth of April in the following year that the first tongues were heard. The speaker was the same Mrs Cardale.

At that time, Irving, who had, it seems, taken no active part in the house meetings, was much occupied with worries about the forthcoming meeting of the General Assembly in May, 1831. When his teaching about Christ's human nature had been adjudged heretical by the London Presbytery the year before, he had referred his cause to the Assembly, and now it was about to be considered. Also to be tried were two of his disciples, his friend Sandy Scott and a certain Hugh Maclean. And together with these Macleod Campbell's doctrine of the universal love of Christ was also to be judged.

Irving had published a great deal in preparation for this moment, in the hope that his jurors would have the clearest possible view of his orthodoxy, but ever the man of prayer as well as the scholar, he started an early morning prayer meeting in his church, which he held daily at 6.30 to pray for a happy outcome to the Assembly's deliberations. About a thousand attended regularly throughout the fortnight before the Assembly met, but to no avail. Macleod Campbell was put out of his church, Scott was deprived of his licence to preach, Maclean was sent for trial by his own Presbytery, and Irving was threatened with proceedings against him if he tried to preach in Scotland again.

However, the early morning prayers had also ranged more widely, into seeking a new outpouring of the Spirit, and so after the Assembly the meetings continued. Others besides Mrs Cardale had now begun to speak in tongues, but Irving was hesitant in permitting them to exercise their gift at the church meetings. He tested the charismata in private and at the house meetings, but while he procrastinated, one or two prophetic utterances were heard in the early morning gatherings proclaiming that he was quenching the Spirit. He had led prayers for renewal of the gifts and he had tried them and found them to be of God, so finally he relented and announced to his congregation that they could be used at the early meetings thenceforth. The decision was heard with alarm by the office-bearers of the church and in view of their opposition Irving refused the prophets permission to speak at the Sunday services.

Thus the prophetic Spirit bubbled like some underground stream beneath the surface throughout the summer of 1831. Prophecy, tongues and interpretation became a regular feature of the week-day meetings, but the Spirit once unleashed could not be held restrained for ever.

*Irving and his Followers Expelled from the Church, 1831-2*

At the end of October, the Sunday service was interrupted and thrown into some momentary confusion when a couple of people rose from their seats, one of them hurrying into the vestry and the other out through the main doors, to give vent in private to the voice of the Spirit that was barred from the church itself. After service, Irving was charged by one of the prophets with being ashamed of following the Master because of opposition and by evening he had decided to permit speaking in tongues and prophesying to be 'added to' the service.

November was consequently a month of turmoil. Crowds filled the church, many out of curiosity, but some to scorn and cause disturbance. Irving, in a moment of uncertainty, forbade further expression to the gifts at divine service, but almost immediately relented, and in mid-November the trustees of the church met to consider what steps they should take. After all his hesitancy, Irving now became fully committed to the movement that was rapidly gathering momentum around him.

The trustees met again in December, but Irving, now fully convinced that the gifts were of the Holy Spirit, refused to heed their pleas to forbid their expression in church. In March they asked the London Presbytery to judge their complaint, which they formulated solely in terms of their church's trust deed, which stated that only persons properly ordained or licensed could lead in public worship. Thus they pleaded that Irving was departing from the terms of the deed, as well as from the discipline of the Church of Scotland, in permitting lay persons to interrupt the constitutional flow of the Sunday services. After a three-day hearing at the beginning of May, the court decided against him, decreeing that he be removed from his charge. On Friday, 4th May, 1832, as he and his people gathered for early prayers, they found the gates of the church locked against them.

That same May the Assembly instructed the Presbytery of Annan, in South-West Scotland, that had ordained Irving, to take proceedings against him on the old charge of heretical Christological doctrine, which it did the following March, in 1833, when Irving was finally deposed from his office of Minister in the Church of Scotland.[342]

By that time Irving had given himself entirely to the new church he had helped to create and was preaching his prophetic gospel both in London and in his Scottish homeland. But presently his health began to fail. He died of consumption in Glasgow on 7th December, 1834, at the age of forty-two.

*Founding the Catholic Apostolic Church*

About eight hundred members of the Regent Square church followed Irving out and in a short time found themselves a new home in a large picture gallery in Newman Street, which they then refurbished as their church. In its foundation we find the confluence of two streams, the Irvingite and the Albury circles. Both already overlapped in considerable measure before 1832, for Irving was a dedicated member of the Albury Conference and some of that circle were regular attenders at his church.

By the time of Irving's death, leadership of the church had already passed into the hands of Henry Drummond and others of the Albury group. In October 1832, at a meeting in Irving's house, Drummond, speaking under prophetic inspiration, nominated Cardale to the office of 'Apostle'. Over the next two years eleven other men were called by prophetic designation to complete the roll of these latter-day Apostles. Others were similarly appointed Prophets, Evangelists, Pastors and Teachers, Elders, Deacons, and to a variety of other assisting ministries. They gave the chief pastors of their congregations the title 'Angel' (after the designation of the recipients of the letters to the seven churches in Rev. 2-3). It was to that office in the Newman Street church that Irving was himself ordained, at the hands of Apostle Cardale.

Naturally the Church's character was Presbyterian at first, but even from its inception the community of believers contained Anglicans, Baptists, Congregationalists and Roman Catholics, including ministers of these denominations. It was from this motley group that the 'Seven Churches of London' were born and the twelve 'Apostles' were drawn. The College of Apostles was formally constituted in July, 1835, and all twelve withdrew to Albury, which was now to become their Church's headquarters. There they lived for a year in quiet retreat along with seven of the Prophets, daily

342. Time changes memories, turning today's heretic into tomorrow's saint. A full-size memorial statue of Irving now stands in the forecourt of the church at Annan.

praying and studying the Bible. Through prophetic leading they came to recognise the Mosaic tabernacle in the Old Testament as the pattern for their Church, which was consequently to become thoroughly liturgical in its worship, something after the style of Anglo-Catholicism.

The Apostles' status and authority also assumed a somewhat Catholic hue, for, like bishops, they were responsible for the doctrines and disciplines of their Church and for the administration of the rites of ordination and 'sealing' (similar to confirmation). In fact the Church that formed itself in the 1830s and '40s was essentially priestly, sacramentarian and ritualistic, an odd child to emerge from a Presbyterian cradle. It is little wonder that Irving was reluctant to see the continued prompting of the Holy Spirit behind every new doctrine and practice that was beginning to take shape during the last years of his life.

*The Place of Spiritual Gifts in the Catholic Apostolic Church*

The gifts of the Spirit continued in use, but in a subdued and controlled fashion now that official spokesmen of the Spirit had been appointed. Prophecy itself fell into disrepute at a very early stage because of its apparent subjectivity. Even Mr. Taplin, who was designated 'the chief of the Prophets', had been shown to be an unreliable mouthpiece for the Spirit, for on one occasion he had uttered a prophetic rebuke to Irving, only to find himself immediately rebuked by another prophet, and then later to admit he had spoken 'by the power of an evil spirit.' The problem of discernment, present from earliest Old Testament times and the bogey of the early Church, still remained unresolved.

Tongues fared a little better and were still to be heard in Catholic Apostolic services even in the twentieth century, though their use was no longer actively encouraged. In Irving's theology they had been regarded as evidence of baptism in the Spirit, but that view never became the accepted doctrine of the Church.

In fact, the movement's general prophetic zeal subsided quite rapidly and within a few years the Church was faced with a spiritual crisis, or rather a 'crisis of apathy'. The Apostles responded in 1847 by instituting the 'rite of sealing', in which they held that the Holy Spirit was imparted to baptised Church members through the laying on of the Apostles' hands to equip them for service. Their view of this rite, as a supplement to water-baptism, finds echoes in Pentecostal 'second-blessing' theology and in Catholic ideas about confirmation:

> 'There the gift of the Holy Ghost which Christ imparts after Baptism, and to those already baptised ... to be distinguished from baptism with water.'[343]

Irving had not himself insisted on such a conscious separation, but by 1847 Catholic Apostolic attitudes had changed considerably. Tongues and prophecy were no longer expected to accompany baptism in the Spirit. Irving's theology had developed as a response to and was concerned to explain spontaneous, charismatic activity, but in the Catholic Apostolic Church the spontaneity was curbed and only echoes of the early enthusiastic, charismatic activity survived. The gift of the Spirit was encapsulated in a formal rite, his worship was framed in stereotyped liturgical modes, and his prophetic voice, once free and unfettered, was channelled through designated officials.

The progression is a familiar one, witnessed in the New Testament Church, in Montanism, in the Quaker and Shaker movements, and again to some extent in present-day Pentecostalism, only the transition from enthusiasm to ecclesiasticism seems to have been much more accelerated than in any of these. Their observation of this progression convinced the Macdonald brothers that the Spirit of prophecy was being driven from the Church, and so they never joined the Catholic Apostolic organisation when it established itself in Scotland.

*Irvingism as a Prophetic Movement*

In the history of Irvingism, as it is often called, though the Catholic Apostolic community did not like the name, we can find many other traits and trends that remind us of earlier movements of the Spirit. Thus, for example, evangelistic zeal and interdenominational ecumenicism went hand in hand with sectarianism, the members being drawn from many different churches, full of enthusiasm for the new work, but forming themselves into a church entirely separate from all others. Like other prophets before them they were not slow to denounce other churches in the land for their spiritual bankruptcy. Or again, as at other times, the voice of prophecy was often heeded among them at the expense of intellectual caution. The miraculous and the supernatural were, of course, cherished, and in like manner their charismatic leaders were respected and revered. The movement was also thoroughly millennarian, believing itself to be the church of the end-times.

343. J.B. Cardale, *Readings upon the Liturgy* II, London, 1878, p. 291.

Irvingism was also different from earlier prophetic movements in many respects and was in some measure like a foretaste of twentieth-century Pentecostalism. For the first time since New Testament days tongues assumed a place of central significance. We hear little about tongues among the Montanists, or any other of the movements after them, until we come to the Shakers, but even they, with their French Prophet and Quaker background, regarded their shaking or bodily agitations as the primary evidence of Spirit Baptism. In a book published in 1831, *The Day of Pentecost, or baptism with the Holy Ghost,* Irving stated his belief that speaking with tongues was the 'standing sign' of baptism in the Spirit. Though he never spoke in tongues or prophesied himself, his theology had become fully Pentecostal in the sense with which we commonly use the word today. None the less, it is one of the strange ironies of history that, when the Pentecostal Movement came to birth at the beginning of the twentieth century, it had no connection with Irvingism, indeed did not even seem to know of its existence.

The Catholic Apostolic Church's prophetic belief that it had been birthed to usher in the last days was strong. That was part of its fundamental reason for existing. The outpouring of the Spirit and the restoration of the gifts to the Church were in fulfilment of Joel's prophecy, quoted by Peter on the Day of Pentecost, that these things would take place precisely 'in the last days' (Acts 2:16-21). This very doctrine, however, became the obituary of the Church, written at its birth. Because of it, the teaching was formulated that there should be no more apostles before the end, and since only apostles had the authority to ordain ministers in the churches, the death of the last apostle in 1901 heralded the approaching demise of the Church itself. 1902 was designated the beginning of 'the Silence', on the basis of the prophecy in Rev. 8:1 that at the opening of the seventh seal, signalling the run in to final end of history, there would be 'silence in heaven for about half an hour.' From that time on the Catholic Apostolics became a waiting people, awaiting the second coming of Christ that their Church existed to herald. Gradually their officiating priests died off, the last one in 1971. Churches gradually closed, or were handed over to other denominations, though some remained open as long as possible, their congregations growing older and smaller. There are still people today who remember the Catholic Apostolic Church services, and those that do tend to reminisce with a fondness that echoes times of considerable blessing among a very faithful people.

*Johann Lutz and the Catholic Apostolic Church in Europe*

The Catholic Apostolic Church was never confined to London. Congregations were quickly established in other towns in England and Scotland, and the movement spread abroad to the Continent and America. Part of the European story is very much worth retelling.

At Irving's early prayer meetings in 1831, he tells us,

> 'We cried unto the Lord for apostles, prophets, evangelists, pastors and teachers, anointed with the Holy Ghost.'[344]

A year earlier, in the Macdonalds' house in Port Glasgow, a similar prayer, 'Send us apostles,' was also being offered. But two years before that, in 1828, these words were already being spoken 'in the power':

> 'Know ye not, ye children of God, that ye are living in the last days, in the days in which the Lord will come? Know ye not that before the Lord comes He will give again apostles, prophets, evangelists, and pastors, and churches as at the beginning?'

This prophecy could have been uttered at Regent Street, but it was not. It was spoken in the town of Karlshuld in the Donaumoos in Bavaria, in a Roman Catholic community that had never heard of Irving, or Drummond, or the Macdonalds.[345]

Unlike the cultured National Scotch Church, they were a poor congregation living in a very rough setting. Johann Lutz had been their priest since August, 1826, and in response to his people's obvious craving for a spiritual nourishment which the Church did not provide, he began to give them what he considered appropriate teaching from the New Testament. Something of a revival started and throughout 1827 people came to him from time to time to tell how they had been touched by the grace of God.

Then on New Year's Eve he preached a very moving sermon, the consequence of which was that he was awakened at 3.15 in the morning of New Year's Day by a crowd of people anxious to make confession. The Mass that day was an unusual one. We read of 'joy', of 'loud sobs and tears', of a sermon that turned to prayer, of prayers unfinished 'on account of the overpowering emotion', of 'the spiritual exaltation and agitation of the congregation', and the

344. W. Harding, *The Trial of the Rev. Edward Irving, M.A. Before The London Presbytery*, 1832, p. 24.
345. The story is told for English readers by L.W. Scholler, *A Chapter in Church History from South Germany*, being passages from the life of Johann Evangelist Georg Lutz, tr. W. Wallis, London, 1894.

like. Then in the evening a certain woman from the congregation came to tell him his heart was not right with God, that he did so much in his own strength that he left little room for the Spirit to work. The scene reads like a replay of the conversation between the Master and the Friend of God in an earlier century.[346]

The spiritual stream continued to flow and prophetic utterances began to be heard both in church and in people's houses towards the end of February. No record was kept of the utterances, but their gist is preserved in the quotation cited above, to the effect that the end was near, that the Spirit was to be outpoured anew, and the spiritual Church was to be restored as at the beginning. The prophecies also encouraged the reading of Scripture and the valuing of the sacraments. No reference is made to tongues, though 'other spiritual communications, such as visions and dreams' are mentioned, and apparently 'to Lutz himself it was revealed, through a vision, that the Lord would again send forth apostles.'[347]

Of course, the revival was not without its problems, but these need not concern us here. The 'speaking in the power' only continued till July and was sporadic thereafter, though Lutz still spoke of the grace experienced by his congregation. In due course he was called to account by the ecclesiastical authorities and had to leave Karlshuld in the autumn of 1831. He sought refuge in Protestantism for a time, but found that too arid in its excessive rationalism, and so he returned to the Roman fold to become curate of Unterroth at the end of 1832. He served the church there faithfully and by 1839 had become priest of Oberroth and was elevated to the office of Archdeacon and Rural Dean.

But the light of the Spirit was still flickering within him when in 1842 he met William Caird, husband of Mary Campbell of Fernicarry, who told that 'in England there were churches such as there were in the beginning,' directed by 'men of discernment' called 'Apostles'. Lutz replied,

'What? Apostles? Is that really so? I have been waiting for apostles, and for a special work of God in the Church for fourteen years.'[348]

The rest of the story hardly needs telling. Lutz and Caird spent much time together and expressed some of their views in writing. Lutz was challenged by his Chapter to declare his attitude to Irvingism and after lengthy proceedings was deprived of his charge and excommunicated in 1856 along with five other Roman Catholic

---

346. See above, p. 213.
347. Scholler, pp. 30-32.
348. Scholler, p. 156.

priests who had espoused his views. He now formally joined the Catholic Apostolic Church and became Angel of the church at Berne. After eleven years there, because of his recognised gift for preaching, he was appointed to an itinerant, evangelistic ministry. One of his great joys must have been his return in this role to the Donaumoos in 1870 and '71 to find many who remembered the events of forty years earlier and were therefore prepared to establish a small Catholic Apostolic congregation there to await the Saviour's return. Lutz died in August, 1882, at the age of 81. It is easy to imagine him comparing happy testimonies with Irving on another shore!

# 27
# Church and Theology in the Nineteenth Century

The radical changes in life style for millions world-wide, as the Industrial Revolution created its new cities, new ways of employment, new forms of transport and communication, as political revolutions and wars caused nations to rise or fall and colonial holdings to change hands and, as expansion continued into newly explored lands. Such changes have continued into our own century leaving the world today a vastly different place from what it was in 1800.

A similar measure of change has taken place in the Christian Church. The revivals of the eighteenth century were followed by other massive changes that have totally altered the face of the Church in our times. Not all of these have by any means resulted from prophetic or revival workings, but they have often influenced such workings and so merit some comment.

It is important to remember that the purpose of this book is to trace the history of movements that show the prophetic qualities of biblical faith. The history of the Church can be written with a very different emphasis, as it commonly is, in which such movements are hardly noticed, some of them not at all. But it is the author's belief that in the story of the Church of the future they will be remembered as works of far greater significance than has been commonly recognised hitherto. Pentecostalism, their present-day successor, embraces one third of the Church world-wide. Two hundred years ago very few would have had any conception of such a possibility.

*Continuing Missionary Work*

In the 1790s Christianity was primarily a white man's religion. Apart from a few vestiges of early times in other parts of the world, the Church was mainly located in Europe (from Russia to the Atlantic), with branches for European settlers in the New World colonies. Today, two hundred years later, it is a world-wide religion in which whites are outnumbered by coloured peoples. The change is due mainly to continued missionary work, increased revival outpourings and the rise of Pentecostal Christianity.

Before the eighteenth century awakening living faith was in danger of being swamped by Renaissance rationalism, but thanks largely to the German Pietists the pendulum began to swing back in the direction of faith. Catholic missionaries were already busy around the world, especially where the Catholic governments of Europe were establishing their colonies. The Protestant churches did undertake some missionary activity, but it was mostly limited to maintaining chaplaincies among colonial settlers. The Society for the Propagation of the Gospel, founded in 1701, was outstanding in this field.

The Moravians started sending out their missionaries in the 1730s and then the Wesleyan revival awakened zeal among other Christians for the evangelisation of peoples who had not yet heard the gospel. At the end of the century the first missionary societies were founded in England and by the 1830s many similar non-denominational societies had been birthed in northern Europe and America. Then the churches began to see the need for having their own societies. By the middle of the nineteenth century missionaries were going out everywhere throughout the world.

Before the missionaries came, churches had already been built in the colonial and trading settlements, either by the trading companies for the benefit of their employees or by the government for the settlers. Though the new missionary societies were truly motivated by evangelical zeal, the political and commercial links remained. Explorers like Livingstone and Stanley are remembered with equal honour by both secular and church historians. Sometimes traders followed missionaries, sometimes the reverse. Both welcomed the opportunities they opened up for each other, and missionaries often welcomed the protection of their governments, while the colonial governments welcomed the civilising work done by the missionaries. The establishment of the 'three C's'—Christianity, commerce and civilisation—became the objective of most missionary societies, which therefore put much energy into founding schools, hospitals, industries, social welfare and the like.

And, of course, hand in hand with all that went the work of translating the Bible. The Religious Tract Society was founded in 1802, the British and Foreign Bible Society in 1804, and since then Bible Societies have multiplied in Britain and abroad. For a time there was some disagreement between them over points of doctrine, but today there is a high degree of co-operation. Thanks to their work, the Bible is now available in all the major languages of the world, and in parts in many tribal languages. Today the word of God is being read all round the globe.

The work of the missionaries, wonderful in its own right, was greatly assisted by the revivals of the nineteenth century and then marvellously expedited by the Pentecostal outpourings of this. In 1900, for example, only two per cent of Africans were Christian, while today between forty and fifty per cent are, the major part of them Pentecostal believers. Comparable figures can be produced for many other parts of the world. The growth rate is quite phenomenal, unparalleled in history since the earliest days of the church, except perhaps in the conversion of Europe in the Middle Ages.

### *Rationalism, Scientific Theory and Liberal Theology*

Alongside this world-wide growth in Christianity, other major changes were taking place in Britain, Europe and the United States. Some of them had already begun before the revivals started, perhaps the most significant and dangerous of all for the Church being the rise of rationalistic thinking that followed in the wake of the Renaissance. As we have seen, it had already influenced the great reformers and the churches they founded, causing Protestantism to have a generally reduced view of supernatural action in daily life and turning faith into a dry system of doctrine. In the eighteenth and nineteenth centuries the trend accelerated in a downward spiral into a rationalistic negativism that eventually saw no place for God any more.

Descartes, a French Catholic, Spinoza, a Dutch Jew, and Leibniz, a German Protestant, laid the foundations for this new rationalism in the seventeenth century, encouraging, in different ways, a reasoning from first principles, rather than from prestated dogmas and doctrines of the Church or of other philosophical systems. None of them denied the existence of God, but they held that belief in God should be tenable on the basis of rational argument. British thinkers adopted a different approach, Locke, Berkeley and Hume arguing in the early eighteenth century that belief depends on experience (empiricism) rather than reason (rationalism).

Continental rationalism led to a view of God that was pantheistic, one in which scarcely any distinction could be drawn between God and nature. British empiricism, on the other hand, led to scepticism. Particularly influential in initiating that process were the writings of David Hume (1711-76), a Scotsman who questioned absolutely everything. In line with the anti-religious bias of the Enlightenment, he found no place for consideration of anything spiritual or miraculous in understanding life. And his arguments were so utterly logical that they led him to view even the miracle stories in the Gospels on a par with the folktales of other ages and societies. His views were to prove pivotal in the development of modern European secular thinking. After his time Protestant theologians became divided into two broad camps, those who sought to accommodate their beliefs to this new scepticism (liberals) and those who resisted its inroads (conservatives). Neither camp, however, sought to revive any prophetic viewpoint, but continued to argue from purely intellectual premises.

In the mid-eighteenth century a third form of philosophy, known as deism, became popular in Europe. It was to prove every bit as dangerous to the Church, though perhaps more on a political than a theological front. Its fundamental belief was that God created everything in the beginning, but since then has left the universe to its own devices and has little or no continuing interest in its present condition. This was broadly the view of a number of Englishmen, but more importantly of the Frenchmen, Rousseau and Voltaire, and the German, Lessing. The logical conclusion of such thinking is that men must not expect God to intervene in history and that they are therefore the masters of their own destinies. It was such thinking, taken up and developed by others, that led to the overthrow of the Church and its political power in much of Europe at the time of the French Revolution.

Philosophers have always asked unsettling questions, even from earliest times, but the thought patterns of the seventeenth and eighteenth centuries were also being influenced by new scientific discoveries, such as those of men like Copernicus, Kepler, Galileo and Newton, who showed the earth was not the centre of the universe, but a planet revolving round the sun along with several other planets, and that the stars, instead of circling the earth, were themselves other suns far flung in space. In earlier days the doctrines of the Church could be re-established over philosophical speculation and scientific discovery by the exercise of ecclesiastical authority, which was also tried in the case of Galileo. But the day when such heavy-handed methods could succeed had passed. Explorers were discovering new worlds, new products were being brought into Europe, new thinking was in the air, and in the light of all these new discoveries man was beginning to look more and more like a small creature in a vast universe, and God more and more remote with every passing decade.

All these things had a radical impact in fields far beyond the philosopher's armchair and scientist's laboratory. In the political and social arena they led, as we have already seen, almost directly to the awakening of the working classes to consciousness of the common dignity of man and that in turn led, after the American Revolution, to the French Revolution and the overthrow of the ancient monarchical and feudal systems of Europe.

The turmoil continued and became even stronger in the nineteenth century. In the world of scientific investigation Charles Lyall published his *Principles of Geology* in 1830, introducing the concept of geological time measured in millions of years, much in contrast with biblical chronology which counted back to creation in thousands. Until then the calculations of James Ussher, a seventeenth century Archbishop of Armagh, had stood unquestioned by most Christians. His dates, often included in the margin of the King James Bible, put creation at 4,004 BC. When Charles Darwin's *Origin of the Species* appeared in 1859 propounding the theory of evolution and his *Descent of Man* in 1871 positing man's affinity with the ape, the Church's dogmatic proclamation was radically challenged and, in the opinion of many, totally undermined.

Alongside all this went a continuing search for a rationalistic understanding of life, ending in the materialism of Karl Marx, for whom there was no divine answer, only a human one, expressed in the class struggle and a call for revolution. His *Communist Manifesto* was published in 1848, the year that revolutions broke out in France, Germany and Italy. The century ended with another atheistic philosopher, Nietzsche, for whom God was dead, calling for a new liberated humanity. His teaching proved particularly acceptable among the Nazis in the 1930s. The socialism of the eighteenth century philosophers prepared the way for the French Revolution which overthrew the power of the Church, the atheism of their nineteenth century successors sought to abolish the very existence of God. Man, in their view, had no more need of God. He was master of his own destiny.

But perhaps the most devastating of all elements in the new thinking was the critical biblical study that came to flower in the latter half of the nineteenth century. Julius Wellhausen and others in Germany taught that Old Testament faith had evolved from a primitive form of tribal religion through various stages of growth in understanding, partly by borrowing from surrounding pagan cultures, and that the Scriptures themselves were the product of much editorial work on the text down the centuries. Such teaching left little place for revelation or for the workings of God. Similarly, David F. Strauss and others after him dismissed all the supernatural elements in the Gospels as myth. The approach caught the imagination of scholars world-wide. It had found its way into British universities by the 1870s and by the end of the century most theological institutions in Britain and America were moving over to this new 'liberal theology'.

The philosophers had argued God out of existence, the scientists had raised huge questions about the reliability of the biblical revelation and were busy developing a thought-system that did not involve God in the discussion at all, and biblical scholars were now doing the same. The very foundations of faith were being shaken and undermined. Nothing was sacred any more, and young men studying theology or training for ministry were being educated in these new forms. The forces ranged against the faith were by no means insignificant. There was urgent need for some intervention from heaven.

*Reaction in the Church*

Of course, the Church argued back. The response of the Catholic Church was to dig in its heels. In 1864 Pope Pius IX, probably the most influential Pope of the nineteenth century, issued a statement known as the *Syllabus of Errors*, which categorically condemned everything that hinted of liberalism, including political liberalism, liberal theology, rationalism of all kinds, religious toleration, and other things similar. In so doing, however, he was expressing his reactions to other, more political assaults as well. His power was then being eroded on almost every front. The authority of the Church in Catholic Europe had already been massively undermined by the French Revolution, but after Victor Emmanuel took the city of Rome in 1870 the process was greatly accelerated, for he also took control of the Vatican States, thus depriving the Pope of his extensive holdings in Italy and leaving him with only the Vatican and the Lateran in Rome, and his villa at Castel Gondolfo, in the hills about eighteen miles south-east of the city. By the end of the century the Catholic Church had lost its political voice and its control over education in France and Germany. It was partly the Papal entrenchment that caused the old Catholic governments of Europe to react so strongly, but, within the Church itself, the decrees of Pius IX[349]

349. His decrees included the famous *Ineffabilis Deus* (1853), promulgating the doctrine of the immaculate conception of the Virgin Mary, claiming that Mary's own conception was free from the taints of original sin. It was he who summoned the First Vatican Council (1869–70), out of which came the statement of the infallibility of the Pope when speaking *ex cathedra* (from his throne) on matters of faith and morals.

established conservative attitudes that were to persist right down to the Second Vatican Council in the 1960s.

The Protestant response was no less reactionary, though inevitably much more evangelical. Many books were written in defence of the faith, most of them forgotten today. Their arguments often seemed quite hollow in contrast with the new learning. One or two more outstanding names are still remembered, such as William Law, Joseph Butler and William Paley, who argued for the reasonableness of faith in the eighteenth century, and, in a very different way, Søren Kirkegaard in the nineteenth.

In 1860 a book called *Essays and Reviews* was published in Britain, containing contributions by seven liberal scholars urging freedom of thought and enquiry in religious matters. It immediately called forth a scathing denunciation from the evangelical Bishop Samuel Wilberforce, and it was condemned by the synodical authority of the Church of England. In Scotland, in 1881, William Robertson Smith was dismissed from his post as professor of Hebrew at Aberdeen University for teaching his students the new 'German Criticism' or 'Higher Criticism' and was tried for heresy by the General Assembly of the Church of Scotland for contributing critical articles on biblical subjects to the first edition of the *Encyclopaedia Britannica*. However, none of these or other similar actions halted the movement's progress.

Much more effective were the work of the Oxford or Tractarian Movement and the Evangelical Alliance. The two approached the challenge from totally different angles. The Tractarians sought to re-establish faith in the Church, the Evangelicals faith in the Bible.

*The Oxford or Tractarian Movement*

The first name derives from the fact that the main leaders were Oxford dons: John Keble, Edward Pusey, John Henry Newman and others. Concerned about erosion of the Church of England's authority that could result from the new thinking, and also from manifest liberal tendencies in the Reform Bills of 1828-9 allowing non-Anglicans and non-Protestants (Catholics) to become members of Parliament, they sought to strengthen its voice by reviving some of its ancient authority structures, particularly the apostolic succession of bishops, the priestly office, and the sacraments. The movement traces its birth to 1833, when John Keble preached a sermon on 'National Apostasy' in St. Mary's, Oxford. That was followed over the next eight years by the publication of some ninety tracts, known as 'Tracts for the Times' (hence the name Tractarian). They were very influential in spreading the views of all three leaders, plus others who contributed to them, but equally influential, if not more so, were Keble's poems and hymns, Newman's sermons and Pusey's scholarship. Because of Pusey's prolific scholarship, the movement was also known as 'Puseyite', but is better known today under the title 'Anglo-Catholic'. Its teaching certainly had strong Catholic leanings, so much so that Newman actually went over to the Roman Church in 1845, where later he became a Cardinal.

The Movement's influence on the Church of England, and indeed on other denominations as well, has been immense. Though its early leaders showed little interest in ritual matters, within a generation it had re-introduced many of the outward trappings of Catholicism that were thrown out at the Reformation. Colour and music were restored to worship. At the beginning of the century hymn-singing was illegal in the Anglican Church and, although it slowly became acceptable after about 1820, it was given a tremendous boost by the Oxford Movement. Personal religious disciplines and the use of devotional manuals became popular, as also did frequent communions, confessions, pilgrimages, retreats and the like. The priests did much good among the working classes of the industrial cities where their ornate churches and rituals brought colour and song into many lives that otherwise knew nothing but daily routine and drabness. That, at a time when many of the churches were losing touch with the masses in the industrial cities, was particularly valuable.

*The Evangelical Movement*

There is no birth-date for this movement, which was mainly Anglican. It grew out of the eighteenth century revivals of Wesley and Whitefield, but it did not follow the teachings of either in their entirety. Nineteenth century evangelicalism was divided into three main streams. The Wesleyan or Methodist branch taught salvation available to all men and perfection or sanctification for those who would pursue it. The Calvinist followers of Whitefield and the Countess of Huntingdon taught salvation for the elect. The Anglican branch, which is the one that mainly inherited the title 'Evangelical', had an embracing view of salvation for the whole world and taught that this would become reality through the missionary work of the Church before Christ's second coming.

The Evangelical Movement produced some outstanding Christian men and women in all walks of life, people like William Wilberforce (1759-1833) whose work in Parliament led to the abolition of slavery and other social and humanitarian reforms; Sir Charles Middleton (1726-1813), who sought to rid the Admiralty of corruption and was largely responsible for the excellent condition of the fleet at the Battle of Trafalgar; Elizabeth Fry (1780-1845), who worked tirelessly for the reform of Britain's prisons; the army general, Sir Henry Havelock (1795-1857), who, as a strong, believing commander and pastor, led his troops in India with exemplary courage and righteousness; Lord Ashley, 7th Earl of Shaftesbury (1801-85), whose works as a philanthropist and social reformer are still maintained today by the society that bears his name.

In the Church's ministry there were people like John Newton (1725-1807), converted slave-trader, who is still remembered for his hymns, particularly 'Amazing Grace'; Charles Simeon (1759-1836), who made evangelicalism a dominant force in Cambridge and indirectly at other universities; Henry Martyn (1781-1812), one of the most outstanding of the early missionaries to India. And so forth—the catalogue is a long one. Their main impact in the nineteenth century was on missionary work and social reform, but also on the Church's attitudes to Scripture and personal salvation. They stood opposed to the trends of both the Oxford Movement and of Liberalism.

In 1846 the Evangelical Alliance was founded

> 'to associate and concentrate the strengths of an enlightened Protestantism against the encroachments of Popery and Puseyism, and to promote the interests of scriptural Christianity.'

The Alliance is still active and strong today, not only in England, but all round the world, now embracing evangelicals of many denominations other than Anglican.

*A Continuing Flow of Revival and Prophetic Longings*

Confrontation and debate, though they did help to preserve the faith of many, were not God's own best answer to the new challenges of the age. He has never needed to defend himself. When the academic, political, religious and social world rages against the Church, and the churches themselves are blinded by its fury, God is always working quietly in his own way, seemingly oblivious to all the debate. He never leaves himself without a witness.

Running like continuous threads alongside and through all these religious movements and rationalistic debates were the ongoing spiritual longings of the prophetically inclined. One thread is traced from the German Pietists, Spener and Zinzendorf, through the heart-moving preaching of Edwards in America and Wesley in England.

Another was found among the Quietists. Their movement started with the teaching of a Spaniard, Miguel de Molinos. In 1663 he went to Rome, where his spiritual counsel was warmly received, and in 1675 he published his *Spiritual Guide*. In it he recommended a form of contemplation that demanded total obliviousness to environment, to religious ordinances, to self, to everything except God, in pursuit of perfect, mystical union with him alone. He was arrested and imprisoned in 1685, when the nuns he directed began refusing to attend to their religious duties, and two years later his teaching was condemned by the Church.

That, however, did not eradicate his teaching, which continued to have a great deal of influence, especially among the Pietists, but on no one more than the Frenchwoman, Madame Guyon. Unhappy in her marriage to an invalid more than twenty years her senior, her beauty destroyed by smallpox, she was driven in on herself and found solace in total passivity, in which she found complete peace with God. After her husband died she began to weigh her religious experiences, encouraged by François Fénelon, Archbishop of Cambrai, and in 1685 published her *Short Method of Prayer*, a book that has been immensely influential, one that is still being reprinted and read today. Meantime she had started travelling through France spreading her mystical teachings, but was arrested and imprisoned in 1687. Thanks to the intervention of Madame de Maintenon, who was then all powerful at the court of Louis XIV, she was released and became well known in court circles. But persecution started again and Jacques Bossuet, Bishop of Maux, set himself to investigate her teaching. Fénelon rose to her defence, but to no avail. In 1695 she was sent to the Bastille where she remained imprisoned until 1702. Fénelon lost his place at court and retired to Cambrai where he spent the rest of his life faithfully caring for his diocese. Madame Guyon spent her latter years quietly at Blois, where she communicated by letter with her followers in France, Germany, England, Scotland[350] and elsewhere. She died in 1717.

---

350. Madame Guyon's writings became particularly popular among a handful of Divinity professors at King's College, Aberdeen, and with other churchmen in the North-East, particularly some of Episcopalian and Jacobite persuasion, who supported and encouraged each other in her quietist ways. (G.D. Henderson (ed.), *The Mystics of the North-East*, Third Spalding Club, Aberdeen, 1934. H.R. Sefton, 'Religious Responses to Revolution in North-East Scotland in the Seventeenth and Eighteenth Centuries,' *Aberdeen University Review*, 186, 1991, pp. 128-34.

It is often thought that Quietism teaches total inaction or complete passivity, but that is not so. What it teaches is passivity as a platform for initiating activity, that the soul must be stilled completely to its environment so that it can become perfectly attuned to the voice of God. Once that voice is heard, then action may be taken. Quietists therefore spurned all human effort, claiming that to attain perfection we must abandon ourselves wholly to God, become personally passive and quiet, so that God could have his way. Fénelon put it this way in his book, *Christian Perfection*,

> 'Let God do all that He wishes with us … To want to serve Him in one place rather than in another, in one way and not another, is to want to serve Him in our own way, and not in His … O man of little faith! What are you afraid of? Let God act.'

In France the Quietists undertook considerable acts of charity and care. Though condemned by the Catholic Church, their influence continued to spread, and some of their writings are classics, still being reissued today. They are particularly popular among Charismatics.

Not entirely unlike the Quietists, and considerably influenced by them, were the Quakers, whose roots lay in the Puritanism of the seventeenth century. The popularity of Madame Guyon's *Short Method of Prayer* and her *Autobiography* among them was one of the chief causes of their turning away from militancy to their own brand of quietism. George Fox, their founder, had been consumed by a strong spiritual hunger. Some of his preaching meetings, as we saw in an earlier chapter, were attended with spiritual visitations not unlike Wesley's in the following century, so much so that many of the Seekers joined him, believing his movement offered the fulfilment of their pentecostal quest. Its anti-church, anti-ritual, anti-establishment views went hand in hand with its focus on the inner light of the Spirit. The movement spread rapidly and widely in Britain and America, and also helped to sustain the witness of the Spirit, without compromise with the popular trends of the age.

Also outstanding in the seventeenth century was the contribution of the French scientist, Blaise Pascal, a man born again in a mystical experience of God. In 1654, while reading the seventeenth chapter of John's Gospel, he found all the emptiness of his former life being wonderfully filled with the presence of God. The experience was one of fire, and was so transforming that he wrote a 'Memorial' of it, jottings on a piece of parchment, which he carried with him ever after, sewed into the lining of his jacket. He started no movement, but when he died he left many notes on scraps of paper, which he had intended to put together in a great apologetic work. It was never written, but his notes were found to contain some remarkable thoughts and were published as his *Pensées* (*Thoughts*). These have been read by many thousands ever since and have had a great impact on their readers. His main preoccupation is with the greatness of God and the incompetence of reason to comprehend his immeasurable universe. Thus he makes statements like these:

> 'We come to know truth not only by reason, but still more so through our hearts.'
>
> 'The heart has reasons which the reason does not know.'
>
> 'The greatness of wisdom, which is nothing if not of God, is invisible to the carnal-minded and to intellectuals.'
>
> 'The saints ... have no need of carnal or intellectual greatness which has no relevance to their domain, for it neither adds to nor detracts from it. They are seen by God and the angels, not by bodies or curious minds. God suffices them.'[351]

There were plenty of others who were spiritually minded besides these. The seventeenth was a century that produced a number of well-known mystics, particularly in France, men like Francis de Sales and Brother Lawrence, who were inspired largely by the Spanish Theresa of Avila and John of the Cross from the century before.

And, of course, there were the French Prophets whom we have already studied in some detail. The theological debates of the age were not unknown to them, but as they had 'met with God' these debates seemed of little relevance. But that is how it always is with prophets and mystics. Their experience may be irrational by man's intellectual standards of assessment, but it is real, none the less, and so transcends all debate. Where man is no longer able to do it, God himself preserves the witness to his own honour. However, he does not do that by apology or debate. He simply reveals his presence, confounding all the arguments of the philosophers and rendering their proofs of his non-existence or non-involvement quite worthless.

The impact of these men and movements left a continuing ripple of longing and hunger in many hearts in the eighteenth and nineteenth centuries that has lingered on even into our own time.

---

351. For a recent edition of the *Pensées*, see J.M. Houston (ed.), *The Mind on Fire*, Hodder and Stoughton, 1991.

### *A Century of Revivals*

While Wesleyan Methodism was settling down into respectability as a denominational church and the Primitives were breaking loose into a new wave of revivalist evangelism in England in the early 1800s, over in America the Wesleyan preachers were facing new challenges that launched them into a whole century marked by waves of revival ministry. By this time the westward movement into the prairies was well under way and some concern was growing that the frontier settlers were passing out beyond the influence of the churches. The Wesleyans and Presbyterians were among the earliest to take up the challenge, sending out 'Circuit Riders', mostly uneducated lay-preachers, to visit them in their settlements. Through their labours revival enthusiasm was kept alive out on the frontiers.

That enthusiasm found its liveliest expression in 'Camp Meetings' at which thousands gathered to hear the gospel preached. These were regularly scenes of mass conversion, but also sometimes of strong emotional and physical experiences similar to those witnessed during Wesley's campaigns in England. Many told of ecstatic utterances, visionary experiences and bodily agitations, not unlike those found among the French Prophets and the Shakers, though such phenomena were generally limited to the times of the revival meetings themselves and did not form a continuing part of the converts' experience, as they did in the prophetic movements.

The campaigns brought a mighty harvest at the beginning of the century and many times of revival visitation were recorded. It all started in May, 1801, when a frontier pastor, Barton Stone, called for four days of special meetings at Cane Ridge in central Kentucky. This proved to be an occasion of great blessing, and so Stone announced a further meeting in August. To everyone's astonishment over 20,000 turned up, complete with waggons and tents, and the leaders had to call in the army to help manage the vast crowds. Where they all came from remains a mystery, for Cane Ridge was then on the American frontier where the settlers were still widely and thinly spread. In the following years, the fire that was set ablaze that autumn spread rapidly through Kentucky and the adjacent south-eastern states. Baptist membership in Kentucky trebled at that time, the Methodists quadrupled, the Presbyterians doubled and the foundations were laid for what is today known as the 'Bible Belt' in America.

The camp meetings at Cane Ridge in 1801-5 were all highly spectacular and were reported far and wide. Similar events were soon being held in many other places and the revival that ran through them radically changed the whole atmosphere in the frontier communities. The reports went even further afield, and one direct result was that the early Primitive Methodists started holding their camps in England after 1807, with a like measure of success. In America, between the camp meetings, many faithful pastors kept the revival flames burning in the towns while the circuit riders did the same among the settlers and in the more remote communities. Then later in the century, from about 1830, the revival meetings were carried into the cities by men like Charles Finney and Asa Mahan of Oberlin College, Ohio, in whose ministries the same high spiritual and emotional flavour remained.

Finney's ministry was particularly outstanding. Soon after his conversion in 1821 he experienced what he called 'a mighty baptism in the Holy Ghost'. He was a lawyer at the time, and he tells how in his office,

> 'The Holy Spirit descended on me in a manner that seemed to go through me, body and soul ... No words can express the wonderful love that was shed abroad in my heart. I wept aloud with joy and love and bellowed out the unutterable gushings of my heart.'[352]

That launched him into one of the most remarkable revival careers any man has known. To him it was a baptism of power from on high, something that every Christian needs, without which their Christianity will be totally ineffective. Though he did not encourage men to seek prophetic gifts, his teaching on the Spirit was otherwise very close to what would become common Pentecostal doctrine, even speaking of this baptism as a 'Second Blessing'. He shone as a revival preacher, not only in his pastorate at the Broadway Tabernacle in New York and during his subsequent time as Principal at Oberlin, but in all his missions both at home in the USA and overseas as well. His *Lectures on Revival* are still highly popular and widely read today. After him, in the latter part of the century and the beginning of this, R.A. Torrey, who was a friend of D.L. Moody, became the strongest advocate of his teaching, that baptism in the Spirit was to be sought as a second blessing after conversion giving power for life and ministry, though again with no special reference to the gifts.

352. From Finney's *Autobiography*, quoted here from V. Raymond Edman, *Finney Lives On*, Bethany, 1971, pp. 35f.

The great wave broke in 1858, the wave that carried a flood of revival right round the globe and rippled on down into the beginning of the twentieth century when the Pentecostal Movement was birthed. This move is sometimes known as the Second Evangelical Awakening.

It started almost simultaneously in New York and Hamilton, Ontario, in the autumn of 1857. It was then that Jeremiah Lanphier, a city missioner in New York, started a lunch-time prayer meeting for businessmen. It got off to a slow start, but by the beginning of 1858 it had outgrown its premises and soon similar prayer groups were springing up in other cities all over America. The movement spread like wildfire; prayer meetings proliferated; at them the Spirit moved in convicting power; there were no apparent leaders; thousands were born into the kingdom of God. All America was touched, in every stratum of society—the business world, the universities, the working classes, the churches. Out of a total population of under thirty million, over one million who had never known Christ were converted and the same number of lapsed Christians were revived.

The movement crossed the Atlantic to Ireland first. In Ulster a certain James McQuilkin started a prayer meeting with three others near Kells, not far from Ballymena. That was the start, but other places were soon affected. Presently the most striking revival visitations were reported in schools, market places, homes, churches, everywhere.

> 'Churches were crowded, families prayed together, all classes, all age groups sought the Lord for salvation and did not seek in vain. Prayer meetings often carried on all night.'[353]

In Wales the revival worked great transformations in the lives of hard, working men in the towns and valleys, causing a significant drop in the crime rate and adding a tenth of the population to the churches. In Scotland there was a powerful move among the lower, illiterate classes, but also in all strata of society.

The English story was somewhat different, focusing more on preaching and evangelistic meetings. That is perhaps because the movement came to England from Canada rather than America. The Canadian revival started at an evangelistic crusade led by Walter and Phoebe Palmer in 1857 in Hamilton, Ontario, where thousands attended their meetings and the whole town, from the mayor right

353. Whittaker, *Great Revivals*, p. 78.

down to the children, were affected. This visitation was headline news in the press at the time and the reports of it gave a great boost to the prayer revival in America.

The Palmers came to Newcastle, England, in the summer of 1859 and the blessing came with them. Soon large gatherings were being held in London and other major cities, but also in towns and villages around the country. Spurgeon's ministry was in its heyday at the time, but he regarded 1859 as its high point. He wrote in 1860,

> 'The times of refreshing from the presence of the Lord have at last dawned upon our land. A spirit of prayer is visiting our churches. The first breath of the rushing mighty wind is already discerned, while on rising evangelists the tongues of fire have evidently descended.'[354]

The revival had very far reaching effects. As well as sweeping millions into the kingdom on both sides of the Atlantic, it raised up some mighty men of God. In America the ministries of Finney, Mahan and the Palmers were able to ride the crest of the wave and flourish for many years afterwards. In Scotland the names of Andrew and Horatius Bonar and Brownlow North are still remembered, as is that of David Morgan in Wales. But also, out of this revival were born new significant movements both at home and overseas. William and Catherine Booth started the Salvation Army, which has done so much among the working classes in Britain; Dwight Moody was launched into his evangelistic ministry in America; Hudson Taylor founded the China Inland Mission; Dr. Barnardo began his work with orphans. Many other philanthropic and evangelistic organisations were born at this time.

It was not only Britain and America that enjoyed the fruits of this revival. The movement spread to Scandinavia, Jamaica, India, Africa and Australia. Missionary societies were re-envisioned and the gospel work took a great leap forward overseas.

It was a veritable work of God and its fruits were lasting. Over the next fifty years there were continuous waves of visitation in different parts of the world. A fountain had been released from heaven and its streams flowed on. Wales witnessed several local revivals in the latter half of the century. In Scotland the Faith Mission, founded in Edinburgh in 1886, brought revival to many rural areas of the land. Sankey and Moody, and then later Charles Alexander, kept the gospel flames burning in the towns and cities of Britain.

---

354. Whittaker, *Great Revivals*, p. 86.

Then came another mighty visitation, in 1904 in Wales and 1906 in Los Angeles, thrusting the work of God mightily forward into the twentieth century. But before we continue with that part of the story, we must return for a moment to the early nineteenth again.

*Millennialist Expectation*

If revivalism came back to Britain from America, so also did dispensationalist, millennial teaching. Before the nineteenth century the general view of the future held by Protestants, or at least by those Protestants who thought about such matters, was that Christ would return at some distant time after the world was rid of the Pope and his Catholicism, and of the Turk and his Islamic empire, and after the Jews were restored to Palestine. Hardly anyone spoke of an imminent return of Christ to establish his millennial kingdom. Most would have thought of the millennium as a period at the end of history before the return of Christ, a time when the Church would rule the earth. There cannot have been many who expected Christ to return soon.

All that changed when the horrors of the French Revolution sent its shock wave of fear rolling through Europe. As we saw when discussing the background of Irvingism, the Revolution and the Napoleonic Wars sparked off a fresh wave of interest in apocalyptic prophecy among British churchmen, who, when the wars were over and peace was restored, began considering seriously what it all signified for the greater purposes of God in history. The shock had awoken them to the possibility that these were already the last days and that the anti-Church, anti-God voices of the revolutionaries were in fact end-time evidences of the appearance of Antichrist, who, of course, was readily identified as Napoleon.

Between 1826 and 1830 a number of conferences on prophecy were held at Albury in Surrey, on the estate of Henry Drummond which was later to become the headquarters of the Catholic Apostolic Church. Their purpose was to consider the end-time prophecies of Scripture to see how they related to the events and spirit of the age.

One of the keenest supporters of these conferences was Edward Irving. In 1826-27 he published an English translation of a Spanish work entitled *The Coming of Messiah in Glory and Majesty*. It was written by an author who presented himself as a converted Jew called Ben Ezra, though he was actually a Chilean Jesuit, Manuel de Lucunza, who had died in 1801. He taught about a coming event (the 'rapture') when Christ would secretly return to gather up the faithful out of the earth to be with himself.[355] Those remaining would live through the Great Tribulation, which for some of them would act as a purifying judgment (Matt. 24:21; Rev. 7:14), and that would be followed by the establishment of the Millennium when Christ and the saints would rule on earth (Rev. 20:4-6), after which the earth's history would end in the great Last Judgment. Today this teaching is widely accepted doctrine in many evangelical and free churches. It is usually referred to as 'Premillennialism' or 'Premillennial dispensationalism'.[356]

Further conferences were held at Powerscourt in Ireland between 1831 and 1834. Though the two did overlap slightly in personnel, the Albury Conferences were interdenominational and gave birth to the Catholic Apostolic Church, whereas the Powerscourt Conferences were attended by Anglican Evangelicals mainly and gave shape to the Brethren Movement.

The Brethren are often known as the Plymouth Brethren since many of their earliest leaders, who were themselves mostly disaffected Anglican Evangelicals, came from the Plymouth area. Their chief theologian and visionary was John Nelson Darby, who was supported in the early days by Benjamin Newton, himself a fine scholar and theologian. However, Darby found his teaching about Christ's human nature was too close to Irving's for his liking and after several disagreements excommunicated him in 1845. The majority of the Brethren followed Darby, but not all. The Bethesda Meeting in Bristol, led by outstanding men like Craik and Müller, refused to denounce Newton and so they were also expelled in 1848. It was at this time that Darby and his followers formed themselves into the Exclusive Brethren. The rest became known simply as the Christian Brethren or the Open Brethren.

The details of the internal history of Brethrenism are not important here, but what is is that Darby adopted and developed the Jesuit de Lucunza's dispensational view of history.[357] Not all the Brethren agreed with him about that either. For his followers among the Exclusives it meant adopting a view of themselves as a holy people

355. 'Rapture' in this context means 'snatching up' or 'catching up', from the Latin *raptus*, meaning 'caught', the past participle of the verb used in the Vulgate (Catholic) translation of 1 Thes. 4:17, the verse on which this doctrine is based.

356. There are many Christians who find this teaching difficult to accept, partly because it is based on quite slender evidence. Some argue that Christ's return will come after the Millennium (Postmillennialism), others that there will be no sudden irruption of Christ into history before its final end and that John's portrait of the Millennialism in Rev. 20 is a visionary symbol of the kingdom of God as it will be established in historical time as we know it through the continuous process of Church growth and expansion (Amillennialism).

357. Darby himself denied that he borrowed this doctrine from him.

set apart from the rest of men and all the corruptions of their society at the end of this world's age awaiting Christ's return. The Open Brethren were much more missionary minded and through their witness Brethren assemblies have been planted all over the world.

At first Darby was unable to rouse much enthusiasm for his dispensationalist beliefs in England, but in the wake of the revival of 1858-60 the Christian world was far more ready to hear its preachers, and so when Darby went on his preaching tours in the United States between 1862 and 1877 he was heard readily and willingly. Dwight L. Moody had certainly adopted his teaching by the time of his crusades in Britain in 1872-5, and he was largely responsible for bringing the doctrine back over from the States and popularising it in this country.

Moody's missions were a great success. At their conclusion clergy of various denominations who had supported and been influenced by him met at Keswick in 1875 and pledged themselves to maintain the momentum of his work of revival in Britain. Thanks mainly to Moody's teaching their view of history was basically the same as Darby's, and so by the end of the century the millennialist theory of a Spanish Roman Catholic had become fundamental doctrine in Protestant circles that stood at the opposite end of the spectrum of churchmanship altogether. Here is one of the strange twists that history can take, but the explanation is not hard to find, for the channel through which the teaching first came was Catholic Apostolic and that circle, because it was a melting-pot for pentecostal people from all denominational backgrounds, embraced everything from Calvinistic Presbyterians to Roman Catholics.

The end result of the process, stretching over most of the century, was that there were many people on both sides of the Atlantic and elsewhere who were living with a keen expectation of Christ's imminent return, believing that these were indeed the last days. Fortunately, though Darby's dispensationalism was widely accepted, it was often adopted with modifications. Though one of his foundational tenets was that the age of miracles was long past, having ended in apostolic times, there were plenty who still longed for its restoration. And as they searched the Scriptures for hints of what would come to pass in these end times, they found there the prophecy of Joel, that in the latter days God would pour out his Spirit on all flesh. Jesus himself had said that this event, 'what the Father had promised,' would be an empowering for witness, the prelude to a new thrust of evangelism carrying the gospel message to all nations (Acts 1:8).

There were therefore many who were beginning to pray for a Pentecost, a fresh outpouring of the Spirit from heaven in these last times, to equip God's people for a world-wide evangelistic work that would herald the return of Christ and the inauguration of the millennium. That was standard teaching at Keswick at the end of the century—and in many other places around the world. The mood of expectancy was high. The Spirit would be given, the church would expand, the harvest of evangelism would be brought in, and history would move to its climax. Pentecostal expectation was in the air.

*Holiness and Baptism in the Holy Ghost*

Intermingled with all this revivalist and millennialist enthusiasm was another strain that became fundamental to the pentecostal expectation of the later nineteenth century—the doctrine of 'holiness', or 'sanctification', or 'Christian perfection'. In the century before, Wesley had encouraged his converts to seek after perfection, to pray for a closer relationship with Christ in holiness, which he saw as something additional that God willed Christians to have after conversion.

The longing for such sanctification remained among his followers, but it did not become a major point of focus until the latter half of the nineteenth century. And then it was brought to public attention mainly through the influence of the Congregationalists and Presbyterians of the Oberlin School in America, people like Finney, Mahan and the Palmers, who developed it along classical Wesleyan lines. This emphasis on the pursuit of holiness was then carried far and wide on the waves of revival that swept America and the rest of the world after 1857. Holiness Churches began to appear in many places. The best known in Britain is the Church of the Nazarene. Its parent body was the Pentecostal Church of Scotland, founded in 1908, which changed its name to Nazarene in 1915 and then united with the International Holiness Mission in 1952 and the Calvary Holiness Church in 1955.

In 1869, out of this revival and holiness background, the National Camp Meeting Association for the Promotion of Holiness was birthed in the United States. Originally founded as a non-denominational venture, it actually gave birth to a number of Holiness Churches, to which many who found themselves no longer at home in the traditional denominations gravitated. Darby's tours preceded its founding by a few years and so his millennialist teaching was still fresh and flowed into it too, in the same way as at Keswick a little later. The holiness strain came over to England with the Palmers and others in the revivals and crusades of the 1860s and '70s. Asa Mahan spoke at the meetings in Oxford and Brighton in 1874-5, out of which the Keswick Movement emerged, and Keswick became to all intents and purposes the English counterpart of the Camp Meeting Association, even named like it, 'The Keswick Conventions for the Promotion of Practical Holiness.' The American body had a stronger Wesleyan background than the English, which was more Evangelical in its conception, and so the two were never in full agreement about all aspects of their teachings. The American ministry most in harmony with Keswick was, inevitably, the Moody Bible Institute. Although the Pentecostal revival in America was birthed out of the Wesleyan Holiness background, the Camp Meeting Association was never as open to the gifts of the Spirit as Keswick.

Wesley himself had never associated Christ's work of holiness with baptism in the Holy Spirit, which he generally related to the event of conversion. But the Oberlin people did. There was some debate among Wesley's followers about how sanctification was to be attained. Some said it would be by a gradual process of growth and development in holy living, but the main teaching that emerged in the revival and holiness movements of the nineteenth century was that it would be in an event like conversion, a 'second blessing' available to Christians once their faith had increased sufficiently to embrace it, in which God would come to a man and fill him with his holiness.

In her crusades from the late 1850s onwards, Phoebe Palmer began referring to this event of sanctifying visitation as 'baptism in the Holy Ghost'. In 1870 Mahan published a book entitled *The Gift of the Holy Ghost* propounding the same view. It was an instant success, widely read and also translated into a couple of other languages. After that the phrase became common currency for describing a second visitation in the life of a believer that would sanctify him thoroughly, making him holy.

Suddenly the floodgates opened and the language of 'baptism in the Spirit' became popular in circles both inside and beyond the Camp Meetings and the Conventions. By the end of the century the word 'Pentecostal' was also very much in vogue, though the reference was still primarily to holiness, with only occasional hints of any reference to spiritual gifts.

*The Influence of Early Healing Evangelists*

Some of the gifts had been witnessed at revival and holiness camp meetings, particularly the prophetic and healing gifts, but it had not yet become part of the general expectation that these gifts would be widely restored, even though one or two individuals were known to exercise them in wonderfully powerful ways. Outstanding among these were a number of early healing evangelists.

In the mid 1860s Dr. Charles Cullis, a medical practitioner from Boston, opened a healing home for tuberculosis sufferers and others. Within a decade he was seeing many healed through prayer at his centre, where he began holding healing sessions for the public in the early 1880s, followed soon after by summer faith camps and conventions focusing on healing ministry. Notable too was the ministry of A.J. Gordon, a Baptist pastor, also from Boston, a disciple of Cullis's, who brought his theological learning to the support of the healing movement. Another who was strongly influenced by Cullis was A.B. Simpson, a Presbyterian minister from New York, and his ministry became very well known in the '80s and '90s. E.O. Allen was yet another outstanding healing evangelist of the day. He presented his hearers with a challenge that many found excessive, to choose between faith and medicine for healing.

But perhaps the most memorable of all was John Alexander Dowie, a Scotsman influenced by the Irvingites, who discovered he had a uniquely anointed healing ministry while living and working in Australia. He held a very low opinion of the medical profession of his day and through his own anointing established a strong ministry in the United States in the 1890s, first in California and then near Chicago where he built his own holy city, calling it Zion. His anti-medical teaching drew a lot of criticism, but he was strong in his views, so much so that in the end pride became his downfall. A day came when he announced to the world that he was Elijah and thereafter his support began to dwindle away. However, by the time he died, in 1907, he had influenced many of the future leaders of Pentecostalism, including Charles Parham, whose story we shall look at in the next chapter.

These healing evangelists did not themselves preach a prophetic gospel, in the sense that they expected all their followers to exercise the same spiritual giftings and anointings as they had. But the very fact of their ministry acted as a powerful encouragement to the prophetically inclined, particularly in an age when liberal scepticism and evangelical orthodoxy were increasingly dominating the Christian scene.

*The State of Pentecostal Expectation at the End of the Century*

Drawing together the various threads we have just traced, we can see that in the founding of the National Camp Meeting Association and the Keswick Convention several streams began to flow together: Millennialism, Revivalism, Holiness perfectionism, Missionary enthusiasm and Evangelical zeal. Thanks to people like Phoebe Palmer and Asa Mahan, the language of baptism in the Holy Spirit became popular and so in the last years of the century there was *a growing expectation of a pentecostal-style outpouring of the Spirit with power that would enable a world-wide mission, taking the Gospel to all men before the return of Christ.* However, despite the fact that spiritual gifts had been exercised in individual ministries in the nineteenth century, sometimes very powerfully, baptism in the Spirit was still so closely tied to Sanctification (Holiness) teaching that, when Pentecostalism broke on the world, many who were thus prepared for the new move of God failed to recognise it and accept it when it came.

The place of the Catholic Apostolics in all this is puzzling. Considering they had been teaching a pentecostal baptism in the Church for two thirds of the century, it is surprising that so little expectation of it was found on a wider front. Strangely the two streams, Irvingite and Holiness, seem to have had very little influence on each other. One suspects they could have been powerful allies, but strangely it was not to be so. God's ways and ours are not always the same.

# 28

# Pentecostalism and the Full Blessing of Pentecost

Twentieth-century Pentecostalism needs little introduction. It has become the most expansive form of Christianity in our times and the Pentecostal denominations, in all their confusing multiplicity, now rank as the 'third force' in Christendom alongside Catholicism and Protestantism.

The literature about the Pentecostals is vast and very diverse. Most of it is sympathetic, sometimes naively so. Much of it reflects the fundamentalistic attitudes of the movement at large, though some of it pretends to forms of psycho-analytical understanding that seem to leave little room for divine action. Indeed, one of the main questions that is never very far from the surface in most writings on Pentecostalism is the ancient question that confronted the Old Testament prophets and the New Testament Christians, namely how much of its so-called inspired activity is of human origin and how much divine. The presuppositions of individual writers are usually easy to discern.

Unlike the other movements we have studied, Pentecostalism takes its origin outside Europe, in the United States. Also, unlike the earlier European movements, it very rapidly became a world-wide phenomenon. What the French Prophets and the Irvingites had hoped to achieve by their missionary activities happened almost spontaneously and today Pentecostalism is found in every corner of the globe, not only throughout North America and Europe, but in South America, Africa, India, China, Russia, Indonesia and elsewhere, albeit flourishing more vigorously in some places than in others. The movement is strong in Russia, Italy and Scandinavia, but some of its most striking successes have been in parts of Africa and in Latin America.

Perhaps the time was not ripe for global expansion before the twentieth century. As we have seen, British and European prophetism had usually become sectarian and sometimes heretical before it undertook its missionary outreaches. The emphases were different in the early 1900s.

*A Fire Ready for Kindling*

Pentecostal historians like to date the birth of the movement right at the beginning of the century, at the turn of the years 1900 and 1901, but it is commonly acknowledged that the soil from which it sprang had been well prepared before that date.

Although the movement sprang up in America, its roots lay in the story we have just traced, the flow starting in Europe, among the Pietists and the Moravian Brethren of the early eighteenth century, from whom Wesley learned the assurance of salvation by faith and the reality of the Spirit's power. Both Moravian settlers and Wesleyan evangelists took this gospel across the Atlantic, generating a revivalist spirit that has been at the heart of most American Protestant churches ever since. Revival ran again in the early nineteenth century in the frontier areas in particular, and later entered the cities where it burst forth in a new flow in the latter half of the century. Then came Pentecost.

Several main ingredients went into the melting-pot in that time. One was the Wesleyan teaching that conversion should be followed by a further definable act of God's grace, commonly referred to as sanctification, in which the power of sin was fully and finally broken in the believer's life. That became an increasingly dominant theme in revival preaching, until by the end of the century the pursuit of holiness as a 'second blessing' became something of an obsession in certain circles, giving birth to a number of Holiness churches.

A similar ingredient was added by other revivalist teachers, like Finney and Torrey, who taught that after conversion believers should seek, as a second blessing, an enduement with power for witness and effective Christian living. At the end of the century both they and the Wesleyan-Holiness people were applying the phrase 'baptism in the Holy Ghost' to their different understandings of this second experience after conversion.

A third main element was the millennialist enthusiasm brought over from Britain by Darby, giving the movement a vibrant sense of urgency. A fourth was the heightened expectation of the miraculous encouraged by the healing ministries at the end of the century, teaching men to look for strong physical effects from the touch of Christ. And then there was the simple longing among many of the Lord's people for a restoration of the vital, Spirit-filled reality of primitive New Testament Christianity.

These strands woven together produced a people with eschatological, revival and holiness longings that they believed would find fulfilment in a pentecostal outpouring of the Spirit that would bestow on them new power for a fresh thrust in world-wide mission before the return of Christ. Moody popularised these views in Britain as well as in America. They found even more zealous exponents in men like Torrey, Simpson and Gordon and soon would be adopted by the Pentecostals.

All the main ingredients of Pentecostalism were already there in the late nineteenth century: revivalist enthusiasm with its emphasis on religious experience and its openness to emotional and ecstatic manifestation, lay-orientated theology with its emphasis on the inner life of holiness and moral perfection, heightened expectation of imminent end-time activity in history and, perhaps most important of all, a widely accepted theology of second blessing. All that was now needed was a light to kindle the pile.

Already throughout the century there had been instances of tongues-speaking and prophecy at revival meetings and, of course, the same gifts were still cherished to some degree among the Shakers and the Irvingites. But none of this was co-ordinated in the theological views of the Holiness people. Similarly, the language of 'baptism in the Spirit' was also in use, though again not yet in any clear co-ordination with other teachings of a prophetic sort. Men like Finney and Torrey taught that there should be some physically recognisable evidence accompanying Spirit-baptism, but they did not see tongues or prophecy as that necessary evidence. Nevertheless, by the end of the century there was a growing expectancy in certain quarters that the world was about to see a new visitation from heaven.

By then that expectation was quite commonly being encapsulated in the word 'pentecostal', while the phrase 'baptism of the Holy Ghost' was popularly used to identify the experience of sanctification. The language of Pentecost and baptism in the Spirit had become commonplace for expressing the hopes and expectations of Holiness people on both sides of the Atlantic. Sadly, however, this baptism was still so closely tied to sanctification that, when Pentecostalism broke on the world, many who were thus prepared for the new move of God failed to recognise and accept it.

*The Dawn of the Twentieth Century and the Birth of Pentecostalism*

The timing is significant. Though instances of baptism in the Spirit with speaking in tongues are recorded in revival settings towards the end of the nineteenth century, Pentecostals traditionally identify the birth of their movement with events that took place at the very beginning of the twentieth century. In the autumn of 1900 a Methodist Holiness evangelist called Charles Parham opened Bethel Bible college in Topeka, Kansas, with about forty students registered. The atmosphere was very much that of the upper room in Acts 1. The students were permitted no other book but the Bible and great emphasis was put on prayer, particularly corporate prayer. At the end of December Parham had to leave the college for three days, but he set the students the task of discovering an answer to the question, 'What is the Bible evidence of the baptism in the Holy Ghost?' Since what was under consideration was the experience of holiness or sanctification, he was much surprised on his return to learn their answer: 'speaking in tongues as the Spirit gives utterance.'

In the process of their research the students began to pray that they too might be baptised in the Spirit as at the first Christian Pentecost. Then in the evening of New Year's Day, 1901, one student, called Agnes Ozman, asked that hands be laid on her, as it was done in various places in the New Testament. She later wrote,

> 'As hands were laid upon my head the Holy Spirit fell upon me, and I began to speak in tongues, glorifying God. I talked several languages and it was clearly manifest when a new dialect was spoken. I had the added joy and glory my heart longed for and a depth of the presence of the Lord within that I had never known before. It was as if rivers of living water were proceeding from my innermost being.'[358]

Presently other students and Parham himself entered into the same experience. Unfortunately the college had to close down that summer when the owners required the building that housed it, but already the new prophets were spending their energies on spreading their charismatic gospel throughout the southern and western states of America.

The movement was slow in getting off the ground at first, but in the autumn of 1905 Parham opened another college, the first Pentecostal Bible school, in Texas and the really startling explosion began in the following year. In the spring of 1906 one of his students, William J. Seymour, a Negro, blind in one eye, came by invitation to Los Angeles to speak in a small Nazarene (Holiness) church. When he preached from Acts 2:4 and the congregation discovered he

358. Durasoff, *Bright Wind of the Spirit*, pp. 57f.

believed in baptism in the Holy Spirit with speaking in tongues, they locked him out. Undaunted, he began to hold meetings in a private house on Bonnie Brae Street and these attracted so many people that he presently rented an old building at 312 Azusa Street, once a Methodist church, but at that time no more than a derelict 'large, unplastered, barn-like room.' It was there, in those humble surroundings, that God performed his gracious work.

*The Azusa Street Revival*

There were none of the expected trappings of revivalism—no music, no choir, no collections, no advertisements, no church organisation, not even proper seats, but only planks set over nail kegs, nor any proper pulpit, just two boxes set on end. And yet the news spread far and wide.

The plank-benches were originally set out in a square so that about thirty people could sit facing each other, but the meetings grew rapidly. They were held from ten in the morning till after midnight daily, with Seymour sometimes preaching or teaching, but more often praying hidden from the congregation with his head inside his box-pulpit. Prophecy, tongues, interpretation of tongues, singing of hymns, singing in tongues, weeping, shouting, dancing, falling into trances—all such were commonly heard and observed, increasingly so as the movement developed.

As the numbers grew, the building was renovated. An upper or 'tarrying' room was set apart where those earnestly seeking salvation or baptism in the Spirit could pray quietly and wait (tarry) for the Lord to come and fill them. This upper room was a place of quiet, having a notice posted forbidding any speech louder than a whisper. It was not a place for ministry, but for drawing close to God, for seeking his face, for those earnestly hungering after the promise of the Father.

The unusual scenes at 312 Azusa Street inevitably attracted the curious, the critical and the cranks, as well as genuine seekers. The result was a fair amount of mockery and opposition and a measure of unfavourable reporting in the press, but that proved to be free advertisement for the movement and drew even larger crowds.

Perhaps the best inside account of the Azusa Street Revival is found in the diaries of Frank Bartleman.[359] He tells of people convicted by the Spirit even out in the street as they approached the building.

359. F. Bartleman, *Another Wave Rolls In*, or *What Really Happened at Azusa Street?*

He also tells us that the greatest threat to the work came from inside the fellowship itself, not from its opponents outside, from 'the religious sore-heads and crooks and cranks' that came seeking a place in the work. However, his main testimony is to a gracious movement of God among people whose hearts were set to seek his face in deep, soul-searching prayer.

Partly thanks to the adverse publicity, but more through the testimony of those who were blessed, the news spread rapidly and far. The Azusa Street revival lasted about three years and in that time people of all ethnic and social strata from all over North America, then from Europe, and indeed from all over the world, came to receive their baptism in the Holy Spirit.

Charles Parham, the man whose ministry had sparked it all off, was immensely popular at the time the revival broke in 1906 and could well have become one of its leaders, but after Alexander Dowie's death he became entangled in a struggle for the control of Zion City, out of which he emerged with a badly tarnished reputation. It is one of the sad facts of history that right down to his death twenty years later he remained outside the main flow of the Pentecostal Movement he had been largely responsible for bringing to birth.

### *The Emergence of the American Pentecostal Churches*

At first the movement was interdenominational, or rather it sat loose to denominational distinctions. Its entire concern was the inner life and the empowering of the Spirit, but gradually it became clear that those who had found this new life were no longer welcomed in their own churches. Also some of the language used by these new Pentecostals about the deadness of traditional Christianity did little to endear the movement to the churches. Local Pentecostal groups and churches therefore began to form, but without any central control or national organisation. Although the Holiness churches were the seed-bed, they were quite unable to host the movement, because most of them split over the new teaching on tongues. While some became fully Pentecostal, others rejected the work so totally that they dropped the 'Pentecostal' language they themselves had popularised over the preceding decades.

In 1914 an 'All Pentecostal Convention' was held at Hot Springs, Arkansas. Its purpose was to seek some sort of stability in the movement, especially with respect to the formulation of its basic doctrines and the co-ordination of its missionary efforts, but no proper unity resulted. The main positive fruit of this convention was the birthing of the Assemblies of God, conceived as a loose affiliation of groups and churches, though today a large and well structured denomination. Many others, however, had had enough of denominations and resisted such 'human' schemes, preferring to remain independent and 'free'. Hence neither doctrinal stability nor practical co-operation resulted, and the subsequent history of American Pentecostalism is one of the proliferation of a multiplicity of denominations and sects.

Amongst the best known of them, apart from the Assemblies of God, are the Church of God in Christ, the Church of God of Prophecy, the Church of God (Cleveland), the United Pentecostal Church, the Pentecostal Holiness Church, and the International Church of the Four-Square Gospel. A greater measure of harmony does exist today, since some of the churches now meet annually as members of the Pentecostal Fellowship of North America, an umbrella organisation that encompasses twenty-four of the main Pentecostal groupings in the United States. It was founded in 1948 to promote fellowship and demonstrate unity among Pentecostals, which it does within certain limitations. Since its members are required to subscribe to Trinitarian doctrine, no Unitarian churches, like the United Pentecostal, have joined it. Nor have any of the black Pentecostal churches, though they have been invited to join.

Most of the denominations became established after 1914, though some were earlier, and a few even before 1906. The Church of God (Cleveland) is historically the oldest. It traces its origins back to the foundation of the 'Christian Union' by R.G. Spurling, his son and seven others in Monroe County, Tennessee, in 1886. Their aim was to see primitive Christianity restored, but they made slow progress over the first ten years. A second fellowship was started in Cherokee County, North Carolina, in 1892, and it was there, in the summer of 1896, that the Spirit fell. People began to speak in tongues and many healings were reported. For the hundred and thirty or so involved, this was the restoration of baptism in the Holy Ghost that they had been waiting for, but for their neighbours in the surrounding hills such things were strange indeed. Suspicion quickly turned to opposition and then to violence. Churches were destroyed, homes burned, people flogged, shot at and persecuted bitterly over the next ten years, but the movement continued to spread in the surrounding counties. Then, in 1907, with its headquarters established in Cleveland, Tennessee, it officially adopted the name 'Church of God'. Though technically it was the first of the Pentecostal Churches, it actually made little impression outside

Tennessee and North Carolina until after 1906, when its evangelists, encouraged by news of the Azusa Street revival, began to become more aggressive in their preaching. Today it is one of the largest denominations. One of its distinguishing features is that it maintains footwashing as an ordinance to be observed at least annually.

Interesting as it would be to trace the stories of all the others, a few brief comments must suffice. The largest, most affluent and most powerful of the white churches is the Assemblies of God. It and the United Pentecostal Church maintain a congregational form of government, each church ruling its own affairs in federation with the others in the denomination. On the other hand, the Church of God in Christ (by far the largest of the black Pentecostal denominations), the Pentecostal Holiness Church and the International Church of the Four Square Gospel adhere to an episcopal form, overseen by bishops. Some of these churches have become fairly formalised in their worship and doctrine over the years, but there is a great deal of variety in the movement overall.

It is not only administrative issues that separate, but also doctrinal and social. For example, the large United Pentecostal Church is Unitarian in doctrine, baptising 'in the name of Jesus' only and denying the doctrine of the Trinity. There are also many ethnic churches, the most prominent being the Hispanic and the African ones. And at the extremes there are many smaller denominations and sects that most main-line Pentecostals refuse to recognise, such as the snake-handling churches. There are many other issues that divide, but these need not occupy us here. Indeed it would give a wrong impression to emphasise them too much, for embracing all there is actually a sense of unity and purpose found in proclaiming a four-fold gospel of Jesus as Saviour, Baptiser in the Holy Spirit, Healer and Coming King, and that by and large overrides the divisions enabling all these groups to be classed together as those giving a unified witness to the power of Pentecost.

Anyhow, the matters of doctrine that divide one Church from another are often quite small and insignificant, or at least so it seems to the outside observer. We might therefore be forgiven for drawing the conclusion that twentieth-century Pentecostalism is a living illustration of the tendency to separation and division we have observed in other movements of the Spirit, except that today, since there are so many more people involved, there are correspondingly more denominations. Perhaps that has been unavoidable, for it is of the very essence of prophetic Christianity to remain open to the Spirit's leading, and in a revivalist setting such openness inevitably entails a suspicion of institutional control, doctrinal conformity and all efforts to impose organisation. This is one of the main points at which Pentecostalism parts company with Irvingism. The Macdonald brothers would have been much more at home in some sectors of the twentieth-century American Pentecostal scene than would Cardale or Drummond.

*Pentecostalism Comes to Europe and Great Britain*

At the beginning of the century the Welsh churches, like most others in Britain, were suffering the depressing effects of liberal theology. The flame of faith, that had burned so brightly forty years before, was growing dim. Then suddenly, in 1904, God broke in on the scene with a revival that shook the whole of Wales and caught the attention of the rest of the world. In just over a year about 100,000 new converts were swept into the kingdom, and thousands of others whose faith had grown cold or weary were stirred to new life and brought back into the churches. All of society was affected. The crime rate fell, as also did alcohol consumption. Hardened men, coal miners and quarry workers, became gentle and God-fearing overnight. Prayer meetings were packed to capacity; men and women in agony cried out under conviction of their sin; then they sang the praises of God for their deliverance, sometimes for hours. And strong workers were won over for the Lord's service, some of whom were to become leaders in the Pentecostal Movement that was to start only three years later.

The Welsh revival was not itself Pentecostal, neither in its genesis, nor its ethos, but its leading evangelist, Evan Roberts, did preach a baptism in the Spirit (though without tongues or prophecy), and that in the long run helped to pave the way for subsequent events. The burden of the work burnt Roberts out emotionally, and he withdrew from ministry. He was cared for by Jessie Penn-Lewis, who had been a keen supporter of the revival, but sadly both she and Roberts opposed the Pentecostal Movement once it got started. Nevertheless, many throughout Britain, and even abroad, on hearing of the dramatic events in Wales, were encouraged to pray for their own Pentecost. When the news of the revival reached Los Angeles it greatly strengthened some of the praying people there who stood behind the Azusa Street move, as also did the news of another revival sparked off by the Welsh one, far away in Mukti in India, where many wonderful visitations were witnessed. When the reports of Azusa Street reached Britain, revival was already in the air.

In 1906, T.B. Barratt, a Norwegian Methodist pastor, a Cornishman by birth, went to America to raise funds for his City Mission in Oslo. The venture proved fruitless, but then he learned of the events at Azusa Street and instead of money brought back the Holy Spirit. His subsequent ministry took Pentecostal revival to Norway itself and also to many other parts of Europe. His meetings in Oslo received extensive publicity and many flocked to them. All of the Western and some of the Eastern European countries where Pentecostalism was established before the war broke in 1914 received the prophetic gospel from Norway, whether through preaching visits by Barratt himself or some of his followers, or through the reports of visitors to Oslo returning from Barratt's meetings to their homelands and taking the fire of the Spirit with them.

The strongest Pentecostal block was established in the Scandinavian countries, Norway, Sweden, Finland, Denmark and Iceland. The record of their subsequent missionary work around the globe is highly impressive. In the rest of Europe the story is less coherent. Strong opposition was encountered from the Roman Catholic Church in the Latin countries, so much so that Pentecostals in Italy, Spain and Portugal have had to cope with a great deal of persecution and hostility, though much of that has eased off in recent years, especially since 1964 when the Second Vatican Council issued its Decree on Ecumenism permitting more open dialogue with other churches. In Germany the antagonism came from the opposite end of the spectrum of churchmanship, from, surprisingly enough, the Pietist-Holiness branch of Evangelical Protestantism, which, in the Berlin Declaration of 1909, denounced the movement as the work of Satan. Though the German Pentecostals replied almost instantly with their Mülheim Declaration, they have had to struggle against Protestant hostility ever since, as also have their brothers in Switzerland and the Slavonic countries. One of the main hindrances to Pentecostalism in Lutheran countries has been the memory of Luther's own hostility to excessive enthusiasts (*Schwärmer*[360]), which is still strong. In many places, however, the situation has changed quite dramatically in recent years, especially since the Charismatic Movement began to make its impact on the traditional churches. And now at last the near-century old divide has been formally bridged in the Kassel Declaration, a joint statement made by the German Evangelical Alliance and the Federation of Free Church Pentecostal Assemblies, in June, 1996. In France, where the opposition

360. See above p. 234.

has been less overt, the Pentecostal is the second largest of the Protestant bodies after the Reformed Church.

In England Alexander A. Boddy, Anglican vicar of All Saints', Monkwearmouth, in Sunderland, a keen supporter of the Keswick Conventions, visited the revival centres in Wales in 1904 and there met and spoke with Evan Roberts. Then, when he heard about Barratt's ministry, he sailed to Oslo to see for himself what was happening there. On his return he wrote to the newspapers:

> 'My four days in Oslo can never be forgotten. I stood with Evan Roberts in Tonypandy, but have never witnessed such scenes as those in Norway.'

That was in March, 1907. At Keswick that summer he enthusiastically distributed thousands of copies of a tract he had written himself, called *Pentecost for England*. It was not received with corresponding enthusiasm among its readers, but, undaunted, Boddy invited Barratt to his church in Sunderland. Barratt came at the end of August and stayed till mid-October, during which time All Saints' became a kind of English Azusa Street. People seeking the experience of baptism in the Spirit flocked to it from all over the country. That first month of Pentecostal grace is commemorated by an inscription on the wall of the parish church hall:

> *September 1907. When the fire of the Lord fell it burned up the debt.*

The Spirit clearly brought more than spiritual blessings!

Barratt returned to Oslo on 18th October, but the fire continued to burn in Monkwearmouth. Only ten days later it birthed one of Pentecostalism's most outstanding luminaries, a Bradford plumber called Smith Wigglesworth, whose subsequent preaching and healing ministry has become a legend in our time. His own testimony is that

> 'At about 11 a.m., on the Tuesday at All Saint's Vicarage … the fire fell and burned in me till the Holy Spirit revealed absolute purity before God… . My body became full of light and holy presence, and in the revelation I saw an empty Cross, and at the same time the Jesus I loved and adored crowned in the Glory in a reigning position. The glorious remembrance of those moments is beyond my expression to give—when I could not find words to express, then an irresistible Power filled me and moved my being till I found to my glorious astonishment I was speaking in other tongues clearly. After this a burning love for everybody filled my soul… . Today I am actually living in the Acts of the Apostles' time … almost I am

persuaded to believe that twenty years is not too long to wait for the holy anointing of the Holy Ghost.'[361]

*The Movement Spreads in Britain*

Soon fires were being kindled in other parts of the country too. At the beginning of 1908 Boddy preached in Scotland and some who heard him took the gospel to a small independent church in Kilsyth where about thirty or forty people experienced a corporate pentecostal visitation and soon their meeting place had become another centre of revival attracting over-capacity crowds. Before long other centres had sprung up all over Scotland, and then in Ireland too.

In England the growth was more co-ordinated, under the leadership of Boddy himself and others who joined him. Fortunately the then Bishop of Durham, Dr. Handley Moule, was sympathetically disposed to revival, being himself a frequent speaker at Keswick, and so raised no objections to Boddy's meetings, which were consequently allowed to continue for some time. Also unhindered were his annual Whitsun conventions, the first of which he convened in 1908. These became a point of focus and co-ordination for the infant movement in this country but, unlike the Hot Springs Convention in America, they did not issue in the formation of any denomination, largely because of Boddy's own insistence that the Spirit-baptised remain in their own churches, as he did himself until the day of his death.

So also did Cecil Polhill, another of the movement's early leaders. Squire of Howbury Hall near Bedford, educated at Eton and Cambridge, he was Pentecostalism's heir to the mantle of Sir Richard Bulkeley and Henry Drummond. In 1885 he had gone to China as one of the famous 'Cambridge Seven', a group of university men (including C.T. Studd) who forsook all the prospects their education offered them in order to become missionaries. He received his Spirit-baptism in Los Angeles and, when the Pentecostal revival began to express itself in missionary zeal, he was the natural person to become President of the Pentecostal Missionary Union, which was formed in 1909 as a loosely organised, non-denominational venture to encourage continuing revival and to co-ordinate missionary work. He retained that position until the Union merged with the Assemblies of God in 1925. But he equally devoted his wealth and energies to the movement's work of evangelism at home by sponsoring conventions in the capital and elsewhere,

361. Donald Gee, *The Pentecostal Movement*, p. 27.

including an annual Whitsun Convention in Kingsway Hall, London, as a southern subsidiary to Boddy's convention in Sunderland.

By some of today's standards Boddy's conventions would seem very restrained. The numbers were never very large, only a few hundred at most. Admission was by ticket and the programme was carefully arranged and controlled. Strict rules governed the place of prayer and singing, which was ordered by the leader of the meeting. Everything was done in a very orderly way, as indeed Paul required it should be (1 Cor. 14:40). None the less, the atmosphere was wonderfully heavenly and the sense of God's presence at times quite overwhelming.

Most of those who attended these early conventions were fairly mature Christians, many of them missionaries or church workers, some with previous experience of the Spirit's workings in revival or holiness settings. But their Spirit-baptisms did not come easily. Many had quite prolonged times of deep soul-searching and waiting on God before they knew he had filled them. They were pioneers, but their spirit was strong and they produced many effective leaders and workers in the kingdom for the establishment of Pentecostalism both at home and overseas.

In this vein the work continued up to the outbreak of war in 1914, with Boddy and Polhill as its leading personalities. But despite the success of the conventions, and also of a magazine called Confidence that Boddy edited, Pentecostal growth in Britain was much more restrained than in America and Scandinavia. Perhaps its leaders' vision of a movement within the Churches somehow dampened freedom-consciousness (or freedom of the Spirit), which is, as we have repeatedly seen, an essential ingredient of prophetic enthusiasm, and thus hindered the possibility of the kind of co-ordinated evangelistic drive that emerged in the United States at an early stage. Be that as it may, others felt a need to separate and organise. After the war new names began appearing in the headlines, like George and Stephen Jeffreys, Smith Wigglesworth and Stanley Frodsham, and alongside them the names of several new organisations and churches.

### *The Founding of the British Pentecostal Churches*

One of the earliest churches to form itself was the Apostolic Church. It came to birth in 1916 at Penygroes in Wales, out of a congregation of Pentecostals who were members of an earlier group known as the Apostolic Faith Church that was founded in Bournemouth in 1908.

Believing that prophecy was not simply for exhortation, edification and comfort, but for the guidance and leading of the Church itself, they established themselves under the authority of two brothers, both converts of the Welsh revival, Daniel P. and William J. Williams, whom they styled Apostle and Prophet respectively. Then, something after the manner of the Irvingites, they created a series of offices (Shepherd, Teacher, Evangelist, Elder, Deacon, Deaconess) to which members were appointed by prophetic designation. At the head of the Church today is a College of Apostles. They are probably the most centrally organised and hierarchical of the Pentecostal denominations in this country, but they are also among the smallest, except in Scotland where they are the most numerous. Their early successes are usually attributed to the fact that they alone were offering a constructive vision of Church government at a time when many were feeling a need for some form of coherent structure. While this Church has spread mainly in Wales and Scotland, it also has branches abroad, in Europe, Australia, and especially Nigeria, where it is the largest of the Protestant churches.

Much larger in size are the Elim Pentecostal Churches. Their origins lie in the 'Elim Evangelistic Band', an organisation created in 1915 by the highly successful Welsh evangelist, George Jeffreys, to further his campaigns in Ireland. As his work expanded, the organisation established itself in several centres, and in 1918 its name was changed to 'Elim Pentecostal Alliance'. In 1919 it began issuing its own magazine, the *Elim Evangel*. Thanks to the continuing, powerfully charismatic ministry of George Jeffreys and his brother, Stephen, both children of the Welsh revival, Elim spilled over into England in the 1920s and soon came to be recognised as one of the major Pentecostal denominations, though it is only in recent times that the name was changed from 'Alliance' to 'Churches'. Again it has a fairly centralised and bureaucratised structure, the tendency to which eventually caused a rift between Stephen Jeffreys and the Alliance he had helped to create.

The Assemblies of God were the next to organise. While the Apostolic Church and the Elim Alliance were developing their distinctive forms, most other Pentecostal groups and congregations found their focus in Polhill's Kingsway Conventions and in his Pentecostal Missionary Union. Although they were often unwilling to accept any overarching structure, they did eventually agree to the formation of a federal organisation that respected their congregational autonomy. In 1925 the Pentecostal Missionary Union was dissolved and absorbed into the Assemblies of God. The years that followed were ones of intensified evangelisation and growth, particularly thanks to the amazingly charismatic ministries of men like Stephen Jeffreys (who joined the Assemblies in 1926), Smith Wigglesworth and John Carter. Though the paths of George and Stephen Jeffreys separated when Stephen left Elim they both continued to blaze the evangelistic trail with ever increasing glory, founding new churches and assemblies in many places. Everywhere they went there were huge crowds running into thousands, outstanding healings and miracles, and hundreds of converts. People often had to queue many hours for a seat at their meetings. Many have considered them England's greatest evangelists since Wesley and Whitefield. Stephen Jeffreys' work dramatically increased the growth rate of the Assemblies of God and changed its character significantly.

1925 marks a significant turning-point in our story. From that date those who refused to leave the traditional churches, like Boddy and Polhill, could no longer find any place in the work of Pentecostalism in this country. What started as a work of revival in the churches had in less than twenty years travelled the same road as most of the other prophetic movements we have studied in this book, into separation and independence. However, Pentecostalism in Britain was not entirely a break-away movement, but rather a revival movement that developed alongside and partly outside the churches, mainly among the working classes, among whom there grew assemblies and meetings of converts who had never had any church affiliations. 1925 therefore represents more a recognition of a status quo than a separation from existing structures, and so, strange as it seems, since they were unable to enter into the fullness of it when it came to pass, that was actually in keeping with the vision of Boddy and Polhill, who never intended that there should be any break-away, but only a revival of faith.

To sum up, the story of Pentecostalism in Britain divides into a number of fairly-well-demarcated phases. From 1907 to the outbreak of war in 1914 was its time of discovery, revival and first enthusiasm. Then the denominations began to form and 1925 marks the end of the revival work of those who were unable to leave their churches to join the new ones. The rest of the 1920s and '30s were times of steady growth, dominated by the ministries of outstanding evangelists like the Jeffreys brothers and Smith Wigglesworth. After the Second World War the fire subsided for a while and the denominations settled into their traditions and doctrines. Then most recently, since the Charismatic Movement got under way in the

1960s, many Pentecostal congregations have been reawakening to the power of the Spirit that is theirs in Christ and a number of them are again leading the way in revival witness in the nation.

*World-Wide Expansion*

Today it is no longer enough to think simply of national churches. Pentecostals have always made powerful missionaries and so it continues to be. In Britain today there are Pentecostal churches that have been planted by missionaries from other parts of the world, some by Americans, some by immigrants, most of them ethnic, Caribbean, African and the like. Equally the British have planted Pentecostal works in other lands, as have European, North American, South American, Asian and other missionaries. It is as if the globe has been criss-crossed from nation to nation by Pentecostal evangelists establishing churches wherever they have been able to do so. Pentecostals have proved brilliant at producing forceful preachers and church-planters.

The result is that Pentecostal churches are now found in most countries around the world. Some are still quite small, some are large and powerful, but world-wide statistics record either steady or phenomenal growth. In South America, particularly in Brazil, Chile and Argentina, but also elsewhere, evangelicals were numbered in hundreds and thousands in the earlier years of the twentieth century, but today in millions and tens of millions, most of them Pentecostal, while the membership of individual churches is now numbered in thousands and tens or hundreds of thousands.

Though the numbers are not as spectacular, the percentage rate of growth in Western and Eastern Europe, Australia and New Zealand, certainly is. In many parts of Africa the story is as phenomenal as in South and Central America. There the foundations laid by the Pentecostal missionaries have been built on by Africans themselves, who have started a plethora of indigenous churches, most of them majoring on prophecy and healing, though not always on tongues, but still thoroughly Pentecostal in ethos.

Similar growth is reported in South East Asia, in the South Sea Islands of the Pacific, in Indonesia, in China, in parts of India, in Nepal. And so the story goes on from nation to nation. Until the 1950s the movement world-wide made its main impact on the lower social classes, but since the advent of Charismatic renewal in the established churches much has changed. Today there are Pentecostal universities, Pentecostals in government, in social work, and in positions of national leadership and authority in many places. The growth is thus not just in numbers, but in maturity and in social and political influence as well.

Some of the stories of the earliest missionaries make heroic reading. Some were simple converts who caught a vision and went out trusting the Lord without any supporting organisation. Their motives were good, but in the early days their wisdom was not yet highly developed and many of these early evangelists suffered terribly or died for lack of financial support. More effective were those who had already been missionaries and got baptised in the Holy Spirit. But in around 1910 missionary societies started to form and the positive thrust of evangelism could then be sustained more effectively. However, it was not their organisational capabilities that converted so many, but rather the power of God at work in them performing signs and wonders and the Spirit of love sustaining them in their search for the lost. The record of the Pentecostal Churches in mission compares well with that of the early Church in the Roman Empire and the European monks in the Middle Ages.

With all this expansion and growth, considerable differences of opinion and practice have entered the movement around the world, so that today Pentecostalism has many different faces, though still unified in purpose.

The old two-blessing or three-blessing debate is not so much a living issue as it once was. The majority of Pentecostals world-wide adhere to a two-stage doctrine, though some, such as the Church of God and the Pentecostal Holiness Church, still preach three.

The 'Jesus Only' or 'Oneness' debate, on the other hand, is still quite heated, particularly in the third-world mission-field. Almost the entire Indonesian Pentecostal Movement is unitarian and the subject stirs much animosity in parts of Africa. By contrast, few in Europe have ever heard about it at all. It is based on the observation that in the Acts of the Apostles baptism was always conducted 'in the name of Jesus' (2:38; 8:16; 19:5), from which it was concluded that, since that was how the apostles interpreted the Lord's command to baptise in Matt. 28, it must be the correct way. The doctrine first emerged in the American Assemblies of God movement, being taught from about 1913 and then properly formulated along with its other unitarian corollaries in 1915. It was rejected by the Assemblies the following year, with the result that 156 ministers, about a fifth of their total number at the time, left and began establishing the Oneness churches. The largest of these in the United States is the United Pentecostal Church, but there are plenty of others with similar doctrines in many parts of the world.

The African scene is very confusing. Pentecostalism has taught Africans to evangelise effectively, to plant and run their own indigenous churches, to operate in prophecy, healing and miracles, but also to dispute and divide. Today there are thousands of independent African denominations of this sort, some thoroughly Pentecostal, others partly or questionably so, some so indigenous that they are overlaid with animistic practice and idolatrous superstition, others also totally indigenous but rigorously biblicist. Some African churches are large and powerful, others are small and local, some have a strong political voice, others stand aloof from social involvement. But all in all the gospel is spreading in Africa with amazing power.

Most Pentecostal churches still cherish congregational freedom and lay participation in ministry, adhering to a doctrine of the priesthood of all believers, and affirming that anointing and gifting are more important than status and position. Some, however, do have more structured systems, overseen by bishops, apostles or other officials. Once more in these matters Africa is perhaps the place with the most confusing mixture of customs, though considerable diversity is also found in Britain, America and elsewhere.

*Pentecostalism as a Prophetic Movement—Spirit-baptism and Tongues*

It seems almost unnecessary to list the prophetic characteristics of Pentecostalism, since they are so obvious. Signs and wonders are of the very essence of the movement, as are prophetic and preaching gifts. What is almost unique, however, is the movement's emphasis on speaking in tongues. At no other time in history before 1900 has this gift loomed as large as it does in twentieth century Pentecostalism. It created a considerable stir in Edward Irving's church and he even regarded it as the 'standing sign' of Spirit-baptism, but in a very short time it faded into the background in the Catholic Apostolic tradition. By contrast, though with a variety of shades of emphasis, tongues has remained the 'scriptural evidence' of baptism in the Spirit for the majority of Pentecostal people. There has, however, been a shift in their understanding of the phenomenon.

Early records of the Azusa Street and Sunderland period cite many instances of xenolalia (tongues as a language that is understood by foreign hearers), so much so that some of the earliest Pentecostals believed they had been given the linguistic capability to evangelise heathen peoples abroad. There are several stories about such persons returning from missionary ventures thoroughly disillusioned after failure to find any tribe or nation able to understand their speech. Though Pentecostals still testify that xenolalia is occasionally instanced, the gift today is most commonly defined as glossolalia (an unintelligible form of speech). In their teaching and experience it subdivides into three functional categories: tongues as the initial evidence of Spirit-baptism (Acts 2:4; 10:46; 19:6), as a continuing gift for purposes of private praise or intercession (1 Cor. 14:2,4), and as a form of public utterance to be interpreted by those who have the gift to do so (1 Cor. 14:13,27f).

The doctrine of baptism in the Holy Spirit has also changed somewhat over the years. Many movements, sects and heresies through the ages have used the language of Spirit-baptism without showing any interest in prophetic or charismatic phenomena. As we have seen, nineteenth-century revivalist preachers tended to use it in connection with either sanctification or power for ministry. The problem of definition became particularly acute at the beginning of the twentieth century. In Britain the Pentecostal revival found some of its earliest criticism on the pages of a magazine called *Tongues of Fire* published by an organisation known as 'The Pentecostal Mission'! Within the Pentecostal Movement itself, particularly in America where the Holiness movement was strongest, there was much dispute whether baptism in the Holy Spirit was a third blessing after conversion and sanctification, or a second blessing after conversion, with sanctification regarded as an on-going process. Third blessing was what was preached at Azusa Street, but the second-blessing doctrine, first widely propounded by W.H. Durham in Los Angeles and Chicago in 1908, won the day and is now the accepted doctrine of most Pentecostals.

In support of their doctrine of baptism in the Spirit as second blessing and with speaking in tongues as its evidence, Pentecostals rely heavily on a handful of passages in Acts (2:1-12; 8:14-19; 10:44-48; 11:15; 19:1-7) and on the teaching of John the Baptist in the Gospels, which seems to contrast baptism in water with baptism in the Holy Spirit. But it must be remembered that theirs is more than just a doctrine. It is also an experience, and it becomes doctrine only because they find their experience corresponds so well with these sections of the biblical narrative.

And, as we have already seen, the New Testament identifies Pentecost, baptism in the Holy Spirit and speaking in tongues with the latter day prophecy foretold by Joel and others, as the fundamental marks of a biblically based prophetic movement.

Having discovered the Bible trustworthy in this respect, Pentecostals tend to be unwilling to question its teaching on other matters, and so their churches are, to a greater degree than most, thoroughly fundamentalist in their attitude to the Scriptures.

Fundamentalism began as a protest against evolutionary theories and biblical criticism among conservative Protestants at the end of the nineteenth century. It started to crystallise as a movement at the beginning of the twentieth century with the publication of *The Fundamentals* between 1909 and 1915, a series of twelve tracts (from which Fundamentalism got its name) propounding the five points of the movement: the verbal inerrancy of Scripture, the divinity of Jesus Christ, the Virgin Birth, a substitutionary view of the Atonement, and the physical resurrection and bodily return of Christ. Then in 1919 'The World's Christian Fundamentals Association' was founded.

Although Pentecostals hold a generally conservative view of Scripture, there is one major point at which they and the fundamentalists disagree, namely in their attitude to miracles and spiritual gifts. Fundamentalists say these belong to a former dispensation in the history of the Church and have no part to play in modern times; Pentecostals, of course, maintain that they belong to every age. While many Pentecostals might therefore maintain that they are 'fundamentalist with a difference,' fundamentalists themselves refuse to have anything to do with them. In a resolution of their Association passed in 1928 they declared themselves 'unreservedly opposed to Modern Pentecostalism.'

*Pentecostalism as the Prophetic End-time Church of the Spirit*

The strong biblicist attitude of most Pentecostals has a number of corollaries. It encourages them to take more seriously than most other Christians the end-time passages in the Bible. That, of course, is also part of their heritage from nineteenth-century apocalypticism, and is a natural ingredient in prophetic thought in any age, but their fundamentalistic views have led some of them to concentrate so much on the minutiae of eschatological teaching that churches have split from each other over differences in opinion about what the future may or may not hold, differences that many would consider trivial and abstruse.

On one point of eschatology, however, most of them agree, namely that the present age of history is the last before the return of Christ. The contemporary outpouring of the Spirit is interpreted in the context of Joel's prophecy, as that which is to come to pass 'in the last days' (Joel 2:28; Acts 2:17) before the final irruption of God. This urgent sense of an imminent end, together with the enthusiasm resulting from charismatic experience, goes a long way to explaining the Pentecostalist zeal for mission and evangelism that has been one of the striking characteristics of the movement from its earliest days. The echoes of New Testament prophetic fervour are quite unmistakable.

Their biblical literalism and heightened spiritual awareness has also encouraged them to adhere to a world-view that regards many forms of suffering and strife as the evidences of spiritual warfare, in the New Testament rather than the Old Testament sense of conflict with Satan and his minions. The healing ministry, which is always much in evidence in prophetic circles, is therefore not only a ministry of faith and miracle, but also regularly one of 'confronting the enemy' in exorcism and deliverance, very much like Jesus' ministry in the Gospels.

The sense of superiority, as the rest of the world sees it, that has characterised other movements that regarded themselves as the elect Church of the Spirit, is also not far from the surface. It shows itself most obviously in a critical attitude to the traditional churches, which are sometimes even viewed as the instruments of Antichrist or Satan. Pentecostals have therefore always been perfectly happy to proselytise among the churches and have for the most part stood aloof from the humanly manufactured (as they see it) Ecumenical Movement.

The veneer of superiority is also evidenced in their higher ethical standards. Like the Montanists, most Pentecostals have maintained a fairly rigid ethical discipline, much of it negative and sabbatarian, but most of it arising from a sense of the awareness of God's awesome reality resulting from their experience of baptism in the Holy Spirit, and perhaps also from their urgent eschatological apprehensions, rather than from any imposed legalistic principle.

Finally, mention must be made of the lay-orientation of most Pentecostal Churches, which is more akin to the ethos of the Zwickau Prophets or the French Prophets than that of the Catholic Apostolic Church, though sometimes their churches are very structured affairs and do have strong hierarchical systems, which is particularly true in parts of Africa. But whatever the outward structures, Pentecostal worship tends to be freely participative, and hence loosely structured, sometimes boisterous, and to the uninitiated observer even at times chaotic. Over the years the charismatic spontaneity has given place in some churches to the acceptance of stereotyped forms, recognisable in frequent interjections of 'Hallelujah,' 'Amen,' 'Praise the Lord,' or the like, that punctuate many services. Even so, the charismatic element has certainly not died. Perhaps it is still kept alive mainly because of continuing insistence on the necessity of the basic Pentecostal prophetic experience of baptism in the Spirit and speaking in tongues as its evidence.

Some present-day Pentecostals lament the passage of their age of miracles, the toning down of eschatological expectation, the relaxation of morals, and so forth, but others affirm that the charismatic Spirit is still as much alive as ever. The fact of the matter is that after the Second World War the Pentecostal revival seemed to have run its course in the Western world and many churches were settling down into styles and patterns that had become stereotyped and traditional. There were few who would have denied that the Pentecostal churches themselves were in need of a revitalising breath of the Spirit once more. Many of them had drawn dangerously close to becoming the very kind of institutional, doctrinal organisations that they themselves once broke with and have continued to criticise. The pattern is a familiar one. Other movements of the Spirit have died as they have travelled this road. But then, because of its sheer size, Pentecostalism is virtually unique in this history and can only profitably be compared with the New Testament Church. However, even there the process was the same.

The Scripture tells us that if we return to the Lord and seek him again then 'times of refreshing' will come from his presence (Acts 3:19). And so it has been in more recent times. There is a new surge of Pentecostal fire running all over the world and many of the traditional Pentecostal churches are being swept into it, coming back to fullness of life. Pentecostalism is still the fastest growing part of the body of Christ world-wide, a wonderful testimony to the power of prophetic Christianity.

# 29
# Charismatic Renewal

This chapter must differ from all the others in this book, for they recount the history and teachings of clearly definable movements, some forgotten today, others still in existence, some of them obscure and off-centre, others flourishing and widely supported, but all of them living in some measure of separation from the rest of the body of Christ. In contrast, the Charismatic Movement is well-known in almost every branch of the modern Church, whether welcomed, rejected or just politely acknowledged. In some parts of the world its story is already a fact of the past, in others its impact is more recent; in some places it is still struggling in infancy, in yet others it has grown and is now seeking a full, mature identity. Our examination of this movement must therefore mix historical analysis with contemporary assessment and, because of the nature of this book, we shall sometimes do that by comparison with the earlier movements of the Spirit that we have studied.

The Charismatic Movement, perhaps more so than any other movement in Christian history, has generated a vast amount of literature on various aspects of its own teaching and experience, much of it popular and inspirational, but also much that is pastoral and theological, most of it readily available in libraries and religious bookshops. The revival spirit was markedly present in the early days of this movement and that is vividly reflected in some its earliest literature.[362] In some places it is still very much alive, in others it has subsided, in still others it has adopted new forms. The story differs from nation to nation, from church to church, from person to person.

---

362. One of the best and most comprehensive outlines of its history is in the article on the 'Charismatic Movement' by Peter Hocken in the *Dictionary of Pentecostal and Charismatic Movements*, pp. 130-160, but to capture the spirit of the movement in its various stages it is advisable to look at some of the original literature. The sense of dawn-time excitement is still best caught in Dennis Bennett's *Nine O'Clock in the Morning*, the freshness of early Catholic Charismatic discovery in Kevin and Dorothy Ranaghan's *Catholic Pentecostals*, the flavour of the early years in England in Michael Harper's *As at the Beginning*, the attitude of the Anglican Church in the General Synod's report, *The Charismatic Movement in the Church of England*, the portrait of a church in renewal in Colin Urquhart's *When the Spirit Comes*, or Graham Pulkingham's *Gathered for Power*, and so forth.

This is a movement of great diversity, but also of considerable unity. It has been truly a move of God.

*Background and Early History*

The way was prepared by two other major movements that started earlier in the century and are still continuing in our time. The first of these, of course, is Pentecostalism. Indeed the links are so close that it seems almost unreasonable to divide the Charismatic Movement from its Pentecostal forerunner by putting them in separate chapters. The two are virtually continuous one upon the other. So much of their experience, aims and theology is the same. The Charismatic's emphasis on tongue-speaking, his adoption of second-blessing theology (especially in certain Protestant circles), his eschatological views, his tendency to fundamentalism, his support for healing and deliverance ministries, and so forth, clearly present him as the direct heir of Pentecostalism. None the less, the Charismatic Movement is a separately definable entity, for its impact has been largely outside the established Pentecostal denominations, more in the traditional Protestant and Catholic Churches.

Even before the Charismatic Movement came to birth in the 1960s there were already people in the traditional churches who knew what it was to be baptised in the Holy Spirit. Some had found the Spirit in the crusades and meetings of the outstanding independent healing evangelists of the '40s and '50s, men like William Branham, Oral Roberts and T.L. Osborn. Others came into blessing through the witness of the Full Gospel Business Men's Fellowship International (FGBMFI), founded by Demos Shakarian in 1953 to promote the work of the Holy Spirit among laymen and businessmen without proselytising for any Pentecostal denomination. Through these and other such channels and ministries there was always a steady trickle of people being baptised in the Holy Spirit in the traditional churches, but none of it was organised, and few ever heard anything about it until 1960.

The second major movement that helped prepare the way is one that few Pentecostals like to acknowledge, and that many Charismatics also spurn, claiming that it is man-made and not of the Spirit, namely the Ecumenical Movement. Its historical origins date back to the end of the nineteenth century and the early years of this, in a search for unity among the Western churches working on the mission field. A Missionary Conference held in Edinburgh in 1910 established the International Missionary Council. That was followed by another Conference on Life and Work in Stockholm in

1925 and then by a third on Faith and Order at Lausanne in 1927. At a second meeting of these two conferences, held in Edinburgh and Oxford in 1937, it was decided they should be fused into a World Council of Churches (WCC). Its constitution was drafted at Utrecht the following year and it was officially inaugurated in 1948. The International Missionary Council merged with it at its third assembly in 1961.

Though a small number of Pentecostal denominations have joined the WCC over the years, most fundamentalist churches have stood aloof from it, including most of the Pentecostal ones, mainly through fear of compromise. However, David du Plessis, General Secretary of the World Conference of Pentecostal Churches from 1949 to 1958 and Donald Gee, Vice-Chairman and then Chairman of the Assemblies of God of Britain from 1934 to 1948, both sought to encourage their Pentecostal brothers to take an interest in the WCC in the 1950s and '60s. The result was that the WCC itself began to show an interest in the Pentecostals, even though most Pentecostals still refused to enter into dialogue with it. The openness that resulted was to be of great help to the Charismatic Movement once it got under way.

Du Plessis and Gee attended the 1961 assembly of the WCC in New Delhi as invited observers, but that meeting got more publicity in the world presses because of the presence of other first-time observers, this time from the Vatican in Rome. A new mood was beginning to sweep through the Roman Catholic Church at the time. Pope John XXIII was in the process of summoning the Second Vatican Council which met over the years 1962 to 1965. Its decisions were totally transforming for Catholics who now found themselves worshipping in their own languages instead of in Latin, encouraged to read their Bibles and to be open to dialogue with other churches, discovering a new openness to the Jews, and praying for 'a new Pentecost' in the Church. In 1964 the Council issued a Decree on Ecumenism and in 1965 Pope Paul VI and Patriarch Athenagoras nullified the ancient anathemas that had kept Catholicism and Orthodoxy at enmity with each other since 1054. The effects of this new openness were to prove very far reaching for the process of Charismatic renewal in the churches.

*The First Protestant Charismatics*

The Charismatic Movement is not the result of conscious promotion in infancy by any particular person or ministry. When recounting the history of earlier prophetic movements we have had to tell about the call and early ministry of one person or a group of people. It is much more difficult to do the same in this chapter, for so many people were involved. Perhaps the best parallel to draw is with the prayer revival that started in America in 1858 and spread almost spontaneously around the globe. The story is, of course, about people, some of them outstanding instruments in the hand of God for the birthing and furthering of the work, but it is difficult to point to any of these as self-conscious founders of the work.

Charismatics generally date the birth of the movement in 1960, when it was reported in the American national press, in *Newsweek* and *Time,* that Dennis Bennett, the rector of St. Mark's Episcopal Church in Van Nuys, a respectable suburb of Los Angeles, California, and some members of his congregation had spoken in tongues. The storm that erupted drove Bennett from his church[363], but it also brought into the open this movement that already had been growing unnoticed in the United States throughout the late fifties. Bennett was offered another appointment in St. Luke's, Seattle, a church the bishop was then thinking about closing, but within a year its congregation had risen from seventy-five to three hundred and it became one of the leading Charismatic churches in the States. Bennett soon found himself being invited to speak in other places and, thanks to his continuing ministry and to the work of others who, like him, were being caught up in this new wave of prophetic revival, the Charismatic gospel spread rapidly through the other Protestant churches in the United States and Canada. From about 1962 it spilled over into Britain and has since then continued to spread in Protestant churches all round the world.

By the early 1960s there were people in virtually every major Protestant denomination who had been baptised in the Holy Spirit. Right from the start, of course, the movement ran into opposition in the churches, but it also won over a number of clergy and other church leaders, some of them theologically articulate and well able to defend the work of the Spirit in language appropriate to the traditions of their own churches. And so the work continued to grow within the denominations.

The movement's growth was greatly helped by some of the books that were written in these early days. Bennett's own account of what happened was only published in 1970 and that gave a fresh boost to the work when it came, but there were other very influential books available long before that, particularly David du Plessis's

363. The story is told in his book, *Nine O'Clock in the Morning*.

account of his call to witness about Pentecost to the traditional churches, *The Spirit Bade Me Go* (1961), David Wilkerson's description of the impact of the Holy Spirit on teenage drug addicts in New York, *The Cross and the Switchblade* (1963), and John Sherrill's record of his findings as a journalist investigating tongue-speaking, *They Speak in Other Tongues* (1964). The effect these and other such books had on their readers was considerable. Unlike early Pentecostalism, which spread mainly among the working classes, Charismatics have by and large been drawn from the more literate, book-reading, church-going middle classes, with the result that books and other literature have done much more to help promote this movement.

In Europe the story differs from place to place. There were already ministries and communities influenced by Pentecost in the Protestant sector in the 1950s, such as the Mary Sisters in Darmstadt, but as in America open consciousness of Charismatic revival only came in the 1960s, after the news of Van Nuys was brought to the world by the press. There is not the space here to tell the story of renewal in each part of the globe. Suffice it to say that progress continued steadily throughout the sixties and into the seventies, though with some marked regional variations. For example, in Germany the emphasis was strongly theological from the start; in Eastern Europe and the communist nations growth was inevitably uncoordinated and attended by mixed degrees of harassment and persecution; in the Scandinavian lands the movement started later, more in the '70s than the '60s, and was influenced by Pentecostalism more so than in most other places.

Beyond North America and Europe, lively stories came from Australia and New Zealand, Singapore and South Africa, indeed from many parts of the world. In South America it has not always been easy to distinguish the impact of the movement from that of the continent's vigorous Pentecostalism. But it would be true to say that by the mid '70s most Protestant denominations around the world had either been influenced by the movement or had at least heard of it.

In Britain co-ordinating leadership and encouragement was given by Michael Harper, an Anglican priest, who established the Fountain Trust in 1964. It undertook the work of organising conferences that fulfilled something of the function of Boddy's and Polhill's conferences at the beginning of the century and they, coupled with the Trust's bimonthly magazine, Renewal, provided a forum for public discussion which helped stimulate further growth. The Fountain Trust's ministry reached its peak between 1971 and 1975 with its major, national conferences at Guildford, Nottingham and Westminster. By then the work was spreading out beyond small prayer groups into whole churches, such as St. Michael-le-Belfrey in York, St. Andrew's in Chorleywood, St. Hugh's in Luton, and a number of others that were experiencing corporate renewal.

In the 1990s it was estimated that some thirty million Protestants have been baptised in the Holy Spirit and about eight million of these are active in their witness to his transforming work in their lives. That statistic can give us little more than a general sense of the movement's size. A more helpful impression of its world-wide impact may perhaps be gleaned from a report such as that of the WCC in 1981, *The Church is Charismatic*, even from the fact that the WCC saw the need to produce it at all. This has indeed proved one of the most dynamic movements to touch the traditional churches in our time.

*Roman Catholics Receive the Holy Spirit*

Perhaps the biggest boost the Charismatic Movement got after 1960 came in 1967 when Pentecost broke in the Catholic Church. The way had been well prepared by Vatican II, which had only recently ended. Its recommendations, that Catholics adopt a positive attitude both to ecumenical relations with other churches and also to the importance of charismatic gifts, opened wide the door for the Holy Spirit to be released in the Catholic Church. The whole face of renewal changed as churchmen and theologians now had to grapple with this new phenomenon that took many of them totally by surprise.

Pentecostals at the time were finding it difficult enough to accept David du Plessis's openness towards the Protestant Churches. Many of them condemned him for it, believing that the Spirit could only be received in the right context which, of course, was their own. Most Pentecostals in the 1950s had little problem with regarding the traditional churches as fields for evangelism, and certainly they viewed the Catholic Church in that way. To most of them the Pope was Antichrist and his church was of the devil. Many of them therefore found it very hard to come to terms with the events of 1967 and after, which Catholics themselves viewed as God's answer to Pope John's prayer for a new Pentecost for their Church.

In complete contrast with almost any earlier prophetic movement, apart from the Amalrician in the thirteenth century, this one started in a university setting among young theologians, priests and other intellectuals. It began when two lay teachers in the theology department at Duquesne University in Pittsburg, a Catholic institution, after reading Wilkerson's and Sherrill's books, sought baptism in the Holy Spirit in a Protestant prayer group. That started a movement that spread rapidly in Duquesne itself, but also out into other universities, and in particular to Notre Dame in South Bend, Indiana, and the University of Michigan in Ann Arbor. All that happened in the spring of 1967 and it established these two campuses as the main centres of renewal for Catholics in the States, and of encouragement for Catholic renewal in many other parts of the world. Growth has been exceedingly rapid in every country, much more so than in the Protestant churches. Thirty years later it was estimated that there may be more than sixty million Catholics who have been baptised in the Spirit, with probably about ten or eleven million of these active in their witness, many of them meeting regularly in prayer groups. The comparable figures for Protestants noted above are considerably smaller.

*The Evidence of Baptism in the Spirit*

While the global and interdenominational aspects of the movement have ensured that its ethos and theology are by no means exact replicas of the Pentecostal, at the heart of its proclamation lies the same, familiar doctrine and experience of baptism in the Spirit that was the focus of the Pentecostal revival. At first, in the 1960s, this experience was described in traditional Pentecostal modes as a second blessing after conversion (among evangelicals), or after water-baptism (among sacramentalists), with tongues as its physical and commonest evidence.

Emotional responses of praise, exuberant joy or even bodily motions were, of course, acknowledged as corroborative evidences, but were scarcely accorded the kind of authority that the French Prophets might have allowed them. Early Charismatics were frequently reminded of the fickleness of emotion and were urged to view non-emotional, supernatural concomitants as the only really reliable evidences of the Spirit's action. While these included healings, prophecies, miracles and the like, it was generally held that speaking in tongues alone was admissible as 'scriptural evidence' when testing the validity of claims about Spirit-baptism, so much so that many readily described the movement as the 'Tongues Movement'.

During the 1970s the emphasis shifted. Like all prophets before them, Charismatics speak warmly of their new awareness of inner joy, peace and the reality of God's love. Increasingly acknowledgment of that awareness came to be accepted as sufficient evidence for Spirit-baptism, that is, without tongues or any of the other spiritual gifts normally associated with prophetic enduement.

Several factors were involved in the change. To begin with, the Charismatic Movement, unlike any other prophetic movement in Christian history, has succeeded in staying, in considerable measure at any rate, inside the denominational churches, but its success in doing so has sometimes been at the expense of its prophetic witness. The tendency to potentially divisive polarisation in the churches led many to play down tongue-speaking and prophecy and to concentrate more on 'the manifold aspects of the Spirit's working'. However, the result has been that the Charismatic gospel has far too often been so weakened that it has become virtually indistinguishable from the non-Charismatic, a trend that is nowhere more clearly discerned than in the desire of many of the movement's adherents to avoid using the expression 'baptism in the Spirit' itself, because of its seemingly offensive implication that Christians should be divided into two groups and that one of these could claim some kind of spiritual superiority. Thus a whole range of alternative phrases came into common use, such as 'release in the Spirit', 'expressing the Spirit', 'being filled with the Spirit', 'yielding to the Spirit', 'receiving the Spirit', some of which are found in the New Testament, but none of which so readily conjure up the Pentecostal notions associated with the more traditional expression.

This shift in terminology was more than just diplomatic. It also reflected modification in the theology of Spirit-baptism. Though most Charismatics probably still think in terms of a second blessing, there was a growing tendency in the 1970s to view Spirit-baptism as something more directly related to water-baptism, an approach perhaps nearer to that of Edward Irving than to that of the Pentecostals. The argument is briefly that the Spirit is already given in water-baptism, but lies dormant in the believer until released in him by a stirring of faith. Evangelicals have not been slow to point out the inadequacy of such a doctrine, claiming that an experience so described is simply what they have always called conversion. Indeed the lines often do seem rather blurred once the overtly prophetic phenomena are pushed into the background.

The logical conclusion of this tendency towards accommodation with traditional modes of theological thinking is found in the oft-expressed desire to drop the term 'charismatic' altogether and speak only of 'Christian experience', the claim being that charismatic experience is what Christian experience ought to be anyhow. The comprehensiveness of such a theological viewpoint may be commendable in theory, and even truer to the New Testament pattern, but in practice there is a distinction to be drawn, and the blurring of that distinction, whilst it may have helped to bring peace to some, has also been a cause of further disruption within Charismatic circles themselves, since not everyone in the movement has approved of such compromising accommodation, as they see it.

*The House Church and Restoration Movements*

People who have experienced pentecostal, charismatic or revival workings of the Spirit have always proved difficult for traditional churches to handle, with the result that they have either been compelled to leave their denominations, have chosen to leave them, or have had to compromise their new-found faith. The drift out into new independent churches is not at all a new thing and has been happening all over the world, not just in Charismatic circles in our time, but in Protestantism since the Reformation. The process has, however, accelerated considerably in the twentieth century, and though the Charismatic Movement has largely remained within the denominations, there have still been plenty who have left in dissatisfaction or been driven out in disgust.

In Britain the fellowships and congregations formed by the 'come-outers' are commonly referred to as the House Churches (though few of them now meet in houses—the name reflects the earliest stages of their history). Their own members have often preferred the title 'Restoration Movement', which reflects their desire to see the restoring of the ministries and systems of the New Testament Church, particularly the fivefold ministry of apostle, prophet, evangelist, pastor and teacher (Eph. 4:11). There are essentially two broad groupings within the movement, those that welcome some form of strong oversight or central control, and those that prefer to maintain congregational freedom and independence. Some of the larger groupings have virtually become new denominations and are led by strong apostolic figureheads such as Bryn Jones, Terry Virgo, Gerald Coates, John Noble. But there are also a fair number of quite small groupings and other entirely independent units. Some of these have sizeable assemblies and powerful ministries too. The scene is a very mixed one, but overall there is a good degree of common mind and purpose throughout it, even though it is also crossed by many disagreements and factions.

The House Church Movement was born in the late 1950s and grew in the 1960s with the encouragement and leadership of some outstanding men such as Arthur Wallis, David Lillie, Dennis Clark and Campbell McAlpine, many of whom were ex-Brethren preachers and so naturally thought in terms of assemblies rather than churches. Because the Charismatic Movement in the traditional churches was also growing rapidly at the same time and claiming most of the limelight, the development of the House Churches went largely unnoticed. Most of its leaders supported the work of the Fountain Trust anyhow (indeed Campbell McAlpine was largely responsible for the choice of the name) and so that and the House Churches were all viewed as part of one great whole, the reviving work of the Spirit of God throughout British Christendom.

Most of that changed in the 1970s. In 1972 Arthur Wallis and six others[364] entered into a covenant agreement committing themselves to support each other and together see the vision of restoration established in Britain during these last days. Seven others joined this group of restoration apostles and, although it was disbanded in 1976, it created a new, more positive self-awareness in the House Church scene. It also led to the emergence and growth of some strong restoration churches, such as that of Bryn Jones in Bradford in the north of England with its own magazine called *Restoration*, its own training centres, publishing and broadcasting ministry, summer camp, missionary work, etc., and the similarly strong work of Terry Virgo in the south, now known as 'New Frontiers', with its comparable programme of ministry, mission and growth.

For a time the restoration leaders were at the centre of a storm about shepherding and discipling. Between 1972 and 1974 they came under the influence of Ern Baxter and others from Fort Lauderdale, Florida, USA. Their teaching, which was itself influenced by the Argentinian, Juan Carlos Ortiz, author of a controversial book entitled *Disciple*, called for a strong system of authoritarian apostolic oversight. That proved too much for some who had broken away from ecclesiastical restriction precisely because they were seeking a new way of liberty in the House Church stream. That, among other things, was largely responsible for the covenanting group breaking up in 1976 and the emergence of other more independent groupings in the 1980s, under the leadership of men like Gerald Coates and John Noble, whose views found expression for a time in a magazine called *Fullness*. The shepherding issue is now largely a matter of history, though it still lives on in some places, mainly in the form of continuing negative reaction to an unhappy memory of the past.

364. Peter Lyne, Bryn Jones, David Mansell, Graham Perrins, Hugh Thompson and John Noble. They were later joined by seven others: George Tarleton, Gerald Coates, Barney Coombs, Maurice Smith, Ian McCullogh, John MacLaughlan and Campbell McAlpine.

In the meantime the House Churches have continued to grow and are one of the largest growth sectors in the British Charismatic/ Pentecostal scene today. Though some have become introverted and lifeless, and others have fallen apart in division, many are active in dedicated works of evangelism, social concern and mission. They have gained a great deal from continuing dissatisfaction among Charismatics in the traditional churches, but they have also grown through primary evangelism among the unconverted.

*The End-Time Church of the Spirit?*

One of the strong teachings in the restoration movement, from which it gets the name, is that God in these latter days is restoring his church as at the beginning, and that he is doing so by pouring out his Spirit afresh to make his people ready for the final harvest of mankind, equipping a Spirit-empowered army in preparation for the last battle, sending down his 'latter rain' on his chosen ones.

'Latter Rain' teaching has been popular in some sectors of Pentecostalism from earliest times. In England it was espoused by George Jeffreys and Smith Wigglesworth, who in the 1920s spoke about a world-wide revival ('the latter rain') that would bring the denominations to an end, inaugurate the universal Church of the Spirit, and herald the return of Christ. It was given a new injection of life through a revival in Saskatchewan, Canada, in 1948, that gave birth to what is sometimes referred to as the 'Latter Rain Movement'. It found a mixed reception among the Pentecostal Churches of America, but some of its teaching was taken up in the Charismatic Movement. The main vehicle used to make it known to the early Charismatics in Britain was Arthur Wallis's book, *In the Day of Thy Power* (1956), reprinted as *Rain From Heaven* (1968). It is based on linking the prophecy in Joel 2:23, which speaks promise of both former and later rain for the people of God, with the prophecy of 2:28, which foretells the outpouring of the Spirit. In Israel the 'former rain' comes in the autumn and softens the soil for cultivation; the 'latter rain' comes in the spring and waters the young crops as they grow for harvest. In Pentecostal interpretation, the 'former rain' came with the outpouring of the Spirit at the first Pentecost in New Testament times, thus enabling the planting of the Christian Church; the 'latter rain' is falling today in these last times of Neo-Pentecostal visitation, empowering the Church for the end-time harvest of mankind.

The consequent view of history is that prophetic life was known in the Church in apostolic times, was lost after Constantine, has gradually been reintroduced since the reformation, and is now running in fullness again today, restoring the kingdom of God on earth to what Christ intended it to be, so that it can expand to all nations in preparation for his return. In this view of things, the main task of the churches today is to bring back the systems of New Testament times that were lost for so many centuries.

Not all Pentecostals and Charismatics have adopted such a view. The more common approach, inherited from nineteenth-century revivalism, is to expect a sudden irruption, believing that already it is the time of the harvest and that the premillennial return of Christ could take place at any moment. It is therefore not for the Church to try restoring the kingdom of God now, for that is what Jesus will return to do by establishing his millennial kingdom.

Few Charismatics within the traditional churches would understand what restoration theology is about, nor would they show as much interest in the teaching about a premillennial return of Christ or about a secret rapture as traditional Pentecostals have done. That is mainly because the formative influences on them had been different, deriving largely from their own denominational church teaching which, while it certainly teaches about a second advent, does so without too close definition of its circumstances.

Despite the differences, all these groupings share one thing in common with each other and with every prophetic movement that has gone before them: the belief that God is ushering in the final age of the Spirit and raising up a renewed and revivified community, the Church of the Spirit, as the organ of his end-time work of salvation and self-revelation. Each movement we have studied began its life in a crusade for revival, in reaction to prevailing decadence or sterility in the Church, to decline of morals in society, and the like. At first its spirit was aggressive, whether for physical or for spiritual combat, and its adherents were regarded as members of God's army which he was equipping with his spiritual armoury in readiness for the last show-down with Satan and all his evil minions.

### *Shift from Eschatology to Renewal*

This general eschatological vision of an end-time Church of the Spirit, however presented in its details, has created a tension with others in the churches in every age, with the result that persecution has ensued and the prophetic movement in question has either been broken by the ecclesiastical authorities or else has branched off in division, sometimes into sectarianism. Almost inevitably something similar was bound to happen in our own time.

Such has indeed been the story for some in the Charismatic Movement, although its own hope has always been rather different. In the early days the sense of last-time urgency was strong and prophetic utterances frequently spoke about the dawning of a new age of the Spirit, or an imminent return of Christ, but over the years these gradually gave way to statements about Christ's abiding presence and the Spirit's continued encouragement for believers. In the flush of first enthusiasm Charismatics spoke about God pouring out his Spirit in these latter days, making them ready for the final reaping of mankind, preparing them as an army for the last battle. However, before too long other voices were also heard, saying that God was granting a new endowment of his Spirit to revitalise and strengthen an ailing Church so that the lamp of faith could continue to burn and give light in our lost world through more effective preaching of the gospel. Today there is a great deal of variety in the views being expressed by the movement's adherents, and both messages can still be heard, but for many the sense of end-time excitement has somewhat abated and given way to more ecclesiastical modes of thinking. The pattern is a familiar one in the chapters of this book.

This change in direction, together with the toning down of language about speaking in tongues and baptism in the Spirit, went a long way to making the movement more tolerable in the Church at large. Rather than being any more an aggressive, prophetic voice calling urgently for its hearers to respond to the word of the Spirit, it became a renewal movement, working for the reform of faith and practice in the churches, and so found itself a place of acceptance in the recognised structures of the Church as simply another movement or pressure group for change alongside the Evangelical, the Catholic, the Liturgical, the Ecumenical and so forth, that seem to proliferate in our time. The change is aptly reflected in the way the movement's name altered during its early history. At first it was 'the Charismatic Movement', or 'the Neo-Pentecostal Movement', sometimes 'the Tongues Movement', then it became 'the Charismatic renewal', then 'the Renewal Movement' and then quite simply 'the Renewal'.

Considering this tendency one might have concluded that there was little danger of the Charismatic Movement causing any major division in the church. But it is perhaps this general drift towards accommodation with the existing systems that, more than anything else besides some continuing non-acceptance in traditionally minded congregations, has encouraged Charismatics to leave their denominations. The drift had already started early in the 1960s, but it accelerated considerably in the 1970s, when many moved over to align themselves with the by then rapidly expanding House Church movement, where prophetic emphasis was allowed greater freedom of expression. Then a double danger faced the Charismatic Movement, the potential of exclusivism, sectarianism and idiosyncrasy, even heresy, in the House Church circles, and the possibility of becoming submerged in and stifled by the ecclesiastical systems of the established churches. In some instances these dangers became reality, but the early 1980s also brought a release of new prophetic vigour in both camps.

One fact that has repeatedly emerged in this history is that a prophetic movement is a movement with a vision of a better world and a better Church, inspired by God's Spirit. Without that vision it ceases to be prophetic and becomes little more than another denomination. There have always been those in the older churches who have held to this dream, though it has been among those who have lost hope for any purposeful renewing of the traditional systems that the more eschatological message has been sounded most clearly. If today the Spirit, rather than ecclesiastical politics and compromise, is allowed to inspire and renew the vision, then perhaps this unique movement that has still largely been able to stay within the churches will in the end succeed in its prophetic task of converting them into the longed-for Church of the Spirit—that is, of course, if its earlier and persistent expectation of the Lord's near return is not realised first! Either way, if its vision for the future is permitted to die, so proportionately must the movement fossilise, as indeed it seems to have done in many places. Surely here is one of the most important lessons this history teaches, that without a living prophetic vision there can be no prophetic movement, only an ecclesiastical system.

*Move from Renewal to Denominational Renewal*

Since the Charismatic Movement (from this point on, for clarity's sake, we shall for the most part use the term to refer to the movement within the churches) is still mainly a renewal movement, its message seldom sounds like an alternative gospel. Baptism in the Spirit is held to be a blessing available to all Christians, not merely to an elect few or to those prepared to join a movement. In some ways it is misleading to think of the Movement as having 'members', because it is almost entirely without structures. Unlike Pentecostalism, it has no churches; unlike Irvingism, it has no hierarchy;

unlike Shakerism, it has no leaders (let alone a Messianic leader); unlike Montanism, it has no central fund or headquarters. In many ways its ethos is not very far removed from that of the French Prophets, or the Friends of God. It is a movement of ministries, miracles, heroes, books, meetings, conferences, prayer groups, personal witness and evangelism. And yet it is not a ragged, incoherent affair, but a clearly definable movement with discernible aims and character.

In Britain the Fountain Trust gave it a point of focus and encouragement, through its conferences, publications and other activities, but that was eventually disbanded in 1980. Its magazine, *Renewal*, continues to be published under independent sponsorship and so still provides a forum for dialogue and some focus for common identity. The Fountain Trust had no membership since it was not an association. It was non-denominational, drawing its support from Catholics, Protestants, Pentecostals and House Churches. Hence it stood apart from the churches, but not in competition with any of them.

The 1980s marked a change in the direction of renewal in more ways than one. It is significant that the demise of the Fountain Trust overlapped with, or was roughly coincident with, the emergence of a number of denominational organisations, such as Anglican Renewal Ministries (ARM, 1981) with its own magazine, *Anglicans for Renewal* (now renamed *ARM-Link*), Baptists for Life and Growth (1978), the United Reformed Church's Group for Evangelism and Renewal (GEAR, 1974), the Methodist Church's Dunamis Renewal Fellowship (1983), also publishing its own magazine, Dunamis (earlier than the Fellowship, since 1972). Better organised and more influential than any of these is the National Service Committee for Catholic Charismatic Renewal (1973). It was partly because the Catholics got themselves well organised at an early date that the other denominations had to follow suit. One of their major contributions was the introduction from America of a group study course called *Life in the Spirit Seminars* which proved highly successful in preparing and leading Catholics into baptism in the Spirit in a biblically informed way. The Anglicans followed after them with *Saints Alive*, which is a modified version of the Catholic course for use by Protestants. It has proved so successful that the Catholics came to prefer using it themselves.

These changes brought new life for a time. The opportunities for a deeper work of renewal at a denominational level were evident, but equally so were the inherent dangers of final absorption into the churches and the consequent loss of identity and vitality. The various organisations continued to arrange national conferences and to issue their publications, though it seemed for a time that the House Churches were taking the lead in these aspects of the work, particularly with their widely circulating magazines, *Restoration* and *Fullness,* and their highly successful Dales Bible Week and Downs Bible Week conferences that attracted thousands every year in the north and south of England respectively, and the large ACTS conferences held at the National Exhibition Centre in Birmingham.

*John Wimber and the Third Wave*

The whole movement in Britain and Europe received a new injection of life in the mid 1980s through the work of John Wimber. From 1975 he lectured along with Peter Wagner at Fuller Theological Seminary on the subject of 'Signs, Wonders and Church Growth' and in 1977 he founded the Vineyard Christian Fellowship of Anaheim, California. His lectures proved amazingly popular and soon he was holding conferences in other places. His ministry has proved particularly popular in Britain and Europe where today there are now many Vineyard Fellowships linked with Anaheim.

His teaching is not normally thought of as Pentecostal or Charismatic, although it is largely in harmony with both and has greatly encouraged their adherents. The term that is usually applied to it is 'Third Wave', on the understanding that it represents a new movement similar but subsequent to the Pentecostal Movement (first wave) and the Charismatic Movement (second wave). Just as the two earlier movements, though in the same flow, differed from each other in many ways, so this third also differs again. The Pentecostal was at first, and for the most part continues to be, mainly a work of evangelism among the working classes and the unchurched, emphasising baptism in the Spirit, usually with speaking in tongues, as a second blessing after conversion. The Charismatic has been chiefly a work among middle-class churchgoers renewing and reviving spiritual life in the churches or calling new spiritually alive churches into being, emphasising the operation of the Holy Spirit, sometimes in the Pentecostal way, sometimes more generally. The Third Wave has been primarily a work of education among evangelicals, teaching and equipping the saints to operate in the ministries of the Holy Spirit, particularly the power ministries of healing the sick, deliverance, word of knowledge and prophecy. Baptism in the Spirit is sometimes seen as a concomitant of conversion rather than its sequel, while openness to many subsequent fillings is encouraged. The gift of tongues is not much emphasised and accommodation to particular church customs is advised, specifically to avoid any of the divisiveness that Pentecostalism engendered among evangelicals. Perhaps the main thrust of the movement is summed up in the phrase 'power encounter'. This age is seen as one in which paganism is again rampant and so the primary need is for Christians to be equipped to fight the Lord's battle against the powers of evil. For that they themselves must be anointed with power from God. It is no longer enough to rely on platform evangelists. The whole body of Christ must now be armed and trained for the battle, which is most commonly held to be in the context of the body of believers itself rather than in the lonely sphere of individual ministry.

This Third Wave movement peaked in the mid and late '80s. It is still powerful in many places, but no longer holds the front line attention it did a few years ago. Even though it self-consciously distinguished itself from the Charismatic Movement, it did actually inject a fresh breath of life into it. Other movements now claim the headlines. They too have injected new life into some Charismatic churches, but most prophetic people agree that we have been needing once more a fresh breath of revival wind to blow through the traditional churches, and even through some of the newer fellowships. God has, of course, been doing precisely that, in his own way, which is quite different from how most people expected it would be. More about that later.

*Charismatic Ministries and Heroes*

Despite the number of people, organisations, conferences, publications and the like that have added impetus to the Charismatic Movement, it is none of these that has been its real driving force. In the 1960s and '70s it grew mainly by word of mouth, by church meetings, by prayer groups, by home cells, by personal witness. The large gatherings and publications were particularly helpful in stimulating a hunger for God that sent people to prayer seeking after him. The first consciousness of the seekers was not usually of meetings, but of their need for a living encounter with Christ and a filling with the power of the Holy Spirit. God was very much at the centre. Men and women rejoiced to find their Father, their Saviour and their Comforter. To be sure the Movement raised up certain personalities and institutions to positions of prominence, but in the hearts of most, in the early days at any rate, the focus was the Lord.

The main Charismatic ministries were therefore biblical administrations of grace, rather than people and organisations.

Pre-eminent among these ministries, of course, has been that of baptism in the Spirit. It is commonly performed through laying on of hands with prayer (in tongues) and has been exercised by clergy and laity alike. Sometimes it takes place in the context of public worship, sometimes in house meetings, sometimes through personal counselling. It is also recognised that this baptism can be received by faith in private with no other person present, though strangely the 'tarrying room' of older Pentecostal times has virtually no part to play. That is partly because Charismatics have been encouraged to believe there is no point waiting for something that has already been given, but that they should reach out to God and receive it by faith from him now. Hence they have generally received their baptism through ministry rather than through tarrying or waiting. This ministry is usually, though not always, quiet and orderly, quite unlike the 'blessing' ceremonies of the French Prophets, or the rather noisy conversion scenes usually associated with Wesley's preaching or American revivalism, but it is effective none the less, and one man's account of his Spirit-baptism to another probably has done more to spread the movement than anything else.

Healing ministry has also been very much at the centre of Charismatic renewal. At first there were plenty of stories about individuals healed through private prayer, or at conferences, or in house meetings, mostly out of sight of the Sunday congregation. But in the 1970s, and particularly in the wake of Wimber's teaching in the 1980s, this ministry, which was once viewed with scepticism and suspicion, found itself a place of respectability in many churches that began to hold regular public 'healing services'. Some saw this change as evidence of man's attempt to harness and channel what ought to be left to the free and spontaneous will of the Spirit, but in many churches the Spirit did honour the work and so it has become a common feature of church life and another focus of renewal, so much so that in some places the special services have been discontinued and ministry for healing has been incorporated into the regular services. Where the life of the Spirit is flowing freely the results continue to be good, but this ministry has often become watered down and ineffective, a mere shadow with little power.

Deliverance, or the casting out of demons, is also an inseparable part of the Charismatic's work. In the eyes of some, it is an unexpected element to find in this age of rationalism and has tended to degrade the movement in their estimation, but it corresponds well with the pastoral needs of our society that has become fascinated with the power of the occult. Like the healing ministry, it has become increasingly harnessed by the churches, many of which now have recognised consultants or advisers on exorcism on their clerical staff, a thing that would have been unheard of before the rise of the Charismatic Movement.

In the movement's early years these ministries tended to be exercised widely by all and sundry, but certain individuals inevitably became prominent in them, men and women who rose to the status of charismatic hero, like Elijah and Elisha, or Barnabas and Philip. In other times such personalities might sometimes have found themselves elevated to Messianic or quasi-Messianic positions, as happened to Montanus, the prophet from Bourges, Nicholas Storch, Ann Lee and Alexander Dowie. Similar things have occasionally happened in the nineteenth century, as in Zaire, where the prophet Simon Kimbangu, after only five months of amazing ministry in 1921, was arrested and held in prison for thirty years until his death in 1951, and is now regarded as God by his followers in the Kimbanguist Church. However, the more common tendency today has been to treat such strongly anointed leaders more like gurus, or men with all the answers.

This veneration of the charismatic hero is in no way better attested than in the success of the charismatic (auto)biography, a type of literature that details the hero's life-changing experience in Spirit-baptism and outlines his or her subsequently successful ministry of miracle, mission, or service. It is of the same literary genre as the prophetic narratives in the book of Kings or in the Acts of the Apostles and probably does as much as they did to encourage the faithful and maintain their vision. It is the existence of literature such as this, more so than of theological treatises, that brings the Charismatic Movement into the same arena of religious life as Old and New Testament prophecy.

In recent years, however, while the prophetic narrative is still published, there has been a movement away from it to more reflective and theological types of writing. In its later years the Fountain Trust started issuing a supplement to *Renewal* called *Theological Renewal*. It never had a very wide circulation, but it marked a trend and today most publications by Charismatics are either of a reflective and theological cast or in the nature of pastoral guides, as witness, for example, the ever increasing flow of books on healing, prophecy, faith, church growth, leadership and the like. Currently the personal biography of the charismatic hero is no longer the main attraction.

Today we hear more and more people call for teaching, and we read more about renewed and growing churches than about renewed individuals. The prayer of most is now for national revival. Charismatic ministry has increasingly passed from the hands of the few to the wider body of Christ, which is where it properly belongs anyhow.

*The Gifts of the Spirit and the Charismatic Church*

As in most earlier prophetic movements, the spiritual gifts are generally used in and for the benefit of the charismatic community itself. Unlike the Old Testament prophets and the French Prophets, Charismatics have not been inclined to publish their inspired sayings and visions for scrutiny by the wider community, either in the Church or in society at large. Rather, they have sought, very much like the New Testament Church, to use every other available means of reaching the public with their message, but to reserve prophecy for their own internal edification. Hence anyone who would study the content of Charismatic prophecy is confronted with an immediate problem posed by the virtual absence of collected sayings of the prophets. Odd utterances are recorded in biographical works, but the only worthwhile way of discovering the message of the prophets is by attending Charismatic meetings, and even then it is possible to be disappointed, since there is no guarantee that prophecy, or any of the gifts for that matter, will he exercised at a particular meeting. This lack of documented material makes systematic study of the subject difficult, though in recent years it has generated a great deal of interest and a number of excellent books are now available on the gift of prophecy.

Charismatics broadly divide into two camps with respect to the prophetic gifts. In more catholic circles there tends to be a readier emphasis on the mystical aspects of religion, on visions and revelations quietly received, rationally tested and then communicated without too much display of emotion. The ethos encountered here is in many ways akin to that found in Tertullian's church, or among the Friends of God. In circles of a more evangelical and Pentecostal bent we are in a world much closer to that of the French Prophet or the Shaker meeting, where direct and immediate utterances, whether in tongues or in English, sometimes accompanied by ecstatic or emotional behaviour, are willingly received and often carry considerable weight with the community.

Either way, the most vibrant locus for the operation of the gifts has been, and probably still is, the home group and smaller meeting, rather than the public assembly of the whole body. That is how it has been in most ages. In New Testament times, it was in the earliest days of the Church, when meetings were generally held in homes, that prophecy flourished most vigorously. The Amalricians, the Friends of God and the Zwickau Prophets all favoured conventicle Christianity, though for them that may have been partly because of the exigencies of the age. The French Prophets and the Shakers tried to create forms of communal expression, but they took their origins in, and to different degrees continued to foster, home gatherings and small group meetings. It was in non-formal settings that the Irvingites discovered their prophetic giftings, which rapidly dwindled away in the formal context of the Catholic Apostolic Church. Similarly today's Charismatics find a more ready outlet for their gifts in the freer atmosphere of the lay group which is unhampered by the necessities of tradition, and so it is in the eclectic atmosphere of the mid-week meeting that the movement finds its most natural expression.

The gifts are also instanced in public meetings, though there the more noticeable effects are usually less ostensibly supernatural. They tend to be more in the nature of increased joy in worship, freer interpersonal contact, greater informality, more extensive lay and corporate participation, stronger scriptural teaching, louder praise and prayer, more contemporary forms of music and song, wider use of drama and dance. All of these are frequently classified under the heading of 'Charismatic (sub)culture' and are dismissed by some as not of the real essence of prophetic Christianity. On the other hand, they are mostly the sort of effects that have accompanied other prophetic outbursts in history and, if they are of the subculture, they are none the less clear hallmarks of prophetism, just as are the more miraculous and spectacular gifts. From the days of Samuel onwards, prophets have usually been free, happy worshippers, revelling in their songs and dances and in a natural, informal enjoyment of the presence of God.

Longing for such freedom, coupled with frustration over ecclesiastical formalism, has ensured a continuing drift from the traditional churches into the House Churches, and now also into some of the Pentecostal churches that are themselves rediscovering their own ancient freedom in the Spirit. That has undoubtedly weakened the charismatic witness and impact in the older denominations but, fortunately, enough has remained to ensure varying degrees of freedom and continuing renewal activity in different places, thus preventing the total exodus that some have predicted. However, the danger remains and the trickle continues to flow.

*The Fruit of the Charismatic Movement*

Given that there are denominational, national and regional variations, some of them quite significant, there have also been some common characteristics that can be identified as the fruit of the movement's impact. Firstly, though baptism in the Spirit lies at the heart of the message, the common witness of the movement has been to Jesus, to a heightened awareness of both his near, personal presence and also his lordship. That has resulted in a new flow of praise, not just in the many new songs that have come out of the movement, but in the discovery of a new ability to worship from the heart. The Bible has come alive for many, not simply as the record of the past, but as something that speaks personally to the heart. That, of course, is coupled with the vital discovery that the Spirit of God communicates revelation and direction to individual believers through prophetic words or personal inspiration as well as through the Scriptures.

Again, as in other movements of the Spirit, moral consciousness has been heightened, matched with a good desire for holiness. Spiritual consciousness has also been intensified, accompanied with a heightened awareness of spiritual battle. That in turn has given expression to new military modes of prayer and ministry, particularly deliverance ministry. Most Charismatics have also found themselves spontaneously witnessing, or at least becoming aware of the need to witness, and discovering that they have been given a new power that enables them to do so in ways they never appreciated before. That same power has also enabled them to pray for healing of the sick with a considerable degree of effectiveness, as well as to exercise many of the other gifts of the Spirit mentioned in the Bible. And then, of course, they have, like all prophets, become conscious of the urgency of the times, that these are indeed the last days and that the Jesus they have rediscovered and learned to love will be coming back very soon.

Because of the strength of their witness, all these things have made an impact on non-Charismatic churchmen as well, many of whom have had to begin taking note, and have consequently been stirred to action. While they have rejected the central message of baptism in the Spirit, they have tried to import some of the adjuncts, such as praying for the sick, singing new songs, praying new prayers, though Charismatics would say that their doing so without baptism in the Spirit makes all they do quite hollow and lifeless. Other churches have tried bringing the Charismatics into line and have rejected the blessings, but one way or another the impression the movement has made is of no mean significance.

The greatest danger confronting the Charismatic Movement today is not hostility, but compromise. The change-over to denominational renewal, in the opinion of some, sounded its death-knell. Others have not abandoned hope but have continued to work for revival within their traditions. Only time will enable us to pass the final verdict. One lesson should, however, already be clear. Much effort was for a time put into renewal of worship, renewal of prayer, renewal of many different aspects of church life. That shifted the focus off Christ onto schemes and programmes. It left Christians with new liturgies, new songs, new words, new forms, etc., but no new life. The testimony of Jesus himself is that the Holy Spirit would take the things that are his and show them to us, that he would glorify him (John 16:14). When the focus shifts off Jesus and the Holy Spirit onto church affairs, practices and doctrines, the life departs. Prophetic witness is to Jesus Christ and to the life that is available in him. That is the heart of the revival message and to compromise it in any way, or fail to preach it, is death. A fresh outpouring of the Spirit will renew that life, and only that will do it.

PART EIGHT

# PROSPECT AND CONCLUSION

History is a strange subject. One generation tells it differently from another, and different groups view it differently. Edward Irving, rejected nineteenth century as a heretic by the churches, estimated little by his own followers in Catholic Apostolic circles, critically reviewed in almost every book written about him, is today studied as a great theologian with understanding beyond his age and highly honoured in Charismatic circles as an outstanding but sadly neglected forerunner of modern Pentecostalism. Opinions change, and not always rationally. Most Pentecostals estimate Martin Luther's contribution to their recovery of primitive prophetic Christianity very highly, although he denounced the only prophetic movement in his time. Similarly John Wesley, though he had no time for the prophets of his day. And they estimate them so even though the Zwickau Prophets and the French Prophets were far closer to them in ethos and aspiration than ever Luther or Wesley were. Macarius' *Spiritual Homilies* was formative for Wesley's understanding of the Gospel, and the mystical *Theologia Germanica* for Luther's, yet neither of these is read by the prophetic Christians who today think so highly of these two men. Charismatics occasionally honour the early Quakers, but they do not remember the Seekers, though their longings were more akin to their own. The Quietism of Miguel de Molinos and Madame Guyon still has a very mixed reception among Pentecostals and Charismatics, some loving it, others despising it. And so we could go on.

Fashions change and men view history now one way, now another. It is not possible to speak of a present-day Pentecostal or Charismatic view of history, nor of a consensus about future tendency. We are therefore passing now over into a world of debate, mixed opinions and varied personal assessment. One thing that history does show is that in relation to present trends such division of opinion is unavoidable, even among kindred spirits. Men who claim to be prophets will continue to make their authoritative pronouncements, but ultimately the sound wisdom of Scripture will prevail: 'If what a prophet proclaims in the name of the LORD does not take place or come true, that is a message the LORD has not spoken. That prophet has spoken presumptuously.' (Deut. 18:22) Perhaps, for the moment at any rate, it is best simply to make an assessment and express a hope, one that will encourage the Lord's people in the light of all he is doing in our times, but with the wisdom of hindsight, not forgetting the realities of the past.

# 30

# Where is the Spirit Leading us Now?

One thing is unquestionable: that God is granting amazing growth and revival in our day and that most of it has a clear, strong prophetic heart.

That, however, has to be set against a world that keeps changing —at breathtakingly accelerated speed. It has been impossible for most people to keep abreast with the rate of technological advances over the past ten years. They have revolutionised our educational, working and home environments. Our systems of communication have so developed that it can be much quicker for our typed messages to reach the other side of the world than for our letters to be delivered in our own home town. For advanced nations the world shrinks daily, while for the undeveloped time moves slowly still.

The flavour of international politics has also changed. Since the death of Mao and the collapse of Russian Communism, the Cold War tensions between East and West have largely disappeared. Wars between nations have become rare, though there has been more fighting and bloodshed than ever. Battles today are mainly fought between ethnic groups quarrelling for independence or for governmental control inside national borders.

Aggression today is probably less often political than religious or cultural in its motivation. Islam is once more intent on world domination and uses every means at its disposal to spread its influence, from oil wealth to terrorism. It is probably the most rapidly advancing ideology in our world today. Other religious groups are also beginning to wake out of complacency and follow Islam's ways, especially in the Indian sub-continent, where many Christians are suffering serious persecution as a result.

Equally aggressive, though in totally different ways, are the pressures of wealth, drugs, moral decadence and the occult, all claiming control over the minds and souls of men. Ours has become an age of strange contradictions and inconsistencies, embracing unprecedented scientific advance alongside a wholesale slide into primitive paganism. These trends are not new, but at the end of the twentieth century the process has massively intensified. It is well that the prophetic church is also experiencing phenomenal growth. It has a central role to play in our times and an even more urgent message to proclaim.

Sometimes when we look at the Church, even the Pentecostal Church, we might be excused for wondering whether it is even aware of the forces ranged against us. We may see little consistency in its proclamation and even find it far too occupied with internal theological issues of no apparent relevance. But still Jesus reigns and is able to use his ragged and divided body, the Church, to wondrously powerful effect. The last two decades have seen more church growth and expansion than ever in history. However, new growth brings new demands. So how have our leaders and thinkers responded to them? What indeed are the challenges that confront today's Church of the Spirit?

At one level they are much the same as they have always been, right from the beginning. The church in Corinth in New Testament times was in many respects a very ragged affair, especially when it came to matters prophetic. It was in the context of his discussion about their use of spiritual gifts that Paul had to write, 'God is not a God of disorder but of peace,' and 'Everything should be done in a fitting and orderly way.' (1 Cor. 14:32,40) He could write the same today if he were alive to survey the Pentecostal/Charismatic scene. There is so much variety of practice and opinion in it that the closer we look, the more confused we can become. Many questions remain unanswered, many questions are given a variety of conflicting answers, and many answers are given to questions that few are asking, all with great zeal and intensity as if our eternal salvation depended on our response to the solutions offered.

Some of the old debates live on and continue to generate animosity. There are still those who say that persons baptised in the name of the Trinity forfeit their salvation unless they are rebaptised in the name of Jesus only. Hot air is still generated by disputes about the premillennial return of Christ. Arguments continue to abound about whether baptism in the Spirit is part of conversion, a second blessing, or what, and whether speaking in tongues is needed as evidence of it having happened. In fact almost every aspect of the work of the Spirit has at some time or in some place generated a new doctrine and, since those baptised in the Spirit speak with such boldness, each man asserts his opinion with authority as if he were right and everyone else wrong.

Today the issues are often more pastoral, whether this way or that is the correct method of praying for the sick, or driving out demons, or discerning whether any demons are there at all, or praying with faith for material provision, or counselling the distressed, or whether there should even be such a thing as counselling ministry, and so forth. To the uninitiated it may all seem totally mysterious and confusing, but even to the initiated much is still utterly confusing.

One result of all this is that Pentecostals and Charismatics have at last started to think more theologically, which in itself raises an enormous challenge in a movement that has traditionally spurned intellectualism.

*The Theological Challenge*

At first Pentecostalism was mainly a working-class phenomenon and so had little natural interest in higher education. The early evangelists emphasised the spiritual and emotional aspects of religion and frequently scorned formal education as a hindrance to faith. Pentecostals therefore refused to establish schools, other than short-term, non-academic Bible schools, and concentrated all their efforts into proclaiming the gospel. That they did very effectively indeed, but with the passage of the century and the rise in cultural status among Pentecostal people, the need for sympathetic educational institutes began to be felt.

In the early 1940s in America the Church of God (Cleveland), and soon after them the Assemblies of God, began to upgrade some of their educational programmes. In the post-war years others followed suit, some of them eventually obtaining regional academic accreditation. Then in 1964 Oral Roberts University opened in Tulsa, Oklahoma, offering a full range of theological and secular studies and other institutions have since followed, not all of them with the same width of syllabus. Nor have they all sought accreditation. Some offer the more traditional Pentecostal-style Bible college education, as, for example, does Christ for the Nations, founded in Dallas, Texas, in 1972, but now with branches in other countries. Since then numerous new Bible institutes have been opened all over America and in the rest of the world. Many of these have been founded by Charismatic leaders to give expression to their own particular brand of teaching. Not all have the same academic calibre, but their very existence signifies a total turn-around from the anti-theological attitudes of the earliest Pentecostals. Teaching and training are now much in demand.

This trend has accelerated greatly since the Charismatic Movement has touched the better educated, middle classes. Catholic Renewal's seminar approach to teaching and John Wimber's fairly academic workshops on the Holy Spirit have also added to the upgrading of theological standards in the Movement today. The main leader of early Charismatic renewal in Germany, Arnold Bittlinger, was a scholar, and he was one of the first to use the methods of biblical criticism in Charismatic exegesis of the Bible. His book, *Gifts and Graces*, appeared in English in 1967, followed in 1973 by *Gifts and Ministries*. Both proved quite popular at the time.

The first major work presenting a critical examination of the theological presuppositions of Pentecostalism appeared in 1970, in a Ph.D. thesis by James Dunn published under the title *Baptism in the Holy Spirit*. Since then there has been a steady flow of theological writing covering all aspects of the movement's life, history and doctrines. Much of it has been descriptive and analytical rather than critical, but more recently dialogue has been opened up with scholars of other traditions. It would be impossible to catalogue the full range of that dialogue here. Suffice it to say that the theological interest has intensified over the past ten or fifteen years, as witness, for example, the fact that *ARM-Link* added a theological supplement and *The Journal of Pentecostal Theology* has been issued regularly since 1992, with several scholarly monographs attached to the series.

### *The Nature of the Theological Challenge*

In some respects the theological interests of the Charismatic Movement differ from those of earlier prophetic movements. For instance, it has no deutero-Messianic leanings and not all its members have a separatist vision for an alternative church. Nor has it on the whole had any political voice, although it has a very profound concern for social and moral welfare and many of its members have been exceedingly active in these fields. In other ways it is very similar to earlier movements, for example, in its biblicist emphasis, its fostering of old-fashioned moral attitudes, and its cross-denominational appeal. Many of its theological emphases arise from its stance as a movement for renewal, such as its openness to ecumenical dialogue, its general support for liturgical revision, its stress on evangelistic outreach and its deep concern for the local church.

It is the theology of baptism in the Spirit and of spiritual gifts that has tended to generate most debate. The emphasis on joy and peace, so marked an element in Jesus' teaching about the Holy Spirit's work in John 14-16, is welcomed in all quarters without any dispute, as also is the desire for growth in the fruit of the Spirit, described by Paul in Gal. 5:22f as love, joy, peace, etc. It is commonly seen as part of the aim of renewal to revitalise these facets of the Spirit's action in the life of believers. With that, by and large, all sectors of the movement are happy and so no theological defence for this aspect of the work has had to be formulated.

By contrast, much has been written about the theology of Spirit-baptism, especially on the apparent tension between Charismatic teaching on the subject and traditional church teaching about conversion, water baptism and confirmation. Similar disputes surround Charismatics' claims about the gifts of the Spirit. There are still many who maintain a cessationist view that these were intended only for first-century Christians to help them get the work of the gospel established and that they therefore became superfluous once the Church was constituted with its episcopal system in operation (say Catholic opponents), or once the New Testament Scriptures were written down and acknowledged as canonical (say evangelical critics). Charismatics respond that they were given at Pentecost for all time (Acts 2:39), but simply fell into disuse with the passage of the years. The argument is as old as the time of the Montanists and has recurred in relation to most of the movements we have reviewed, but still it is hotly debated today.

One feature of Charismatic theology that is different from anything that has gone before, and one that has not yet had a proper airing, is its view of the inspiration of Scripture. It is not that Charismatics are saying anything much different from what earlier prophets have said on this matter, but rather that they are saying it against a background of widely accepted liberalism that tends to conflict with their viewpoint. While Pentecostals are mainly fundamentalist, many Charismatics have been drawn from liberal circles and so have an in-built tendency to question things, particularly the miraculous and the supernatural. Their discovery of the world of the Spirit is often so cataclysmic that many of them reject their liberal upbringing completely and adopt Pentecostalist ways of thinking. Some remain puzzled and torn in two directions, others refuse to think about the problem, a few claim to have some kind of solution to it, but the general cry from the Charismatic Movement is a reactionary one, that theology in the churches is decadent, like worship, faith, ethics, prayer and so forth, ailing or dead, and urgently needing to be renewed and revitalised.

Renewal to a Charismatic seldom means reinstating old ways. It usually means new wineskins as well as new wine. Liberal theology is deeply entrenched in our universities and colleges and shows few signs of being affected by either Pentecostal or Charismatic renewal. To be sure, a number of theological teachers in the older teaching establishments have been personally touched by the Spirit and are beginning to contribute to theological debate. But by and large the work of the new theologians is being done outside the old universities, in some of the Pentecostal Bible schools or the new colleges that have come into being in the wake of the Charismatic revival. Many of the theological writings and teaching manuals now available are of a high quality, but they are still very mixed. Some simply plough the old evangelical furrow, acknowledging charismatic aspects as necessary. Few enter into dialogue with existing theological systems. Many are aimed at practical application rather than theological reflection. There is still a vacuum to be filled.

*The Need for a New Approach to Bible teaching*

None of our earlier chapters can be of much help to us in tackling this issue, for liberal theology is unique in the nineteenth century. It was already in existence when the Pentecostal Movement began, but was then still in infancy and hardly represented the common approach to Scripture, certainly not in the background from which Pentecostalism emerged. On this front the Charismatic Movement is on its own. It has little to learn from fundamentalism, for it is not a doctrinaire movement fighting to establish a particular view of the Bible, but rather a movement that has discovered a spiritual reality which compels its adherents to review their attitude to the Bible in the light of their new-found experience of God in the Spirit. The need is urgent.

Our age has seen a massive erosion of Bible knowledge and consequently of faith in God. The cry of Hosea, 'my people are destroyed for lack of knowledge' (Hos. 4:6), is as true today as it was in his time. More than a century of liberal teaching and preaching has wrought havoc in the churches, in our schools and in society at large. Never since Wycliffe's time has the Bible been so little read and taught. We can thank God for the evangelicals who have kept up a faithful flow of Bible teaching down the long decades of arid rationalism, but in today's church, where the Spirit is powerfully reviving the faithful, the older form of evangelical exposition often seems rather dry and irrelevant. That is because it is not geared to the revival flow of the Spirit's working in our times, and so a new thrust is called for—urgently.

The Pentecostal Movement discovered basically the same revival dynamic as we know today, but it did not produce a form of Bible teaching to match its life and experience. Instead it adopted the nearest thing available at the time, namely evangelical and fundamentalist exposition. That served well in many ways, but it has always fallen short of the needs of Holy Spirit inspired ministry and living. Today something new and encouraging is beginning to emerge on the Bible teaching front. Our need is not just for books, but for men trained as Bible teachers and preachers, who have caught the living, life-transforming dynamic of Scripture, applying it to themselves and introducing others to it, just like Wycliffe's Lollards did in their day, men grounded in the revival life of God's word, equipped to promulgate new revival moves in our time.

What is needed is not just another version of the kind of academic study we have had for the past hundred and fifty years, but something that feeds the heart as well as the head, which has been of the very essence of revival and prophetic faith in every age. Jesus did not ask his disciples to get theology degrees, but he did teach them the Scriptures and they loved it, and became teachers themselves—more effective ones for fulfilling his kingdom purposes than many of our learned expositors today. Wycliffe also found that too much theological learning could hinder his Lollards' appreciation of the Word and undermine its proclamation.

The danger in making a statement like this is that it sounds anti-intellectual, which is the very criticism frequently levelled, and not without some justification, against Pentecostal and Charismatic people. However, the road that Pentecostalism travelled in the middle of the twentieth century warns of the opposite danger. The traps of fundamentalism and doctrinalism are very real and very deadly, leading to argument, dispute, hardened attitudes and spiritual dryness. Sadly too many Charismatics still fall foul of them. It is with thoughts like these in mind that I have produced *The Way of the Spirit Bible Reading Course*, which is, to my great joy, indeed proving successful in training people to read their Bibles carefully, in an informed way, and at the same time to be edified in the revival life of the Spirit that comes from its pages. The hunger for such teaching is there and much more is desperately needed.

*The Need for Pastoral and Doctrinal Teaching*

Another large area of theological urgency unparalleled in earlier history is that of healing, counselling and deliverance ministry. Every prophetic movement has had its catalogue of miracles, but healings have tended to be isolated, spontaneous events, or else the work of particular individuals whose spiritual endowment to perform them has been generally recognised. Today it is different. Renewal has taken this ministry into the churches, into healing services, into homes of healing, and into the regular ministry of parish clergy, even into churches and congregations that have no clear affiliation with either the Charismatic or the Pentecostal Movement. The problems resulting have been many and the pastoral theologies of the past offer little help to those involved in these ministries.

Liberals generally shy clear of the subject, since it involves discussion about supernatural action they are often unwilling to handle and, if they do, they tend to employ a largely psychological framework which hardly meets the challenge presented by the claims of the Charismatics. Equally little help is forthcoming from non-Pentecostal conservative and fundamentalist theologians, for their premiss, that the age of miracles ended with the passage of the apostolic Church, has prohibited them from even acknowledging the reality of what happens today, let alone analysing it.

In recent years there has been quite a lot of teaching and publishing by Charismatics on various aspects of healing. That has tended to be of a pastoral nature, some of it of very high quality. The subject, however, continues to raise problems and conflicts in the minds of Christians everywhere. Pentecostal healing tended to be mainly physical and that brought it into conflict with the medical profession. The ailments of the better fed, more leisured, middle classes the Spirit has been touching in recent times in the West tend to be more emotional, and so the debate today is as much with psychiatrists as with physicians. Just as the doctors at the beginning of the century objected to the healing ministry then as treatment by medically unqualified persons, so today psychiatrists object to a healing ministry that is unqualified in their skills. That would be less of a problem if the Charismatics agreed on their methods, but they do not. Instead the approaches of the healers often conflict with each other quite radically, particularly on matters of inner healing and deliverance. The details of the disputes need not occupy us here, but the very fact that they exist is a clear indication that again there is much work for our pastors, teachers and theologians to do.

The questions of good and evil, of health and suffering, of divine power and human frailty, of faith and unfaith, indeed of the very nature of faith as it is exercised in healing, these and so many other questions need to be more fully understood and explained for the benefit of so many perplexed and puzzled Christian clergy and people who have come into contact with this ministry.

The problem of true and false prophecy, over which the early Church stumbled, also needs more airing. Again liberals do not discuss it because their premises hardly permit them to do so. Prophecy for them is reduced to forms of intuition, clever reading of the times, heightened perceptivity and the like. Conservatives would probably retort along with Filastrius of Brescia,

'They do not seem to know that "the law and the prophets were until blessed John the Baptist" and that the complete and utter end of the law and the prophets came with the presence of Christ.'[365]

Only quite recently have Charismatics begun to explore and write on the issue. Again some of their works are excellent, but many Christians are still puzzled. More than once have they heard a 'Thus says the Lord,' and have had no theological yardstick by which to measure the utterance. Not a few have been hurt by naive acceptance of every spoken word, and Paul's injunction to 'test everything' (1 Thes. 5:21) remains as insistent today as it did nineteen centuries ago. History suggests that we neglect this issue to our peril. It is the very bedrock on which the movements of the Spirit we have studied in this book are founded, and yet also the rock on which many of them have foundered.

Many other pastoral and theological topics need fuller attention from Pentecostal and Charismatic teachers, particularly moral, political and social issues, about which many young Christians are quite confused, imagining that attitudes they have gleaned from their general environment and education are Christian when they are not at all so. Perhaps too exclusive attention has been paid to the more churchy doctrines of Spirit-baptism and spiritual gifts. There is still much work for the Charismatic scholar to do.

*Decline or Growth?*

It would be misleading, however, to think that the challenges facing today's prophets are mostly academic. Rather the opposite, for the strength of Pentecostal work has always lain more in its witness than in its thought processes. No nation has ever been won for Christ by reason, but rather the converse, for reason has often weakened witness, as has been evidenced again by the record of the past decade. Today there is far more dialogue between Charismatic and non-Charismatic biblical scholars than there was in the 1970s.

365. See above, p. 101.

In some ways that is good, but in others quite damaging, for compromise resulting from dialogue has so often weakened the witness of Charismatics that the name now prompts correspondingly weak notions about experience of the Holy Spirit.

Depending on who one listens to, the picture today can look depressing or encouraging. In some parts of the world it might seem that the Charismatic Movement has run its course and the much hoped-for revival has not followed in its wake. Instead the fire of the Spirit has subsided, churches have continued to decline and evil in society has continued to increase. The renewal of the churches has proved little more than cosmetic and has had no great impact on political and social structures. In other places, by contrast, the Charismatic Movement is still quite young and vibrant, particularly in parts of Europe, both east and west, and all over Asia.

It is not always called by that name today. Many new churches and ministries have been birthed out of it and so the nomenclature varies from place to place. Some of these new ministries are proving very powerful all around the globe, such as *Youth with a Mission* (YWAM), *Teen Challenge* (David Wilkerson), *Christ for the Nations International* (Dallas), *Vineyard Ministries International* (John Wimber), *Christ for all Nations* (Reinhard Bonnke), *Word of Life* (Ulf Ekman, Sweden), *Rhema* (Kenneth Hagin), *Kingdom Faith* (Colin Urquhart, England) and so forth. There are many other independent ministries, indeed a seemingly limitless proliferation of them, some better known than others, some local, some national, some international; some evangelistic, some providing training, some pastoral care. But all of them have a basically pentecostal/charismatic framework for belief and action, and through them a great deal of encouraging growth is indeed taking place. Some of them have generated new movements that their followers and adherents have called by new names, as if they embodied the next and most important thing the Spirit is doing in our time, for example, the Restoration, Third Wave and Faith Movements. These new movements have tended to emphasise the restoring or fostering of some particular aspect of Christian witness or ministry in the church, such as healing, faith, revival, prophecy, five-fold ministry, prosperity, deliverance, and the like. So much have these ministries and movements grown in recent years that many now talk about our day as the Post-Charismatic Era.

Even more impressive than all this, however, is the phenomenal, almost spontaneous, world-wide growth of Christianity through continuing revival.

*Continuing World-wide Revival*

Pentecostalism has revival in its background and was itself birthed in revival. The spark that ignited the flame was struck in Wales in 1904 and in Los Angeles in 1906 and since then Pentecostalism has always flourished best in revival settings. The very expectation expressed by the early pioneers of a further wave or rain after the first at the beginning of the century attests to that fact. Even more, the course of history itself has confirmed it to be so.

The first flowering was mainly before the Second World War, when Pentecostalism established itself in many countries, sometimes in small ways through hard-working evangelists, as in Europe, for example, and at other times in massive ways through revival visitations, as in South America (particularly Brazil), or East Africa (in 1935 in Rwanda, Burundi, Uganda, Kenya), but by far the most phenomenal growth has been in the latter half of the twentieth century, since about 1950.

One of the early tremors of this second wave was witnessed in 1949-52 on the Island of Lewis, in the Outer Hebrides, off the West of Scotland, where a local revival among the small communities of Gaelic-speaking Presbyterians caught the attention of many in Britain and set them praying again. This was not a Pentecostal revival, but more in the tradition of Wesley or Finney, though the heart of the *Faith Mission* evangelist who enabled it (Duncan Campbell) and of the people who were touched by it was in many ways much the same.

Shortly after that, but not in any way connected, in the early 1950s, revival broke out in Argentina through the work of an American Assemblies of God pastor, Edward Miller. (Paradoxically his enthusiasm for the revival got him and his followers expelled from the Assemblies!) This revival peaked in 1954 when Tommy Hicks, an American evangelist, filled the 110,000 seat Huracane Football Stadium daily for two months. Up to that time evangelical Christianity had struggled to maintain a meagre existence in Argentina, but since then revival has broken again in the nation and today many living Pentecostal/Charismatic churches count their membership in thousands and tens of thousands, some more than a hundred thousand.

Similar stories can be told about other South and Central American countries besides Brazil and Argentina, such as Bolivia, Peru, Chile and Guatemala. In 1900, it is estimated, there were about 50,000 Evangelicals in the whole of Latin America. Today the estimate is well over 100 million. These figures bear comparison with those for Africa, where in 1900 only two per cent of Africans were Christians at all and today between forty and fifty per cent are. Again most of the growth has been Pentecostal or related, and much of it has come through revival moves.

In the East there have been waves of revival in Korea throughout the century, and today the largest churches in the world are found there. Particularly famous is the massive Yoido Full Gospel Church of Seoul founded and pastored by Yonggi Cho. Similar stirrings are now reported in Thailand; Singapore has seen a wonderful move of renewal and evangelism in recent years; since 1965 a powerful revival has been running in Indonesia; the small state of Nagaland in northern India is today almost a hundred per cent evangelical Christian, about half of that Charismatic, and rapidly extending its influence into surrounding states and countries, such as Assam and north Burma; Nepal has witnessed some wonderful church growth since restrictions against the gospel were eased in 1990. And so we could go on, from country to country. Of course there are many places where the church still struggles for its very existence, let alone for growth, but the overall picture is more than encouraging.

Probably the most exciting revival story of all comes from China. It is estimated that there were about a million Christians there altogether in the 1940s, but after Mao came to power in 1949 all missionaries were expelled and most of the churches were closed, apart from one or two in the major cities that were kept open to impress foreign diplomats and visitors. As Mao's cultural revolution progressed, the persecution intensified and living Christianity was forced underground. Then in 1966 the government set itself to annihilate the underground church altogether, and many began to fear that the persecution and massacre had obliterated Christianity from the nation. However, during those later years the church was still growing underground, despite the terrible persecution. After Mao's death in 1979, the political mood changed and now an indigenous church has emerged that is running with phenomenal revival power. Today it is estimated, as far as that is possible in China, that there are probably over one hundred million Christians in that vast nation, most of them in unregistered charismatic House Churches that are aggressively gathering new converts into the kingdom of God at a phenomenal rate, one statistic says at about two and a half thousand converts a day. The stories of sacrificial dedication and courage among the evangelists and leaders of this revival make some of the most inspiring and faith-building reading in our day.

Also most exciting are some of the recent, though still small, stirrings in Orthodox and Islamic contexts, both of them historically very difficult for revival to influence. Orthodoxy is a religion of tradition in which anything new is instantly suspect. Nevertheless, since the early 1970s, an American Orthodox priest, Eusebius Stephanou, though he has been bitterly opposed, has sought to foster renewal in the Church. Today, there is a lively revival church in Egypt led by a former Orthodox monk extending its witness to other Arab-speaking countries, and Spirit-filled missionaries are at work among Greeks, Iranians and other peoples who have known little else besides Orthodoxy, often in an Islamic environment.

Christian witness is prohibited in Islamic countries, sometimes with severe legal penalties attached. That in itself reduces the potential for Christian growth instantly, but on top of that many Islamic states have become aggressive in seeking to expand their own faith, which they are doing quite successfully in many parts of the world. Nevertheless, in some strong Islamic areas the gospel is making a lively impact. There are vibrant and rapidly growing churches in Malaysia, some of them with memberships of thousands. The bulk of the population of Indonesia is Muslim, in name at any rate, but revival there has left an indisputable mark. In 1900 less than two per cent of the total population was Christian; today the figures estimated range between eleven and twenty per cent. In some parts of Africa the church is making excellent progress among Muslims in a number of areas. In other places, of course, we still wait to see any initial movement of new life in the churches, many of them struggling for their very existence under oppressive political governments.

Revival continues to be a spreading phenomenon. Reports keep coming in from all over the globe. There are new awakenings taking place among Christians in atheistic states, communist countries, Hindu societies, tribal communities, and Islamic lands. The world may be raising its satanic horns, but the Church of Christ is also on the move. And most of this revival growth is prophetic/charismatic/pentecostal in nature. It seems that the original Keswick vision of a latter-day, pentecostal outpouring of the Spirit to enable a final thrust of world evangelisation before the coming of Christ was not far off the mark!

*Britain in the 1990s—first tremors of Revival?*

Something fresh and new has been stirring in Britain as well—so new, indeed, and so different, that it has generated the same enthusiasms, debates and criticisms as attended most earlier prophetic and revival moves of the Spirit. In 1994, in many churches of varied traditions, mostly, though not exclusively, those already touched by Charismatic renewal, pastors, leaders and lay people alike have experienced convulsive laughter and such uncontrollable bodily movements as would have graced any French Prophet meeting. Scenes not unlike those reported in the early 1800s at Cane Ridge, Kentucky, have been witnessed in churches on Sundays, as well as at mid-week meetings and home groups, such as falling, shaking, jerking, shouting, weeping, laughing. People have spoken about being drunk in the Spirit, so utterly so that they sometimes have had to be physically carried home after meetings. These outward manifestations are so reminiscent of revival scenes in other times, that the question they raised at the start was whether they indicated the birthing of a new revival move in Britain, one that would call the nation back to Christ. Not so, it seems, for two years later the fire was already subsiding.

What is certainly clear is that the Lord's people were thoroughly refreshed by it all. After the depression of the later '80s, when it seemed to many that the enthusiastic hopes of the early Charismatics were not going to be fulfilled and statisticians were still gloomily recording declining numbers in the mainline congregations, this new move proved welcome indeed, particularly among leaders, who had to carry the load of the depression more than anyone else. The laughter may have subsided, but the atmosphere in the churches is quite different today.

All this, of course, is not unrelated to what has gone before. Since the Charismatic Movement came to Britain, many new things have been birthed in the Christian scene, all of which have helped to prepare the way for what God is doing now and is about to do further. Some denominational churches have found a new lease of life, Pentecostals have been recapturing the life their founding fathers once knew, many Catholics have discovered it for the first time, Evangelicals have been stirred to take more positive action, hundreds of new churches have been birthed, Black Pentecostals have raised their profile massively. Wimber's teaching, as well as birthing Vineyard churches, has impacted thousands of others with encouragement to see evidence of the power of God at work, faith teachers have raised the expectancy level of Christians everywhere, Restorationists have taught us to look for a good future for the church, healing evangelists have continued to exhort us to hope for the miraculous and, of course, the millennialist voice has been far from silent, constantly reminding us that these are urgent times in which we live.

A lively enthusiasm has been sustained among young people, generating many new ventures in youth evangelism, particularly notable being the work of Youth With A Mission. In the professional community, the Full Gospel Businessmen's Fellowship International has continued to maintain its wholesome witness. We could go on and on, for the list is long. A mere glance at the advertisements on the back pages of any Pentecostal or Charismatic magazine tells an instant story of the many who have given themselves and their livelihoods to support the work of the gospel in this nation. Para-church organisations have multiplied considerably in our time.

But it is not only institutions that testify to a change; a new atmosphere has also been emerging among believers. Of that there are many evident barometers. New songs abound, many full of purposeful praise, others quite militant, though there are still plenty that are dreamy and introverted. Bible weeks and family camps have continued to prove increasingly popular, attended by thousands of Christians every summer. Particularly spectacular is the record of Spring Harvest, which started in 1979 with 3,000 people attending and now has to run over nine weeks at four sites to accommodate the 70,000 that attend it. Similarly indicative of today's mood is the annual March for Jesus. The first march was held in London in 1987, supported by about 2,000, by 1990 some 250,000 were marching all over the country, by 1994 some 10 to 12 million marched all round the world.

What is equally telling is that all of this has been relatively well received among the national presses and broadcasting companies. Reporting has been generally very favourable, which was particularly striking in their accounts of the laughter and attendant blessings. When we think of how the shaking that accompanied Fox's preaching was received, or how the French Prophets were publicly mocked in the puppet shows, or how 'enthusiasm' has been despised by influential Christian writers even in recent times, the public reception of Christian witness today is little short of miraculous. And all this is starting to make an impact in the political arena. Members of Parliament who are Christian are becoming less afraid to express their stance, and some of them have begun to meet for informal prayer. Businessmen give up lunch breaks to attend prayer meetings and prayer break-fasts are multiplying. There is an overall change in the atmosphere of the nation with respect to the believing Church.

This has not come without a great deal of prayer, but even that is itself a barometer of the spiritual climate among Christians. Intercessors for Britain, Prayer for Revival, the Lydia Fellowship, and other praying organisations have been encouraging their members to call out to God for revival in this nation. Prayer gatherings for revival have been held in many places, the largest being in the National Exhibition Centre in Birmingham. Prophetic voices have been heralding and proclaiming its coming for several years now, outstanding among them being that of Colin Urquhart. In 1990 John Wimber and Paul Cain caused quite a stir by forecasting that first tokens of revival would be released in England that autumn. Others have argued that there must first be judgment, and considerable debate has been aroused over the issue. But all of that has simply increased the longing in the hearts of the Lord's people for a new move of God in our time.

Meanwhile the work of evangelism has not slacked, but rather intensified. The churches announced that the 1990s would be a decade of evangelism, which set many discussing what to do, others praying and others taking action. Among the evangelistic highlights that followed were the Morris Cerullo missions in Earls Court, London, and the Minus-to-Plus initiative co-ordinated by the Reinhard Bonnke organisation. As with most evangelistic ventures, it is difficult to assess results until long after, but what has certainly become manifest is that there has been a rising longing in the hearts of Christians to see God move powerfully again in our time and to reap a harvest.

There is much more that could be told, and certainly plenty that could be debated about or criticised in the majority of the ministries and tendencies just listed. Some of them have even been accused of heretical leanings, but the very fact that they are there exerting the degree of influence they do is witness enough that a spiritual fire has been laid and arranged over the past twenty or thirty years. It is already smouldering, but also still waiting for the flame that will set it ablaze. Though so much has happened, and there has been much fruit from it, the longed for revival has still not come. Violence, lawlessness, immorality, superstition, paganism and atheism have continued to increase, and overall the church has not yet made the massive inroad into society that is needed to turn the tide in its favour. The general mood has, therefore, continued to be one of hardness and depression, though interlaced with increasing hope among many Christians.

*'The Toronto Blessing' or 'The Refreshing'*

The news broke on the nation in both the religious and the secular presses in the middle of June, 1994. They reported astounding scenes in highly respectable churches, of people convulsed with near hysterical laughter, weeping uncontrollably, shaking violently, falling and writhing on the floor. And it was all traced back to a small Vineyard fellowship about a hundred yards from the end of the runway at Toronto Airport in Canada, where pastors and people from England had been going to 'get the blessing' (as they put it) and bring it home to their congregations.

It started at a conference in the Airport Vineyard in January, 1994, led by its own pastor, John Arnott, and the pastor of another Vineyard fellowship in St. Louis, Randy Clark. Arnott had been blessed two months earlier at a conference in Argentina where Claudio Freidzon, an Assemblies of God pastor, had prayed for him. Both Arnott and Freidzon had been ministered to a year earlier by the American evangelist, Benny Hinn, and that had made an immense difference to Freidzon in particular. Meantime, Randy Clark had been receiving ministry from Rodney Howard-Browne, a South African evangelist, who tells that he has been operating with an anointing of joy and laughter since 1989, though only in full flood since he moved his ministry to the United States in 1993.

Laughter was therefore already reported in South Africa and the United States in 1993. Australia also was hit by it in the spring of 1993, but none of that touched Britain significantly until after the January '94 conference in Toronto turned the Airport Vineyard into a kind of Azusa Street, a centre of pilgrimage from which thousands returned to their churches, not only in Britain, but also in Europe and elsewhere, taking 'the blessing' with them.

The movement has no particular leaders. Toronto remained the main centre throughout 1994 and '95, and so the blessing is commonly referred to as 'the Toronto Blessing', though it is equally available in many local churches. The Toronto pastors travelled extensively speaking and ministering at conferences, as also did Rodney Howard-Browne and the several from Argentina. But others were also used widely in the same national and international ministry. It operated without central administration, headquarters, journal, or central fund. It was primarily a move of the Spirit sweeping through churches wherever Christians were open to receive it. It never permitted leaders to loom large, because they too were humbled by the Spirit's touch. Not many can entertain illusions of personal grandeur when they are spending much of their time laughing and rolling on the floor, quite unable to preach or hold centre-stage, seeming utterly foolish in the eyes of those that might otherwise idolise them!

The phenomenon quickly became world-wide, not just American, Canadian and British. Though it only affected a small proportion of the churches, its influence became amazingly extensive. At first it was thought this might be the flame that would set ablaze the bonfire laid throughout the century, but now it is remembered as simply a 'refreshing' for the saints. Some have compared it with past revivals, but in actual fact there is nothing quite comparable in the history of revival. Agitations and fallings in the revivals of the past have tended to be linked with conviction of sin, and laughter with release into the knowledge of forgiveness and salvation, all for the most part related to conversion and new birth. By contrast, those touched in this move were mainly people who were already born again, and what they experienced was mainly a refreshment of faith and renewal of spirit, though, of course, as in any move of God, significant numbers were also born into the kingdom for the first time as well.

Perhaps it is best to compare what happened with some of the prophetic movements we have studied. These were mostly moves of the Spirit among the Lord's people, equipping them for the prophetic task of building up the church and spearheading the work of evangelism into the heart of pagan society. Probably the closest parallels are found among the French Prophets, which is one of the reasons why our study of them was a little more detailed than of any other movement. They too delighted in strong awarenesses of the divine presence and in the resulting bodily manifestations, and their testimonies often sound very similar to those from Toronto. There are, of course, many differences, but it is worth remembering the lessons they had to learn so that some of the pitfalls may be avoided and some of the positive benefits may remain.

To counter the resurgent paganism of our times some such strengthening has been urgently needed in the churches. Thanks to the preparatory work done by Pentecostals and Charismatics, the spiritual gifts have been able to operate quite freely in these recent moves. Visions, revelations, tongues, prophecies, healings, miracles and the like are as much part of it all as are the laughings and the bodily movements. The context is unquestionably prophetic. We must therefore pray that the testimony will continue to be to the Lordship of Jesus Christ, for 'the testimony of Jesus is the spirit of prophecy (Rev. 19:10). If that testimony ever ceases to be central, the movement will cease to be prophetic in the Biblical sense.

Perhaps now is the time when we should take seriously, more so than ever before, the lessons to be learned from the record of prophetic movements of the past. The Lord's blessing is clear enough, but the hazards are still there, as dangerous as ever. It is therefore urgent that we return to the Bible, study its prophetic thrust, and take the word more earnestly to heart than ever before. If God is pouring out his Spirit anew, we should study his ways afresh, and learn to live by them.

One very recent, encouraging development should be mentioned here, one that contains within itself the potential and hope for co-ordinating the very diverse prophetic and pentecostal voices that surround us, thus enabling a more united approach to the revival needs of the twenty-first century. For most of the past thousand years prophetically minded Christians have prayed for a restoration of apostles to the Church. That has led to the formation of a number of Apostolic churches and movements, none of which have survived the vicissitudes of history until recently.

Today, by contrast, we watch the Lord raising up apostolic ministries all over the world. In recent years a number of the apostles involved have begun meeting and consulting with each other, so that something of an apostolic network has been developing. We must pray that this will not end in division and further confusion, but will somehow bring a sense of co-ordination and coherence to the prophetic voice, so that the Lord's latter-day prophets can stand united in the battle of faith in which they are presently engaged.

# 31
# Pentecost and History

How should we view the whole sweep of Christian history now? Something momentous is clearly happening in our day, something quite unparalleled in the history of Christianity. So what does it all mean? What is God doing with his world through the Church?

*Popular Pentecostal and Charismatic Views of History*

One of the simplest understandings of history expressed in Pentecostal and Charismatic circles says that God blessed the Church with the fullness of the Holy Spirit in New Testament times enabling its rapid growth through the Roman Empire, and that that blessing was quickly lost, but is now at last being restored enabling the present rapid growth through the rest of the world. A basic form of Latter Rain teaching encapsulates this view well. The main problem with it is that it assumes that virtually the whole of history between the first century and the twentieth is one great hiatus, which, as we have seen, is clearly not correct at all.

A more common view today is a modification of this one, a developed form of Latter Rain teaching that speaks of preliminary showers before the second great outpouring, a view that is espoused in Restoration circles. It sees the first-century pentecostal blessing being slowly eroded and finally lost soon after the time of Constantine, the medieval period right down to the Reformation being one long dark age for the Church, and then the recovery starting gradually and progressing with increasing rapidity until it has reached full flood today. In this scheme the sixteenth and seventeenth centuries saw the recovery of faith and the Bible, with the invention of the printing press and the establishment of Protestantism, the eighteenth and nineteenth centuries restored revival, mission, evangelism, eschatological hope, holiness and the like, and the twentieth century restored Pentecost and everything that followed from it, very much 'as at the beginning'. This view is very popular, but it is also deficient, for, again as we have seen, the Middle Ages was far from devoid of lively Christian witness.

A third view still sometimes encountered is the more Dispensational one of the three ages: the age of the Father or Israel, which was dominated by the systems of the law; the age of the Son or the Church which, though a time of grace, has been regulated by intermingled doctrine and tradition; and the age of the Spirit, which is characterised by the outpouring of prophetic, pentecostal anointing on the latter-day Church of God. This view has been around for a long time. We met it in Montanism, in the teaching of Joachim of Fiore, among the Amalricians and the Zwickau Prophets, and echoes of it in other movements, such as the French Prophets and the Shakers. It implies that God is doing 'a new thing', something quite new, and that this is a new age different from any before, the last in history, in which the birthing of a new Church, the end-time Church of the Spirit, marks the prelude to Christ's return. Though there are echoes of this view in both circles, there is more of a sense of it among Pentecostals than among Charismatics. The expectation of a premillennial outpouring of the Spirit inherited by Pentecostals from the nineteenth century is broadly in harmony with it, since that relates primarily to the end stage of the threefold process, not the full sweep of earlier church history. The main problem with it, however, is that it takes little account of the earlier, medieval and reformation movements which also witnessed the Spirit's action and knew of the same expectation.

### *The Need for a More Comprehensive Approach*

To explain the facts as we have studied them a different approach is needed altogether. In this book we have detected a persistent flow of inspired activity, at times increased in power, at others diminished, but regularly traceable. Sometimes it was little more than a longing. At other times it burst forth only to be quenched. Occasionally it found fuller expression for a period and destroyed itself through its own folly. Latterly it has blossomed and flourished. But mostly it has been there somewhere, and our main purpose here has been to trace its stream. However, in doing so it has never been sufficient to write a simple account of the movements we have sought to study, but we have also had to look at the wider history of the Church, and beyond that at the even wider history of Europe and the rest of the world. For obvious reasons it has not been possible to treat all three streams as exhaustively as some might like us to do, but the fact that we have had to do so at all is in itself indicative. Some have written histories of the Church without too much reference to the affairs of the world, others have written secular histories with little reference to the affairs of the Church. It is perfectly possible to write a history of spiritual movements in a similar way but, as we have seen, the three are quite intricately intertwined. That observation itself is one important key to understanding the ways of God's working by his Spirit.

Part of the problem with the popular Pentecostal views is that they turn a blind eye on vast tracts of Christian history, treating them as if they had never happened, or at the very least as if wishing they never had. But the fact is that they did. To dismiss them as aberrations not worthy of much notice is to falsify history and create a distortion. G.K. Chesterton once commented,

> 'To write history and hate Rome, both pagan and Papal, is practically to hate nearly everything that has happened. It comes near to hating humanity.'[366]

We cannot, without imbalance, dismiss secular or pagan history, nor equally ecclesiastical history, whether Papal or otherwise, as if unrelated to the seemingly more enlightened understanding of the prophetic Church. Secular history and church history provide the context for the prophetic, which cannot therefore be understood properly unless related to them. The equivalent folly would be to read the stories of Elijah and Elisha without any reference to the paganism of Ahab and Jezebel, or to the wars between Aram and Israel, or again to tell of Hezekiah's or Josiah's reformations without reference to either the paganism of their respective fathers, or the backdrop of Assyrian imperialism. The biblical authors themselves do not make that mistake; nor must we. To them the pagan and political contexts are as important as the revivals necessitated by them.

### *Interaction of the Secular, the Ecclesiastical and the Prophetic*

Christianity is a historical faith. When God acts through men of the Spirit, he generally does so in a context of social decadence or deviant religion. Pentecostal history is not just about evangelical reformers and prophetic preachers, but about the ebb and flow of faith among fallen men in a fallen world that God has purposed to redeem from its folly. Prophets are, as we have seen over and over again, God's shock-troops for revival and for bringing in the Church of the Spirit. If pentecostal, charismatic Christians are not functioning to that end, then they have either ceased to be, or else

366. G.K. Chesterton, *St. Francis of Assisi*, Doubleday, 1924, p. 24.

they never were, prophets in the succession of their biblical precursors. One of the clear evidences that a prophetic move is of God is its militancy for true, living faith. Pentecostal, prophetic Christianity is precisely to do with revival—awakening both the Lord's people and their secular environment to the things of God, combating the powers of both religiosity and paganism, redeeming both the ecclesiastical and the profane. History shows us clearly enough what happens when the prophetic fire goes out among the faithful—Rome falls to Gothic tribesmen and its churches to Islamic invaders, theologians give way to rationalists and churchmen to unbelieving, multi-faith philosophers.

But then God raises up his men to the Spirit once again to perform their aggressive works—ascetic and mystical monks to rescue medieval hoards from pagan darkness, Bible preaching reformers to restore faith amid superstitious blindness, revival evangelists to stir great awakenings among somnolent churchmen, pentecostal pioneers to establish spiritual works in a world dominated by liberal rationalism. The expressions may vary from age to age, but there is a spiritual heart-longing that is much the same each time.

If we accept that the story of the Church in Europe in Roman Imperial times and in the Middle Ages is part of God's universal plan and purpose and therefore not unimportant in the history of prophetic Christianity, a different appreciation of the place of Pentecost in the total history of the Church begins to emerge.

*The History of Paganism and the Catholic Church*

Let us first consider briefly the history of paganism and the Church. Since earliest times the two have been at war with each other. It is the express purpose of the Church to win back the world from the power of Satan and all the other gods that are seen as his demonic lackeys, and so to establish the reign of God's kingdom on earth. In the first centuries the Church successfully invaded the enemy occupied territories of Greek and Roman paganism, establishing kingdom bases everywhere in the civilised world of the time. Despite much persecution, Christianity slowly won the battle and by the fourth century had conquered the Roman political machine. The old gods of the empire then had to bow out before the rule of Christ.

To be sure, a measure of pagan influence crept into the Church, but on the whole it was the name of Jesus, not Jupiter, that dominated the later years of the Empire. The inroads of paganism in the Dark Ages, when the heathen tribesmen of the north plundered and pillaged, in the long run proved no more than a temporary, albeit brutal and dangerous, setback in the battle, from which the Church emerged triumphant in the later Middle Ages. The war to settle who ruled in Europe was long and often bitter, but by the time of the Crusades, the old gods of Graeco-Roman times and the more recent gods of Germanic and Norse invaders were little more than a faded memory of the past. Christ and his Church reigned supreme.

The system may have been far from perfect. The voices of dissent were many, not all of them as heretical as the authorities regularly supposed, but often rightly expressing a deep yearning for a purer Church. We may want to condemn the hierarchy for silencing them as it did, but its policing methods also very effectively restrained paganism. The late medieval church may be criticised for its corruption and ruthless methods, but still it held Europe for Christ. The power of paganism had been very effectively broken and the Church unquestionably reigned.

*The History of Enlightenment and the Reformation Church*

The new and exciting day that dawned with the Renaissance turned the tables of power. Historians commonly tell how Europe shook itself loose from the shackles of the medieval Church, discovered the liberty that learning and culture brought, and then progressed into the fullness of modern civilisation. Renaissance art, architecture, literature and music all reflect this new freedom and release from the stiffness of the medieval Church.

All of that, however, was gained at a cost. The Renaissance was not just a breaking free, but at root a resurgence of paganism. Its foundation was a revival of interest in the literatures of ancient Greece and Rome, which brought with it a renewed interest in the old gods and their fables, and a fascination with their pre-Christian cultures. The myths of Apollo and Aphrodite, of Mars and Venus, soon took their place alongside the stories of Jesus and the Apostles in the classroom, while the writings of Homer and Virgil were studied as assiduously as those of Isaiah and John. The battle for the mind of European man was being waged once more.

After the Reformation the Church no longer had a united voice, and soon other new and persuasive voices were being heard, uttering their reasonable philosophies, impressing men to turn away from God, in much the same way as the serpent once deceived Eve. The process has accelerated with time, from the scepticism of Hume and Descartes, to the deism of Rousseau and Voltaire, and then the atheism of Marx and Nietzsche. Rationalists, socialists, liberals, humanists, atheists and many others have progressively dethroned

God and elevated man, but that has not led to his satisfaction. Rather the converse, for man cannot be his own answer. He is far too feeble and helpless. Even the ancient pagans had learned that, for when they grew tired of their immoral and capricious gods, they sought to regulate their own lives by their home-spun philosophies, but these had also failed to satisfy, and so they turned to Christ.

In our own day the process has been reversed and the pendulum has swung right back to its ancient position. The Renaissance asserted the dignity of man, but that myth has been totally exploded by the sheer inhumanity of the wars of the twentieth century and the many continuing brutalities of modern society. Having jettisoned Christianity, enlightened European man has had nothing to fall back on except the paganism he once rejected in favour of faith. Today the ancient gods are worshipped again. Spiritualism, oriental religion, the occult, with all their attendant immorality, violence and decadence, have broken loose in our midst. Paganism flourishes once more, as never since ancient Roman times. Men talk about our Post-Christian Era, or a New Age, and sadly that is how it seems to be. The verdict is plain. The Reformation Churches have proved far less effective in our time in this battle for the faith than the old Catholic Church was in the Middle Ages.

But God still has the answer, and to see what that is we must turn again to the prophets.

*The Place of the Prophets in the Battle of Faith*

Prophets have always been at the sharp edge of this battle. Ever since Samuel called Israel back out of Canaanite paganism (1 Sam. 7) and Nathan warned David against forsaking God's call in favour of a religious building project (2 Sam. 7), the battle has been fought mainly on two fronts, against alternative faiths or philosophies and against ecclesiastical religiosity. Elijah's confrontations with the prophets of Baal, or Ezekiel's denunciations of idolatry in the temple, epitomise the first, Amos' clash with the priest at Bethel, or Jeremiah's with the authorities in Jerusalem, the second.

By Jesus' day the pagan gods had been driven from Judaism, but he still had to battle on two fronts, against the theological systematisations of the scribes and the religious establishment of the Pharisees.

When the Church moved out into the Gentile world, the battle with other faiths and philosophies was resumed with vigour. The witness of the New Testament is that it was engaged, 'not with wise and persuasive words, but with a demonstration of the Spirit's power, so that your faith might not rest on men's wisdom, but on God's power' (1 Cor. 2:4-5). But then the early Christians were prophets too.

That, of course, as in Old Testament times, brought them into conflict with the ecclesiastically minded, the Pharisaic party within their own ranks, as well as in Judaism. The choice was then to fight or to compromise. Paul chose to fight, others to compromise, and sadly over the centuries that followed the easier path was the one taken by the majority. Religious practice became stereotyped and hedged around with rules and traditions of men, and the faith was interpreted in terms of the Greek philosophical context of the time, particularly the Platonism of Alexandria. Slowly but steadily, the prophetic fire dwindled, though it never properly died. There were always the enthusiasts, though increasingly even they had to operate within the context of the structured Church and its Neo-Platonic world view.

The more prophetically inclined sought refuge in the desert and then in the monasteries. Out of them came the missionaries and evangelists that conquered Europe for Christ in the Dark Ages. Then followed another phase of compromise, when the Church adopted the new Aristotelian logic of the later Middle Ages.

Whenever the Church has let go of the supernatural dimension of its prophetic faith and compromised with paganism or its philosophies, it has weakened, and with it the society it has influenced. Hence it was a fairly easy matter for the barbarian hordes to conquer sickly Rome, for Islam to overrun the effete eastern and southern Mediterranean nations, and for the Reformation to overtake the governments of northern Europe weary of their corrupt religious advisers. By contrast, whenever prophetic men, or men with a prophetic heart, have risen up, so also has the church and after it the state, as in the first centuries, in the dark ages, and at the Reformation.

It is not always right, however, to think of these things happening in alternating waves and troughs of revival and decline, for sometimes the two processes have been simultaneous, as in the days of Augustine, Francis, Wycliffe and Hus. In fact, the medieval Church, even though it constantly suppressed its prophets, was much more open to the supernatural than the Reformation churches have been. It is probably this basic openness that has enabled Catholics to adopt the charismatic dimension so readily today. Protestants tend to have greater intellectual barriers to overcome. If anything, modern Pentecostalism could be described as a movement among the

Reformation churches seeking to recapture the supernatural that got lost from among them after the sixteenth century.

Anyhow, the patterns are clear enough, and they have continued much the same in post-Reformation times as before.

*The Prophets and Modern Ecclesiasticism, Rationalism and Paganism*

The reformed churches in the main rejected the prophetic way in favour of the doctrinal and the moral which, though biblically founded, came to be set in the context of Enlightenment rationalism. The result was academic aridity and ethical legalism in the church. The situation was exacerbated as theological correctness and moral uprightness became the acknowledged tokens of respectability—and hence a source of pride. But God continued to preserve the Spirit's witness through men like Fox, Spener, Zinzendorf, Edwards and Wesley who, along with others like them, blazed the revival trail for God in their day. Some of these, however, were themselves shy of anything too overtly prophetic, and so the movements they spawned also fell into compromise and eventually ran dry.

Then the new rationalism became stronger, invading the church itself, so that its theological system became more and more liberal and unbelieving. But at the same time the voices of the prophets and the prophetically inclined grew correspondingly stronger. God was raising up his army to wage war against the forces of compromise ranged against the faith.

God's timings are highly instructive. While the French Revolutionaries were dethroning God and the Church, Protestants were beginning to send out their missionaries. As Napoleon carried the new socialism through Europe, America was experiencing waves of revival visitation. In the year that Darwin published his *Origin of the Species,* releasing a furore of debate in the churches, only eleven years after the *Communist Manifesto* appeared, releasing a wave of revolutions in Europe, one of the greatest ever world-wide awakenings started almost spontaneously in America and Ireland. While Marxist atheism was spreading its tentacles over Europe declaring God obsolete, he was sending wave after wave of revival into many parts of the world, particularly in America and Britain. As liberalism became more entrenched in our universities and colleges, denying the supernatural workings of God in our time, Pentecostalism was coming to birth in another flurry of revival attended by many miraculous signs and wonders. And as liberals have continued to promote their compromising theologies, flirting not only with rationalism but also with other religions, and as their churches have correspondingly declined throughout the twentieth century, the prophetic, pentecostal church has been growing more phenomenally than ever before in history.

The strange thing is that by and large the two sides seem to be unaware of each other's existence. While philosophers argue that God is dead, he shows his miraculous power daily, but the philosophers seem quite oblivious to the fact, and if they encounter it, they explain it away. Similarly, while evangelical churchmen argue to defend the faith, God is constantly showing that he can defend his own reputation far better than they can by raising up another prophetic ministry or generating another revival. And strangely the evangelical church very often refuses to recognise it. While many Christians argue much and achieve little, God pours out his Spirit on his prophets and their churches grow wonderfully.

And the more our cultured society rushes headlong into paganism, inter-faith, rationalism, superstition and the occult, so the more does God pour out his Spirit and send forth his prophets.

*The Challenges Confronting the Prophets of Today*

Surely the message is clear. Christian history is essentially the story of the Church doing battle with paganism. Time and again it has lost ground when it has let go of the supernatural, prophetic dimension and become religious, doctrinaire or rationalistic. But then God has raised up a new generation of prophetical men working for a revival of faith and the lost territory has been regained. Sadly, the Church itself has turned against its prophets, betrayed them, sought to control them and suppressed them. And every time that has happened, the Church has sold itself to paganism. The greatest enemies of the prophets and of the work of God itself have always been compromising churchmen and Christian Pharisees. So it has been since the time of Jesus himself, and before (cp. Matt. 23:29-34,37).

However, God keeps on sending his prophets, and the more they rise up, the more paganism is defeated. The future of Christianity lies in the hands of the prophetic Church. That is how it has always been, and how it always will be. That is why Jesus came to make his disciples prophets in the first place. It is God's way.

But it is not ours, for ours is to seek favour with men by explaining ourselves to them in their own terms, which leads inevitably to the erosion of faith and thence directly, whether through rationalism or ecclesiasticism, into paganism and aridity. God's way is entirely different: to wash us of our sins through the blood of Jesus by faith (not reason, doctrine, or religious ritual), and send us out equipped with his Spirit by faith, to speak his creative, prophetic word of life by faith, calling men out of the immorality of paganism that destroys them, the delusion of liberalism that erodes their hope, and the Pharisaism that enslaves them in legalism, into the full life that faith in Christ can give, through the working of the Spirit of God alone.

Ours is no longer a day for compromise. The prophetic way is different from man's way, so much so that it seems strange to many. That is why we may be mocked by the public, as were the French Prophets in England, or excluded from the churches, as Fox, Irving and Seymour were in their times, or violently persecuted, like the men of Bourges and the Amalricians, or rejected by the very evangelical church leaders we support and admire, as the Zwickau Prophets were by Luther. So let it be. We must not allow such things to turn us from the battle we wage for Christ and the gospel.

The Lordship of Jesus Christ will again be established in Europe. There will surely be a cost, though mainly to our pride, which will smart when our friends and neighbours say jeeringly of us, 'Is Saul also among the prophets?' That we must carry, for in the end we shall hear a different voice say, 'Well done, good and faithful servant! You have been faithful with a few things; I will put you in charge of many things. Come and share your master's happiness!' (Matt. 25:21)

Much of our hesitation and compromise results from fear. Perpetually we question, 'Who will win?' To the man of faith the issue is not in doubt. History is being made by today's prophets. The call goes forth loud and clear: Rise up, O Prophets of the Lord. As in the days of Deborah, the battle is again being waged in the heights of the field (Judg. 5:18). The hour of victory is at hand, but let us make sure that in the muster roll afterwards our names are numbered with those who came out with the armies of heaven.

As we go, let us heed the lessons of history and not end in folly, like so many prophetic movements of the past. This is a day for sending men out to the field, yes, but not untrained in the Word of God and sound doctrine, lest they run into excess and strange heresy. This is a day for evangelism and revival, yes, but not without strong support from the prophetic home church, lest it all fall for lack of reinforcement and end in despair. This is a day for uncompromising warfare against the rising forces of darkness, but not without the encouragement and discernment of good prophetic friends and leaders, lest we fall into the immoral snares of Satan ourselves. This is a day for the prophets of the Lord to stand united, as in the earliest church in Jerusalem, lest we fall into the trap of schism and division like so many prophets before us and so lose all we shall have fought to gain. This is a time for right perception of the flow of history, that the prophets are indeed God's front-line fighters in the work of world-wide revival, preparing his Church of the Spirit for the last ingathering before the return of Christ. Without such a perspective we can all too quickly become wearied and find ourselves returning to the comfortable pew of the lifeless church.

Pentecost is not just an event of the ancient past, or a nice option for those who like that sort of thing. It is of the very essence of the purpose of God in the work of redemption to equip his saint for war. It lies at the heart of revival, so much so that for countless millions today pentecostal and revival Christianity are one and the same thing. In the Middle Ages men like Joachim dreamed about the coming of the Church of the Spirit, many others sought to establish it, yet others, like the Seekers in Puritan England, longed profoundly for it. A few found something of it, but their movements were crushed in infancy by the Church or the state. Today the child is well and truly birthed and is now growing towards a measure of maturity. Pentecost has now a stronger place in the church than ever, and in times to come, judging by present trends, will have a yet greater place. The battle is certainly not over, but the prophetic Church of the Spirit is alive and vibrant.

### *And in the End*

End-time awareness has been a constant mark of prophecy ever since Old Testament times, but today there is something different. Montanus, Joachim, Storch, Ann Lee, Irving, and most other prophetic leaders have believed that their church was somehow connected with the ushering in of the end. That has resulted in them encouraging perfectionist attitudes and evangelistic activity. The precise interpretation of the stages of history has varied from movement to movement, with Darbyite premillennialism or a latter rain theology proving more popular in recent times than the older third age view. But all have agreed that these are now the last days.

The important difference today does not lie so much in any of these observations as in the fact that the scale of the movement is so vastly greater. We have noted how prophets or prophetically inclined people have come to the fore in the Church at times when the faith has been most threatened, whether by paganism or rationalism. Such men were the out-front leaders in winning Europe for Christ and then in the later Middle Ages and at the Reformation they were active again. As liberalism and atheism have increased, so also has prophetic activity, until in our time, when rationalism and paganism are stronger than ever, so also is prophetism. Two great armies have been massing in a great struggle for the conquest of the world. And that is precisely what the prophets of Old and New Testament times foretold concerning the last days before the end.

The prophetic Church of today is more of an end-time church than any other before it in history. We cannot, of course, say when the end is to be, but the signs of the times are clear enough. The urgency to reap for the kingdom is more positive now than in any earlier prophetic movement, and hence the spread of mission and revival as never before. These are certainly not days for the prophets of the Lord to sleep. Sadly too many Pentecostal churches have slipped into formalism and too many Charismatic fellowships have become introverted, but the Lord continues to stir in the hearts of those who are open to receive his Spirit and go reap in the harvest.

John, in his vision on Patmos, heard Jesus say, 'Behold, I am coming soon!' The day of his coming is now closer than it was when these words were first spoken. The evidence of the times is in harmony with that rather simple observation. Now is surely the time, as never before in history, for every prophetic Christian to stay alert and to pray with fervour, as John himself did in his day, 'Come, Lord Jesus.' (Rev. 22:20)

# 32
# The End-Time Prophetic Church

By way of conclusion, let us consider more closely the present state of the Church in the light of the Bible's prophetic vision of the future. Prophetic Christianity has normally shown some kind of interest in its present status in relation to the future. Indeed, most of the movements we have looked at in this book have considered themselves in some way or other an end-time movement. But then, end-time consciousness is an intrinsic part of prophetic consciousness, as it has always been, ever since Old Testament days. The prophets of Israel taught that history would run on to a time when there would be a last uprising of the forces of evil, after which God's kingdom would be fully and finally established on earth. The vision is unfolded in greater detail in the book of Revelation in the New Testament.

John begins in his prologue by emphasising that Jesus is the focus of his prophetic vision about what was soon to take place. His book is not just a catalogue of end-time events, but an account of the workings of Jesus Christ in these latter days of Christian history. Hence his opening vision is of Jesus himself, the risen ascended Lord revealed in all his glory, 'the First and the Last', the Lord of the nations, of history, and of all time, even of life and death. And his first instruction is to his people in the churches about how to conduct themselves under the pressures of latter-day living.

When we looked earlier at the New Testament's teaching about the Holy Spirit and prophecy we saw that the witness of the Spirit is always first and foremost to the glory of the Son of God in Jesus Christ. John sums that up beautifully in one short sentence in Rev. 19:10, 'The testimony of Jesus is the spirit of prophecy.' The prophetic Spirit will always bear testimony or witness to Jesus first, which is what Jesus himself told his disciples just before Pentecost, 'You will receive power when the Holy Spirit comes on you; and you will be my witnesses ...' (Acts 1:8)

The first vivid demonstration of the power of that testimony was in what happened on the day of Pentecost itself. It was then that

Peter defined the gift they had received as the last-days Spirit of prophecy Joel had spoken about, and immediately he proceeded to give a testimony to Jesus that led to some three thousand being added to the Church. We see this same power at work again through the Church in the unfolding vision of the end-times in the book of Revelation.

John's first impression of heaven is rather solemn, even frightening. His vision in ch. 4 is reminiscent of the visions Ezekiel and Isaiah saw, that overwhelmed both these ancient prophets with awe and dismay (Ezek. 1; Isa. 6). John's picture of the throne, the rainbow, the flashes of lightning, the rumblings of thunder, the strange living creatures covered with eyes all over, their unending, majestic cry, 'Holy, holy, holy', the twenty-four elders around the throne laying down their crowns before the Creator or all things—all of that reminds us that we are in the presence of God, the King of kings and Lord of lords, the Almighty. The vision is indeed majestic, but it holds little comfort for a lost sinner who longs to be right with God. His only cry must be that of Isaiah: 'Woe to me! I am ruined! For I am a man of unclean lips, and I live among a people of unclean lips, and my eyes have seen the King, the LORD Almighty.' John's own desolation is manifest when he sees a scroll in the right hand of him who sits on the throne, sealed with seven seals, and he realises that there is no one anywhere worthy to approach that fearful throne and take the scroll (5:1-4).

The vision thus far is of the Creator God, the Eternal God of the Old Testament. Christ is found nowhere in it. But suddenly that all changes as we watch the Lamb approach the throne. At that moment all heaven erupts in praise. The living creatures and elders burst into song, a *new* song, and John becomes aware of far more life around him than he noticed before—thousands upon thousands of angels, and every creature in heaven and on earth and under the earth and on the sea, all praising the Lamb. The appearance of Christ on the scene alters everything and the solemnity gives way to total joy.

What makes Christ worthy to take the scroll is his sacrificial death (v. 9). The Lamb comes 'looking as if it had been slain' and the effects of his death are utterly comprehensive, embracing all men and all creation everywhere. Hence the scroll contains the record of history, not just of names, dates and events, but of the full sweep of history and the revelation of God's great purposes in it. But before learning about its progress, the first thing we are shown is that a new phase in its outworking began with the crucifixion—hence the great 'Amen' of the living creatures.

*The unfolding of history in Christian times.*

As the Lamb begins to open the seals some fairly horrifying scenes are reviewed in rapid succession, all samples of the kind of thing that has happened regularly throughout history: (1) war, (2) civil war, (3) famine, and (4) death, affecting a fourth of the earth (v. 8). Then follow two more detailed scenes with slightly more of an end-time feel about them: (5) martyrs crying out, 'How long?', and (6) earthquake that puts terror in the hearts of men, the first rumblings of the day of 'the wrath of the Lamb'. But the end is not yet. Martyrdom, earthquake and such terrors are in our world today. The seventh seal must still to be opened. The accounts of these horrors that ravage our earth are fairly factual. We are told little about their theological significance at this stage, but later we learn that God allows and causes such things to stir men to repentance (9:20-21).

For a refreshing moment John's attention is drawn away from the earth's tumult and he is shown the redeemed, the 144,000 of the tribes of Israel and 'a great multitude that no-one could count, from every nation, tribe, people and language,' all robed in white, praising God and the Lamb along with the angels, the elders and the living creatures, with the martyrs in particular already enjoying Paradisal bliss.

At the beginning of ch. 8 we return to the progress of history, to the opening of the seventh seal. Since it is the last on the scroll, we are now brought right into the last chapter of human history. The silence that follows its opening may be hard to interpret, but one thing is clear, the story of this phase is not yet completed, for the end does not yet come; it must conclude with the return of Christ and the winding up of history as we know it.

Jesus and Paul both said angelic trumpets would herald the end (Matt. 24:31; 1 Thes. 4:16), and so the vision moves on to show us seven angels with trumpets. As they are sounded, we still watch history unfold, just as when the seals were opened, but now there is a strong sense of end-time urgency about what we are shown. History has moved on and these are now truly the last days. The impact of wrath is more widespread, for a third of everything is affected: (1) parts of the earth become desert, (2) sea-water turns to blood and fish die, (3) fresh-water springs and rivers become undrinkable, (4) a third of the sky is darkened. Whatever John thought of all that, we cannot help but think today about the effects of pollution on our environment. However, it is the symbolism that is most striking, for here we find clear echoes of the plagues that were God's ultimatum to Egypt. The trumpets now sound forth God's ultimatum to earth.

Then most dramatically, before the fifth trumpet sounds, our thoughts are interrupted by an eagle screeching 'Woe! Woe! Woe!' in mid-heaven, warning the inhabitants of earth about the urgency of the times. These woes are sounded again just before the sixth and seventh trumpets.

The fifth trumpet (5) heralds the unleashing of monstrous locust-scorpion-like creatures with limited power to kill and torture. Significantly 'their faces resembled human faces' (9:7), for they represent the hellish brutality with which men treat each other. This is not a vision of persecution against the Church (v. 4), but of man's inhumanity to man. The sixth trumpet (6) unveils world war with armies so large John would hardly have been able to estimate their size, but he is told it (9:16). These two visions reveal times of terrible warfare with vast, frightening armies quite unlike anything known in John's own times.

Then finally we are told why God allows such things. Just as Amos had seen so long before, they should stir men to repentance, but as in his day, so still men will not heed the lesson (9:20f; cp. Amos 4).

*Christian prophetic witness before the end.*

With only one trumpet left to be sounded we are brought right to the very last moments of earth's history. Now we are well and truly in the end-times. What we are about to be shown at this point belongs in the last hour before the final outpouring of God's wrath, his showdown with evil and the victory procession of Christ and the saints at the end of historical time.

Before the opening of the seventh seal there was an interlude in which John was granted a refreshing vision of the redeemed at rest in glory. Before the seventh trumpet, there is another interlude, but one with a different feel altogether, full of activity and urgency. This time John is shown, not the saints in heaven, but the latter-day Church on earth, operating in the power of prophetic witness. These final hours of human time afford it the last opportunity to preach the gospel before the end comes, and what John sees happening in them is a dramatic upsurge of end-time prophetic witnessing.

It is in this last period before the end that we live today. We already know the suffering, the pollution and the inhumanity of the first six seals and trumpets, but with God's saints and martyrs we pray and long for the seventh to be fulfilled. At the start we were told that time is near (1.3), now we are reminded of its urgent nearness again (10:6). The challenge to John, and to us, is therefore to receive

God's prophetic word ourselves and take it to our fellow men now.

Our Church is the vehicle of God's prophetic voice for the last days. That was personally symbolised for John in his vision, when a voice bade him take the 'little scroll' from the hand of the angel (distinct from the large scroll the Lamb holds), eat it and go prophesy again. His experience was virtually identical with Ezekiel's when he was given his scroll of prophecy to eat (Ezek. 2:9 – 3:3). And again the message is sweet for the faithful, but bitter for the world.

In ch. 11 we are given a glimpse of the end-time prophets at work. It is a chapter in which we have to interpret John's symbolic language almost more than anywhere else. The 42 months, or 1,260 days, or three and a half days (= three and a half years) are the 'time, times and half a time' of Dan. 7:25 and 12:7, signifying the duration of the last days before the end, times of oppression, persecution and suffering for the saints of God. The two olive trees are found in Zech. 4 and symbolise the Messianic anointing of Jesus that Christians share. The lampstands are the symbols of the churches we have already seen in John's visions (1:20). The fact that there are only two here and not seven, as in ch. 1, indicates that this kind of witness by martyrdom will only ever be the calling of a proportion of Christians.

Now the ministry of the two witnesses is called prophesying in vv. 3, 6 & 10 and is said to be enabled by power given directly from God, reminding us of the pentecostal promise of Acts 1:8 noted earlier in this chapter. Their ministry is exercised with divine anointing, backed up with a display of signs and wonders they are enabled to perform, nature-miracles reminiscent of those performed by Elijah and Moses, both of whom were great prophets who had to stand in their prophetic witness in the teeth of opposition that sought to eradicate the faith of Israel from among men. Like some of their Israelite prophet-forebears, so also the Christian prophet-witnesses will experience persecution and even martyrdom, but God will vindicate them and raise them up to be with him in heaven (vv. 1-12).

What is more, their ministry is followed by many being terrified and giving glory to God (v. 13). To be sure, we read about an earthquake and a mighty shaking of the peoples as well, but earlier cosmic upheavals had not had the same effect at all. By contrast they had caused men to try hiding from God (6:15-17), seeking refuge in death (9:6), and had certainly not brought them to repentance in any way (9:20f). God's later judgments would even cause them to curse him (16:9,11,21), but here, when coupled with this end-time prophetic proclamation, the effect is a wholesale turning to God and giving him glory. The latter days are not just days of prophetic activity, but also of massive conversion.

Now at length we begin to hear the rumblings of the end itself and, after a final warning woe, the seventh trumpet sounds. Thereupon we hear again the praises of heaven, rejoicing because the hour has fully come, and we see God's wrath flashing in the sanctuary in heaven (vv. 13-19).

The vision after this point (chs. 12-22) tells of the final fury of Satan, how he rouses the hordes of evil and the pagan body politic, the consequent oppression of the saints, the harvest of the earth, the outpouring of God's wrath, the last battle, the fall of pagan imperial power (Babylon), the victory procession of Christ, the establishment of God's reign on earth, the great last judgment, and the creation of a new heaven and new earth. We do not need to follow that part of the story here. Suffice it to note that all these end-events are prefaced by this massive and highly effective movement of latter-day prophetic proclamation and ministry among the witnesses of Christ.

*And in the last days, God says …*

Now at length we are in a position to review our place today in the fuller purposes of God in history. The church was birthed at Pentecost with a clear consciousness that its calling and function was to be a latter-day prophetic voice in the society. That is the manifest import of Peter's citation of Joel's prophecy when asked for the meaning of all that was happening that day.

*In the last days, God says,*
*I will pour out my Spirit on all people.*
*Your sons and daughters will prophesy,*
*your young men will see visions,*
*your old men will dream dreams.*
*Even on my servants, both men and women,*
*I will pour out my Spirit in those days,*
*and they will prophesy.*
*I will show wonders in the heaven above*
*and signs on the earth below,*
*blood and fire and billows of smoke.*
*The sun will be turned to darkness*
*and the moon to blood*
*before the coming of the great and glorious day of the Lord.*
*And everyone who calls*
*on the name of the Lord will be saved.* (Acts 2:17-21)

The Church at its beginning was indeed like that. Its prophetic proclamation truly resulted in all who called on the name of the Lord being saved—and most effectively, in large numbers, so much so that within a couple of decades Christians were being spoken of as 'these that have turned the world upside down' (Acts 17:6, AV). But the portrait applies equally well to the Church of the end-time, and also to the Church of the twentieth century. Today's gospel proclamation is undergirded by the most massive outpouring of prophetic, pentecostal power that history has ever witnessed, and its fruit in conversions and revivals world-wide is equally phenomenal and unique. In fact today's testimony is so effective that almost half the Christians in the world are living with some degree of persecution. More martyr blood has flowed in the last century than in the whole of the rest of the Church's history altogether. The gospel today is causing a mighty shaking.

Supernatural earthquakes and such like were known in the days of the apostles, as when the place where Peter and John was praying with others in Jerusalem was shaken (Acts 4:31), or when an earth tremor burst open the prison for Paul and Silas at Philippi (16:26). Tales of similar phenomena pour in from many of today's mission and revival regions too, some of them exceedingly spectacular in the telling.

But many monks had similar tales to tell in the Dark Ages, as also had some sectaries and mystics in later medieval times, and more recently many of our early missionaries. As we have so clearly seen, pentecostal gifting was never withdrawn from the Church. It is equally true, however, that there is something unique about the Spirit's working in our own time, and that that finds its closest parallel in the ministries of the apostles. The Church's true prophetic nature, seen clear and fresh at its birthing, was obscured for many centuries with all kinds of ecclesiastical, political and philosophical overlay, but now is again being made manifest. The process of removing the overlay started in the twelfth century and continued thereafter with mounting vigour, until now at length the prophetic Church has been restored in a wonderful measure of fullness. The result is that almost everything spoken about in Rev. 10-11 is now happening—the prophetic commission and witness, the signs and wonders, the persecutions, the martyrdoms, the cosmic upheavals and the conversions. The Church today is more identifiable than at any time since the first century as the Church of the latter days.

John was made aware of the broad sweep of this process in his vision. The letters to the churches in chs. 2-3 reveal how the fire of the Spirit was already dwindling in them at the end of the apostolic age and that other church concerns and activities were beginning to dominate. His review of history through the opening of the seals and the sounding of the trumpets reveals little evidence of any prophetic activity in the world or the church. Then in 10:11 he hears the angel with the little scroll command him, 'You must prophesy again.' That one word, 'again', speaks of a second wave of prophetic activity in the Church's history, the last—and that is what we are living with today.

The true prophetic nature of Christianity was never forgotten in the Church's middle history. There were always those who caught sight of it and called it to remembrance. But today we are living in it once more, in unprecedented global fullness. Perhaps a 'latter rain' interpretation of history is not without value in helping us to understand the significance of these things. Pentecost in the New Testament was the first rain, softening the soil of humanity to enable the planting of the seed of the word. Today's pentecostal outpouring is the latter rain filling out the grain for the end-time harvest. Of course these patterns are discernible in other ways and at other times. Some have said that the early years of the twentieth century were a time of former rain and that now is the time of the latter rain. God's patterns apply at many levels, but clearly we are today, in one way or another, right in the heart of the action of Rev. 10-11 and in the fullness of the end-time harvest.

One final observation. We have seen repeatedly that the prophets are God's shock-troops for revival and his front-line fighters in the battle of faith against all the forces of paganism and evil. Alongside their latter-days' prophesying John saw a global resurgence of evil (ch. 12), and then, at the time of the harvest (14:14-19), the preparation of two great armies, the militia of heaven in glory (14:1-5) and the demonically inspired hordes of earth, roused in anger for a massive confrontation with the saints of God (16:12-16). When we actually come to it, the last battle, so called, at Armageddon, proves to be no battle at all, for the Lord God Almighty simply utters his word, 'It is done!' and it is suddenly all over (16:17).

This picture of the run up to the last battle is a very apt portrait of our present times too. Not only have Christians been unusually empowered by the Spirit of God in our days, but the powers of paganism and evil have also grown and become exceedingly strong, probably more so than at any time before in history. The stream of Pentecost was suppressed for centuries, but so also was the stream of paganism, both of them by the power of the Church itself. Just as men began to reach out for the Spirit and the word in the late Middle Ages, so also did others begin to reach out for the ways of humanism and paganism. The two streams, which had always been there in some measure, began to surface and display their colours in the Reformation and the Renaissance. The one has grown through the recovery of faith, the Bible, revival power, missionary zeal, and now through pentecostal enduement and prophetic anointing. The other has proceeded through neo-Platonism, Aristotelianism, the renewing of interest in Graeco-Roman paganism and culture, into scepticism, socialism, humanism, atheism, and now coming full cycle into the present flood of superstition, oriental and western paganism, and all manner of evil and occult practices.

The scene is being well and truly set for the last showdown between good and evil. While the Church that once ruled the world has recently stood confused, often not knowing which way to turn, now siding with the one in liberal compromise, now with the other in dogmatic doctrinalism, the battle has been and is being fought on the heights of the field. Souls are being won for the kingdom of God in greater numbers than ever before. Heroes of faith are winning glorious victories and also dying as martyrs. God is surely empowering his people. Our church today is indeed the Church of the latter days, and its nature by divine foresight and actual fact is utterly prophetic.

# Epilogue

Swept down to Roffey Place in the wake of the Toronto blessing in 1994, freshly caught up in a passion for the Lord and newly introduced to heady talk of revival and great awakenings, I found myself in awe sitting under the teaching of Colin Urquhart and John McKay, men who had for years sought true revival.

As John taught, the bible came alive (note: not 'relevant' but alive!) We students were drawn into its pages, whether ascending Mount Sinai beside Moses, hearing God break in out of the storm with Job or caught up in a vision of the Lord in the Temple alongside Isaiah; revival became so intensely personal.

John's history lessons were no less exciting and I welcome the publication of this extraordinary volume. Anointed, informed, accessible, and deeply inspiring it needs to be widely read by all Christians interested in understanding their faith in a bigger context: that of God's dealings with men through biblical and church history.

What has been happening in the church since John's untimely death in 2001? John referred to apostolic ministries potentially advancing the goal of a less fragmented church scene towards the end of this manuscript, and since then churches and ministries have increasingly sought to be linked to apostolic ministries, though the whole 'apostolic movement' remains inevitably controversial elsewhere. There has been progress across denominations of getting the church out of buildings and into the marketplace. Anglicans, for instance, talk easily of 'fresh expressions' of church, somewhat radically planting churches outside the parish system. There has been much written about a 'post-modern' church, in a 'post-missional' and even 'post-Christian' society. People are openly challenging sacred cows of previous generations with a desire to try something new, as the excitement associated with the early years of the charismatic movement has waned where the foundations have been shallow. Mega-churches abound (especially in the USA); though those with Pentecostal roots remain wary of 'seeker friendly' services and sermons that can seem more like worldly motivational speaking than the preaching of the Christian gospel. A plethora of 'Christian' leadership manuals are available and can be quite indistinguishable from their secular counterparts on the 'self-help' and 'management' shelves of bookstores. Talk of reformation these days has largely replaced that of revival.

The question of what, if anything, in all this has been inspired by the Holy Spirit remains crucial.

Though John didn't get as far as mentioning Pensacola in this work, crowds were already flocking there (in the same way they did to Toronto) in 2001. No doubt he was waiting to see what they would produce. More recently, during April-June 2008, outpourings of the Holy Spirit were reported at meetings in Lakeland, Florida and many went there too (140,000, from 40 nations, are said to have visited during the first two months) as night after night football stadiums were filled. As I write, IHOP (International House of Prayer, Kansas City) are experiencing what they describe as a 'student awakening' after ten years of 24/7 prayer.

Predictably enough opinions are divided about these events. If many accept them as moves of the Holy Spirit, others do not. Certain leaders involved in the so-called 'outpourings' have very publicly fallen from grace. The inward looking 'bless me' attitudes present in the way the church handled Toronto are suspected by many of continuing to hinder what might have been.

Even among those who see these as moves of the Spirit, many would stop short of identifying them with revival. As John would surely have continued to urge us, each will be judged according to its fruit, and perhaps that shouldn't be done too hastily.

Since 2001 technology has considerably changed how people participate in such global events. Christian TV broadcasted meetings in Lakeland night after night live to an audience around the globe (in addition to a reported audience of 1.2 million who watched via internet), IHOP meetings can be seen on internet pretty much as they happen. Many bigger churches broadcast live today, and many more podcast their meetings. Facebook, twitter and other instant media tools mean that nothing happens anywhere without the potential for the whole world to know about it instantaneously.

Maybe we should look more globally for glimpses of true revival in the church today, to where there is no media coverage, to the persecuted Christians – in parts of India, Indonesia, Nigeria to name but a few; those working in other Muslim nations, and the faceless leaders of the Chinese church that continues to thrive under persecution. It seems that wherever there is persecution there surely will be a reviving of God's people!

While the coming together of Word and Spirit in the way John McKay talks of it remains largely elusive, his legacy *The Way of the Spirit* continues to develop and impact people in different countries. Many bible teachers in the UK have been trained, initially through the part-time course but more recently in full-time training which has resumed in Norwich, Norfolk. In Africa some years ago John and Marguerite McKay stood at the source of the Nile and God spoke to them of how he would use *The Way of the Spirit* in Uganda. Years later, with others now leading, a door opened into East Africa and since then many teams have gone into Uganda, Rwanda and – to a lesser extent so far – Kenya and Burundi. Groups of leaders and pastors in each of these nations have been introduced to the material in their own vernacular and are keenly working with it in their own churches. Two years ago Fifty Ugandan pastors graduated from the part-time prophetic bible teacher training held just outside Kampala.

New *The Way of the Spirit* bible study materials have been produced, keeping the work and vision of The Way of the Spirit alive and growing. One of the short courses was recently produced in Korean, another in Kinyarwanda and still another is in progress in Burmese. Five different nations were represented during the full-time training that restarted in earnest this year.

This is an all too brief attempt to bring this important work up to date. I suspect John wouldn't have been bogged down into whether this or that series of meetings were revival or not, his horizons were broader. I imagine he would have been excited to hear all the claims of moves of the Holy Spirit around the world (even if some of them didn't stand up to close scrutiny). He would have continued teaching the bible, in the anointing God had given to him, with a deep longing in his heart for all men to know Jesus – to see what Moses, Job, Isaiah and many others had seen. Without relaxing his eagle-eyed discernment, he would have nevertheless looked ahead eagerly to the next outpouring of the Holy Spirit, and to the ever greater strengthening of the prophetic church by what an early theologian called the 'two hands of God', his Word and his Spirit.

*Richard C George,*
*Norwich, England,*
*Spring 2010*

# BIBLIOGRAPHY

# General works containing historical surveys


R.A. Knox, *Enthusiasm. A Chapter in the History of Religion with special reference to the XVII and XVIII centuries*, Oxford, 1950.

R.M. Jones, *Studies in Mystical Religion*, London, 1919.

G.B. Cutten, *Speaking with Tongues, historically and psychologically considered*, New Haven, 1927.

D. Christi-Murray, *Voices from the Gods. Speaking with Tongues*, London & Henley, 1978.

B. Yocum, *Prophecy. Exercising the prophetic gifts of the Spirit in the Church today*, Michigan, 1976.

G.H. Williams & E. Waldvogel, "A History in Tongues and Related Gifts," *The Charismatic Movement*, ed. M.P. Hamilton, Grand Rapids, 1975.

# I. The Prophets of Israel

Although there is no book in which the history of Israel's prophets is studied as a development of successive movements in exactly the same way as in this chapter, there are many excellent works on Old Testament prophecy. The following is but a selection of some of the more useful to read as general introductions to the field.

J. Lindblom, *Prophecy in Ancient Israel*, Blackwell, 1963.

E.W. Heaton, *The Old Testament Prophets*, Penguin Books, 1958.

A.J. Heschel, *The Prophets*, Harper & Row, 1962.

H. Mowvley, *Guide to Old Testament Prophecy*, Lutterworth, 1979.

G. von Rad, *The Message of the Prophets*, SCM, 1968.

R.B.Y. Scott, *The Relevance of the Prophets*, Macmillan, 1968.

H.W. Robinson, *Inspiration and Revelation in the Old Testament*, Clarendon Press, Oxford, 1946.

M.D.R. Willinck, *The Prophetic Consciousness*, SPCK, 1924.

L. Neve, *The Spirit of God in the Old Testament*, Seibunsha, 1972.

# II. Prophetism in the New Testament Church

(a) Very few books have been written specifically on this subject.

D. Hill, *New Testament Prophecy*, Marshall, Morgan & Scott, 1979.

T.M. Crone, *Early Christian Prophecy*, St. Mary's University Press, Baltimore, 1973.

H.A. Guy, *New Testament Prophecy*, Epworth Press, London, 1947.

(b) On the wider aspects of prophecy and charismatic experience in the New Testament, the following may be found useful.

F.D. Brunner, *A Theology of the Holy Spirit*, Hodder & Stoughton, 1970 (Part II).

E. Cothénet, "Le prophétisme dans le Nouveau Testament," *Supplément au Dictionnaire de la Bible* VIII, cols. 1221-1337, Paris, 1971 (also published separately in book form.)

O. Cullmann, *The Christology of the New Testament*, SCM, 1959.

J. Dunn, *Baptism in the Holy Spirit*, SCM, 1970.

J. Dunn, *Jesus and the Spirit*, SCM, 1975.

J. Friedrich, (art.), *Theological Dictionary of the New Testament* 6, ed. G. Friedrich, Eerdmans, Grand Rapids, Michigan, 1968, pp. 859-61.

Ed. J. Panagopoulos, *Prophetic Vocation in the New Testament and Today*, Brill, 1977.

# III. Charismatic Christianity in the Early Catholic Church

Though the works of Weinel and Lombard (neither available in translation) remain the most complete studies of early charismatic Christianity, a great deal of useful information can be gleaned by English readers from the other works listed here.

H. Weinel, *Die Wirkungen des Geistes und der Geister im nachapostolischen Zeitalter bis auf Irenäus*, Freiburg, Leipzig & Tübingen, 1899.

E. Lombard, *De la glossolalie chez les premiers Chrétiens et des phénomènes similaires. Étude d'exégèse et de psychologie*, Lausanne, 1910.

E.C. Selwyn, *The Christian Prophets and the Prophetic Apocalypse*, London, 1900.

J. Reiling, *Homes and Christian Prophecy. A Study of the Eleventh Mandate*, Brill, 1973.

J. Friedrich, (art.), TDNT 6, pp. 859-61. (See last section.)

J. Laporte, "The Holy Spirit, Source of Life and Activity according to the Early Church," *Charismatic Renewal*, ed. E.D. O'Connor, 1978, pp. 57-99.

# IV. Montanism

(a) The most recent complete study of Montanism in English was published over 100 years ago:

J. de Soyres, *Montanism and the Primitive Church*, London, 1878.

• By far the most useful and up to date account of Montanism is in French:

H. Bacht, "Montanisme," *Dictionnaire de Spiritualité* X, Beauchesne, Paris, 1980, cols. 1670-76.

(b) Otherwise the English reader must unfortunately rely on dictionary articles and the odd few pages in general histories of the Christian church or similar works, where some of the views expressed are no longer those of current scholarship, such as:

R.A. Knox, *Enthusiasm*, pp. 25-49.

R.M. Jones, *Studies in Mystical Religion*, ch. III.

E.C. Selwyn, *The Christian Prophets and the Prophetic Apocalypse*, Macmillan & Co, London, 1900.

(c) Original sources:

N. Bonwetsch, *Texte zur Geschichte des Montanismus*, Bonn, 1914. (Texts without translation.)

P. de Labriolle, *La Crise Montaniste*, Paris, 1913.

*Les Sources de l'histoire du Montanisme*, Paris, 1913.

# V. Charismatic Tendencies in the Middle Ages

There is no single study of this aspect of medieval Christianity; information must be gleaned from more general works, such as:

M.D. Lambert, *Medieval Heresy. Popular Movements from Bogomil to Hus*, Arnold, London, 1977.

N. Cohn, *The Pursuit of the Millennium*, Secker & Warburg, London, 1957.

J.B. Russell, *Dissent and Reform in the Early Middle Ages*, Berkeley and Los Angeles, 1965.

W.L. Wakefield & A.P. Evans, *Heresies in the High Middle Ages. Selected sources translated and annotated*, New York & London, 1969.

R.I. Moore, *The Birth of Popular Heresy*, London, 1975.

H.C. Lea, *A History of the Inquisition in the Middle Ages*, New York, 1955 (originally published in 1888.)

G. Leff, *Heresy in the Later Middle Ages. The Relation of Heterodoxy to Dissent c.1250-c.1450*, Manchester & New York, 1967.

R.M. Jones, *Studies in Mystical Religion*, London, 1919.

G.A. Maloney, *Intoxicated with God. The Fifty Spiritual Homilies of Macarius*, Dimension Books, Denville, New Jersey, 1978.

B. Ward (tr.), *The Sayings of the Desert Fathers*, Mowbray, London & Oxford, 1981.

E. Ensley, *Sounds of Wonder. Speaking in Tongues in the Catholic Tradition*, Paulist Press, New York, 1977.

(a) Celtic Christianity

• There has been an increase on interest in recent years. I have found the following particularly well-balanced and helpful:

Anthony Duncan, *The Elements of Celtic Christianity*, Element Books Ltd., Shaftesbury, 1992.

Esther de Waal, *A World Made Whole. Rediscovering the Celtic Tradition*, HarperCollins, London, 1991.

W. Douglas Simpson, *The Historical Saint Columba*, 3rd edn., Oliver & Boyd, Edinburgh & London, 1963.

A.O. & M.O. Anderson, *Adomnán's Life of Columba*, Clarendon Press, Oxford, 1991.

T. Taylor, *The Life of St. Samson of Dol*, Llanerch Publishers, Felinfach, Dyfed, 1991. Facsimile Reprint of S.P.C.K. edn. of 1935.

Ed. by D.C Munro, *The Life of St. Columban by the Monk Jonas,* Llanerch Publishers, Felinfach, Dyfed, 1993. First published in 1895 (Philadelphia) as Vol. II, no. 7 Translations and Reprints from the Original Sources of European History.

(b) The Earlier Local Movements

Apart from occasional references in some of the above works, there is a particularly useful article in French:

P. Alphandéry, "De quelques faits de prophétisme dans les sectes Latines antérieures au Joachinisme," *Revue de l'histoire des religions* 52, 1905, pp. 177-218.

(Not all the movements he studies are included in this book, because, whilst they all had some kind of prophetic element in them, very few of them regarded it as their purpose to propagate prophetic experience.)

Original sources:

Gregory of Tours, *The History of the Franks* X.25, tr. by O.M. Dalton, Clarendon Press, 1927, vol.2, pp.461-3 (on the prophet of Bourges, in translation.)

ed. G.H. Pertz, *Monumenta Germaniae Historica. Scriptorum* I, Hanover, 1926, p.365. (Annals of Fulda, 847 AD, on Thiota, in Latin.)

*P.L.* 142, cols. 643-4 (Ralph Glaber, *A History of His Times* II. 11, on Leutard, in Latin.)

Wakefield & Evans, *Heresies*, pp.72-3 (ibid, in translation.)

Wakefield & Evans, *Heresies*, pp.96-101 (on Tanchelm, in translation.)

(c) The Amalricians

Apart from very useful sections on the Amalricians in Jones and Cohn, and the translations of the main sources in Wakefield & Evans, most of what has been written about them is not available in English.

H. Grundmann, *Religiöse Bewegungen,* 2nd edn., Hildesheim, 1961, pp.355-73.

M.Th. d' Alveray, "Un fragment du Procès des Amauriciens," *Archives d'Histoire doctrinale et littéraire du Moyen Age* XXVI, 1951, pp.325-36

F. Vernet, "Ameury du Bène et les Amauricièns," *Dictionnaire de Spiritualité* I, 1937, cols 472-5.

G.L. Capelle, *Autour du décrit de 1210, III: Amaury du Bène*, Paris, 1932.

Original sources, in English translation:

Wakefield & Evans, *Heresies*, pp.258-63.

ed. J.B. Russell, *Religious Dissent in the Middle Ages,* New York, London, Sidney, Toronto, 1971, pp.83f.

(d) Joachim and his successors

• They have been fully researched in recent years. Particularly useful, apart from the works of Leff and Lea listed above, are a number of publications by Marjorie Reeves, especially:

M. Reeves, *The Influence of Prophecy in the Later Middle Ages. A History of Joachimism*, Oxford, 1969.

M. Reeves, *Joachim of Fiore and the Prophetic Future*, London, 1976.

Original sources:

Wakefield & Evans, *Heresies*, pp.404-39 (in English).

ed. L.A. Muratori, *Racolta degli Storici Italiani* IX. 5: *Historia Fratris Dulcini Heresiarche*, pp.21-24 (= Bernard Gui, *De Secta illorum qui se dicunt esse de ordine Apostolorum*, in Latin.)

(e) The Friends of God

They have received very little attention in English. Apart from a most useful chapter in Jones, *Studies in Mystical Religion*, there is a section on them in the rather dated work:

R.A. Vaughan, *Hours with the Mystics. A Contribution to the history of Religious Opinion*, London, 1856.

Also very old, and mostly of popular value, though it does offer translations of some texts, is:

F. Bevan, *Three Friends of God. Records from the Lives of John Tauler, Nicholas of Basle, Henry Suso*, London, 1887.

(f) On Eckhart et al.:

Jeanne Ancelet-Hustache, *Master Eckhart and the Rhineland Mystics*, tr. by Hilda Graef, Men of Wisdom Books, Longmans, London, 1957.

# VI. The Zwickau Prophets

There is no complete study of the prophets in English, and those who do write about them generally rely on:

P. Wappler, *Thomas Müntzer in Zwickau und die "Zwickauer Propheten"*, Schriften des Vereins für Reformationsgeschichte 182, Gütersloh, 1966 (first published in 1908.)

The most useful account in English is in:

J.S. Oyer, *Lutheran Reformers against Anabaptists*, The Hague, 1964, pp.6-16.

Otherwise there are some remarks about the prophets in:

C.L. Manschrenck, *Melanchthon. The Quiet Reformer*, Westport, Conn., 1975, pp.77-81.

S.E. Ozment, *Mysticism and Dissent*, New Haven & London, 1973, pp.61-97.

E.G. Rupp, *Patterns of Reformation*, Epworth, London, 1969, pp.157-68.

G.H. Williams, *The Radical Reformer*, London, 1962, pp.44-47.

R.A. Knox, *Enthusiasm*, pp.126-35.

Original sources:

(i) The only continuous history of the prophets is found in Joachim Cameraius' *Life of Philip Melanchthon* (*Vita Philippi Melanchthonis*), 1604 and various later editions. There is no English translation of this work. References are to the 1655 edition of the Latin text.

(ii) The only formal presentation of this teaching is in Marcus Wagner's *Einfeltigem Bericht, wie durch Nicolam Storcken der Aufruhr in Thüringen etc. angefangen sei worden*, Erfurt, 1596. The relevant texts are reprinted in Wappler, pp.81-6. For the quotation on p.136f, see Wappler, pp.85f. Wappler claims to have obtained his information from Johann Chiomusus who apparently knew Storch quite well.

(iii) Further historical details are contained in some of Melanchthon's commentaries; see especially his

*Notes on Matthew's Gospel*, 1544, on Matt.7.15 (*CR* XLV, cols 766f)

*Commentary on I Corinthians*, 15xx, on I Cor. 14 (*CR* XV, cols 1160f)

(iv) Otherwise most of our information comes from letters:

Nicholas Hausmann and Colleagues to the Royal Court, 18 Dec., 1521; see Th. Colde, "Ältester Bericht über die Zwickauer Propheten." *Zeitschrift für Kirchengeschichte* 1881, vol.5, pp.323-5.

Johann Agricola(?) to Reusch, 1525(?); see J. Brecher, "Johann Agricola(?) an Reusch, 1525(?)," *Zeitschrift für Historische Theologie*, 1872, pp.398-410.

Melanchthon to Frederick, 27 Dec 1521 = *CR* I, col 513.
to Spalatin, 27 Dec 1521 = *CR* I, cols 514f.
to Frederick, 1 Jan 1522 = *CR* I, col 533
to Camerarius, 17 Apr 1525 = *CR*

Amsdorf to Frederick, 1 Jan 1522 = *CR* I, cols 534f.

Frederick to Melanchthon, 2 Jan 1522 = *CR* I, cols 535-8.

Luther to Melanchthon, 13 Jan 1522 =
to Spalatin, 17 Jan 1522 = *BW*
to Nicholas Hausmann, 17 March 1522 = *BW*
to Spalatin, 12 Apr 1522= *BW* 2, no.472.

Müntzer to Luther, 9 July 1523; see G. Franz, "Thomas Müntzer, Schriften und Briefe," *Quellen und Forschungen zur Reformationsgeschichte* 33, Gütersloh, 1968, p.391.

(v) For the various accounts of Luther's interviews with the prophets, as he told them to his students at table, see *WA* I (*Tischreden*) no. 362; II, no. 2049; II, no. 2060; II, no. 2837a; III, no. 2837b; IV, no. 5018; V, no. 5568.

*WA* = *Weimarer Ausgabe*

(vi) Other sources referred to:

Minutes of Zwickau town council, as cited in Wappler, p.46, notes 195,196.

J.K. Seidemann, *Thomas Müntzer*, Dresden & Leipzig, 1842, p.110, as cited in Wappler, p.32, note 127.

# VII. Seekers and Early Quakers

There is no single book in English on the Seekers, and the only well documented account readily accessible to modern readers is in Jones, *Studies in Mystical Religion*, ch. 19, pp.449-66.

Other helpful, though mostly sketchy notes, are found in Knox, *Enthusiasm*, pp.139-75 and in W.C. Braithwaite, *The Beginnings of Quakerism*, 2nd ed., Cambridge, 1961, pp.25-27.

The quotations from Saltmarsh, Baxter, Edwards & Carlyle are all taken from Jones. Jones also gives some useful descriptions of other sects of the time, as also does Cohn in his *The Pursuit of the Millennium*.

On Quietism:

H.R. Sefton, "Religious Responses to Revolution in North-East Scotland in the Seventeenth and Eighteenth Centuries," *Aberdeen University Review* 186, 1991, pp. 128-34.

G.D. Henderson, *Mystics of the North-East*, Aberdeen University Press, printed for the Third Spalding Club, 1934.

# VIII. The French Prophets in Southern France

(a) The reminiscences of the prophet-refugees form the main source of information for this chapter. They are found in:

Pierre Jurieu: *The Pastoral Letters of the Incomparable Jurieu directed to the Protestants in France groaning under the Babylonish Tyranny*, London, 1689.

ibid: *Reflections of the Reverent and Learned Monsieur Jurieu upon the Strange and Miraculous Exstasis of Isabel Vincent the Shepherdess of Saon in Dauphiné, etc.*, London, 1689.

John Lacy, *A Cry from the Desart*, London, 1707.

More recent appraisals in English sympathetic with the above material will be found in:

R. Heath, "The Little Prophets of the Cevennes", *The Contemporary Review* 49, 1886, pp.117-31.

G. de Felice, *History of the Protestants of France*, London, 1853, pp.354-63.

G.B. Cutten, *Speaking with Tongues*, New Haven, 1927, pp.48-66 (almost entirely dependent on Heath's article.)

Ch. Tylor, *The Huguenots in the Seventeenth Century*, London, 1892.

(b) Contemporary Catholic accounts are naturally critical of the movement. Among the more important are:

V.E. Flechier, *Lettres Choisies de M. Flechier, Evêque de Nismes, avec une relation des formatiques du Vivarez*, Paris, 1715.

D.A. de Brueys, *Histoire du formatisme de nostre temps et le dessein que l'on avoit de soulever en France les mécontens Calvinistes*, 1692. (Reprinted in *Archives Curieuses de l'Histoire de France depuis Louis XI jusqu'à Louis XVIII*, ed. F. Danjou, 2nd series, vol.11, Paris, 1840.)

J.B. Louvreleuil, *Le fanatisme renouvelé, ou histoire des sacriléges... que les Calvinistes révoltés ont commis dans les Cévennes*, 1704

A recent representation of the Catholic viewpoint is to be found in Knox's *Enthusiasm*, pp.356-71.

(c) Detailed accounts of the Camisards and their views are contained in two books:

Ch. Tylor, *The Camisards*, London, 1893.

Mrs. E. Bray, *The Revolt of the Protestants in the Cevennes*, London, 1870. (Mrs. Bray attaches little importance to the activities of the prophets; she scarcely mentions them.

# IX. The French Prophets in England

(a) For the English reader who does not have access to the extensive 18th century literature on the prophets, there are very few useful sources of information.

Apart from a few lines or pages in some of the more general books, the best of which is Knox's *Enthusiasm*, pp.365-9, there is:

J. Symonds, *Thomas Brown and the Angels. A Study in Enthusiasm*, Hutchinson & Co, London, 1961, pp.13-42.

The most useful recent literature is in French, especially:

G. Ascoli, "L'Affaire des Prophètes Français à Londres," *Revue du dix-huitieme Siècle* 3, 1916, Part I, pp.8-28; Part II, pp.85-109.

P. Vesson, *Les Prophètes Camisards à Londres*, Toulouse, 1893.

Ch. Bost, *Mémoires inédites d'Abraham Mazel et d'Elias Marion sur la guerre des Cévennes, 1701-1708*, Publications de la Societé Huguenote de Londres 34, Paris, 1931.

(b) From the 18th century, the most detailed historical account is:

S. Keimer, *A Brand Snatch'd from the Burning: Exemplify'd in the Unparallel'd Case of Samuel Keimer*, 1718. (A number of pages were missing in the copy available to me, but much of this book is reprinted in D. Hughson, *A Copious Account of the French and English Prophets, who infested London during 1707, and the following years*, 1814.

• For an assessment of Keimer's work and personality, see

C.L. Carlson, "Samuel Keimer. A Study in the Transit of English Culture to Colonial Pennsylvania", *The Pennsylvania Magazine of History and Biography* 61, 1937, pp.357-86.

• The other most informative sources are in the writings of Spinckes and Bulkeley, cited in the text from the following editions:

Geo. Hickes, *The Spirit of Enthusiasm Exorcised (4th enlarged ed.) with Two Discourses occasioned by the New Prophets Pretensions to Inspiration and Miracles. The First: The History of Montanism, by a Lay-Gentleman. The Other: The New Pretenders to Prophecy Examined. By N. Spinckes, A Presbyter in the Church of England*, 1709.

N. Spinckes, *The New Pretenders to Prophecy Examined and their pretences shown to be groundless and false. And Sir R. Bulkeley and A. Whitro convicted of very foul practices, in order to the carrying on their imposture*, 1710.

R. Bulkeley, *An Answer to Several Treatises lately published on the subject of the Prophets*, 1708.

R. Bulkeley, *An Impartial Account of the Prophets of the Cevennes. In a letter to a Friend*, 170, reprinted in a series entitled *Prophetical Extracts*, vol.I, 1794-5.

(c) Other sources cited, in the order to which they are referred:

Earl of Shaftesbury, *A Letter Concerning Enthusiasm to My Lord ...*, 1708.

E. Marion, *Prophetical Warnings of E. Marion, one of the Commanders of the Protestants, that had taken arms in the Cevennes: or discourses uttered by him in London, under the operation of the Spirit; and faithfully taken in writing while they were spoken*, 1707.

J. Lacy, *Squire Lacy's Reasons why Dr. Emes was not raised*, 1708.

E. Smedley, *History of the Reformed Religion in France* III, 1834.

J. Lacy, *The Prophetical Warnings of John Lacy, Esq; pronounced under the operation of the Spirit and faithfully taken in writing, when they were spoken*, 1707.

J. Lacy, *Warnings of the Eternal Spirit by Mouth of his Servant John, sirnamed Lacy. The Second Part*, 1707.

J. Lacy, *Warnings of the Eternal Spirit by Mouth of his Servant John, sirnamed Lacy. The Third Part*, 1707.

T. Hearne, *Reliquiae Heranianae: The Remains of Thomas Hearne, M.A., of Edmond Hall. Being Extracts from his M.S. Diaries, collected, with a few notes* by Philip Bliss, 1869.

art. "French Prophets of 1711," *The Baptist Quarterly*, 1924, pp.169-79.

J. Lacy, *The General Delusion of Christians, touching the Ways of God's revealing Himself to and by the Prophets, evinc'd from Scripture and Primitive Authority*, 1713.

J. Wesley, *The Journal of the Rev. John Wesley*, 1827.

For further bibliographies, see esp. Bost, pp.xv-xvii and Symonds, pp.163-9.

# X. The Shakers

Early Shaker works are difficult to find in this country. Glasgow City Library has a copy of Youngs' *Testimony* which has a useful section on the early English Shakers. Evans' *Compendium* is also readily available, because reprinted in 1975. Whiston's *The Shakers* is a very useful source book of selected excerpts from Shaker writings (mainly 19th century).


Giles Avery (ed.), *Testimonies of the Life, Character, REvelations of Mother Ann Lee, and the Elders with her . . .* (2nd edn.), Albany, New York, 1888. (Alternate title: *Precepts of Mother Ann Lee and the Elders.*) A revision of Rufus Bishop, *Testimonies, &c.*, 1816.

F.W. Evans, *Shakers, Compendium of the Origin, History, Principles, Rules and Regulations, Government, and Doctrine of the United Society of Believers in Christ's Second Appearing, with biographies of Ann Lee,* et al., 4th ed., New Lebanon, 1867, reprinted by AMS Press Inc., New York, 1975.

Calvin Green, *Atheism, Deism, Universalism and Fatalism Refuted, &c . . . A Discourse,* 1830. Ms. Sabbathday Lake Society Library.

Calvin Green, *A Summary View of the Millennial Church, or United Society of Believers, Commonly Called Shakers*, Albany, New York, 1823 & 1848.

William Haskett, *Shakerism Unmasked*, Pittsfield, Massachusetts, 1829.

Richard McNemar, *The Kentucky Revival; or, a Short History of the Late Extraordinary Outpouring of the Spirit of God in the Western States of America,* John W. Browne, Cincinnati, 1807.

Seth Wells, *Testimonies Concerning the Character and Ministry of Mother Ann Lee and the First Witnesses of the Gospel of Christ's Second Appearing; Given by Some Aged Brethren and Sisters of the United Society, Including Sketches of their own Religious Experience. Approved by the Church*. Albany, New York, 1827.

R.E. Whiston (ed.), *The Shakers. Two Centuries of Spiritual Reflection*, Classics of Western Spirituality, SPCK, London, 1983.

Benjamin S. Youngs, *The Testimony of Christ's Second Appearing,* Lebanon, Ohio, 1808.

*The Manifesto,* a monthly journal in 29 vols, 1871-99. It was launched in 1871 as *The Shaker,* but the title changed in 1873 to *Shaker and Shakeress Monthly,* in 1876 back to *The Shaker,* in 1878 to *The Shaker Manifesto,* and finally in 1883 to *The Manifesto.*


Useful information can be gleaned from more recent, general studies, such as:


A. White and L. Taylor, *Shakerism, Its Meaning and Message,* Columbus, Ohio, 1904.

C.E. Sears, *Gleanings from the Old Shaker Journals*, Boston & New York, 1916.

E.D. Andrews, *The People Called Shakers. A Search for the Perfect Society*, OUP, New York, 1953.

M.F. Melcher, *The Shaker Adventure*, Cleveland, Ohio, 1968.

G.H. Williams and E. Waldvogel, "A History of Speaking in Tongues and Related Gifts," ed. M.P. Hamilton, *The Charismatic Movement*, Eerdmans, Grand Rapids, 1975, pp. 81-4.

D. Sasson, *The Shaker Spiritual Narrative*, University of Tenessee Press, Knoxville, 1983.

S.J. Stein, *The Shaker Experience. A History of the United Society of Believers*, Yale UP, New Haven & London, 1992.

Harrison, *Second Coming*

For further bibliography, see Whiston, pp. 352-5.

# XI. Edward Irving and the Catholic Apostolic Church


(a) General works:

Mrs. Oliphant, *The Life of Edward Irving, Minister of the National Scotch Church, London*, London, 1862.

(This is the fullest biography of Irving, on which all others draw heavily. Carlyle called it "a loyal and clear, but feeble kind of book.")

A.L. Drummond, *Edward Irving and his Circle; including some consideration of the "Tongues" Movement in the light of Modern Psychology*, London, 1937.

P.E. Shaw, *The Catholic Apostolic Church, sometimes called Irvingite. A Historical Survey*, New York, 1946.

H.C. Whitley, *Blinded Eagle. An Introduction to the Life and Teaching of Edward Irving*, London, 1955.

G. Strachan, *The Pentecostal Theology of Edward Irving*, London, 1973.

• A list of other biographical works, a full bibliography of Irving's own writings and a selection of other related historical works can be found in Strachan's book, pp.232-40.

(b) For a comparison of the Irvingite and the modern Pentecostal and Charismatic Movements, see:

L. Christenson, *A Message to the Charismatic Movement*, Dimension Books, Minneapolis, 1972.

ibid., "Pentecostalism's Forgotten Forerunner," *Aspects of Pentecostal-Charismatic Origins*, ed. V. Synan, Plainfield, New Jersey, 1975, pp.15-37.

(c) Other works cited as mentioned in this chapter:

E. Irving, *Sermons, Lectures and Occasional Discourses, vol. I: The Doctrine of the Incarnation Opened in Six Sermons*, London, 1828.

ibid., *The Coming of Messiah in Glory and Majesty, by Juan Josafat Ben-Ezra a converted Jew. Translated from the Spanish, with a Preliminary Discourse*, London, 1827.

ibid., "Facts Connected with Recent Manifestations of Spiritual Gifts," *Fraser's Magazine* 4, January 1832, pp.754-61.

ibid., *The Day of Pentecost or the Baptism with the Holy Ghost*, Edinburgh, 1831.

W. Harding, *The Trial of the Rev. Edward Irving, M.A., before the London Presbytery*, London, 1832.

R. Story, *Peace in Believing. A Memoir of Isabella Campbell of Fernicarry, Rosneath, Dumbartonshire*, Greenock, 1829.

R. Norton, *Memoirs of James and George Macdonald of Port Glasgow*, London, 1840.

L.W. Scholler, *A Chapter in Church History from South Germany, being passages from the life of Johann Evangelist Georg Lutz*, tr. W. Wallis, London, 1894.

J.B. Cardale, *Readings upon the Liturgy*, London, 1878.

Not referenced:
Graham McFarlane, *Edward Irving*, St Andrews Press,
Graham McFarlane, *Christ and the Spirit*, Paternoster Press, 1996, 204pp.

# XII. Pentecostalism

The following is only a small selection of some of the more readily available or more useful introductory works on various aspects of the subject. Most of the books listed here have fuller bibliographies.

W.J. Hollenweger, *The Pentecostals*, SCM, London, 1972. (The most comprehensive, recent introduction, with an international perspective.)

S.H. Frodsham, *With Signs Following*, Gospel Publishing House, Springfield, Missouri, 1946. (An earlier account of the world-wide history of Pentecostal growth.)

Nils Bloch-Hoell, *The Pentecostal Movement*, Scandinavian University Books, Allen & Unwin, 1964. (On the movement's growth in America and Europe.)

R. Martin, *The Early Years of American Pentecostalism, 1900-1940. Survey of a Social Movement*, (Dissertation submitted to the University of N. California, 1975) University Microfilms International, High Wycombe. (On the movement's origins.)

Steve Durasoff, *Bright Wind of the Spirit. Pentecostalism Today*, Hodder & Stoughton, London, Sydney, Auckland, Toronto, 1972.

ed. V. Synan, *Aspects of Pentecostal-Charismatic Origins*, Logos International, Plainfield, New Jersey, 1975. (Collected essays.)

D. Gee, *The Pentecostal Movement*, Victory Press, London, 1941. (A history of British Pentecostalism.)

F.D. Brunner, *A Theology of the Holy Spirit*, Hodder & Stoughton, London, 1970. (Part I gives an excellent outline of Pentecostal history and doctrine.)

M. Harper, *As at the Beginning*, Hodder & Stoughton, 1965. (A more popular account.)

E. Evans, *The Welsh Revival of 1904*, Evangelical Press, 1969. (As the title suggests!)

Frank Bartleman, *Azusa Street*, Logos International, S. Plainfield, New Jersey.

# XIII. The Charismatic Movement

Out of the flood of publications over the past twenty years, I have found the following most useful and informative:

(a) History:

M. Harper, *As at the Beginning*, Hodder & Stoughton, 1965.

ibid., *Charismatic Crisis*, Hounslow Printing Co., Middlesex, 1981.

K. & D. Ranaghan, *Catholic Pentecostals*, Paulist Press, New York, 1969.

(b) Biographical, but also giving information about the movement's growth and history:

D. Bennett, *Nine O'Clock in the Morning*, Coverdale, 1971.

D.J. du Plessis, *The Spirit Bade me Go*, Logos, Plainfield, New Jersey, 1972.

M. Harper, *And None Can Guess*, Hodder & Stoughton, 1971.

ibid., *Bishop's Move*, Hodder & Stoughton, 1978.

G. Pulkingham, *Gathered for Power*, Hodder & Stoughton, 1973.

D. Shakarian, *The Happiest People on Earth*, Hodder & Stoughton, 1977.

D. Wilkerson, *The Cross and the Switchblade*, Lakeland, London, 1967.

(c) Theology:

A. Bittlinger, *Gifts and Graces. A Commentary on I Cor. 12-14*, Hodder & Stoughton, 1967.

ibid., *Gifts and Ministries*, Hodder & Stoughton, 1974.

J.D.G. Dunn, *Baptism in the Holy Spirit*, SCM, 1970.

D.L. Gelpi, *Charism and Sacrament*, SPCK, 1977.

K. McDonnell, *Catholic Pentecostalism: problems and evaluation*, Dove Publications, Pecos, New Mexico, 1970.

H. Mühlen, *A Charismatic Theology*, Burns & Oates, 1978.

E.D. O'Connor, *The Pentecostal Movement in the Catholic Church*, Ave Maria Press, South Bend, Indiana, 1971.

T. Smail, *Reflected Glory*, Hodder & Stoughton, 1975.

L.-J. Suenens, *A New Pentecost?*, Darton, Longman & Todd, 1975.

S. Tugwell, *Did You Receive the Spirit?*, Darton, Longman & Todd, 1972.

(d) Reports and Collected Essays:

ed. A. Bittlinger, *The Church is Charismatic*, World Council of Churches, Geneva, 1981.

*The Charismatic Movement in the Church of England,* published for the General Synod of the Church of England by CIO Publishing, 1981.

K. McDonnell, *Charismatic Renewal and the Churches,* Seabury Press, New York, 1976.

ibid., *Presence, Power, Praise: Documents of the Charismatic Renewal.* 3 vols. Liturgical Press, Collegeville, Minn., 1980.

ed. M.P. Hamilton, *The Charismatic Movement,* Eerdmans, Grand Rapids, 1975.

ed. E.D. O'Connor, *Charismatic Renewal,* SPCK, 1978.

ed. R.P. Spittler, *Perspectives on New Pentecostalism,* Baker Book House, Grand Rapids, 1976.

S. Tugwell & others, *New Heaven? New Earth? An Encounter with Pentecostalism,* Darton, Longman & Todd, 1976.

(e) Doctrine, Practice and Spiritual Gifts:

D. Bennett, *The Holy Spirit and You,* Kingsway, 1971.

L. Christensen, *The Gift of Tongues,* Bethany Fellowship, Minneapolis, 1968.

ibid., *The Renewed Mind,* Bethany Fellowship, 1972.

M. Harper, *Prophecy, a gift for the Body of Christ,* Fountain Trust, 1964.

ibid., *You Are My Sons,* Hodder & Stoughton, 1980.

M.T. Kelsey, *Tongue-Speaking. An Experiment in Spiritual Experience,* Doubleday, New York, 1964.

J.P. Kildahl, *The Psychology of Speaking in Tongues,* Harper & Row, New York, 1972.

W.J. Samarian, *Tongues of Men and Angels: the religious language of Pentecostalism,* Macmillan Co, New York, 1972.

J.L. Sherrill, *They Speak with Other Tongues,* Grune and Stratton, New York, 1970.

D. Watson, *One in the Spirit,* Hodder & Stoughton, 1973.

B. Yocum, *Prophecy,* Ann Arbor, Michigan, 1976.

E. Ensley, *Sounds of Wonder. Speaking in Tongues in the Catholic Tradition,* Paulist Press, New York, 1977.

(f) Comparisons with earlier Movements:

R. Wild, "Is the Charismatic Renewal in the Church an New 'Montanism'?", *Homiletical and Pastoral Review* 73, 1972, pp.67-72.

L. Christenson, *A Message to the Charismatic Movement,* Dimension Books, Minneapolis, 1972.

ibid., "Pentecostalism's Forgotten Forerunner," *Aspects of Pentecostal-Charismatic Origins,* ed. V. Synan, Plainfield, New Jersey, 1975, pp. 15-37.

***Postscript***

• Some comparison of O.T. prophecy with revivalist, charismatic, prophetic and mystical phenomena in Christian history and experience:

J. Lindblom, *Prophecy in Ancient Israel*

M.D.R. Willinck, *Hebrew Prophetic Consciousness*

N. Ndiokwere, *Prophecy and Revolution*

***Additional books consulted***

David Allen, *The Unfailing Stream. A Charismatic History in Outline*, Sovereign World, 1994.

G.K. Chesterton, *St. Francis of Assisi*, Doubleday, New York, 1924.

William DeArteaga, *Quenching the Spirit*, Creation House, Florida, 1992.

F.W. Farrar, *The Life of St. Augustine*, ed. by R. Backhouse, Hodder & Stoughton, London, Sydney, Auckland, 1993.

Paul Johnson, *A History of Christianity*, Penguin Books, 1990.

Brynmor Jones, *The King's Champions. Revival and Reaction 1905-1935*, Christian Literature Press, Cwmbran, 1968.

Brynmor Jones. *Voices from the Welsh Revival 1904-1905*, Evangelical Press of Wales, 1995.

Rick Joyner, *The World Aflame. The Welsh Revival and its Lessons for our Time*, Morning Star Publications, Charlotte, N. Carolina, 1993.

Paul Kauffman, *Fire on the Rim*, Sovereign World, Chichester, 1990.

Tony Lambert, *The Resurrection of the Chinese Church*, Hodder & Stoughton, London, Sydney, Auckland, Toronto, 1991.

David Pawson, *Fourth Wave*, Hodder & Stoughton, 1993.

Preserved Smith, *The Life and Letters of Marin Luther*, ed. By Robert Backhouse, Hodder & Stoughton, London, Sydney, Auckland, 1993.

Ed. Kevin Springer, *Riding the Third Wave*, Marshall Pickering, 1987.

Bill & Amy Stearns, *Catch the Vision 2000*, Bethany House Publishers, Minneapolis, 1991.

J.W.C. Wand, *A History of the Early Church to A.D. 500*, 4th edn., Methuen, London, 1965.

Colin Whittaker, *Great Revivals. God's Men and Their Message*, Marshall Pickering, 2nd edn. 1990.

Colin Whittaker, *Seven Pentecostal Pioneers*, Marshall Pickering, 1983.

William Williams, *The Experience Meeting. An Introduction to the Welsh Societies of the Evangelical Awakening*, The Evangelical Movement of Wales, Glamorgan, 1973.

***The Toronto Blessing***

Patrick Dixon, *Signs of Revival*, Kingsway, Eastbourne, 1994.

Dave Roberts, *The Toronto Blessing*, Kingsway, 1994.

Mike Fearon, *A Breath of Fresh Air*, Eagle, 1994.

Guy Chevreau, *Catch the Fire. The Toronto Blessing – an Experience of Renewal and Revival*, Marshall-Pickering, 1994.

V. Raymond Edman, *Finney Lives On*, Bethany, 1971.

ABBREVIATIONS

PL = Patrologia Latina

# BOOKS ON REVIVAL

**General**

C. Whittaker, *Pioneers of Revival*, Fountain Trust, London, 1971.
C. Whittaker, *Great Revivals*, Marshall, Morgan & Scott, 1984.
W. Pratney, *Revival*, Whitaker House, 1983.
A. Wallis, *In the Day of Thy Power*, Christian Literature Crusade, 1956.
A. Wallis, *Rain from Heaven*, Hodder & Stoughton, 1979.
C. Wadey, *Spiritual Revival*, H.E. Walter Ltd, Worthing, 1982.

**18th Century**

Jonathan Edwards, *A Faithful Narrative of the Surprising Work of God*, Baker Book House, 1979.
Jonathan Edwards, *Jonathan Edwards on Revival*, Banner of Truth, 1984.
O.J. Smith, *David Brainerd, Man of Prayer*, Marshall, Morgan & Scott, 1978.
Howell Harris, *His own Story*, Bridge Publishing UK, 1984.
A. Skevington-Wood, *Inextinguishable Blaze*,
J. Robe, *When the Wind Blows*, Ambassador Publications, 1985.

**19th Century**

W. Haslam, *From Death into Life*, Good News Crusade Publications, 1976.
C. Davey, *The Glory Man. A New Biography of Billy Bray*, Hodder & Stoughton, 1979.
C.G. Finney, *Power from on High*, Victory Press, 1944.
*Finney on Revival*, Dimension Books.
V.R. Edman, *Finney Lives On*, Bethany Fellowship Inc, Minnesota, 1971.

**20th Century**

Frank Bartleman, *Another Wave Rolls In*, Voice Publications, 1970.
E. Evans, *The Welsh Revival of 1904*, Evangelical Press, London, 1969.
W. Blair & B. Hunt, *The Korean Pentecost*, Banner of Truth, 1977.
R. Monod, *The Korean Revival*, Hodder & Stoughton, 1969.
D. Coomes, *The Flame Still Spreads*, Lutterworth, 1974
P. St. John, *Breath of Life*, Norfolk Press,
Bill Butler, *Hill Ablaze*, Hodder & Stoughton,
Mel Tari, *Like a Mighty Wind*, Kingsway,
A. Woolsey, *Duncan Campbell, A Biography*, Hodder & Stoughton, 1974 (reprinted in 1982 as *A Channel of Revival*.)

**Theology of Revival**

Paul Y Cho, *The Fourth Dimension*, Logos,
*Prayer: Key to Revival*, Word Publishing, 1984.
L. Ravenhill, *Why Revival Tarries*, Send the Light,
A. Wallis, *Rain from Heaven*, Hodder & Stoughton, 1979.
A. Skevington Wood, *Baptised with Fire*, Pickering & Inglis, 1981.
N. Grubb, *Continuous Revival*, Christian Literature Crusade, 1984.
C. Wadey, *Spiritual Revival*, H.E. Walter Ltd., 1982.